WORD BIBLICAL COMMENTARY

General Editors
David A. Hubbard
Glenn W. Barker †

Old Testament Editor
John D. W. Watts

New Testament Editor
Ralph P. Martin

WORD BIBLICAL COMMENTARY

VOLUME 13

2 Kings

T.R. HOBBS

WORD BOOKS, PUBLISHER • WACO, TEXAS

Word Biblical Commentary.
2 KINGS
Copyright © 1985 by Word, Incorporated

All rights reserved. No portion of this book may be reproduced in any form without the written permission of the publisher.

Library of Congress Cataloging in Publication Data
Main entry under title:

Word biblical commentary.

  Includes bibliographies.
  1. Bible—Commentaries—Collected works.
BS491.2.W67   220.7'7   81-71768
ISBN 0-8499-0212-6 (vol. 13) AACR2

Printed in the United States of America

Scripture quotations in the body of the commentary marked RSV are from the Revised Standard Version of the Bible, copyright 1946 (renewed 1973), 1956, and © 1971 by the Division of Christian Education of the National Council of the Churches of Christ in the USA and are used by permission. Those marked NIV are from the New International Version of the Bible, copyright © 1973 by New York Bible Society International. The author's own translation of the text appears in italic type under the heading "Translation."

5 6 7 8 9 9 AGF 9 8

This volume is dedicated to Heather,
Catherine, and Gregory, whose love is
a source of joy and strength

Contents

Author's Preface	ix
Editorial Preface	xi
Abbreviations	xii
INTRODUCTION	xvii
Outline	xvii
General Observations	xix
The "Double Redaction" of 2 Kings	xxii
On Reading 2 Kings	xxvi
2 Kings and History	xxx
The Milieu and Thought of 2 Kings	xxxiii
2 Kings and Old Testament Chronology	xxxviii
The Text of 2 Kings	xliv
MAIN BIBLIOGRAPHY	xlvi
TEXT AND COMMENTARY	1
Ahaziah and Elijah (1:1–18)	1
Excursus: 2 Kings 1:17–18	3
The Ascension of Elijah (2:1–25)	13
Excursus: On the Term בני הנביאים *"Sons of the Prophets"*	25
Jehoshaphat and Joram against Moab (3:1–27)	28
Excursus: The Moabite Stone and 2 Kings 3	39
Elisha's Works (4:1–44)	41
Naaman's Cure (5:1–27)	55
Excursus: The Form of the Letter in 2 Kings 5	62
Elisha and the Syrians (6:1–33)	69
The Lepers and the Syrians (7:1–20)	82
Hazael, King in Damascus (8:1–29)	93
Jehu (9:1–37)	106
The Reign of Jehu (10:1–36)	120
The Revolt against Athaliah (11:1–20)	133
The Reign of Joash (12:1–22 [11:21–12:21])	145
Excursus: The Account of Joash's Reign and the Account of Idri-mi of Alalakh	156
Syrian Oppression and the Death of Elisha (13:1–25)	159

Amaziah and Jeroboam II (14:1–29)	173
Excursus: The Chronology of 2 Kings 13–15	184
Kings of the Eighth Century B.C. (15:1–38)	186
Excursus: Additional Note on the Chronology	204
The Apostasy of Ahaz (16:1–20)	207
The Fall and Resettlement of Samaria (17:1–41)	219
Hezekiah and the Siege of Jerusalem (18:1–37)	241
Excursus: 2 Kings 18:17	260
Isaiah's Prophecy and the Assyrian Retreat (19:1–37)	264
Hezekiah and Isaiah (20:1–21)	284
The Reigns of Manasseh and Amon (21:1–26)	297
The Reign of Josiah (22:1–20)	312
The Reign of Josiah, Continued (23:1–37)	328
Attack and Deportation (24:1–20)	343
Jerusalem Destroyed and Second Deportation (25:1–30)	356
Indexes	371

Author's Preface

The past five years during which time this commentary has come into existence have been years of challenge, discovery, and satisfaction. The challenge came late in 1978 in the form of an invitation to contribute a volume to the *Word Biblical Commentary* series. It was a challenge to commit myself to the careful and concentrated work of writing such a work in the midst of what appeared to be an increasingly busy schedule of teaching and administration. It was also a challenge merely to attempt such a work. It bore a frightening resemblance to jumping into the pool at the deep end, since a commentary has always been (in my mind at least) the kind of work which one completes after a lifetime of reflection, and with the preparation of numerous monographs.

The discovery has come through living so closely to a part of the Word of God for so many months. Although one can study and even teach sections of the Scriptures to generations of students, there is a marvelous sense of thrill when new insights are gleaned, when new perspectives are constructed, and the familiar text takes on a freshness which is nothing short of delightful. At times, in the detailed and often pedantic work which must go into the preparation of such a volume as this, this freshness has been experienced and gratefully appreciated.

The satisfaction, of course, comes from the completion of the task. But while the author alone must take responsibility for the contents of the volume, there are numerous persons to whom thanks are rightly due. Dr. John D. W. Watts, the Old Testament Editor of the series, deserves thanks for the initial invitation to write the commentary and for his encouragement and understanding during some difficult times. I owe a debt of gratitude to the publishers of the series, Word Books, who have been generous to a fault in their extension of the original contract because of illness. Numerous colleagues and friends have also contributed much to my work through their encouragement, their patient listening to my tedious obsession with 2 Kings, and their comments. Several classes of students in my graduate seminar on the Hebrew Bible (Religious Studies 706B) have been a constant source of satisfaction as they have wrestled with many of the issues of interpretation raised in this commentary. To them I say thank you. I also acknowledge the help and encouragement of many "lay" friends, whose interests and work lie far outside the strange world of the late Israelite monarchy and the Old Testament prophets, but who nevertheless shared my excitement and offered the necessary encouragement.

My family, Heather, Catherine, and Gregory, who, I am sure, were baffled by the details of such a work, but who remained constant through the frustrations and shared the joys of progress, are deserving of special mention. Their support and help were precious. To them the book is gratefully dedicated.

T. R. HOBBS

McMaster University
Hamilton, Ontario, Canada
Summer 1983

Editorial Preface

The launching of the *Word Biblical Commentary* brings to fulfillment an enterprise of several years' planning. The publishers and the members of the editorial board met in 1977 to explore the possibility of a new commentary on the books of the Bible that would incorporate several distinctive features. Prospective readers of these volumes are entitled to know what such features were intended to be; whether the aims of the commentary have been fully achieved time alone will tell.

First, we have tried to cast a wide net to include as contributors a number of scholars from around the world who not only share our aims, but are in the main engaged in the ministry of teaching in university, college and seminary. They represent a rich diversity of denominational allegiance. The broad stance of our contributors can rightly be called evangelical, and this term is to be understood in its positive, historic sense of a commitment to scripture as divine revelation, and to the truth and power of the Christian gospel.

Then, the commentaries in our series are all commissioned and written for the purpose of inclusion in the *Word Biblical Commentary*. Unlike several of our distinguished counterparts in the field of commentary writing, there are no translated works, originally written in a non-English language. Also, our commentators were asked to prepare their own rendering of the original biblical text and to use those languages as the basis of their own comments and exegesis. What may be claimed as distinctive with this series is that it is based on the biblical languages, yet it seeks to make the technical and scholarly approach to a theological understanding of scripture understandable by—and useful to—the fledgling student, the working minister as well as to colleagues in the guild of professional scholars and teachers.

Finally, a word must be said about the format of the series. The layout in clearly defined sections has been consciously devised to assist readers at different levels. Those wishing to learn about the textual witnesses on which the translation is offered are invited to consult the section headed "Notes." If the readers' concern is with the state of modern scholarship on any given portion of scripture, then they should turn to the sections on "Bibliography" and "Form/Structure/Setting." For a clear exposition of the passage's meaning and its relevance to the ongoing biblical revelation, the "Comment" and concluding "Explanation" are designed expressly to meet that need. There is therefore something for everyone who may pick up and use these volumes.

If these aims come anywhere near realization, the intention of the editors will have been met, and the labor of our team of contributors rewarded.

General Editors: *David A. Hubbard*
Glenn W. Barker†
Old Testament: *John D. W. Watts*
New Testament: *Ralph P. Martin*

Abbreviations

1. PERIODICALS, SERIALS, AND REFERENCE WORKS

AB	Anchor Bible
AcAnt	Acta Antiqua
AION	Annali dell'istituto orientali di Napoli
AJA	American Journal of Archaeology
AJSL	American Journal of Semitic Languages and Literature
ANEP	J. B. Pritchard (ed.), Ancient Near East in Pictures
ANESTP	J. B. Pritchard (ed.), Ancient Near East Supplementary Texts and Pictures
ANET	J. B. Pritchard (ed.), Ancient Near Eastern Texts
Antiq	Josephus, Antiquities of the Jews
AOAT	Alter Orient und Altes Testament
ASTI	Annual of the Swedish Theological Institute
ATANT	Abhandlungen zur Theologie des Alten und Neuen Testaments
AUM	Andrews University Monographs
AusBR	Australian Biblical Review
AUSS	Andrews University Seminary Studies
BA	Biblical Archaeologist
BAR	D. N. Freedman and G. E. Wright (eds.), Biblical Archaeologist Reader. 2 vols.
BASOR	Bulletin of the American Schools of Oriental Research
BDB	F. Brown, S. R. Driver, and C. A. Briggs, Hebrew and English Lexicon of the Old Testament
BHS	Biblia hebraica stuttgartensia
Bib	Biblica
BK	Bibel und Kirche
BM	British Museum
BMik	Beth Mikra
BN	Biblische Notizen
BTB	Biblical Theology Bulletin
BWANT	Beiträge zur Wissenschaft vom Alten und Neuen Testament
BZ	Biblische Zeitschrift
BZAW	Beihefte zur ZAW
CAH	Cambridge Ancient History
CB	Cultura biblica
CBC	Cambridge Bible Commentary
CBQ	Catholic Biblical Quarterly
CBSC	Cambridge Bible for Schools Commentary
CeB	Century Bible
CTA	A. Herdner, Corpus des tablettes en cunéiformes alphabétiques

DTT	Dansk teologisk tidsskrift
EAEHL	M. Avi-Yonah and E. Stern, *Encyclopedia of Archaeological Excavations in the Holy Land*
EHAT	Exegetisches Handbuch zum Alten Testament
EstBib	*Estudios Biblicos*
EvT	*Evangelische Theologie* (*EvTh*)
FRLANT	Forschungen zur Religion und Literatur des Alten und Neuen Testaments
GKC	*Gesenius' Hebrew Grammar*, ed. E. Kautzsch, tr. A. E. Cowley
HAT	Handbuch zum Alten Testament
HKAT	Handkommentar zum Alten Testament
HSM	Harvard Semitic Monographs
HTR	*Harvard Theological Review*
HUCA	*Hebrew Union College Annual*
IASHP	Israel Academy of Sciences and Humanities, Jerusalem
IB	*Interpreter's Bible*
ICC	International Critical Commentary
IDB	G. A. Buttrick (ed.), *Interpreter's Dictionary of the Bible*
IEJ	*Israel Exploration Journal*
JANESCU	*Journal of the Ancient Near Eastern Society of Columbia University*
JAOS	*Journal of the American Oriental Society*
JBC	*The Jerome Biblical Commentary*, R. E. Brown et al. (eds.)
JBL	*Journal of Biblical Literature*
JBR	*Journal of Bible and Religion*
JCS	*Journal of Cuneiform Studies*
JJS	*Journal of Jewish Studies*
JNES	*Journal of Near Eastern Studies*
JPOS	*Journal of the Palestine Oriental Society*
JQR	*Jewish Quarterly Review*
JR	*Journal of Religion*
JSOT	*Journal for the Study of the Old Testament*
JSOTSup	Supplements to *JSOT*
JSS	*Journal of Semitic Studies*
JTS	*Journal of Theological Studies*
KD	*Kerygma und Dogma*
KeH	Kurzgefasstes exegetisches Handbuch zum Alten Testament
KHAT	Kurzer Hand-Commentar zum Alten Testament
Leš	*Lešonénu*
LTQ	*Lexington Theological Quarterly*
MBA	Macmillan Bible Atlas
NCB	New Century Bible
NICOT	New International Commentary on the Old Testament
NRT	*La nouvelle revue théologique* (*NRTh*)
NTT	*Nederlands Theologisch Tidsskrift*
Or	*Orientalia*
OTL	Old Testament Library

OTS	*Oudtestamentische Studien*
PEQ	*Palestine Exploration Quarterly*
PJ	*Palästina-Jahrbuch*
RA	*Revue d'assyriologie et d'archéologie orientale*
RB	*Revue biblique*
RevExp	*Review and Expositor*
RevistB	*Revista biblica*
RGG	*Religion in Geschichte und Gegenwart*
RHR	*Revue de l'histoire des religions*
SANT	Studien zum Alten und Neuen Testament
SAT	Die Schriften des Alten Testaments
SBLDS	Society of Biblical Literature Dissertation Series
SBLMS	SBL Monograph Series
SBM	Stuttgarter biblische Monographien
SBT	Studies in Biblical Theology
SEÅ	*Svensk exegetisk årsbok*
Sem	*Semitica*
SJT	*Scottish Journal of Theology*
ST	*Studia theologica (StTh)*
TAik	*Teologinen Aikakauskirja*
TDOT	G. J. Botterweck and H. Ringgren (eds.), *Theological Dictionary of the Old Testament*
TGUOS	*Transactions, Glasgow University Oriental Society*
TRu	*Theologische Rundschau (ThR)*
TS	*Theologische Studien*
TToday	*Theology Today*
TTZ	*Trierer theologische Zeitschrift (TThZ)*
TynB	*Tyndale Bulletin*
TZ	*Theologische Zeitschrift (ThZ)*
UF	*Ugaritische Forschungen*
UT	C. H. Gordon, *Ugaritic Textbook*
VT	*Vetus Testamentum*
VTSup	Supplements to *VT*
WBC	Word Biblical Commentary
WMANT	Wissenschaftliche Monographien zum Alten und Neuen Testament
ZAW	*Zeitschrift für die alttestamentliche Wissenschaft*
ZDMG	*Zeitschrift der deutschen morgenländischen Gesellschaft*
ZDPV	*Zeitschrift des deutschen Palästina-Vereins*
ZRGG	*Zeitschrift für Religions- und Geistesgeschichte*
ZTK	*Zeitschrift für Theologie und Kirche (ZThK)*

2. MODERN TRANSLATIONS

KJV	King James Version
NEB	New English Bible
RSV	Revised Standard Version
RV	Revised Version

3. Texts, Versions and Ancient Works

Eth	Ethiopic
G	Septuagint (the text cited in this volume is from A. E. Brooke, N. McLean, and H. St. J. Thackeray, *The Old Testament in Greek*, II, ii [Cambridge, 1930])
G^A	G MS, Codex Alexandrinus
G^B	G MS, Codex Vaticanus
G^L	G MSS, Lucianic recension consisting of boc_2e_2
G^N	G MS, Codex Basiliano-Vaticanus and Codex Venetus
K	Kethib
MT	Masoretic Text
OL	Old Latin
Q	Qere
1QIsa[a]	The Dead Sea Scroll of Isaiah from Qumran Cave 1
6QReq	Dead Sea Scroll fragment of 2 Kgs from Qumran Cave 6
Syr	Syriac
Tg	Targum
Theod.	Theodotion
Vg	Vulgate
α'	Aquila
σ'	Symmachus

4. Biblical Books

Gen	Hab	Luke
Exod	Zeph	John
Lev	Hag	Acts
Num	Zech	Rom
Deut	Mal	1–2 Cor
Josh	Ps(s)	Gal
Judg	Job	Eph
1–2 Sam	Prov	Phil
1–2 Kgs	Ruth	Col
Isa	Cant	1–2 Thess
Jer	Eccl	1–2 Tim
Ezek	Lam	Titus
Hos	Esth	Philem
Joel	Dan	Heb
Amos	Ezra	James
Obad	Neh	1–2 Pet
Jonah	1–2 Chr	1–2–3 John
Mic	Matt	Jude
Nah	Mark	Rev

5. Miscellaneous

ANE	Ancient Near East
chap(s).	chapter(s)

constr	construct
ed(s).	editor(s)
EV(V)	English verse(s)
fem	feminine
Gr.	Greek
Grid	refers to map by survey of Israel
Heb.	Hebrew
hiph	hiphil
hithp	hithpael
lit.	literally
masc	masculine
MS(S).	manuscript(s)
n.d.	no date
pl	plural or plate
ptcp	participle
sec.	section
sg	singular
tr.	translator, translated by
v(v)	verse(s)
vol(s).	volume(s)
yr	year

Introduction

OUTLINE

Chapter

1. The end of the reign of Ahaziah (I) in fulfillment of the prophetic word through Elijah (vv 1–17). Closing formula to the reign of Ahaziah (v 18).
2. The ascension of Elijah and the succession of Elisha (vv 1–18). The "healing" of the waters at Jericho (vv 19–22). The taunting by the boys and their punishment (vv 23–25).
3. The campaign of Jehoshaphat (J) and Jehoram (I) with Edom against Moab.
4. The widow's jar of oil (vv 1–7). The Shunemite woman and her son (vv 8–37). The sweetening of the sour stew (vv 38–41). The feeding of the sons of the prophets (vv 42–44).
5. The cure of Naaman (vv 1–19). The duplicity of Gehazi (vv 20–27).
6. The recovery of the lost axe head (vv 1–7). Elisha's encounter with the Syrians (vv 8–23). The siege and famine at Samaria (vv 24–33).
7. The relief from famine and the flight of the Syrians at the appearance of the lepers (vv 1–20).
8. The Shunemite's flight to Egypt (vv 1–6). Hazael's accession to the throne of Damascus (vv 7–15). Introductory formula to reign of Jehoram (I) (vv 16–18). Characterization of Jehoram's reign (vv 19–22). Closing formula to reign of Jehoram (I) (vv 23–24). Introductory formula to reign of Ahaziah (J) (vv 25–27). Ahaziah's and Jehoram's fight with Hazael (vv 28–29).
9. Anointing of Jehu (vv 1–13). Death of Jehoram, Ahaziah, and Jezebel at hand of Jehu (vv 14–37).
10. Jehu's elimination of the royal house (vv 1–11). The incident at Beth Eked (vv 12–14). Jehu's meeting with Jehonadab ben Rekeb (vv 15–17). The massacre of Baal worshipers (vv 18–27). Comment on four generations of Jehu's dynasty (vv 28–31). Loss of Israelite territory (vv 32–33). Closing formula for reign of Jehu (vv 34–36).
11. Reign of Athaliah (J) and Jehoiada's coup (vv 1–20). Brief reference to Jehoash (J) (v 21).
12. Introductory formula to reign of Jehoash (J) (vv 1–3). Jehoash's reform (vv 4–16). Invasion by Hazael (v 17). Payment of bribe to Hazael by Jehoash (v 18). Closing formula to reign of Jehoash (J) (vv 19–21).
13. Introductory formula to reign of Jehoahaz (I) (vv 1–2). Attacks by Hazael and respite for Israel (vv 3–7). Closing formula to reign of Jehoahaz (I) (vv 8–9). Introductory formula to reign of Jehoash (I) (vv 10–11). Closing formula to reign of Jehoash (I) (vv 12–13). Death of Elisha and the promise to Jehoash (vv 14–19). Revival of corpse touching Elisha's bones (vv 20–

21). Hazael's attacks on Israel (vv 22-23). Reversal of Syria's fortunes (vv 24-25).
14. Introductory formula to reign of Amaziah (J) (vv 1-4). Exploits of Amaziah (vv 5-7). Amaziah's challenge to the north and the battle at Beth Shemesh (vv 8-14). Closing formula to reign of Jehoash (I) (vv 15-16). Closing formula to reign of Amaziah (J) (vv 17-22). Introductory formula to reign of Jeroboam (I) (vv 23-24). Exploits of Jeroboam (vv 25-27). Closing formula to reign of Jeroboam (I) (vv 28-29).
15. Introductory formula to reign of Azariah (J) (vv 1-3). Characterization of Azariah's reign (vv 4-5). Closing formula to reign of Azariah (J) (vv 6-7). Introductory formula to reign of Zechariah (I) (vv 8-9). Shallum's coup and closing formula to reign of Zechariah (I) (vv 10-12). Menahem's counter-coup (vv 13-16). Introductory formula to the reign of Shallum (I) (v 13). Closing formula to reign of Shallum (I) (v 15). Introductory formula to reign of Menahem (I) (vv 17-18). Tiglath Pileser III in Israel (vv 19-20). Closing formula to reign of Menahem (I) (vv 21-22). Introductory formula to reign of Pekahiah (I) (vv 23-24). Pekah's coup (v 25). Closing formula to reign of Pekahiah (I) (v 26). Introductory formula to reign of Pekah (I) (vv 27-28). Invasion by Tiglath Pileser III (v 29). Hoshea's coup (v 30). Closing formula to reign of Pekah (I) (v 31). Introductory formula to reign of Jotham (J) (vv 32-34). Characterization of Jotham's reign (v 35). Closing formula for reign of Jotham (J) (vv 36-38).
16. Introductory formula to reign of Ahaz (J) (vv 1-2). Characterization of Ahaz's reign (vv 3-4). Attack by Syria and Israel (vv 5-9). Ahaz visits Damascus and finds new altar design (vv 10-18). Closing formula to reign of Ahaz (vv 19-20).
17. Introductory formula to reign of Hoshea (I) (vv 1-2). Assyrian invasion and collapse of Israel (vv 3-6). Theological comment on collapse of the north (vv 7-23). Resettlement (vv 24-28). Comment on conditions in Samaria (vv 29-41).
18. Introductory formula to reign of Hezekiah (J) (vv 1-3). Reform of Hezekiah (vv 4-8). Review of the situation (vv 9-12). Assyrian invasion of Judah (vv 13-16).
19. Sennacherib's first diplomatic mission (vv 18:17-19:9a). Letter from Sennacherib (vv 9b-14). Hezekiah's prayer (vv 15-19). Isaiah's response (vv 20-34). Sennacherib's withdrawal from Jerusalem (vv 35-36). Death of Sennacherib (v 37).
20. Hezekiah's sickness (vv 1-7). Sign of the shadow (vv 8-11). Visit of Merodach Baladan (vv 12-115). Prophetic word of warning to Hezekiah (vv 16-19). Closing formula to reign of Hezekiah (J) (vv 20-21).
21. Introductory formula to reign of Manasseh (J) (vv 1-2). Characterization of Manasseh's reign (vv 3-16). Closing formula to reign of Manasseh (J) (vv 17-18). Introductory formula to reign of Amon (J) (vv 19-20). Characterization of Amon's reign (vv 21-22). Assassination of Amon (vv 23-24). Closing formula to reign of Amon (J) (vv 25-26).
22. Introductory formula to reign of Josiah (J) (vv 1-2). Beginning of temple repairs (vv 3-7). Finding of lawbook (vv 8-10). Hearing of law by king (vv 11-13). Huldah's oracle (vv 14-20).

Introduction

23. Reading of law to the people (vv 1–3). Reform and purging of Jerusalem (vv 4–14). Purging of Bethel (vv 15–20). Celebration of the passover (vv 21–23). Abolition of wizardry, etc. (v 24). Characterization of Josiah's reign (v 25). Additional comment on forthcoming judgment (vv 26–27). Closing formula to reign of Josiah (J) (v 28). Death of Josiah (vv 29–30). Introductory formula to reign of Jehoahaz (J) (vv 31–32). Pharoah Neco's control over Judah (vv 33–35). Introductory formula to reign of Jehoiakim (J) (vv 36–37).
24. First Babylonian attack on Judah (vv 1–4). Closing formula for reign of Jehoiakim (J) (vv 5–6). Comment on the extent of Babylonian control (v 7). Introductory formula to reign of Jehoiachin (J) (vv 8–9). Nebuchadrezzar's attack on Jerusalem (vv 10–17). Introductory formula to reign of Zedekiah (J) (vv 18–19). Editorial comment (v 20).
25. Second invasion by Babylon (vv 1–7). Death of Zedekiah's sons and the blinding and exile of the king (vv 6–7). Destruction of the city (vv 8–12). Removal of temple treasures (vv 13–17). Killing of the officials (vv 18–21). Appointment of Gedaliah and his death (vv 22–26). Release of Jehoiachin from prison (v 27–30).

GENERAL OBSERVATIONS

When we remember that the division between 1 Kings and 2 Kings was somewhat arbitrary—based on the amount of material readily contained on one scroll—the balance of material within the twenty-five chapters of 2 Kings is striking. First, a considerable amount of space is devoted to the activities of the prophet Elisha. This is comparable with the ending of 1 Kings where Elisha's predecessor, Elijah, is the subject of chaps. 17–21. The first two chapters of 2 Kings concern Elijah. He confronts the sick Ahaziah about his search for healing from a foreign god, and he prophesies the king's demise. This prophecy is fulfilled. In chap. 2 the first half of the chapter is devoted to Elijah's journey to the site of his ascension. However, the two chapters do form a proper transition between the collection of material about Elijah and the collection about Elisha. The smooth and clever transition provides a perfect introduction to the activities of Elisha as successor to Elijah, which go on to fill chaps. 3–8. Even narratives that appear to deal with history (e.g., chap. 3) are so shaped as to draw attention to the prophet and the divine word he bears.

Second, although the remainder of the book is at first glance a history of the closing decades of the monarchy in Israel and Judah, on closer examination there is seen an unevenness in the presentation of the various kings. Relatively unimportant kings, such as Ahaziah of Israel, are among the main characters of certain chapters. Ahaziah figures prominently in chap. 1, Athaliah in chap. 11. The battle between Israel and Judah and Moab receives a lengthy treatment when compared to the summary treatments of the battles between Israel and Syria (8:28–29), or Judah and Syria (12:17; 13:3–7). Similarly, the fight between Judah and Israel at Beth Shemesh (14:8–14) is given more space than that devoted to the Assyrian invasions of Israel (15:29; 17:3–6). The reform of Jehoash of Judah (chap. 12) occupies much more space than the lengthier reign of Jeroboam of Israel (14:25–27). Three chapters are dedicated to the reign and reform of Hezekiah (chaps. 18–20) and two to those of Josiah (chaps. 22–23). At times the writer can be quite discursive when commenting on events (17:7–23), and at others quite cryptic (13:26–27).

Third, there is a certain thorough consistency in the way some things are expressed. Legitimate rulers of Israel and Judah are introduced and dismissed with formulaic statements that vary little in form. Kings of Judah are synchronized with their contemporaries in Israel at the beginning of their reigns. The king's age is given at his accession, followed by the length of his reign. The name of the king's mother is provided, and this is followed by an evaluation of the reign. For Israel the pattern is similar, but the age of the king and the name of his mother are not given. The dismissal formula is equally as firm. Reference is made to the source of additional information on the reign. The death, and sometimes the burial, are mentioned to be followed by the name of the successor. This pattern is the same for both kingdoms. There are, however, some slight exceptions to this. Following the fall of Israel, naturally no synchronization appears for subsequent kings of Judah. Further, Jehoash of Judah's reign is introduced with all the necessary elements but in a slightly different order (see 12:1–4), and in 16:1–4 the name of the king's mother is absent. Other more interesting variations are to be seen in the absence of a concluding formula for Hoshea of Israel (17:1–6) and Jehoahaz (23:31–35), Jehoiachin (24:8–17), and Zedekiah (24:18–19) of Judah. In each case an invasion, an untimely death, or a deportation takes place, thus bringing an air of abnormality to the conclusions of these reigns. The most blatant example of the absence of such concluding or introductory formulae is the reign of Athaliah (chap. 11), which is clearly presented as an aberration in the smooth progress of the Davidic line.

Further, the writer tends to move back and forth regularly between Israel and Judah. The brief description and assessment of the reign of an Israelite king is completed first before a Judean king is introduced. So, for example, Jehu's reign ends (10:34–36), and the incident with Athaliah takes place (chap. 11) and is fully described. Only then does the attention shift to the legitimate king of Judah (12:1–3, 19–21), even though Jehoash of Judah was a contemporary of Jehu. Because of this distinctive way of organizing the material, the narrative exhibits a sense of disjointedness. An exception is the concluding formula to the reign of Jehoash of Israel, which appears in 13:12–13 before the introductory formula to the reign of Amaziah of Judah (14:1–4), but which is repeated again in 14:15–16. Discussions of "primary" and "secondary" material abound here in commentaries, but the most plausible explanation for the repetition is the unusual circumstances which pertained to the reigns of the two kings. They fought against each other, and careful note is made of the length of time that Amaziah outlived Jehoash (14:17). Thus a repetition of the concluding formula is not necessarily out of place here. An unusual presentation of the ending of a reign is also found in the case of Josiah. The concluding formula (23:28) appears in the narrative before the reference to the king's death at Megiddo (23:29–30).

Apart from the obvious interest the writer has in presenting an interpretation of the end of the monarchy in Israel and Judah, certain other concerns emerge from the narrative. The writer has a particularly strong interest in cultic matters, especially when they concern the temple in Jerusalem. Although the first ten chapters of the book retell incidents that are set in the north, at chap. 11 and beyond the writer betrays a careful attention to detail when he is describing cultic activities in Jerusalem. In the plot to overthrow Athaliah (chap. 11), a wealth of detail is found in the narrative concerning the shifts of the temple guards and their divisions, the ritual for coronation in the temple, and indeed the temple furnishings. In the following chapter, which recounts the reorganization of the system for collecting for temple repairs and running costs, the details are again at the fore (12:9–16). Ahaz's introduction of a Syrian altar into the temple at Jerusalem receives similar detailed attention (16:10–16). Hezekiah's reform (18:4–5) is not so carefully presented, but it does add to our knowledge of the Jerusalem cultus. In the reform of Josiah (23:4–14) and his purging of Jerusalem, the detail reemerges and to a certain extent is repeated in tragic circumstances in 25:8–17. In the body of the *Commentary* we have suggested that the source of this information is the careful record kept at the temple with the kind of detail so loved by bureaucrats.

Conversely, the writer shows a keen interest, albeit a negative one, in the cultic activities associated with local Canaanite worship. Here, however, there is not so much interest in specific details as there is in the repetition of generalizing slogans which the writer uses to characterize such activity. Little precise information is provided in chaps. 1, 9, 10 about Canaanite worship, although it is perfectly clear that the writer is opposed to it. A similar observation can be made on 11:17–18. However, in chaps. 17, 21, 22, 23, which concern the fall of Israel, the reign of Manasseh, and the nature of the purge initiated by Josiah, respectively, more details are provided. The comments still tend to be in the nature of a strong polemic inspired by the prohibitions of the book of Deuteronomy, but much is learned from these passages about the state of apostasy in both Israel and Judah at certain periods of the divided monarchy.

This interest in the cultic activities devoted to Yahweh and Baal is matched by similar interest in the role of the prophetic figure in the history of Israel and Judah. This much is obvious from the amount of space devoted to the careers of Elijah and Elisha. It is customary among commentators to distinguish between those stories about Elisha in which he deals with unimportant issues and people, and those stories in which he encounters kings, deals with matters of state, and becomes involved in overt political activity; such distinctions are not necessary for an appreciation of the clear fascination the writer has with prophetic characters. However helpful such theories of composition might be for recreating the history of the traditions prior to their incorporation into the present book, the writer makes no such distinctions and portrays the prophet as dealing with all, both rich and poor, high and low, as an example of Yahweh's activity with Israel. In some cases a local incident becomes a metaphor for the larger political activity. This is particularly true of chaps. 1–2 (see *Comment* on these chapters).

Of prime importance to the writer in his presentation of prophecy is the fulfillment of the prophetic word in the history of the two nations for good or ill. Thus judgment takes place because of the prophetic word (1:17; 9:36;

17:13-14; 20:16-19), yet judgment is also delayed and respite is given because of the prophetic word (2:19-22; 13:14-19; 20:8-11). Elisha's widespread activity in the north, Isaiah's connection with the reign of Hezekiah, and the repetition of the sum of prophetic proclamation during the reign of Manasseh (21:10-15) serve as illustrations of this point. The grand model with which the writer works is that of the archetypal prophet, Moses.

An additional important emphasis in the book is that the standard by which people are judged (nation and king) is the law of Moses, specifically the deuteronomic version of that law. This is seen not only in the style and vocabulary of the author, which is best characterized as "deuteronomistic," but also in the repeated references and allusions to that law. The issue of the language of Joshua-2 Kings has been carefully examined by numerous scholars, and the details need not be repeated here. Suffice it to say that the vast majority of commentators agree that, to varying degrees, the writer uses a distinct language and style whose closest parallels are to be found in the book of Deuteronomy. In the body of the *Commentary*, where necessary, such details will be discussed. Readers are also referred to Volumes 7 and 12 in the Word Biblical Commentary series, *Joshua*, by Trent C. Butler, and *1 Kings*, by Simon J. DeVries, as well as the works of Driver, Hyatt, Bright, Weinfeld, Thiel, and Nicholson that are mentioned in the *Bibliography*.

It comes as little surprise, then, that the writer should use the "Torah of Moses" as the standard of behavior by which he judges both nations and kings. The manner in which he refers to the standard is sometimes quite general (10:31; 16:3-4; 18:4-6), but where more specific allusions or precise quotations are needed, he leaves one in no doubt that the law which is found in the book of Deuteronomy is in mind (14:5-6; 17:2-23; 21:3-9). The measures taken by Josiah in chap. 23 are the clearest example of this and are widely recognized as dependent upon the prohibitions of the book of Deuteronomy.

From this brief summary of introductory observations we now turn to an introduction of some of the more important issues connected with the book.

THE "DOUBLE REDACTION" OF 2 KINGS

Bibliography

Alt, A. "Die Heimat des Deuteronomiums." *Kleine Schriften.* Vol. 2. München: C. H. Beck, 1953. **Brueggemann, W.** "The Kerygma of the Deuteronomic Historian." *Int* 22 (1969) 387-402. **Cross, F. M.** "The Themes of the Books of Kings and the Structure of the Deuteronomistic History." *Canaanite Myth and Hebrew Epic: Essays in the History and Religion of Israel.* Cambridge, MA: Harvard University Press, 1973. **Dietrich, W.** *Prophetie und Geschichte: eine redaktionsgeschichtliche Untersuchung zum deuteronomistischen Geschichtswerk.* FRLANT 108. Göttingen: Vandenhoeck und Ruprecht, 1972. **Jepsen, A.** *Die Quellen des Königsbuches.* 2nd ed. Halle: M. Niemeyer, 1956. **Nelson, R. D.** *The Double Redaction of the Deuteronomistic History.* JSOTSup 18. Sheffield: JSOT Press, 1981. **Noth, M.** *Überlieferungsgeschichtliche Studien: Die sammelnden und bearbeitenden Geschichtswerke im Alten Testament.* 3rd ed. Tübingen: M. Niemeyer, 1967. **Polzin, R.** *Moses and the Deuteronomist: A Literary Study of the Deuteronomic History.* New York: Seabury, 1980. **Smend, R.** "Das Gezetz und die Volker: Ein Beitrag zur deuteronomistischen Redaktionsgeschichte." *Probleme Biblischer Theologie. Gerhard von Rad zum 70.* Ed. H. W. Wolff. Munich: C. Kaiser, 1971. **Soggin, J. A.** "Der Entstehungsort der deuteronomistischen Geschichtswerk." *TLZ* 100 (1975) 3–8. **Wolff, H. W.** "Das Kerygma des deuteronomistischen Geschichtswerks." *ZAW* 73 (1961) 171–86.

In spite of the very important work of Martin Noth on the single authorship of the Deuteronomistic history (*Überlieferungsgeschichtliche Studien*), the theory of the "double redaction" of the work has persisted and shows little sign of dying. For the more recent presentations of the theories, the term "double redaction" is in fact a misnomer, since the theory is that an original historical work completed during the time of Josiah has undergone one substantial exilic redaction which altered its original ideological purpose. The more recent advocates of the theory have been F. M. Cross, Jr., in his work "The Themes of the Book of Kings and the Structure of the Deuteronomistic History," which was published as part of *Canaanite Myth and Hebrew Epic* in 1973, and R. D. Nelson, whose doctoral dissertation was published in 1981 under the title of *The Double Redaction of the Deuteronomistic History*. Nelson's work represents a refinement of and a detailed apologia for Cross's original thesis.

As Nelson points out, the theory of more than one redactional stage of the deuteronomistic history has had a "long respectable history" (*Double Redaction*, 19). However, such appeals to antiquity ought to be greeted with caution, especially when the great variety of the forms of the theory is surveyed. While many important commentators have argued for a double and even a multiple redaction of the work, there has been no unanimity on the precise nature of the original and its main ideological point, or the nature and purpose of the redaction(s). A number of attempts have simply distinguished between a pre- and post-exilic edition of the work, and Nelson has correctly shown some of the problems of identifying the precise historical situation in which certain parts of the work were written (*Double Redaction*, 25–26). Others have sought more carefully to identify the underlying ideology of the various strata. For Jepsen, an original priestly cultic history was reworked by someone with a greater interest in prophecy. For Smend, an original historical work was edited by someone with a strong concern for the law, and Dietrich has refined this to insert a prophetic stratum between the historical and legal. Eissfeldt argued for a multiplicity of sources, including a pre-deuteronomic history which was reworked by the deuteronomist, but without affecting the basic outline.

Cross has offered a persuasive version of the theory that presents a consistent explanation of some of the tensions in style and ideology found within the book. It forms the starting point for Nelson's work and is more widely accepted. As we will see, however, this theory is not without its serious difficulties. Cross's well-reasoned argument states that there are two main themes apparent in the history, the first being the sin of Jeroboam I and its disastrous effects on Israel. A crucial passage is 1 Kgs 12:25–33, which describes Jeroboam's crime as the establishment of pagan shrines. In the earlier promise of Ahijah (1 Kgs 11:29–39), a concession is made to the durability of Judah (v 39). The inference Cross draws from this is that the avoidance of such shrines in Judah, or their destruction, should they be established, is an important element in this durability. The link with Josiah is formed in 1 Kgs 13. "The string of oracles and judgments which make up this theme in Kings is completed in the great peroration on the fall of Samaria in 2 Kings 17:1–23" (Cross, *Canaanite Myth and Hebrew Epic*, 281).

A complementary theme appears in the promise of an everlasting dynasty for David, found originally in Nathan's oracle in 2 Sam 7 and developed to a climax in the reform of Josiah in 2 Kgs 22:1–23:25 (see *Canaanite Myth and Hebrew Epic*, 283). The juxtaposition of judgment (on the north) and hope (for the south) is an important literary device within the history. In complete contrast to this is the "subtheme" represented in the comment on Manasseh found in 2 Kgs 21:2–15, which portends judgment now, not only upon the north, but also upon Judah. This subtheme, because of its conflicting ideology, and many other passages which agree with its point of view are assigned to the exilic redactor of the work who wrote *ca*. 550 B.C. His purpose in writing was to update the history by adding a chronicle of events subsequent to the reign of Josiah, and to preach a "sermon" to the exiles. Among the earlier editorial comments in this style are 2 Kgs 17:19 and 20:17–18.

The argument is attractive mainly because of its consistency. It seeks to explain the historical context of the "original" work and thereby offer a suitable reason for the popularity of the Josianic reform by the writer. Granted the presuppositions of the approach, it also offers a reasoned explanation for the passages which contradict the detected main themes. As noted above, the essay provides the starting point for the more detailed analysis by Nelson.

But in spite of the very positive aspects of the theory, the position adopted in this commentary is different. The work of the deuteronomist (Joshua to 2 Kings) is, we believe, the work of one author. The relationship of the history to the Book of Deuteronomy is that the writer uses the lawbook as the model standard of behavior for people and kings and continually refers to its legislation. The relationship of the history to the deuteronomistic passages in the Book of Jeremiah is much more complex, although there is undoubtedly a relationship. The nature of the Book of Jeremiah, with its distinctive poetry and distinctive deuteronomistic prose, is still very much under discussion, but the presence of so much prose within the book, which in both vocabulary and theology resembles much of what is found in the history, cannot be overlooked. One aspect of this will be developed later. For the moment we return to a discussion of Cross.

An important beginning for Cross is a recognition of the unconditional nature of the Davidic covenant as presented in the history beginning at 2 Sam 7. However, that it is unconditioned is to be questioned. 2 Sam 7:14, with its allusion to possible punishment for wrongdoing, would argue against a view of the covenant as unconditional. This impression is very much strengthened by a glance at the occasional repetitions of the demands of Davidic kingship which occur at various points throughout the narrative. David's advice to Solomon (1 Kgs 2:1–4), the anonymous prophetic word to Solomon (1 Kgs 6:11–13), and the divine word to him in 1 Kgs 9:1–9 demonstrate that for the historian the perpetuity of the covenant is dependent upon the king's faithfulness to the deuteronomic law. Without a doubt, the subsequent kings of Judah are compared often with David, but the image of this ideal king is dominated by the understanding that he adhered to the law.

Josiah's reform plays a major role in the structure of the deuteronomistic history. The sheer length of the account of the reform, which must have taken up only a small amount of time during his complete reign, would attest to this judgment. However, in spite of Cross's high assessment of the reform and its place in the history, an important event in the full account of the reign of Josiah is his abrupt demise in battle with Neco at Megiddo (2 Kg 23:29–30). When viewed within the context of the complete book of 2 Kgs, the important point about the reign and reform of Josiah is their failure. Within a very short span of time the southern kingdom was brought to an end. An explanation of this quick demise is found at the end of the reign of Josiah (23:26–27), but to assign this to the later exilic editor (so Nelson, *Double Redaction*, 123) is begging the question. This conclusion is in fact impossible when it is noted that this pattern of reform and disaster is one well established in the history. Jehoash's reforms in chap. 12 end with the selling off of the temple and palace treasures to an invader (12:17–18), and Hezekiah's reforms end with the king's showing off the temple and palace treasures to acquisitive foreigners (20:12–19). Josiah's reform is a climax, but is it of a promise now forfeited? After it, the fall of Judah is only a matter of time. The rationale the writer offers us for this state of affairs is the abominable nature of the reign of Manasseh.

Cross and others are correct in drawing attention to the role of Jeroboam ben Nebat and his misdeeds in the structure of the history. The character cannot be overlooked, and, as if to drive the point home, the repeated references to his sins "with which he caused Israel to sin" bring him before the reader again and again. He is the prototypical apostate, the one who initially led Israel astray. To be sure, 1 Kgs 13 and 2 Kgs 22–23 are balanced. The apostate actions of Jeroboam are countered by the reforms of Josiah, in part. But beside Josiah and Jeroboam there are two other characters in the narrative who are no less important than these two. They are Ahab of Israel and Manasseh of Judah. They too are balanced, but the balance is of two (im)moral equals, not of opposites. 2 Kgs 21:3 makes the reflection clear when Manasseh is compared to Ahab, and indeed mimics the activity of the northern monarch in 1 Kgs 16:31–34. It cannot be overlooked that the sins for which Israel is condemned in 2 Kgs 17:7–23 are a combination of those committed by both Jeroboam and Ahab.

It makes good sense, then, to view the end of the nation of Judah as precipitated by the actions of Manasseh, in the same way that the end of the nation of Israel was brought about, in part, by the activities of Jeroboam, compounded by those of Ahab. Ahab is to Manasseh what David is to Josiah— a model. At several points in the narrative the writer sees in the activity and fate of Israel a portent of the fate of Judah. There is an inevitable delay, but the ultimate destruction of the south is only a matter of time. The delays at various places in the narrative are because of Yahweh's love for David, but the message is loud and clear: the delay is only temporary.

On Reading 2 Kings

Bibliography

Alter, R. *The Art of Biblical Narrative.* New York: Basic Books, 1981. **Culley, R. C.** *Studies in the Structure of Hebrew Narrative.* Philadelphia: Fortress Press, 1976. **Fokkelman, J. P.** *Narrative Art in Genesis.* Amsterdam: Van Gorcum, 1975. **Kawin, B. F.** *Telling it Again and Again: Repetition in Literature and Film.* Ithaca: Cornell University Press, 1972. **Licht, J.** *Storytelling in the Bible.* Jerusalem: Magnes Press, 1978. **Miscall, P. D.** *The Workings of Old Testament Narrative.* Philadelphia: Fortress Press, 1983.

A methodological presupposition of this commentary is that 2 Kings is the work of one writer whose intention was to tell the story of the failed experiment of monarchy in Israel and Judah, and to interpret that failure. Unless absolutely forced to do otherwise by the weight of evidence, we shall not speculate about "primary" or "secondary" material within the book. Even in those cases where such speculations are deemed necessary, the reader must always be aware of the possibility of error. In other words, our judgment on a line, a verse, or a word as an editorial gloss (e.g., on 1:17–18) is no guarantee of the accuracy of that judgment. The approach is admittedly cautious and has led throughout the commentary, to an ongoing dialogue with those who see their task of interpretation as heavily dependent upon the recognition of earlier sources within the present book. Our approach, in recent years, has found sound precedent and noble advocates (see the works of Alter, Fokkelman, Licht, and Miscall listed in the *Bibliography*).

Our writer has crafted a work with remarkable skill and perception, and in the execution of that task he has employed a variety of literary techniques. In the body of the commentary attention is frequently drawn to those techniques, so the present aim of this introduction is to anticipate and to summarize some of the more obvious demonstrations of the writer's literary skill.

Our task is aided by an attitude that sees the text of 2 Kings not so much as a collection of disparate parts, but as a well-constructed whole. Many times in the book, when we encounter signs that have been traditionally identified as pointers to joints and seams in the narrative, demonstrating the narrator's clumsiness instead of his skill, we shall seek an alternative understanding of them. Frequently, the fascination with an analytical approach to the biblical text has bequeathed a portrait of an editor or editors whose work can only be characterized as of the utmost awkwardness and insensitivity. It has become almost a cliché, but nevertheless true, that if some of the methods of traditional biblical critics were applied to some of the masterpieces of modern literature, then they too would have to be "relegated to the dustbin of shoddily 'redacted' literary scraps" (Alter, *The Art of Biblical Narrative,* 21).

The modern understanding of what constitutes a "contradiction" of logic within a narrative cannot be superimposed upon the ancient writer. Such dramatic shifts of plot and direction within a biblical narrative (and there are many in 2 Kings) are viewed as deliberate. Choice of vocabulary is exactly that, a choice by the writer. Although this material is generally classified (and we believe correctly) as "deuteronomistic" because of its tendency to favor certain words, phrases, and concepts, no author works within a rigid lexical straitjacket that hampers all attempts at creativity. Repetitions are not to be seen as automatic indicators of a clumsy attempt by a second author to improve upon the first, but, on the contrary, are to be seen for what they are—a common literary device that has a variety of applications within a story (see Kawin, *Telling It Again and Again*).

The story told by the writer of 2 Kings is dramatic. Its subject matter is the stuff of tragedy. The nation, chosen by God, saved by God from slavery, settled by God in a land of plenty, loses everything because of its consistent tendency to chase after other gods. From the vantage point of the exile, the writer seeks to make some sense of this tragedy and to integrate the experience of exile and destruction into Israel's theology of a God of salvation and deliverance who had originally brought them out of the land of Egypt. Along the way, in the careful execution of this task, the writer shows himself to be masterful in his manipulation of words and phrases, in his use of literary techniques, and in his juxtaposition of the two major themes with which Israel now has to come to terms: salvation and judgment.

In the general observations above, we noted a sense of imbalance in the complete narrative with its apparent overattention to the activities of Elisha and certain kings to the detriment of a comprehensive picture of the last century and a half of the history of Israel and Judah. The consistent nature of this "imbalance" identifies it as deliberate. In other words, there is a clear *selection* of certain materials from historical sources to the exclusion of others, and the emphasis that the writer places upon the activities of Elisha, Hezekiah, Jehu, Isaiah, and Josiah betrays a preference for certain themes and examples of those themes in the actions of historical persons. Hence we are continually reminded that additional information may be gathered on the reign of King X from the royal records of the Israelite or Judean courts. In that additional information our writer shows no interest at all, and, to a very large extent, the reader is left at the writer's mercy since those documents to which he refers are no longer extant. On the rare occasions where comparative accounts of incidents are available (e.g., chaps. 3; 15–17; 18–20; 24–25) the amount of additional historical data gathered is minimal.

Within this basic framework of selectivity the writer demonstrates a clear skill in the individual narratives that he offers. The techniques employed range over a number of different categories, and those covered below are by no means an exhaustive list. Jacon Licht (*Storytelling in the Bible*) and Robert Alter (*The Art of Biblical Narrative*) both draw attention to the fundamental feature of biblical narrative—its scenic nature. It is a dominant form of biblical narration and is clearly present in the stories of 2 Kings. For example, the stories of Elisha are rarely extended tales, but, instead, confine themselves to a relatively small collection of sentences for each incident. Chaps. 1–8 have a distinct episodic quality. Description is minimal, and comments by the author are rare. Instead, dialogue and action predominate. The pace of the Elisha stories is therefore swift, and, with the possible exceptions of chaps. 3 and 5, the narrative moves the reader along at a rapid pace.

Although the material dealing more specifically with the kings of Israel and Judah (chaps. 9–25) covers a much longer period of time and more complicated matters of internal and foreign politics, the swift pace is maintained, only to be slowed at those particular junctures in the narrative where an important point needs to be made with care. So the reader pauses over the activities of Jehu and their side-effects, the reign of Hezekiah and, above all, the reign of Josiah. As for most of the others, the reader is forced to be content with swift and predictable characterizations of various monarchs according to established patterns of behavior. A major impression that one receives from the reading of 2 Kings is that of the speed with which the narrative proceeds, but coupled with this is the occasional "retardation" (the phrase is Licht's, *Storytelling in the Bible*, 105) of the narrative.

Within the stories of the kings in the book, two other characteristics are worthy of note. The first is the dominance of "models" in the depiction of successive kings, and the second is the disappointing twist which the writer appends to the stories of potential success. Archetypical of the apostate kings of Israel is her first, Jeroboam ben Nebat, whose actions led Israel astray again and again. Many subsequent kings commit "the sin of Jeroboam with which he caused Israel to sin," for which they are roundly condemned. The figure tends to dominate the narrative. However, Ahab also assumes large proportions as a model of apostasy in the mind of the writer, so much so that the activities of Ahab become a model for the reign of Manasseh (21:3), who is the only Judean king to be so "honored." Manasseh assumes the role of Judah's "Ahab." Nothing that he does is worthy of the slightest commendation. The point is taken further following the reign of Josiah (23:26–27). It is precisely because of the excesses of the reign of Manasseh that Judah's punishment is inevitable. On the positive side, the model of David as the ideal king is evident in the portrayal of many other kings of Judah. Kings are judged frequently by the standard of piety achieved by David (14:3; 16:2; 18:3). The enforced absence of a Davidide from the throne of Jerusalem during the reign of Athaliah (chap. 11) betrays many similarities to the presentation of David's rise to power, and it has frequently been acknowledged that over the reign and reform of Josiah was cast a great shadow—that of David. On this see Cross, *Canaanite Myth and Hebrew Epic*, 283–84.

The second theme under discussion is more overt and has been the occasion for much discussion because it seems to contradict what is seen to be a major optimistic thrust to the book. The events in the history of both Israel and Judah which have the potential of redemption are colored by the presence of ultimate failure. The reform of Jehu, which began as an attempt to restore the northern kingdom to Yahweh, eventually founders because Jehu cannot follow the law (10:28–31). The result is a limited dynasty which will eventually die out. The restoration of the Davidic dynasty in the south, with the coronation of Jehoash (chap. 12) ends in near disaster when the very innovations of temple financing inaugurated by the king are used to pay off a foreign invader (12:17–18). The reform of Hezekiah, a promising king, which reaches a climax with the deliverance of Jerusalem from the Assyrians (chap. 18–19), ends with the king foolishly displaying the temple and palace treasures to the acquisitive eyes of a Babylonian pretender (20:12–19). The point is stressed in the prophetic condemnation of the action. Finally, the reign and reform of Josiah, which is undoubtedly a dramatic climax in the course of the narrative, ends with the untimely and unnecessary death of the king at Megiddo. Again, the comment of the author stresses the point (23:28–30).

The consistent nature of this pattern in 2 Kings, and also in 1 Kings, demonstrates that it is neither an accident nor a cause for speculation about primary and secondary material in the present book. It is a convention used by the author, the effect of which is to remind the reader of the inevitability of judgment.

Within the stories of Elisha (chaps. 2–8; 13) there are also a number of items of style that warrant brief notice. As with the kings, one model dominates the traditions concerning Elijah and Elisha. That model is Moses. This is nowhere more evident than in the transition from the ministry of Elijah to Elisha in chaps. 1–2. The narrative is so constructed as to present a smooth transition from one to the other, but the narrative is also dominated by allusions to incidents from the career of Moses, and indeed Joshua. This is especially clear in the location of the ascension of Elijah and the actions which accompany that ascension.

Repetition also plays an important role in the stories. Moreover, the repetition is of a particular kind. Events and series of events take place in threes. In chap. 1 the judgment on Ahaziah is found three times, but within this story is another which tells of three attempts to arrest the prophet. In chap. 2, Elisha is reminded three times that his master will leave him and he is also instructed to leave his master. He responds abruptly to the reminders and steadfastly refuses to leave Elijah. In chap. 4 three attempts are made to raise the dead boy, and in chap. 9 three scouts are sent out to the approaching rebels headed by Jehu. Such threefold repetition is not accidental, but deliberate, and is a common feature of folk literature, offering a rhythm to such stories. Always, on the third "beat," the story comes to some kind of conclusion.

Our writer also plays with words with great effect. In chap. 5, in the story of Naaman, there is a play on the Hebrew sounds *ka-ra*, which can be translated in a variety of ways depending on the context and precise spelling (see 5:5–8). Deliberate spelling mistakes or clumsy grammatical forms are not to be seen as evidence of poor language skills on the part of the writer, but add a certain amount of color to the narrative. For example, 1:2 contains an awkward expression (אם־אחיה מחלי זה) "whether I shall recover from this illness," which most commentators try to emend to the more correct אם אחיה מחליי הזה. But exactly the same expression occurs in remarkably similar circumstances in 8:8. The difference is that whereas in 1:2 an Israelite seeks healing from a foreign god, in 8:8 a foreign king seeks healing from Yahweh. The link between the two is established by the same "marker," the grammatically imperfect questions of the kings. It is important to note also that all expressions of this kind are in direct speech. In chap. 4 an awkward and frequent addition of the *yodh* to feminine participles is a possible sign of a northern dialect, and in chap. 9 the very awkward language of the watchman, a frequent candidate for emendation, is a delightful touch. It is precisely the kind of tortured language one might expect from an uneducated private soldier.

Broader devices, such as drama and comedy, are very much a part of the narrative of 2 Kings, and chaps. 6–7 even approach farce. Woven through the narrative is the standard convention of the creation of a tension and the move toward the resolution of that tension, which is the structure of all good tales. Throughout the *Commentary*, these and many other devices are noted, but the above summary is sufficient to show that the writer of 2 Kings was an artist in the fullest sense of the word. His skill in language is unquestioned. The conventions he uses are not those of the modern writer, but they are nevertheless conventions to be recognized, examined, understood, and enjoyed.

2 KINGS AND HISTORY

Bibliography

Bloch, M. *The Historian's Craft.* Tr. P. Putnam. New York: Knopf, 1953. **Bright, J.** *A History of Israel.* 3rd ed. Philadelphia: Westminster Press, 1981. **Dentan, R. C.**, ed. *The Idea of History in the Ancient Near East.* New Haven, CT: Yale University Press, 1955. **Donner, H.** "The Separate States of Israel and Judah." In *Israelite and Judean History.* Ed. J. H. Hayes and J. M. Miller. Philadelphia: Westminster Press, 1977. **Gay, P.** *Style in History.* New York: McGraw-Hill, 1974. **Harvey, V. A.** *The Historian and the Believer: The Morality of Historical Knowledge and Christian Belief.* New York: Macmillan, 1966. **Herrmann, S.** *A History of Israel in Old Testament Times.* Tr. J. Bowden. London: SCM, 1975. ———. *Time and History.* Tr. J. L. Blevins. Nashville: Abingdon, 1977. **Jagersma, H.** *A History of Israel in the Old Testament Period.* Tr. J. Bowden. Philadelphia: Fortress Press, 1983. **Renier, G. J.** *History, Its Purpose and Method.* New York: Harper Torchbooks, 1950 (1965). **Seters, J. van.** *In Search of History: Historiography in the Ancient World and the Origins of Biblical History.* New Haven: Yale University Press, 1983.

This is not the place to enter into a detailed discussion on the nature of "history." Nevertheless it is appropriate to spend some time in reflection on the genre of material found in 2 Kings. In the light of the above comments on the literary sophistication of the writer, a possible conflict emerges between the two roles of the book—good prose fiction and yet history. In fact, Alter accepts such a distinction and opts for the former as a suitable definition of biblical narrative in general. Miscall, in his concentration on the "close reading" of the text, sets aside the question, and Licht attempts a synthesis of the two. Such a distinction, however, cannot be pressed too far. Historians have been known to be good writers, and while a modern novelist is careful about matters of style, the subject matter of the finished product might well be historical event.

Any attempt at a definition of history is problematic, and working definitions abound. One must be careful not to superimpose modern views of knowledge, the relationship between "fiction" and "non-fiction," and philosophical presuppositions informed by modern experience upon the ancient writer. At times the ancient writers adopt attitudes and agendas that are embarrassing in their simplicity and that border on propaganda. For example, the self-imposed limitations on the writer of the Gospel of John (John 20:31) betray a clearly evangelistic purpose to which the reader must respond with his or her whole being and not the intellect alone. To force such works into narrowly defined categories of history is to do them a disservice and to miss the main point of their production. The whole matter is extremely complex, and the lines drawn by modern critics between what happened, what was seen to have happened, and what was recorded to have happened, while real, are often blurred and difficult to detect. In the case of 2 Kings the problem is particularly acute. While it is customary to call this material "History" and to assign it to the "historical books" of the Old Testament, one must never lose sight of the fact that its initial designation was as part of the "Former Prophets." Prophecy is overtly an interpretive art. The term is important.

John van Seters (*In Search of History*, 4–5) has provided a helpful set of criteria with which one can identify history-writing in the OT. The list is here repeated in full;

1. History writing is a specific form of tradition in its own right. Any explanation of the genre as merely the accidental accumulation of traditional material is inadequate.
2. History writing is not primarily the accurate reporting of past events. It also considers the reasons for recalling the past and the significance given to past events.
3. History writing examines the causes of the present conditions and circumstances. In antiquity these causes are primarily moral—who is responsible for certain states of affairs?
4. History writing is national or corporate in character.
5. History writing is part of the literary tradition and plays a significant role in the corporate tradition of the people.

As a working definition, the five points are adequate, but they are not likely to meet with universal approval. Alter's approach to the OT is different, as we have noted. The notion of "history" as a distinct genre is helpful, but limited. It does not allow for the conventions of imitation of form and style. And the alternative van Seters establishes—that the traditions were accumulated accidentally—is hardly a fair one. The second point raises an even more sensitive issue. History, even the dullest, is a matter of interpretation. It is an attempt to find in an event or series of events meaning that will fall within the world-view of the intended readers. It is essentially a task of synthesis and integration, and at times meanings which were not immediately apparent to the original participants will be found in events. A serious question is, how far can this license be taken? Deliberate distortion of events, if it is found within the biblical material, raises serious questions for the believer.

In reading 2 Kings one must avoid coming to the material with a desire to see rigid chronological sequences of events, as though that constituted history. It does not. The frequent shifts back and forth in time, which are dictated more by a thematic approach than chronological interest, ought to be noted. Numerous histories of Israel attempt such a historical reconstruction of events but are frequently frustrated by the shape of the extant biblical material and see it as a major stumbling block in the way of this task. See the comments of J. Bright, *A History of Israel* (3rd ed.) 67.

The dichotomy between literary artistry and history is a false one, although a common one. Good history is not an exact representation of the past. It is that and more. Good history has a resounding impact upon society because it is well presented, and because it dares to present truth as forcefully as possible. "The historian's use of elevated diction, compression or elongation of time spans, synecdoche, anaphora, indirect free style, or whatever devices he may use, perform (*sic*) reportorial functions. To use words for their own sake, to make jokes that are not instrumental to the presentation, to employ emphasis in the interests of drama not inherent in the material, are sheer self-indulgence, mere fine writing" (Gay, *Style in History*, 216).

However, when one turns from a consideration of our writer as an artist to our writer as a historian of craft and skill, one encounters some interesting phenomena. Critical historical scholarship would demand that some attention be paid to the author's use of sources. Our writer is notoriously selective in his use of sources. The notes he appends to his accounts of the reigns of kings of Israel and Judah, to the effect that additional material can be found in the court records, are less than helpful. He is controlled by the principle of selectivity to such a degree that the full amount of historical data one can gather from his accounts of the reigns of the kings—apart from the synchronizations, etc.—is very little indeed. What did Josiah do for the rest of his reign? The reform, which is the focal point of our writer's attention, took place in a segment of the king's eighteenth year. Little else is offered. Chronicles provides additional material on the reigns of Manasseh, Hezekiah, and Josiah, all of which our writer did not include. In the interests of full historical investigation we are forced to turn to inferences drawn from the Book of Amos for a fuller account of the reign of Jeroboam II, which our writer fails to supply.

Without a doubt our writer used sources of some kind. Since the scope of his work is so large—Israel from conquest to exile—he was dependent upon records of events and recollections of events that he did not witness. Traditional OT scholarship has insisted upon collections of "legends" connected with the careers of Elijah and Elisha. (For precise definitions, see Burke O. Long, *1 Kings*, FOTL, vol. 9 [1984] 257–58.) These legends or stories have been divided into two separate sources, those which deal with prophet and kings, and those which deal with prophet and commoners. The source of these stories is regarded as the circle of disciples who followed the prophets. But that is obvious enough not to need stating, although the division between the two groups of stories is not as clear-cut as one might be led to expect.

From the reigns of the kings, various materials would have been available to the writer. Apart from the records to which he refers, there are other sources. The details of the various temple reforms (chaps. 12; 18–20; 22–23) betray all the signs of careful bureaucratic records that reflect accurately the measure of innovation that occurred at various times throughout the monarchy. Campaign records provide an additional source of information of the battles between Israel and Judah and their neighbors, and at times the writer lapses into the use of military jargon (8:20–22; 10:12–17). On the other hand, the accounts of the humiliation of the failure of the joint venture to subdue Moab (chap. 3), of the rapid rise of Jehu in chaps. 9–10, and of the downfall of Athaliah in chap. 11, all of which are highly critical of many of the leading actors, have the appearance of eyewitness descriptions of the events. For a recent attempt to delineate the sources of the deuteronomistic history, see van Seters, *In Search of History*, 291–321.

From these diverse sources of information, our writer has crafted a story in which he offers reasons for the events of the past. He lays blame, he offers praise, he comments, and at times he preaches to uncover the truth of the exile. He is an editor in the sense that he carefully selects his material and shapes it to his purpose. But above all he is an author who is burdened by a multiple responsibility. He is responsible to the facts he reports not to distort them; he is responsible to his readers to offer them a coherent and meaningful narrative; he is also responsible to the future Israel that they may read and learn from the past. Above all, he is responsible to God, whose hand he has seen in the past events and whose word he now delivers.

The Milieu and Thought of 2 Kings

Bibliography

Ackroyd, P. R. *Exile and Restoration: A Study of Hebrew Thought of the Sixth Century* b.c. London: SCM, 1968. **Carroll, R. P.** *From Chaos to Covenant: Prophecy in the Book of Jeremiah.* New York: Crossroads, 1981. **Douglas, M.** *Natural Symbols: Explorations in Cosmology.* Harmondsworth: Penguin Books, 1970. **Heschel, A.** *The Prophets.* 2 vols. New York: Harper Torchbooks, 1961 (1969). **Klein, R. W.** *Israel in Exile: A Theological Interpretation.* Philadelphia: Fortress Press, 1979. **Mol, H.** *Meaning and Place: An Introduction to the Social Scientific Study of Religion.* New York: The Pilgrim Press, 1983. **Nicholson, E. W.** *Deuteronomy and Tradition.* Oxford: Blackwells, 1962. **Raitt, T. M.** *A Theology of Exile: Judgment/Deliverance in Jeremiah and Ezekiel.* Philadelphia: Fortress Press, 1977. **von Rad, G.** *Studies in Deuteronomy.* Tr. D. Stalker. SBT 9. London: SCM Press, 1953. **Shils, E.** *Center and Periphery: Essays in Macrosociology.* Chicago: University of Chicago Press, 1968. **Thiel, W.** *Die deuteronomischtische Redaktion von Jeremia 1–25.* WMANT 41. Neukirchen: Verlag des Erziehungsvereins, 1973. **Weinfeld, M.** *Deuteronomy and the Deuteronomic School.* Oxford: Oxford University Press, 1972.

2 Kings, with the rest of the deuteronomistic history, was written in Babylon shortly after the release of Jehoiachin from prison in 560 b.c. This much is evident from 25:27–30, and comparison with Jer 52:31–34 would suggest that, when the historian wrote, the king was still alive. It seems most plausible to hold that the work is a product of the exiles in Babylon, Noth's theory of a Palestinian origin notwithstanding. For Noth's viewpoint, see his *Überlieferungsgeschichtliche Studien,* and for a discussion on the origin see Ackroyd, *Exile and Restoration,* 65–67. If these assumptions of date and place are correct, the writer worked during a time which was a period for Judah both of intense political and social turmoil and of creative literary activity.

The conditions of the exile can be partly reconstructed from available sources and partly inferred from contemporary documents. In Judah, as our writer so clearly informs us, the city of Jerusalem, with its temple and houses of note, had been destroyed by the Babylonians. This action was precipitated by the unnecessary rebellion of Zedekiah against the Babylonians (2 Kgs 24:20–25:7). As a result, not only was the capital city destroyed, but any connection with the Davidic lineage on the part of the rulers of Judah was severed by the installation of Gedaliah, a member of the civil service, as governor (25:22–26). The complete breakdown in order, illustrated by the assassination of Gedaliah, was symptomatic of the severe crisis that faced the Judeans who remained in Judah, as well as those who had been deported to Babylon. The temple was no more, the king was in exile, and a monarchical society that lacked such important symbolic centers was doomed to chaos.

More than a political disaster, the loss of temple, city, land, and king was a serious religious and theological crisis for the exiles. Each of the items lost represented a form of the concrete assurance of God's election of Israel and his presence with her. The land was a gift of God. The city was the dwelling-place of God (Pss 2; 48). The king was a living representation of God's grace (Pss 110; 132; 2 Sam 7). All were now lost, and with them the visible symbols of the ordering of Judean society under God. Without such centers the people lacked cohesion, and without a land it could be argued that the people lacked an identity.

But, remarkable though it seems, the exile did not signify the end of the people of God. The people survived, albeit in a markedly different form; but they nevertheless survived. A new focus was found for the religious center of their lives. The hope of the return from exile remained alive, and a considerable number of creative persons emerged from the exile to interpret the past events for the people of God and to fuel their hopes for restoration. Among them were prophets like Ezekiel, Deutero-Isaiah, and the later producers of the Book of Jeremiah, the later editors of the Pentateuch, the Chronicler, and most important for our purposes, the writer of the deuteronomistic history. (For a general survey of the period, see Ackroyd, *Exile and Restoration;* Klein, *Israel in Exile: A Theological Interpretation;* Raitt, *A Theology of Exile;* and Carroll, *From Chaos to Covenant.*) The task of these writers and thinkers was to interpret the past in the light of the collective experience of the people and to integrate the two. In so doing they constructed a platform of a different shape upon which the future could be built.

But for our purposes, how can this be more sharply focused in such a way as to provide an outline of the major orientation of 2 Kings? In his picture of the past, what ideals are cherished as those necessary for the restoration, and, more importantly, why? As a general and sound observation, it can be said that for those living in times of insecurity and instability, order becomes exceedingly attractive (see Mol, *Meaning and Place,* 111). The Exile was a time of such disorder. The people of Judah had suffered a forced removal from their sacred land and a subsequent loss of identity which was reinforced by the destruction of many central symbols of their world. One might expect then that the literature of such a period would exhibit a stronger interest in order, conformity, and social solidarity. These values are certainly evident in 2 Kings.

To assist us further in this brief investigation, we shall borrow a model from the work of the cultural anthropologist Mary Douglas. Douglas offers a graph of two intersecting lines, one horizontal and the other vertical. On the horizontal axis she plots the amount of pressure exerted upon an individual in a given society. The axis is a continuum from zero upward. Along the vertical axis she plots the relative amounts of shared classifications in a society. Zero on this axis would be an individual completely isolated and alienated from his fellows. The higher the score, the greater is the correspondence between an individual's system of classification and that of the group of which he is a member. For convenience, the horizontal axis is labeled "group," and the vertical "grid." (See Douglas, *Natural Symbols: Explorations in Cosmology*, 81-85.)

Douglas's theory is that the relative position in which a group or society can be located on the graph indicates the group's understanding of several general concepts (purity, ritual, personal identity, body, sin, cosmology, and suffering). Of course, such a model is by nature a general pattern constructed out of the detailed analysis of many specific societies. Although it is in this form highly abstract, it can be concretely applied. It is a tool for analysis, and its verification comes from its suitability to specific cases. In this case, the model proves most helpful.

A simple illustration is provided to show how the model works. A society identified as "weak group-low grid" would be one in which fragmentation would be the order of the day. Group pressure to conform would be minimal, and individual systems of classification would abound and be unshared. Such a society or group would be very difficult to conceive since its main characteristic would be anarchy. At the other end of the scale, a "strong group-high grid" society would be one like the military where uniformity to established ideals is demanded and nonconformity is not tolerated. Modern North American society (itself a generalization) would be classified on the graph as "weak group-high grid" because of its widely accepted ideal of individual freedom. Whatever the reality of the situation in detail, the larger model does serve as a convenient conceptual framework within which societies can be examined.

In a situation like the Exile, where central symbols have been destroyed and the continuation of a society's life is seriously threatened, one might expect the elevation of order. (On the concepts of "center" and "periphery," see Shils, *Center and Periphery*, 93-109.) In the interests of survival there would be strong pressure to conform, but the immediate experience of the Exile would not correspond entirely to the society's patterns of perception and evaluation. Out of this latter fact comes the literature of confusion and despair which was also current during and after the exile (see Lamentations, Ps 89, etc.) Broadly speaking, then, one would expect a society within which and for which the writer of 2 Kings wrote to fall into the general classification of "strong group-low grid." The general concepts seen by Douglas as characteristic of such groups are most enlightening:

a. Purity—strong concern for purity but the inside of the social and physical body is under attack; pollution is present and purification rituals are ineffective.
b. Ritual—a society of fixed rituals; ritual is focused on group boundaries with great concern to expel pollutants from the social body; fluid sacred place.
c. Personal identity—located in group membership, not in the internalization of roles, which are confused; distinction between appearance and internal state, dyadic.
d. Body—social and physical bodies are tightly controlled but under attack; invaders have broken through bodily boundaries; not a symbol of life.
e. Sin—a matter of pollution; evil is lodged within the individual and society; sin is much like a disease deriving from the social structure; internal state of being is more important than adherence to formal rules, but the latter are still valid.

f. Cosmology—anthropomorphic; dualistic; warring forces of good and evil; universe is not just and may be whimsical; personal causality.
g. Suffering and misfortune—unjust; not automatic punishment; attributed to malevolent forces—may be alleviated but not eliminated.

Within this cultural context there is room for creativity. If this were not so then there would be no room for change. No writer should be regarded merely as a "product of his time," although there is certainly a great deal of truth in that cliché. The relationship of a society and its shared concepts to a creative individual within that society is a delicate one and at times indefinable. Bach is clearly a Baroque composer, yet to limit one's description of him to that categorization is to miss so much of his musical genius. Artists, be they writers, painters, or musicians, demand room to question as well as to affirm, to challenge as well as to encourage. They do not always conform. This is certainly true of the writer of 2 Kings. If the above list bears any resemblance to the reality of the Judean Exile, then he does not conform to it entirely, although he does share some of the fundamental attitudes reflected in the list. By comparing 2 Kings to the list, what is seen is that, if anything, he tends to be more conservative on those points where he departs from the model. In his attempt to reconstruct order out of chaos, he tends to be backward-looking.

From within the book we can extract many sentiments which echo the general concepts listed above. On the question of purity (a), the body (d), and sin (e) there is a large amount of correspondence. As the king's person symbolizes the nation and its fate, so often does the king's physical body become a more precise symbol. The health of the king reflects the health of the nation, and a constant theme running through the book is that of sickness-healing, especially of royal figures. The book begins with Ahaziah, sick and seeking aid from a foreign god. He is warned of his impending death. This incident takes place within the context of the deterioration of Israel, begun now with the rebellion of Moab. A clever balance in the first two chapters juxtaposes the death of the king with the "healing" of the waters at Jericho. Similarly, Hezekiah's sickness, which receives a temporary remission, corresponds to the delay in the final judgment on the nation (20:1–11).

Closely connected with this notion is that of sin as pollution, i.e., invasion from outside the social and physical body. Limits then become important, since limits not only define the extent of the body, but strong limits protect. Leprosy, a skin ailment, features in a number of incidents. Hezekiah suffers from a skin sore. This attack on the royal physical body is balanced by frequent attacks on the territorial limits of both Israel and Judah. This is seen as judgment. Judah loses Edom and Libnah. Israel loses Moab, Gilead, and Galilee. And both are repeatedly invaded by Syria, Egypt, Assyria, and eventually Babylon. At each point, limits are broken down and the attack moves further into the social body. On this theme, see Douglas, *Purity and Danger*.

On the question of ritual, surprisingly little is said in 2 Kings. A Passover celebration is mentioned in connection with the reform of Josiah (23:21–

23), but little else, apart from the occasional reference to sacrifice. The writer's position on ritual must be inferred more from the negative stance he adopts toward Canaanite practices than from any clear description of what he would like to see in its place. But perhaps this is sufficient. For him it is clear that there is only one way to worship Yahweh, and that way (by implication) is in accordance with the deuteronomic law. Expulsion of pollutants, in the light of the reforms of Jehu, Hezekiah, and Josiah, is clearly high on his agenda.

Personal identity is most certainly a matter of group membership. The writer exhibits a strong sense of Israel and Judah as one people of God, under one law, and bound by one covenant. All, king and commoner alike, are subject to this law, and the consistent standard of behavior he applies is that of the law in Deuteronomy. Out of this interest emerge his ideal models of behavior. The prophet is a true prophet insofar as he conforms to the model of Moses, the archetype, and the king is a true king insofar as he conforms to the model of David, the archetype, who followed the law. These characters are not individualistic heroes but true examples of absolute conformity.

It is in the matters of cosmology and sin and punishment that our writer parts company with the model. The consistent role played by the prophet and the word in the history of the nation (see von Rad, *Studies in Deuteronomy*, 74–91), together with the intimate connection established at the outset between this word and the misfortunes of Israel and Judah, demonstrates that the history of the two nations, even toward decline and exile, is not out of control but is unfolding as an expression of the will of God. The universe, if such can be conceived by the writer, is entirely just. Therefore suffering and misfortune are not accidental or the result of caprice. Instead, Israel and Judah are punished for wrongdoing. That wrongdoing is given explicit form in the breaking of the law of Moses. At times the punishment is delayed (8:19; 13:14–19; 14:25–27; 17:18; 20:1–11), but the delay is never interpreted as the result of force of circumstance. It is an expression of God's patience for his own sake or for the sake of his servant, David. Conversely, even the actions of a good king like Josiah are not sufficient to avert the inevitable judgment (23:26–27).

The theological point thus made is important. On the model of Douglas, the writer shows a distinct affinity with the "strong group–high grid" quadrant, which is a move towards stability and order. Theologically it is an attempt by the writer to integrate the experience of exile with Israel's understanding of her history. Incorporated into the past "great acts" of God is now the judgment upon Israel and Judah for apostasy. It was not an abandonment by God. That God himself was active in the Exile alone gives hope for the future. If God were seen to be not in control of history then despair would be a legitimate response to the recent events. In the words of one scholar:

> The task of the hour was for Israel . . . to acknowledge God's justice, to listen to his voice, and to do his law. And then, though Dtr even in its final form is short on details, Israel could hope that Yahweh, in his unpredictable freedom would act as Savior once more (Klein, *Israel in Exile*, 43).

Questions of a "positive" or "negative" outlook of the writer which were raised by Noth's important study of the deuteronomistic history, and which have been debated ever since, are misdirected without two important qualifications. First, although the precise relationship of the history to the prose passages of the book of Jeremiah is much discussed, and not yet fully understood, the relationship exists and is a close one. To a large extent they share the same language, the same style, and the same narrative interests and theological preferences. (On this in much more detail, see Weinfeld, *Deuteronomy and the Deuteronomic School*, and Thiel, *Die deuteronomistische Redaktion von Jeremia 1–25*, among many others.) In keeping with the traditional genre of a prophetic book, Jeremiah in its present form offers plenty of hope for the future. The oracles of judgment (1–25) are followed by oracles of hope (30–33), biographical narratives which also offer some hope (34–45), and oracles against the enemies of Israel and Judah (46–51) in which a strong message of hope can be heard. The book is a product of deuteronomists who have reworked the traditions of the prophet to support the themes to be found in the history. (On this see Nicholson, *Preaching to the Exiles*, and Carroll, *From Chaos to Covenant: Prophecy in the Book of Jeremiah*.) The book then provides a concluding chapter to the work of the deuteronomist, which began with the present form of Deuteronomy.

Second, one must be careful to see "positive" and "negative" solely in terms of the survival of institutions such as monarchy, city, temple, sacrifice, etc. Nor should one expect the writer to answer some of the questions put to him by the twentieth-century historian. Noth's insistence that the historian answer the question why he did not include a more fully developed image of the future is such a question. In the situation current at the Exile, the theological affirmation that Israel and Judah were in exile as a result of God's punishment of their sin is a profound one. The "anger" of God was roused and nothing could abate it. The alternative to such an "angry" God is, as Heschel has argued, an apathetic one, untouched by the breakdown of the order established by Moses (see Heschel, *The Prophets*, 2:59–86). The writer is not content to leave matters there. Instead he offers a firm platform upon which others could build.

2 KINGS AND OLD TESTAMENT CHRONOLOGY

Bibliography

Andersen, K. T. "Die Chronologie der Könige von Israel und Juda." *ST* 23 (1969) 69–112. **Albright, W. F.** *Archaeology and the Religion of Israel*. 4th ed. Baltimore: Johns Hopkins, 1942. **Begrich, J.** *Die Chronologie der Könige von Israel und Judah und die Quellen des Rahmens des Königsbucher*. Tübingen: Mohr, 1929. **Campbell, E. F. and Freedman, D. N.** "The Chronology of Israel and the Ancient Near East." In *The Bible and the Ancient Near East: Essays in Honor of William Foxwell Albright*. Ed. G. E. Wright. Garden City, NY: Doubleday, 1961. **Finegan, J.** *A Handbook of Biblical Chronology*. Princeton: Princeton University Press, 1964. **Gibson, J. C. L.** *Textbook of Syrian Semitic Inscriptions. Hebrew and Moabite Inscriptions*. Vol. 1. Oxford: Clarendon Press, 1971. **Grayson, A. K.** *Texts from Cuneiform Sources: Assyrian and Babylonian Chronicles*. Vol. 5. Locust Valley, NY: J. J. Augustin, 1975. **Hall, E. T.** *The Dance of Life: The Other Dimension of Time*. Garden

City, NY: Doubleday, 1983. **Jepsen, A.** "Noch einmal zur israelitsiche-jüdischen Chronologie." *VT* 18 (1968) 31–46. **Kitchen, K. A.** "Late Egyptian Chronology and the Hebrew Monarchy." *JANESCU* 5 (1973) 225–33. **Klein, R. W.** "New Evidence for an Old Recension of Reigns." *HTR* 60 (1967) 93–105. **Kutsch, E.** "Zur Chronologie der letzen jüdaischen Könige (Josia bis Zedekia)." *ZAW* 71 (1959) 270–74. **Larsson, G.** "Is Biblical Chronology Systematic or Not?" *RevQ* 6 (1969) 499–515. **Luckenbill, D. D.** *Ancient Records of Assyria and Babylonia.* 2 vols. Chicago: University of Chicago Press, 1926–27. **Miller J. M.** "Another Look at the Chronology of the Early Divided Monarchy." *JBL* 86 (1967) 276–88. **Meer, P. van der.** *The Chronology of Ancient Western Asia and Egypt.* 2nd ed. Leiden: E. J. Brill, 1963. **Oates, J.** "Assyrian Chronology 631–612 B.C." *Iraq* 27 (1965) 135–59. **Shenkel, J. D.** *Chronology and Recensional Development in the Greek Text of Kings.* HSM 1. Cambridge, MA: Harvard University Press, 1968. **Thiele, E. R.** *The Mysterious Numbers of the Hebrew Kings.* Rev. ed. Grand Rapids: Eerdmans, 1983.

No problem associated with 2 Kings, and indeed the OT in its entirety, is more complicated than that of chronology, that is, the placing of events recorded in the OT in their proper sequence and assigning them their proper moment in the broader history of the ANE. In books which have their own internal chronologies (e.g., Exodus), but which contain little or no reference to other known events, the problem is serious. However, even in those books of the OT that do contain a large number of events datable by our exacting contemporary standards and allusions and direct references to events in other countries, the problem is not lessened. Into this latter category falls 2 Kings. Even to the casual reader it is clear that the author works within a certain chronological framework. The repeated synchronizations between rulers of Israel and Judah illustrate this well. There are also references to rulers of other lands, such as Mesha, Ben Hadad, Hazael, Tiglath Pileser, Shalmaneser, Sennacherib, and Nebuchadrezzar, but only rarely is there precise synchronization with events from their reigns (e.g., 25:8, 27).

Externally there is an increasing amount of data from contemporary sources which aid in the chronological endeavor. For 2 Kings an alternative account exists for the events described in chap. 3, namely, the Moabite Stone (for a commentary on the stone see Gibson, *Syrian Semitic Inscriptions* 1:71–83). Campaign records of Shalmaneser, Tiglath Pileser, and Sennacherib, among others, exist (see Luckenbill, *Ancient Records of Assyria and Babylonia*, 2 vols.) as well as chronicles from Babylon (see Grayson, *Assyrian and Babylonian Chronicles*). Matters of interpretation remain on many points, such as the order and dating of the Assyrian invasions into the Levant during the reign of Tiglath Pileser III, and this means that the problems of chronology are compounded by these sources as much as helped.

In any study of a book which has traditionally been classified as "history," such as 2 Kings, matters of chronology are important, but the study of chronology often tends to be overladen with as many modern philosophical and cultural presuppositions as any other historical critical discipline. When approaching an ancient text one must be careful to appreciate the full scope (or perhaps it is better to say the limited scope) of the work. For 2 Kings the scope is certainly not international politics, and there is a paucity of references to other nations of the ANE. They are brought into the story only insofar as they impinge directly on the fortunes of Israel and Judah. The fates and fortunes of Tyre, Syria, Moab, Ammon, and Philistia do not provide the framework within which our writer sees the history of Israel and Judah. They are mentioned only incidentally as their fortunes either reflect or affect that history. There is no concept in the mind of the writer of an international political context within which the history of his nation must be seen. It might be implied, but it is not a major item. Yet one of the important presuppositions of the modern historian is that this history makes sense only in such a context. This presupposition is most evident in John Bright's grand work, *A History of Israel.*

Even in the use of non-Israelite events in the history our writer is not consistent. There are some remarkable omissions. What modern historian would omit any reference to the battle of Karkar (853 B.C.) in his presentation of ninth century B.C. Palestine? Yet our writer does just that, in spite of the known participation of Ahab in the battle. It is from Assyrian sources, not biblical ones, that we are informed of Jehu's submission to Shalmaneser III of Assyria (see *ANEP*, pl. 351). Our writer deems the details of the conversation surrounding Jehu's approach to Jezreel (9:17–20) to be more important for his story. Similarly, it is from an alternative source (2 Chr 33:10–33) that we learn of an important journey of Manasseh to Assyria to give an account of himself before his Assyrian overlord. The perspective of the writer of 2 Kings is different from that of the modern investigator. This fact alone, of course, does not mean that investigation of history or chronology is unimportant, or that our writer was sloppy about the details of what he did include in his work, but it does mean that the modern historical investigator must reckon with frustration at many turns.

Another important point to bear in mind is the different understandings of time which the modern has when compared to the ancient writer. This is not so much a philosophical one as a cultural one. The understanding of time with which the nonsophisticated Western person works is quite different from that of the skilled ancient writer. This is not a judgment upon the relative values of each understanding, but simply a statement of fact. In an age of digital watches which provide the average wearer with a highly formal, almost technical use of time, seconds can be split by the schoolboy with the press of an electronic button. (The terms "formal" and "technical" are borrowed here from Hall, *The Dance of Life: The Other Dimension of Time.*) Against this background, it is difficult to appreciate fully that the word for "hour" does not occur in the Hebrew Bible, although it does appear in the later Aramaic of Dan 3:6. The smallest unit of formal time with which the ancient had to work was the day, but it was a day framed within the availability or nonavailability of light, not a day of twenty-four hours. Within the day, activity took place such as sacrifices, rising, eating, working, and other daily functions. Anything smaller than the day is referred to solely in terms of the length of a given activity. In 2 Kings the closest one comes to a more formal division of time below that of the day is the rhythm of the change of temple guards in chap. 11. Life and its rhythm are determined more by the activities done, the tasks accomplished and their quality, rather than by hours, minutes, and seconds. Timetables, which determine transport schedules, class allotments, and a host of other activities that are part and parcel of Western life, were completely beyond the experience of the ancient Israelite or Judean.

This has led in 2 Kings to a greater stress upon what happens and the general characterization of what happens rather than on the precise location of an event in a larger time frame. The reform of Josiah, for example, began at a very specific time in the reign of the king, but its exact duration is not given. Presumably it took a matter of weeks, but that is not important. Another example of this is the use of very general temporal expressions to preface important events in the reigns of certain kings. The revolt of Edom from Judah (8:20), the invasion of Tiglath Pileser (15:29), the Egyptian incursion along the coastal plain during the reign of Josiah (23:29), and the Babylonian attack on Judah (24:1) are events of great national and international importance. Each one is introduced with the very vague statement "In his days. . . ." Precision is completely lacking. But on examination it is clear that the point being made is that the reigns of the various kings concerned were a time of invasion, of loss of territory, and therefore judgment. To alert the reader to this, the writer uses this general temporal expression. It is of course on these hints at synchronization with international events that the student of chronology will concentrate.

It cannot be ignored that the writer of 2 Kings did use chronological annotations. Kings of Judah and Israel are frequently synchronized. It then follows that if fixed dates can be found to pin down one or more of these kings to definite times in ANE history, then a reasonably accurate chronology of the monarchy in Israel and Judah can be established. It appears to be a matter of simple addition and subtraction. But the matter, on closer examination, proves to be far from that simple. Let us look at some illustrations of the initial difficulties.

Even within the present Hebrew text some of the reigns of the kings are difficult to calculate. For most of the kings the length of a reign is given in years. This means that the smallest unit of time with which the writer works in his record of the kings presents a problem. No king is considerate enough to die on New Year's Eve, so at times there is the possibility of overlap in the reckoning of the lengths of reigns, and at others of a shortfall. If one resorts to the simple task of adding the numbers of years given for successive kings in Judah, and then compares this with a similar total for Israel, the two rarely fit. For example, 2 Kgs 8:16 indicates that Jehoram of Judah became king in the fifth year of his namesake, Jehoram of Israel. But this seems impossible when compared with other figures.

The first three kings in Judah after the death of Solomon were Rehoboam, Abijah, and Asa, who reigned for 17, 3, and 41 years respectively. The total is 61. Roughly contemporary with these kings are the first six kings of Israel, Jeroboam (22), Nadab (2), Baasha (24), Elah (2), Zimri (less than 1), and Omri (12). This is a total of 63, slightly larger than the total for their Judean contemporaries. This would suggest that Omri's successor, Ahab, began his reign after the death of Asa of Judah and early in the reign of Jehoshaphat. 1 Kgs 16:29 states that Ahab began to reign in the 38th year of Asa. G and G^L offer a variant (2nd year of Jehoshaphat), but the traditions part company at 1 Kgs 22:41 where the beginning of Jehoshaphat's reign is given as the

4th year of Ahab (MT, G) or the 11th year of Omri (G^L). The figures are not matching.

A number of differences between the various manuscript traditions make matters more difficult. In the various versions of 1 Kgs 15:1 the length of the reign of Abijah of Judah differs. MT states it was 3 years, G^{BL} have 6, and G^A lengthens it to 10. At 2 Kgs 8:16 MT and G^L give the length of the reign of Jehoram of Judah as 8 years. G^{AB} raise the number to 40. One possible explanation of this is that somewhere in the transmission of G the age of the king at his accession, 32, was added to the original length of his reign, making a total of 40. In this case the explanation is plausible but cannot be applied indiscriminately. A final example of variants is 2 Kgs 15:23 where MT and G^B give Pekahiah's reign as 2 years, whereas G^{AL} offer 10.

Not all of the problems of Israelite and Judean chronology have to do with the different textual traditions or with the comparative chronologies of Israel and Judah. For example, 2 Kgs 1:17–18 states that Jehoram of Israel began his reign in the second year of the reign of his namesake, Jehoram of Israel. 2 Kgs 3:1 alternatively states that Jehoram of Israel began his reign in the eighteenth year of Jehoshaphat, i.e., some nine years before. This would tend to be supported by 2 Kgs 8:16. G at this point omits the contradiction, so the problem is an internal Hebrew one. The oft-applied solution of positing a co-regency in cases like this is attractive, and a common device of Thiele, but it has serious limitations and, again, cannot be used without a great deal of care.

The above examples are representative of internal difficulties with the text, either in Greek or Hebrew. They can be classified as follows. First, there are difficulties over the use of the year as the smallest unit of time in the reckoning of the reigns of kings. Of course, there are some minor exceptions to this, such as the case with Jehoiachin. But the general pattern is to use the year. What then constitutes the first year of a king's reign? What is meant by the final "year" of a king's reign? In either case, is the year the first twelve months of the reign, or the first full year (New Year to New Year) of the reign? The matter is complicated further by the difficulty in determining when the year began. Second, the different textual traditions often disagree, and to complicate matters, different versions of one tradition (G) often disagree among themselves. Third, there are occasions, admittedly few, where the Hebrew text disagrees with itself.

The external difficulties have already been hinted at and revolve around the problem of interpreting accounts of events mentioned in the OT. Questions concerning nonbiblical texts are no less complicated than those of the biblical sources. For example, how literally can one understand the statement in the Moabite Stone (line 8) that Omri occupied Moab "forty years"? Mesha too uses the general, imprecise statement "In his/my days . . ." (lines 6–8) to characterize Omri's occupation of Moab and his own reign. Such an imprecise term seems to be a standard device of ancient semitic historiography.

Attempts at making sense of the chronology of 1–2 Kings have varied in design and result, but most are characterized by a serious grasp of the problems outlined above. On the matter of the understanding of the "year" in the book, the following ought to be noted.

Month reckoning in Israel can be seen in the Gezer Calendar, a document from approximately the eleventh century B.C. (For a translation and description, see Gibson, *Syrian Semitic Inscriptions* 1:1–4.) Twelve months of the agricultural year are listed, and certain activities associated with those months are given. Exod 13:4, which dates the passover in the month of Abib, corresponds to the seventh month of the calendar. However, Ziv (1 Kgs 6:1), Ethanim (1 Kgs 8:2), and Bul (1 Kgs 6:38) are the second, seventh, and eighth months respectively. The Babylonian calendar was organized as follows:

1. Abib (Nisan)	Mar/April
2. Ziv (Iyyar)	April/May
3. Sivan	May/June
4. Tammuz	June/July
5. Ab	July/Aug
6. Elul	Aug/Sep
7. Ethanim (Tishri)	Sep/Oct
8. Bul (Heshvan)	Oct/Nov
9. Kislev	Nov/Dec
10. Tebeth	Dec/Jan
11. Shebat	Jan/Feb
12. Adar	Feb/Mar

The difference between Abib reckoned as the first month and as the seventh month is caused by the difference in the dating of the New Year.

Added to this is the reckoning of the beginning of a reign. The method in Egypt was to count the accession year as the first of the new king, but also the last of the late king. This resulted in an extra year being added to the length of the reign. This system is known as the ante-dating system. The alternative (post-dating) system was to count the first full year (New Year to New Year) after the death of the previous king—complicated, of course, by the year beginning in either Tishri or Nisan. In general, the post-dating system was practiced throughout the rest of the ANE. Thiele (*The Mysterious Numbers of the Hebrew Kings*) argues that, in the early years of the divided monarchy (from Rehoboam to Jehoshaphat), Judah used the post-dating system, whereas Israel (from Jeroboam to Jehoahaz) used the ante-dating system. He further argues that, from Jehoash to Hoshea, Israel changed to the latter, whereas in Judah, between the reigns of Jehoram and Jehoash, the opposite was the case. Finally, from Amaziah to Zedekiah, Thiele posits the return to the postdating system in Judah.

This hypothesis certainly helps to clarify a number of possible contradictions and variant numbers, as Thiele's work demonstrates in great detail. However, it is offered as a working hypothesis to accommodate the obvious difficulties. On many points, where the figures still remain out of line, Thiele resorts to the theory of numerous co-regencies. On this point, in the *Commentary* we take issue with his method. The evidence for numerous co-regencies is lacking. Thiele's approach is gaining in popularity but is certainly not as solid as it might seem at first. While it does help preserve the integrity of the Hebrew text and provides a refreshing change from many of the conjectural emendations which have characterized other works on chronology (see

Albright, "The Chronology of the Divided Monarchy in Israel," *BASOR* 100 [1945] 16–22, and J. Begrich, *Die Chronologie der Konige von Israel und Juda*), it remains a hypothesis.

Thiele has been rightfully criticized for not taking seriously the textual variants in the books of Kings. This is certainly true of the earlier editions of his work, but it is partly dealt with in the latest edition. A work which takes the variants very seriously is that of J. D. Shenkel, *Chronology and Recensional Development in the Greek Text of Kings*. Shenkel argues for the superiority of the "proto-Lucianic" recension found in the minuscules boc_2e_2 on the matter of dating, especially in 1 Kings, but also in the early part of 2 Kings. The argument is carefully worked out and adds to the discussion a dimension that was lacking in many previous works, notably those of Albright and Thiele. But caution should be registered toward the thesis. It is based on the hypothesis of Cross and others on the development of Hebrew *Vorlage*, which are evident in various recensions of the Greek text. The theory has by no means received widespread acceptance, and in many places in the *Commentary* we enter into discussion with Shenkel.

THE TEXT OF 2 KINGS

Bibliography

Biblia Hebraica Stuttgartensia (BHS), ed. K. Elliger and W. Rudolph. Stuttgart: Deutsche Bibelstiftung, 1967/77. **Brooke, A. E.; MacLean, N.; and Thackeray, H. St. J.** *The Old Testament in Greek According to the Text of Codex Vaticanus.* Vol. 2. Cambridge: Cambridge University Press, 1930. **Burney, C. F.** *Notes on the Hebrew Text of the Books of Kings.* Oxford: Clarendon Press, 1903. **Cross, F. M.** "The History of the Biblical Text in the Light of the Discoveries in the Judean Desert." *HTR* 57 (1964) 281–99. **Ehrlich, A. B.** *Randglossen zum hebraischen Bibel: textkritisches, sprachlisches und sachliches.* 7 vols. Hildesheim: G. Olms, 1914 (1968). **Field, F.** *Origensis Hexapla.* Oxford: Oxford University Press, 1875. **Goshen-Gottstein, M.** "The Theory and Practice of Textual Criticism: The Text-critical use of the Septuagint." *Textus* 3 (1963) 130–58. **Jellicoe, S.** *The Septuagint and Modern Study.* Oxford: Oxford University Press, 1968. ———. *Studies in the Septuagint: Origins, Recensions and Interpretations.* New York: Ktav Publishing, 1974. **Kahle, P.** *The Cairo Geniza.* London: The British Academy, 1947. **Rahlfs, A.** *Septuaginta.* Stuttgart: Württembergische Bibelanstalt, 1935. **Tov, E.** *The Text-critical Use of the Septuagint in Biblical Research.* Jerusalem Biblical Studies 3. Jerusalem: Simor, 1981.

In the textual *Notes* which accompany the *Commentary* the reader will notice a conservatism in favor of the Hebrew text upon which the commentary is based. That text is the Codex Leningradensis of the Ben Asher family of manuscripts, which is represented in the most popular printed versions of the Hebrew Bible, the *Biblia Hebraica Stuttgartensia*, published by the Württembergische Bibelanstalt of Stuttgart, and in the version published by the United Bible Societies without a critical apparatus. The reasons for this conservatism are varied and are not based on a rigid theory of the historical priority of the Leningrad Codex. The majority of variants to this version are to be found among the many Greek versions of the OT (G). It has now long been recognized that G is not a uniform translation but, like the Hebrew, is the product of a long process of recension and refinement. (In the present work, G refers to the Vaticanus text as presented by Brooke, MacLean, and Thackeray in the Cambridge edition.)

Studies of G are in a state of flexibility and growth, and as yet there is no universally acceptable theory of its development and of the significance of its variants. Earlier scholarship tended to be too quick to alter the Hebrew text on the basis of a Greek reading without providing sufficient rationalization for the emendation. This changed with Paul Kahle's theory of the "targumic" quality of the Greek, which relegated it to the status of little more than a paraphrase of the Hebrew and tended to rob it of any value as an important and reliable alternative to the Hebrew. For some this reversed the trend to indiscriminate emendation.

In more recent years, because of the work of Lagarde, Albright, Cross, and others, there has been a decisive shift toward the rehabilitation of G as a reliable alternative witness to the Hebrew, and this has led to increasing confidence in the ability to reconstruct the history of G. Cross and his students have turned to the many early biblical manuscripts that were found at Qumran and have outlined a persuasive theory of the development of the OT text. Cross suggested that the Old Greek (OG) version was subsequently revised in the light of extant localized Hebrew versions. These local texts are reflected frequently in the manuscripts which comprise the Lucianic recension of the historical books (boc_2e_2). Further revisions are detected in the so-called *Kaige* recension, and in the final stage which resulted in Aquila. For the first few chapters of 2 Kings, the Lucianic minuscules are thought to represent the earlier localized Hebrew texts. The variants in this recension are then of great value in textual criticism.

This brief outline of the theory of Cross must suffice at this stage. This is not the place to enter into a detailed discussion of the merits or lack of merits of the theory. It is an attractive one, but it does have its weaknesses and is far from being accepted by all textual critics. The works of Goshen-Gottstein, Jellicoe, and Tov listed in the *Bibliography* provide a detailed assessment of the theory, pointing out its obvious strengths and weaknesses. It is a convenient working hypothesis but remains such, and at some points in the *Commentary* we enter into discussion with it.

The practice in the textual *Notes* in the commentary has been to offer the important variants from MT and to comment upon them where necessary, but we have avoided emendation unless it is deemed absolutely necessary. The caution expressed by Tov (*The Text-critical Use of the Septuagint in Biblical Research*, 277–311) is well heeded. The most important work for our purposes has been the study of Shenkel, and consideration is taken of his contribution. A guiding principle throughout is to comment on the Hebrew text and where necessary to discuss and emend it. But this is kept to a minimum.

Main Bibliography

Commentaries

Bach, R. "Königsbucher." *RGG*. Vol. 3. Tübingen: Mohr, 1929. **Barnes, W. E.** *The Second Book of Kings.* CBSC. Cambridge: Cambridge University Press, 1908. **Benzinger, I.** *Die Bücher der Könige.* KHAT 9. Freiburg, Leipzig, Tübingen: Mohr, 1899. **Craigie, P. C.** *Deuteronomy.* NICOT. Grand Rapids: Eerdmans, 1976. **Driver, S. R.** *A Critical and Exegetical Commentary on Deuteronomy.* ICC. Edinburgh: T. & T. Clark, 1903. **Ellis, P. F.** "1-2 Kings." *JBC*. Ed. R. E. Brown. Englewood Cliffs, NJ: Prentice Hall, 1968. **Fricke, K. D.** *Das Zweite Buch von den Königen. Die Botschaft des Alten Testaments* 12/11. Stuttgart: Calwer Verlag, 1972. **Gray, J.** *I and II Kings, A Commentary.* OTL. 2nd ed. Philadelphia: Westminster Press, 1970. **Kaiser, O.** *Isaiah 13-39.* OTL. Philadelphia: Westminster Press, 1974. **Kittel, R.** *Die Bücher der Könige.* HKAT 1.5. Gottingen: Vandenhoeck und Ruprecht, 1900. **Mauchline, J.** "I and II Kings." *Peake's Commentary on the Bible.* Eds. H. H. Rowley and M. Black. London: Thomas Nelson, 1962. **Montgomery, J. A.** *A Critical and Exegetical Commentary on the Books of Kings.* ICC. Ed. H. S. Gehman. Edinburgh: T. & T. Clark, 1951. **Myers, J. M.** *I Chronicles.* AB 12. Garden City, NY: Doubleday, 1965. **Robinson, J.** *The Second Book of Kings.* CBC. Cambridge: Cambridge University Press, 1976. **Rudolph, W.** *Jeremia.* HAT 12. 2nd ed. Tübingen: Mohr, 1968. **Sanda, A.** *Die Bücher der Könige.* EHAT 9. 2 vols. Munster: Aschendorff, 1911-12. **Skinner, J.** *The Books of Kings.* CeB. 2nd ed. Edinburgh: T. C. & E. C. Jack, 1904. **Snaith, N. H.** "The First and Second Books of Kings." *IB*. Vol. 3. Nashville: Abingdon Press, 1954. **Thenius, W.** *Die Bücher der Könige.* KeH 9. 2nd ed. Leipzig: Hirzel, 1873. **Wifall, W.** *The Court History of Israel: A Commentary on First and Second Kings.* St. Louis: Clayton Publishing House, 1975.

Books

Abel, F. M. *La géographie de la Palestine.* 2 vols. 2nd ed. Paris: Gabalda, 1933-38. **Aharoni, Y.** *Arad Inscriptions.* Jerusalem: Israel Exploration Society, 1981. ———. *The Land of the Bible.* Tr. A. F. Rainey. 2nd ed. Philadelphia: Westminster Press, 1979. **Albrektson, B.** *History and the Gods: An Essay on the Idea of Historical Events as Divine Manifestations in the Ancient Near East and in Israel.* CB/OT 1. Lund: Gleerup, 1967. **Albright, W. F.** *Archaeology and the Religion of Israel.* 4th ed. Baltimore: Johns Hopkins, 1942. **Baillet, M.; Milik, J. T.; and de Vaux, R.** *Discoveries in the Judean Desert of Jordan III. Les Petites grottes de Qumran.* Oxford: The University Press, 1962. **Beyerlin, W.** *Near Eastern Religious Texts Relating to the Old Testament.* Tr. J. Bowden. Philadelphia: Westminster Press, 1978. **Blank, S. H.** *Of a Truth the Lord Hath Sent Me: An Inquiry into the Source of the Prophet's Authority. The Goldenson Lecture for 1955.* Cincinnati: Hebrew Union College, 1955. **Bronner, L.** *The Stories of Elijah and Elisha.* Leiden: E. J. Brill, 1968. **Brueggemann, W.** *The Land.* Philadelphia: Fortress Press, 1977. **Butler, T. C.** *Joshua.* WBC 7. Waco, TX: Word Books, 1983. **Dever, W. G. and Paul, S. M.** *Biblical Archaeology.* Jerusalem: Keter, 1973. **DeVries, S. J.** *1 Kings.* WBC 12. Waco, TX: Word Books, 1985. **Eisenstadt, S. N.** *The Political Systems of Empires.* New York: Macmillan, 1963. **Eissfeldt, O.** *The Old Testament: An Introduction.* Tr. P. R. Ackroyd. Oxford: Blackwells, 1965. **Engle, J.** "Pillar Figurines of Iron-Age Israel and Asherah." Diss., University of Pittsburgh, 1979. **Fohrer, G.** *Die symbolischen Handlungen der Prophe-*

ten. 2nd ed. ATANT 54. Zurich: Zwingli Verlag, 1968. **Fokkelman, J. P.** *Narrative Art and Poetry in the Books of Samuel. A Full Investigation based on style and structural analysis.* Vol. 1. Assen: Van Gorcum, 1981. **Frick, F. S.** *The City in Ancient Israel.* SBLDS 36. Missoula MT: Scholars Press, 1977. **Gichon, M. and Herzog, C.** *Battles of the Bible.* London: Wiedenfield and Nicholson, 1978. **Ginzberg, L.** *The Legends of the Jews.* 7 vols. Tr. H. Szold. Philadelphia: Jewish Publication Society, 1913. **Knott, J. B.** "The Jehu Dynasty: An Assessment Based upon Ancient Near Eastern Literature and Archeology." Diss., Emory University, 1971. **Koch, K.** *The Growth of the Biblical Tradition: The Form-critical Method.* Tr. M. Cupitt. London: A. & C. Black, 1969. **Lemaire, A.** *Inscriptions hébräiques. Les ostraca.* Vol. 1. Paris: Les Édition du Cerf, 1977. **Lidzbarski, H.** *Handbuch der neue Epigraphik hebst ausgewahlten Inschriften.* 2 vols. Hildesheim: G. Olms, 1962. **Lind, M.** *Yahweh Is a Warrior: The Theology of Warfare in Ancient Israel.* Scottdale, PA: Herald Press, 1980. **Long, B.** *The Problem of the Etiological Narrative in the Old Testament.* BZAW 108. Berlin: W. de Gruyter, 1968. **McKay, J. W.** *Religion in Judah under the Assyrians.* SBT 2. London: SCM Press, 1973. **Marcus, R.** *Josephus, with an English Translation. Antiquities Books IX-XI.* Loeb Classical Library. Cambridge, MS: Harvard University Press, 1937. **Martin-Achard, R.** *From Death to Life: A Study of the Development of the Doctrine of the Resurrection in the Old Testament.* Tr. J. P. Smith. Edinburgh: Oliver & Boyd, 1960. **Mettinger, T. N. D.** *King and Messiah.* Lund: CWK Gleerup, 1977. **Miller, P. D.** *The Divine Warrior in Early Israel.* HSM 5. Cambridge, MS: Harvard University Press, 1973. **Ringgren, H.** *Israelite Religion.* Tr. D. E. Green. Philadelphia: Fortress Press, 1966. ———. *Religions of the Ancient Near East.* Tr. J. Sturdy. London: SPCK, 1973. **Robinson, E.** *Biblical Researches in Palestine and the Adjacent Regions: A Journal of Travels in the Year 1838 by E. Robinson and E. Smith.* 2 vols. Boston: Crocker and Brewster, 1857-60. **Robinson, H. W.** *Inspiration and Revelation in the Old Testament.* Oxford: Clarendon Press, 1946. **Rogerson, J. W.** *The Supernatural in the Old Testament.* London: Lutterworth Press, 1976. **Rowley, H. H.** *The Growth of the Old Testament.* New York: Harper Torchbooks, 1963. **Saggs, H. W. F.** *The Greatness that was Babylon.* New York: Hawthorn Books, 1962. **Schmitt, H. D.** *Elisa: Traditiongeschichtliche Untersuchungen zur vorklassischen nord-israelitischen Prophetic.* Gütersloh: G. Mohr, 1972. **Simons, J.** *Jerusalem in the Old Testament: Theories and Research.* Leiden: E. J. Brill, 1957. **Smend, R.** *Elemente alttestamentlichen Geschichtsdenkens.* TS 95. Zürich: EVZ Verlag, 1968. **Smith, G. A.** *Jerusalem: The Topography, Economics and History from the Earliest Times to A.D. 70.* 2 vols. London: Hodder & Stoughton, 1907-1908. **Soggin, J. A.** *Introduction to the Old Testament from Its Origins to the Closing of the Alexandrian Canon.* Tr. J. Bowden. London: SCM Press, 1976. **Thackeray, H. St. J.** *The Septuagint and Jewish Worship.* London: The British Academy, 1923. **Yadin, Y.** *The Art of Warfare in Biblical Lands.* 2 vols. New York: McGraw-Hill, 1968. ———. *Hazor: The Rediscovery of a Great Citadel of the Bible.* New York: Random House, 1975. **Yamashita, T.** "The Goddess Asherah." Diss. Yale University, 1964.

ARTICLES

Canosa, A. C. "Panorama critico del ciclo de Eliseo." *EstBib* 23 (1964) 217-34. **Couroyer, B.** "Le litige entre Josias et Nechao." *RB* 55 (1948) 388-96. **Croatto, J. S. and Soggin, J. A.** "Die Bedeuting von '*sdmwt*' im Alten Testament." *ZAW* 74 (1962) 44-50. **Cross, F. M. Jr.** "The Contribution of the Qumran Discoveries to the Study of the Biblical Text." *IEJ* 16 (1955) 81-95. **Crüsemann, F.** "Kritik an Amos im deuteronomistischen Geschichtswerk: Erwagungen zu 2 Kon. 14:27." In *Probleme biblischer Theologie, Gerhard von Rad zum 70.* Ed. H. W. Wolff. München: C. Kaiser, 1971. **Deltombe, L. F.** "Josias, heros de l'independence judéene." *BTS* 63 (1945) 2-5. **Dietrich, W.** "Die Aramaer sudbabyloniens in der Sargoniden zeit (700-648)." *AOAT*

7 (1970) 1–232. **Driver, G. R.** "The Modern Study of the Hebrew Language." *The People and the Book: Essays on the Old Testament.* Ed. A. S. Peake. Oxford: Clarendon Press, 1925. **Eakin, F. E.** "Yahwism and Baalism before the Exile." *JBL* 84 (1965) 407–14. **Ephal, I.** "Assyrian Dominion in Palestine." *World History of the Jewish People.* Vol. 4, *The Age of the Monarchy.* Ed. A. Malamat. Jerusalem: Masada Press, 1979. **Fohrer, G.** "Das Geschick des Menschen nach dem Tode im Alten Testament." *KD* 14 (1968) 249–62. **Fowler, M. D.** "The Israelite *bama:* A Question of Interpretation." *ZAW* 94 (1982) 203–13. **Gese, H.** "Geschichtliches Denken im Alten Orient und im Alten Testament." *ZTK* 55 (1958) 127–45. **Geva, H.** "The Western Boundary of Jerusalem at the End of the Monarchy." *IEJ* 29 (1979) 84–91. **Klein, R. W.** "New Evidence for an Old Recension of Reigns." *HTR* 60 (1967) 93–105. **Kraus, H.-J.** "Die Geschichte des Passah-Mazzot Festes im Alten Testament." *EvT* 18 (1958) 47–67. **Kutsch, E.** "Salbung als Rechtsakt im AT und im Alten Orient." *BZAW* 87. Berlin: B. Topelmann, 1963. **Lance, H. D.** "The Royal Stamps and the Kingdom of Judah." *HTR* 64 (1971) 315–32. **Lemaire, A.** "Note sûr le titre *bn-hmlk* dans ancien Israel." *Sem* 29 (1979) 59–65. **Lindars, B.** "Commentaries on Samuel and Kings." *Theology* 47 (1964) 11–15. **Lipinski, E.** "Le Ben Hadad II de la Bible et l'histoire." *Proceedings of the 5th World Congress of Jewish Studies.* Jerusalem: World Congress of Jewish Studies, 1969. ———. "The Egyptian-Babylonian War of the Winter of 601–600 B.C." *AION* 22 (1972) 235–41. **Malamat, A.** "Doctrines of Causality in Hittite and Biblical Historiography." *VT* 5 (1955) 1–22. **Mastin, B. A.** "Was the *SLS* the Third Man in the Chariot?" *SVT* 30 (1979) 125–54. **Miller, J. M.** "The Moabite Stone as a Memorial Stela." *PEQ* 106 (1974) 9–18. **Mitchell, H. G.** "Isaiah on the Fate of His People and the Capital." *JBL* 37 (1918) 149–62. **Mowinckel, S.** "Israelite Historiography." *ASTI* 2 (1963) 7–12. **Noth, M.** "Jerusalem und die israelitische Tradition." *OTS* 8 (1950) 28–46. **Oded, B.** "The Historical Background of the War between Rezin and Pekah against Ahaz." *Tarbiz* 38 (1969) 205–44. **Talmon, S.** "The History of the 'am-ha'aretz in the Kingdom of Judah." *BMik* 12 (1966–1967) 27–55. **Thackeray, H. St. J.** "The Greek Translators of the Four Books of Kings." *JTS* 8 (1907) 262–78. **Thomas, D. W.** "The Age of Jeremiah in the Light of Recent Archaeological Discoveries." *PEQ* 82 (1950) 1–15. **Vaux, R. de.** "Le sens de l'expression 'peuple de pays' dans l'AT et le role politique du peuple en Israel." *RA* 58 (1964) 167–72. **Vogelstein, M.** "Nebuchadnezzar's Reconquest of Phoenicia and Palestine and the Oracles of Ezekiel." *HUCA* 23 (1950–1951) 197–220. **Watts, J. D. W.** "The Deuteronomic Theology." *RevExp* 74 (1977) 371–87. **Weinfeld, M.** "The Origin of the Apodictic Law: An Overlooked Source." *VT* 23 (1973) 63–75. **Weippert, H.** "Die deuteronomistische Beurteilung der Könige von Israel und Juda." *Bib* 53 (1973) 301–39. **Welten, P.** "Kültohe und Jahwetempel." *ZDPV* 88 (1972) 19–37. **Wevers, J. W.** "Principles of Interpretation Guiding the Fourth Translator of the Books of Kingdoms." *CBQ* 14 (1950) 40–56. **Wifall, W.** "David, Prototype of Israel's Future." *BTB* 4 (1974) 94–107. **Willis, J. T.** "Redaction Criticism and Historical Reconstruction." *Encounter with Texts: Form and History in the Hebrew Bible.* Ed. M. J. Buss. Philadelphia: Fortress Press, 1979. **Yeiven, S.** "Who Was So, the King of Egypt?" *VT* 2 (1952) 131–36.

Ahaziah and Elijah (1:1–18)

Bibliography

Buchholz, W. "Thisbe: Ein Erklärungsvorschlag." *ZRGG* 22 (1970) 80–81. **Fensham, F. C.** "A Possible Explanation of the Name of Baal-Zebub of Ekron." *ZAW* 79 (1967) 361–64. **Gilead, C.** "וידבר ויען ויענה" in II Kings 1:9–13." *BMik* 52 (1972) 46–47. **Juon, P.** "Le costume d'Elie et celui de Jean Baptiste: étude lexicographique." *Bib* 16 (1935) 74–81. **Lundbom, J. R.** "Elijah's Chariot Ride." *JJS* 24 (1975) 39–50. **Rofé, A.** "Baal, the Prophet and the Angel (II Kings 1): A Study in the History of Literature and Religion." *Beer Sheba* 1 (1973) 222–30. **Rudolph, W.** "Zum Text der Königsbücher." *ZAW* 63 (1951) 201–15. **Steck, O. H.** "Die Erzählung von Jahwes Einschreiten gegen die Orakelbefragung Ahasjas." *EvT* 27 (1967) 546–56.

Translation

¹ Moab rebelled [a] against Israel after the death of Ahab.
² Now Ahaziah fell through the lattice work of his upper chamber which was in Samaria, and became ill. Then he sent out messengers and gave them the following order, "Go. Ask [a] Baal-Zebub, god of Ekron [b] whether I shall recover from this sickness." [c]
³ But the angel of Yahweh had said to Elijah the Tishbite, [a] "Get up! Go to intercept the messengers of the king of Samaria, and say to them, 'Is there no God in Israel [b] that you go to seek out Baal-Zebub, god of Ekron?' ⁴ Therefore, thus has Yahweh declared, 'You shall not come down from the bed which you have mounted, because you will most certainly die.' " [a] So Elijah went. [b]
⁵ The messengers then returned to the king, and he said to them, "Why have you come back?" ⁶ They replied, "A man came to meet us and said to us, 'Go return to the king who sent you, and say this to him: Thus has Yahweh declared, "Is there no God in Israel that you go to seek out Baal-Zebub, god of Ekron? Therefore the bed to which you have retired, you shall not come down from it, because you will most certainly die." ' " ⁷ He said to them, "What is the description [a] of this man who came to meet you and said to you all these things?" ⁸ They replied, "He was a hairy man, [a] with a leather belt around his middle." Then he said, "It is Elijah the Tishbite!"
⁹ᵃ The king then dispatched an officer with his company of soldiers to him. The officer went up [b] to Elijah and found him [c] sitting on top of the hill, and he said to him, "Man of God! The king says, 'Come down!' " ¹⁰ But Elijah answered the officer by saying, "If I am a man of God may fire come down from the skies and consume both you and your company!" Fire did come down from the skies, and it consumed both the officer and his company.
¹¹ So a second time [a] the king sent an officer and his company to Elijah. The officer went up [b] and said to him, "Man of God, thus has the king spoken, 'Come down quickly!' " ¹² Elijah's response to these men [a] was, "If I am a man of God may fire come down from the skies and consume both you and your company!" And fire [b] did come down from the skies and consume both the officer and his company of men.

13 *Yet again the king* ª *sent a third* ᵇ *officer and his company, but the third officer went up, approached and fell on his knees in front of Elijah and implored him with these words, "Man of God, may my life and the lives of these fifty servants of yours be precious in your eyes.* 14 *See already, fire from the skies has come down and devoured the first two officers and their companies.* ª *Now, please let my life be precious in your eyes!"* 15 *Then the angel of Yahweh said to Elijah, "Go down with him.* ª *Do not be afraid of him." So he arose and went down with him to the king.*

16 *He then said to the king, "Thus has Yahweh declared, 'Because you have sent messengers* ª *to seek out Baal-Zebub, god of Ekron, Yet is there no God in Israel that you may seek his word? Therefore, you shall not come down from the bed which you have mounted. You will most certainly die!' "* 17 *And he did die, according to the word of Yahweh which Elijah spoke, and Jehoram reigned in his place, (this was in the second year of Jehoshaphat, king of Judah) because he had no son.* 18 *Now the rest of the acts of Ahaziah which he did, are they not written in the record of the daily deeds of the kings of Israel?*

Notes

1.a. The G translation of פשע "rebel" in 2 Kgs 1:1 is ἀθετεῖν, the meaning of which is to reject authority. Although this Gr word is used as a translation of seventeen different words in G, it is mainly in 1 and 2 Kings that it translates פשע (1 Kgs 8:50; 12:19; 2 Kgs 1:1; 3:5, 7; 8:20, 22). This would reflect the individual style of the translator of this part of the Heb text into Gr.

2.a. G^AL translate דרש "seek" with ἐπερωτήσατε and OL and Syr follow this pattern with "interrogate." This need not presuppose an original Heb of שאל "ask," rather, it brings the verb into line with the addition found in G at the end of the verse, καὶ ἐπορεύθησαν ἐπερωτῆσαι δι' αὐτοῦ.

2.b. בעל זבוב אלהי עקרון is interpreted by G and Josephus (*Antiq.* ix.19) as "lord of the flies" (Βααλ μυῖαν θεον Ακκ. or τον Ακκαρον θεον μυιαν), a meaning of זבוב which is also found in Isa 7:18 and Eccl 10:1. On this see the *Comment* below. The interpretative process seen in G is continued in some of the versions which add προσοχθίσμα "abomination" to the name of the god of Ekron. In G this term is usually reserved to translate שקוץ "detested thing" or תועבה "an abominable thing" (Deut 7:26; 2 Kgs 23:13).

2.c. The expression אם־אחיה מחלי זה "whether I shall recover from this illness" is a little unusual, the more regular form of such a phrase being מחלי הזה, which appears to be presupposed by G (ἐκ τῆς ἀρρωστίας μου ταύτης). However, Mic 7:12 (יום הוא) and Ps 80:15 (גפן זאת) both preserve similar forms of expression. G and Vg also presuppose מחלי.

3.a. For התשבי G offers Θεσβείτης or Θεσβών (1 Kgs 17:1). Josephus (*Antiq.* vii.319) gives Θεσβων or Θεσσεβων. See further the *Comment* below.

3.b. המבלי אין־אלהים בישראל "Is there no God in Israel?" The double negative serves for emphasis. Between MT vv 3 and 4 G adds καὶ οὐχ οὕτως either as a preface to v 4 (Rahlfs) or as a postlude to v 3 (CGOT). A translation of ". . . it shall not be . . ." seems in order, but whether this refers to the recovery of Ahaziah, or the journey to the God of Ekron is not clear. G^L reads διὰ τοῦτο as an introduction to v 4. It is superfluous.

4.a. With its translation of θανάτῳ ἀποθάνῃ for מות תמות "surely die," G appears to have mistaken the Heb מות "dying" for a noun rather than an inf ab.

4.b. וילך אליה "and Elijah went" is expanded by G with καὶ εἶπεν πρὸς αὐτούς "and he said to them," thus filling out the rather abrupt ending of MT at this point. The abruptness of style in this narrative is stressed by the absence in MT of an antecedent to אליו "to him" in v 5. Clearly the king is in mind.

7.a. The term משפט "description" is used in an unusual way here. Normally it is associated with the practice of justice, and its most common meaning is a legal judgment. This meaning is carried by G in its translation of τίς ἡ κρίσις "what is the judgment" and by G^L with its rendering of τὶ τὸ δικαίωμα "what is the right," which is even more specific.

8.a. איש בעל שער "a hairy man" is translated by G with δασύς. See further the *Comment* below.

9.a. Throughout this verse there is a confusing lack of antecedents in the Heb. G^L attempts to clear up the confusion with καὶ ἀποστέλλει Ὀχ. πρὸς Ἠλ.

9.b. No clear subject exists for ויעל "and he went up," and in view of the previous sentence G^L makes the verb pl. Such an emendation is not necessary.

9.c. MT is literally והנה ישב "behold he sat," for which G^L offers αὐτὸς δὲ which might presuppose והוא "and he was sitting." This is entirely possible and the change is a minor one.

11.a. MT is literally וישב וישלח "and he turned and sent." While not common, the use of the verb שוב in sequence to indicate the repetition of an action is found in biblical Heb. (Gen 26:18).

11.b. MT reads ויען "and he answered," which is omitted by G. It is possibly a dittography from either v 10a (ויענה אליהו וידבר) or v 12a (ויען אליה וידבר) "and Elijah answered and said"). However, G^L reads καὶ ἀνέβη which presupposes the reading of ויעל. The repetitive style of the narrative would favor an original ויעל. See vv 9, 11, 13.

12.a. G here reads πρὸς αὐτόν (אליו).

12.b. MT reads אש־אלהים "fire of God," which is probably a dittography from the previous line's איש האלהים "man of God."

13.a. So G. MT has no subject. This abbreviated Heb. style is difficult to render literally into English, so the variant is adopted.

13.b. G omits שלשים "third" although G^L and Vg retain it. G and Vg omit חמשים "fifty."

14.a. G omits חמשיהם.

15.a. MT reads אותו, which makes no grammatical sense. The G reading of μετ'αὐτοῦ (אתו) "with him" is to be preferred. G^L here adds ἐπορεύθη (וילך) "and he went."

16.a. G omits any reference to the messengers, thus bringing the verse into conformity with vv 3–4, 6. The same motivation appears to be behind the G omission of the whole sentence המבלי אין־אלהים בישראל לדרש בדברו.

Excursus: 2 Kings 1:17–18

The textual problems associated with 2 Kgs 1:17–18 are notorious. The solution to the problems involves not only decisions regarding the priority of textual traditions represented by the variants, but also the difficult question of the synchronization of the reigns of the kings of Israel and Judah. The latter part of v 17 (MT) is omitted entirely by G. Further, after v 18 (MT) G adds four more verses which occur in substantially the same form in 3:1–3 (MT). G^L offers some additional material for discussion by adding some of what G omits in v 17b, but without reference to the second year of Jehoshaphat of Judah. However, this chronological note is added later by G^L at v 18a (G), instead of G's reference to the eighteenth year of Jehoshaphat. At the end of this verse G^L adds the sentence "Joram son of Ahab reigned in Samaria." Finally, some of the versions (G^A) conflate this collection of variants at the end of v 18d (G).

The possibility that G^L here has preserved the OG reading (Shenkel, *Chronology and Recensional Development,* 64–82) is an unlikely one. Although this would preserve the reading of the second year of Jehoram ben Jehoshaphat, thus making the reading of the eighteenth year of Jehoshaphat secondary, there are other possibilities. First, the expansionary characteristics of G^L, which would indicate a later tradition, are present throughout this chapter, and in these verses. Whether G^L here, and only here, preserves the OG reading of 2 Kings is questionable. Second, the form of MT at this point needs some attention.

No finite verb exists in the phrase בשנת שתים ליהורם בן יהושפט מלך יהודה, and this has led to a certain clumsiness in the syntax. In the translation this has been accommodated by placing the whole phrase in parenthesis. The standard formula for the concluding of the reign of a particular king in 1 and 2 Kings is

(a) reference to "the rest of the acts of . . ."; (b) reference to his death and burial, followed by the name of his successor; (c) an attempt to synchronize introduced by the phrase בשנת. After 2 Kgs 17 another element is added, (d) the age of the Judean king at his accession.

A slight variation of this order to *b-a-c* occurs in 1 Kgs 15:28–33; 2 Kgs 15:10, 14, 30. The order of 2 Kgs 1:17 as it stands (b-c-a) is quite unique. The phrase, not found in G, bears all the marks of an insertion. It violates the usual form, it is grammatically clumsy, and there is textual support for its omission. See also Dietrich, *Prophetie und Geschichte*, 125–26.

Form/Structure/Setting

2 Kgs 1:1 is neither dislocated from 1 Kgs 22:51–52 (Burney, *Notes*, 260–261), nor is it a deliberate copy of 2 Kgs 3:5 (M. Noth, *Überlieferungsgeschichtliche Studien* 1, 2nd ed. [Tübingen: Max Niemeyer, 1957] 83), but stands as an editorial introduction from the hand of the deuteronomist, in a style found elsewhere in the Deuteronomistic History (cf. Josh 1:1; Judg 1:1; 2 Sam 1:1). In its immediate context the verse introduces two originally separate narratives concerning the prophet Elijah. These two narratives in turn serve to begin the transition of prophetic authority and power from Elijah to Elisha, who is to be the prophet active during the revolt of Moab described in more detail in chapter three, and referred to here. The transition is complete by the end of chapter two.

The verse also serves the wider purpose of closing off one era in the history of Israel, and opening up another. This is certainly the intention behind the use of the similar statements noted above. The model for this seems to be Gen 25:11. In such periods of change, a significant epoch in the history of Israel is ended with the deaths of Abraham, Moses, Joshua, and Samuel. The present text has no intention of elevating the apostate Ahab to the level of these others, but simply indicates that the "age of Ahab" is either over or fast drawing to a close.

2–17a The two stories which follow this introductory statement, the reaction of Elijah to Ahaziah's search for healing outside Israel (vv 2–8, 16–17*a*) and the confrontation between the prophet and the authority of the king (vv 9–15), are told in an extremely vivid fashion, and a close analysis reveals a sophisticated narrative composition. It has long been customary to regard as originally independent these two narratives (Koch, *Biblical Tradition*, 187). There is merit to this suggestion, the objections of DeVries notwithstanding (S. J. DeVries, *Prophet against Prophet*, 62). Two different themes are dealt with. In the first story (vv 2–8, 16–17*a*) the center of the narrative is the prophetic word of Elijah which foretells the death of Ahaziah. The second story (vv 9–15) concerns the confrontation between the prophet and state authority. It will be seen below that in the present structure the first story embraces the second and places it in a new context. DeVries' classification of the chapter as "prophetic authorization narrative" is suitable for the final form of the chapter. Each of the two stories contains a threefold repetition of its respective theme in the following way.

In the first story the repetition revolves around three basic elements in the narrative:

I. *The Command to the Prophet*
   (v 3a) ומלאך יהוה דבר אל אליה התשבי קום עלה לקראת
   "But the angel of the Lord had said to Elijah the Tishbite, 'Get up! Go to intercept . . .'"
   (v 6) איש עלה לקראתנו
   "A man came to meet us."
   (v 15) וידבר מלאך יהוה אל־אליהו רד
   "Then the angel of the Lord said to Elijah, 'Go down.'"

II. *The Question about the Existence of God in Israel*
   "Is there no God in Israel" המבלי אין־אלהים בישראל (v 3b)
   "Is there no God in Israel" המבלי אין־אלהים בישראל (v 6)
   "Is there no God in Israel" המבלי אין־אלהים בישראל (v 16)

III. *The Oracle of Judgment*
   (v 4) המטה אשר־עלית שם לא־תרד ממנה כי מות תמות
   "From the bed which you have mounted, you will not go down, for you will die."
   (v 6) המטה אשר־עלית שם לא־תרד ממנה כי מות תמות
   (v 16) המטה אשר־עלית שם לא־תרד ממנה כי מות תמות

V 17 then provides the climax to this sequence by its emphasis upon the proper fulfillment of the prophetic work, וימת כדבר יהוה אשר דבר אליהו "and he died according to the word of the Lord which Elijah spoke." Thus is Elijah's ability and authority to utter the word of Yahweh vindicated.

In the second set of verses (vv 9–15) the repetition revolves around the confrontation between the man of God and the representative of the king, namely, the captain and his company of soldiers. In a meticulous way the story is repeated almost word for word. Vv 9–10 provide the first account of the confrontation, with what becomes characteristic vocabulary. The first repetition appears in vv 11–12, and the second in v 13. Here, however, the ending changes with the officer's appeal for mercy. The writing or telling of a story by repeating the main elements at least twice is a common feature of the narrative art of 2 Kings.

Stories about prophetic characters like Elijah and Elisha clearly come from the followers of such men. That these circles of followers were restricted to the "sons of the prophets" is an assumption often made, but one which is inaccurate. Not all of the prophets' followers and admirers were part of this grouping. (On this further see *Introduction.*) The shape and the purpose of these stories in 2 Kgs 1 are closely connected. In the first story the stress is upon the prophet, Elijah the Tishbite, as bearer of the word of Yahweh. In the unfolding of the narrative this aspect of the prophetic task is clearly vindicated. Three times the oracle is repeated, and its fulfillment is stressed. In the second story the emphasis is upon the prophet as "man of God," a term reserved for characters as Moses (Deut 33:1), Samuel (1 Sam 9:6), Elijah, and Elisha. Although not restricted to the miraculous activity of such men, the term is frequently associated with such activity (1 Sam 9; 2 Kgs 4). This second story is in keeping with this trend. Before each dramatic act of power Elijah speaks of his role as "man of God." Implicit in these statements is the theme of the word of the prophet. In this chapter the combination of these two stories serves to enhance this twofold aspect of the activity of Elijah. Underlying each is the clash between the authority of Yahweh and the authority of the king.

The time of the origin and preservation of these stories and their eventual committal to writing is impossible to determine with any degree of certainty. In their present form and position they owe much, if not all, to the compiler of the Former Prophets, the Deuteronomist. To be more specific would be hazardous. The historical circumstances which caused such narratives to be preserved can only be hinted at since the themes of the fulfillment of the prophetic word and the clash between the prophet as Yahweh's representative and civil authority run throughout the history of the prophetic tradition. Such narratives as these could represent one or more of the frequent attempts to recall examples of true prophecy and prophetic characteristics by the heirs of such prophetic giants. (See DeVries, *Prophet against Prophet* 54–55.) More precision cannot be offered.

It is also important, however, to understand the final form of the stories set in the larger body of literature, the Former Prophets, as well as in their supposed setting in life. What relationship does this chapter have to the narrative in 2 Kings? An additional question would be: What rhetorical links are there to connect the narrative to what follows and to what comes before? Such questions are answered not only by examining the structural similarities with other passages in the same literature, but also by the examination of the specific choice of language within the text.

The themes and language of the first story are repeated in 2 Kgs 8:7–15. The similarities are close enough to be deliberate. DeVries (*Prophet against Prophet*, 64) notes the formal similarities between the two chapters, but then argues that they are minor, and that after 8:9 the chapter "goes its own way." However, the similarities are deeper than this and need attention. First, the question of Ben Hadad via Hazael to Elisha is mentioned three times (8:8, 9, 14). Second, the precise linguistic form of the question is exactly the same as that found in 1:2, including the unusual form of מחלי זה "this illness." Third, the outcome of the enquiry is expressed in the same way, כי מות תמות "for you will surely die" (1:4) and כי מות תמות (8:10). Fourth, the overall theme of the inquiry about a monarch's health in a foreign country is common to both narratives. Such similarities cannot be ignored. They are not simply the result of a common origin, common form and common intention in their original life-setting. A literary motivation is at work. This motivation will be explored later.

A second set of similarities, this time not as overt but evident nevertheless, concerns the theme of the presence of God and his prophet in Israel. It is expressed by the question in vv 3, 6, 16 (המבלי אין אלהים בישראל "Is there no God in Israel?"). The theme is picked up again in 3:11–12 האין פה נביא ליהוה ונדרשה את יהוה מאותו "Is there no prophet of Yahweh here that we may enquire of Yahweh through him?" and in 5:15 ידעתי כי אין

אלהים בכל הארץ כי אם בישראל "I know that there is no God in all the earth except in Israel." 5:3 is reminiscent of 3:11. Chapter five also deals with the search for healing in a foreign country. The anticipation here of these themes which occur later in 2 Kgs in association with the successor of Elijah, Elisha, is important, since it enhances the theme to be found in the following chapter, namely, נחה רוח אליהו על־אלישע "the spirit of Elijah rested on Elisha" (2:15). The broader relation of the form of chapter one to the form of chapter two will be treated in the discussion of that chapter.

Comment

The narrative of 2 Kgs 1 is an exposition of the summary of the reign of Ahaziah found in 1 Kgs 22:51–53. The reign was a very brief one, two years, but it was characterized by the kind of evil which had become the hallmark of the reign of Ahaziah's father, Ahab. Among other things, it is said of Ahaziah that he "served Baal" (1 Kgs 22:53). This is an accusation found rarely in the Former Prophets. It is the accusation reserved for Ahab himself (1 Kgs 16:31), and is also found in the catalog of sins and apostasies of the nation of Israel which eventually led to its downfall (2 Kgs 17:16). Such activities of the house of Ahab become notoriously significant until the fall of that house at the hand of Jehu (see 1 Kgs 22:53; 2 Kgs 8:18, 27). In other words, Ahaziah continues the pattern of national life established by his father. There is no improvement during his short reign. The story of the events surrounding Ahaziah's sickness provides a sordid example of that continuing apostasy.

1 The opening editorial comment begins a new epoch in the history of the nation of Israel, and what follows becomes extremely important. One of the most apostate periods in the history of the nation has just drawn to a close, but no subsequent improvement is seen. Ahaziah, son and successor to Ahab, reigns for only two years, and the selection of this comment to begin his reign is a careful one. The comment serves to introduce again into the narrative of the history of Israel the nation of Moab as a decisive historical force. (Apart from incidental references to Moab in 1 Kgs 11:1, 33, no mention has been made of Moab since its defeat at the hands of David in 2 Sam 8:12.) Anticipated in 2 Kgs 1:1 is the rebellion of Moab, dealt with in greater detail in chapter three. Subsequently, Edom (2 Kgs 8:20) and Libnah (2 Kgs 8:22) made similar moves toward independence from Israel. The significance of these events is that they show, after the death of Ahab, the disintegration of the Israelite empire. There is no conflict between this reference to Moab and the detailed treatment of the revolt in chapter three.

ויפשע מואב "and Moab rebelled." The noun פשע is normally associated with the concept of sin or transgression against God. This is seen in the combination of the terms פשע "trangress" and חטאה "sin" in Gen 31:36. The verbal form of פשע is never used in this sense in the Pentateuch. The most common meaning of the verb is political rebellion (cf. 1 Kgs 8:50; 12:19).

2 Exactly when during his reign Ahaziah met with his accident is not clear. Josephus (*Antiq.* ix.18) places it at the end of his reign and coincident with the revolt of Moab against him. Josephus also embellishes the account of the accident, indicating that the king tripped while descending from the roof top via the stairway. The many additional characterizations of the participants in the account and the padding of the narrative with small details by Josephus would cast doubt on his dating. The OT offers no certainty on this point; nor is it clear, since v 1 is editorial, that Moab rebelled during the reign of Ahaziah.

שבכה is literally to be translated "network," as in the decorative work used in the construction of Solomon's temple (1 Kgs 7:17, 18, 20, 41, 42; 2 Kgs 25:17). In Job 18:8 the term is translated "net." Apart from this the term is restricted to the Former Prophets. G translates with the two words δικτυον, which is the most common, and δικτυωτος, which is used only here of the Hebrew שבכה. Normally this second Greek word is reserved for אשנב (Judg 5:28). The latticework was probably made of reed or wood strips and was designed to keep out the sun, and the prying eyes of neighbors, yet allow whatever breezes there were to cool the occupants of the "upper chamber."

לכו דרשו "Go. Ask . . ." The asyndeton is not unusual in biblical Hebrew, especially in commands or pronouncements (cf. GKC § 120g-h). דרש "ask" is the normal expression for an enquiry of a god or an oracle (Gen 25:22; Exod 18:15; Deut 4:29). O. H. Steck (*EvT* 27 [1967] 548) makes reference to the ZKR stele (cf. Beyerlin, ed., *Near Eastern Religious Texts Relating to the Old Testament*, 229–30) in this connection. Oracles are certainly given by Baalshemayim to ZKR but ZKR's own activity is not related to the same vocabulary of Ahaziah's search.

בעל זבוב אלהי עקרון "Baal-Zebub god of Ekron." G, followed by Josephus (*Antiq.* ix.19), interprets the deity's name as "lord of the flies" (βααλ μυῖαν or τον θεον μυῖαν), a meaning of זבוב which is also found in Isa 7:18 and Eccl 10:1. The reading of זבל for זבוב, which is retained in the later NT tradition (Mk 3:22), has provided a possible alternative of "Baal prince" (H. Ringgren, *Religions of the Ancient Near East*, 132–33; G. R. Driver, *Canaanite Myths and Legends*, 149). A similar word in Ugaritic means "plague-stricken" or "diseased" (KRT 1:1:17). A further appeal to Ugaritic is made by Fensham (*ZAW* 79 [1967] 361–64). According to Fensham, Anat 111:42–43 contains <u>d</u>bb as a synonym for išt (flame, fire). The fire motif in 2 Kgs 1 is evident and Fensham suggests that the chapter is a polemic against the Philistine/Canaanite god of fire. To be sure, the Philistines were influenced by Canaanite culture, but it is equally possible that the term "lord of the flies" is a pejorative epithet (T. H. Gaster, "Baal-Zebub, *IDB* 1:332). Such a use of corrupted names conveying more of the writer's or speaker's opinion of the character than its proper meaning is common in the OT (cf. J. F. A. Sawyer, *A Modern Introduction to Biblical Hebrew* [Boston: Oriel, 1976] 73).

Ekron was one of the five Philistine cities in the southwest of Palestine. In 1 Sam 6:16–17 it also appears in the OT in connection with sickness when the Philistines possessed the Ark of the Covenant. The reason why Ahaziah should choose this particular god for the desired oracle is unclear since the precise meaning of his name and nature is unknown. That the king of Israel should seek after healing from a foreign god, while an act of apostasy, is hardly out of character with the descendants of Ahab. Later in 2 Kgs this motif of the search for healing from a foreign deity becomes common (cf. 2 Kgs 5, 8). The point of these stories is to demonstrate that only in Israel is the true God to be found. Such a notion of deities as the source of healing was common in the ancient Near East (see Beyerlin, *NE Religious Texts* 23;109–10). Further, the activity of Ahaziah clearly violates any belief that Yahweh is the sole God for Israel, and the specific prohibition for such activity is found in the writer's blueprint for the perfect Israelite society (see Deut 12:30).

3 מלאך יהוה "angel of Yahweh" is an uncommon phrase in the prophetic literature (so K. Koch, *The Growth of the Biblical Tradition,* 187), but this is no reason for seeing the occurrence here as editorial. The figure of the "messenger of Yahweh" plays an important role in the Elijah stories (1 Kgs 19:7). The contrast in the present narrative between the "messenger of Yahweh" who commands Elijah and the "messengers of the king" who run errands for Ahaziah cannot be overlooked.

אליה התשבי "Elijah, the Tishbite." The name Elijah also occurs as אליהו, a common alternative ending to such theophoric names (cf. M. Noth, *Die israelitischen Personennamen,* BWANT III, 10 [Hildesheim: Georg Olms, 1966²] 101–13). The name means "the LORD (Yahweh) is my God," and the vast majority of occurrences of the name in the OT refer to the main character in the chapter under discussion. Others are found in 1 Chr 8:27 and Ezra 10: 21, 26.

With Josephus, most modern interpreters regard התשבי "the Tishbite" as a reference to the locality from which Elijah originated. This has been identified, somewhat unsatisfactorily, with modern Listib in the northeast of biblical Gilead. The word is very infrequent in the OT, occurring only in 1 Kgs 17:1; 21:17, 28; 2 Kgs 1:3, 8; 9:36, and only in connection with the prophet Elijah. That it was used as a decisive designation for the prophet might indicate that the term was far more common in ancient Israel than would appear from the number of occurrences in the OT. 1 Kgs 17:1, where the complete phrase is מתשבי גלעד "from Tishbe of Gilead," might provide a clue for an alternative interpretation of the term. The consonants can be pointed to render the phrase מִתֹּשָׁבֵי גלעד "from the inhabitants of Gilead." But this does not apply to all occurrences. Glueck's suggestion that the phrase should be emended to read מִיָּבֵשׁ גלעד "from Jabesh Gilead" is interesting because so much of Elijah's activity took place in that general area (cf. also L. Ginzberg, *The Legends of the Jews,* 6:316, n. 2). But such an emendation is difficult to envisage, and has no substantial textual support. The theory that Elijah was from the so-called "toshab-class" of Israel, i.e., an immigrant, is also attractive, but this is a very late interpretation. The form of the word תשבי is in keeping with the naming of places of origin or domicile (2 Sam 11:6 החתי "the Hittite," Mic 1:1 המרשתי "the Moreshite"). This being the case, the exact location of Tesheb or Thisbe is unknown. Buchholz's suggestion (*ZRGG* 22 [1970] 80–81) that Elijah had some connection with the Hurrian weather god, Tashub, has little to commend it.

קום ועלה "Get up. Go . . ." is a repetitive, but normal, expression in biblical Hebrew (see Gen 35:1; Deut 17:18; Josh 8:1). Elijah's response to the activity of Ahaziah is interesting. He adopts the role of legal accuser and uses the classic judgment speech against an individual (see C. Westermann, *Basic Forms of Prophetic Speech*, 142–63), with the accusation in the form of a question, followed by the announcement of judgment. The announcement of judgment contains legal language found elsewhere in the OT (see Num 15:35; Ezek 18:13; Jer 26:8).

אתם הלכים is a participial expression which can be translated as indicating an immediate future action (cf. W. Stinespring, "The Participle of the Immediate Future," in *Translating and Understanding the Old Testament*, ed. H. T. Frank and W. L. Reed [Nashville: Abingdon, 1970] 64–70).

7 The term משפט is unusual here. It normally means "judgment" or "justice" (see *Notes* above). A similar usage is found in Judg 13:12.

8 איש בעל שער "a hairy man." In spite of the development of the Jewish and Christian traditions concerning Elijah, there is no justification for the translation of this phrase as "he wore a garment of haircloth" (RSV). On its own the word שער simply means "hair," and when it is used adjectivally of clothing there is no ambiguity at all (cf. Gen 25:15; Zech 13:4). Further, the use of the construct form of בעל indicates that שער is descriptive of a person. A perfect parallel exists in Dan 8:6, 20 in the use of בעל הקרנים "a baal with horns." If Elijah were to be characterized by his head of hair then this would certainly be a distinguishing feature, since it would set him apart from Elisha, who was bald! On the other hand, if "hair garments" were the uniform of all prophets, this would not identify Elijah the Tishbite. The speaker of the oracle could have been any one of the prophets (cf. A. B. Ehrlich, *Randglossen zum hebräischen Bibel* 7:278–79). In the Jewish tradition, the appearance of Elijah as long haired was a source of ridicule (see Ginzberg, *Legends of the Jews*, 4:295).

The reaction of Ahaziah to the pronouncement of judgment touches on a common theme in the prophetic literature, namely, the desire of those in authority to silence an unfavorable prophetic word.

9 שר־חמשים וחמשיו is to be translated literally as "an officer of fifty and his fifty." Such a unit is one of the many unit designations of the Israelite army during this period. It corresponds roughly to a company of men. The use of "fifties" in military matters is found elsewhere in the OT (1 Sam 8:12; 2 Sam 15:1; 1 Kgs 1:5). Units of one hundred (2 Sam 18:1) and units of one thousand staffed in a similar way (1 Sam 8:12) are also known. Such ranks and units correspond to similar ones in other countries of the ancient Near East (cf. H. W. F. Saggs, *The Greatness That Was Babylon*, 254.) The commander-in-chief held the rank of שר צבא "commander of an army" (2 Kgs 5:1).

והנה ישב על ראש ההר "and behold, he was sitting on top of a mountain." Since the mountain is definitely indicated it is most likely to be identified with Carmel. Carmel is an abode of Elisha (2 Kgs 2:25; 4:25) and was the scene of Elijah's conflict with the prophets of Baal (1 Kgs 18). The similarity of motifs and themes between this latter incident and the events of 2 Kgs 1 cannot be overlooked. In both the theme is a conflict between the prophet and the royal representatives, and the agent of divine judgment is fire.

איש האלהים "man of God" is a term used of selected characters within the prophetic tradition. In 1 Sam 2:27 it is used of an anonymous prophet and in 1 Sam 9:6, 10 it designates Samuel. 1 Kgs 12–14 contains a cluster of stories concerning prophets and a "man of God" who stand in opposition to the policies of Jeroboam (cf. J. Gray, *I and II Kings,* 318–22). In 1 Kgs 13:14–18 the terms "prophet" and "man of God" are closely related. While others are given the title, it is used most frequently of Elisha. On the use of the term cf. N. P. Bratsiotis, "אשה איש," *TDOT* 1:222–35, esp. 233–35. עלה ירד. The movement introduced into this narrative by the frequent use of the verbs ירד and עלה is noteworthy. See vv 3, 4, 6, 9, 10, 11, 12, 13, 14, 15, 16, and 2:1, 11. Cf. also J. R. Lundbom, *JSS* 24 (1973) 46.

10 אם איש אלהים אני "If I am a man of God." These words are both a riddle and a challenge. What follows provides an authentication of Elijah as "man of God" over against the royal authority. The question recalls that of Jesus in Mark 11:27–33.

11 כה אמר המלך "Thus the king has spoken." The precise choice of these words by the officer highlights the theme of the prophet's conflict with the authority of the king. This "messenger formula" is that adopted by the prophetic tradition (see Westermann, *Basic Forms,* 90–128).

12 האלהים "the God." The use of the definite article of the divine is unusual for this narrative.

15 וידבר מלאך יהוה "then the angel of Yahweh said." The source of the prophet's authority and the motivation for his action in this story is the will of Yahweh mediated through his messenger. Only on this command does Elijah deign to come down from the mountain, where he is in control, and allow himself to be arrested.

16 The repetition of the word of Yahweh by the prophet emphasizes its content. The narrative continues with a minimum of detail. In what follows there is no hint of any harm to the prophet, although it is to be expected that Elijah did not escape lightly from any consequences of his opposition to Ahaziah and his confrontation with the soldiers. This is to be compared with 1 Kgs 12–14. The suggestion that there was a retaliation in the form of an attempted kidnapping (so Lundbom, *JJS* 24 [1973] 39–50) is speculative.

17 כדבר יהוה "according to the word of the Lord." In the history narrated in 1 and 2 Kings the fulfillment of the prophetic word is the hallmark of the prophet (1 Kgs 14:18; 22:13; 2 Kgs 2:22; 10:17; 24:2). On this, cf. G. von Rad, *Old Testament Theology,* 1:334–46. The precise "fulfillment formula" used here is not regarded as characteristic of the deuteronomist (cf. Dietrich, *Prophetie und Geschichte,* 22–26). The notice concerning "the second year of Jehoshaphat" has been dealt with above (cf. *Excursus: 2 Kgs 1:17–18*). A note of tragedy and condemnation is introduced by the reference to the absence of progeny for the king. A similar note is sounded in Jer 22:30 regarding Coniah of Judah.

18 The treatment of Ahaziah is brief, but telling. The chapter ends with a typical summary statement concluding his reign. On the slight change in form, cf. above (see also C. F. Burney, *Notes,* ix–xii).

Explanation

Although it is tempting to restrict the search for meaning in 2 Kings to the historical, textual, or literary, one has to keep in mind continually that

2 Kings is a part of the scriptural inheritance of the people of God and its exposition is incomplete without an acknowledgment of this fact. This is in no way to be interpreted as though any given text, pericope, or chapter contained scriptural themes or patterns of thought *in toto*, but rather that the function of any passage moves beyond the purely historical or textual to the theological, and even kerygmatic, level. Yet, caution must be exercised lest theological issues foreign to the text are imported into it (see *Introduction*).

Several issues are raised in this chapter and receive comment in the precise way they are presented. Beyond the clear presentation of Ahaziah "following in his father's footsteps" lies the deeper implication of the inherent connection between the collapse of the Omride dynasty, the political misfortunes of Israel, and the apostasy of its leaders. This perspective is stated decisively in the book of Deuteronomy (4:25–28) and echoed again in the rhythmic presentations of the fortunes of Israel in the book of Judges. It is a tenet of the deuteronomistic history that political events are always seen from a very distinct perspective, namely, that of the nation and its leaders in relationship to God. The climax of this presentation is seen in the demise of Israel in 2 Kgs 17 and the subsequent exile of Judah in 2 Kgs 24–25. These disasters are not seen simply as political accidents, but as expressions of the will and purpose of God. Thus it is that the writer of 2 Kgs 1 introduces the closing years of the Omride dynasty with a signal of its demise. It stands under the judgment of God.

The apostasy of Ahaziah in 2 Kgs 1 is both illustrative of the general decay of the house of Ahab, and also an exposition of his brief reign mentioned in 1 Kgs 22:51–53. His apostasy consists, in the present example, of the request for an oracle from a foreign god. The other misdeeds mentioned in the summary statement are not developed. There is a subtle point made in the narrative between the king's search for the healing word and the response to the king by Yahweh. The implication behind the word of Yahweh, repeated three times in the chapter, "The bed to which you have retired, you shall not come down from it, but you shall surely die!" (vv 4, 6, 16), is that even if the word of the God of Israel had been sought, it would have contained no guarantee of salvation. In fact, the word of Yahweh comes uninvited, and it is a word of death and judgment, not a word of life. In this way Yahweh, the God of Israel, maintains his integrity by remaining apart from and uninfluenced by human decisions. He is unable to be manipulated.

A second issue raised in the chapter is that of the clash of divine authority in the person of the prophet with the secular authority in the person of the king and his agents. The analysis of the form demonstrated the clever juxtaposition of the two authorities. But the struggle is not simply a clash of wills, which would allow for an uncertain outcome. The conflict is one-sided. The awful power of the God of Israel makes mockery of the attempts of the king to arrest and silence Elijah with his soldiers. The appeal of the third captain makes this clear. The outcome of such a conflict is predictable, in spite of the apparent odds. Before the power of the God of Israel and his prophet ("man of God") no one can stand. In the broader context of the stories of the prophets in 1 and 2 Kings the clash is between two opposing views of Israel as the people of God. Both here and elsewhere (e.g., 1 Kgs 18) the question of loyalty is posed. Will Israel be Yahweh's people or not? Will due homage be paid to the God of Israel even in the light of the possibility of the word of judgment? Ahaziah chose to escape this possibility. In the midst of this conflict stand the prophets, the "servants of Yahweh." In the broader view of the history of Israel presented in the OT, this cannot be construed as a power struggle, but rather a conflict over the very survival of Israel as the people of God and the role of the prophets in that crisis. It is in this light that the terrible excesses of the narrative are to be seen. In the role exemplified here, Elijah is remembered in subsequent history. He is a worker of miracles, a bearer of the word of God, but also one who ". . . in all his days did not tremble before any ruler, and no one brought him into subjection" (Sir 48:12).

The Ascension of Elijah   (2:1–25)

Bibliography

Beek, M. A. "The Meaning of the Expression 'The Chariots and the Horsemen of Israel' (2 Kings 2:12)." *OTS* 17 (1972) 1–10. **Blake, I. M.** "Jericho (Ain es-Sultan): Joshua's Curse and Elisha's Miracle—One Possible Explanation." *PEQ* 99 (1967) 86–97. **Carroll, R. P.** "The Elijah-Elisha Sagas: Some Remarks on Prophetic Succession in Ancient Israel." *VT* 19 (1969) 400–415. **Galling, K.** "Die Ehrenname Elisas und die Entrückung Elias." *ZTK* 53 (1956) 129–48. **Grill, S., and Haag, E.** "Die Himmelfahrt Elias nach 2 Kg. 2:1–15." *TTZ* 78 (1968) 18–32. **Kraus, H.-J.** "Gilgal." *VT* 1 (1951) 181–91. **Lundbom, J. R.** "Elijah's Chariot Ride." *JSS* 24 (1973) 39–50. **Messner, R. G.** "Elisha and the Bears." *Grace Journal* 3 (1962) 12–24. **Reiser, W.** "Eschatologische Gottesprüche in den Elisa-legenden." *TZ* 9 (1953) 321–38. **Sperber, A.** "Weak Waters." *ZAW* 82 (1970) 114–16. **Williams, J. G.** "The Prophetic 'Father.'" *JBL* 85 (1966) 344–49.

Translation

> [1] *Now when it came time for Yahweh to take Elijah up to the heavens in the whirlwind, both Elijah and Elisha went from Gilgal.* [2] *Elijah said to Elisha, "Please stay here* [a] *for Yahweh has sent me on to Bethel." But Elisha retorted, "As Yahweh lives, and as your soul lives, I will certainly not forsake you!" So they descended* [b] *to Bethel.* [3] *The sons of the prophets who were in Bethel came out to Elisha and said* [a] *to him, "Do you know that this day* [b] *Yahweh will take your master from being in charge over you?"* [c] *He replied, "Of course I know! Be quiet!"*
> [4] *Again Elijah said to him, "Please stay here for Yahweh has sent me on to Jericho." And again Elisha retorted, "As Yahweh lives and as your soul lives, I will certainly not forsake you!" So they came to Jericho.* [5] *Then the sons of the prophets who were in Jericho approached Elisha and said to him, "Do you know that this day Yahweh will take your master from being in charge over you?" He replied, "Of course I know! Be quiet!"*

⁶ Yet again Elijah said to him, "Please stay here for Yahweh has sent me on to the Jordan," Again Elisha replied, "As Yahweh lives and as your soul lives, I will certainly not forsake you!" So they both went on together. ⁷ Then fifty men from among the sons of the prophets went and stood opposite them at a distance, and the two of them stood facing the Jordan.ᵃ ⁸ Then Elijah took his garment, rolled it and struck the waters, and they parted. The two of them crossed over on the dry land.ᵃ

⁹ When they had crossed over,ᵃ Elijah said to Elisha, "Ask what I can do for you before I am taken from you." Elisha said, "May a double share of your spirit be mine." ¹⁰ He replied, "You ask a hard thing. If you see me taken upᵃ from you, you shall have it thus. But if not, it shall not be yours." ¹¹ Then, as they were proceeding on their journey and talking, a fire chariot and fire horses came between them. Then Elijah went upᵃ in the whirlwind to heaven. ¹² Elisha was witness to this, and he cried out,ᵃ "My father! My father! The chariot of Israel and its horses!" Then he saw it no more, so he gathered up his garments and tore them into two pieces.

¹³ He lifted up Elijah's garment which had fallen from him,ᵃ and he returned to stand on the bank of the Jordan. ¹⁴ Then he took Elijah's garment which had fallen from him, and struck the waters and said, "Where is Yahweh,ᵃ the God of Elijah, even he?" Then he struck the waters,ᵇ they parted and he crossed over.ᶜ ¹⁵ The sons of the prophets who were opposite in Jericho saw himᵃ and said, "Elijah's spirit has rested upon Elisha." Then they went forward to meet him and bowed down to the ground before him. ¹⁶ Then some of them said to him, "Now look, there are here with your servants fifty strong men. Please let them go and look for your master. Perhaps the spirit of Yahweh has lifted him up and dropped himᵃ upon some mountain or in some valley." But he replied, "Do not send them!" ¹⁷ But they pleaded with him to the point of embarrassment, so he said, "Send them." So they sent out the fifty men, who looked for him for three days without finding him. ¹⁸ They returned to Elisha who was staying in Jericho. He reminded them, "Did I not tell you not to go?"

¹⁹ The men of the cityᵃ said to Elisha, "See now, the location of the city is good, as you see sir. But the waters are bad and the land is barren." ²⁰ He said, "Fetch me a new, shallow bowl, and put some salt in it." They brought it to him. ²¹ He then went out to the sourceᵃ of the water and threw the salt there, and said, "Thus has Yahweh declared, 'May these waters be cleansed, and may there come from them no more death or barrenness.'" ²² The waters are clear even to this day, according to the word which Elisha spoke.

²³ He went up from there to Bethel, and as he was going up in the road some small boys came out of the city and tauntedᵃ him and said, "Up you go, baldy! Up you go, baldy!" ²⁴ He turned around and fixed his gaze upon themᵃ and cursed them in the name of Yahweh. Then two she-bears came out of the forest and devoured forty-two of the boys. ²⁵ From there he went on to Mount Carmel, and thence returned to Samaria.

Notes

2.a. Here and in v 4 פה "here" is rendered by G as ἐνταῦθα. This is not common in G, and occurs only in the Former Prophets (Judg 4:20; 1 Sam 16:11; 21:8; 2 Sam 11:22; 1 Kgs 19:9 and 2 Kgs 2:4). G^B translates with the more normal ὧδε.

2.b. Here G reads ἦλθεν (וילך "and he went") perhaps in an attempt to smooth out some of the obvious geographical difficulties of the passage (see below *Comment*).

3.a. G^L adds here the phrase οἱ υἱοὶ τῶν προφητῶν "the sons of the prophets" which appears to be a typically Lucianic expansion.
3.b. G correctly renders the MT היום with σήμερον "this day." Cf. S. J. DeVries, *Yesterday, Today and Tomorrow*, 133–277, esp. 233–34.
3.c. The MT מעל ראשך "from over your head" is rendered very literally by G with ἀπάνωθεν τῆς κεφαλῆς σου.
7.a. With the phrase על הירדן "at the Jordan" Syr attempts an assimilation with v 13 by the addition of the equivalent of שפת "lip," "bank." Some Gr. MSS read ἐνώπιον "before."
8.a. MT reads חרבה "wadi," a word normally reserved for dried-up water courses (Gen 7:22; Exod 14:21–22; Josh 3:17; 4:18; Ezek 30:12; Hag 2:6). G offers ἔρημος, which can have the same meaning, but apart from here and Ezek 30:12 the word is never used as a translation of חרבה. G^L offers ξηράς "parched land," which is the more normal rendering.
9.a. G reads ἐν τῷ διαβῆναι (possibly כעברם).
10.a. MT reads לקח "take." The absence of the מ on the ptcp is permissible. See GKC § 52s.
11.a. G reads here καὶ ἀνελήμφθη for ויעל "and he went up." This is an exegetical interpretation of the ascent of Elijah as an ascension in the later religious sense. In the NT the verb becomes a standard term for exaltation (cf. Mark 16:19).
12.a. For the MT והוא מצעק Syr offers the equivalent of והנה מצעק. G offers the simple καὶ ἐβόα.
13.a. MT clearly implies that the garment had fallen from Elijah. However, G reads as though the garment had originally landed upon Elisha. This is probably another example of exegetical interpretation anticipating the comment of the sons of the prophets in v 15.
14.a. The first part of the question is omitted by G which has instead Ποῦ ὁ Θεὸς Ἠλιοὺ ἀφφώ "where is the God of Elijah Apho," thus understanding the MT אף־הוא "also he" as a proper name. α' reads καίπερ αὐτός and σ' καὶ νῦν (איפה "where"). The difficulty of reading אף הוא as a proper name is recognized by Θ who added the explanatory note, ἄλλου ἑρμηνεύται κρυφίως "by another a secret is interpreted" (cf. Ehrlich, *Randglossen* 7:281–82).
14.b. G^L here adds ἐκ δευτέρου "a second time."
14.c. Some MSS add διὰ ξηρᾶς "on parched land" in conformity to v 8.
15.a. G^L adds here καὶ ἀναστρέφοντα αὐτόν "and he returned."
16.a. G adds here καὶ ἔρριψεν αὐτὸν ἐν τῷ Ἰορδάνῃ "and thrown him in the Jordan," which is omitted by G^L.
19.a. The changes offered by G^L in the next few verses are clearly in the nature of expansionary interpretive comments which do not presuppose a different original text. For example, after העיר "the city" (v 19) is added ταύτης "same."
21.a. The preposition ἐπί "upon" is added after מוצא. "source" and at the end of v 21 the explanation διὰ ταῦτα "through the same" is given.
23.a. Almost as if to make the taunting of the prophet by the boys more deserving of punishment G^L adds here καὶ ἐλίθαζον αὐτόν "they stoned him."
24.a. In the same spirit as the above G^A describes the boys as παραβάσεως καὶ ἀργίας "a transgression and idle deed."

Form/Structure/Setting

2 Kgs 2 contains three distinct stories about the prophet Elisha, who now assumes the role of his former master Elijah. Vv 1–18 recount the story of the journey toward the point where Elijah is taken up "in the whirlwind," and the beginning of the journey retracing the steps of the pair. The "sons of the prophets" witness to the fact that Elisha is indeed the rightful successor of Elijah. Vv 19–22 tell of the "healing" of the waters of Jericho and vv 23–24 recount the strange incident of Elisha and the taunting boys. V 25 is a redactional comment to direct the itinerary of Elisha back to where Elijah was in chapter one. This final verse also places Elisha in Samaria, the place from which the narrative of chapter three begins.

DeVries (*Prophet against Prophet*, 53–54, 116–23) has suggested the following history of the chapter. Vv 19–22 are secondary and not a part of the original collection to which the other stories of the chapter belong. The phrase משם "from there" of v 23 cannot refer to the "city" of v 19 "since Gilgal and Jericho do not fit the description of having foul water or lying in a barren land" (DeVries, *Prophet against Prophet*, 120). Vv 1–18 and vv 23–24 originally had different life settings, the first as a "prophet-legitimation narrative." Characteristic of this genre is a marvelous story demonstrating the scope and nature of the prophet's power, the purpose of which is to identify a particular prophet as genuine. Vv 23–24 is a "power-demonstration narrative" which is a marvelous story exemplifying charismatic power. Its purpose is to provide illustration of what a model prophet can do. This genre has a subclassification of "prophetic word story." Vv 19–22 come under the same general heading, but are subclassified as an "interpreted act story."

The first stage in the collection of these narratives, according to DeVries, is an early legitimation collection, one of the "several elemental collections attributed to Elisha and developed among his disciples" (*Prophet against Prophet*, 117). In this collection DeVries includes parts of 1 Kgs 19–21; 2 Kgs 2:1–18, 23–25, with v 23a and v 25 being redactional. An independent collection of narratives, composed sometime after the death of Elisha, it also included 4:8–37; 5:1–27; and 8:1–6. In the first stage of collection it was not attached to the Elijah tales. DeVries notes that the geographical framework might have provided the connecting link for these stories.

The lone narrative, vv 19–22, belonged to a second collection of stories, also dealing with the legitimation of the prophet, but containing more spectacular miracles. It included 4:1–7; parts of 4:39–41, 42–44; and 6:1–7. In distinction from the first collection, these narratives share "a common style, a common elemental structure, and a common theme of wonders worked in the realm of nature" (*Prophet against Prophet*, 121). Details of location are vague.

Detailed though such an analysis is, and helpful for the categorization of such stories, a reconstruction of the pre-history of the chapter rests on two unprovable assumptions. The first is that all common literary forms have a common life-setting, and the second is that the original life-setting of such stories is necessary for an interpretation of the narratives in their present setting. While the first assumption inevitably involves a certain amount of uncertainty regarding the oral and early literary stages of the development of the tradition, the second assumption involves a circular argument. From the shape of the story an original life-setting is posited, but it can be no more than hypothetical. From this the form is interpreted. Such a position is best avoided.

Rofé's attempt at the classification of these stories (*JBL* 89 [1970] 427–40) provides a possible alternative. 2 Kgs 2:1–24 are "simple legends" originating from within the circle of the prophet's followers. The purpose of such tales was to enhance the prophet's ability to perform miracles. Lacking in such stories is any moral content. They are brief and immediate responses to given situations. In chap. 2 the situations are a pressing need and ridicule of a man of God. They are abbreviated forms of longer oral tales.

Vv 1–18 are the result of a "biographic drive" behind the collection of such tales and are probably the end-product of the process of compilation. In distinction from the following two tales, the miracles in vv 1–18 "do not come about in order to solve any contingent need; no redemptive act is required by the circumstances. . . . Here the miracles are necessary for a much broader end" (Rofé, *JBL* 89 [1970] 438).

Attempts such as these to search behind the present narratives for (1) a classification of forms and genres and (2) a clearer understanding of the history of such forms are valuable to a point. Certain "breaks" do exist in the present narrative which might indicate the joining together of originally separate tales. But there can never be certainty in such ventures. First, in the light of the fact that most narratives of this kind are restricted to the histories of Elijah and Elisha, is there ever sufficient comparative material with which to compile a catalog of forms and genres? Rofé's comparable material, the "lives" of the saints, presents a serious anachronism. Second, do such stories in their present literary forms betray any traces of their oral stage? Form-critics like Koch (*Biblical Tradition*, 5) would argue that certain stereotyped features of each story reveal an original oral setting. But it is precisely the abrupt, simple style of the stories which leads Rofé to suggest exactly the opposite, namely, that they are literary abbreviations of a longer oral form! Third, whether such a detailed, yet hypothetical, reconstruction of the pre-literary stage of the stories in 2 Kgs 2 is of any help in the understanding of the chapter in its present form and in its wider literary context is a question still worth posing. The answer must be that such a reconstruction is of marginal significance (see D. Greenwood, "Rhetorical Criticism and Formgeschichte," *JBL* 89 [1970] 418–26).

Both the analyses referred to above agree on the separation of the stories in the chapter (vv 1–18, vv 19–22, vv 23–24). Each story represents a stage in the progression of the early ministry of Elisha. The abrupt change of pace between v 18 and v 19, the linking comment in v 23a (ויעל משם בית־אל "and he went up from there to Bethel"), and the editorial conclusion of v 25 all speak to the composite nature of the chapter. But to what purpose? It is with this level of the question that the interpreter of Scripture *qua* Scripture is ultimately concerned. Taken as it stands, the chapter does "round off" the journey embarked upon by Elijah and Elisha. But the following analysis takes the matter further, and sees the chapter as an integral part of the opening stages of the ministry of Elisha encompassed by both chapters one and two.

The focal point of chapter two is v 11, which describes briefly the departure of Elijah. Chapters one and two are so structured that what precedes v 11 leads inevitably to it and what follows v 11 moves decisively away from it, while at the same time repeating in reverse order the stages leading to the ascension. In other words chapters one and two form an inverted narrative, an extended chiasmus. In 2:10, Elisha's request for the double portion of the spirit of Elijah is made dependent upon his witnessing the ascension (אם תראה אתי לקח) "if you see me taken"). 2:12 states simply ואלישע ראה "and Elisha saw." 2:9 includes the request for the spirit; 2:13 tells how Elisha picked up the garment, the symbol of succession (1 Kgs 19:19), which had fallen from Elijah. 2:8 and 2:14 are almost identical:

2:8		2:14	
ויקח את אדרתו		ויקח את אדרת	"and he took his garment"
ויכה את המים		ויכה את המים	"and he struck the waters"
ויחצו הנה והנה		ויחצו הנה והנה	"and they parted"
ויעברו שניהם	"and they two crossed over"	ויעבר אלישע	"and Elisha crossed over"

In 2:7 and 2:15 mention is made of the "sons of the prophets" who are situated "opposite" (מנגד) the site of the ascension. 2:2–6 tell how three times the sons of the prophets ask Elisha whether he knows that his master will be taken from him. This is balanced in 2:16–18 by their request to confirm the departure of Elijah.

Although 2:19–22, 23–24 appear to be outside this scheme of inversion, this is not so. To complete the journey begun in chapter one from Carmel they must be included (cf. Lundbom, *JTS* 24 [1973] 39–50). But this geographical interest is not the only one. The themes and phrases found in these remaining stories reflect those found in 1:1–8, 16–17, and 9–15. The balance is between 1:1–8, 16–17, and 2:19–22 and 1:9–15 and 2:23–24. The common theme in the first pair of stories is of sickness and healing. In the one, the king seeks out a foreign god to ask to be healed; in the other, the men of Jericho seek Elisha's help. Both situations are greeted with a word of God—in the first a word of judgment and death, in the second a word of healing. Both stories end with a fulfillment formula וימת כדבר יהוה אשר־דבר אליהו "and he died according to the word of Yahweh which Elijah spoke" (1:17); וירפו המים עד היום הזה כדבר אלישע אשר דבר "and the waters are clear even to this day, according to the word which Elisha spoke" (2:22). There appears to be a deliberate link between the fact that Ahaziah dies without progeny, and the original state of the land which Elisha heals.

In the second pair of stories three points of similarity are worth noting. In both a challenge is offered to the status of the prophet. In 1:9–15 Elijah is ordered by the king to "come down," and in the second Elisha is taunted by the boys to "go up." The response in both is drastic and decisive. Death comes, but through a third party, the agent of judgment. The syntax of each description of the judgment is identical:

1:10		2:24	
ותרד	"and came down	ותצאנה	"and came out
אש	fire	שתים דבים	two she-bears
מן־השמים	from the skies	מן היער	from the forest
ותאכל	and consumed"	ותבקענה	and devoured"

To be noted also is that in 2 Kgs 1 and 2 are found the only physical features of the prophets. The one is "hairy" and the other "bald."

The purpose of this literary retracing of the steps of Elijah by Elisha is to identify the latter as the rightful successor of the former. The narrative contains several overt statements to this fact (2:15) and the literary structure of the two chapters offers further support. The two chapters together form the "succession narrative" of Elisha and as such, should be included as part of the Elisha material. They provide a fitting end to the ministry of one prophet and a good beginning to the ministry of another.

Comment

2 Kgs 2 tells the story of the last event in the life and ministry of Elijah and the succession of his servant and follower, Elisha. The two embark upon a journey from Gilgal to Bethel and thence to the Jordan near Jericho where they cross the river. On the east bank of the river Elijah departs in a spectacular way. Much has been said as to whether this narrative belongs strictly to the Elijah or the Elisha collection of stories (see *Introduction*). It seems unnecessary to make such a distinction when the present context is taken seriously. The narrative of the chapter provides a fitting conclusion to the stories concerning Elijah—a conclusion certainly not provided by the material in 2 Kgs 1—and a fitting opening to the ministry of Elisha as his rightful successor.

A point of note in this chapter is an overt reminder of the traditions connected with Moses and Joshua (cf. Montgomery/Gehman, 354; Gray, 475.) The similarities are quite extensive between this narrative, the narrative of the crossing of the Reed Sea (Exod 14), and the narrative of the crossing of the Jordan (Josh 3). They are expounded in the comments below. The similarities extend beyond the use of common words. The relationship of Elijah to Elisha is like that of Moses to Joshua, and both successors are appointed in similar fashion (Num 27:18–23; 1 Kgs 19:15–21). Further, the location of the crossing of the Jordan is identical, and the cities of Bethel, Gilgal, and Jericho are common to both. Whether this connection is due to the preservation of the Reed Sea traditions and the first crossing of the Jordan by the custodians of the shrine at Gilgal (so Gray, 475, following H.-J. Kraus, *VT* 1 [1951] 190–91), who later became the followers of the prophet, or whether it is a deliberate echo created by the writer is difficult to determine.

1 מִן־הַגִּלְגָּל "from Gilgal." The identification of Gilgal here is problematic. The Gilgal mentioned in the Conquest narrative (Josh 4:19) is clearly a site immediately to the west of the Jordan between the river and Jericho. It is normally identified with Khirbet al-Maffjir (cf. J. Muilenburg, "Gilgal," *IDB* 2:398–99). This identification, however, would necessitate an ascent, not a descent from Gilgal to Bethel as indicated in the following verse. Alternative sites for Gilgal are Qalqilya or Jajljulya, both situated in the central highlands north of Bethel. This might solve the puzzling geographical details of the journey. On the other hand, the OT makes no distinction between different Gilgals. The suggestion of Lundbom (*JJS* 24 [1973] 39–50) that the journey was indeed much longer than is indicated by the narrative is possible, but supporting evidence is lacking. Further, it does not solve the problem of the journey from Gilgal *down* to Bethel. The same objection is to be leveled against the notion of Galling (*ZTK* 53 [1956] 139) that the repeated attempts of Elijah to leave Elisha behind lend themselves to the kind of zig-zag journey indicated in the narrative. The departure from Gilgal has no link with the preceding narrative and demonstrates the originally separate context of the two stories.

2 חי־יהוה וחי־נפשך "as Yahweh lives and as your soul lives." Such an oath is common in the OT and is found also in the Lachish Letters (111:9; Cf. J. C. L. Gibson, *Syrian Semitic Inscriptions*, vol. 1, 38). The difference in pointing between the two exclamations חֵי is to preserve the uniqueness of the divine name (so Burney, *Notes*, 264). The form חַי is used only of יהוה (see also GKC § 93aa).

אם אעזבך "I will certainly not forsake you." The emphatic denial is idiomatic and a similar "semitism" is found in *koine* Greek (Mark 8:12). On the construction cf. GKC § 149c. The repetition of this verse anticipates the "taking up" of Elijah later in the narrative (v 11). Elisha's persistence ensures that a witness is present at both the ascension and the sign of succession (v 15).

3 The important place given the sons of the prophets in this narrative is noteworthy. Of the eleven references to them in the OT, four are found here. They function as corroborating witnesses to the succession of Elisha.

אשר בית אל is to be compared with the אשר ביריחו in v 5. The lack of the preposition is due either to an omission of the original ב from בבית־אל or the use of an "accusative of place" (so Burney, *Notes*, 264). G makes no distinction with its translation of both as ἐν "in." Cf. *GKC* § 118d-g. Rudolph, *ZAW* 63 (1951) 209, recommends a reading of אשר מיריחו "who (were) from Jericho," but this is without any foundation. If Bethel was one of the dwelling places of the sons of the prophets, then this verse sheds some light on one aspect of the prophetic tradition. It had clearly experienced a rather rapid growth since the days of Ahab and Jezebel, since there are now groups in many of the cities of Israel. Galling, however, believes the group had no formal connection with Bethel (cf. *ZTK* 53 [1956] 13). החשו the hiphil perfect should better be read as an imperative (הֲחֲשׁוּ) or emended to qal imperfect with the waw consecutive (וַיֶּחֱשׁוּ). See Ehrlich, *Randglossen* 7:280. As an imperative it reflects the very strong sense of urgency Elisha felt during this period. The persistence of Elisha shows his attempt to see through to the end the journey he and his master have embarked upon.

7 וחמשים איש מבני הנביאים "and fifty men of the sons of the prophets." The first mention of a specific number of the sons of the prophets brings to mind the spared company of fifty soldiers from the previous incident. That the two groups are to be identified (so Lundbóm, *JJS* 24 [1973] 46–47) is most unlikely. The first incident took place on Carmel and was probably removed from the ascension of Elijah by some considerable period of time. In the present narrative, these fifty men serve as further corroborating witnesses to the final disappearance of Elijah.

8 ויגלם "and he rolled them up." The use of a verbal form is a *hapax legomenon* in the OT, although it does occur in later Hebrew. Common nouns with a similar root are מגלה "scroll" and גלגל "circle." The form here is very awkward; Ehrlich (*Randglossen* 7:280) suggests ויגלה חרבה. The word is rare, appearing in Exod 14:21 and Josh 3:17. That the two prophets crossed the Jordan into the territory of Moab is important. It is the region of the death of Moses. The connection is fully exploited by Josephus. The G translation of Deut 34:6 reads: καὶ οὐκ οἶδεν οὐδεὶς τὴν ταφὴν αὐτοῦ ἕως τῆς ἡμέρας ταύτης "and no one knows the place of his burial to this day." Josephus (*Antiq.* ix.24), referring to the departure of Elijah, echoes this with the statement: καὶ οὐδεὶς ἔγνω μέχρι τῆς σήμερον αὐτοῦ τὴν τελευτήν "and no one even today knows his end." Later, he links the departure of Enoch with that of Elijah, and unconsciously with that of Moses, by stating: θάνατον δ'αὐτῶν οὐδεὶς οἶδεν "the death of them no one knows." Ignorance of the place of burial is a motif found in the OT only in connection with the death of Moses.

9 The phrase פי שנים "a double share" is found elsewhere in Deut 21:17 and indicates that Elisha is asking for the status as rightful heir to the prophetic leader's role. The phrase indicates twice as much as any other heir, not double the amount Elijah had. V 15 states simply that "the spirit of Elijah" came upon Elisha. This allusion to Deut 21:17 keeps to the fore in this narrative the motif of rightful succession.

10 The persistence of Elisha is now given explanation. His right to the succession is dependent upon his witnessing the departure of his master.

11 This verse completes the thought introduced in v 1, and from this point on in the narrative the focus of attention is now placed upon Elisha. רכב־אש וסוסי אש "a chariot of fire and horses of fire." The literary link with the "fire from heaven" in the previous chapter is obvious. What precisely a רכב אש "chariot of fire" was or a סוס אש "horse of fire" is unknown. It might refer to a "fire chariot" and "fire horses," i.e., specialized weapons of war, although such weapons are unknown elsewhere. The translation could also be "fiery chariot," as though it were some kind of apparition, or a relic of an ancient tradition (so J. W. Wevers, "Chariot," *IDB* 1:553–54). The term reappears in 6:17. See also below on v 12. The image is undoubtedly military, and the combination of chariots and horses in this way is scattered throughout the OT. The background to such allusions as these has been identified, with some merit, with the tradition of Holy War; cf. P. D. Miller, *The Divine Warrior in Early Israel*, 134–35; G. von Rad, *Der heilige Krieg im alten Israel*, 55–56; F. Stolz, *Jahwes und Israels Kriege* (ATANT 60 [Zürich: Theologischer Verlag, 1972]) 151–52. A connection with the "horses of the sun" in 2 Kgs 23:11 is a tenuous one.

בסערה "in the whirlwind." The definite article indicates a well-known tradition (cf. Amos 1:1). Of the fifteen occurrences of the term in the OT, and the eight occurrences of the shorter סער, only here in the Former Prophets is סערה found. The term is used frequently by the Latter Prophets as a symbol of judgment. Gray's (475) cautious appeal to the theophany tradition in connection with this incident is unnecessary. No elements of the classic theophany are present, with the exception of the allusion to fire (see Jeremias, *Theophanie*, for a full treatment of the topic). To be noted also is that God does not appear in this incident. Gray's rationalization of the incident as being inspired by Elijah's disappearance in a dust storm is to be rejected. Clouds, or dust of any kind, are absent from the description.

12 אבי אבי רכב ישראל ופרשיו "My Father! My Father! The chariots of Israel and its horses!" This cry of Elisha at the climax of the chapter reappears again in 13:14, this time on the lips of the king. Attempts to show a literary dependency of the present text on the latter (Williams, *JBL* 85 [1966] 346; Phillips, *Words and Meanings*, 188; A. Rofé, *JBL* 89 [1970] 436) are unsuccessful. They are based on the presupposition that the term "father" was not used of prophets, except by kings. The cry is best treated in two parts.

The double expression is distinctive. That it signifies an address of respect (Ehrlich, *Randglossen* 7:281; H. Ringgren, *TDOT* 1:7–8) is obvious. It has also been interpreted as the title of the leader of the prophetic group (so Williams, *JBL* 85 [1966] 348), as a professional title for an interpreter of ecstatic utterances (so Phillips, *Words and Meanings*, 194), or even an expression of mild anxiety parallel to the Italian *"mama mia!"* (so T. H. Gaster in a private communication to Lundbom, *JJS* 24 [1973] 47). Because of its repetition, Galling (*ZTK* 53 [1956] 130) sees it as an expression of sorrow at the loss of his leader. Some comparable texts are 1 Kgs 13:2 and Jer 22:29. This double form is not restricted to the lament, although it does occur as such in 2 Sam 19:4, and is adopted as such by Luke 13:34. The repetition is a simple means of attracting attention (cf. Gen 22:11; 46:2; Exod 3:4 and 1 Sam 3:4).

Elisha's reference to the "chariot(ry) of Israel and its horses" is puzzling. There is little to commend the suggestion that it was used in contrast to the Aramaic war god "Rekeb-el" mentioned in the Senjirli inscriptions (Galling, *ZTK* 53 [1956] 146–48). It is a deliberately chosen military image and can only reflect what Elisha saw during this incident, a vision of a chariot and cavalry. The possible link with the Passover liturgy (Beek, *OTS* 17 [1972] 4–7) seems unnecessary.

13 Now begins Elisha's journey back to the other witnesses. The idea of the cloak as a symbol of succession is first seen in 1 Kgs 19:19 in connection with the two men.

14 איה יהוה אלהי אליהו "Where is Yahweh, the God of Elijah?" The performance of this miracle by Elisha answers his own question. Since he is able to duplicate what Elijah had done, the true succession is confirmed. There is no need to see it as a question born of anxiety (Ehrlich, *Randglossen* 7:281–82). A link with Deut 32:37 is perhaps implied in the question.

15 The function of the initial questions from the sons of the prophets is now clear in the narrative. Their questions serve to confirm and their attitude to support Elijah's succession.

The following incident offers additional confirmation of the departure of Elijah. Elisha's word is found to be true. He was a true witness to the ascension of his master. With this incident, the focus of attention now moves completely to the new prophet.

16 בני־חיל "sons of power." The phrase can be used of soldiers, although not exclusively so. They are so described because they are capable of carrying out a three-day search for the departed Elijah. This search, and its results, again confirm the word of Elisha.

רוח יהוה "the spirit of Yahweh." The link between the whirlwind and the spirit of Yahweh is in keeping with the presentation of the spirit of God in the OT as an instrument of power (cf. H. W. Robinson, *The Christian Experience of the Holy Spirit* [London: Nisbet, 1928] 8–14). The reference is a deliberate allusion to 1 Kgs 18:12, in which mention is made of the unpredictability of the prophet's activity under the guidance of the spirit of God. Ezekiel's frequent references to being "lifted by the spirit" (Ezek 3:12, 14; 8:3, etc.) for a visionary experience can be seen as a development of this. This development continues into the apocalyptic tradition (cf. *Asc Isa* 6:14).

17 עד בש "to the point of embarrassment" is an expression found again in 8:11 and earlier in Judg 3:25.

18 The confirmation of the disappearance of Elijah and the truth of the word of his successor is now complete.

The following two incidents present the first characteristic miracles of the prophet Elisha. They are marked by both kindness and severity. On the rhetorical links with the incidents of chap. 1, see *Form/Structure/Setting*.

19 מושב העיר טוב "the location of the city is good." "The city" is usually identified with Jericho and, although that is not stated, it is certainly implied from the context. The story is preserved today in the tradition of the spring of Elisha situated to the east of Tell es-Sultan.

המים רעים "the waters (are) bad." The reason for the toxicity of the waters is not given. I. M. Blake (*PEQ* 99 [1967] 86–97) has suggested that periodic contact with radioactive matter released during earth tremors gave rise to the tradition of Joshua's cursing the spring (Josh 6:26) and its subsequent "healing" by Elisha.

משכלת "barren." The Hebrew root שכל means "to be bereaved." Its form, a piel participle, is a problem. Grammatically, the first occurrence is adjectival, qualifying הארץ, "the land is barren." This can be taken either as understanding the piel as causative, "the land causes barrenness," or as understanding the term "land" to include its people. While causative meanings can be given to certain words pointed piel (e.g., לִמֵּד "to teach," i.e., "to cause to learn," see GKC § 52g), the causative meaning of this verb in the piel is not found elsewhere in the OT. The use of הארץ for the inhabitants of the land is found in 1 Sam 17:46, but this is not common, and the more normal understanding of the term in a context such as 2 Kgs 2 is "ground" in the agricultural sense. G^L offers a reading of ἀτέκνουντα "be childless," which might suggest a prior Hebrew reading of מְשֻׁכָּלִים. But this could also be an attempt by the Greek to smooth out the grammatical difficulty noted above.

21 The occurrence of מְשַׁכָּלֶת again as a piel participle is difficult. Gray, 7) suggests that it be pointed as a substantive noun. However, the piel participle can assume a nominal function in a sentence, as in Isa 40:9 (מְבַשֶּׂרֶת יְרוּשָׁלָם . . . מְבַשֶּׂרֶת צִיּוֹן).

The pointing of רִפֵּאתִי "I have healed" is on the analogy of a *lamedh he* and not a *lamedh aleph* verb. This is not impossible, though not very common (see Burney, *Notes*, 267). The correct pointing should be רִפֵּאתִי.

The use of salt as a healing agent is unknown elsewhere in the OT. It can be used as a food flavoring (Job 6:6) and is used in some sacrifices (Lev 2:13). Abimelech's "sowing" of a city with salt (Judg 9:45) is to demonstrate the opposite of that intended by Elisha's gesture, namely, to curse the city.

22 The pointing of וַיֵּרָפוּ is also problematical since the verb is *lamedh he* and pointed as such. The root, therefore, could be רפה "to sink," "to weaken," and not רפא "to heal." Many, e.g., Burney, *Notes*, 267, regard it as a *lamedh he* form of רפא "to heal," and so it is translated in most versions. A. Sperber (*ZAW* 82 [1970] 114–16) takes the above difficulty seriously and argues that two events are being described in this story: (1) the curing of the toxicity of the waters by the use of salt, (2) the subsequent desalination (i.e., the weakening) of the waters so that they once again become potable. This would be, in effect, a miracle within a miracle. However, the subtleties in the pointing of the consonantal text are representative of a late stage of interpretation. G clearly understands both verbs as variant forms of רפא "to heal." Such combinations of form and pointing occur elsewhere with this verb in the OT. The consonantal form of רפה, as a synonym for רפא "to heal," occurs in Jer 3:22; 19:11; 51:9; Ezek 47:8; and Ps 60:4. Pointed as a *lamedh aleph* verb it is found in Jer 3:22 (ארפה); 19:11 (להרפה); and Ps 60:4 (רפה). Pointed as a regular *lamedh he* verb it is found in Jer 51:9 (נרפתה) and Ezek 47:8 (נרפאו). Therefore, neither the combination of *lamedh he*, pointing with a *lamedh aleph* verb, nor the use of the *lamedh he* רפה as a synonym for רפא "to heal" is unique to 2 Kgs 2:21–22.

כדבר אלישע "according to Elisha's word." The repetition of a phrase similar to that found in 1:17 confirms Elisha's role as the successor to Elijah as prophet.

The final story in this chapter raises some serious questions which are not answered by the writer. The death of forty-two boys is hardly to be seen as a characteristic prophetic activity. Suffice it to say that, like the incident of Elijah and the soldiers of Ahaziah, this incident is characterized by excess. Like the touching of the Ark of the Covenant (2 Sam 6:6–7), the ridicule of sacred persons is rewarded by the harshest of punishments. The incident is reminiscent of 1 Kgs 13:20–24 and 20:35–36.

23 With the ascent to Bethel the journey of Elisha is taken a step further. He is now retracing the steps both he and Elijah took earlier in the chapter.

עלה קרח "go up, baldy." The paucity of references to the physical characteristics of prophets in the OT throws this into sharp relief. It is in direct contrast to the identifying features of Elijah (1:8). Since artificial baldness was legislated against in Israel (Deut 14:1), Elisha's condition was a natural one.

24 With the utterance of a curse "in the name of the LORD," the focus of attention in this incident is the word of the prophet. It is, however, in direct contrast to the preceding word of healing.

ארבעים ושני "forty-two" is hardly likely to contain any symbolic significance (contra Gray and Montgomery) since the term is quite uncommon in the OT. The connection with the forty-two fellow officers of the king of Judah in 2 Kgs 10:14 is coincidental.

25 אל הר הכרמל "to Mount Carmel" makes the journey complete, and Elisha returns where Elijah was first encountered in chapter one. His movement from there to Samaria would indicate a previous residence in that city. It also places Elisha in a position to be involved in the military expedition which presumably originated in Samaria, and which is described in the following chapter.

Excursus: On the Term בני הנביאים *"Sons of the Prophets"*

With the exception of 1 Kgs 20:35, the phrase בני הנביאים is found for the first time in the OT in 2 Kgs 2. It occurs eleven times in the OT (1 Kgs 20:35; 2 Kgs 2:3, 5, 7, 15; 4:1, 38 [2x]; 5:22; 6:1; 9:1), and all but the first occur in connection with the figure of Elisha. Other groupings of prophets are also found in the OT. Saul encountered a "band of prophets" (חבל נביאים) descending from a high place, presumably after worship (1 Sam 10:5, 10). Organized prophets appear in connection with the court (1 Kgs 22) and as the object of attack by the "classical" prophets (Jer 23:9–40; Mic 3:5–8). A further collective title is "my servants the prophets" (2 Kgs 9:7; Amos 3:7, etc.). The statement in Amos 7:14 that he is "neither a prophet nor the son of a prophet" has furthered the opinion that the prophets of the early monarchy were banded together into guilds, and organized for the propagation of professional prophetic activity (so J. Lindblom, *Prophecy in Ancient Israel* [Philadelphia: Muhlenberg, 1962] 69–71). The idea is that such "guilds" were carefully organized under a leader, whose title was "father." Lindblom states, "It seems that the leader had to train members of the guild in ecstatic exercises and ecstatic practice and also instruct them in matters belonging to the true Yahwistic religion and cult" (*Prophecy*, 69). The analogy for such guilds is found among the dervish guilds of Islam (see G. von Rad, *Old Testament Theology*, 2:25–32; Gray, 474).

The earliest interpretation of the "sons of the prophets" in this way is that of Josephus (*Antiq.* ix.28), who refers to Elisha as the "disciple" (μαθητής) of Elijah. This is the same word used of the man sent to anoint Jehu in 2 Kgs 9:1. The phrase אחד מבני הנביאים "one of the sons of the prophets" he renders ἕνα τῶν αὑτοῦ μαθητῶν "one of his disciples" (*Antiq.* ix.106). However, Josephus is not consistent in his use of the word μαθητής. In *Antiq.* ix.68, in paraphrasing 2 Kgs 6:32, he states that Elisha καθιζόμενος δὲ οἴκαδε παρ'αὑτῳ σὺν ταῖς μαθηταῖς "was sitting in his house with the disciples." However, for "disciples" MT reads "elders" (הזקנים).

The fact that the term "sons of the prophets" is only used, with one exception, in connection with the ministry of Elisha and the fact that most of the data used for the reconstruction of the prophetic "guilds" is found in the same collection of material should caution against hasty conclusions regarding the nature of the entire prophetic movement in the mid-ninth century in Israel. Further, deductions based upon 1 Kgs 20:35; 2 Kgs 1:8; and 2 Kgs 2:22–24 that the prophets all wore some kind of distinguishing tattoo, a uniform, and a tonsure (so Lindblom, *Prophecy*, 69–71; Gray, 480) are generalizations based upon limited pieces of evidence. Whether the "sons of the prophets" were anything more than admirers or lay supporters of the prophet Elisha (so Rofé, *JBL* 89 [1970] 437) must still be shown.

An understanding must be gained of the term בני הנביאים "sons of the prophets" by looking at its use in the OT, the use of the terms בן "son" and בני "children of" in an analogous form, and what light, if any, Amos 7:14 throws on the debate. Regarding the first point, the limitations of the term have already been mentioned. 1 Kgs 20:35 is difficult to date. Although it is incorporated within the Elijah material, the prophet does not figure in the story at all. The only prophet directly associated with the group is Elisha. Sometimes the term "father" (אב) is found in the Elisha material. It is spoken by Elisha at the departure of Elijah (2:12) and again by Joash at the death of Elisha (13:14). In 6:21 it is found on the lips of the king of Israel, presumably Joram. Nowhere is it found as a form of address used by the "sons of the prophets." The likelihood of its being the group title for the leader

(Williams, *JBL* 85 [1966] 344–49) is therefore remote. No evidence exists to show that Elisha himself was one of the "sons of the prophets" before he was named as Elijah's successor. The more common form of address, and the one used exclusively by the "sons of the prophets," is "lord" (אדני).

The term "son" (בן) in the singular and plural construct is used in a bewildering number of ways in the OT. It can designate progeny (Gen 21:10); it can designate national groupings (Gen 23:18; Lev 27:34, etc.); and it can also be used to characterize persons or groups in a derogatory fashion (Gen 35:18; 1 Sam 10:27; 2 Kings 6:32; Ps 89:22; Hos 10:9; Job 41:26). It is used of certain professional groups such as priests (Lev 3:13; Ps 42:1). In Gen 5:32 age is indicated with the phrase בן־חמש מאות שנה "five hundred years old," and in Gen 15:2 an heir is called a בן ביתי "son of my house." In Ps 79:11 those under sentence of death are בני תמותה and men of valor are בני חיל (1 Sam 14:52; 18:17). Mankind is also referred to as בני האדם (Ps 33:13; Eccles 1:13). In Zech 4:14 persons anointed for a special purpose are בני היצר, a synonym for משיחים. In Gen 6:2, 4 the enigmatic בני אלהים "sons of God" are encountered. With the exception of this last reference there are no other occurrences of the structure: plural construct noun, article plus plural noun.

At this point Amos 7:14 should be mentioned. The text reads לא נביא אנכי ולא בן־נביא אנכי "I am no prophet, nor am I a son of a prophet" and is a simple denial by Amos of any prophetic status. Amos' reply is in parallel form comparable to Ps 22:6 or Ps 8:5. The expression בן נביא "son of a prophet" is unique and a synonym for נביא "prophet." It is therefore to be distinguished from the plural form of the phrase (contra Williams, *JBL* 85 [1966] 344–49). The translation of "prophet's disciple" (H. W. Wolff, *Joel and Amos*, Hermeneia [Philadelphia: Fortress, 1977] 306) is unjustified. When one member of the group is singled out, the expression is "one of the sons of the prophets" (1 Kgs 20:35) and not "a son of a prophet." Further, to designate the "sons of the prophets" as a professional group on the basis of a supposed parallel between them and the "sons of Aaron" or the "sons of Korah" begs the question.

That the "sons of the prophets" were a well-known group can be assumed by the way they are introduced without explanation in 1 Kgs 20:35. A full picture of the group could only be gained by the biblical description of them, but the picture is sketchy indeed. 1 Kgs 20:35 offers little by way of description. There is no suggestion in the narrative that the man revealed a tattoo, or some other distinctive badge of his prophetic office when he removed his bandage. The impression left by the story is that the king recognized him. The oft-cited connection of the groups with shrines on the basis of texts such as 2 Kgs 2:3, 5, 15 can only be sustained if the group present in Jericho was really the group from Gilgal (so Gray, 474)!

In 2 Kgs 4, one of the sons of the prophets dies and leaves his wife and sons destitute. Whether family life was the norm for the others is not stated. The narrative does imply that this man lived alone with his family apart from the group and that Elisha's response to her need was something out of the ordinary. The same is true of 4:38. In time of famine some of them come to Elisha for help and nothing is suggested concerning a permanent dwelling place. The phrase "sitting before him" (ישבים לפניו) is ambiguous. 2 Kgs 6:1 suggests a temporary meeting place. In 2 Kgs 5:22, the "servant" might indicate that some of the sons of the prophets had servants, or it might be a synonym for one of the group (cf. 2 Kgs 9:1–13). To be noted is that the prophets killed during the reign of Ahab are designated by the term "servants," not "sons of the prophets" (cf. 2 Kgs 9:7).

Since the evidence does not support the kind of highly organized group of prophetic "disciples" envisaged by some scholars, what can be concluded? Since the group disappears after the death of Elisha, they must have had some special connection with him. We conclude that they were the "lay supporters" of the successor of Elijah who offered encouragement after the decimation of the Yahwistic prophets during the reign of Ahab. They were scattered throughout the country and associated with Elisha to varying degrees, some even assuming the rare function of prophecy (2 Kgs 9:6–10).

Explanation

Of all the stories about the prophets in the OT, the first two chapters of 2 Kings are unique in that they offer the only detailed account of the succession of one prophet by another. The uniqueness of the stories preserves the "charismatic" nature of biblical prophecy. The prophetic function is not to be seen as related to an office in the professional sense. To be sure, there are professional prophets in the OT (cf. Jer 23:9–40) and the many references to "my/his servants the prophets" (e.g., Amos 3:7, etc.) emphasize the continuing nature of the prophetic tradition. But the OT makes clear that this tradition is created by the will of God and through the call of God, not by inheritance. It is a true gift, hence a "charisma" (cf. Jer. 1:5). The earlier choice of Elisha from outside even the "sons of the prophets" (1 Kgs 19:10, 19–21) illustrates this point and sets in motion the series of events which culminates in his succession as depicted in this chapter.

Mention has already been made in the *Comment* above of the connections between the succession of Elisha in place of Elijah and the succession of Joshua in place of Moses. Joshua is chosen as successor to Moses (Num 27:12–23) and, as a result of his "ordination" by Moses, is "full of the spirit of wisdom" (Deut 34:9). Joshua performs actions similar to those of Moses (Exod 14; Josh 3–4) and Elisha performs actions similar to those of Elijah (vv 9–14). These links were exploited by later traditions concerning these men and were most carefully forged by Josephus.

That the writer of the story of the ascension of Elijah wished to emphasize the element of the succession of Elisha is made apparent by the role he assigns the "sons of the prophets" in the narrative. They act as witnesses to Elisha's receiving the mantle of Elijah (v 15) and, by their questioning of the departure of Elijah and the outcome of that incident (vv 16–18), they add confirmation to the fact that Elijah has departed and that his successor's word is true. This purpose of the writer is further demonstrated by the careful construction of the opening two chapters of the book (see *Form/Structure/Setting* above).

Why such a point should be so important can only be guessed. That there was originally some question about the validity of Elisha's succession is certainly a possibility. The presentation of the departure of Elijah and the succession of Elisha would then be an attempt at legitimating the succession. But this is speculative. It moves us into areas of historical reconstruction for which clear evidence is lacking. The literary effect of the presentation of the succession of Elisha in this way is more easily seen. Throughout the following chapters of 2 Kings, frequent mention is made of the presence of "the prophet in Israel" or similar phrases (cf. 3:11; 5:3, 8; 6:12). Furthermore, the presence of this particular prophet, Elisha, is contrasted with the availability of other prophets, notably those of the apostate house of Ahab (3:13).

In the years following the decimation of the Yahwistic prophets under the evil reign of Ahab and Jezebel, the prophetic tradition is not allowed to fail. There remained a faithful witness to the God of Israel after the departure of Elijah. It is this to which the sons of the prophets give witness. The interlocking design of the two chapters makes the smooth transition from the ministry of Elijah to that of Elisha.

According to both Jewish and Christian tradition, Elijah's ministry did not end with his ascension. He assumes the role of the "prophet like Moses" (Deut 18:15-18) who will be the forerunner of the Messiah at the end of time (Mal 4:4-6). His mission is to preach repentance. On the basis of Sir 48:9, a Jewish tradition developed that Elijah did not ascend to heaven, but waited in an interim state to return as forerunner of the Messiah. It is no wonder that the early Christian interpreters saw in Elijah the model for John the Baptist. His preaching of repentance, his relationship to Jesus, and even the misunderstanding of the dress of Elijah (2 Kgs 1:8) were all reflected in the Christian understanding of John (cf. Mark 9:9-13).

In light of the treatment accorded Elijah by later tradition, it is easy to overlook the important role Elisha played in the development of the prophetic tradition. Apart from the illustrative use of an incident from his ministry in Luke 4:27, the NT ignores Elisha. He is completely overshadowed by his predecessor. Similarly, Jewish tradition devoted far more attention to Elijah.

Jehoshaphat and Joram against Moab (3:1-27)

Bibliography

Bernhardt, K. H. "Der Feldzug der drei Könige." *Schalom: Studien zur Glaube und Geschichte Israels*. Stuttgart: Calver Verlag, 1971. 11-22. **Derchain, P.** "Le plus anciens témoignages de sacrifices d'enfants chez les Semites occidentaux." *VT* 20 (1970) 351-55. **Geus, C. H. J. De.** "The Importance of Archaeological Research into Palestinian Agricultural Terraces, with an Excursus on the Hebrew Word *gbī*." *PEQ* 107 (1975) 65-74. **Liver, J.** "The Wars of Mesha, King of Moab." *PEQ* 99 (1967) 14-31. **Long, B. O.** "2 Kings III and the Genres of Prophetic Narrative." *VT* 23 (1973) 337-48. **Rost, L.** "Erwägungen zum israelitischen Brandopfer." *BZAW* 77 (1961) 177-83. **Sales, R. H.** "Human Sacrifice in Biblical Thought." *JBR* 25 (1957) 112-17. **Schweizer, H.** *Elischa in den Kriegen. Literaturwissenschaftliche Untersuchung von 2 Kön. 3; 6:8-23; 6:24-7:20.* SANT 37. Munich: Kosel Verlag, 1974. **Shafer, B. E.** "מבחור/מבחר = 'Fortress.'" *CBQ* 33 (1971) 389-96.

Translation

¹ Then Joram became king in Samaria [a] in the eighteenth year of Jehoshaphat king of Judah, and he reigned twelve years. ² But he committed evil in the eyes [a] of

Yahweh, but not as his father or his mother because he turned aside the pillar of Baal which his father [b] *had made.* ³ *But the sins* [a] *of Jeroboam son of Nebat, with which he caused Israel to sin, he clung to, and did not turn aside from it.* [b]

⁴ *Now Mesha, king of Moab, was a sheep-breeder* [a] *and was responsible for sending* [b] *to the king of Israel one hundred thousand lambs, and the wool of one hundred thousand rams.* ⁵ *But now that Ahab* [a] *was dead the king of Moab rebelled against the king of Israel.* ⁶ *So Joram the king went out and mustered* [a] *all* [b] *of Israel.* ⁷ *And as he went* [a] *he sent* [b] *word to Jehoshaphat, king of Judah, saying, "The king of Moab has rebelled against me. Will you come with me to Moab to do battle?" He replied,* [c] *"I will go up, and I will match you man for man, horse for horse."* [d] ⁸ *Then he asked, "Which way shall we go up?"* [a] *The response* [b] *was, "By the Way of the Desert of Edom."*

⁹ *So the king of Israel went* [a] *together with the king of Judah* [b] *and the king of Edom, and they circled round by this route for seven days. There was no water for the camp or for the animals who accompanied the foot soldiers.* ¹⁰ *Then the king of Israel said, "Ah! It is because Yahweh has called out these* [a] *three kings to hand them* [b] *over* [c] *to the king of Moab!"*

¹¹ *But Jehoshaphat* [a] *said, "Is there not here a prophet of Yahweh from whom* [b] *we might enquire of Yahweh?" And one of the servants of the king of Israel said, "Elisha ben Shaphat* [c] *is here, the one who poured water over the hands of Elijah."* ¹² *Jehoshaphat said, "The word of Yahweh* [a] *is with him." So the king of Israel, accompanied by Jehoshaphat and the king of Edom, went down* [b] *to him.*

¹³ *Elisha then said to the king of Israel, "What do we have in common?* [a] *Go to the prophets of your father, or the prophets of your mother!"* [b] *But the king of Israel said to him, "No! Yahweh has called these* [c] *three kings out to hand them over to the king of Moab!"* ¹⁴ *Then Elisha said, "As the LORD of hosts lives, before whom I stand, were it not that I respected* [a] *Jehoshaphat* [b] *king of Judah, I would neither glance at you nor have any respect for you!* ¹⁵ *Now bring me a minstrel!" And it happened* [a] *that as the minstrel played the hand* [b] *of Yahweh came upon him,* ¹⁶ *and he said, "Thus has Yahweh declared, 'Make this riverbed* [a] *into deep pools.'* [b] ¹⁷ *Because thus has Yahweh declared, 'You shall see neither wind nor rain, but this riverbed shall be filled with water, and you and your camp and your animals shall drink.'* ¹⁸ *This is an easy thing in the eyes of Yahweh, and he has given Moab into your hands.* ¹⁹ *You shall strike down their fortified cities, and all their choice cities.* [a] *Their best trees you shall chop down and you shall stop up their water holes. Then you shall despoil every good piece of land with rocks."* ²⁰ *Then it happened in the morning, shortly after the offering of the sacrifice, that water came from the Way of Edom,* [a] *and the whole land was full of it.*

²¹ *Now all of Moab had heard that the kings had come up to fight them, and they called together* [a] *men, all those wearing belts and upward, and they mustered along the border.* ²² *They rose up early in the morning and the sun was shining on the water, and the Moabites saw from the opposite side that the water was red like blood.* ²³ *Then they exclaimed, "This is blood! The kings* [a] *must have taken up the sword against each other,* [b] *and each man has killed his partner! Now Moab, to the spoil!"*

²⁴ *They came to the Israelite camp but Israel rose up and defeated Moab, and they fled before them, and the Israelites closed in on Moab for the final blow.* [a] ²⁵ *The cities they overthrew, and on all the good land each one threw a rock until it was*

full. They stopped up all the springs of water, cut down all the trees until there was nothing left but Kir Haresheth. ᵃ *Then the slingers surrounded it and took it.*

²⁶ *The king of Moab saw that the fight was going badly for him, so he took with him* ᵃ *seven hundred swordsmen to break out through the king of Edom's line, but he failed.* ²⁷ *So he took his firstborn son, who was to reign in his place, and offered him as a sacrifice upon the wall. At this there was great wrath upon Israel, so they withdrew from him and returned home.*

Notes

1.a. "Samaria" is omitted by G, but included by several minor MSS.
2.a. G^L translates this with the term ἐνώπιον, regarded as a relic of the OG (see Shenkel, *Chronology and Recensional Development,* 71–72). G renders it with the more literal phrase ἐν ὀφθαλμοῖς.
2.b. The second reference to "father" is omitted by some minor MSS.
3.a. G does not follow MT here, but offers the smoother sg. G^L reads ἐν ταῖς ἁμαρτίαις.
3.b. Consistent with the pl, G^L reads αὐτῶν.
4.a. G transliterates the Heb. נקד "sheep-breeder" into ἦν νωκηθ and there are several minor variations of this practice. A mistakes it for a proper name, "Menachoth." On this term see *Comment.*
4.b. G makes the reference more specific with the phrase ἐν τῇ ἐπαναστάσει, "at the rising up (turn) of the year." Tg adds the phrase "year by year."
5.a. G^L reads Jeroboam.
6.a. MT = ויפקד "appointed." G renders ἐπεσκέψατο.
6.b. כל "all" is omitted by G.
7.a. וילך "and he went" is omitted by G.
7.b. After וישלח "and he sent" G^L adds Joram. This is entirely in keeping with the G^L tendency to rename the kings and to redate the event. In this incident G^L identifies the Judean king as Ahaziah.
7.c. G^L adds Ahaziah.
7.d. MT reads כמוני כמוך כעמי כעמך כסוסי סוסיך "mine like yours, my people like your people, my horses like your horses."
8.a. G reads ἀναβῶ "I go up," G^L retains the second pers pl.
8.b. G^L again adds Joram.
9.a. Again here G^L identifies Joram.
9.b. Some MSS add "to his servants," which is an unnecessary expansion.
10.a. G omits האלה "these."
10.b. G^L reads the first pers pl pronoun.
10.c. G reads παρερχομένους δοῦναι "pass on to give," G^L offers παραδοῦναι ἡμᾶς "to give us over."
11.a. In keeping with his identification of the monarchs in this story, G^L omits any reference to Jehoshaphat.
11.b. MT reads מֵאוֹתוֹ, which is better read מֵאִתּוֹ "from him."
11.c. G renders υἱὸς Ἰωσαφάτ "son of Jehoshaphat," Josephus adds τὸν Ἠλία μαθητὴν "the disciple of Elijah."
12.a. G omits יהוה "Yahweh."
12.b. G reads "he went down."
13.a. MT reads מה לי ולך "what to me and to you." This is a common semitic expression, which is also found in *koine* Greek (John 2:4).
13.b. G omits ואל נביאי אמך "to the prophets of your mother."
13.c. G omits האלה "these."
14.a. MT reads פני יהושפט מלך יהודה אני נשא, literally, "the face of Jehoshaphat king of Judah I lift up." The same concept is found in 5:1. See also Job 22:8; Isa 3:3.
14.b. Omitted by G^L.
15.a. The expression והיה "and it happened" is awkward, and normally would read ויהי. Burney (*Notes,* 269) adopts the suggestion that this is a continuation of the speech of Elisha,

and reads it as a *waw* consecutive with the pf. He restores the text as: והיה בהיות עלי יד יהוה
והגדתי אליך את אשר ידבר יהוה ויקחו לו מנגן ויהי "and it happened when the hand of Yahweh
is on me, I shall reveal to you what Yahweh says. And so they took a minstrel to him and it
happened." This seems an unnecessary lengthening of the text, the sense of which is retained
without it.
15.b. Tg here reads "spirit."
16.a. G makes explicit the MT נחל with a translation of χειμαρρου, "a fast flowing winter
stream."
16.b. MT = גבים גבים "pools, pools."
19.a. G^B omits the first Heb clause, but G^A retains it. B. E. Shafer (*CBQ* 33 [1971] 391–92)
notes that Tg retains the double reading (ותמחון כל כרך תקיף וכל קריא כריכא), thereby
interpreting the phrase עיר מבחור not as "choice city," but rather as "walled city," a synonym
for עיר מבצר. This evidence is not conclusive, although, as Shafer points out, the double
reading is a very early phenomenon in the Palestinian textual tradition. Burney's emendation
(*Notes*, 270) to תאבדו "you shall destroy" is not necessary.
20.a. G^L adds "in the wilderness of Sour."
21.a. The G tradition is confusing. For the MT ויצעקו מכל חגר חגרים ומעלה ויעמדו על
הגבול, "and they called together of all those wearing belts and upward, and they mustered
along the border," G reads και ανεβοησαν εκ παντος περιεζωσμενοι ζωνην και ειπον Ω "and they
cried out from all those girdling on a belt and said 'Oh!' " G^L however, retains the sense of
MT with its use of επανω "above" for ומעלה "and upward." This is a mistake which could
only have come about in the G tradition with the confusion of επανω for ειπεν Ω.
23.a. G^L adds here "three."
23.b. MT = הָחָרֵב נחרבו. "attacking they attack." LXX, Syr. = הַחֶרֶב "sword."
24.a. Here MT is badly preserved. The text reads יבו בה, which is rendered by G as εισηλθον
εισπορευομενοι "they came in intervening." G clearly understands an original of ויבאו בא. Tg
and Q understand ויכו as "and they struck" and בה as "them."
25.a. MT is again confusing. *BHS* suggests an emendation to השאר לבדה קיר חרשת "was
left only Kir Haresheth." G interprets with εως του καταλιπειν τους λιθους του τοιχου καθηρμενους.
Rudolph (*ZAW* 63 [1951] 210) offers (אגפיהם) בקיר הרשת עד השאר אגפיה. The term אגף
is a loan word meaning wing or flank of an army formation. Further, see Burney, *Notes*, 272.
26.a. MT אותו is better read as אתו.

Form/Structure/Setting

2 Kgs 3 is a chapter which falls into three easily discernible sections. Vv
1–3 comprise a chronological introduction typical of so many found in the
books of Kings. Vv 4–25 offer a version of the combined Israelite, Judean,
and Edomite invasion against the rebel Moabites. Vv 26–27 tell of a quick
reversal of the fortunes of the allies and of the retreat of the invaders from
the field of battle to their homeland. Although the narrative has a "substantial
unity" (Long, *VT* 23 [1973] 337–48), there are underlying tensions of style,
content, and ideology of sufficient visibility in the chapter to lead many to
detect the composite nature of the narrative.

For example, Elisha figures in the story only in vv 11–19, and there he
performs an action which is subsidiary to the main plot of the story (cf. Gray,
468–69). Vv 4–5a seem to be an unnecessary duplication of 1:1, and it is
argued that it is unlikely that Ahab would have been named in the original
account of the Moabite campaign (so DeVries, *Prophet against Prophet*, 88–
89). Further, vv 25b–27 appear to add nothing to the preceding narrative.
The prophecy of v 19 receives its emphatic fulfillment in v 25*a* (cf. Long,
VT 23 [1973] 339). It is also noted that there is a stylistic shift between vv
16 and 17, and that the miracle has a double thrust. It satisfies the thirst of
the army and also signals the defeat of the Moabites (Long).

Such observations have led many commentators to posit a complex preliterary history for the chapter. Whether Gray wishes to conclude that the section dealing with Elisha (vv 11–19) is secondary is not clear. His language is ambiguous at this point. However, both DeVries and Long see at least three layers of tradition in the chapter. Vv 1–3 are regarded as a deuteronomistic introduction. Long's conclusion is that the remainder of the chapter is to be divided into vv 4–9a, 16, 20–24 (and vv 26–27), on the one hand; and vv 9b–15, 17, 18–19 on the other (*VT* 23 [1973] 341). The first is a regular account of the military campaign, over which the second layer of tradition has been laid. DeVries sees vv 4–5a and vv 25b–27 as redactional, altering the intention of the core of the chapter (vv 5b–25a), characterized as an "instrumental fulfillment narrative" (*Prophet against Prophet,* 88–89, 122–23). Most are agreed that the naming of the kings is secondary.

The phenomena noted above do exist. There are some apparent stylistic and theological, as well as historical, inconsistencies in the chapter. But whether these features *necessarily* imply such composition is not proven. To argue at one time that vv 25b–27 are secondary because they add nothing to the "emphatically fulfilled" prophecy in v 25a, and at another that they are secondary because they radically change the outcome of the prophecy, would imply the impossible. That the tensions exist is taken for granted, but that the detailed literary pre-history outlined above is the only reason for their existence is an assumption in need of proof. Before one resorts to the existence of sources, the possibility of the *deliberate* creation of such tensions by the writer must be explored. There might well be some literary artistry at work which can be appreciated by examining the story in its present form. Historical reconstructions on the basis of the analysis of a document into sources are, at best, hypothetical.

For example, the material in Long's stratum one is regarded as part of an official account of the Moabite campaign "long since lost." Yet it is sufficiently unlike similar accounts to warrant the conclusion that it has undergone such extensive reshaping and editing. For DeVries the process is reversed. The prophetic core of the chapter has been reshaped into political propaganda by the addition of the "framework" of vv 4–5a and vv 25b–27. Of the two, Long admits to the precarious nature of such analysis, and allows for the importance of the interpretation of the narrative in its present form.

Both form critics cited above see the intention of the narrative as the emphasis upon the fulfillment of the prophetic word. Long, however, treats the complete narrative, minus vv 1–3, while DeVries deals only with vv 5b–25a. Their classifications are "oracle actualization story" (Long) and "instrumental fulfillment narrative" (DeVries). For Long, the three main ingredients to the plot are the opening situation (vv 4–9a), the crisis (vv 9b–10), and the resolution (vv 11–27). For DeVries, the main elements are the crisis (vv 5b–13), the complex oracle and its instrumental fulfillment (vv 14–20), and the ultimate fulfillment (vv 21–25a). Both point to the formal similarities of this chapter with others, such as 2 Kgs 8:7–15 (Long) and 2 Kgs 8:29b–9:36a (DeVries). For Long, the key word of the story is דרשׁ "seek."

One major problem with such analyses is the material which both omit. Neither treats the place of vv 1–3 in the completed structure, other than to

Form/Structure/Setting

designate it as a deuteronomistic introduction. Of the two, only Long includes a treatment of vv 25b–27; but they both note that the verses stand in contradiction to the oracle in vv 19–21. That they do is plain. Why they do cannot be left unanswered.

First, some comments are in order concerning the items of "tension" noted above. That the kings are not named after v 12, except for the passing reference to Jehoshaphat in v 14, is worth noting; but this need not indicate the additions of such names in the early part of the story (cf. Noth, *Überlieferungsgeschichtliche Studien* 1:83–84). The same characteristic is found in the Mesha Stone. There, after the reference to Omri and his son in line 7, the enemy is simply referred to as "the king of Israel" or "Israel." Second, that vv 25–27 comprise part of an official account of the raid into Moab is highly unlikely. Official accounts do not contain defeats; they are rarely that honest. The origin of this material must be seen in the light of the other OT stories of the defeat of either Israel or Judah. Almost without exception, such stories of defeat have a theological purpose. Defeats are explained as punishments for disobedience. It is valid to inquire whether the same motivation is to be found here.

Can the complete chapter be understood in its present form? Although DeVries classifies the prophetic core of the narrative as chiastic, that can only be maintained by the omission of vv 1–3, 4–5a, and 25b–27. Vv 1–3, which provide the chronological introduction to the narrative, are similar to many others in the books of Kings, but this fact does not exempt the introduction from further comment. There is an interesting addition to the introductory formula which is not found in the others (vv 2–3). Stylistically it provides an example of assonance with the line which follows:

ויעשה הרע בעיני יהוה רק לא כאביו וכאמו ויסר את־
מצבת הבעל אשר עשה אביו
רק בחטאות ירבעם בן נבט אשר החטיא את ישראל דבק
לא־סר ממנה

Note the underlined words "but not," "he turned aside," "but," and "did not turn." In other words, even though Joram could not be seen as an exact duplicate of his father Ahab, there was little in his reign that could be spared condemnation. The downward trend in the fortunes of the nation continues under Joram, the successor to the unfortunate Ahaziah. A qualified judgment is made of him. This introduction sets the stage for the account of the Moabite expedition.

Vv 4–5 introduce the historical context of the following story. It is a major crisis brought about by the audacious rebellion of Moab against Israel. The deliberate echo of 1:1 cannot be avoided. Vv 6–8 tell of the extensive preparations made to deal with the rebellion of Moab. The king of Israel is joined by both Judah and Edom and echoes of chapter one resound here. *Three kings go up* to teach Moab a lesson in a manner similar to that of the *three* company commanders who *go up* to take Elijah under the authority of the king. In the same tradition, the odds are with those who ascend.

But as the story develops, no sooner had the campaign begun than it starts to go wrong. Two crises develop. There is no water to drink and an army thus weakened will be easy prey to the Moabites. Both these crises are addressed by the prophet in vv 11–19. Drinking water will be supplied and Moabite territory will be devastated. This prophecy, in turn, receives a response from Moab, by the mustering of the army along the border to protect their territory (vv 21–23). Finally, though the prophecy receives a rather literal fulfillment in vv 24–25, the apostate King Joram is denied complete victory and has to return home with his troops because of an act of worship made by his opponent to a foreign God, Chemosh.

The overall design of the narrative is alternative themes of plot and counter plot. Each successive section of the narrative forces a change in direction of the narrative. The result is that the story oscillates between the promise of success for Israel, assured by a large army and a word from Yahweh, and the threat to that success, seen in the Moabites and the lack of water. Ironically, the success is short-lived. The reign of Joram, begun in rather an inauspicious way in vv 1–3, continues the pattern of the house of Ahab and receives the same judgment.

Comment

1 The chronological and textual problems of 3:1–3 have been alluded to elsewhere in the commentary. It was argued above that 1:17*b* is an addition to the text. There is therefore no need to revert to attempts at synchronization of the reigns of Jehoram of Judah and Jehoshaphat his father (cf. E. R. Thiele, *The Mysterious Numbers of the Hebrew Kings*, 61–74; S. J. DeVries, "Chronology," *IDB* 1:587; Gray, 460).

2 The definite article on רע "evil" does not imply some specific evil. In Num 32:13, when רע is used as the object of עשה, it is prefixed with the article.

The pillar which Joram is said to have turned aside is a puzzle, since there is no record in the reign of Ahab of that king's ever having erected one. The use of such pillars seems more characteristic of Judah, not Israel (1 Kgs 14:23). If the word is to be retained it refers either to the setting up of cultic pillars by Ahab—an action overlooked by the biblical writer—or the establishment of a commemorative stele by Ahab in honor of Baal. But given the obvious dislike of the author of 2 Kgs for Ahab, it is strange that there is no previous reference to either of these actions. The word could also be emended to מזבח "altar," such as the one erected at the beginning of Ahab's reign (1 Kgs 16:32).

4 Moab's subservience to Israel was of long standing. David had effectively humiliated Moab during his reign (2 Sam 8:2). Since that time Moab had enjoyed a degree of religious independence, as is implied by Solomon's allowing his Moabite wife to build a high place in Jerusalem (1 Kgs 11:7). Recent excavations have shown that Dibhan (Dibon) was occupied in the period shortly after the middle of the ninth century B.C., possibly coinciding with Mesha's annexation of the city. The Mesha Stone is ambiguous regarding Dibon and appears to have in mind a general area rather than a specific city.

The name "Mesha" is known from the Moabite record of the rebellion against Israel (cf. Gibson, *Syrian Semitic Inscriptions* 1:71–83). The versions offer various forms of the name, from Mosab to Amos.

The Hebrew word נקד appears here and in a plural form in Amos 1:1. From both contexts it is clearly something to do with sheep, hence the translation "sheep breeder" above. The Akkadian word for sheep is *nakidu*. Line 30 of the Mesha Stone contains a barely discernible נ; the following line mentions צאן הארץ "flock of the land." This is in connection with Mesha's campaign to Beth Baal-meon, a site located some twenty-five kilometers southwest of Heshbon (cf. Y. Aharoni, *The Land of the Bible*, 306). Gibson proposes the restored word נקדי (*Syrian Semitic Inscriptions* 1:82). The Hebrew והישב, literally, "caused to return," is presumably a reference to regular tribute paid to Israel. The status of Moab as a vassal of Israel is well attested in Mesha's own account.

5 The revolt of Mesha is difficult to date. The OT states simply that it was "after the death of Ahab," who died approximately 850 B.C., and during the reigns of Joram and Jehoshaphat. According to Mesha's own account the revolt gave rise to an extensive territorial enlargement.

6 The preparations made by Joram in the following verses are impressive. The mustering (פקד) of the whole army would not have been difficult in Israel. What is interesting is the mustering of "all Israel," which probably included the local militia as well as the regular army. The retaliatory action was clearly taken very seriously by Joram.

7 The fact that Jehoshaphat matches Joram's army exactly and the fact that they allied themselves with Edom shows that the allies were dealing with a considerable threat to their eastern borders. The preparations are weighty, and the sheer force of numbers was on the side of the allies. The introduction of Jehoshaphat into the narrative at this point brings in a third party who, in turn, introduces the prophet Elisha.

The use of the verb עלה "go up" for the attack on Moab need not be taken literally, although the way the allies chose to travel would have entailed an ascent from the Wadi Arabah to the Plain of Moab. The verb is often used in a technical sense of the approach of an army to do battle or to lay siege. In many cases the "going up" is neither to the north, nor does it have anything to do with land elevation. Cf. Judg 6:3; Josh 10:33; 2 Kgs 18:9; 24:1; 2 Chr 16:1. On these texts see the NEB translations.

That the allies chose to go around via the difficult "Way of Edom" is understandable (cf. Aharoni, *Land of the Bible*, 41, 54, 57). The Mesha Stone indicates that the whole of the northern approach to the Moabite Plain was in the hands of the rebels. The "Way of Edom" went south through Arad and into the Wadi Arabah and it would provide a southern approach to Moab, linking first with the "Way of Horonaim" (Isa 15:5) via Zoar (Jer 48:34) to join the "King's Highway," the second major thoroughfare in this area.

9 The crisis which begins to affect the expedition develops in vv 9–10. The impression given by the use of the verb סבב "surround" is not that the allies wandered aimlessly around in the desert and became lost. Such a possibility for a well-equipped army is remote. Rather, the enforced detour took longer than anticipated. The large force would have been quite unwieldy.

The verb is used in the same sense in Judg 11:18. The beasts accompanying the army would be the supply animals and those used either for food or sacrifice (cf. v 20). The initial lack of water for the expedition and the miraculous supply in v 20 are not simultaneous with the foolish behavior of the Moabites in vv 22–23. In some ancient treaty texts, such as that between Ashurnirari V and Mati'ilu of Bit-Agusi, wandering around in the desert "like an ass or a gazelle" is seen as a divine curse for disobedience to the treaty stipulations (see D. J. McCarthy, *Treaty and Covenant*, AnBib [Rome: Pontifical Biblical Institute, 1963] 196, 201).

10 Elisha the prophet is now introduced. That the prophet is introduced in response to a crisis seems to be typical of the Elisha stories. The king of Israel fears the worst; he sees the failure of his army's water supply as divine judgment.

11 Jehoshaphat provides the salvation from the immediate crisis through the prophet Elisha. Here, and later in chapter five, it is an innocent third party who opens the way for the activity of Elisha. That he should be called upon during such a time of crisis possibly reflects the role prophets played during campaigns of this kind. Elisha is identified by his relationship with Elijah. The precise meaning of pouring water on the hands is unknown since it is without parallel in the OT. Later rabbinic interpretation connected it to the incident with the prophets of Baal in 1 Kgs 18 (see Ginzberg, *The Legends of the Jews* 4:199).

12 It is Jehoshaphat, not Joram, who confirms that Elisha is a worthy prophet. The apostate character of Joram is highlighted by the prophet's subsequent response.

13 The utter disrespect for the house of Omri is rarely more clearly expressed.

15 This incident is unique in the stories of the prophets and provides one of the very few glimpses at the mechanics of prophetic inspiration. To generalize from this lone incident to a theory of prophetic inspiration, even for this early period of prophecy, would be unwise (cf. von Rad, *Old Testament Theology* 2:59). Music and musicians play a role in the activity of the band of prophets descending from the high place in 1 Sam 10:1–16, but other means of inspiration such as vision and audition are also found in the OT (Jer 1:11–15, etc.). That this was typical, or that one can appeal to the analogy of the dervish guilds of a much later age for parallels (so W. R. Smith, *The Prophets of Israel*, 2nd ed. [London: A. C. Black, 1895] 391–92), are unwarranted conclusions. Cf. also J. Lindblom, *Prophecy in Ancient Israel*, 59.

Generally speaking, the hand is a symbol of power in the OT (1 Kgs 2:46). It is also the power of judgment (Exod 9:3, etc.). With Ezekiel, the hand of the LORD becomes a regular symbol of prophetic inspiration (Ezek 1:3; 8:1; 13:9). B. O. Long (*VT* 23 [1973] 339) saw the stylistic differences between vv 16 and 17 as evidence of the composite nature of the chapter. However, this type of "double oracle" is certainly not unusual within the prophetic tradition, and v 16 needs the kind of conclusion offered by v 17. For a comparison, cf. Jer 27:2–11.

18 Vv 18–19 deal with the secondary threat which results from the lack of water, namely, that the expedition will have to abort and Moab will be victorious. However, the prophet assures the kings that it is as easy to hand over Moab into their power as it is to supply water for the armies.

19 The systematic way in which the defeat of Moab is described is reminiscent of the ordered way in which holy war is described elsewhere in the OT.

The Hebrew כאב is sometimes translated "to be in pain" or "to give pain," physical or mental. Unless a rhetorical use is intended, the verb seems out of place. A similar personification of the land is found in Jer 23:10 and Joel 1:10.

The prohibition of cutting down trees, found in Deut 20:19–20, does not apply here. The law in Deuteronomy is designed to ensure that the army's food supply would not be cut off since non-fruit-bearing trees are excluded.

20 The miracle is one of timing, with the land being filled with water from the flash floods caused by rainfall on the higher ground. The effect would be the same if the allies were in the Arabah or on the leeward side of the Plain of Moab. The former seems more likely from the text. Since the reaction of Moab to the pending invasion is described in the following verses, it is unlikely that the allies had penetrated the Moabite territory to any great extent.

21 The reaction of Moab is swift. "All of Moab" is mustered to the defense of the land.

The use of the verb צעק "call out," while indicating a general call to arms, might also indicate a call mingled with a small degree of panic. The wearing of belts, as opposed to loose-fitting garments, might indicate young men of military age (so Gray, 489). However, the Hebrew גדוד "raiding party" is translated into Greek with μονοζωνος (2 Sam 22:30; 2 Kgs 5:2), i.e., "one belted," indicating a lightly armed skirmisher. This might be the meaning here, although it is not certain. In any event, the Moabites have a general draft of all able to carry arms. In Moab's early days of independence a highly organized army would have been unlikely.

The border along which the Moabites stood is the southern border between Moab and Edom, normally identified with Nahal Zered (Wadi Hasa) south and east of the Dead Sea (cf. Deut 2:13).

22 The Moabites were initially outmaneuvered by the allies, since to see the reflection of the sun in the morning they would be looking east. The allies had outflanked them.

24 The devastation of the land fulfills the prophecy of Elisha almost word for word, but not completely, since Kir Haresheth is left. Kir Haresheth is not mentioned in the Moabite Stone, but is usually identified with El Kerak, to the southeast of the Dead Sea (see Burney, *Notes*, 272). See also Isa 16:7; 2 Kgs 16:11; Jer 48:31, 36.

25 The city finally fell to the slingers, but eventually the battle turned against Israel.

26 The phrase להבקיע אל מלך אדום "to break through to the King of Edom" is ambiguous. Some interpret it as meaning that the Edomites had deserted to Moab during the campaign (Long, *VT* 23 [1973] 340–41). The analogy would be the emendation suggested of 2 Kgs 23:29 by *BHS*. However, the preposition can have the opposite meaning, as in Gen 4:8 (ויקם קין אל

הבל "Cain rose up *against* Abel"). Montgomery, 363, suggests an emendation of אדם "Edom" to ארם "Aram." But such seems unnecessary.

27 The sacrifice of the first-born son of Mesha on the walls of Kir Haresheth was the turning point for the campaign. The meaning of the "great wrath" which came upon Israel is uncertain. Either the battle suddenly went against them or they withdrew from the field in disgust. The campaign ends in a similar way as that earlier one undertaken by Ahab and Jehoshaphat (1 Kgs 22).

Explanation

The story of the abortive attempt by the kings of Israel, Judah, and Edom to quash the revolt of Mesha of Moab as told in 2 Kgs 3 has received substantial historical support from Mesha's own account of his revolt (see above). However, in keeping with the nature of the material in these early chapters of 2 Kings, the writer's purpose is not to record the fact of history, but rather to explain the role of the prophets, Elisha in particular, in that history. In the service of this presentation much detail is omitted, either because such detail would be understood by the original reader or because it is irrelevant to the main thrust of the narrative.

The particular role of Elisha in this story of the revolt and the attempt to suppress it is told briefly. He accompanies the army of the allies into battle. Why he is present is not explained. He offers an oracle of victory to the allies, which is fulfilled (vv 16–19), and a reassurance that they would be supplied with water, which also comes true (vv 16, 20). This activity of Elisha is interwoven with the account of the expedition, which finally ends in a retreat for the allies.

The introduction to the chapter (vv 1–3), with its conventional summary of the reign of Joram, appears to interrupt the flow of Elisha stories which begins in chapter two and continues to chapter nine without a break. However, the point of the introduction is to present the consequences of the activities of the descendants of the apostate Ahab "after the death of Ahab." Joram is introduced as one who continues in the fashion of his father. The account of the abortive expedition into Moab supports the thesis that apostasy brings with it defeat. This thesis is established by the writer of the "deuteronomistic history" as early as the book of Judges with its rhythm of apostasy, defeat, and deliverance for Israel. The decisive change in the history of Israel, which was promised by the opening phrase of 2 Kings "after the death of Ahab" (cf. 1:1; 3:5), was not for the better. The venture into Moab, which was spurred on by prophetic encouragement, presents the final judgment on the apostasy of Joram. He returns defeated and loses control of Moab in the process.

The "deuteronomist," both here and elsewhere, makes a strong connection between the territorial gains of the Israelites and the blessing of God on the one hand, and the losses of territory by Israel and the judgment of God on the other. Just as "Yahweh gave victory to David wherever he went" (2 Sam 8:6), including the subjugation of Moab (2 Sam 8:2) and the taking of the weapons of gold from Hadadezer (2 Sam 8:7), so now the process is reversed as Moab is lost. Later the temple treasures are given as a bribe to the Syrians (2 Kgs 12:17–18). In the scheme of the "deuteronomist" the beginning of the end of Israel is now seen, and the gradual fulfillment of the threat in Deut 4:25–28. The monarchy is disintegrating. Whatever respites are ahead are only temporary.

The prophet's involvement in a military venture such as this ultimately raises the question of war in the OT. Is there an implicit sanction of war by the Scriptures with their record of such an event and the prophet's participation in that event? The focus of the OT at this point is elsewhere. Prophetic involvement with war is found at many stages of Israel's history. Samuel's activity bears witness to this (1 Sam 15:1–3). As elsewhere in the ANE, Israelite prophets were often consulted before a battle (1 Kgs 22). They often offered oracles of victory. Such is the role of Elisha in the narrative (cf. v 18). In later prophecy of the eighth, seventh, and sixth centuries B.C., the older war oracle of the early prophetic tradition is transformed into the conventional "oracle against the nations" (cf. Amos 1–2; Jer 46–51; Isa 13–23; Ezek 25–29). But at this juncture of the narrative a distinction is to be made between an historical "given," the prophetic involvement in war, and the theological interpretation of history being made. The writer is concerned to point out that there is an unbreakable connection between the faithfulness of the nation of Israel and its fortune. For a king of the character of Joram to venture into battle, even though he sought an oracle of victory from a prophet of Yahweh, was virtual suicide and was bound to have serious repercussions upon the fortunes of the people as a whole. There is, of course, much within this interpretation of history which is open to criticism, but it is the interpretation with which the "deuteronomist" works and which dictates his presentation of events in the history of Israel and Judah. This understanding of history is much more clearly expressed as the end of Israel draws closer. From the time of David, when Moabite, Syrian, Ammonite, and Edomite were subject to the power of Israel (2 Sam 8:12), the narrative has reached a point in the history of Israel where the borders of Israelite power are being whittled down.

Excursus: The Moabite Stone and 2 Kings 3

The Moabite Stone (or Mesha Stone) Inscription, discovered at Dibon toward the end of the last century, offers an account of the war between Mesha, king of Moab, and the Israelites during the mid eighth century B.C. It both confirms and raises questions about the account of the expedition of Joram, Jehoshaphat, and the king of Edom into Moab which is found in 2 Kgs 3. A recent transliteration and translation of the inscription is found in Gibson, *Syrian Semitic Inscriptions* 1:71–83, and a clear reproduction of the original can be found in Beyerlin, *NE Texts*, 236. Gibson also supplies a full bibliography on the inscription.

Mesha's account speaks initially of building a "high place" in honor of victories given him by his god, Chemosh. Oppression of Moab by Israel had lasted forty years under Omri and his "son." But Mesha threw off the Israelite yoke (l 5) and "Israel perished utterly forever" (l 7). Mesha then recounts, probably in chronological order, a list of campaigns which secured for him the expulsion of Israel from the territory of Moab. In these lines the "king of Israel" is referred to, but not named. A list of cities and the repairs Mesha made upon them is given in this section. Generally, the Moabite Stone confirms the expansion of Israel into the Transjordan and the control Israel exercised over that area after the time of David. According to some interpreters, the reference to the "son" of Omri and the "perishing" of the house of Israel sets Mesha's revolt between Ahab's reign and the destruction of the Omrides under Jehu, and nearer the latter. This need not be the case. It was the practice in the ancient Near East to refer to Israel as the "house of Omri" long after the Omrides had disappeared, and the term "son" can simply indicate "descendant."

The genre of the inscription is a war report designed to enhance the reputation of the national deity and that deity's loyal servant, the king. Such reports are common inside and outside the OT. As such, the Stone is a piece of political and religious propaganda. In documents of this kind, all that would tarnish the national and the divine image is omitted. No defeats are mentioned. The number of Moabite casualties is not given, the cost of the campaign Mesha undertook is ignored. Only the victories, the rewards, and the grand achievements are named. The record of an incursion into southern Moab by three enemies, as described in 2 Kgs 3, which was almost successful, would be completely out of place in the Moabite Stone. The variant accounts of Sennacherib's abortive attempt to take Jerusalem in 701 B.C. reflect the same kind of ideological tendencies. Both the Assyrian and the Judean accounts claim victories of sorts!

Any attempt at synchronization between the Moabite Stone and 2 Kgs 3 is impossible. Although the Moabite record appears to date Mesha's revolt during the reign of Ahab, this is not clearly stated. That Mesha "saw his desire in Ahab and his house" offers no precision, and indeed allows for the revolt to have begun after the death of Ahab (2 Kgs 1:1; 3:5). The reference throughout the inscription to "the king of Israel," without naming him, allows for considerable flexibility in dating.

The raid carried out by the three kings was a retaliatory one, presumably made after the revolt was well under way. The fact that the allied expedition had to go via "the Way of Edom," under the southern extremity of the Dead Sea, would indicate that the northern approaches to Moab, across the Jordan near Jericho, were firmly in Mesha's hands. All of the cities mentioned by Mesha as having fallen to him in battle, such as Madeba, Ataroth, Nebo, and Jahaz, are located in the northern tableland of Moab (see Aharoni, *Land of the Bible,* 306). Building programs were carried out at Aroer, Beth-diblathaim, Beth Baal-meon, and Kiria thaim. Presumably they fell into Moab's hands during the course of the revolt through siege, or capitulated when the Israelite garrisons would have had to withdraw. They are in the same general area. Only Horonaim is in the south, since Mesha "went down" to fight against it. Lines 31-33 of the inscription are in a bad state of preservation. Gibson's reconstruction (*Syrian Semitic Inscriptions* 1:75) is:

31. די.י.לרעת.את.(צאן.הארץ וחורנן.ישב.בה.ב---וק--אש-
32. --------(וי)אמר.לי.כמש.רד.הלתחם.בחורנן וארד.ו(אל
33. תחס.בקר.ואחזה.וישב.(בה.כמש.בימי.ועל-דה.משם.עש---

31. (in order to tend the) sheep of the district. Then in Horonaim there had settled ....
32. ....; and Chemosh said to me, Go down, fight against Horonaim. So I went down (and
33. fought against the town and took it), and Chemosh (dwelt) there in my days. As for ...., from there.........

Clearly, some emergency had arisen which caused Mesha to move south and deal with it. According to his account, he was successful. This might not have been the time of the invasion, but it does allow for the possibility. From the inscription, it is clear that there was a southern campaign as well as a northern one for Mesha.

Elisha's Works (4:1–44)

Bibliography

Haller, E. "Märchen und Zeugnis. Auslegung der Erzählung 2 Kön. 4: 1–7." *Probleme biblischer Theologie.* Munich: Chr. Kaiser, 1971, 108–15. **Heller, J.** "Tod im Topfe." *Communio Viatorum* 10 (1967) 71–76. **Kilian, R.** "Die Totenerweckung." *BZ* 10 (1966) 44–56. **Lemaire, A.** "Le sabbat à l'époque royale israélite." *RB* 80 (1973) 161–85. **Schmitt, A.** "Die Totenerweckung in 2 Kön. 4:8–37." *BZ* 19 (1975) 1–25. **Wishlicki, L.** "The Revival of a Boy by the Prophet Elisha: A Case of Hypothermia." *Koroth* 5 (1972) 876–78.

Translation

[1] *A certain woman, from the wives of the sons of the prophets, complained to Elisha saying, "Your servant* [a] *my husband is dead. You well know that your servant feared Yahweh, but the creditor has come to take my two sons into slavery."* [2] *Elisha said to her,* [a] *"What shall I do for you? Tell me,* [b] *what do you have* [c] *at home?"* [d] *She replied, "Your maidservant has nothing* [e] *but an oil jar."* [f] [3] *Then he said, "Go and borrow vessels from all your neighbors,* [a] *empty vessels,* [b] *and many of them.* [c] [4] *Then go in and shut the door upon yourself and your sons, and pour it out into all these vessels. When one is full, set it aside."* [5] *Then she went from him,* [a] *and shut the door upon herself and her sons. They were bringing jars to her as she poured.* [b] [6] *When the vessels had been filled,* [a] *she said to her son, "Bring me more vessels!" But he replied, "There are no more." Then the oil stopped flowing.* [7] *Then she went and told the man of God, and he* [a] *said to her, "Go sell the oil, and pay your creditors, and you and your sons can have the rest."* [bc]

[8] *On the same day Elisha traveled to Shunem where a woman of substance lived who used to encourage him to eat bread with her. So each time he passed by he would turn aside and eat* [a] *with her.* [9] *She said to her husband, "Now look, you know that this person is a holy man of God who frequently passes through here;* [10] *let us make for him a small walled upper room, and let us furnish it with a bed, a table, a chair, and a lamp. Then, whenever he comes to visit he can stay there."*

[11] *So it happened one day that he came* [a] *by, turned aside to the upper room, and slept there.* [12] *Then he said* [a] *to Gehazi, his young servant, "Call this Shunemite!" So he called* [a] *her and she stood before him.* [13] *And he said to him, "Tell her now, 'Look, you have gone to all this* [a] *trouble on our behalf,* [b] *what can be done for you* [c] *in return? Is there something to be said* [d] *on your behalf to the king or to the military commander?'" But she replied, "I live among my own people."* [14] *But Elisha persisted, "What can be done for her?" Then Gehazi said, "Look, she has no son, and her*

husband is getting old." ¹⁵ So Elisha said, "Call her!"ᵃ So he called her and she stood in the doorway. ¹⁶ He said,ᵃ "At this season, when it is time, you shall embrace a son." She then said, "No sir! You, a man of God,ᵇ would not lie to your maidservant!" ¹⁷ But she did conceive, and did bear a son, at that season when the time had come, just asᵃ Elisha had told her.

¹⁸ The boy grew and one dayᵃ he went out to his father, to the reapers.ᵇ ¹⁹ He said to his father, "My head! My head!"ᵃ and his father said to his servant, "Take him to his mother!" ²⁰ He took him up and brought him to his mother,ᵃ and he slept upon her lap until noon. Then he died. ²¹ She went up and laid him on the bed of the man of God, shut the door upon him, and left. ²² She then called to her husband and said, "Send for me one of your young men and one she-ass, and I will hurry to the man of God and return." ²³ But he responded, "Why are you about to go to himᵃ today? It is neither a feast day nor a sabbath." But she said, "It is all right." ²⁴ Then she saddled the ass and said to her servant, "Lead on. Do not slow down unless I tell you to." ²⁵ So she set out on her journey and cameᵃ to the man of God on Mount Carmel.

When the man of God saw her oppositeᵇ he said to Gehazi, "Look, that is the Shunemite! ²⁶ Run to meet her, and say, 'Is it well with you and your husband and your son?'ᵃ And she replied, 'It is well.' " ²⁷ When she came to the man of Godᵃ on the mountain she grabbed hold of his feet. Gehazi approached to stop her, but the man of Godᵃ said, "Let her be! Her soul is bitter and Yahweh has hidden the reason from me. It has not been told me." ²⁸ She said, "Did I ask a son from you sir? And did I not ask you not to deceive me?" ²⁹ Then he said to Gehazi, "Prepare yourself. Take my staff in your hand and get going. If you encounter anyone do not greet him, and if anyone greets you, do not reply. Set my staff on the face of the boy." ³⁰ Then the boy's mother said, "As Yahweh lives, and as your soul lives, I will not leave you!" So he arose and went after her.

³¹ Gehazi went on in front of themᵃ and set the staff on the face of the boy, but there was no sound, no response. So he returned to meet him and said, "The boy did not wake up." ³² Then Elisha came into the house and the boy was dead, lying upon his bed. ³³ He went in,ᵃ shut the door on the two of them and prayed to Yahweh. ³⁴ He climbed up and lay down on top of the boy, face to faceᵃ and eye to eye, and nestled down on top of him and warmed his flesh. ³⁵ Then he returned, walked back and forthᵃ in front of the house, went up and leaned over the boy, and the boy sneezedᵇ seven times and opened his eyes. ³⁶ Then he calledᵃ to Gehazi, "Call thisᵇ Shunemite!" He summoned herᶜ and she came to him and he said, "Take up your boy." ³⁷ She then approached and fell at his feet and bowed in worship,ᵃ then took up her son and went out.

³⁸ Now Elisha returned to Gilgalᵃ and the land was hit by famine. The sons of the prophets were assembled before him, and he said to his servant, "Prepare a largeᵇ pot and cook some vegetables for the sons of the prophets." ³⁹ Oneᵃ of them went out into the open country to gather plants, and he found a wild vine,ᵇ took from it a wild gourd,ᶜ and filled his pockets. He came back, cut it up, and threw it into the pot unwittingly.ᵈ ⁴⁰ The stew was poured outᵃ for the menᵇ to eat, but as they ateᶜ from the pot theyᵈ cried out and said, "There is death in the pot, man of God!" They were not able to eat. ⁴¹ So heᵃ said, "Fetchᵇ some flour!" And he threwᶜ it into the pot. Then he said,ᵈ "Pour it out for the people to eat." They ate it and there was nothing badᵉ in the pot.

⁴² *Now a man had come from Baal Shalishah,* ᵃ *and he brought with him to the man of God bread of the first fruits, twenty barley loaves, and produce from his harvest.* ᵇ *He said, "Give to the people to eat."* ⁴³ *But his servant said, "How can I set this before one hundred men?" He insisted,* ᵃ *"Give to the people to eat! Thus has Yahweh declared, 'Eat and have some left.'"* ⁴⁴ *So he set it before them,* ᵃ *they ate and had some left according to the word of Yahweh.*

Notes

1.a. Tg identifies this servant as Obadiah, probably on the basis of 1 Kgs 18:3, 12.
2.a. אליה "to her" is omitted by G.
2.b. הגיד לי "tell me" is omitted by G.
2.c. MT reads לכי "to you," either a dittography from the next line, or an Aramaism (so Gray, 492). Such peculiarities of style are often found in reported speech of this kind.
2.d. MT בבית "at home," G^L adds αὐτου "it."
2.e. G omits the second בבית "at home."
2.f. אסוך is either a noun in apposition to שמן "oil," or a first pers sg impf of סוך "hedge" (so G). G^L combines both readings.
3.a. שְׁכֵנָכִי "your neighbors" is either better pointed as שְׁכֵנָיִךְ, or understood as another Aramaism.
3.b. רקים "vessel" is translated correctly by G^B as κενα "empty jar," but several minor G MSS (B*Negjosuvwy) mistakenly read καινα "new." Others read και ινα "and if."
3.c. Heb. lit., "make not a few." In the G tradition there are several variations of the reading of ὀλιγωσης. G^L offers further diversity. G^B reads θεασης.
5.a. Many MSS from G add και εποιησεν ούτως "and he did thus," or something similar.
5.b. The piel ptcp מיצקת "poured" is extremely rare, and many suggest it be pointed as a hiph.
6.a. In G the first sentence of v 6 is appended to v 5 in a slightly different form, ἕως ἐπλησθησαν τα σκευη "until they had filled the vessels."
7.a. After ויאמר "and he said," G adds Elisha's name, which is common for G in this chapter.
7.b. G adds ἐλαιῳ "olive oil."
7.c. MT reads here ואת בניכי תחיי בנותר "and you shall live with your remaining sons." G reads και συ και οἱ υἱοι σου ζησεσθε ἐν τῷ ἐπιλοιπῳ ἐλαιῳ "and you and your sons shall live on the remaining oil."
8.a. Here we have adopted the G reading, which omits the second occurrence of לחם "bread," in the interest of smoother language, not textual priority.
11.a. G^L again in typical fashion, adds the name of Elisha.
12.a. G again adds the proper name.
13.a. הזאת "this" omitted by G.
13.b. MT אלינו, lit., "to us."
13.c. MT מה לעשות לך "What is there to do for you?"
13.d. MT reads דבר "word or matter," rendered by G as λογος, i.e., "Is there a matter (case) before the king?"
15.a. G^L omits.
16.a. Again G^L adds the proper name.
16.b. איש האלהים "a man of God" is omitted by G.
17.a. For the MT אשר "which," G reads ὡς ἐλαλησεν "as he spoke" (כאשר).
18.a. G renders ἡνικα "when."
18.b. G^L adds ἡμερα θερισμου "day of harvest."
19.a. G^L adds ἐγω ἀλγω "I am in pain!"
20.a. G here is much shorter, omitting much of the first part of the verse.
23.a. MT pointing is confusing אַתִּי הֹלֶכֶתִי "you go to him," and could be emended to אַתְּ הֹלֶכֶת. The possibility of another Aramaism is still present.
25.a. MT ותלך ותבוא "you come and go" is conflated by G to δευρο και πορευση και ελευση "come, you will journey and you will go."
25.b. Omitted by G.
26.a. G^L repeats the instructions here.

27.a. In both cases איש האלהים "man of God" is omitted by G and substituted by the proper name.
31.a. G reads ἐμπροσθεν αὐτης "before her," G^L reads αὐτου "him."
33.a. At the beginning of this verse G adds the beginning of the previous verses (και εἰσηλθεν Ἐλισαιε εἰς τον οἰκον "and Elisha entered the house"). G^L follows MT.
34.a. The variants in the versions are many. MT כפו "his palm" is better read כפיו "his palms." G^L adds "and his mouth upon his mouth." Others extend further with the mention of other parts of the body.
35.a. MT וילך בבית "and he went in the house" is rendered by the RSV, "He walked once to and fro in the house" (cf. G). The Heb idiom אחת הנה ואחת הנה "here and there " is similar to that used in 2:8.
35.b. G omits any reference to the boy's sneezing and reads instead, "Elisha stretched himself on the boy seven times." This brings a measure of conformity with Elijah's healing of a boy in similar circumstances (1 Kgs 17:17–24). The variety of translations and interpretations of the verb for "sneezing" is great. Burney (*Notes*, 276) suggests an emendation, arguing that ויזרר "and he sneezed" is a dittography for ויגהר "and he bent." This is unnecessary.
36.a. Here, as in many other places in this narrative, G supplies the proper name of the prophet.
36.a. G omits אל "to" and הזאת "this."
36.c. Omitted by G.
37.a. G^L expands considerably with ἐπι τα γονατα αὐτης "upon her knees," and προσεκυνησεν αὐτω "she did obeisance to him."
38.a. The variations upon the name of Gilgal in the versions are many.
38.b. Omitted by G.
39.a. OL, undoubtedly influenced by the reference to נערו "his servant" in v 38, adds here "Giezi."
39.b. MT ארת "wild vine" is transliterated by G as ἀριωθ. G^L renders it ἀγριαν "wild plant."
39.c. G translates τολυπην "ball of yarn"; one manuscript offers βοτανην δηλιτηριον "poisonous grass."
39.d. MT ידעו is pl, but the subject is sg. G^L, Vg, and Syr keep the verb sg.
40.a. MT "then they poured out," G renders as sg.
40.b. Omitted by Syr.
40.c. MT כאכלם "as they ate," but G renders ἐν τῳ ἐσθιειν "in the food."
40.d. MT והמה "and they" rendered by G as ἰδου "behold," Heb והנה. G^L reads αὐτου "his."
41.a. G^L typically adds the proper name.
41.b. MT וקחו is better read קח "take."
41.c. So MT. G retains what follows as part of the command of Elisha, ἐμβαλετε "throw." G^L adds και ενεβαλον "and they threw."
41.d. G adds Ἐλισαιε προς Γιεζι το παιδαριον (αὐτου) "Elisha to Gehazi his servant."
41.e. MT דבר רע "an evil word" which is translated literally by G ῥημα πονηρον.
42.a. The confusion of the exact location of Baal Shalishah is reflected in the vast variety of translations and interpretations of the name in the versions. OL and G^L identify it with Bethlehem.
42.b. MT reads וכרמל בצקלנו "produce from his harvest," but the meaning of the second word is unclear. G omits it. Vg supports our translation, although the precise meaning is lost. Cf. Burney, *Notes*, 277. See also *Comment*.
43.a. MT ויאמר "and he said."
44.a. The Heb. ויתן לפניהם "and he put before them" is omitted by G.

Form/Structure/Setting

According to Gray (465–71), who follows the analysis of Sanda, the stories about Elisha are from two sources: the Elisha-saga, dealing mainly with the prophet and his contact with various individuals, and the collection about Elisha in the broader context of Israelite history. The stories in this chapter are classified under the first heading. The first two, the stories of the widow's oil and of Elisha's dealings with the Shunemite woman, are "anecdotes of the individual Elisha" (Gray, 467). The last two, the sweetening of the stew and the feeding of the one hundred, are "anecdotes . . . of Elisha among the prophets." The common feature consists of miracles performed, and "they have generally no point beyond demonstrating the miraculous power and authority of Elisha" (Gray, 466).

Eissfeldt (*Introduction*, 37, 46) identifies 1–7 as both "fairy tale" and "prophetic legend." DeVries (*Prophet against Prophet*, 53–54) classifies all the stories in the chapter as "power demonstration narratives" which are designed to illustrate what a model prophet can do. All of these analyses presuppose an original setting of the stories among the circle of prophetic followers, the sons of the prophets. This can hardly be disputed; it is true of vv 1–7 and vv 8–37, even though the groups are conspicuous by their absence from the stories. But to identify the original setting as being among the sons of the prophets needs some amplification. Is it as true as stating that the stories of the Gospels originated with the disciples of Jesus? The intention attributed to this group of prophets by DeVries, for example, is a more serious matter since it colors the interpretation of the narratives. They are designed to edify. The perpetual danger in the search for common formal features is that the common elements are stressed to the detriment of the individual features. It is precisely in the particulars of a given story that the genius and intent of the writer can be seen (Cf. R. C. Culley, *Studies in the Structure of Hebrew Narrative*, 110–15).

There are some common features of these stories which are offered initially without interpretation. The timing of the stories is quite imprecise beyond the general statement that one of the incidents happened "one day" (vv 8, 11, 18). The other stories are lacking even this feature. The date of the famine in v 38 is unrecorded and the other stories in the chapter begin with the imprecise conjunction (vv 1, 38, 42). Also in these stories, there is a distinct lack of important characters such as kings or soldiers as prime actors in the plots. This provides a sharp contrast with both the preceding and following chapters. To be sure, the Shunemite has nothing to do with the king or the commander in chief (v 13). There is also an absence of proper names, with the exception of Elisha and Gehazi. Although they are of some importance the Shunemite and her husband are unnamed. The wife of one of the sons of the prophets is not given a name, nor is the stranger from Baal Shalishah. This feature is all the more noticeable in MT because of the many attempts of the G tradition to supply such names. Finally, the first two stories have some linguistic features which have suggested to some (e.g., Gray) that the narratives have a distinct Aramaic influence in them.

The classification of these stories as "prophetic" is not sure. Whether they are "prophetic legends" (Eissfeldt, *Introduction*, 46) or designed to enhance the reputation of the prophet (Gray, 466–67) or designed to encourage other prophets (DeVries *Prophet against Prophet*, 53) is uncertain, but doubtful. Nowhere in the stories is Elisha called "prophet." The most frequent designation is "man of God" (vv 7, 9, 16, 21, 22, 25, 27, 40, 42). Further, only in the final story and in the final verse of the chapter is the notion of the prophetic word of the LORD prominent. Again, this is in sharp contrast to the preceding narratives in chapters one, two, and three. Dominant in these stories is the ability of Elisha, the man of God, to perform miracles of varying types.

In the interest of this main theme the narrator has used the basic literary device of dramatic tension. It is wrong to argue for a common form on the basis of this common formal element or a prototype genre, because dramatic tension is the most fundamental element of story-telling and is included in such diverse stories as the Exodus and Jack and the Beanstalk! A central character is presented with a problem, and the problem is solved by various means. (See D. Jobling, *The Sense of Biblical Narrative,* passim.) In the present collection, the means to this end is miracle, not the prophetic word. The exception to this is the final story. Even the classification of "miracle story" is based on a study of content, not form. The formal characteristics are as much a part of the modern detective novel as they are of such ancient stories.

The stories in the chapter then are of the very fundamental type of "problem to solution." The artistry of the narrator is to be found in the way this progression is made, through the building up of the tension between problem and solution, and with the use of certain rhetorical devices and phrases. The final stage is to see how the stories fit together, their setting in the literature.

1-7 The story of the widow's supply of oil is reminiscent of the story of Elijah in 1 Kgs 17:8-16, but whether it is a strict "doublet" with only the main character changed is certainly not clear. In the final analysis such a question is unanswerable. In this first story, the writer moves from problem to solution by the means of a continuous dialogue, broken only for the moment by some action on the part of the woman. The verb which begins the sequence is צעקה "she cried" (v 1). The continuation of the sequence with the waw consecutive and imperfect is ויאמר "and he said" (v 2), ותאמר "and she said" (v 2), ויאמר "and he said" (v 3), ותסגר . . . ותלך "then she went and shut" (v 5), ותאמר "and she said" (ויהי) (v 6), ותבא ותגד ויאמר "and he came, and told, and he said" (v 7).

As the dialogue progresses, the focus of attention falls upon Elisha, the man of God, not upon Elisha the prophet. The two questions which Elisha asks the woman highlight this feature, "What can I do for you?" "Tell me, what do you have at home?" The woman's response to this is followed by direct commands, which she dutifully obeys. The result is that the oil provides her and her family with sufficient money to pay her debts and for her sons to remain free. The simplicity of the narrative is seen in the way in which no details are given concerning the second command of Elisha in v 7b. It is understood that the woman carried out these orders. Her obedience to the man of God is constant. What he commands is done, even without his presence.

8-37 This story is more complicated with its development of subsidiary characters such as Gehazi and the husband and the extended plot which gives the impression of an added tension within the narrative. In the first story (vv 1-7), the solution to the widow's problem is easy and swift. In the second story, the woman first is reluctant to accept any payment for her kindness to the prophet, and then loses what the prophet had promised her. Even the raising of the boy is initially frustrated by both Gehazi and Elisha. Rofé's comment (*JBL* 89 [1970] 430-33), that with this narrative the reader moves out of the realm of oral tradition into literature, is perceptive insofar as it points to these added features of this second story.

Four main divisions can be detected: vv 8–11, vv 12–17, vv 18–28, and vv 29–37. Each builds on the preceding one to create the final narrative form. In vv 8–11 the style is tight and displays the features seen in the first story, swift moving action and the repetition of key words. Elisha's habitual journeys through the southern part of Galilee are made more comfortable by the generosity of the wealthy woman of Shunem. "One day" (ויהי היום) he stops by (יסר שמה) her home and this precipitates the wife's suggestion that he should be made more comfortable when he stops on his journeys (יסור שמה). The result is that "one day" (ויהי היום) he stops by (ויסר . . . שמה) and takes advantage of this home away from home.

In vv 12–17 the narrative reverts again to dialogue, but it is a dialogue in which Gehazi plays a very important role as an intermediary between Elisha and the woman. These verses are also swift in their movement, although the action is speaking, not doing. However, in this dialogue the character of the Shunemite woman is clearly drawn. There is a quiet dignity in her stance before the prophet (v 12 ותעמד לפניו "and she stood before him") and this dignity is enhanced by her refusal to take advantage of Elisha's attempt at influence peddling. It is at this point that the authority of the man of God tends to work against him; it is rebuked by her declaration of self-sufficiency (בתוך עמי אנכי ישבת ותאמר "But she replied, 'I live among my own people,'" v 13b).

Elisha and Gehazi together then become the focus of the dialogue (v 14) and decide to grant her a son. Her standing at some distance from the prophet (v 15 ותעמד בפתח "and she stood in the doorway") and her suggestion that Elisha might be deceiving her (v 16b) raise a shadow over the confidence with which Elisha and Gehazi present their gift to her. The point at this juncture of the story is made by the woman's rhetorical question in v 28. The reluctance of her initial response to the gift is brought out in the form of the question (השאלתי בן מאת אדני "Did I ask a son from you, sir?" v 28a). In vv 13–14 there is an echo of Elisha's dealings with the woman of the first story in the questions he asks both women, מה אעשה לך "What shall I do for you?" (v 2). The conclusion to this section of the chapter, with its straightforward announcement of the fulfillment of the promise Elisha made to the woman, reflects the repetitive style of vv 1–7 and vv 8–11. It ends this brief story well. In the broader context of the chapter this ending of the episode is deceptive in its presentation of apparent well-being.

In vv 18–28 the scene shifts to some years later, but the initial episode is remarkable for its brevity. Within the space of a few sentences the boy grows up, becomes sick, and eventually dies on his mother's lap. Thus is another serious element of tension introduced into the story. The originally unsolicited gift is now lost.

From this point on in the narrative it is the woman who dominates. In contrast to the compression of years into a few words (vv 18–20), vv 21–25 give considerable detail of the woman's determination to confront the man of God with the outcome of his promise. The woman shows no signs of grief; in fact, her actions are characterized by a degree of cold, efficient control.

She ascends the stairs, lays the boy down on Elisha's bed, closes the door behind her, then informs her husband that she will visit her erstwhile benefactor. His objections are brushed aside with a simple שלום "peace!" Although she asked for a servant, it is the woman who saddles the ass and through her instructions to that servant shows that she is in control. She eventually arrives at Carmel.

In the same way that she dismisses her husband's objections to her visit she brushes aside the polite preliminaries offered to her by Gehazi. As is her intention, she comes right into the presence of the man of God on the mountain (vv 25, 27). Her questions pick up two points. First, it was not her request for a son that prompted Elisha's action. Second, she had warned the man of God not to deceive her. The relationship established by the woman's gratuitous hospitality at the beginning of this section is now at the point of being completely destroyed, and a dark cloud hangs over both Elisha and Gehazi.

From vv 29–37 Elisha and Gehazi seek to make amends, yet the character of the woman is by no means forgotten. Elisha's commands to Gehazi in vv 28–29 show the urgency of the situation and the seriousness with which Elisha treats the situation. The woman insists on accompanying them, or more precisely, Elisha, perhaps to be a reminder of his responsibility in the whole affair (v 30). The repetition here of the oath Elisha had once sworn to his master Elijah is a touch of literary genius, and irony.

Gehazi's attempts to revive the boy fail (v 31), even though he has carried out Elisha's orders to the letter (vv 30*b*, 31*a*). It is only when Elisha himself takes personal control of the situation that things begin to happen. He enters the house, shuts the door to ensure privacy, and prays. For the first time in the chapter is divine aid sought by Elisha. Now the tension begins to be resolved, although even from this point the solution does not come easily. The embellishment by a later tradition of the sinful activity of Gehazi (see *Comment*, v 12) is out of place, since it absolves Elisha of any responsibility. The involvement of Elisha now centers on the contact he makes with the body of the boy (v 34), and finally, on the second attempt, the boy wakes. The significance of this action is that at the beginning of the story Elisha is introduced as "a holy man of God" (v 9). In such actions as these he risks his holiness (cf. Num 19:11).

When the boy wakes, the action shifts once again to the woman. She comes to Elisha, falls at his feet as before (vv 27, 37), but this time in worship. She also carries her son, this time not as a dead body (vv 21, 37).

38–41 In the first story the problem was caused by external circumstances, namely, the indebtedness of a dead husband. The problem was beyond the control of both the widow and her sons. In the second story the problem was inadvertently caused by the actions of Elisha and solved by a deed on the part of the man of God at cost to himself. In the present story the problem is a simple mistake, and the solution comes about by the man of God who intervenes with the exercise of remarkable power and authority.

Elisha returns to Gilgal to be with the "sons of the prophets." His command to the unnamed servant (v 38*b*) is motivated by the concern for the welfare of the group during a time of famine. The small scene change in v 39 is clever and serves to explain the reaction of the rest of the men who tried to eat the bitter stew. Their response carries with it a touch of irony in light of Elisha's previous encounter with death. But his response is swift and full of authority. His commands are obeyed, the meal is saved, and his care and concern for the welfare of the group are not thwarted.

42–44 The final story is as abrupt as vv 38–41 and vv 1–7. Generosity is again the theme of the story, this time generosity through a stranger identified only as "a man of Baal Shalishah" (v 42). The subject of ויאמר "and he said" in v 42*b*, although it appears to be the same as in v 42*a*, is thought by most commentators to be Elisha. This would be supported by the command תן לעם ויאכלו "give the people and they shall eat," which echoes the command of Elisha in v 41. An objection is raised to this command by an unnamed servant who indicates that the generosity of the stranger is insufficient. Elisha repeats the command and supports it by a word from Yahweh. V 44 states that the word was fulfilled. Again, the care and concern of Elisha for the group is maintained, and his authority is restored.

If the individual stories in this chapter had existed separately before their inclusion in the present context, such an observation would add little to their function as a collection. The chapter itself contains numerous themes and motifs throughout and individual stories within it are connected by style and phrasing. For example, the question asked of the widow in v 2 (מה אעשה לך "What shall I do for you?") is echoed by virtually the same question asked of the Shunemite woman in v 13 (מה לעשות לך "What to do for you?"). Both stories are connected by the common theme of privacy and the "shutting of the door" upon various activities (vv 4, 5, 21, 33). Further, vv 1–7 and vv 38–41 find common vocabulary in "pouring out" (vv 4, 5, 40, 41) to provide for certain needs. Vv 38–41 are connected by vv 42–44 with the expressions צק לעם ויאכלו "Pour it out for the people to eat" (v 41), and תן לעם ויאכלו "Give to the people and they will eat" (vv 42, 43). In addition, the first, third, and fourth stories make mention of the "sons of the prophets."

Additional motifs are seen in the chapter. The authority of the man of God, especially in the first, third, and fourth stories, is clear. He acts decisively and his results are certain. In stories one and two, Elisha's relationship with women and their sons is prominent. In both stories there is a movement from death or near-death (slavery) to life (v 7). In stories two and three, Elisha's ability to overcome "death" is prominent. Another common motif presents Elisha in the context of his servants, either Gehazi or ones unnamed. That these common features and recurring themes signify a common source or original collection of such stories before their inclusion in the present context is a very tempting conclusion, but not a necessary one. It can be drawn if there is a predisposition toward the identification of sources. Far more important, however, is the function that such stories have in their literary setting (see *Introduction*).

Comment

The opening story in this chapter is told in tight style, with an economy of words and background details. Nothing beyond the minimum necessary detail is given.

1 The reference to אשה אחת מנשי בני הנביאים "a certain woman from the wives of the sons of the prophets" would indicate that the "sons of the prophets" lived reasonably independent lives and were not a monastic-like order. See *Excursus* above. The targumic identification of עבדך היה ירא את־יהוה "your servant feared Yahweh" with the royal servant Obadiah of 1 Kgs 18:3, on the basis that both were God-fearing men, need not be taken too seriously. Josephus (*Antiq.* IX. 47–48) also adopts the tradition, claiming that in feeding the fugitive prophets (1 Kgs 18:4) Obadiah had incurred the debts mentioned here. A further embellishment is added by Josephus in his claim that the woman herself was also in danger of being sold into slavery.

The term הנשא "the creditors" is also written הנאה (Q Neh 5:7; GKC § 75). Ancient Israel had strict laws governing the practice of lending money. Whether the laws were intended to correct abuse or whether they represented an initial ideal is difficult to say. Two versions of the laws are found in Exod 22:24–26 and Deut 24:10–13. The sabbatical year and the year of Jubilee forgave all debts. It is possible that the sons had been pledged in payment of a debt the father had incurred. See G. A. Barrois, "Debt, Debtor," *IDB* 1:809–10.

4 Throughout this section the motif of the "shutting of the door" (סגרת הדלת בעדך ובעד־בניך) is common. Cf. 4:5, 21, 33; 6:32. The use of the preposition על "on" with the verb יצק "pour" is unusual, but not unique. The combination is used for the practice of anointing (Lev 2:1, 6; 2 Kgs 9:3). In 9:6 the preposition אל "to" is also used. A translation of יצק על as "to pour into" is rare. Some of the Peshitta MSS regard this as a miracle of turning water to oil.

8 ויהי היום, literally, "there was the day. . . ." It indicates the specific day on which an incident took place, and corresponds to the English "one day." The same phrase occurs in vv 11, 18. See DeVries, *Yesterday, Today and Tomorrow*, 153, 235.

שונם "Shunem" is identified with the modern village of Sulam on the slopes of Mt. Moreh, overlooking the eastern end of the Plain of Jezreel from the north. It is situated about seven kilometers north of the village of Jezreel. In Josh 19:18 it is assigned to the tribe of Issachar (*MBA*, Map 72) and its proximity to Gilboa brought it into the battle between Saul and the Philistines (1 Sam 28:4). It was an ancient site, mentioned in the list of cities conquered by Tutmoses III in the fifteenth century B.C. (cf. *ANET*, 243). It figures in the Amarna letters (*ANET*, 485) and in the list of cities captured by Shishak in the tenth century B.C. (*ANET*, 243). Two women of the Bible are mentioned as coming from Shunem, the "woman of substance" of the present story and Abishag (1 Kgs 1:3).

אשה גדולה "a woman of substance." Apparently the woman was wealthy, although not independently so. Reference is made to the servants of her husband (v 22) and she consulted with her husband before the construction of the upper room for the prophet. The distance from Shunem to Carmel would not normally necessitate a stop at the village, hence the narrator emphasizes the constraint the woman exercised over the prophet. Rabbinic tradition embellishes the story a great deal. The woman is identified as the sister of Abishag and wife of Iddo the prophet (2 Chr 9:29). She would then be over one hundred years of age. See Ginzberg, *Legends of the Jews* 4:242–44.

Comment

9 תמיד "continually" would suggest that Elisha habitually journeyed through this area from Carmel. Most of the activity of the prophet recorded in 2 Kings takes place south of Carmel. Probably Elisha, like Samuel, went on regular trips like this.

10 עלית קיר קטנה "a small walled upper room," as opposed to Ahaziah's upper room (1:2), which was surrounded by lattice work, Elisha's room was walled and clearly of a more permanent nature. This indicates something of the respect in which he was held by the woman. The careful way in which the furnishings are described also reflects this concern. All his basic needs were met. The furnishings were simple, but adequate. The מנורה "lamp" referred to is not the liturgical lamp of later Judaism. Lamps of this period (Iron, 11b) were simple turned bowls with a pinched neck for holding a wick. The שלחן "table" might have been a simple floor covering, like the modern Bedouin *sufra*.

12 ויאמר אל גחזי נערו "then he said to Gehazi his servant." For the first time in the Elisha stories the servant Gehazi is encountered. In chapters 4, 5, and 8 he plays a prominent role, and he becomes a rather tragic figure. His status in relation to Elisha is interesting. Elijah had an unnamed servant (1 Kgs 18:43), and Elisha had more than one such attendant (2 Kgs 6:15; 9:4). Unlike this other servant, Gehazi is not given any prophetic status. Josephus omits all references to those incidents in which Gehazi plays a prominent role. This reflects the disrepute which accompanied the memory of Gehazi in the later tradition. Rabbinic tradition blackens him to the point of caricature (see Ginzberg, *Legends of the Jews* 4:244–45). The name "Gehazi" has been interpreted as meaning "Valley of Vision" (so BDB; J. M. Ward, *IDB* 2:361). Gray (495) connects the name with the Arabic *jaḥida*, "to be avaricious," "greedy." His further suggestion that this and other stories were told to explain such a name misses the central place afforded to Elisha in these narratives. Thenius (*Könige*, 286) thought the name contained the place of Gehazi's birth.

13 היש לדבר לך אל המלך "Is there something to be said on your behalf to the king?" This expression indicates that the woman might have had a case before the chief magistrate, the king, at this time. G has it that Elisha wished to put in a good word for her to the king. The reference to the commander in chief is puzzling, unless a military governor is in mind. The influence Elisha had with those in authority must have been considerable, equal to that of Elijah.

בתוך עמי אנכי ישבת "I live among my own people." This response is one of complete security. Later when the woman is encountered again (8: 1–6) her fortunes have changed radically.

16 למועד הזה כעת חיה literally means "at this time, at the time of living," i.e., when the land comes to life again in the spring. See also Gen 18:10, 14; 17:21. An alternative way of expressing such precise points of time is found in the Lachish letters (11:3) עת כיום עת כיום "even this day, even this day" (cf. Gibson, *Syrian Semitic Inscriptions*, vol. 1, 37).

חבקת בן "embracing a son" is an unusual expression, reserved for emotional reunions (Gen 29:13; 33:4; 48:10) or for sexual caressing (Eccl 3:5).

23 לא חדש ולא שבת "It is neither a feast-day nor a sabbath" could involve one of several elements. Elisha might have received visitors only on feast days or sabbaths. The visit of the woman would then be out of order. The woman herself might have visited the prophet on a regular basis on such days. Another possibility is that festive days and sabbaths were those on which no work was done, therefore the woman would be free to make journey on those days only. Whatever the reason for the husband's comment, it displays a certain amount of callousness toward the woman's feelings. Her reply was intended to reassure her husband that the visit would not be an inconvenience for either him or the prophet.

25 The forty kilometer journey to Carmel necessitated speed.

השונמית הלז "that is the Shunemite." The rare form of the demonstrative is found only here with a feminine noun. See also Judg 6:20; 1 Sam 14:1; 17:26; 2 Kgs 23:7; Zech 2:8.

27 יהוה העלים ממני "Yahweh has hidden the reason from me" is an unusual admission of ignorance on the part of the prophet, especially in the light of the following narrative of Naaman and the actions of Gehazi.

28 תשלה "to deceive" is a rare verb in biblical Hebrew, occurring only here and in 2 Chr 29:11.

29 לא תברכנו "do not greet him." The extremely discourteous behavior which Elisha encouraged serves to highlight the extreme urgency of the situation being dealt with. The concern of the prophet is clearly seen in these words. On the many uses of the root ברך, cf. J. Scharbert, "ברך," *TDOT* 2:279–308; also J. Pedersen, *Israel: Its Life and Culture, I–II*, 202–4.

ושמת משענתי על פני הנער "Set my staff on the face of the boy." This symbolic action which Elisha asks Gehazi to perform is reminiscent of some forms of the treatment of ailments involving sympathetic magic in the ancient Near East (cf. R. C. Thompson, *Semitic Magic*, 206–8). On the prophetic symbolic actions, cf. G. Fohrer, *Die symbolischen Handlungen der Propheten*. In Exod 7:19, Moses' staff possessed miraculous powers, but there is little here to indicate that Elisha thought his staff had similar powers. The use of the staff could have been a gesture of his intention to arrive later (so Barnes, 19). The hypothetical parallel cited by Gray (498) of the sending of a lock of hair to accompany a prophetic message in Mari (cf. Beyerlin, *Near Eastern Religious Texts*, 124) is no parallel at all. In this narrative no prophetic word is given, and the likely recipient of such an oracle, the woman, remained with the prophet.

30 חי־יהוה וחי־נפשך "as Yahweh lives and as your soul lives" is the oath given by Elisha to his master Elijah (cf. 2:2, 4, 6).

33 ויבא ויסגר הדלת "he went in and shut the door." The motif of the shutting of the door reappears. Gray's suggestion (469–97) that it was an attempt to retain the spirit of the boy is unlikely. Secrecy and private miracles are a distinctive part of the ministry of Elisha.

34 Elisha's activity is described in more detail than the activity of Elijah in 1 Kgs 17:21. Elisha seems to wish to measure himself to the exact size of the boy. Whereas Elijah "stretched himself" (ויתמדד) over the boy, Elisha matches him limb for limb. This is a point fully exploited by the versions. Elisha thus attempts to do what the servant was unable to do, and a living body takes the place of the staff.

35 וילך . . . אחת הנה "and he walked . . . back and forth" reflects a

Comment

sense of agitation on the part of the prophet at the failure to wake up the dead boy.

אחת הנה ואחת הנה "back and forth." The use of the feminine אחת is due to the absence of the noun פעם (cf. Josh 6:3).

ויזורר . . . עד־שבע פעמים "and he sneezed seven times." The suggestion that this is a secondary comment has been dealt with in the *Notes* above. That its exclusion would bring the narrative into conformity with 1 Kgs 17: 17–24 would be evidence for its originality. The fact that זרר is a *hapax legomenon* would also support this. Sneezing is a most appropriate sign of life.

37 ותפל על־רגליו "and she fell at his feet." The action of the mother is in contrast to her initial scolding of the prophet (v 27). Now her gesture is one of gratitude and praise (cf. also 1 Sam 25:24; Esth 8:3).

38 שב הגלגלה "He returned to Gilgal." The location of Gilgal has been discussed in connection with 2:1. The Gilgal near Jericho would have been an unlikely place to go in times of famine, but the sentence gives no indication that he went there because of the famine. His visit and the famine are simultaneous, but unconnected. The image conjured up in this brief narrative becomes characteristic of later views of the prophets. It is a sign of their asceticism (cf. 4 Ezra 9:26; 12:51; *Asc. Isa.* 2:11).

ובני הנביאים ישבים לפניו "and the sons of the prophets were assembled before him." Such a gathering of the "sons of the prophets" is rare in the OT and generalizations cannot be made on the basis of this.

ויאמר לנערו "and he said to his servant." Although Gehazi is not mentioned, OL identifies the servant as Gehazi. The theme is similar to that of the preceding narrative, namely, the inability of the prophet's servant to accomplish something, with the situation being served by the prophet himself.

39 ארות "plants" is a *hapax legomenon*, which might be derived from the root ארה "to pluck" (cf. Ps 80:12).

גפן שדה "a wild vine." For the use of שדה as "wild," cf. Exod 22:30.

פקעת "gourds" are probably to be identified with *citrullus colycinthus*, a wild vine with a fruit the size and shape of an orange, but with an extremely bitter taste. Such a fruit would certainly have elicited the reaction described in the story. See J. C. Trever, *IDB* 2:450–51.

40 ויאמרו מות בסיר "and they said, 'Death is in the pot'" is not to be taken literally, but is a natural reaction to something which tasted bitter.

41 וקחו קמח "fetch some flour." Such a use of flour would absorb any excessive salt in the stew.

42 מבעל שלשה "Baal Shalishah." The exact location is unknown, although it is generally identified with Kfar Tilt (Thult) twenty kilometers west of Shechem. Such an identification would correspond with Eusebius' (*Onomasticon*) location of the site fifteen miles north of Lydda (Diospoleos). In 1 Sam 9 the territory of Shalishah is mentioned in the search for the asses of Saul's father. Later tradition comments favorably on the fertility of this area.

לחם בכורים "bread of the first fruits" locates the event during the time of harvest when the famine would be most severely felt.

בצקלנו is a *hapax legomenon* normally translated "sack." Major versions omit the term, although the Vg *in pera sua* provides the RSV translation. On an analogy with a Ugaritic text, Gray (501) suggests that וכרמל בצקלנו should be emended to ובצקלנו כרמלו "fruits from his orchard."

43 Again the servant (משרתו) of Elisha (?) proves unable to rise to the occasion. This motif runs through these stories like a thread. The term עם "people" used of the prophetic group is unusual, unless this particular gathering was larger than the "sons of the prophets" themselves.

מאה איש "a hundred men." The numbering of the "sons of the prophets" in multiples of fractions of one hundred (1 Kgs 18:4; 2 Kgs 2:7, 16, 17) might reflect a well-organized network of such persons or might reflect the colloquial use of such round figures by the narrator.

44 כדבר יהוה "according to the word of the Lord." Only here does a reference to the word of Yahweh appear in the whole chapter and it comes at the end of a relatively minor incident.

Explanation

The four stories presented in this chapter offer a sharp contrast to the type of story that precedes them in chap. 3 and follows them in chap. 5. Here we see Elisha's care for individuals. The contents of the chapter illustrate the extremely complicated phenomenon of early Israelite prophecy. Only in the last of these incidents is there anything approaching what has come to be understood as traditional prophetic activity. Elisha orders the feeding of his companions with a word of God (v 43). However, the word is no judgment, nor does it have any wider historical significance outside the immediate grouping of men around Elisha. It constitutes an immediate response to their pressing need during the famine.

Any attempt to restrict the nature of the Israelite prophetic tradition to one source or to one type of character must be carefully avoided. It includes a variety of types of men and a variety of activities.

Clearly one of the activities attributed to early prophets, notably Elijah and Elisha, was the ability to perform miracles. Any decision on the "historicity" of such actions is out of order at this point. By their very nature miracles are not susceptible to proof in the scientific sense. To believe in the ability of Elisha to perform such miracles requires an act of faith in which the normal processes of logic are suspended. But, to argue at this level is to miss the point of such stories. Their origin might be similar to many such tales attached to famous men and women throughout the history of religion. But, properly seen, such miracles are the results of faith, not the inspiration of faith. The Synoptic image of Jesus is of one who evoked faith before the performance of miracles (cf. Mark 5:36). What is important in the literary presentation of such incidents is not the miracle-working power attributed to Elisha, since the ability to perform miracles is not necessarily a sign of the power of God (cf. Exod 7:8–13). As if to make this point clear the narrator reveals a weakness on the part of Elisha during the performance of his most spectacular miracle, the raising of the Shunemite's son. Only on the third attempt is the miracle successful. What is of great importance in these stories is the motivation of the miracle worker. Are the miracles an attempt at self aggrandizement or do they have another purpose? In the case of Elisha in chap. 4, the motivation is the desire to respond to pressing human needs. The motivation is compassion.

The picture of Elisha's responding in this way to human need is one of great tenderness. The narrator has included human characteristics of excessive zeal (vv 13–16) as Elisha presses upon the unwilling Shunemite woman the gift of a son. There is also a fumbling sense of inadequacy, as he repeatedly tries to raise the son to life.

This contact between Elisha, a threatened widow and orphans (vv 1–7), a bereaved woman (vv 18–37), and hungry companions (vv 38–42) has echoes elsewhere in the OT. It reflects the ideal society in which such care is commonplace (cf. Deut 14:29; 16:11, 14, etc.). But it is also a reflection of the very character of God himself, who "executes justice for the fatherless and the widow, and loves the stranger, giving him food and clothing" (Deut 10:18). A king could do well to seek such an ideal of true justice (Ps 72:1–19).

It is a short step from this ideal, exemplified in the actions of Elisha, to the later prophetic voice raised on behalf of the poor and oppressed and those victims of monarchical society. The voice God has given to the poor is that of the prophet.

The actions of Elisha find echo in the ministry of Jesus. Like Elisha, Jesus responded to the needs of unfortunate women (Mark 7:24–30; 5:24–34); like Elisha, Jesus raised the dead (Mark 5:21–24; 35–43; Luke 7:11–17); and like Elisha, Jesus fed the hungry (Mark 6:30–44).

Naaman's Cure (5:1–27)

Bibliography

Fitzmyer, J. A. "Some Notes on Aramaic Epistolography." *JBL* 93 (1974) 201–25. **Heller, J.** "Drei Wundertaten Elisas." *Communio Viatorum* 2 (1959) 83–85. **Pardee, D.** "An Overview of Ancient Hebrew Epistolography." *JBL* 97 (1978) 321–46. **von Rad, G.** "Naaman: Eine kritische Nacherzählung." *Gottes Wirken in Israel.* Neukirchen-Vluyn: Neukirchener Verlag, 1974. **Schult, H.** "Naamans Übertritt zum Yahwismus (2 Kön. 5,1–19a) und die biblischen Bekehrungsgeschichten." *Dielheimer Blätter zum Alten Testament* 9 (1975) 2–20. **Wevers, J. W.** "Double Readings in the Books of Kings." *JBL* 65 (1946) 307–10.

Translation

¹*Naaman, commander-in-chief*[a] *of the army of the king*[b] *of Syria was a great man according to his master. He was well-respected because through him Yahweh had provided deliverance for Syria. Although he was a great warrior*[c] *he was also a leper.* ²*Now Syria had sent out raiding parties, and had brought back from the land of Israel a young girl, and she was the attendant of Naaman's wife.* ³*She said to her mistress, "I wish*[a] *my lord would go before*[bc] *the prophet who is in Samaria. He would surely cure him of his leprosy."* ⁴*Someone came*[a] *and told his master, saying, thus and so did the young girl from the land of Israel speak.* ⁵*Then the king of Syria said, "Go on your way, and I shall send a letter to the king of*

Israel." So Naaman went [a] and took in his hands ten talents of silver, six thousand shekels [b] of gold, and ten fine robes. [6] Eventually he brought the letter to the king of Israel which said, "Now when this letter arrives, see I have sent you Naaman my servant, that you may cure him of leprosy." [7] And when the king of Israel read [a] the letter, he tore his clothes and exclaimed, "Am I a god, to kill and make alive, that this man sends me a message to cure someone of leprosy? Know full well that he is looking for an excuse to quarrel with me!"

[8] Now when Elisha, the man of God [a] heard that the king of Israel [b] had torn his clothes, he sent word to the king saying, "Why have you torn your garments? Let the man come to me and let him know that there is a prophet in Israel." [9] So Naaman came with his horse [a] and his chariot and stopped at the door of Elisha's house. [10] Elisha sent out a messenger to him saying, "Go and wash seven times in the Jordan, and your flesh shall be restored and cleansed." [11] At this Naaman was furious and made to leave. He said, "I thought that he would surely come out, stand here and call on the name of Yahweh [a] his God, wave his hand over the infected place, and cure the leprosy! [b] [12] Are not Abana and Pharpar, rivers of Damascus, better than all the rivers of Israel? Could I not have washed in them and have been cleansed?" He turned [a] and went away in a rage.

[13] Then his attendants drew close to him, and said, [a] "Father [b] if the prophet had told you to do some great thing, would you not have done it? Now all he says to you is, wash and be cleansed." [14] So he went down, dipped in the Jordan seven times, according to the word of the man of God, [a] and his flesh was restored like that of a small child's, and he was cleansed.

[15] He [a] then returned to the man of God, [b] both he and his entourage, and he came and stood in front of him [c] and said, "Now I do know that there is no God in all the earth, save in Israel. Now please accept a gift from your servant." [d] [16] But the reply was, "As Yahweh lives, before whom I stand, I will not accept." He urged him to accept, but he refused. [17] Then Naaman said, "If not, [a] then let your servant be given two mule-loads of earth, [b] because your servant will no longer offer sacrifice to foreign gods, only to Yahweh. [18] [a] Concerning this matter, may Yahweh forgive your servant when my master enters the temple of Rimmon to worship there, [b] and he leans upon my hand, and I worship in the temple of Rimmon—I have to worship in the temple of Rimmon—may Yahweh forgive your servant for this thing." [19] And he [a] said to him, [b] "Go in peace." So he [c] went away from him a short distance.

[20] Then Gehazi, the servant of Elisha the man of God, [a] said, "Now my master has refrained from taking from the hand of Naaman this Syrian what he brought. As Yahweh lives, I shall certainly run after him and take something from him." [21] So Gehazi pursued Naaman, and Naaman saw him running after him. He jumped down from his chariot to meet him and said, "Are things well?" [22] He replied, [a] "All is well, but my master has sent me to say that now these two young men have come from the hill country of Ephraim, from the sons of the prophets. Donate a talent of silver, and two fine robes." [23] Naaman's response was, "Please take two talents!" He urged him, and he tied two talents of silver in two bags, and two fine robes. Then he handed them to two of his servants who carried them on ahead. [24] Gehazi came to the Ophel, [a] and he took the gifts from their hands, and set them in his house. He then sent the men away, and they departed. [25] Then this man went and stood before his master. Elisha said to him, "Have you been anywhere [a] Gehazi?" He replied, "Your servant has been nowhere in particular." [26] But he [a] said to him,

"Did not ᵇ my heart travel with you when the man ᶜ alighted from his chariot to meet you? Did you not take ᵈ silver and robes for orchards, vineyards, sheep and cattle, men and maidservants? ²⁷ Now may the leprosy of Naaman cling to you and your offspring forever." He went out from his presence, snow-white with leprosy.

Notes

1.a. G reads τῆς δυναμεως Συριας "the power of Syria," Gᴸ offers ἀρχιστρατηγος "the chief soldier."
1.b. מלך "the King" is omitted by G.
1.c. MT חיל גבור "a great captain" is omitted by Gᴸ which reads simply "the man was a leper" (ὁ ἀνθρωπος ἦν λεπρος). Burney (279) believes the Heb. to be a marginal gloss upon the preceding איש גדול "a great man," but this hardly seems necessary. The contrast in MT between the גבור חיל "a strong hero" and the מצרע "was a leper" is deliberate.
3.a. The pointing of אַחֲלַי "I would that," which occurs only here and in Ps 119:5, is analogous to אַשְׁרֵי "blessed is." But the Ps 119:5 pointing is אַחֲלַי, which is paralleled by the G reading of ὄφελον "oh that." In its present form the term seems to be a pl constr, possibly indicating some idiomatic expression, like the oath beginning with אם "if." Syr and Tg read it so.
3.b. G adds here του θεου "the God."
3.c. Gᴸ adds και δεηθειη του προσωπου αυτου "and would beg before him."
4.a. The subject of ויגד ויבא "someone came and told" is ambiguous and can be rendered as in the translation. Vg, apparently taking into consideration the named subject of the following sentence, removes the ambiguity by reading *ingressus est itaque Naaman ad dominum suum.* G and Tg take the subject to be the wife of Naaman, thus identifying the אדני "lord" as Naaman. Burney (279) opts for Naaman as the subject, but MT is not clear.
5.a. Gᴸ adds Νεεμαν προς τον βασιλεια Ισραηλ "Naaman to the king of Israel."
5.b. Gᴸ adds ἐξ ταλαντα.
7.a. The Heb preposition כ "as" is consistently translated with the Gr ὡς "as" here.
8.a. איש האלהים "a man of God" is omitted by G, and Gᴸ omits אלישע "Elisha."
8.b. Gᴸ reads simply ὁ βασιλευς "the king."
9.a. MT בְּסוּסָו, which is better read בְּסוּסָיו "with his horses" or בְּסוּסוֹ "with his horse."
11.a. G omits יהוה "Yahweh."
11.b. Gᴸ adds ἀπο της σαρκος μου "from my flesh."
12.a. G translates with ἐξεκλινεν "turned," which is rare for פנה "turn." Gᴸ offers ἐπεστρεψεν "turned," normally reserved for שוב "return."
13.a. G omits ויאמרו "and they said."
13.b. MT is confusing since it states the opposite of what is given in the translation. The intention seems to accord with the translation. Gᴬ includes אבי "my father," although Gᴮ and others omit it. Gᴸ reads εἰ "if," which provides an original אם "if." Such a corruption from אם "if" to אבי "my father" is possible.
14.a. איש־האלהים "man of God" is omitted by G.
15.a. In typical fashion, Gᴸ adds the proper name Naaman.
15.b. Gᴮ reads "Elisha."
15.c. לפניו "to his face" is omitted by Gᴮ. Gᴬ offers εἰς προσωπον αυτου "to his face," whereas some MSS of the Lucianic recension read ἐνωπιον "before."
15.d. Gᴸ renders מאת עבדך "from your servant" as παρα ἐκ χειρος "from the hand" (מאת ידיך).
17.a. MT ולא is rendered by G as εἰ μη (אם לא) "if not."
17.b. Some minor MSS add και συ μοι δωσεις ἐκ της γης της πυρρας "and you shall give me red clay from the ground."
18.a. G and others appear to presuppose a conjunction, ולדבר, "But in this matter. . . ." This makes better grammatical sense.
18.b. MT בהשתחויתי "when I bow down." But G, Gᴸ, and Vg presuppose a third pers masc sg suffix, "When he comes to worship. . . ." The change need not reflect an original reading. It is more likely to be a tendentious reading, since Naaman has already foresworn the worship of a foreign god.

19.a. G adds Ἐλισαιε "Elisha."
19.b. G adds Ναιμαν "Naaman."
19.c. Many translations add this last part of the verse to the succeeding story.
20.a. אִישׁ הָאֱלֹהִים "man of God" is omitted by G, not by G^L.
22.a. וַיֹּאמֶר שָׁלוֹם "and he said, 'peace,'" is omitted by G, probably because of the similar conclusion to v 21.
24.a. G renders the Heb עֹפֶל "Ophel" as το σκοτεινον "the darkness" (אֹפֶל "darkness"). See *Comment* below.
25.a. MT reads מֵאָן "anywhere," which is better read as מֵאַיִן.
26.a. G adds Ἐλισαιε "Elisha."
26.b. G reads לֹא "not" as הֲלֹא and adds the equivalent of עִמָּךְ.
26.c. G^L adds "Naaman."
26.d. MT הָעֵת לָקַחַת "Now did you take?" which is rendered by G as και νυν "and now," probably understanding וְעַת "and then." With v 26 the Dead Sea Scrolls fragments of the books of Kings (6QReg) become important. See M. Baillet, J. T. Milik, and R. de Vaux, eds., *Les Petites Grottes de Qumran: Textes,* 108. In the 6QReg fragment on v 26 an interrogative is present (הֲעֵת). Cf. also Burney, 283.

Form/Structure/Setting

Many form-critical classifications of the story of Naaman in 2 Kgs 5 are unsatisfactory insofar as they fail to do complete justice to the unique features of this particular narrative. DeVries (*Prophet against Prophet,* 54, 57, 118) designates the narrative as "power demonstration narrative," illustrating a model prophet's activity and further classifies it under sub-type III, "prophetic word story." Similar stories are found in 2:22–24 and 8:1–6. It is also regarded as part of an early legitimation collection with 2:1–18, 23–24; 4:8–37; and 8:1–6, and some additional redactional phrases. Common to chapters four, five, and eight is the figure of Gehazi. In 5:1–27, the motif of tension (DeVries: "opposition") occurs between the prophet's potential to do both good and evil, heal and afflict. The stories are seen to move from problem to solution.

On the other hand, Eissfeldt (*Introduction,* 295) identifies 5:1–27 as an "historical narrative" because of the presence of the two kings in the story. Contrary to DeVries, Eissfeldt sees the figure of Gehazi—the common element in chaps. 5 and 8—as an argument against a common literary form or source for both chapters. In chap. 8, Gehazi is not a leper; and yet the sequence is correct, since chap. 8 presupposes the demise of the prophet, Elisha. They appear to come from different sources.

Such confusion and contradiction demand a fresh approach to the story. The problem-resolution structure, noted by DeVries, is a fundamental feature of the story form. Because of its universality, this structure provides no clues as to the specific genre of story being told. While the prophet is introduced as נָבִיא "prophet" (vv 3, 8), other prophetic characteristics are absent. Nowhere in the story do the traditional prophetic speech formulas occur, and nowhere in the story is any word or promise fulfilled as it is in 1:4, 17; 2:21, 22. The confusion as to the identification of a specific genre for this story brings to the fore another feature overlooked by both DeVries and Eissfeldt, namely, the complicated plot structure which moves beyond the intricacies of chap. 4. To place the story under a single heading along with 2:23–24 does not do justice to this feature.

All of the stories found in 2 Kgs 2:22–5:27 move from problem to solution.

In most of the stories, however, the crispness of the plot is demonstrated by the small number of main characters and the lack of characterization. For example, in 2:19–22, two main characters appear, Elisha and the men of the city. In 2:23–24, there are three, Elisha, the boys, and the bears. In 4:1–7, there are four—Elisha, the widow, and her two sons. With these latter figures Elisha has very little to do. In 4:8–37 there are five characters, Elisha, the Shunemite, her husband, her son, and Gehazi; but Elisha has no contact with the husband in the narrative. In 4:38–41 only Elisha and the sons of the prophets appear, and one of the sons is singled out for his unwitting mistake. In 4:42–44 Elisha, the sons of the prophets, who remain very passive, the man from Baal Shalishah, and an unnamed servant appear.

In the story of Naaman (5:1–27) no less than *ten* characters, or groups of characters, appear in the cast. There are Naaman, his wife, her maid, the king of Syria, the king of Israel, Elisha, Gehazi, Naaman's servants, Elisha's unnamed messenger, and the additional unidentified servants who carry Gehazi's loot for him. With the marked increase in characters comes an increase in the number of subplots and "scene changes" which enhance the main incident of the encounter between Naaman and Elisha. The complexity of the narrative is seen in the incidental way in which Elisha figures in some of the subplots (cf. vv 2–3; vv 5–7; vv 20–24). To identify the form of the story with that of 4:1–7 and 4:38–41 among others is to overlook these very distinctive features of the story. The effect of this complexity is to stall temporarily the smooth movement from problem to resolution of the problem. Eventually the chapter ends with Naaman cleansed and Gehazi judged, but the plot entails many twists and turns before that point is reached.

There are two major stories in the chapter that deal with separate but related issues (contra Montgomery, 373). The stories concern the healing of Naaman and his offer of a gift to the prophet (vv 1–19) and the duplicity of Gehazi (vv 20–27). The latter story is clearly dependent upon the former, which "sets the stage" for the activity of Gehazi. The link between the two is Naaman's attempt to pay for his healing (vv 15–19). In dramatic terms, the three episodes are like three acts of a drama, each with their individual scene changes and entrances and exits of the subsidiary characters upon the stage.

The first incident involving the setting up of the problem can be further subdivided into vv 1–7; vv 8–12; and vv 13–14. The first two subdivisions are well balanced and deal with the frustration of Naaman's attempt to find healing. The third provides the needed resolution to the problem of Naaman's sickness.

V 1 begins the story on a note of tragedy. In spite of all his achievements, the high official, Naaman, is a leper. This state of affairs is made more harsh by the comment that many of Naaman's achievements were made by the help of Yahweh. In vv 2–3 the first subsidiary characters are introduced. They appear here, help move the plot along, then disappear. A young girl from Israel had found her way into the household of the afflicted man. She reports to Naaman's wife concerning the "prophet in Samaria" who could heal the leprosy (v 3). Now a glimmer of hope is seen. The literary problem is how to bring the two together.

In vv 4–6 this is taken a step closer toward resolution. The report of the young girl is brought before the king, and with this an additional subsidiary character is introduced who takes over the role played by the wife and the maidservant. His action is typical. He sends a letter to his Israelite counterpart concerning Naaman. This scene ends on the same note as the previous one. It echoes the young girl's hope for her master. When the king has fulfilled this obligation, he too disappears from the story.

The optimism is lost when the king of Israel (the next subsidiary character) receives the letter. He reacts to it with suspicion and fright. The possibility of healing is rejected (v 7), because of the mistrust and misunderstanding of bureaucracy. The move toward the resolution of Naaman's problem is stalled.

In vv 8–12 the move is now through almost exactly the same stages traveled thus far, as a second attempt is made to find healing for Naaman. Here Elisha is introduced. In his reaction to hearing the king of Israel's response to the letter, he recalls the words of the young girl, יבא נא אלי וידע כי יש נביא בישראל "Let him come to me and let him know there is a prophet in Israel." Naaman obeys by coming (ויבא) to Elisha's door to be healed. Elisha's response is to send (וישלח) a messenger with a simple solution to one problem—washing in the Jordan seven times. This would provide him with his desire (וישב בשרך לך יטהר "your flesh will be restored and cleansed"). Again, v 3 is echoed, only with more promise.

Whether through pride or a sense of insult, Naaman himself becomes an obstacle to his own healing by his angry, disappointed reaction (vv 11–12). His anger parallels the fright of the Israelite king. An additional frustration results.

In the third act the resolution is found. Additional characters now appear in the persons of Naaman's servants, who repeat Elisha's commands (v 13). By consenting to this, Naaman finds healing as promised. The reference to Naaman's flesh as being like the flesh of a "small youngster" (נער קטון) in v 14 provides an *inclusio* with its reminder of the "young lass" (נערה קטנה) of v 2. The servants of Naaman and the young girl have similar roles in the story. The girl begins the process of healing and the servants help to complete it.

Vv 15–19 provide transitional dialogue between the opening "act" and the closing "act." That they could have existed as a separate story is unlikely since they are dependent on what precedes and anticipate what follows. Here Naaman is the main actor. He returns to Elisha, who remains unnamed in this section. He comes to the prophet and stands before him. His confession in v 16 certainly accords with the intention of the healing as seen by Elisha in v 8. After having offered a gift, and after having been refused, Naaman makes a touching request. He asks for forgiveness—whether for offering the gift or the future religious compromise is not clear—then asks for a souvenir of Israel. In v 19 he is sent on his way in peace, which is in direct contrast to his initial journey (v 5) as a sick man. Thus is the scene set for the following episode with Gehazi. Naaman returns home grateful. He is grateful enough to be tricked into giving some of his gift away when approached by Gehazi.

A different kind of problem emerges in vv 20–27, and a radical solution is offered by Elisha. The problem is created by the deceit and greed of Gehazi, Elisha's servant. The end-note of the story is tragedy. The main actor is Gehazi and his character is filled out by the portrayal of his actions. The story moves in three stages, identified in part by the other characters in the plot. The first concerns Gehazi and Naaman (vv 20–23), the second Gehazi and the servants (v 24), and the third Gehazi and Elisha. In the first two Gehazi is successful in his deceit, but in the third he is punished for it.

In vv 20–23 Gehazi self-consciously establishes himself as the opposite of his master. Whereas Elisha had refused a gift from "this Syrian," Gehazi is determined to profit. The justification of these opposite reactions to Naaman's generosity is prefaced with the same device, an oath (vv 16, 20). Even the use of the term מאומה "anything" in v 20 gives to Gehazi an air of reckless greed. This greed is enhanced by the narrator's use of וירדף "so he pursued" in v 21. Gehazi actively pursues this goal. In vv 21–23 Naaman remains the innocent who is lied to repeatedly. The description of his enthusiasm in unwittingly helping Gehazi in his deceit (v 23b) is touching. To impress the reader with this obvious contrast, Naaman "urges" now as he had done earlier (cf. v 16b). The lack of trust that an attitude such as Gehazi's engenders is seen in the next episode. Gehazi carefully hides the loot, after having sent the servants away (v 24).

The climax of this story is brought about by the dialogue between Gehazi and his master in which the deceit is compounded further. A simple yet penetrating exchange takes place in which Gehazi's actions are exposed for what they are. Gehazi's reward is to receive from Naaman, not any part of his gift intended originally for Elisha, but the sickness which began the general's search in the first place.

To speculate on the original life-setting for this story is ultimately fruitless, since it must remain speculation. The story holds together well in its present form, which was what was intended. Three main themes dominate the story: Elisha's ability to heal, Israel's relations with Syria, and Gehazi's greed and punishment. But whether these warrant the epithets of "power demonstration narrative," (DeVries), "historical narrative" (Eissfeldt), or even "deception-action sequence" (Culley, *Time Structure of Hebrew Narrative*) is doubtful. Each concentrates on one of the three themes to the exclusion of the other two. Further, to locate such stories among the circles of the prophet's disciples is not helpful.

The literary setting of the chapter is much more certain. It is one of Elisha stories which make up the greater part of 2 Kgs 2–13. More important is the relationship of this chapter to the preceding one. It provides an interesting study of contrasts with many of the themes and motifs already seen in chap. 4. Mentioned above is the "role reversal" in which characters of chap. 4 now play roles in which they are the recipients of similar actions they performed earlier. Elisha offers a gift once, now refuses one himself. Gehazi acts like the Shunemite in a search for satisfaction; but, whereas she did it for the health of her son, he does it for selfish gain. Both are greeted with השלום "is it well?" and both reply שלום "it is well," none too honestly. Elisha's ignorance in 4:27 is in sharp contrast to his knowledge in 5:26. In both chapters persons are frequently "standing before" a person of authority, usually Elisha. Whereas chap. 4 ends with the satisfaction of all concerned, chap. 5 ends with judgment for Gehazi.

Such similarity of themes and expression, however, does not interpret the *distinctive* features of chap. 5. These features make this story one of greater complexity than the others in the collection and enable it to stand as a unique contribution to our knowledge of the life and ministry of Elisha.

Excursus: The Form of the Letter in 2 Kings 5

Under a treatment of form, one must refer to the correspondence which passed between the king of Syria and the king of Israel. In the story, only the general intention of the letter is given, not its complete contents. Sufficient detail is provided to make some observations about its relationship with standards of diplomatic correspondence of the ancient Near East.

Two articles by Fitzmyer and Pardee have appeared in *JBL* (see Bibliography) which deal with known Hebrew and Aramaic correspondence. Known Hebrew letters, particularly, are later than the events of 2 Kgs 5. There are nine characteristics of such letters outlined by these authors. Letters are called ספרים "scrolls" or its equivalent; the praescriptio includes the name of the recipient and some use of the verb "to send"; an initial, formal greeting follows; then a secondary greeting. The contents of the letter are often introduced by the phrase ועתה "and now." A concluding formula, the name of the scribe, the date, and an exterior address are also common.

In 2 Kgs 5 the correspondence is named ספר "scroll" (vv 5, 7) and it is dispatched (שלח) from one king to another (v 6). In v 6*b* the contents of the letter are introduced by the phrase ועתה "and now." The narrative disallows any other detail of the letter, but what appears conforms to known ANE letter forms.

Comment

1 Naaman is a name attested in texts from Ugarit and is derived from a word meaning "fair," "gracious." Cf. Gray, 504; Driver, *Canaanite Myths and Legends*, 156. שר צבא "commander for the army"; for a discussion of Naaman's rank, see the comment on 1:9 above.

מלך־ארם "The king of Syria" here is unnamed, although in 6:24 and 8:7 he is identified as Ben Hadad (presumably Ben Hadad I). The incident recorded in this chapter must have taken place during a rare time of peace between Syria's many conflicts with Israel.

איש גדול "a great man." This reference to Naaman echoes the description of the אשה גדולה "woman of substance" of Shunem in the previous chapter. Also common to both narratives is the role of Gehazi. The combination reappears in 8:1–6.

ונשא פנים "and lifted of face" is an idiomatic expression of respect. It might have its origin in the action of one in authority literally lifting the face of a subject (so Gray, 504), although the term comes to mean general respect (cf. 3:14).

תשועה לארם "deliverance for Syria." The first word is a variant spelling of ישועה from the root ישע "to save." The comment is remarkable, although not unusual in the OT. The belief in the sovereignty of God over nations other than Israel is a logical outcome of monotheism. Cf. also Amos 9:7; Isa 10:13. The specific deliverance in mind has been interpreted as a victory over Israel. According to Josephus (*Antiq.* xv.5) Naaman was the slayer of the apostate King Ahab. The Targum on 2 Chr 18 makes the same identification.

מצרע "a leper." There are many forms of leprosy; the exact affliction of Naaman is not easy to determine. It is clear from the story that Naaman's disease was a skin disease and that it resulted in a whiteness, possibly dryness of the skin tissues (v 27). It is unlikely to have been what modern medicine understands by leprosy ("Hansen's disease"). The symptoms and result of Hansen's disease are pain, blotchy, wide-spread infection of the joints causing eventual loss of limbs, and gross disfigurement. Apparently, Naaman's affliction was such that he was not forced to live in quarantine. It was also of a temporary nature. There is no indication that he was ritually unclean and subject to regulations, such as those in Lev 13. For a comprehensive study of leprosy and its nature cf. R. G. Cochrane and T. F. Davey, eds., *Leprosy in Theory and Practice.* Of particular interest to students of the OT is the first chapter, "The History of Leprosy and Its Spread Throughout the World," 1–12. Cf. also R. G. Cochrane, *Biblical Leprosy: A Suggested Interpretation.*

2 גדודים "raiding parties." The Hebrew is from a root גדד "to cut," "penetrate," and is often used as a term for a raiding party (1 Sam 30:8, 15). G translates with μονοζωνος "one-belted," that is, soldiers who were lightly armed for quick raiding activity. Cf. above the comments on 3:21. A number of lesser Greek MSS add the term πειρατηριον "gang of pirates."

לפני "before" is a characteristic phrase in these stories. In conjunction with the verb עמד "stand" it is a sign of reverence, even worship. It forms part of an oath (5:16) and designates an attitude of respect (4:12, 15).

3 אז יאסף "surely he would cure." It is apparent that the reputation of Elisha as a miracle worker was fairly widespread, even to the point of becoming the subject of talk by young maidens of Samaria. Since this is presupposed in this story, there is obviously much about the activity of Elisha which is not included in this collection of material on his ministry.

4 כזאת כזאת "thus and so." As a general expression for conversation this is common in the Former Prophets (cf. Josh 7:20; 2 Sam 7:15; 2 Kgs 9:12).

5 אשלח ספר אל "I will send a letter to" is a reference to the sending of diplomatic letters. It is an interesting glimpse at the niceties of international protocol in the ANE.

מלך ישראל "the king of Israel." As with the king of Syria, no name is given this monarch. Elisha was active during the reigns of Joram (ca. 849–42 B.C.), Jehu (ca. 842–15 B.C.), Jehoahaz (ca. 815–802 B.C.), and part of the reign of Jehoash (802–776 B.C.). If these narratives are in any semblance of chronological order, which is by no means sure, then the Ben Hadad of chapter eight must be Ben Hadad I, who was assassinated in approximately 842 B.C. The king of Israel would then be Jehoram.

The amount of the gift taken by Naaman is excessively large. One talent is approximately thirty-two kilograms, and a shekel weighs approximately thirty milligrams. Naaman's total gift would then amount to approximately three hundred and forty kilograms of silver and ninety kilograms of gold. By any standards, this is an enormous amount.

6 The language used in the communication between the Syrian and Israelite kings conforms to what is known of formal Aramaic correspondence (cf. Fitzmyer, *JBL* 93 [1974]201–25). See below.

7 להמית ולהחיות "to kill and to make alive" is an unusual pair of words which occurs only here in the OT. The hiphil infinitives of either verb are not used with God as the subject elsewhere, so this cannot be a formulaic designation of God. However, in Deut 32:39 hiphil indicatives are used:

ראו עתה כי אני אני הוא	"See now that I, I am he,
ואין אלהים עמדי	and there is no god beside me.
אני אמית ואחיה	I will kill and I will make alive
מחצתי ואני ארפא	I wound and I heal
ואין מידי מציל	and there is none who can deliver from my hand."

The language of this hymn is certainly reflected in the cry of the king of Israel.

8 כשמע אלישע "when Elisha heard." We are probably to understand that Elisha was still at Gilgal when this incident occurred. Its proximity to the Jordan would certainly be in keeping with the narrative of Naaman's cleansing.

וישלח אל המלך "he sent word to the king." This could be a play on the earlier reference that the king of Syria sent word to the king of Israel, thus causing the problem, and Elisha now sends word to the king of Israel suggesting a solution. In this narrative there is a definite play on words between קרא "to read" and קרע "to tear." See above: *Form.* וידע כי יש נביא בישראל "and he will know that there is a prophet in Israel." This theme, closely associated with the uniqueness of God, is found also in 1:6; 3:11; and 8:7–15.

9 ויעמד פתח "and he stood in the door." This action of Naaman's, so similar to that of the Shunemite, is a sign of his respect for the prophet (cf. 4:15).

10 The regulations governing leprosy (Lev 13–14) are reflected in much of the vocabulary of this verse, but the associations and intentions are different. Washing (רחץ) is part of the ritual of cleansing; but, whereas in Lev 14: 8–9 it is symbolic of cleansing, here it precipitates the cleansing. The number seven is found frequently in the regulations, but there is no indication that a leper must bathe seven times. Rather, it is the period of quarantine (Lev 13:4, 5, etc.). It is not necessary to see the figure as evidence of the "saga-form" of the story (cf. Gray, 506).

ורחצת שבע פעמים בירדן "wash seven times in the Jordan." It has been suggested (R. C. Thompson, *Semitic Magic,* liv) that the washing for ritual cleansing in rivers such as the Jordan had its origin in the primitive worship of river gods in the ANE. But none of the semitic gods of healing (Resheph, Enlil, and, on occasion, Ishtar) is associated with water. Even if the connection could be made, there is little parallel with the Naaman story. Water is an obvious symbol for cleansing in the OT and in the ANE (cf. Thompson, *Semitic Magic,* 159–61, 212). There are also many features of the ritual incantations for cleansing which are absent from this story.

11 ויקצף "but he was angry." Naaman's anger is occasioned by what he thinks is the perfunctory treatment he has received from Elisha. His preparations for the journey—the diplomatic involvement of the king, the gift he has brought—all seem rejected in the most off-hand way by the prophet.

וקרא בשם יהוה "and call on the name Yahweh" is a traditional formula for prayer and worship (see Gen 4:26; Exod 23:19; Deut 15:9; etc.). On the lips of Naaman, however, such an expression is in keeping with one of the major themes of these chapters, namely, the "God in Israel" who is the source of healing.

והניף ידו "and wave his hand" is a rare expression in the OT. The verb occurs mainly in connection with the ritual of "waving" offerings before their presentation (Lev 14:12). In prophetic literature (e.g., Isa 11:15; 30:28) such an action is a synonym for judgment.

12 הלא־טוב אבנה ופרפר נהרות דמשק "Are not Abanah and Pharpar, rivers of Damascus, better?" Qere, Syr, and Tg read אמנה "Amana," and this river is identified with the modern Barada River which flows east from the Anti-Lebanon mountain range to the region of Damascus. The legendary beauty of Damascus in the Abanah/Amanah Valley is well described by G. A. Smith, *The Historical Geography of the Holy Land,* 25th ed. (London: Hodder & Stoughton, 1931) 429–30. The Pharpar is usually identified with the Wadi 'A'waj a few miles south of Damascus, although this is not certain. See A. Haldar, *IDB* 3:781.

13 The confusion in the statement of the servant is dealt with in part in the *Notes* above. The intention of the question is clear, and centers around Naaman's pride. Naaman, the powerful and wealthy, is asked to accept a gratuitous healing simply by washing himself. The gift which he had brought now fades into insignificance.

14 וירד "So he went down." A double meaning might be intended. Naaman descended to the Jordan and also demonstrated his humility. ויטבל "and he dipped." The use of the verb טבל is unusual. The verb is not frequent in the OT (sixteen times) and means simply "to dip." With few exceptions in the Pentateuch (Num 19:18; Deut 33:24) it refers to objects dipped in blood (e.g., Lev 14:6). Even when it refers to objects dipped in water (2 Kgs 8:15) or in other liquids (Deut 33:24; 1 Sam 14:27) it is not a synonym for washing (רחץ).

כבשר נער קטן ויטהר "like the flesh of a small child and he was cleansed." This statement cannot but remind the reader of the innocent young girl (נערה קטנה) who began Naaman's search for cleansing (v 2).

15 וישב "Then he returned." The cleansed Naaman with his entourage returns to the man of God. This time he approaches in gratitude. ידעתי כי אין אלהים בכל־הארץ כי אם־בישראל "I know there is no God in all the earth except in Israel" are words which accord closely with Elisha's words in v 8. Following a major theme of these chapters, Naaman realizes that only in Israel, and through Israel's God, is healing to be found. Following this confession, Naaman's actions support his new-found faith.

קח נא ברכה מאת עבדך "accept now a gift from your servant." The dialoque which follows between Naaman and Elisha is reminiscent of that between Elisha and the Shunemite in the previous chapter. The roles are reversed. It is Elisha who now refuses to accept payment for what had happened to Naaman.

16 חי־יהוה אשר־עמדתי לפניו "As Yahweh lives before whom I stand." Naaman had come to "stand before" the prophet (v 15). Elisha declares with this oath that he "stands before" (i.e., worships) Yahweh. Elisha's refusal to accept Naaman's gift is particularly remarkable, since the story is set in a time of famine (4:38; 7:1–20).

ויפצר־בו לקחת "and he urged him to accept." In Hebrew there are two closely related words for "to urge," פצר and פרץ. The second has a secondary meaning of "to break out" (cf. BDB, 829). This verb is used in v 23. Naaman's urging and Elisha's refusal to accept any gift echoes the encounter between Jacob and his alienated brother (Gen 33:11). Esau, however, finally accepts the gift as a token of reconciliation.

17 Naaman's strange request for two loads of dirt from Israel introduces into the story a mixture of monotheism and universalism with the notion of the localization of Yahweh in Israel. A conflict appears between Naaman's statement and the author's comment in v 1. Sentiment, rather than superstition, motivates Naaman. Altars were to be made of earth or unhewn stone (Exod 20:25) and Naaman wished to establish his own shrine to the LORD in Syria.

עלה וזבח "offering and sacrifice." The עלה was the whole burnt offering which ascended as a symbolic prayer. The זבח was a general offering consumed by the worshiper after the sacrifice. Cf. R. de Vaux, *Ancient Israel*, 415–23; *Studies in Old Testament Sacrifice*. For a general survey of the use of the two terms in the OT cf. BDB, 257–58.

18 The text of v 18 is confusing (see *Notes*), although the basic sense is clear. Even with the emendations suggested, the text still remains grammatically clumsy and repetitive. Naaman clearly asks for forgiveness for the resumption of his duties as the king's "right hand man," which would involve him in compromise. He would be forced to accompany the king to worship.

בית רמון "the temple of Rimmon." Rimmon was the national god of the Syrians. He is also known as Hadad, the storm god, a common figure in many ancient Near Eastern pantheons. Later he became identified with Zeus, the all-powerful Hellenistic storm god. See H. Ringgren, *Religions of the Ancient Near East*, 154–56; *IDB* 4:99. Presumably the Syrian king, especially if he were Ben Hadad, would have worshipped regularly at the temple of his divine patron.

19 Elisha's reassurance sends Naaman on his way.

20 The story of Gehazi's deceit, which follows, diverts the plot to a different track from what it has traveled thus far. The contrast is cleverly drawn between the selfless action of Elisha and the selfish conniving of Gehazi. Naaman now assumes the role of a naive dupe.

גחזי נער אלישע "Gehazi, the servant of Elisha." Gehazi now becomes the main actor. It is not clear, although it is often assumed, that the servant of v 10 was Gehazi.

חי יהוה "as Yahweh lives." Gehazi's exclamation, although in the form

Comment

of an oath, stands in direct contrast to the oath of Elisha (v 16). The contrast is seen in the purposes to which the oaths are put. Gehazi's oath borders on blasphemy and can be equated with the English expression, "By God!" מאומה "anything." Gehazi's greed is such that he is determined to get "anything" from Naaman.

21 ויאמר השלום "and he said, 'Are things well?'" There is an interesting reversal of roles for Gehazi here. In 4:26 this was the question he asked of the Shunemite woman. Both responses were untrue since the woman was very distressed. Her intention, however, was to get to the one man who could help her. Gehazi is out to deceive for personal gain.

22 הר אפרים "Mount Ephraim." In mind here is the central mountain range of Israel. The territory was originally allotted to Joseph (Josh 17:15) and became the final settling place for Joshua (Josh 19:50; 24:30). Its capital was Shechem (Josh 20:7). In the Former Prophets the area assumes importance as the place of origin of famous judges (Judg 4:5; 7:24; 10:1; 17:1; etc.) and it was the home of Elkanah, the father of the prophet-judge Samuel (1 Sam 1:1).

מבני הנביאים "from the sons of the prophets." Gehazi's cunning is shown by this allusion. Since the story is set in a time of need, Elisha's care for such persons would have been quite natural.

23 ויפרץ בו "and he urged him." It cannot escape attention that Gehazi finds himself in the same position as Elisha. Unlike Elisha (v 16), he accepts the gift. The added detail of the way the gift is secured is a fine literary touch.

ויתן אל שני נעריו "and he handed them to two of his servants." The reference is ambiguous. Either Gehazi's own servants are intended (so Skinner, 301, et al.) or Naaman's servants. Since Gehazi's actions are secretive, they are likely to be the servants of Naaman.

24 ויבא אל העפל "and he came to the Ophel." The change in G from עפל "hill" to אפל "darkness" is most effective, and perhaps deliberate. It exploits the homonyms to the full, and draws out the theme of the "dark deed" of Gehazi. However, it serves no purpose as an attempt to identify precisely where this "ophel" was located. The term is used exclusively elsewhere of the "Ophel" of Jerusalem (cf. 2 Chr 27:3; Isa 32:14; Mic 4:8; Neh 3:26, 27; 11:21). But it is unlikely that Jerusalem is in mind here. Gehazi would not hide his loot in the capital city of a foreign country, nor would he live there. Most commentators suggest an etymology of "hill." The word occurs in the Moabite Stone (1:22), and is translated by Gibson as "acropolis" (cf. *Syrian Semitic Inscriptions*, vol. 1, 76). Albright's translation (*ANET*, 320) is "citadel." The precise city is still unknown. The modern "Ophel" of Jerusalem is the "city of David," which can hardly be called an "acropolis" since it is the lowest of the Jerusalem hills. See further F. S. Frick, *The City in Ancient Israel*, 53.

25 ויעמד אל אדניו "and he stood before his master." The use of the preposition אל "to" with the verb עמד "he stood" is rare in the OT and can indicate antagonism (cf. 1 Sam 17:51). It stands in contrast to the more usual עמד לפני "he stood before." אנה ואנה "nowhere in particular." Cf. 1 Kgs 2:36, 42.

26 (ה)לא לבי הלך "did not my heart go?" Elisha's claim to knowledge of Gehazi's actions is in sharp contrast to his confession of ignorance in 4:27. העת לקחת את הכסף "did you not take silver?" Elisha pinpoints the greed of Gehazi in his self-seeking at a time of hardship for others. Such comprehensive catalogs of wealth and prosperity are a common feature of the Former Prophets (cf. Deut 6:11; 8:8; Josh 24:13; 1 Sam 8:14–17) and elsewhere (Neh 5:11; 9:25). They are seen as a gift from God (Deut 8:8; Josh 24:13), a temptation to apostasy (Deut 6:11; Neh 9:25) or a sign of self-seeking greed (1 Sam 8:14–17).

27 ויצא מלפניו מצרע כשלג "He went out from his presence, snow-white with leprosy." Gehazi's punishment for his greed shows two things. First, his leprosy is not that dealt with in the regulations in Lev 13–15. In 8:1–6 Gehazi is still able to enjoy social contact and is not ceremonially unclean. Second, Naaman's affliction, contracted by Gehazi, was contagious. It is reminiscent of Moses' temporary leprosy in Exod 4:6–7. On the absence of the symptoms of what is medically described as leprosy today cf. V. R. Khanolkar, "The Pathology of Leprosy" (*Leprosy in Theory and Practice*, 125–51).

Explanation

2 Kgs 5 contains a more complicated story than has appeared thus far in the book, and these features of the narrative have been dealt with above. The story moves in two directions and the common element in each is the figure of Naaman. The tragic figure of Naaman receives healing for his condition in the first part of the chapter, then is used for personal gain by the deceitful Gehazi. For his deceit Gehazi is rewarded. The conditions pertaining to Naaman's journey to Israel in search of healing must have been such that the journey was possible. Israel and Syria must have been enjoying a certain relaxation of hostilities.

In contrast to the miracles performed in chapter four, the healing of Naaman was motivated by something other than a pressing human need. The miracle clearly has an "apologetic" aim, and Naaman is expected to learn something from the miracle, namely, that "there is a prophet in Israel" (v 8). The miracle then becomes a witness to Elisha's status as a prophet. With the action of Naaman after his healing, this goal is achieved (vv 15–18).

In the context of the Elisha stories the miracle takes on added significance. To call the miracle "ordinary" because Elisha performs no spectacular actions, as some have done, is in error. In fact, few of Elisha's miracles are spectacular, if by that is meant some ostentatious gesture. The actions of Elisha almost always consist of the ordinary, such as the use of the chemical salt to "heal" waters (2:19–22) or a rather uncanny sense of timing (cf. 3:16). In some, the prophet takes no active part (4:1–7), and even in those miracles which tax the imagination (4:32–37) the prophet acts behind closed doors. The results of the miracles are important, not necessarily how the results are achieved; although it must be noted that in the story of Naaman, Elisha did not live up to the expectations of the visitor since he avoided any gestures at all (v 11).

There is a second element to the miracle of healing in this chapter, and that is the obedience of Naaman. At first he is reluctant to follow the instructions of the prophet, and only on the advice of one of his own servants does he obey and thereby receive healing (vv 13–14). When he finally "descends" (v 14) he is healed.

Beyond these incidental features of the story, the miracle draws back to the forefront the theme already encountered in chapter one and again in chapter eight, namely, the search for healing in a foreign country. In chapter one, Ahaziah, the apostate son of Ahab searches for healing from Baal-Zebub, god of Ekron, and later, in chapter eight, Ben Hadad seeks help from Elisha. Only Naaman, however, is healed. Ahaziah searches in the wrong place and in chapter eight, other, more important, historical events must take place. Coupled with this theme is that of the presence of Yahweh's prophet in Israel, which is established in chapter two and repeated in chapters three, five, and eight.

Beyond the immediate context of the stories dealing with the activities of Elisha other links can be seen. The book of Deuteronomy makes much of the love Israel is to show the stranger and foreigner (Deut 10:19). Such love and care are motivated by Israel's own experience as a stranger in Egypt (Deut 23:7). It is also a theme kept alive during the period of the monarchy with Solomon's prayer at the dedication of the Temple (1 Kgs 8:41–43). That prayer, too, has an apologetic aim which is echoed in Naaman's confession of his new-found faith (vv 15–18) and in the dream to which expression is given in Isa 56:8:

> "Thus says Yahweh God,
>   who gathers the outcasts of Israel,
> I will gather yet others to him
>   besides those already gathered."

Elisha's action for Naaman receives the supreme affirmation from the lips of Jesus himself. In justification of his gentile ministry, Jesus cites, among others, the healing of Naaman, acknowledging fully the aspect of universalism embedded in the narrative and also making the incident a model for his own ministry (Luke 4:27).

Elisha and the Syrians (6:1–33)

Bibliography

Cummings, J. T. "The House of the Sons of the Prophets and the Tents of the Rechabites." In *Studia Biblica,* ed. E. A. Livingstone. Vol. 1, JSOTSup 11. Sheffield: Sheffield University, 1978. 119–26. **Miller, P. D.** "The Divine Council and the Prophetic Call to War." *VT* 18 (1968) 100–107. **Schweitzer, H.** *Elischa in den Kriegen.* SANT 37. Munich: Kösel Verlag, 1974.

Translation

¹ The sons of the prophets said to Elisha, "See now, the place where we stay with you is too confined for us. ² Let us go to the Jordan, and let each one take from there one plank, then let us make for ourselves a meeting place."[a] So he said,[b] "Go." ³ Then one of them said, "Be sure[a] to accompany your servants." And he replied, "I am coming." ⁴ So he went with them, and they came to the Jordan and began cutting wood. ⁵ But it happened[a] that as one of them was felling a beam, the very iron[b] fell into the water, and he called out[c] and said, "Oh sir, it was borrowed!" ⁶ But the man of God said, "Where did it fall?" He showed him the place, and Elisha chopped off some wood and threw it in there, and the iron floated. ⁷ Then he said, "Pick it up for yourself!" So he stretched out his hand and took it.

⁸ Now the king of Syria was fighting against the king of Israel, and he took counsel with his advisers saying, "I will make my camp at such and such a place."[a] ⁹ Then the man of God[a] sent word to the king of Israel saying, "Take care! Do not pass over at this particular place because the Syrians have made their camp there."[b] ¹⁰ Then the king of Israel sent word to the place of which the man of God[a] had told him. He warned him,[b] and he took such precautions on more than one occasion.[c]

¹¹ Now the king of Syria was bothered by this, so he complained to his advisers and said to them, "Will you not tell me who of us is working[a] for the king of Israel?" ¹² Then one of his advisers said, "No my lord king. It is Elisha, the prophet in Israel. He informs the king of Israel of even the things you say in your bedroom!" ¹³ So he said,[a] "Go and see where he is, and I will send someone there to kidnap him." It was then told him that he was in Dothan. ¹⁴ So the king dispatched horses,[a] chariotry comprising a large force. They arrived by night and surrounded the city.

¹⁵ Now the servant[a] of the man of God had arisen early, and he went out. But the army had surrounded the city, both horse and chariot, and a young man said to him, "Ah sir, what[b] shall we do?" ¹⁶ But he replied, "Do not be afraid, because those who are with us are more numerous than those with them."[a] ¹⁷ Then Elisha prayed, and said, "Yahweh, please open his eyes and let him see." And Yahweh opened the servant's eyes and he looked, and the hill was filled with horses and chariots of fire surrounding Elisha. ¹⁸ When they began to descend toward him Elisha prayed to Yahweh and said, "Please strike this people with blindness." He struck them with blindness as requested. ¹⁹ Elisha called out to them, "This is not the way![a] This is not the city! Come on, follow me, and I will lead you to the man you seek!" And he led them right to Samaria.

²⁰ When they had come to Samaria, Elisha then said, "Now open these eyes and let them see!" So Yahweh opened their eyes and they looked, and they were[a] right in the middle of Samaria. ²¹ Then the king of Israel said to Elisha[a] when he saw them, "Shall I strike them down, strike them down,[b] my father?" ²² But he replied, "You shall not strike them down! Would you strike down those you had captured with the sword and bow? Set food and water in front of them, and let them eat and drink. Then let them return to their master." ²³ So he prepared for them a large meal,[a] and they ate and drank. Then he dismissed them and they returned[b] to their master. No more did raiding bands from Syria come into the land of Israel.

²⁴ It was after this that Ben Hadad[a] king of Syria mustered all his forces, and went up and besieged Samaria. ²⁵ Because of their siege[a] there was a serious famine in Samaria, to the point where an ass's head was sold for eighty shekels of silver,

and a pint of dove's dung [b] *was sold for five shekels.* [26] *It happened that the king of Israel* [a] *was passing by on the wall, and a woman cried out to him, "Help* [b] *my lord king!"* [27] *He replied, "Yahweh cannot save you,* [a] *how much less can I?* [b] *We are caught between the threshing floor and the wine vat!"* [28] *Then the king said to her, "What problem do you have?" She answered, "This woman said to me, 'Give your son so that we can eat him today, then tomorrow we can eat my son.'* [a] [29] *So we did cook my son, and we ate him. The following day I said to her, 'Give your son so that we may eat him.' But she had hidden her son."* [30] *Now when the king heard the words of the woman,* [a] *he tore his clothes. He did this as he was passing along the top of the wall, and the people saw* [b] *that he had sackcloth on underneath.* [c] [31] *He said, "May God do this to me and more if the head of Elisha son of Shaphat* [a] *stays on his shoulders this day!"*

[32] *Elisha happened to be sitting at home,* [a] *and the elders were staying with him. But before the messenger came to him (the king had already sent a man out),* [b] *he said to the elders, "See this murderer* [c] *has sent to cut off my head. Now when the messenger* [d] *comes, shut the door and hold it against him. Is that not the sound of his master's footsteps after him?"* [33] *Even while he was speaking with them, the messenger came down to him, and he said, "See this evil is from Yahweh! What more should I expect from Yahweh?"*

Notes

2.a. MT מקום לשבת "a place to rest." The G MS b offers σκεπειν "shelter," c₂ reads σκεπην, and e₂ reads σκηνην "dwelling place."
2.b. G[L] adds here the proper name, Elisha.
3.a. MT הואל "be willing." G translates always with ἐπιεικως "considerately," "fairly."
5.a. The Heb ויהי "and it was" is omitted by G, which reads και ιδου (והנה) "and behold." G[L] retains and follows with a genitive abs.
5.b. MT precedes הברזל "the iron" with the direct object sign (ואת). However, the verb נפל "fall" is not transitive in the Qal. G ignores the direct object, although G[L] adds του στελεου "from the handle." However, there are a few instances in which the sign of the direct object can indicate a subject with emphasis (Num 3:46; Judg 20:44, 46; Dan 9:13; et al.). See GKC § 117m. GKC regards the case under discussion as "derived from a text which read the Hiph'il instead of נפל Qal." 1 Sam 13:20 might suggest a possible reading of אֵת as "axe head," derived from its meaning there as an agricultural cutting tool.
5.c. G omits ויאמר "and he said."
8.a. The Heb פלני אלמני "a certain one" is rendered by G as τονδε τινα ἐλιμωνι, obviously interpreting אלמני as a proper noun. Subsequent variants follow this suggestion. In Dan 8:13 a conflation of the two appears as למני (*RSV* "separate one"). See S. R. Driver, *Notes on the Hebrew Text of the Books of Samuel*, 137. G[L] has confused this verse with Dan 8:13 with its reading of φελιμουνι.
9.a. Omitted by G, but retained by G[L].
9.b. MT נחתים "hiding" is rendered by G as "are hiding" (κεκρυπται). On the basis of this, and G's translation of תחנתי as παρεμβαλω "to form a line (of troops)," Burney (285) and others suggest an emendation to נחבאים "be hidden." Gray (514) suggests נחתים "hide," "an Aramaism appropriate to this passage."
10.a. G reads "Elisha."
10.b. MT הזהירה "he warned him" is omitted by G.
10.c. MT לא אחת ולא שתים "more than one occasion."
11.a. MT מִי מִשֶּׁלָּנוּ אֶל־מֶלֶךְ יִשְׂרָאֵל, which G translates as "Who has betrayed me?" Burney (285) therefore suggests a pointing of מַשְׁלֵנוּ "Who has misled us?" See 4:28.
13.a. G[L] adds "the king of Syria."
14.a. G reads sg. G[L] follows MT.

15.a. MT משרת, which is a rare word for "servant." G translates with ὁ λειτουργός "the minister." The phrase לקום . . . וישכם "now the servant arises" is "at best extremely harsh." (Burney, *Notes*, 286). Burney adopts the emendation בבקר . . . ממחרת in accord with G^L (τὸ πρωί "the morning"), and offers the translation "and the man of God rose early on the morrow in the morning." The harshness, however, still remains.

15.b. איכה is unusual. G reads τι (מה) "what?"

16.a. MT אותם "them" is better pointed אַתָּם "with them."

19.a. G reverses the order of דרך "way" and עיר "city."

20.a. MT reads הנה "behold," better read as הנם "they were." G offers a combination with ἰδοὺ ἦσαν "behold, they were."

21.a. אל־אלישע "God of Elisha" is omitted by G.

21.b. הַאַכֶּה אַכֶּה "shall I strike them down?" can be pointed as in MT, or as an inf abs הַחֲכֵּה אַכֶּה (Burney, *Notes*, 287). If the text is left as in MT it is indeed clumsy grammar, but could well reflect the inarticulate excitement of the king at his good fortune.

23.a. MT ויכרה "he prepared a feast." G is a paraphrase. The verb כרה "give a feast" is used only here in this sense, and the meaning is gathered from the context. It is possibly connected with the Akkadian *kiretu* "feast."

23.b. וילכו "they returned" is omitted by G and retained by G^L.

24.a. G confuses ר for ד in הדד "Hadad" and reads υἱὸς Ἀδερ "son of Hader."

25.a. MT והנה צרים עליה "because of their siege," which is perhaps better read as "because of the siege of the city," והנם צרים על העיר although G retains והנה "behold."

25.b. The Heb חרייונים is possibly a compound word from הריאה and יונים "dung of doves," and is so understood by G. Cf. Isa 36:12; 2 Kgs 18:27. Gray (518) refers to a plant known in Arabic as *hara' al-hamām* "dove's dung."

26.a. G identifies the king as Joram.

26.b. G^L adds the pronoun "me."

27.a. RSV translates this as a conditional sentence, however MT is more a direct statement. GKC § 109h interprets this passage as "a jussive in a negative protasis" and offers the translation, "If Yahweh do help thee. . . ."

27.b. MT מאין אושיעך "cannot save you." G paraphrases with πόθεν σώσω "whence shall I save."

28.a. G^L adds καὶ οὐκ ἔδωκεν αὐτὸν ἵνα φάγωμεν "and she did not give him that we might eat."

30.a. With G^L καὶ αὐτὸς εἰστήκει "and he stood with," some emend to והוה עמד "and he stood" (cf. Burney, *Notes*, 289).

30.b. הנה "behold" omitted by G.

30.c. MT מבית "from the house" is translated by G as ἔσωθεν "from beneath," "within."

31.a. בן שפט "Son of Shaphat" omitted by G.

32.a. Vg reads "Bethel."

32.b. In MT there is no direct antecedent to this verb, therefore the identity of the subject is in doubt; is it Elisha or the king? To clear up the ambiguity G transposes the clause to the beginning of the verse, and G^L makes it explicit by naming the king.

32.c. Josephus (*Antiq.* ix.68) translates בן המרצה, literally, having in mind Ahab, the father of Joram.

32.d. *BHS* suggests a reading of מלך "king" for מלאך "messenger," but the textual evidence is unanimous for retaining מלאך. Burney (*Notes*, 290) makes the same emendation, but this is not necessary. Of the versions, only Josephus (*Antiq.* ix.68) interprets מלאך as מלך.

Form/Structure/Setting

1–7 Difficulties with the classifications of "power demonstration narrative" (DeVries) and "prophetic legend" (Eissfeldt) have been expressed elsewhere in the commentary. These verses, as is so common in the Elisha collection, move from stating a problem to the final resolution of the problem. This is a fundamental element in any good story. The artistry of the narrator is seen in the way in which the problem is described, and the way in which the central character of the story deals with the problem.

Form/Structure/Setting

The problem in this story is briefly described in how Elisha found his way to the banks of the Jordan. Much incidental detail is offered, detail which is not developed in the story. It takes the reader nowhere. The meeting place is too small. Why this is, is not stated. Perhaps it was because of a growing interest in the prophet and his ministry. The group moves toward the Jordan to obtain materials for a new meeting place. Even this is puzzling. Elisha is invited to go along, and the group begins their work (vv 1–4). The problem is briefly described in v 5. One of the sons of the prophets loses his iron tool in the water. The seriousness of the problem is indicated by his statement that he had borrowed the tool from someone else.

Elisha ascertains the iron's whereabouts by asking the unfortunate worker, and he then performs a simple action. He throws a stick in the water and recovers the lost tool (vv 6–7). In its simplicity, much is left unsaid in the story. Did they finally build another meeting place? If so, where was it situated? Such details are unimportant to the narrator because the spotlight falls upon the central character of Elisha and his actions.

However, more than this is missing from the story. The prophetic characteristics, found in 3:1–27; 5:1–14 and in the earlier stories, are absent here. There is no word to be fulfilled. There is no judgment stated, no promise given; nor is there an attack on the prophet because of his activity. The name "prophet" is not used throughout. That it is a "power demonstration narrative" is also open to question, since there is little in the story which would be classified as powerful or miraculous. Elisha has to ascertain the spot where the iron fell in the water by asking, thereby admitting a certain ignorance. The follower is himself instructed to pick up the iron.

No other story in the Elisha material is quite the same (contra Culley, *The Structure of Hebrew Narrative*). In 4:1–7 Elisha asks a question, as here, but the subsequent action is more akin to the actions accompanying the miracles in 2:19–22 and 4:38–41. In all three, something is "thrown" to effect a change. To argue for a genre on the basis of a selection of features from different stories is unsound methodology. This story presents Elisha as one who responds immediately and decisively to need. It has this feature in common with 4:1–7; 2:38–41; and others. In such brief stories, an additional feature which distinguishes them from other "prophetic" stories is the variety of epithets given to the main actor. He is "Elisha" (2:19, 23; 4:1, 2; 6:1), addressed as "sir" (אדני) (6:5; 2:19), and described as "man of God" (4:7; 6:6). Never is he referred to as "prophet" (נביא). In contrast to the story of Naaman, or the revolt of Mesha, this story is not balanced. The description of the problem is long, but the solution is told abruptly. Decisiveness on the part of Elisha is the purpose to which the form is put.

8–23 There is a marked contrast in the story that follows. The detail offered is a distinguishing feature. The development of the plot is sophisticated, and the brief character sketches are full of color. DeVries's classification of the tale as "prophet-authorization narrative" and "supplicatory power story" (*Prophet against Prophet*, 55) is helpful in that it points to certain features of the story. But there is also an element of humor.

Using the dramatic analogy, the story moves forward in five scenes and deals with Elisha's response to the warring of Syria against Israel. Important in the story is the absence of some detail and the presence of other detail. There is no date for the story. No names are given for the kings involved. They appear almost as background for the main character. How he reacts to them becomes important. Yet, in the plot development the inclusion of small details fills out the story to a remarkable degree.

The first stage of the story opens with the vague information that the Syrians are warring against Israel and are camping at "such and such a place." This vague introduction invites the figure of Elisha into the story as he warns the king of Israel of these facts and averts the danger (vv 9-10). A touch of humor enters the narrative as the king of Syria, furious at the misfiring of his plans, accuses one of his own of betrayal. This offers a perfect lead into the second stage of the story (vv 12-14). The cause of the king's misfortunes is the "prophet who is in Samaria" whose powers of knowledge differ very sharply from those in chapter four and in 6:1-7. The antagonists are now Syria and Elisha, not Syria and Israel. The preparations for the kidnapping of Elisha in v 14 are reminiscent of the preparations for war in chapter three. Again, the humor is evident. "Horses, chariots and a large attacking force" (v 14) are dispatched to take one man! One is reminded of the one hundred and fifty men sent to take Elijah in chapter one.

In the third stage of the story (vv 15-18), the panic of the servant of Elisha is perfectly understandable. He reacts as any human being would when faced with such odds. He is afraid. The coolness of Elisha in the face of such danger (v 16) is to be noted. But in spite of Elisha's reassurance and prayer, all that the young man can see is the enemy surrounding them and about to attack (v 17b). Their attack is stalled as they are struck with "bedazzlement" (סנורים) and follow into captivity the very one they had come to arrest!

The fourth stage of the story (vv 19-20) now turns the tables upon the Syrians as they realize that they are in the middle of Samaria. The fifth and final stage of the story (vv 21-23) demonstrates the humor of the narrator. The king is confused at his good fortune and overreacts. Instead of allowing the prisoners to remain in custody, Elisha humiliates them by having them fed and sent on their way. The acquiescence of the king of Israel in this gesture reflects the major feature of Elisha's character thus far in the story. He is full of self-confidence. He is in complete control.

If any genre of literature must be seen in the narrative thus far it is comedy (cf. A. Nicholl, *The Theory of Drama*, 175-229). This is not to argue that the story was told as the well-designed comedy of modern theater, but rather that basic features of comedy are present. In this story is the "comedy of manners" in which the institutional might of the Syrian court and its army are ineffective against the lone man of God. Elisha's tricking of the kidnapping force is a case of mistaken identity which borders on caricature. Even the king of Israel emerges as something of a fool with his excited babbling about the slaying of the prisoners. Elisha's generosity, which leads to the chastising of the king and the release of the prisoners, provides the comic ending. Throughout the story, controlling events, is the man of God, Elisha.

24-31 In direct contrast is the complete change of mood in the next story. It is more a testimony to the writer's artistry than a sign of separate sources. The two incidents are thematically linked by the phrase ויהי אחרי כן "and it happened after this," which opens v 24. Following this is a rapid sequence of scenes, each introduced by the clause ויהי "it was" (vv 25, 26, 30). The reaction of Ben Hadad is a massive display of power which results in a siege of the capital and serious famine for its inhabitants (v 25).

In v 26 the king experiences an example of the depths to which his people have sunk because of the famine. He emerges now as a man of sympathy who wears mourning dress (v 29), and his anger at Elisha is understandable (vv 30–31). He vows to have the head of the prophet before the day is done. The rather light-hearted way in which the prophet had dealt with the Syrians initially has now backfired and he is forced to take other measures. The utter self-confidence with which he acted in vv 1–7 and vv 8–23 is now completely eroded.

Commentators often think vv 24–31 belong to chapter seven, because of the clear way in which the kings are portrayed. The king of Israel emerges as a real threat for the prophet and assumes strength as a character. The king of Syria is named. It is possible that the original contexts for the two stories were different, but the alternative is equally possible. The development of the characters of the two kings by naming them or providing them with strong emotions is illustrative of a clever piece of writing. The reversal of roles for these kings from foils of the prophet's wit and activity (vv 8–23) to real threats to the prophet (vv 24–31), and the similar reversal for Elisha from controller to victim of events bring to the story a real element of drama and suspense. The prophet has both kings against him.

32–33 No independent form can be identified for these verses, since they are integrally related to what precedes. They provide a contrast to the confident Elisha who begins the chapter. Now he is at home, surrounded by the elders (for protection?) and threatened by the king, who has sent someone to kill him. The motif of "shutting the door," formerly used in connection with the miraculous actions of the prophet, is now used to indicate how terrified he is. He asks others to protect him behind a closed door as they hold it against the assassin. The contrast is almost painful. The man who entrapped the Syrian army so confidently is now cowering behind a door, hiding from the furious intentions of one man! The end of the chapter, with its statement and question, brings to the narrative its first theological rationale, namely, Elisha's renewed dependence upon Yahweh.

Comment

1 This story, like most of those from the Elisha-collection, is not dated. Its context places it during the great famine. The sons of the prophets figure again and, often, an opening comment of one of them precipitates an action by Elisha. Cf. 1 Kgs 20:35; 2 Kgs 2:3, 5; 4:1.

אנחנו ישבים שם לפניך "we are staying with you." The verb ישב is often translated here as "dwell" (KJV, RSV) or "live" (NEB), but the phrase לפני "before" implies something more formal. With the prepositions ב or על the verb is translated "live," but with the preposition לפני the meaning is distinctive. Joseph's brothers "sit before" him at an organized court meal (Gen

43:33). David "sits before" Yahweh in an act of worship (2 Sam 7:14). The elders "sit before" Ezekiel to hear his advice (Ezek 8:1; 14:1). That the phrase implies a "prophetic community" of a highly organized nature (so Gray, 511) is an over-interpretation of the phrase, although it does allow for formal gatherings.

צר ממנו "too confined for us." The adjectival form צר (root צרר "to tie up") is not common in the OT and occurs only in Num 22:26; Isa 49:20; Prov 23:27; 24:10; and here.

2 עד־הירדן "to the Jordan." Why the group decided to go to the Jordan is not clear. Two possibilities exist. Either they went to the Jordan to obtain wood, or they wished to relocate their meeting place. For the former, the location is strange. The land of Israel was undoubtedly better supplied with wood in biblical times than it is today (cf. D. Baly, *The Geography of the Bible* [New York: Harper Bros., 1957] 92–95), and yet the Jordan has never been famous for its supply of wood. That one would have been able to obtain "beams" of a size suitable for building is unlikely. A better source of timber would have been available on the western slopes of the central highlands. Montgomery's appeal (381) to F. Abel (*La Geographie de la Palestine*, vol. 1, 213) is a little misleading. The general growth in the Jordan Valley between the Sea of Galilee and the Dead Sea does not yield much in the way of building materials. Cf. E. Orni and E. Efrat, *Geography of Israel*, 167–77. If the second possibility is the more likely then the phrase משם "from them" poses a problem since it could refer to the Jordan or to the current meeting place. Cf. Gray, 510n.

קורה אחת "one plank." The work קורה "rafter," "beam" is rare, occurring only in Gen 19:8; Cant 1:17; and 2 Chr 3:7. In the first of these, it is generally translated "roof."

5 והיה האחד מפיל הקורה "it happened as one of them was felling a beam." The argument that one cuts trees, not beams, and therefore the text should be emended to הקרדם "axe" (so Burney, *Notes*, 284), is entirely speculative.

6 ויקצב עץ וישלך שמה "and he cut off some wood and threw it in there." This is open to different interpretations. A similar action occurred in both 2:21 and 4:41, and it is possibly a literary motif of the writer. The action could be a form of sympathetic magic, or Elisha could have fished the iron out with the stick. The grammar, however, would argue against such a rationalization. For a symbolic interpretation of the event cf. J. T. Cummings, *Studia Biblica*, 1:119–26.

8 ומלך ארם היה נלחם בישראל "now the king of Syria was fighting against Israel." Again, the incident is not dated. It is located here in the narrative for thematic rather than chronological reasons. The lack of interest in dating is shown by the absence of the names of the kings involved. Josephus (*Antiq.* ix.51–78) identifies them as Joram and Ben Hadad. However, the statement in v 23 would indicate that it was a time when Israel was stronger than Syria. The impression in the following story and in 13:3, 14–19, 22 is the opposite. Gray (513–14) separates this incident from the one following by reason of the miraculous element and the imprecision of historical details. He dates the story in ca. 797 B.C., after a period of decline in Israel's fortunes. The Syrian king is therefore identified as Hazael. However, during the reign of

Joram conditions were not uniformly stable and such a raid by Syrian forces, especially at night (v 14), would not be unusual.

תחנתי "I will make my camp." On this word see the *Notes* above. Josephus (*Antiq.* ix.51–78) tends to embellish this story. The Syrian plan was to kill Joram; when the king hears of this he does not go hunting.

9 Elisha's role as a spy is unusual since he appeared to be on good terms with the kings of both Israel and Syria at times (cf. 8:1). נחתים "hiding"; on this word, see *Note* 9.b.

10 והזהירה ונשמר שם "and he warned him." With most translations, Elisha is to be seen as the subject of the first verb. This translation is a paraphrase of difficult and ambiguous Hebrew.

12 כי־אלישע הנביא אשר בישראל "that Elisha is the prophet who is in Israel." Elisha's reputation, not only for healing, but also for other supernatural powers, was widespread.

בחדר משכבך "in your bedroom" is an idiomatic expression for secrecy (cf. Eccl 10:20). Again, the closeness of the relationship between Elisha and the king of Israel is noteworthy. He has access to the king (5:8), warns the king of impending danger, and is addressed by the king as "father" (6:21). All of this, however, is soon to change.

13 ואשלח ואקחהו "I will send and kidnap him." The Syrian's motivation was either to get revenge or to secure for himself such a valuable source of intelligence.

הנה בדתן "see, in Dothan." Dothan is modern Tell Dothan situated at the southeastern edge of the Valley of Dothan, about eighteen kilometers north of Samaria.

14 The most convenient access for a force of this size to the city of Dothan would be up the Wadi Faria from the southeast after crossing the Jordan near modern Deir Alla, or across the Jordan further north at Beth Shean, around Gilboa then south into the Valley of Dothan. In spite of the statement in v 23 that this was a "raiding band" (גדוד), it was large enough to set siege to the capital city. Like most battle plans in these stories, they are characterized by excess. The sole purpose of this force was to capture one man!

15 וישכם משרת "Now the servant rose early." Cf. the emendations noted above (*Note* 15.a.). The same verb is used of the younger Elisha (1 Kgs 19:21) and of Samuel (1 Sam 2:11).

ויקפו על העיר "and they surrounded the city." If Dothan is identified correctly, the city was very vulnerable to siege since the valley floor surrounding the city is flat.

16 אל־תירא כי רבים אשר אתנו מאשר אותם "Do not be afraid because those who are with us are more numerous than those with them." This language is reminiscent of the regulations for Holy War in Deut 20:1–4 (cf. von Rad, *Der Heilige Krieg im Alten Israel,* 9–10). However, Elisha's response to his companion was hardly in the classic tradition of Holy War. Rather than stress the unimportance of the size of his forces, Elisha does exactly the opposite. The whole incident is told with a great deal of sarcasm, since the chariots and horses seen by the young man are the enemy's, not Israel's.

17 ויתפלל אלישע "then Elisha prayed." Only here and in 2 Kgs 4:33

does Elisha pray. והנה ההר מלא סוסים ורכב אש "and behold, the hill was filled with horses and chariots of fire." The prayer is answered in a most unexpected way. The chariots and "fire horses" which fill the hills can hardly have been Israelite. They are the same ones that move down to attack Elisha. That which the servant "sees" is the entrapment of this attacking force by the prophet.

18 בסנורים "with blindness." The word occurs only here and in Gen 19:11. Its derivation is unknown. That it is related to "light" (ניר) would contradict the intended meaning of "blinding," unless a meaning of "dazzle" can be found. Both biblical uses of the term involve a spectacular or miraculous act, and both are used in the context of deliverance from danger. Since the "opening of the eyes" in both the case of the servant and the Syrians (v 20) is to be interpreted metaphorically, physical blindness need not be implied.

כדבר אלישע "according to the word of Elisha." Once again the word of the prophet becomes important, although it is not as prominent as in the earlier chapters.

19 ויאמר אלישע לא זה הדרך לא זה העיר "Elisha said, 'This is not the way! This is not the city!'" Elisha's tricking of the attacking force shows that they were more deceived than blinded. They could hardly have followed the prophet without seeing.

וילך אותם בשמרון "and he led them to Samaria." The road from Dothan to Samaria rises steeply through the central hill country, following a winding route. That the Syrians allowed themselves to be led astray in this way shows their lack of intelligence and their foolishness to trust a local scout.

21 האכה אכה אבי "shall I strike them down, my father?" (On this construction, see n. 21.b.) Only kings called Elisha "father," whereas the normal form of address for one of the prophets was "lord" (אדני). The king's enthusiasm for such slaughter was fed by the good fortune of having been handed such a prize of war without a fight.

22 ויאמר לא תכה "but he replied, 'You shall not strike them down.'" Under normal circumstances of war, prisoners would be spared as the spoils of war. They would be used as slaves. In several campaign records of ancient kings from the third millennium on (cf. *ANET*, 277–322) thousands of prisoners are so dealt with. In the OT, only rarely were prisoners killed out of hand (2 Sam 8:2). In a Holy War prisoners were subject to the "ban" (חרם), which meant their complete annihilation (cf. von Rad, *Der Heilige Krieg im alten Israel*, 13–14; Craigie, *The Problem of War in the Old Testament*, 45–54). Elisha, however, seems more intent upon embarrassing his foes with kindness than sparing them for purely humanitarian reasons.

23 ויכרה להם כרה "so he prepared a meal for them." Elisha's advice to the king was followed, much to the king's later dismay.

ולא־יספו עוד גדודי ארם "no more raiding parties from Syria were sent." The size of the force was not small. In the light of what follows, this cannot be taken as a respite for Israel. The reaction of the king of Syria shows that he was in earnest about subduing Israel. Later he sends his whole army.

24 בן־הדד "Ben Hadad." This is presumably the same Ben Hadad who had attacked Ahab (1 Kgs 20). The chronology of this incident is not clear, adding to the confusion. Three Syrian kings named Ben Hadad have been identified. The Ben Hadad of 1 Kgs 15:18 was the son of Tabrimmon, better identified by his throne name Hadad-ezer (Adad-idri). He was active in the tenth century B.C. during the reign of the Israelite Baasha (ca. 909–885 B.C.). During the reign of Ahab, Ben Hadad I was captured after an abortive raid on Samaria (1 Kgs 20:1–22). This king was present at the battle of Qarqar. It is also possible, though not certain, that this was Ben Hadad of 1 Kgs 22, and the Syrian king of the early activities of Elisha (cf. Herrmann, *The History of Israel in Old Testament Times*, 214). However, others distinguish between the two kings and regard the latter as Ben Hadad II. He was killed by Hazael, who in turn was succeeded by Ben Hadad III in ca. 798 B.C. (2 Kgs 13). Cf. R. A. Bowman, *IDB* 1:381–82.

ויקבץ . . . את־כל־מחנהו "and he mustered all his forces." This implies a complete mobilization of the Syrian army by the king in revenge for the humiliation of the preceding incident.

25 ויהי רעב גדול "and there was a serious famine." As it stands, this clause implies two coincidental happenings. With the small suggested emendation (see *Note* 25.b.) the siege becomes the reason for the famine, which is restricted to the city of Samaria.

ראש חמור "an ass's head" is a most unappetizing dish, but history is replete with stories of the extremes to which human beings are driven in times of such deprivation. Dogs, cats, and even vermin were eaten during times of starvation in Europe following the surrender of the German army at the end of World War II.

ורבע הקב. The exact size of a "kab" is unknown. Josephus (*Antiq* ix.62) interprets it as a ξέστη (possibly a Latin sextarius). In *Antiq* viii.57, he offers a more precise measurement, stating that one "bath" equals seventy-two ξέστα. Since a "bath" was the equivalent of about thirty-six liters, the ξέστη was half a liter, or just over one pint.

חרייונים "doves' dung" is to be translated either *Kethib* or *Qere* as "pigeon dung." Attempts of commentators to interpret the term as some kind of unappetizing vegetable are unnecessary. The fate of people under siege is adequately expressed in 18:27, and there is no need to make pigeon dung into a kind of delicacy. The writer is showing that this material, whatever its use (food or fuel), was an extremely expensive item on the black market which would have developed under such conditions. Josephus (*Antiq* ix.62) comments that the dung was used as salt, but this is an imaginative interpretation. The writer is trying to show how desperate were conditions under siege.

בשמנים כסף . . . בחמשה כסף "eighty shekels of silver . . . five shekels of silver." The cost of these items is exhorbitant by any standards.

26 The utter hopelessness of the situation is seen by the following incident. In the light of what the woman narrates, her appeal to the monarch is understandable. Gray (522) and others date the incident during the reign of either Jehoahaz (ca. 815–801 B.C.) or Jehoash (ca. 801–786 B.C.). There is nothing in the story which would deny it to the time of Joram.

27 המן הגרן או מן היקב "between the threshing floor and the wine vat" is a strange expression which has no parallel in the OT. Three interpretations are possible. First, the גרן "threshing floor" and the יקב "wine vat" are often paired as the source of produce in the OT (cf. Num 18:27, 30;

Deut 15:14; 16:13), and the king could be stating a simple fact. There is nothing left to feed the people. In Hos 9:1–2 such circumstances are even seen as a sign of the judgment of God. The threshing floor in Samaria was at the gate (1 Kgs 22:10) and access to it would have been blocked during the siege. Second, the king might be using imagery which became common in later prophetic literature which sees a threshing floor as a place of judgment (Hos 13:3; Mic 4:12; Jer 51:33). Third, the expression might be an idiom, depicting the utter hopelessness of the situation (cf. *Translation* above). It would parallel the English expression "Between hell and high water!"

28–29 The sheer pathos of the situation is seen in the woman's report. The woman had been forced to eat the corpse of her dead son. Her complaint is a purely legal one. Her neighbor had lied to her and deceived her. The seeming lack of feeling for the death of her son emphasizes the horror in the narrative. In such circumstances both the best and the worst of humanity are revealed. Deut 28:56–57 echoes similar circumstances. See also Lam 2:20; 4:10; Ezek 5:10. During Assurbanipal's siege of Babylon (*ANET*, 298), similar things happened.

ויאמר מה לך "and he said, 'What is there for you?'" This question is the same asked of the Shunemite in 4:13. The prophet aided that woman, but the king is at a loss to help his subjects.

30 ויקרע את בגדיו "he tore his clothes." This is the second time the king has made this gesture. Here he has the reader's sympathy.

31 The threat against Elisha's life makes sense only if vv 8–23 and vv 24–33 are seen as consecutive. Elisha's clemency to the first Syrian force, and their humiliation, gives rise to this second punitive expedition by Ben Hadad. This led in turn to the siege. Indirectly Elisha is held responsible by the king for the current state of affairs.

32 בביתו "in his house." Presumably this was in the capital city, Samaria. Elisha then had dwelling places in various locations in Israel.

The הזקנים "the elders" are the leading citizens of the capital. There is no need to regard these gatherings as habitual (so Gray, 523). Such a gathering does indicate the high regard in which Elisha was held by important people in Samarian society. Such people appear willing to protect the prophet from danger.

וישלח איש מלפניו "he sent a man before him" probably refers to the action of the king and can be read parenthetically (see *Translation*). The epithet בן־המרצח "murder" is either a literal reference to the king's father, Ahab, or a pejorative comment on his character. In view of the king's intentions, the latter is more likely.

סגרו הדלת "shut the door." This motif appears again. This time, however, it does not concern miracles done in secret, but the ignominious rescue of the prophet from the anger of the king by the elders of the city. Were it not for the tragedy of the circumstances surrounding the incident, it would appear comical.

33 מלאך "messenger" (cf. *Notes* above). A number of translations (NEB, RSV) accept the reading "king," but this is a mistake. The appeal to the reference in 7:2, as though he were present, is unconvincing.

ויאמר הנה זאת הרעה מאת יהוה "and he said, 'See! This evil is from

Yahweh.'" Elisha is interpreted as the subject of the verb ויאמר "and he said." Modern English translations regard the king as subject (RSV, NEB), the KJV is ambiguous. The syntax would make Elisha the subject. What he states is in reply to the arrival of the king's messenger, which he sees as a threat to his life. Elisha understands that the crisis comes from Yahweh and he senses that it has served God's purpose.

Explanation

The stories concerning Elisha in this chapter are unusual. The miraculous element is minimal. No miracles are performed of the type seen thus far. The first story is open to rationalization (see above) and the two stories which follow display a decided turn for the worst in the fortunes of Elisha. He quickly becomes victim rather than controller of circumstance, and every vestige of the confident prophet is lost by the end of the chapter.

In the incident of the lost axe-head (vv 1–7), unusual features are seen. More questions are raised than are answered; although the prophet solves the problem of the lost tool for the sons of the prophets, his control over the situation is not complete. He has to ask where the tool was lost (v 6). The story is characterized by brevity and economy of words which hint at the confidence of the prophet. But as the chapter continues, such confidence is seen to be misplaced.

In the incident of Elisha and the Syrians (vv 8–23) the miraculous element is completely lacking, other than the incidental reference to Elisha's special knowledge of the affairs of the king of Syria (v 12). The incident represents a clever and rather high-handed treatment of the Syrians by the prophet. The Syrian army is made to look like a collection of fools as they are "bedazzled" and led astray by the prophet, ending up right in the middle of the city of Samaria in the hands of the excited Israelite king. As if to add insult to injury, Elisha advises a demonstration of largess rather than a display of power (vv 20–23), and the Syrians are sent on their way.

Israel's relations with Syria had changed sharply and apparently change again by chapter eight when Ben Hadad seeks Elisha's word. The cause of this change is not given, nor is the reason for the renewal of hostilities.

In the closing incident of the chapter (vv 24–33) Elisha's actions rebound, and the consequences of what he did earlier now threaten his very life. The chapter ends with Elisha's cowering behind a door held by the "old men" of the city against the angry king. The prophet is humiliated. At this point Elisha sees the hand of Yahweh in the events (v 33).

The quick change in the attitude of Elisha from complete confidence to severe insecurity is quite surprising. The confirmed successor of Elijah, who is remembered for his confidence before kings, the confident miracle-worker of chap. 2 and chap. 4, and the healer of the foreigner Naaman is now reduced to hiding because of the repercussions of his actions against the Syrian army. His actions become the cause for the mobilization of the whole of Syria to invade Israel (v 24), which had dire consequences for the city of Samaria. There was, however, some foreshadowing of this in chapter four. Not all went smoothly for the Shunemite and her son. Elisha had urged a gift on her that she did not want. The gift had been lost, and Elisha was not at first successful in his attempt to regain the gift. There, too, his confidence weakened.

There are, however, some additional issues involved in this chapter which were of concern to the Deuteronomist. These issues involved the reappearance of Syria as a strong threat to the security of Israel. Syria took on the role in this and succeeding chapters that Moab played in chapter three. The Syrian threat becomes a symbol of the disintegration of the Israelite territory and the serious weakening of Israelite military and political power. In 2 Sam 8:6 David defeats Syria and brings her under Israelite domination. Although during the reign of Solomon, Rezon and Hadad become a source of irritation for Israel (1 Kgs 11:23, 25) they pose no serious danger to the security of the nation. In 1 Kgs 22 Israel and Judah react to a Syrian capture of Ramoth Gilead. Syria is contained and her king captured. But by 2 Kgs 6 matters have changed. Already, mention has been made of the growing power of Syria at the hand of Naaman and with the blessings of Yahweh (5:1). In 6:11–23 a punitive expedition is sent in, only to be followed by a much larger force (cf. v 24). From this point on relations between Israel and Syria deteriorate. Although Syria is contained in chapter seven, the respite is brief. With the accession of Hazael, the eastern border of Israel is eaten away.

Syria again becomes a symbol of judgment upon Israel. The nadir of Israel's religious life under the Omride dynasty now affects the history of the nation.

The Lepers and the Syrians (7:1–20)

Bibliography

Gurney, O. R. *The Hittites.* London: Penguin Books, 1952. **Herzog, C.** and **Gichon, M.** *Battles of the Bible.* London: Weidenfeld and Nicolson, 1978. **March, W. E.** "Prophecy." In *Old Testament Form Criticism*, ed. J. H. Hays. San Antonio: Trinity University Press, 1974.

Translation

¹ *Elisha had said, "Hear the word of Yahweh! Thus has Yahweh declared, 'By this time tomorrow, a measure of meal for a shekel, and a double measure of barley for a shekel,* ᵃ *in the gate* ᵇ *of Samaria.'"* ² *Then the lieutenant,* ᵃ *the king's righthand man,* ᵇ *said to the man of God,* ᶜ *"Yahweh is the one who makes windows in the heavens. Shall this thing be?" And he replied, "You are about to see for yourself, but you shall not eat of it."*
³ *Now there happened to be four lepers in the gateway, and they said to each other, "Why should we wait here until we die?* ⁴ *If we say, 'Let us go into the city, there is a famine in the city and we shall die there. But if we sit here we shall die.*

So let us desert to the Syrian camp, perhaps we shall live, but if we die we would have died anyway!" ⁵ *So they arose at twilight* ᵃ *to go to the Syrian camp, but when they came to the perimeter of the Syrian camp there was no one there.* ⁶ *Yahweh had caused the Syrian army to hear the noise of chariots* ᵃ *and cavalry* ᵇ *and a great army, so they said to each other,* ᶜ *"The king of Israel has hired the Hittite kings and the kings of Egypt* ᵈ *to come against us!"* ᵉ ⁷ *So they too arose at twilight and fled, leaving behind their tents, their horses and their donkeys. The camp* ᵃ *was just as they had left it.* ᵇ *They had fled* ᶜ *for their lives.* ⁸ *Now these lepers had come to the perimeter of the camp, and they entered one tent, and there they ate, drank, and carried off from there silver, gold, and garments, and they went and hid them.* ᵃ *Then they returned and came to another tent,* ᵇ *and carried stuff from there and went and hid it.* ᶜ ⁹ *Then they said to each other, "We ought not to be doing this. Today is a day of good news and we are silent. If we wait until morning light and remain silent, we will be found out.* ᵃ *Come on, let us go and tell in the king's palace."* ¹⁰ *So they went and called to the city gatekeepers* ᵃ *and said to them, "We came upon the Syrian camp, and there was no one there, not even the sound of anyone, except the tethered horses and mules and the tents* ᵇ *just as they were."* ¹¹ *Then the gatekeepers* ᵃ *called out and it was relayed to the king's palace.*

¹² *Then the king got up in the night,* ᵃ *and said to his advisers, "I will tell you what the Syrians have done to us. They know we are starving, and they have gone out of their camp to hide in the open country,* ᵇ *saying, 'If they come out of the city we can take them alive, then we can enter the city.'"* ¹³ *One of his advisers responded by saying, "Let some men take five of the horses that are left—since those that remain are to be like the whole mass* ᵃ *of Israel left in her,* ᵇ *they will be like the whole mass of Israel, already doomed* ᶜ *—let us send* ᵈ *and let us see."* ¹⁴ *So they took two chariots* ᵃ *and horses, and the king* ᵇ *sent them to the Syrian camp,* ᶜ *and said, "Go and see."* ¹⁵ *They followed their tracks as far as the Jordan, and the road was full of clothing and weapons which the Syrians had discarded in their haste.* ᵃ *The messengers then returned and told the king.* ᵇ

¹⁶ *The people then went out* ᵃ *and plundered the Syrian camp, and so it happened that a measure of meal was sold for a shekel, and a double measure of barley for a shekel, according to the word of Yahweh.* ᵇ ¹⁷ *Now the king had appointed his lieutenant, his righthand man, to be in charge of the gate,* ᵃ *but the people trampled upon him in the gate, and he died.* ᵇ *(It was just as the man of God had said—which he spoke* ᶜ *when the king* ᵈ *came down to him.)* ¹⁸ *It took place according to the word of the man of God to the king, saying, "Two measures of barley for a shekel, a measure of fine grain for a shekel, this time tomorrow in the gate of Samaria."* ¹⁹ *But the lieutenant had responded to the man of God by saying,* ᵃ *"Now Yahweh makes windows in the heavens. Shall this thing be?" And he had replied, "You shall see with your eyes, but you shall not eat of it."* ²⁰ *And it happened to him* ᵃ *in precisely this way, the people trampled upon him in the gate, and he died.*

Notes

1.a. The MT וסאתים שערים בשקל "and a measure of meal for a shekel" is omitted by G by homoioteleuton, although retained by the versions and Josephus (*Antiq.* ix.71) in reversed order (cf. v 18).

1.b. G reads pl, although G^L follows MT with the sg. The Heb שערים "barley" and שערים "gates," unvocalized, are identical and the mistake in G is a simple one.

2.a. MT שליש "lieutenant" (cf. Exod 15:4; 2 Sam 23:8). Josephus (*Antiq.* ix.72) reads "commander of the third division" (ὁ τῆς τρίτης μοίρας ἡγεμενων). G^L offers ὁ ἀπεσταλμενος "the messenger," probably mistaking שליש for שליח "one sent."
2.b. For MT למלך "to the king," G reads ὁ βασιλευς "the king."
2.c. Omitted by G.
2.d. G^L reads και εαν (ואם) "and if."
5.a. Only here and in Job 24:15 is נשף "twilight" translated with σκωπος "goal," "mark."
6.a. MT רכב "chariotry," a collective sg. G^L offers the pl ἁρματων "chariots."
6.b. G adds και φωνη "and a voice."
6.c. MT איש אל־אחיו "a man to his brother," G^L reads πλησιον "neighbor" in harmony with v 9.
6.d. Most commentators (Burney, Gray, Montgomery, Skinner, Snaith, et al.) point מִצְרִים "Muṣrites" rather than מִצְרַיִם "Egypt." The same emendation is made in 1 Kgs 10:28. Muṣri was regarded as Cilicia, the plain of northern Syria (Cappadocia), which would have been a natural place for rearing horses. Furthermore, Hittites and Muṣrites would have been natural allies, and the reference to the "kings" of Egypt is thereby dealt with. The identification of Muṣri with Cilicia, however, is not universally accepted. Cf. S. Parpola, *Neo-Assyrian Toponyms*, AOAT 6 (Neukirchen-Vluyn: Neukirchener Verlag, 1970) 405 and map. See also W. Barnes, *The Second Book of Kings*, 33.
6.e. The frequent use of the phrase הנה in the narrative of 2 Kings, and especially in chapter six, can be irritating if always translated as "look" or "behold." For the variety of uses of the term cf. T. O. Lambdin, *Introduction to Biblical Hebrew*, 135–36.
7.a. MT המחנה כאשר היא "the camp as it is," which G renders ἐν τῇ παρεμβολῇ "in the camp" and G^L as ὡς ἦσαν ἐν τῇ παρεμβολῇ "as it was in the camp," understanding במחנה "in the camp." The final statement is a separate clause.
7.b. With המחנה (masc) it is better to read הוא 3 m.s. than היא 3 f.s. Cf. Burney, *Notes*, 291.
7.c. After וינוסו "they fled." G^L adds οἱ Συροι "the Syrians."
8.a. G omits the first ויטמנו "they hid."
8.b. These verses differ in MT and G and yet again in the Dead Sea Scrolls fragments (6QReg). In three points G disagrees with MT: (1) in the omission of the first ויטמנו "they hid" (v 8); (2) in the addition of ἐκειθεν "there" (משם) "from there" after ויבאו "and he went" (v 8b); (3) in the addition of the preposition εἰς "into" before τον οἰκον (בית) "the house" in v 9b. In two places, independently of G, G^L disagrees with MT but finds support in 6QReg: (1) in v 8b משם "from there" of MT is matched by ἐκειθεν "there" of G, but 6QReg has משום "from there" which is closer to the G^L ἀρσω αὐτων; (2) in v 9b the MT ועתה "and now" is matched by G's και νυν "and now," but G^L omits the conjunction, and 6QReg reads עתה "now." This latter reading is not certain.
8.c. There is no direct object in MT, but loot is certainly understood.
9.a. MT עוון "guilt," for which G has ἀνομιαν "lawlessness" and G^L offers the more normal ἀδικιαν "unrighteous." Cf. Shenkel, *Chronology and Recensional Development*, 115.
10.a. G^L adds here και ἐκαλεσεν τους στρατηγους της πολεως "and they called the magistrates of the city," to retain the pl.
10.b. G's reading of αἱ σκηναι αὐτων "their tents" would possibly suggest an original of ואהליהם "their tents." This would make sense, although the indefinite אהלים "tents" would express something of the chaos left behind by the Syrian flight.
11.a. With G, G^L, Tg, and Vg the pl is adopted.
12.a. לילה "night" is omitted by G^L.
12.b. MT בְּהַשָּׂדֶה "in the open fields," is better read as בַּשָּׂדֶה "in the land." See GKC 35n.
13.a. For חמשה "five" G^A reads παντες "all."
13.b. MT בה "in her" is translated by G as ὧδε (פה?) "here."
13.c. From the second occurrence of בה "in her" to תמו "are doomed" is omitted by G. It is repetitive and might well be regarded as superfluous, although the repetition can indicate the panic of the event reflected in the servant's speech. Burney (*Notes*, 292) suggests an emendation on the basis of Tg ואם אבידו הנם "and if they perish there." But this might well represent an attempt by Tg to smooth out a difficult text.

13.d. G adds ἐκεῖ "there."
14.a. G mentions "mounted horses" but omits any reference to chariots.
14.b. After הָמֶּלֶךְ "the king" G adds a qualifying "of Israel."
14.c. G offers τοῦ βασιλέως "the king" for מַחֲנֵה "camp." G^L agrees with MT.
15.a. MT בְּהֵחָפְזָם "in their haste" is better read as בְּחָפְזָם "in their haste."
15.b. After לַמֶּלֶךְ "to the king" G^L adds Ισραηλ "Israel."
16.a. In typical expansive fashion, G^L adds ἐκ τῆς πόλεως "from the city."
16.b. The order in G is changed. The reference to the double measure of barley follows the allusion to the word of the LORD.
17.a. G^L omits the phrase "in the gate."
17.b. In Syr^{Hex} the clause וַיָּמֹת "and he died" is under the asterisk, possibly indicating a secondary insertion here. The last clause of the chapter is the same and might have been included here through dittography.
17.c. The text, as it stands, is extremely clumsy. It is possible that כאשר דבר איש האלהים "according to the word of the man of God" is a dittography from the following verse. Burney's suggestion (*Notes*, 292) that אשר דבר "which he spoke" be read כדבר "according to the word" makes for a smoother text, but does not solve all the difficulties of repetition in these verses. 6QReg would suggest an ending for chap. 7 with an enclitic mem. Either the phrase כדבר איש האלהים "according to the word of the man of God" was added to the end of the chapter in 6QReg (so Baillet, Milik, de Vaux, *DJD* 3:109), or the chapter originally ended at v 17*b*.
17.d. Here G reads τοῦ ἀγγέλου (המלאך) "the messenger" in keeping with the Heb of 6:33.
19.a. Omitted by G.
20.a. Omitted by G, but included by G^A.

Form/Structure/Setting

DeVries's analysis of this chapter leaves 6:24*aβ*–30, 32*a*–33; 7:1–2, 6–7*aα*, and 14–17 as a unit. The remaining verses are assigned to a redactor (R) (cf. *Prophet against Prophet*, 118). This division seems arbitrary with its omission of the small and amusing story of the lepers, since it forms part of the progression of the complete narrative from problem to resolution, and from word to fulfillment of the word. In its present form the chapter moves through four distinct stages: vv 1–2, 3–11, 12–15, and 16–20.

V 1 contains the elements of the classic prophetic speech style with its summons to hear, its introductory formula, and its announcement. Such patterns of speaking are numerous in the prophetic literature. The concluding statement is a verbless clause in distinct contrast to the existing state of affairs. The contents depict a dramatic improvement of circumstances for the inhabitants of Samaria.

Whether the verse can be classified as a prophetic oracle of salvation is doubtful. Westermann (*Basic Forms*) does not include it in his catalogue of original forms. The examples of this form cited by Koch (*Biblical Tradition*, 207–8, 213–15) and March (*Old Testament Form Criticism*, 162) are not similar enough in content to make the identification. What similarities there are between 2 Kgs 7:1 and oracles of salvation, such as the summons to hear and the introductory formula, are common to many types of prophetic utterances, including those of judgment. The oracle proper is the verbless clause סאה־סלת בשקל וסאתים שערים בשקל בשער שמרון "a measure of meal for a shekel and a double measure of barley for a shekel, in the gate of Samaria," which is only understandable in the immediate context. Its cryptic form suggests the citation of a vendor's cry, "A measure of meal for a shekel! Two measures of barley for a shekel!"

V 2 is a statement of Elisha to an individual bystander, but cannot be seen as a formal judgment speech to an individual as outlined by Westermann (*Basic Forms*, 130). Of the four main characteristics of such a form—summons to hear, accusation, formal introduction, and a personal announcement of judgment—only the last is present. This statement is not introduced as a word from the LORD. An accusation is implied in the context of the saying, but this does not make the saying a formal judgment speech to an individual. The meaning of the statement is derived from its context, not from a preconceived form. There are some noteworthy stylistic features of the prophet's statement to the officer. The word הנה "behold," followed by a participle, is used in a similar way in Jer 20:4 and the reference to "eyes about to see" is duplicated in the same verse. Although הנה features prominently in prophecies of personal disaster (so Koch, *Biblical Tradition*, 205) it introduces an action of God in judgment, as in Jer 32:37, rather than a general statement of the reversal of fortunes as here. A close parallel to Elisha's statement is God's statement to Moses in Deut 32:52 כי מנגד תראה את־הארץ ושמה לא תבוא אל־הארץ אשר אני נתן לבני ישראל "for you will see the land before you, but you will not go there into the land which I give to the children of Israel." This idiom of eyes seeing, but not being satisfied, could well be a stylistic trait of the Deuteronomist.

The word of God which the prophet announces in v 1 presents a sharp contrast to the preceding narrative. The oracle announces deliverance for the stricken city by a huge drop in the price of staples, and the prophet's confidence is regained with the utterance of the words. The second statement to the lieutenant is a reinforcement of the divine word. On another level, it serves to bring back the theme of official skepticism.

3–11 This incident, which is omitted by DeVries from the original story (*Prophet against Prophet*, 118), is vital to the plot. The contrast between scarcity and plenty is shown by the opening words of the chapter. The narrative moves on to show the process by which the fulfillment takes place. As with the story of the water in the desert of Edom in 3:20, there is nothing necessarily miraculous about the process of fulfillment, except the timing of the events.

The fulfillment of the word of Yahweh and the judgment of the king's officer in v 1 now move forward in three distinct stages. There are some changes of scene and three changes in the direction of the story. As with chap. 5, the king of Israel plays a minor role which halts the fulfillment temporarily. In the first scene, the four lepers at the gate of the city, with simple logic, desert to the Syrians. When they arrive at the enemy camp the enemy has run away, frightened by a rumor (vv 3–7). The style is reminiscent of 3:22–24. With their stroke of good fortune, the lepers begin the plunder of the camp (v 8). The detail of the Syrians leaving their camp at the moment when the four lepers arrive brings to the story an element of farce.

The second stage of the fulfillment shifts the scene from the camp back to the city and the palace (vv 9–11). The lepers cause this shift by their decision to tell the king. The chain of narration from lepers to gatekeepers, from gatekeepers to palace reflects custom since lepers would not have had access to the palace in their condition. It also serves as a narrative device to bring the story back to the palace and the king. The chapter began with Elisha's offering a promise to the king. The narrative moved in a circle from the palace to the gate of the city (v 3), from the gate of the city to the Syrian camp (vv 5–8), from the Syrian camp back to the gate (v 10), and from the gate of the city finally back to the palace (v 11). The device is one seen before in these stories, inversion or chiasmus.

The third stage of the fulfillment opens with a setback (vv 12–15). The king refuses to believe the good fortune of the Syrians' retreat. Official skepticism, first of the king's officer, now of the king himself, echoes the problems encountered by Naaman in his search for healing, and there is a danger of the word's not being fulfilled. To break this barrier a servant suggests a common sense course of action (v 13). Such a solution is a common one (cf. 3:11; 5:13; 6:12). In vv 14–15 the confirmation of the retreat reinforces the previous narrative and convinces the king of the fact. At this point in the narrative the focus shifts back to the beginning of the story. The actors who have played a decisive role in the fulfillment of the word, the lepers, the gatekeeper, even the king, are left behind. The restatement of the oracle and the word of the prophet concludes the chapter.

16–20 The fulfillment is repeated twice in a slightly different form in these verses. In vv 16*b*–17 the clause ויהי "and it was" introduces the fulfillment of the word of Yahweh and repeats the promise of abundance word for word:

סאה סלת בשקל	"a measure of meal for a shekel"
סאתים שערים בשקל	"and a double measure of barley for a skekel."

The balance of these lines is good, with the fulfillment of each word being introduced with the waw consecutive, and concluded by a comment introduced with the preposition ב:

		והמלך תפקיד	"Now the king had appointed
		השליש אשר נשען	his lieutenant to be in charge
		על ידו	on his right hand
		על השער	of the gate."
ויהי	"and it was"	וירמסהו	"but they trampled him"
סאה סלת	"a measure of fine flour"	העם	"the people"
בשקל	"for a shekel"		
וסאתים שערים	"and two measures"		
בשקל	"for a shekel"		
בשער שמרון	"in the gate of Samaria"	בשער וימת	"in the gate and he died"

כדבר יהוה	"according to the word of the Lord."	כאשר דבר איש אלהים	"just as the man of God said."
		(כאשר דבר)	"as he had spoken this word"
		(ברדת המלך אליו)	"when the king came to him."

The material in parentheses provides necessary supplementary details. The grammatical clumsiness of the second parenthesis provides possible evidence of its secondary nature. For the textual difficulties see above.

Vv 18–20, while providing a duplication of the fulfillment of the two words uttered at the outset of the narrative, do not display the same balance. The introduction with the clause ויהי "and it happened" followed by the phrase כדבר "according to the word" is unique among the fulfillment clauses in the Former Prophets. The closest parallel is 1 Kgs 15:29, but there the two elements are separated by additional words. The other fulfillment clauses of the Former Prophets are either as in vv 16*b*–17, or use waw consecutive and the imperfect followed by a phrase prefixed by the preposition (cf. 1 Kgs 13:26; 14:18; 16:12, 34; 17:16; 22:38; 2 Kgs 1:17; 2:22; 5:14; 6:18; etc.).

Further, the statement אל המלך "to the king" is hardly consistent with the plural in the appeal for attention in v 1 (שמעו "hear it"). A third peculiarity is the reversal of the order of "a measure of meal" and "two measures of barley." The phrase כעת מחר "this time tomorrow" is also displaced. The repetition of the comment of the king's officer is almost exact, except for the omission of the subordinate clause and some changes in orthography.

If these verses are intended to emphasize the fulfillment by repetition, then they are a clumsy attempt. In view of the fact that the last word records the fate of the king's officer, then the weight of the final verses should be seen there. The differences would suggest a secondary addition, to stress again the death of the officer and the prophet's judgment upon officialdom and its skepticism. In this it echoes 1:17.

Nothing definite can be stated concerning the prehistory of the story. Vv 18–20 display the marks of a secondary addition, but the further separation of the narrative into an original "prophetic authorization narrative" and redactional material (vv 3–5, 8–13) (so DeVries, *Prophet against Prophet*, 55) seems arbitrary. As it stands, the narrative moves smoothly from the initial problem—the giving of a prophetic word in contrast to existing circumstances—to the solution of the problem. The circuitous route taken, via the lepers to the Syrian camp and back again to the palace, is not evidence of secondary additions to an original form, but rather is integral to the progress of the plot. The chiastic device is common in these stories, and, it has been argued, in the Books of Kings in general (cf. Y. T. Radday, "Chiasm in Kings," *Linguistica Biblica* 31 [1974] 52–67).

Comment

1 שמעו דבר יהוה "hear the word of Yahweh." This is the first time in the stories of Elisha where he uses the classic introduction to a prophetic speech. This "summons to hear" is a common introduction to certain collections of prophetic utterances (Jer 2:4; 10:1; 11:2; 19:3; 17:20; 21:11; Mic 2:1; 3:1, 9; 6:1; Amos 7:16–17). The plural form is common when a prophet is addressing a group (Mic 3:9) or when the group is treated as one (Jer 2:4). Individuals within groups are addressed with the singular (Jer 22:2). See *Form/Structure/Setting*.

כה אמר יהוה "Thus has Yahweh declared." This is the most common introduction to prophetic utterances. What now becomes important is that the deliverance of the city of Samaria from the Syrian threat comes about through a word from Yahweh, whereas the original problem was caused through the hubris of man.

כעת מחר "by this time tomorrow." The noun עת "time" preceded by the preposition כ is rare in the OT (Num 23:23; Josh 11:6; Judg 13:23; 21:22; 1 Sam 4:20; 9:16; 1 Kgs 20:6; 2 Kgs 4:16, 17; Isa 8:23). It designates specific time.

סאה סלת בשקל "a measure of meal for a shekel." The exact measurement of a סאה "seah" is unknown, although it is thought to be about one-sixth of a bushel (cf. Sellers, *IDB* 4:828–39). In contrast to the terrible privations of the siege depicted in chap. 6, abundance will be the order of the day. Cf. 6:25. A *kab* is approximately one-sixth of a *seah*, yet the *seah* of meal is to be one-fifth the cost of a quarter *kab* of dove's dung. A double measure of barley will be the same price. The contrast is well made.

בשער שמרון "in the gate of Samaria." Why trade of this kind should take place in the gate of the city is unclear. If this was a place of much commerce it was probably unsuitable. The city gates of this period were reasonably large, but not large enough for a sizable market. The G translation of ἀγορά is rare, and is more an interpretation than a translation of certain terms (cf. Cant 3:2; Ezek 27:12, 14, 16, 18).

2 ויען השליש "then the lieutenant answered." The precise meaning of the term שליש in this context is unclear, although it appears to be derived from the word for "three" (שלש). That it is to be translated as "third man in the chariot" (BDB) is unlikely. Even the heavy four-wheeled chariots depicted in a Sumerian relief from the third millennium (cf. Yadin, *Art of Warfare* 1:132–33) do not have more than two crew members. Most hunting chariots were designed for speed and manned by one man. Gurney (*The Hittites*, 105–6) mentions heavy Hittite war chariots which were manned by three men, but these seem to be a form of armored personnel carrier designed to take as many men into battle as quickly as possible. The same appears true of the Hittite chariots which fought against Ramses II at Kadesh (cf. Yadin, *Art of Warfare* 1:104–5). Often depicted is one of the three men dismounted with shield or spear. In any event, it is highly unlikely at this time that the king was riding in a heavy war vehicle. In the OT the term שליש "lieutenant" appears in a variety of contexts, not all of them associated with the military. In Exod 15:4 the RSV translates the term more generally with "picked officers." In Ezek 23:23, government officials are intended.

אשר למלך נשען על ידו "who was the king's righthand man." Like Naaman, this particular officer was an important person in the court of the king of Israel. The expression cannot be taken literally, since there is no indication that either the Israelite or Syrian kings were infirm. It occurs only here and in chap. 5.

הנה יהוה עשה "behold, Yahweh makes." On the frequent use of the term הנה cf. Lambdin, *Introduction to Biblical Hebrew*, 168–72.

3 וארבעה . . . מצרעים "and four lepers." The rabbinic tradition has these four as sons of Gehazi. This tendency to blacken the character of Gehazi has already been mentioned. They are never shown holding normal conversations with others. All communication is done by shouting. They might have been in quarantine for their sickness.

4 ונפלה אל "let us desert to." On the use of this verb in this kind of context, cf. Jer 38:19. It is best translated "desert to. . . ." This incident of the lepers reflects a humorous common-sense which had escaped others in the city.

5 The usual word for evening is ערב "evening," not נשף "twilight." The latter term is ambiguous and can also indicate early morning light (1 Sam 30:17; Jer 13:16; Ps 119:147; Job 3:9; 7:4) as well as twilight (Isa 5:11; 21:4; 50:10; Prov 7:9).

קצה מחנה "the perimeter of the camp." Normally, when on campaigns which involved siege, armies would prepare armed encampments with protecting walls and guards. Illustrations of such camps used on large expeditions by the armies of Mesopotamia can be found in Yadin, *Art of Warfare*, 2:291–93, 432.

6 אדני השמיע את ארם "The Lord has made the Syrian hear." The sentiment here is that God is the first cause of history. Yahweh was also the giver of victory to Syria through Naaman (cf. 5:1). There is also a strong contrast, however. In 5:1 victory is given. Here defeat is the result.

מלכי החתים ומלכי מצרים "Hittite kings and Egyptian kings." The rumor fled through the Syrian camp that an alliance of Hittite and Egyptian mercenaries had come to the aid of Israel. The "kings of the Hittites" referred to here were not the emperors of the early Hittite empire which had spanned most of the territory covered by modern Turkey. In 1200 B.C., and again a few centuries later, the Hittite empire had received some serious blows from the Sea Peoples and the Assyrians and its vast power was broken. Hittite culture was then perpetuated in numerous small principalities in northern Syria, which were gradually becoming assimilated into the semitic culture. It is these small principalities which are represented by the "kings of the Hittites." Cf. Gelb, *IDB* 2:612–15, Astour, *IDBSup*, 411–13; O. R. Gurney, *The Hittites*, 39–46.

The identity of the "kings of Egypt" is more problematic. The same state of affairs did not pertain in Egypt, hence the plural "kings" is difficult. The textual change from "Egyptians" (מִצְרַיִם) to "Musrites" (מֻצְרִים), suggested by a number of commentators, is possible. During the period following the invasion of the Sea Peoples, the area of Cilicia was also occupied by a mixed group of princes (cf. Gurney, *The Hittites*, 42–43). Further, in the eleventh year of his reign (ca. 846 B.C.), Shalmaneser attacked and defeated an alliance of Syrians and Hittites (cf. *ANET*, 279–80). The alarm of the Syrians could then be explained as distress that their former allies had deserted them. However, the term "Musri" refers invariably to Egypt in Assyrian records. An

Comment

alliance of Hittites and Egyptians, rumored in the Syrian camp, was not impossible at this time (cf. Herzog and Gichon, *Battles of the Bible*, 233).

7 וינוסו בנשף "so they fled at twilight." The coincidence of the Syrian army's fleeing from a rumor in the twilight offers a sense of rapid movement to the story, which now borders on the comic. The Syrians flee out the back door as the four harmless lepers arrive at the front! ויעזבו את . . . סוסיהם "and they abandoned their horses." Why horses and mules were left behind during the flight is unknown. They would have made excellent animals for a quick getaway. Even chariot horses could have been used for this purpose. The haste which must have characterized the flight and the abandoning of all the equipment gave rise to the statement וינסו אל נפשם "they had fled for their lives."

8 The lepers, after satisfying their most pressing need for food and water, now begin a systematic plundering of the Syrian camp, tent by tent.

9 היום הזה יום בשרה "today is a day of good news." The term translated "news" (בשרה) is not always good news (cf. 2 Sam 18:20). The conscience of the lepers was pricked not simply because of their patriotism, but because of their fear of reprisals. True to their declared intention to keep out of as much trouble as possible, they decide to spread the good news of the Syrian flight. The term ומצאנו עוון "we will be found out" is unusual. Nowhere else in the OT does the noun appear as the subject of this verb. In Gen 44:16 it functions as the object of the verb (cf. also Deut 4:30; 31:17).

10 ויקראו אל שער "and they called to the gatekeepers." Presumably because of their condition, the lepers did not have access to the inside of the city. The good news is relayed from one herald to another until the chain is complete (v 11).

12 The king of Israel reacts with skepticism. Such an attitude is common among officials in these chapters. He suspects a trick. The tactics he describes are those of the "feint," in which part of an army withdraws to give the impression of defeat and to lure the enemy on to more favorable ground. The unsuspecting enemy is then surrounded and beaten. The tactic had been used before to Israel's advantage in Joshua's defeat of Ai (Josh 8) and in Abimelech's capture of Shechem (Judg 9). Cf. Yadin, *The Art of Warfare* 2:318–20; Herzog and Gichon, *Battles of the Bible*, 30–34.

13 ויען אחד מעבדיו "and one of his advisors responded." As is often the case in these stories, the lesser figures, such as servants, bring an element of common sense to the situation (cf. also 3:11; 5:15; 6:12). The textual problems of the servant's comment are impossible to solve. The advice, however, seems plain: "Send someone to see!"

14 ויקחו שני רכב סוסים "so they took the chariots and horses." The dispatch of two chariot horses on a scouting expedition is strange, and the versions, notably G and Vg, attempt to smooth out this difficulty. It is possible that this was all that was available to the king at this time. A small change from רכב to רכבי would offer "two riders" (cf. *BHS*).

15 וילכו אחריהם עד־הירדן "they followed their tracks as far as the Jordan." The Syrian flight to the Jordan was along a well-known route (הדרך "the way") and could have taken two directions. The army could have moved farther south and east to Shechem, then joined the route through the Wadi Faria and crossed the Jordan at the "Bridge of Adam" and escaped via Jabbok; or the army could have returned the way the first expedition came into Israel from Syria, that is, north to the Valley of Dothan, past Jenin and east to Beth Shean to the Jordan, escaping via the Yarmuk. Either route is indirect and would have taken the fleeing soldiers through a great deal of hostile territory. This would have added to the panic which afflicted the Syrian force.

כלים "weapons." Although most occurrences of this term are translated "vessels," the alternative of "weapons" is possible (cf. Gen 27:3; Deut 1:41; Judg 9:54; 18:11, 16, 17). For the Syrians, this was an igniminious end to their campaign against Samaria. The annals of history offer frequent illustrations of an army in similar flight. Some commentators omit vv 18–20 as secondary (cf. DeVries, *Prophet against Prophet,* 55; Montgomery, 388). However, Gray suggests that if vv 18–20 were original to the narrative, they "may indicate the way in which the prophetic anecdotes, though dealing with the stuff of history, were told over with due emphasis upon the prophetic word and its fulfillment" (525). The emphasis in vv 16–20 is clearly upon the fulfillment of the prophetic word of promise and threat, which provides a suitable ending to the chapter which opens in the same way. See above on *Form/Structure/ Setting.*

17 אשר דבר ברדת המלך אליו "which he spoke when the king came down to him." Which incident this refers to is not clear. A distinct possibility is the ending of chap. 6 (33*b*). But there the Hebrew is "messenger," not king. G deliberately links the two. The comment is the only part of vv 18, 20 which might be superfluous. The whole chapter, while it deals with the "stuff of history" with its account of the Syrian defeat, also places strong emphasis upon the course of the fulfillment of the word of Yahweh through the prophet.

Explanation

2 Kgs 7 contains the well-executed tale of the lifting of the siege by the Syrians from the Israelite capital, Samaria. The dramatic fulfillment of the prophetic word promising plenty for the inhabitants of the city, and disaster for the official who doubted the word of God, gives to the chapter both literary "color" and a sense of inevitability. The word of God will not fail. No less color is found in the tale of the four lepers, which is sandwiched between the pronouncement of the prophetic word (vv 1–2) and its fulfillment (vv 16–20). But it is color of a different hue. The tale is told with a great deal of humor and the writer sketches the characters of the lepers with sensitivity. They are not idealized into heroes who save the city, but are men, who by a series of accidents open the way for the city to be relieved. The action of the narrative is built up by the device of dialogue.

The relief of the city, brought about by the four lepers, brings to mind several other occasions in these stories in which a person of low social standing provides a solution to a serious problem. The young girl introduces Naaman's wife to the possibility of the general's healing (5:2–3). Naaman's own servant persuades him to obey the prophet's command (5:13–14). An attendant of the king of Israel brings Elisha to his attention on the expedition into Moab (3:11). And in the incident of the lifting of the siege, one of the servants of the king suggests the common-sense solution to the king's anxiety of sending out a patrol for reconnaissance (7:13).

In direct contrast to this, both here and in other stories from the collection, the role of officialdom is to frustrate the movement of the stories from problem to solution. This is exemplified in chap. 7 by the reaction of the officer to the word of God in vv 1-2, and the reaction of the king of Israel to the good news of the Syrian flight in v 12. The reaction of each is understandable, and to a certain extent predictable. Echoes of such reactions are found in the panic with which the king of Israel faced the difficulties in the desert of Edom (3:9-12), the suspicion with which the king of Israel reacted to the letter sent by the king of Syria on behalf of Naaman (5:5-7), and the suspicion of the king of Syria of his own men when his plans regarding Israel were thwarted (6:8-14). It is the officer who stands out in this story, however, since the results of his skepticism toward the word of God are far reaching.

Throughout the prophetic tradition the conflict between prophet and authority is a consistent theme. It is seen in Samuel's relationship with Saul (1 Sam 15), Elijah's relationship with Ahab (1 Kgs 21), Amos' confrontation with Amaziah (Amos 7), and Jeremiah's clash with Passhur (Jer 20:1-6), Jehoiakim (Jer 36), and the scribes (Jer 8:8-12). In each case the attitude of officialdom to the word of God is greeted with judgment. The word of God through the prophet is seen as the ultimate interpretation of history for the "deuteronomist."

The control of God over history and the power of the prophetic word in the shaping of history are common themes in the Former Prophets. They are evident here. Just as Yahweh had given Syria victory (5:1) and set Syria as a threat to Israel, so the brief respite from that threat is also seen as a result of the will of God. The panic of the Syrian army and their temporary withdrawal from Samaria happened because God willed it (v 6).

Hazael, King in Damascus (8:1-29)

Bibliography

Albright, W. F. "The Chronology of the Divided Monarchy in Israel." *BASOR* 100 (1945) 16-22. **Bin-Nun, S. R.** "Formulas from Royal Records of Israel and Judah." *VT* 18 (1968) 414-32. **Katzenstein, H. J.** "Who Were the Parents of Athaliah?" *IEJ* 5 (1955) 194-97. **Strange, J.** "Joram, King of Israel and Judah." *VT* 25 (1975) 191-201.

Translation

¹*Now Elisha had said to the woman whose son* [a] *he had brought back to life, "Get ready, and go, both you* [b] *and your household,* [c] *and live for a while somewhere*

else. Yahweh has summoned a famine,^d and it will come upon^e the land for seven years." ² So the woman made ready and acted in accord with the command of the man of God. ^a She went with her household, and stayed in the territory of the Philistines ^b for seven years. ³ Then, at the end of seven years the woman returned from the territory of the Philistines,^a and went to lodge a complaint to the king about her house and her land. ⁴ The king happened to be speaking to Gehazi, the servant of the man of God,^a saying, "Tell me ^b now the great deeds Elisha did." ⁵ And as he was speaking to the king about the raising of the dead boy,^a the very woman whose boy had been raised ^b was complaining about her house and her land. Gehazi said, "My lord king, that is the woman, and that is her son whom Elisha brought back to life." ⁶ The king interrogated the woman, and she told him everything. So the king appointed a eunuch for her, and told him, "Restore to her everything that belonged to her, including all the produce of her land ^a from the day she left the country until now."

⁷ Now Elisha went to Damascus, and Ben Hadad, the king of Syria, was sick. Someone told him, "The man of God has arrived."^a ⁸ So Ben Hadad told Hazael,^a "Take a gift ^b and go to the man of God, and inquire of Yahweh through him saying, 'Shall I recover from this sickness?' " ^c ⁹ Hazael went to meet him and took in his hand a gift of all the good things ^a of Damascus; in all, forty camel loads. He came and stood before him, and said, "Your son, Ben Hadad king of Syria, has sent me to you with a message, 'Shall I recover from this sickness?' " ¹⁰ Then Elisha said to him,^a "Go, say to him, ^b 'You shall indeed recover.' But Yahweh has shown me that he will most certainly die." ¹¹ Hazael stared him in the face ^a until he was embarrassed, and the man of God began to weep. ¹² Hazael asked, "Why do you weep sir?" And he replied, "Because I know what evil you will do to the children of Israel. You will put their forts to the torch, slay their best men with the sword, dash in pieces their infants, and rip open their pregnant women." ¹³ Hazael retorted, "What is your servant? A dog ^a that he should do such an enormity?"^b Elisha replied, "Yahweh has shown me you as king over Syria."^c ¹⁴ He departed ^a from Elisha ^b and came to his master, who said to him, "What did Elisha say to you?" He replied, "He said you would definitely recover." ¹⁵ But on the following day he took a coverlet,^a dipped it in water and spread it over his face, and he died. Then Hazael became king in his place. ^b

¹⁶ In the fifth ^a year of Joram, son of Ahab, king of Israel (and Jehoshaphat king of Judah),^b Jehoram, son of Jehoshaphat reigned as king of Judah. ¹⁷ He ^a was thirty-two years old at his accession, and he reigned eight ^b years in Jerusalem. ¹⁸ But he behaved as did the kings of Israel, in the same manner as the house of Ahab, because he had married the daughter of Ahab. He behaved badly in the eyes of Yahweh. ¹⁹ But because of his servant David, Yahweh did not want to destroy Judah. He had promised to David ^a to give him a lamp for his sons forever. ^b

²⁰ In his days Edom rebelled from under the control of Judah and appointed their own king. ²¹ So Jehoram ^a crossed over to Seir ^b with all his chariot force. One night ^c he mustered and defeated the Edomites who had surrounded him and his chariot force. But his people fled home. ²² Edom rebelled from under the control of Judah ^a until this day. Even Libnah ^b rebelled in that day. ²³ Now the rest of the deeds of Jehoram, and all he did, are they not written in the book of the daily acts of the king of Judah? ²⁴ Then Jehoram slept with his fathers, and was buried with his fathers in the city of David. ^a Ahaziah his son reigned in his place.

²⁵ In the twelfth year ^a of Joram, son of Ahab, king of Israel, Ahaziah, son of Jehoram king of Judah, ^b began to reign. ²⁶ Ahaziah ^a was twenty-two years old at

his accession, and he reigned one year in Jerusalem.[b] His mother's name was Athaliah, daughter of Omri [c] king of Israel. [27] He behaved like the house of Ahab, and acted badly in the eyes of Yahweh like the house of Ahab, because he was a son-in-law to the house of Ahab.[a] [28] He supported [a] Joram, son of Ahab in his war with Hazael king of Syria at Ramoth Gilead, but the Syrians defeated Joram. [29] So Joram returned to Jezreel [a] to be healed of the wounds the Syrians [b] had inflicted [c] upon him at Ramah [d] in his war with Hazael king of Syria; and Ahaziah, son of Jehoram, king of Judah, [e] came down to see Joram, son of Ahab, in Jezreel because he was sick.

Notes

At this point in the text of 2 Kings, the Dead Sea Scrolls fragments become important. A fragment of 2 Kgs 7:20(?)—8:5 is reproduced in Baillet, Milik, and De Vaux, *DJD* 3:109. In several cases the 6QReg 15 agrees with G against M.

1.a. The possessive is missing from G, but retained in G^L.
1.b. MT אתי "you" and G renders συ "you." 6QReg 15 offers את.
1.c. G^L adds independently και ὁ υἱος σου "and your son."
1.d. G adds here ἐπι την γην "upon the earth."
1.e. MT reads וגם בא אל־הארץ "and surely it will come to the earth." 6QReg 15 reads וגם בא על הארץ "and surely it will come upon the earth," which accords with G ἐπι την γην "upon the earth."
2.a. G reads the proper noun.
2.b. G offers γη ἀλλοφυλων "land of the foreigners" for the MT פלשתים "Philistines." Elsewhere G uses this word of Syria (2 Kgs 8:28), Kedem (Judg 8:10), and "foreign" (נכר) (Isa 61:5). 6QReg 15 uses the preposition אל "to" and G^L expands with "as the man of God said to her."
3.a. After ארץ פלשתים "the land of the Philistines" both G and 6QReg 15 add אל העיר "to the city."
4.a. 6QReg 15 here reads אל־שע. G combines both readings.
4.b. For ספרה נא "tell it, please" 6QReg 15 reads ספר נא "tell it, I pray."
5.a. Both G^L and G add to this statement τον υιον αὐτης τον τεθνηκοτα "her son who had died" and υἱον τεθνηκοτα "son who had died" respectively.
5.b. G adds the proper noun here.
6.a. G adds ἐπιστρεψον παντα αὐτης τα γενηματα του ἀγρου "return everything of hers, the produce of the field."
7.a. G^L offers the slightly different reading of ἐνταυθα ὁ ἀνος του Θυ̅ "the man of God arrived."
8.a. MT reads חזהאל "Hazael," although there is a variant in v 9 (חזאל "Hazael") which is supported by G (᾽Αζαηλ "Hazael").
8.b. For the MT מנחה "gift," G offers the transliteration of μαανα.
8.c. As with 1:2 G reads ἐκ της ἀρρωστιας μου (מחלי) "from my sickness."
9.a. For a smoother translation we adopt the reading of G^L (מכל "from all") rather than the MT כל "all" followed by G.
10.a. G omits אליו "to him."
10.b. MT has the negative, although Qere is undoubtedly correct with לו "to him." Burney suggests (*Notes*, 293) that the alteration to the negative was due to the desire to avoid the impression that Elisha lied. The confusion between לו "to him" and לא "not" is common in the OT. Josephus (*Antiq.* ix.92) also avoids the impression that Elisha lied by having Hazael inform Ben Hadad that he would recover.
11.a. MT ויעמד את פניו וישם עד־בש, lit., "And he caused his face to stand, and he set until shame." G^L tidies the text up by stating "Hazael stood in front of him, and set before him the gifts" (ἐστη ᾽Αζαηλ κατα πρωσοπον και παρεθηκεν ἐνωπιον αὐτου τα δωρα). It is clearly a paraphrase. Josephus (*Antiq.* ix.90) interprets with και ὁ μεν οἰκετης του βασιλεως ἐλευπειτο ταυτ᾽ ἀκουσας "and while the king's servant was grieving at what he heard," which reverses the text's intention. Burney (*Notes*, 293–94) lists the numerous suggestions of the versions. Burney's own comment that the subject of עד בש "until shame" is Hazael also seems contrary to the intention of the text. Since it is Elisha who reacts to this stare, and offers an explanation for his embarrassment (v 12), it is better to have Elisha as the subject.

13.a. G offers ὁ κυων ὁ τεθνηκως "the dead dog."
13.b. הגדול "the great" is omitted by G.
13.c. G offers σε βασιλευοντα ἐπι Ἰσραηλ, which could be translated, "you, lording it over Israel."
14.a. G^L adds "Hazael."
14.b. G^L replaces the proper noun with "man of God."
15.a. The Hebrew מַכְבֵּר "a netted cloth" is a *hapax legomenon*, the normal word being the related מִכְבָּר "grating" (Exod 27:4). G transliterates, whereas Josephus (*Antiq.* ix.92) offers δίκτυον "net," possibly understanding מכמר "snare" or מכמרת "fishing net."
15.b. G^L adds "over Syria."
16.a. So MT and most of the versions. One G MS reads "first."
16.b. The phrase ויהושפט מלך יהודה "and Jehoshaphat, King of Judah" is found in MT and in G^BAL but is omitted by some. Burney (*Notes*, 294) and Skinner (*Kings*, 316) see it as a scribal error.
17.a. In typical fashion, G^L adds "Joram."
17.b. G reads "forty" and G^L reads "ten." G seems grossly enlarged, and results from an addition of the reign (eight years), and his age at accession (thirty-two years).
19.a. MT אמר לו "he said to him." The preposition is included in G^AL, but omitted from G^B.
19.b. The phrase לבניו "for his sons" is omitted by most MSS of G, although included in G^N, Syr,A. Burney's suggestion (*Notes*, 295) that the phrase should be read לפניו "to his face," instead of לבניו "for his sons," is attractive.
21.a. Although MT has "Joram" in vv 21, 23, 24, the *Translation* uses "Jehoram" in order to clarify that Joram of Judah (Jehoram), not Joram of Israel, is the primary subject of 8:16–24.
21.b. For צעירה "to Sair" G reads Σειωρ "Seir" and G^L offers ἐκ Σιων αὐτου "from his Zion." See the comments below for the location and identification of the place.
21.c. לילה "night" is omitted by G.
22.a. G^L paraphrases the idiom with μη δουναι Χειρα "not under the control of." G tends to be more literal with ὑποκατω της χειρος Ἰουδα "under the hand of Judah."
22.b. G^B offers "Senna," and a great variety of forms occur in the versions. Josephus identifies it with Lebanon.
24.a. G adds "David his father."
25.a. G^L reads either "eleventh" (G^bc2e2) or "tenth" (G^o).
25.b. The phrase מלך יהודה "king of Judah" is omitted by G^B, but retained by G^A.
26.a. G^L adds "son of Jehoram."
26.b. G reads "Israel," which is in error. The mistake is easy to make because of the common names of the kings (Joram/Jehoram).
26.c. Although G^L reads "Ahab," which would make better chronological sense, all the versions apart from this read "Omri." The term could mean "female descendant."
27.a. The comment "because he was the son-in-law to the house of Ahab" is omitted by G^B, and is absent from 2 Chr 22:4.
28.a. MT reads וילך . . . למלחמה "and he went . . . to battle," but this need not be taken literally since Ahaziah's fate in the battle of Ramoth Gilead is not mentioned in the narrative. Hence the more general translation.
29.a. Throughout v 29 G reads "Israel."
29.b. Omitted by G.
29.c. MT יכהו "they inflicted" would read better with 2 Chr 22:6 הכהו "they inflicted."
29.d. G harmonizes with "Ramoth Gilead" by rendering the term "Remmoth."
29.e. Omitted by G^B.

Form/Structure/Setting

1–6 Eissfeldt's classification of this pericope as a "prophetic legend" (*Introduction*, 46) is less than helpful. Such a classification suggests more the hypothetical source of the story than a description of its form. DeVries's grouping of this with other stories designated "power demonstration narratives" (*Prophet against Prophet*, 54) sub-type III, "prophetic word stories," and his placing it in an early "legitimation collection" (118) is weak. An examination of the story and a comparison with others so designated (2:23–24; 5:1–27) reveals few, if any, formal similarities. That the story "legitimates" Elisha in any sense is unlikely.

In its present form the story moves through four "scenes" involving Elisha and the woman (v 1), the action of the woman (vv 2–3), the king and Gehazi (vv 4–5), the king and the woman (v 6). The common factor in each of the scenes in the story is the woman. This is true even of the third, since, even though she does not appear in person, she is the subject of conversation between the king and Gehazi. The construction of the story is tight and each scene has some distinctive stylistic characteristics. V 1 is introduced by a conjunction and a proper noun plus the simple perfect (ואלישע דבר "and Elisha spoke"), which in turn is followed by *lamedh* and the infinitive construct (לאמר "saying"). Vv 2–3 move through a series of *waw* consecutives (ותקם, ותשב, ותצא לצעק "she made ready, returned, went to lodge a complaint"). Vv 4–5 are introduced with a noun plus a participle (והמלך מדבר "Now the king was speaking"), and vv 5–6 begin with ויהי "and it was" plus participle, then continue with a series of *waw* consecutives (ותספר, ויתן, ויאמר, וישאל "and she told . . . and he gave . . . and he said . . . and he inquired"). These formal features are not found in either 2:23–24 or 5:1–27, but are found in 4:1–7, as the following breakdown shows:

8:1–6	4:1–7
ואלישע דבר	ואשה . . . צעלה
לאמר	לאמר
ותקם כדבר איש אלהים	ויאמר
ותשב	ותאמר
	ויאמר
ותצא לצעק	ותלך ותסגר
והמלך מדבר	הם מגשים
ויהי מסכר . . . הנה	ויהי כמלאת
ויאמר	ותאמר
וישאל	ויאמר
ותספר	ותבא ותגד
ויתן לאמר	ויאמר

In this first example (4:1–7) the prophet emerges as a problem-solver par excellence, the problem being the destitute state of the woman. Elisha's original advice and the action of the woman in obedience to that advice relieve her situation to a miraculous degree. There the action moved from the woman to Elisha, to whom she appealed (צעקה) for help, thence to the woman and her sons and back again to Elisha. In 8:1–6 it is to the king, not Elisha, to whom the woman appeals (ותצא לצעק) for help. Her problem, in fact, is caused by following the advice of the prophet to leave her country. In this narrative it is the king, not the prophet, who provides a very practical solution to her problem of dispossession. The prophet inadvertently caused the problem, and his role in the solution to the problem is a passive one. If anyone is legitimized in this narrative, it is the king, not Elisha. Prophetic legitimation cannot be the motive behind the story, nor can it dictate its form. By imitating the form of 4:1–7, this story provides a clever reversal of the prophet's power and reduces the prophet to a very human level (cf. 6:33).

7–15 Eissfeldt again designates this pericope as "prophetic legend" (*Introduction*, 46). DeVries's "superseding oracle narrative" (*Prophet against Prophet*, 64–65) provides an alternative genre and Long's "oracle actualization story" (*VT* 23 [1973] 347) offers yet a third possibility. All, however, establish the genre on the basis of external criteria, and the parallels used (2 Kgs 3—Long; 1 Kgs 22—DeVries) are not enough to establish a firm genre. The passage must first be analyzed in its present form.

This story moves through five successive stages. In vv 7–8, the scene is set. Elisha had traveled to Damascus coincident with Ben Hadad's seeking an oracle concerning his sickness. The section ends with the all-important question האחיה מחלי זה "shall I recover from this illness?" V 9 tells of Hazael's obedience to his king's wishes, and ends with the same question. V 10 provides Elisha's response to the question, which is quite ambiguous. He first suggests to Hazael that he inform the king that he will recover, then offers a revelation that the king will die. This is not a "superseding oracle," since the first statement is not given as an oracle. A stylistic feature is the balance between the first response (חיה תחיה "you shall indeed recover"), and the oracle (מות ימות "he will certainly die"). Vv 11–13 offer explanation for the double answer in the previous verse. The reality of brutal war between Israel and Syria drives Elisha to tears. Why this should be is explained by a further revelation הראני יהוה אתך מלך על ארם "the Lord has shown me you as king over Syria" (v 13*b*). In vv 14–15 is a repetition of the language of Hazael's to the prophet, this time reversed as he retreats to his king. In v 15, which is introduced with the fulfillment formula ויהי "and it was" (cf. 7:16*b*, 18*a*, 20*a*), the oracle concerning the death of Ben Hadad is fulfilled, as is the revelation concerning the succession of Hazael. This latter point is important, since Hazael was not in the normal line of succession, being a "son of nobody." The balance between vv 9–13 and vv 14–15 is clear and can be illustrated in the following way:

Vv 9–13	*Vv 14–15*
וילך חזאל לקראתו ויקח מנחה "and Hazael went to meet him"	וילך "and he went"
ויבא ויעמד לפניו ויאמר "and he came and stood before him and said"	ויבא אל אדניו ויאמר "and he came to his master and said"
ויאמר אליו אלישע "and Elisha said to him"	מה אמר לך אלישע "What did Elisha say to you?"
לך אמר לו "Go and say to him"	ויאמר לי "and he said to me"
חיה תחיה והראני יהוה כי "You shall certainly live but Yahweh has shown me that"	חיה תחיה "you will certainly live"

Form/Structure/Setting

מות תמות	ויהי ממחרת . . . ימת
"he shall certainly die."	"But on the following day he died"
הראני יהוה	
"Yahweh has shown me"	
אתך מלך על ארם	וימלך חזאל תחתיו
"that you will be king over Syria."	"and Hazael reigned in his place."

The links between these two sections of the story tempt one to think of chiasmus, but this cannot be sustained. While vv 9 and 14 provide a framework for v 13, the stress on the succession of Hazael dominates in the final verse. Out of the original question of Ben Hadad come four answers, not one as suggested by DeVries and Long. Elisha states that Ben Hadad will recover, then that he will die. He speaks clearly of war and oppression, and finally says that Hazael will succeed to the Syrian throne. All of these statements, with the exception of the first, are fulfilled. The peculiarities of this narrative, such as the naming of Hazael as opposed to the unnamed messengers of chapter one, arise out of the context. With its climax of the oracle in the succession of Hazael and the climax of the series of fulfillments in the succession of Hazael, the purpose of the story becomes clear. It explains how Hazael became king of Syria and how this affects the subsequent history of Israel. From this point on in 2 Kings, Hazael assumes the role of the main oppressor of Israel (cf. 9:14; 10:32; 12:17–18; 13:3, 22).

16–24 The account of the reign of Jehoram of Judah is a mixture of types of literature. The "death and burial formula" in vv 16–18 is a common one in 1 and 2 Kings. V 19 is an editorial comment in which the delay of Judah's punishment is justified theologically. V 21 bears all the marks of an official campaign report. It alludes to the direction of the military expedition, including the verb "to cross over" (ויעבר), to the "rising up" to fight, to the outcome of the battle, and to the flight of the vanquished. A parallel is found in the campaign record from the fourteenth year of Shalmaneser III (*ANET*, 280). There the formal elements are present in the same order. A major difference is that the biblical account records the defeat for Judah, not its victory. V 22 is an allusion to the continuing disintegration of the Judean kingdom under Jehoram, and the pericope ends with the formal conclusion to his reign of the type found throughout the books of Kings.

Vv 25–27 constitute a formal introduction to the reign of Ahaziah of Judah (cf. Burney, *Notes*, ix–xiii). The language of v 28 is again the precise and dispassionate language of the military report (cf. *ANET*, 279–81). This incident of Joram's abortive attempt to defeat Syria and Ahaziah's visit to the wounded Israelite king place both kings at one place, and prepare for the events of chapter nine.

The prehistory of the section is unclear. That the stories about Elisha come from circles of his supporters can be taken for granted. But that these supporters were as diversified in their interests as DeVries indicates (*Prophet against Prophet*, 118–19, 121–22) is difficult to imagine. The thesis that the chapter grew from independent sections drawn from an "early legitimation collection" (vv 1–6), an "early Syrian war collection" (vv 7αβb–15), a Jehu "accession narrative" and a "later Syrian war collection," all bound together with redactional cement, begs several questions. In such distinctions as "early" and "late" Syrian war collections, DeVries has moved out of the realm of form, genre, and plot analysis, into value judgments on content which are unrelated to form.

The annotations of the compiler concerning the exploits of two neighboring kings (vv 20–22, 28–29) do resemble ancient battle reports and could well be assigned to such archival sources, save for one detail which betrays the artistry of the writer. These accounts record the defeat of the chief protagonists, and the further disintegration of their kingdoms. Defeats are not the subject of such ancient battle reports, unless they involve enemies of the writer. Only victories are recorded, for obvious purposes. In mimicking this style of writing with which the author was familiar, the material borders on parody.

Comment

The incident recorded in vv 1–6 rounds off the dealings of Elisha with the Shunemite woman.

1 וגורי באשר תגורי "and sojourn for a while somewhere else." See the translation above. This use of the imperfect implied indefiniteness. Cf. S. R. Driver, *Tenses*, 42–43; Driver, *Deuteronomy*, 31. The woman who had so confidently announced to Elisha her self-sufficiency in 4:13 is now forced to flee her homeland in time of great need. There is a note of tragedy here.

כי קרא יהוה לרעב "for Yahweh has summoned a famine." The famine referred to here is the one caused by the siege of Samaria in chap. 6. The former was apparently short-lived and the direct result of the attack of the Syrians on the capital city. There is no indication that that famine was widespread.

אתי וביתך "you and your household." Since Elisha implies that the woman is responsible for the welfare of her household would suggest that her husband, described as old in 4:14, was now dead. Her property was probably held in trust by the crown during her absence (so Gray, 527; de Vaux, *Ancient Israel*, 1:124). On the complicated business of property and property rights cf. Pedersen, *Israel I–II*, 81–96; de Vaux, *Ancient Israel*, 1:166–77.

2 בארץ פלשתים "in the land of the Philistines." That the woman should choose to go to the territory of the Philistines is understandable. It was situated on the southwest coastal plain of Judah where rainfall was quite adequate to support a good agricultural life. Even today the area is renowned for its fertility (cf. Aharoni, *The Land of the Bible*, 23; Orni and Efrat, *Geography of Israel*, 45–47).

3 ותצא לצעק "and she went to lodge a complaint." This is a legal procedure. The king was also the chief magistrate of the country, responsible for the welfare of his subjects. On this cf. Whitelam, *The Just King*. See also 2 Sam 8:15.

4 This conference between the king and Elisha's former servant is most interesting. Presumably, Gehazi had found some kind of refuge at court after his deceit of chap. 5. There is no reason to place this episode earlier than chap. 5, since it is quite possible that by this time Gehazi had been cured of his leprosy (so Skinner, 314). Jewish tradition did not deal kindly with Gehazi (cf. *Comment* above on 5:20–28). This incident demonstrates the widespread interest in the activities of Elisha even during his lifetime. To assume that the prophet was dead by this time (so Gray, 529; DeVries, *Prophet against Prophet*, 120–21) is unnecessary. There is no hint of this in the story.

6 The subject of the king's interrogation could have been the activities of Elisha or the plight of the woman, or both. The story continues by dealing solely with the latter.

ויתן . . . סריס "and he appointed a eunuch." Although the term is normally translated "eunuch," and can be understood as such here, it did have a wider application. Potiphar is so named in Gen 39:1, and the Rab Saris of 2 Kgs 18:17 is a high military official. Cf. C. U. Wolf, "Eunuch," *IDB* 2:179–80. The king took the woman's plight seriously enough to appoint one of his own officials to be in charge of the restoration of her property. This is in sharp contrast to the land-grabbing activities of his predecessor, Ahab. Expropriation of land by the powerful is a constant target of the prophets' attack (e.g., Isa 5:8).

7 The incident which follows raises some interesting questions. What was the precise relationship between the prophet and the king of Syria, who is called his "son"? Did Elisha deliberately lie? Josephus embellishes this account considerably by having Ben Hadad fall sick on learning that the Israelite God had worked against him in the expedition of chap. 6 (cf. *Antiq.* ix.87).

ויבא אלושע דמשק "and Elisha went to Damascus." In light of the Syrian king's ignorance of the prophet in 6:8–23, the king's subsequent request of the prophet is unusual. It betrays a remarkable increase in goodwill between the two men, and this in turn might explain Elisha's otherwise inexplicable journey to Damascus. Elijah had skirted the Syrian desert to escape capture by Jezebel (1 Kgs 19:15).

ובן הדד "and Ben Hadad." On the possible identification of this king cf. the *Comment* above on 6:24. Gray (528) does not identify Hadad-eser of the Assyrian inscriptions with the Syrian king mentioned here. Identifying him with the son of Hazael in 6:24–7:20 would imply that this text has been displaced from before chap. 6.

8 חזהאל "Hazael." In Assyrian inscriptions (cf. *ANET*, 280) reference is made to a battle between Shalmaneser III and Hazael. The latter's name is Haza'il, which supports the spelling in v 9. However, variants in proper nouns are not unusual in the OT. An additional inscription of Shalmaneser III (858–824 B.C.) mentions a serious defeat of Hadadeser (Ben Hadad I) at his hands, in which 20,900 Syrian troops were killed. The text reads "Hadadezer perished. Hazael, son of nobody, seized the throne. . . ." (Cf. *ANET*, 280.) Since the Assyrian text is unclear about the exact nature of Ben Hadad's demise, there need be no conflict with the biblical account.

האחיה מחלי זה "Shall I recover from this sickness?" The request of Ben Hadad echoes the request of Ahaziah of Israel in chapter one, and a thematic link is established between the two chapters.

9 בִּנְךָ בֶן־הֲדַד "your son, Ben Hadad." Elisha's relationship with this king had changed dramatically. The reasons are not given. The social relationship between kings and prophets warrants the use of the term "father" for the prophet (cf. 6:21; 13:14).

10 וְהִרְאַנִי יהוה "but Yahweh has shown me." The association of "seeing" and prophecy is a long-standing one (cf. G. von Rad, *Old Testament Theology* 2:50–69; J. Lindblom, *Prophecy in Ancient Israel,* 122–37). In 4:27, knowledge through vision is hidden from the prophet. It is in later prophetic literature that the literary form of vision becomes well-developed (cf. Amos 7:1–8:3; 9:1; Jer 1:11–13; etc.).

11 וַיָּשֶׂם עַד־בּשׁ "until he was embarrassed." Hazael is the subject here. He obviously wished for a solution to the puzzle presented to him by Elisha's response to Ben Hadad's inquiry. It is certainly not an allusion to Elisha's trance (so Skinner, 316).

12 The language is the stereotyped language of the description of the horrors of warfare in the ancient Near East. No one was safe from the ravages and the excesses of the victor (cf. Lam 5:6–22; Hos 10:14; 14:1; Nah 3:10).

13 מָה עַבְדְּךָ הַכֶּלֶב "What is your servant? A dog?" The reference to Hazael as a "dog," which was misunderstood by Josephus, is not necessarily a gesture of humility, but a common form of self-designation when a person is addressing a superior. The same is found in the Lachish Letters (ii:3–4; v:3–4; vi:2–3). Cf. Gibson, *Syrian Semitic Inscriptions* 1:37, 43–45.

15 Gray (528, 532) acknowledges no assassination of Ben Hadad by Hazael in this action. The "coverlet" is regarded as a kind of mosquito net, which when dipped in water would act as a cooler for the person in bed. He sees here nothing more than the discovery of Ben Hadad's death in the morning when the coverlet was removed. While the Assyrian records (*ANET,* 280) do not mention the mode of death, they do allow for a violent death. The assassination might have been to rid Syria of a weak and ailing king. In other Assyrian records (*ANET,* 280–81) Hazael fared no better than his predecessor. According to Josephus (*Antiq.* ix. 93–94), the Syrians deified both Hazael and Ben Hadad. The source of this tradition is unknown, but it might be Josephus' own ignorance of the northwest Semitic god, Hadad, whose existence is now well known. Josephus also adds considerable color to the narrative by exaggerating Joram's relief at Ben Hadad's death.

16 There is a briefer summary of Jehoram's reign in 9:14*b*–15*a*. That the latter text is more original is likely, but doublets do not automatically indicate literary and chronological dependency of one text upon another.

בִּשְׁנַת חָמֵשׁ לְיוֹרָם "in the fifth year of Joram." This dating for Jehoram of Judah conflicts with other data. In 1:17*b* Joram of Israel becomes king in the second year of Jehoram of Judah. In 3:1 Joram of Israel becomes king in the eighteenth year of Jehoshaphat of Judah, Jehoram's predecessor, and 1 Kgs 22:42 states that Jehoshaphat reigned for twenty-five years. V 1:17*b* has been dealt with elsewhere. Even if 3:1 and 1 Kgs 22:42 were accepted at face value, the present text would conflict since the fifth year of Joram would then be the twenty-third of Jehoshaphat. Three solutions have been suggested.

First, W. F. Albright (*BASOR* 100 [1945] 20–21) suggests a rewriting of

2 Kgs 3:1 as the twenty-fifth year of Jehoshaphat. Then Shenkel (*Chronology and Recensional Development*) argues that the references which place Jehoshaphat during the ministry of Elisha are secondary. They represent attempts by the Hebrew text to make Elisha the contemporary of a "good" king. Finally, Thiele (*The Mysterious Numbers of the Hebrew Kings*, 65) and Gray (65–67, 532) would argue for a coregency of Jehoshaphat and Jehoram.

1:17*b* is secondary. Albright's emendation of the text is arbitrary and without any textual support. Shenkel's arguments on the priority of 1:17*b* and the secondary nature of the references to Jehoshaphat can be used either way, and are inconclusive. If the theory of a co-regency is adopted, no emendation of the text is needed. 1 Kgs 22:42 can also stand, and it permits the reference to Jehoshaphat in 8:16 to remain intact.

18 כי בת אחאב היתה לו לאשה "because he had married Ahab's daughter." The daughter of Ahab was the notorious Athaliah of 11:1. According to 2 Chr 21:4, Jehoram killed off all possible rivals to the throne. Josephus (*Antiq.* ix.95–96) mentions that this was done at the prompting of Athaliah. The purge would have silenced any opposition to the pro-Israelite policies of the king and his wife. It also presages the activities of this queen in chap. 11.

כאשר עשו בית אחאב "just as the house of Ahab had done." The standard of evil established by Jeroboam I (cf. 1 Kgs 15:34) is temporarily displaced by the sins of the house of Ahab.

19 ולא אבה יהוה להשחית "but Yahweh did not want to destroy." The narrator explains the delay in the punishment of the Judean royal house by an appeal to a theological motif, the Davidic covenant. This gives the impression of ambivalence on the part of God. The aspect of longevity was basic to the promise to David (cf. 2 Sam 7:12–17; Pss 89:27–37; 132:11–12). However, the initial condition attached to the covenant in 2 Sam 7:14 is expanded in subsequent repetitions of the covenant and includes obedience to the Mosaic law (cf. 1 Kings 2:1–4; 9:1–9). On the Davidic covenant cf. M. Noth, "David and Israel in 2 Sam 7," *The Laws in the Pentateuch and Other Studies*, tr. D. R. Ap-Thomas (Edinburgh/London: Oliver & Boyd, 1966) 250–59; and more recently Mettinger, *King and Messiah*, 42–63. The image of the lamp is found in 1 Kgs 11:36; 15:4.

20 וימלכו עליהם מלך "and they appointed their own king." This accords with 1 Kgs 22:48 which refers to the "deputy" (נצב) who governed Edom on behalf of Judah. It conflicts with 3:9, which refers to an Edomite "king" who accompanied Jehoshaphat and Joram on their abortive mission against Moab. According to Josephus (*Antiq.* ix.30, 97), the Edomites had by this time killed their ruler who was loyal to Jehoshaphat. The term מלך "thing" in 3:9 might be a general term for "ruler" (so Gray, 533).

21 ויעבר . . . צעירה "so he crossed over to Seir." The identification of צעיר is unknown, although it is safe to assume that it was close to the border between Judah and Edom. The reference to "crossing over" might well indicate that it was beyond the border. The form of צעירה is unusual. It is either a locative ending, or a form of the diminutive (so Montgomery, 396–98). Some identify it with Zoar of Gen 13:10 (so Montgomery, 398; Aharoni, *Land*, 309). The problem with this is that G consistently translates

צעיר as Σιγωρ not Σειρ as it is here. The G rendering is normally reserved for שעיר (Seir), but the change in the Hebrew is considerable, although not impossible. Gray's identification of the site with ציער located in southeast Judah, not far from Hebron (Josh 15:54) is possible, but again involves an emendation of the Hebrew, and does not accord with G. According to the *Onomasticon* of Eusebius, Σειωρ is to be identified with the mountains of southern Edom (Gen 14:6). The confusion is reflected in 2 Chr 21:9, which arbitrarily offers עם שריו "people of Seir."

הוא קם לילה "one night he mustered." The verb קם in this context is best understood as a technical military term, in the same way that עלה is used in similar contexts. Cf. Deut. 19:11; Judg 7:15; 8:20, 21; 9:32; 2 Sam 23:10; Isa 14:22; and Amos 7:9.

The second part of this verse is confusing (cf. Burney, *Notes*, 295–96). A small change from ועת to ועתו would make better sense. Apparently the nighttime attack by Jehoram against the Edomites failed and he escaped with his chariot force. The latter part of the verse would suggest that either his infantry (העם) were left to fend for themselves and were routed, or that the whole army deserted and returned home from the field of battle. Cf. 3:24. For an alternative cf. Herzog and Gichon, *Battles of the Bible*, 160–61.

22 Josephus (*Antiq.* ix.98) exaggerates the depravity of Jehoram by having him force the Judeans to worship foreign gods.

ויפשע אדום "and Edom rebelled." The writer now begins to document the apostasy of Judah by linking the rebellion of Edom and Libnah to that fact. The location of Libnah is unknown, although Tel Barnat is a likely candidate (cf. Aharoni, *Land*, 199, 292–93). It is frequently mentioned as being in southwest Judah (Josh 15:42) along with Lachish and Gezer. In 1 Chr 6 it is listed as a levitical city. Skinner's suggestion (318) that it was a Philistine city is strange. Its rebellion reflects the uncertain state of affairs that periodically afflicts border towns.

On death and burial formulas such as this, cf. Smit, "Death and Burial Formulas in Kings and Chronicles Relating to the Kings of Judah," *Biblical Essays*, 173–77. 2 Chr 21:19 adds the detail, from an unknown source, of the death of Jehoram by some horrible sickness.

25 According to v 16 Jehoram of Judah began to reign in the fifth year of Joram of Israel and reigned eight years. The chronologies do not accord. A radical solution is offered by Strange (*VT* 25 [1975] 191–201) who suggests that the two Jehorams are to be identified, and that the Joram of Israel is a ghost invented by the deuteronomist. On this see the *Introduction*.

26 עתליהו בת עמרי "Athaliah, daughter of Omri." On the reading "Omri" see the *Notes* above. The term בת could mean "female descendant," rather than biological daughter. The masculine בן has the same broad application. Cf. Haag, *TDOT* 2:332–38.

27 הוא ... כי חתן "because he was a son-in-law." Strictly speaking, Jehoram was son-in-law to the house of Ahab, but the term can indicate a person related by marriage (cf. BDB, 368).

28 וילך את־יורם בן־אחאב "and he went with Joram, son of Ahab." Since no record of Ahaziah's fate in the war with Syria is given, the precise meaning of his "going with" Joram is unclear. It could mean that Ahaziah, related by marriage to the northern king, gave general support to the policies of Israel. Athaliah would certainly encourage this kind of activity. Herzog and Gichon suggest (*Battles of the Bible*, 127–28) that the campaign was part of an ongoing war between the allies and Syria which was started with the repulsion of Israel and Judah from Moab some years before.

ברמת גלעד "in Ramoth Gilead." Ramoth Gilead became a perpetual fighting area between Israel and Syria and is usually identified with Tel Ramith, some forty-five kilometers southeast of the Sea of Galilee. A major approach to this site would be across the Jordan and along the Yarmuk valley. With the recounting of this incident, the writer is beginning to establish the circumstances which would see the fulfillment of the prophecy against the house of Ahab.

29 ברמה "in Ramah." Cf. *Notes* above. This is not to be identified with the Ramah of Samuel's activity, but is another rare name for Ramoth Gilead (cf. Cohen, *IDB* 4:10).

ביזרעאל "in Jezreel." Although the versions differ on this reading, Jezreel is a perfectly obvious place for the wounded king to stop. En route from Ramoth Gilead to Israel, it is the first major city which would provide refuge from Joram. It also serves a dramatic purpose. It puts the king at the very place where Ahab expropriated Naboth's vineyard, and it sets in motion the series of events which culminate in the destruction of that apostate dynasty.

Explanation

The two sections of chap. 8, vv 1–6 and vv 7–29, appear to be records of disconnected events. The adaptation of the pattern of 4:1–7 in the first section (see above) has provided an interesting twist to the narrative in which the prophet, although motivated by his concern for the welfare of the Shunemite, is the unwitting cause of additional problems for her. It is finally the king who is able to restore to her what she had lost. Interesting also in this brief narrative is the reappearance of Gehazi. His deceit is now behind him, and he is apparently cured of his leprosy. Contrary to his earlier appearances, he now acts for the benefit of someone other than himself. He did not fare as well in subsequent tradition.

What purpose does the story have in its present position? It does not provide a fitting introduction to the historical events which follow in that the woman is quite unconnected with kings and wars. But the themes of the story, of exile, loss and restoration, do in fact provide a suitable beginning for the tales which follow, of loss, exile, and restoration on a much broader political scale. The narrative acts as a prefiguring of the adventures of King Joash (cf. chaps. 11 and 12) who is exiled, or dispossessed for seven years, only to be reinstated. The narrative also foreshadows the larger exile of Judah, her return and restoration (cf. Jer 32:44; 33:11, 26; 49:3, 6). The deterioration of the fortunes of Israel and Judah has already begun and is hastened in the stories which follow.

The story of the death of Ben Hadad recalls many of the themes of chap. 1. Even the peculiar spelling of the monarchs' requests is repeated (cf. 1:2; 8:8–9). Elisha's relationship to Ben Hadad has changed markedly from chap.

7. The prophet is sought out by the king, and warrants the greatest respect from the ailing monarch. The details and problems of the story have been discussed above and need not be repeated here. What is important about the story is its introduction of the figure of Hazael to the stage of history. In many ways he was a perfect counterpart to his contemporary, Jehu. Both were usurpers, not from the line of royalty, and both took their respective thrones by force. Both actions had a profound effect upon the subsequent history of Israel. From this point on Hazael emerges as the most serious Syrian threat to date to both Israel and Judah. Hazael's reign inaugurated a period of political chaos in which Syria moved outward and eastward to threaten the borders of both Israel and Judah.

In the chronological and archival notes at the end of the chapter, the theological judgments upon the various kings of Judah and Israel are important. They bring to mind again the writer's motivation for presenting this material, namely, to offer a theological interpretation of the history of Israel and Judah according to the standards of the book of Deuteronomy. With this in mind, the writer draws clear lines between the activities of the kings of Israel and Judah and the fate of the nations during their reigns. The sins of Ahab now influence the southern kingdom of Judah in the accession of Jehoram ben Jehoshaphat, who married Athaliah, and Ahaziah ben Jehoram, the son born of that union. Both are influenced by their pedigree, and their nation suffers the consequences of their misdeeds. Israelite and Judean power continues to be whittled away.

The additional losses of territory and the growing threat of Syria bring the two monarchs, Joram and Jehoram, together as they wage war against Hazael at Ramoth Gilead. The wounds inflicted by the Syrians upon Joram of Israel eventually cause the action to be shifted back to the city of Jezreel, the scene of Ahab's crime against Naboth. The next act in the drama is inevitable.

Jehu (9:1-37)

Bibliography

Elat, M. "The Campaigns of Shalmaneser III against Aram and Israel." *IEJ* 25 (1975) 25–35. **Frost, S. B.** "Judgment on Jezebel, or a Woman Wronged." *TToday* 20 (1964) 503–17. **Gehman, H. S.** "The Burden of the Prophets." *JQR* 31 (1940) 107–21. **Ishida, T.** "The House of Ahab." *IEJ* 25 (1975) 135–37. **Miller, J. M.** "The Elisha Cycle and the Accounts of the Omride Wars." *JBL* 85 (1966) 441–54. ———. "The Fall of the House of Ahab." *VT* 17 (1967) 307–24. **Napier, B. D.** "The Omrides of Jezreel." *VT* 9 (1959) 366–78. **Parker, S. B.** "Jezebel's Reception of Jehu." *Maarav* 1 (1978) 67–78. **Parzen, H.** "The Prophets and the Omride Dynasty." *HTR* 33 (1940) 69–96. **Rad, G. von,** "Royal Ritual in Judah." In *The Problem of the Hexateuch and Other Essays.* Edinburgh: Oliver & Boyd, 1966. 222–31. **Rendtorff, R.** "Erwägungen zur

Fruhgeschichte des Prophetentums in Israel." *ZTK* 59 (1962) 145–67. **Smith, C. C.** "Jehu and the Black Obelisk of Shalmaneser III." In *Scripture in History and Theology,* ed. A. L. Merriland and T. W. Overholt. Pittsburgh: The Pickwick Press, 1977. 71–106.

Translation

[1] *Now Elisha the prophet had called to one of the sons of the prophets and said to him, "Put on your traveling clothes, and take this flask* [a] *of oil in your hand, then go to Ramoth Gilead.* [b] [2] *You will arrive there and see Jehu son of Jehoshaphat son of Nimshi.* [a] *You shall go in and take him from among the group of his brother officers, and bring him into the inner room.* [3] *Then you shall take the flask of oil, pour it out upon his head, and say, 'Thus has Yahweh declared, "I have anointed you as king for* [a] *Israel." ' Then open the door and run away. Do not wait around."*
[4] *Then the young man, the prophet's young man that is,* [a] *went to Ramoth Gilead.* [5] *When he arrived the officers were settling in, and he said, "Captain, I have a word* [a] *for you." Jehu replied, "For me, out of all who are here?" He said, "Just for you, captain."* [6] *So he arose and went into the house,* [a] *and the servant poured the oil upon his head and said, "Thus has Yahweh declared, the God of Israel, 'I have anointed you as king for the people of Yahweh, for* [b] *Israel.* [7] *Now you shall strike* [a] *the house of Ahab your master* [b] *and avenge the blood* [c] *of my servants the prophets, and the blood of all the servants* [d] *of Yahweh who suffered at the hand of Jezebel.* [8] *The whole of the house of Ahab shall be destroyed,* [a] *and I shall cut off for Ahab those who piss against the wall, and even those locked up and forsaken in Israel.* [9] *I shall make the house of Ahab like the house of Jeroboam son of Nebat and like the house of Baasha son of Ahiah.* [10] *And as for Jezebel, the dogs shall devour her in the allotment of Jezreel,* [a] *and there shall be no one to bury her.' " Then he opened the door and fled.*
[11] *Then Jehu went out to his master's servants, and someone said to him, "Is everything all right?* [a] *Why did this crazy man visit you?" He replied, "Oh, you know the man and his babble."* [12] *But they persisted, "Do not lie. Tell us." So he said,* [a] *"Thus and so he spoke to me, 'Thus has Yahweh declared, "I have anointed you king for Israel." ' "* [13] *Then to a man they rushed out and grabbed their garments, and set them down underneath him on the uncovered* [a] *steps. They blew the shophar and declared, "Jehu has become king!"*
[14] *Thus it was that Jehu son of Jehoshaphat son of Nimshi* [a] *plotted against* [b] *Joram. (Now Joram had been keeping watch in Ramoth Gilead with the whole Israelite army in front of Hazael king of Syria.* [15] *But Joram had returned to be healed in Jezreel of the wounds which the Syrians inflicted upon him during the war with Hazael king of Syria.) Jehu said, "May this not enter your minds,* [a] *let no one escape secretly from the city to go and broadcast* [b] *this in Jezreel."*
[16] *Then Jehu mounted his chariot and set off toward Jezreel, because Joram* [a] *was resting there, and Ahaziah king of Judah had gone down to see Joram.* [b] [17] *Now there was a watchman standing in the watchtower at Jezreel, and he saw the commotion Jehu caused as he approached, and he said, "I can see a commotion."* [a] *Joram said, "Select a rider and send him out to meet them, and to ascertain whether everything is all right."* [18] *So the rider set out on horseback to meet him, and said, "Thus has the king said, 'Is everything peaceful?' " Jehu replied, "What is peace to you? Turn*

about and fall in behind!" Then the watchman reported, *"The messenger has reached them,* ᵃ *but he has not returned."* ¹⁹ *So he sent a second rider, and he approached them* ᵃ *and said, "Thus has the king said, 'Is everything peaceful?' " And Jehu replied, "What is peace to you? Turn about and fall in behind me!"* ²⁰ *So the watchman reported, "He has reached them* ᵃ *but has not come back. The driving is like that of Jehu son of Nimshi, because he drives like a madman."* ᵇ
²¹ *Then Joram said, "Make ready!" So they made ready his chariot.* ᵃ *And Joram king of Israel and Ahaziah king of Judah, each in his chariot, went out to meet Jehu. They found him at the allotment of Naboth the Jezreelite.* ²² *When Joram met Jehu he too asked, "Is everything at peace Jehu?" and Jehu replied, "What peace is there so long* ᵃ *as there exist the harlotries and the many sorceries of your mother Jezebel?"* ²³ *Then Joram reined about and fled and shouted to Ahaziah, "It is a trap Ahaziah!"* ²⁴ *Jehu took his bow into his hand and struck Joram between the shoulder blades and the arrow went through into his heart and he sank down in his chariot.* ᵃ ²⁵ *He then said to Bidkar, his lieutenant,* ᵃ *"Pick him up,* ᵇ *and throw him onto the allotment of Naboth the Jezreelite, in the open. Remember, you and I* ᶜ *rode together as a team* ᵈ *behind Ahab his father, and Yahweh pronounced this oracle,* ᵉ ²⁶ *'Oh, if I did not see yesterday the blood of Naboth and the blood of his sons,' says Yahweh. 'I shall requite you* ᵃ *in this place,' says Yahweh. Now, throw him upon the allotment, according to the word of Yahweh."* ²⁷ *Now when Ahaziah king of Judah saw this he fled away by the road to Beth Haggan,* ᵃ *and Jehu pursued him and said, "Him too!" So they struck him down in his chariot on the ascent of Gur* ᵇ *at Ibleam, and he fled to Megiddo and died there.* ²⁸ *His servants* ᵃ *then transported him to Jerusalem and buried him in his tomb with his ancestors* ᵇ *in the city of David.* ²⁹ *It had been in the eleventh year of Joram son of Ahab that Ahaziah had become king over Judah.*
³⁰ *As Jehu was on his way to Jezreel, Jezebel heard the news and daubed paint on her eyes and fancied up her hair. Then she looked out of the window.* ³¹ *Jehu arrived at the gate, and she called out, "Is everything well Zimri, you master's assassin?"* ³² *He raised his face* ᵃ *toward the window and said, "Who is on my side,* ᵇ *who?" Then two or three eunuchs* ᶜ *looked in his direction.* ³³ *He said, "Throw her down!"* ᵃ *So they threw her down, and her blood spattered on the wall and on the horses, and they trampled over her.* ᵇ ³⁴ *Then he went inside, ate, and drank, then said, "Take care of this cursed woman and bury her. After all, she is the daughter* ᵃ *of a king!"* ³⁵ *They went to bury her, but found nothing of her except her skull, her feet and the palms of her hands.* ³⁶ *They went back inside and told him. He said, "This is the word of Yahweh which he spoke by the hand of his servant,* ᵃ *Elijah the Tishbite, 'In the allotment of Jezreel shall the dogs eat the flesh of Jezebel,* ³⁷ *and the corpse of Jezebel shall be like manure on the topsoil* ᵃ *of the allotment of Jezreel,* ᵇ *so that no one can say, This is Jezebel.' "* ᶜ

Notes

1.a. One Lucianic MS (e₂) suggests τῶν φακῶν "of the throne."

1.b. Variously spelled in many of the versions. Josephus (*Antiq.* ix.105) emphasizes its Syrian flavor with his rendering of Ἀραμώθη ἐν Γαλααδίτης "Ramoth in Gilead."

2.a. Josephus (Antiq. ix.105) follows G^L in changing the order to "Jehu son of Nimshi son of Jehoshaphat." That this is an accommodation to v 20 is clear. 6QReg 16 reads נמשי בוא,

Notes

which suggests that Nimshi was the last of the two names. Most of the versions have variant spellings for the names.

3.a. Many MSS read על "upon" for אל "toward." The two often become confused. Cf. 5:11; Burney, *Notes*, 297.

4.a. The article before the constr of הנער in the appositional phrase is clumsy. Many versions, including G^B, transpose the two, reading "the prophet, the young man," or leave them as two nouns in apposition, "the young man (that is) the prophet." Cf. G^{AN}.

5.a. G^L adds color with λογος μου κρυφιος "word of my lord."

6.a. G^B adds αὐτου "his."

6.b. G translates על "upon" for אל "toward."

7.a. G reads ἐξολεθρευσεις "utterly destroy." *BHS* suggests an original of והכרתה "you shall cut off" instead of הכיתה "you shall smite." Both verbs are violent enough, and the Gr is normally used for the Heb אבד.

7.b. G^B reads ἐκ προσωπου σου "from your face," possibly to balance the G opening of v 8.

7.c. G reads second pers sg.

7.d. עבדי is omitted by G and Josephus.

8.a. For ואבד "and it is destroyed" G reads και ἐκ χειρος = ומיד "and from the hand." Others (Syr, Tq) offer ואבדתי "I have destroyed."

10.a. Consistently in this narrative G^{BAo} reads "Israel" for "Jezreel."

11.a. G^L adds και εἰπον αὐτω "and said to him."

12.a. G^B adds και εἰπεν "and he said."

13.a. G^{BL} transliterate the Heb גרם with γαρεμ. G^{AN} and several miniscules offer various interpretations which are dependent upon the above transliteration (e.g., γαρ μιαν ἑνα, γαρ των ἑνα, γαρ ἑνα). G^L conflates the readings with ἐφ ἐν των γαρεμ ἐπι μιαν των ἀναβαομιδων.

14.a. *BHS* suggests the omission of the phrase בן־יהושפט "son of Jehoshaphat," but the evidence in support of this is slight.

14.b. Again G^L renders על "upon" for אל "to." The word קשר "conspire" is rare, but takes על "against" as a preposition (cf. 2 Chr 24:25, 26).

15.a. G renders Εἰ ἐστιν ἡ ψυχη ὑμων μετ᾽ ἐμου "if your soul is with me" while G^L offers the command ἐχετε ὑμεις την ψυχην "have your soul." Josephus (*Antiq.* ix.113), taking his cue from G, sees Jehu's comment as a reference to the support of his followers in the revolt and the subsequent assassination of Joram.

15.b. לגיד "to tell" is better read להגיד "to make known." Cf. Burney, *Notes*, 298.

16.a. G adds βασιλευς Ἰσραηλ "king of Israel" after יורם "Joram."

16.b. G^B here adds much of v 14, indicating why Joram happened to be in "Israel" (i.e., Jezreel) at this time.

17.a. G translates the Heb שפעת "multitude" with κονιορτος "dust cloud," and G^L adds του ὀχλου "of the multitude," which appears to have influenced Josephus (*Antiq.* ix.114). On reading שפעה for שפעת cf. Burney, *Notes*, 298.

18.a. With *BHS*, read "to them."

19.a. G^B reads προς αὐτον "to him."

20.a. MT is clumsy, *BHS* suggests עדיהם "as far as they."

20.b. MT בשגעון "with madness," which G renders ἐν παραλλαγη "swinging from side to side," although this hardly reflects the urgency of Jehu's mission. Josephus's comment (*Antiq.* ix.117) that Jehu "was going along rather slowly and in good order" (Marcus) seems entirely out of keeping with the sense of MT.

21.a. G^L reads pl, indicating that a larger force went out to meet Jehu. MT implies that the two kings suspected nothing until the very last minute, therefore they went out alone.

22.a. MT עד "until," G^B reads ἐτι (עוד) "yet."

24.a. G adds "upon his knees" (ἐπι τα γονατα αὐτου).

25.a. MT שלשה "lieutenant," which is better read שלשו "his lieutenant."

25.b. Omitted by G^B.

25.c. MT is awkward, Burney (*Notes*, 300) suggests following G, G^L, Vg, and Syr which all presuppose an expanded text כי זכר אני כי אני "For remember me that I." The MT lacuna would then be a result of homoioteleuton. But this argument cuts both ways.

25.d. MT את is awkward and ungrammatical. While צְמָדִים "paired together" might be better pointed צְמָדִים, it can stand. Cf. Burney, *Notes*, 300.

25.e. G translates with λημμα "burden," from λαμβανειν "to take."
26.a. G's αὐτω "to him" is to smooth out the text.
27.a. The place name is variously rendered by the versions. G reads Βαιθαν "Bethany?" G^L offers "Beth Horon" and G^A and S transliterate.
27.b. A number of variations on this name also exist.
28.a. G expands with "on his chariot."
28.b. This phrase is omitted by G^B, but retained by G^A, A, Syr.
32.a. For פניו "his face," G^L reads עיניו "his eyes."
32.b. For the question מי אתי מי "who is with me?" G offers Τις εἰ συ = מי אתך "who is with you?"
32.c. G reads only δυο "two." The double numeral is not unusual. Cf. Isa 17:6.
33.a. Better read as שמטוה "throw her down."
33.b. MT וירמסנה "she was trampled," which is better read וירמסוה "they trampled her" with G^L.
34.a. A minor MS (G^X) reads "mother."
36.a. עבדו "his servant" is omitted by G^B, but included by G^L.
37.a. For שדה "field," Syr and Vg read the equivalent of אדמה "soil."
37.b. בחלק יזרעאל "in the allotment of Jezreel" omitted by G^L.
37.c. For this clause G^B offers μη εἰπειν αὐτους Ἰεζαβελ "no one will say this is Jezebel."

Form/Structure/Setting

As with most of the Elisha stories, DeVries has offered a detailed analysis of this chapter (*Prophet against Prophet*, 56, 67–69, 90, 119, 122). He sees the chapter as having four redactional stages: (1) an original prophetic narrative ("prophetic fulfillment") contained in vv 1–8a, 10–14a, 15b–16a, 17–25a, 27, 30–36a, and prefaced by 8:29b; (2) the stage of incorporation into a "Jehuite accession narrative" consisting of vv 8a, 25b–26, 36b–37; 10:1–28; (3) deuteronomistic additions in vv 8b–9, 14b, 28; 10:29–31; and (4) a "late chronological gloss" (v 29). The original oracle came from those prophetic circles who honored Elisha and who wished to record vengeance upon Jezebel for her treatment of the prophets. The Jehuite accession narrative seeks to glorify the downfall of the house of Ahab, and to legitimize Jehu. The deuteronomistic material would bring the narrative into accord with similar statements elsewhere.

Details of this redactional process are vague and the reasons for the breaks in the narrative are unclear or ambiguous. For example, that 8:29b shows no awareness of 8:29a is a value judgment. That the second half of the verse repeats the first half or its substance is a critical observation which might be open to one or more interpretations. That it automatically presents evidence of sources begs the question. The delineation of such "sources," whether redactional additions or subsidiary narratives in the chapter is not necessarily helpful in the attempt to understand the chapter in its present form. The following analysis will demonstrate that the chapter has a distinct character to which the language and style of its composition lend themselves well.

1–10 These verses consist of two main sections, vv 1–3, the command of Elisha to the young prophet, and vv 4–10, the carrying out of the command. Each section moves swiftly and a strong sense of balance is maintained between the two.

The syntax of the opening (conjunction + subject + verb + object) expresses either contemporaneity with the previous incident, or temporal priority to it (cf. R. J. Williams, *Hebrew Syntax*, 96–97). This construction is also found in the opening verses of chaps. 3, 4, 5, 6, and 8. Vv 2–3 follow a sequence of *waw* consecutives + perfects, instructing the young man to go to Ramoth Gilead, take Jehu, anoint him, give a confirmation of his kingship, and retreat quickly. With some minor alterations, the verb sequence in vv 4–10 is precisely the same.

The effect of such a balance of verbs is to give to the narrative a sense of inevitability. Absolutely nothing goes wrong in the young man's carrying out of the orders of Elisha. They are carried out to the letter. Unlike the narratives of chaps. 4 or 5, there are no plot surprises or possible frustration of plans.

The oracle given by the young man in vv 7–10 is the subject of some debate. For DeVries, v 8*a* is part of the Jehuite redaction and vv 8*b*–9 are deuteronomistic redaction (*Prophet against Prophet*, 90, 119). Such texts contain theological or political tendencies and vv 8*b*–9 have affinities with previous texts. V 8*a* is in keeping with much that is critical of Ahab's dynasty. However, it is doubtful whether these texts are to be interpreted as part of fortuitous redactional activity. The text must be understood in its present shape.

Vv 7–10 contain two elements: (1) the statement concerning the striking down of the house of Ahab and the vengeance because of the prophets (v 7); (2) the stereotyped expansion in which all males, bond or free, will be cut off, and Ahab's house will suffer the same fate as that of Jeroboam. It is clear that these verses have much in common with 1 Kgs 14:4–11; 16:1–3; and 21:17–24. The common element, however, is not the so-called "deuteronomistic" element, the second part, but the complete structure. Each of the oracles contains the same two elements, the oracle which has immediate relevance to the situation addressed; the stereotyped expansion concerning the cutting off of all males and the making of that particular dynasty like that of a destroyed predecessor. Exactly the same device is found in vv 7–10. An oracle relevant to the immediate situation is followed by the stereotyped curse (vv 7, 8–9). That the young man expanded on the words of the prophet Elisha is not unique. It brings to a climax the accumulation of sins on the kings of Israel and the judgment upon those kings from Jeroboam to Joram. This is not accomplished by haphazardous redactional activity, but by purposeful narrative writing.

11–37 It is customary to break this second major section down into smaller paragraphs (vv 11–13, 14–15, 16–29, 30–37). This is quite proper since each of these sections describes a "scene" in the ongoing drama of the downfall of the house of Ahab. Such natural divisions do not necessarily reveal the hidden sources of the narrative.

Vv 11–13 are a dialogue between Jehu and his fellow officers. Until the final verses, the action moves only at the level of conversation. The officers ask for an account of the young man's words and will not be diverted by Jehu's generalities. In v 12, Jehu repeats the oracle in its briefest form. This repetition provides an echo of vv 1–10 (cf. vv 3, 6). The response of Jehu's fellow officers is immediate and enthusiastic. It lends confirmation to the revolt and the subsequent accession of Jehu.

The action of the officers bears some resemblance to other accounts of coronations in the OT, that of Solomon (1 Kgs 1:38–40) and that of Jehoash of Judah (2 Kgs 11:9–12). In both these other accounts the circumstances are similar, namely, a secretive coronation in the face of opposition. Those who anoint the king perform a symbolic action (1 Kgs 1:38*b*–39*a*; 2 Kgs 11:12*a*), make a noise to proclaim their new king. In spite of von Rad's statement to the contrary ("Royal Ritual in Judah," *The Problem of the Hexateuch and Other Essays*, 222–31, esp. 223), the action of the officers in this text is a parallel. But whether it reflects a literary parallel, and therefore provides evidence of a literary genre, or whether it shows that the royal ritual in the north was similar to that in the south is not clear. The latter is the more likely. The institutions of the two nations would not have been so different.

Vv 14–15, which introduce the next scene, sketch the chronological background of what follows. With few minor exceptions, v 15*a* repeats 8:29*a* word for word. DeVries (*Prophet against Prophet*, 90, 119) identifies v 14*b* as deuteronomistic and v 15*a* as part of the Jehuite accession narrative, as an explanation of the repetition. It has therefore been included, but is superfluous. However, the deliberate nature of the narrative thus far cannot be ignored. These annotations serve to fix the precise temporal and circumstantial background for the events which follow. They provide an excellent transition to the second stage of the fulfillment of the oracle, namely, the death of the present leaders of the house of Ahab. The syntax of v 14*b* is quite regular, forming a circumstantial clause (Driver, *Hebrew Tenses*, 199, 232) and does not betray an insertion. With the *waw* consecutive which follows, a permissible translation is "Now Joram had been guarding. . . ." The statement "And Joram had returned to be healed in Jezreel . . ." sets up the next scene perfectly. Within the context of the present narrative, the verses find a valid place and aid in the inevitable movement of the story to its conclusion.

Vv 15*b*–29 present the next stage in the fulfillment of the young prophet's oracle, the end of both Joram and Ahaziah. This section moves with a rhythmic alternation between swift moving narrative sequences and brief reflective and explanatory comments. Syntactically, this is achieved by the use of (1) *waw* consecutives plus the imperfect, and (2) subordinate clauses consisting of the subject plus the perfect. The "rhythm" can be seen as follows:

(1)	(2)
vv 15*b*–16*a*	
	vv 16*b*–17*a*α
vv 17*a*β–20*a*α	
	vv 20*a*βb
vv 21–25*a*	
	vv 25*b*–27*a*
vv 27*b*–28	
	v 29

This rhythm does not imply the presence of secondary insertions, redactional or otherwise, but provides an outline of the narrative, which shows the speed at which the narrative proceeds and the presence of such explanatory pauses.

Comment 113

If this alternation is deliberate, then the judgment that vv 16*b*, 25*b*–26, 28, 29 are secondary to the original narrative (DeVries, *Prophet against Prophet*, 90, 119) is false. In each of the explanatory comments, the sense of inevitability is enhanced as each part fits into place.

Within this section one sequence is worthy of comment on its own. It is the threefold cycle which comprises Jehu's approach to Jezreel in vv 17–21. Twice riders are sent to meet the approaching party with the same result. On the third time the kings go out to meet Jehu (who has now been identified in v 20). A confrontation takes place. As this third revolution of the cycle develops, the climax of the narrative is reached with the murder of the kings and the fulfillment of the second part of the prophet's oracle. Already this device has been seen. In 1:9, 11, and 13 is the threefold cycle of the approach of the soldiers to Elijah on the mountain. The climax is reached on the third approach and a confrontation takes place. In 2:2–3, 4–5, 6 Elijah is nearing the end of his life and three times asks Elisha to leave him to go on alone. The climax is reached with Elisha's third oath in v 6*b*. Finally in 4:29–31, 32–34, and 35–36, only on the third attempt does the dead son of the Shunemite revive. This latter example is not as stylized as the others. The use of this type of writing betrays an important stylistic characteristic of the writer of these narratives.

Finally, the oracle which Jehu recalls in vv 25*b*–26 is unusual for a prophetic oracle. It bears little resemblance to classic prophetic oracles, save for the use of שלם "to requite" with יהוה "Yahweh." Its form is that of an oath, but in the light of the contents it might be a rather free recollection of an oracle of Elijah (1 Kgs 21:19?) where the principle of recompense is very much in evidence.

30–37 Apart from the circumstantial clauses (ואיזבל שמעה "Jezebel heard" v 30; ויהוא בא בשער "Jehu arrived at the gate" v 31), this narrative moves swiftly to its inevitable conclusion. It completes the third aspect of the prophet's oracle, namely, the ignominious death of Ahab's wife, Jezebel. The sequence of the narrative is built up through the use of *waw* consecutive plus imperfect. The gruesome details of the death provide a fulfillment of 1 Kgs 21:23 and 9:10, which are in turn the specific application of the general curse on the houses of Jeroboam, Baasha, and Ahab. The final verse completes the fulfillment with its reference to no memorial to Jezebel.

In its present form then, the narrative of chapter nine is a self-contained story in which each component has an important place. It demonstrates the relentless and inevitable fulfillment of the word of judgment uttered against the house of Ahab.

Comment

This chapter recounts the end of the dynasty founded by Omri (1 Kgs 16:15–28) and perpetuated by his infamous sons Ahab, Ahaziah, and Joram. The narrative is vivid and contains much of historical value. The dynasty is bloodily destroyed with the deaths of Joram and Jezebel.

1 ואלישע הנביא "Now Elisha the prophet." The combination of the proper noun and the designation "prophet" in this way is unique among the Elisha stories. Either the name is given, or the epithet "man of God." In his dealings with kings, however, the term "prophet" is preferred. לאחד מבני הנביאים "to one of the sons of the prophets." See above, *Excursus* on "Sons of the Prophets."

חגר מתניך "put on your traveling clothes" is usually translated "gird up your loins." It indicates preparation for some special task (cf. 4:29). לך רמת גלעד "go to Ramoth Gilead." Cf. the comments above on 8:28.

2 יהוא בן יהושפט בן נמשי "Jehu son of Jehoshaphat son of Nimshi." The name "Jehu" reflects the conservative religious circles from which the soldier came, as does the name of his father Jehoshaphat. The name means possibly, "The LORD is the one."

מתוך אחיו "from among the group of his brother officers." On the broad meaning of the term "אחי," in the OT cf. H. Ringgren, "אחי," *TDOT* 1:188–92. In this particular context the term has a meaning overlooked by Ringgren. Neither physical brothers, nor a religious community (Deut 1:16), but a military comradeship is intended. Cf. Deut 20:8; Judg 9:26, 31, 46, 56; 1 Sam 30:23. See also below on 10:13. חדר בחדר "the inner room." The prophet clearly intends the deed to be done in private. Cf. 6:12.

3 משחתיך "I have anointed you." Anointing of kings is not recorded often in the OT (1 Sam 10:1; 2 Sam 2:7; 1 Kgs 19:15; 2 Kgs 11:12; and 23:30). Without the anointing the order to the young man is almost identical to that in 1 Kgs 11:23–43. That anointing signified a charismatic succession in the north (so Gray, *I & II Kings*, 540) is unlikely, since the action was common to both north and south. The religious significance is that it designates persons and objects for a special purpose. Cf. K. H. Bernhardt, *Das Problem der altorientalischen Königsideologie im Alten Testament*, 84, 232–34.

4 הנער הנביא "the prophet's young man." Although the phrase is awkward, there is no reason to see it as a gloss (so Montgomery, *Kings*, 400–401).

5 שרי החיל "officers." These are the officers of a more junior rank than the commander-in-chief.

ישבים "settling in." Either the officers were resting during a lull in the fighting, while the armies "faced each other," or more is intended. There is merit to Gray's suggestion that they were already plotting the coup d'etat. The verb ישב is used to indicate consultation (cf. Ezek 8:1; 14:1; 20:1; etc.). השר "captain" is a polite form of address. Cf. 6:12.

6 אל עם יהוה "for the people of Yahweh." The use of this phrase echoes the traditions surrounding the choice of David as king (2 Sam 7:8) and of Jeroboam I (1 Kgs 11:23–43). Cf. R. Rendtorff, "Erwägungen zur Fruhgeschichte des Prophetentums in Israel," *ZTK* 59 (1962) 145–67, esp. 152–54.

7 Most commentators regard vv 7–10 as a deuteronomistic addition, but what happens in these verses is too important to be dismissed as a mere "intrusion" (Montgomery, *Kings*, 400). It is an accumulation of the curses against the evil kings of Israel, Jeroboam and Baasha, now coming to a climax with the judgment of the house of Ahab. The added feature is the judgment upon the woman Jezebel. Cf. 1 Kgs 14:6–11; 16:1–14; 21:21.

דמי עבדי הנביאים "the blood of my servants the prophets" is a reference

Comment

to 1 Kgs 18:4, 13. The use of the verb והכרתי "and I shall cut off" (v 8) might also echo the same incident. The tables are now turned.

8 משתין בקיר "those who piss against the wall." To the modern reader this is a rather crude way of expressing the death of the male members of the house. It appears to be an old form of threat (cf. 1 Sam 25:22). The second expression, incorporating "those locked up and forsaken," indicates the widespread nature of the coming purge. Not even prisoners are safe. Cf. 2 Kgs 14:26.

10 The reference to the fate of Jezebel is a specific application of a general threat found in 1 Kgs 14:11. In all of the preceding threats there is no reference to the lack of burial. Such a thing would follow from the nature of the death. In the later prophets the lack of burial is a disgrace. Cf. Jer 8:2; 16:4, 6; 22:19; 25:33.

11-13 Jehu's anointing as king is received enthusiastically by his fellow officers. This shows perhaps that the seeds for revolt were widely sown before this series of events was set in motion.

11 המשגע "crazy man." This is a word with a wide meaning. In Deut 28:34 it is madness following trauma. David feigns insanity, which resembles mental retardation (1 Sam 21:13). In Hos 9:7 and Jer 29:26 it is used as a derogatory term for prophets, good or bad. To see the expression in terms of prophetic ecstasy (so Montgomery, *Kings*, 401; Gray *I & II Kings*, 541-42) misses the point. Ecstatic behavior, such as that displayed by the prophetic band in 1 Sam 10, would not have been considered unusual in Israel, any more than the behavior of the ecstatic *mahhu* in Mesopotamia. In Jer 29:26 the use of the term applies not to the behavior of the prophets, but rather to their message (cf. also Mic 3:5-8). The term is used here simply as a demeaning and derogatory reference to one who was already known to be somewhat crazy. Jehu's comment reveals that the man was well known by the group of officers.

13 There is no other reference to an action such as this. Its echo in Matt 21:8 is irrelevant. The outer cloak was a symbol of personality and power (cf. chap. 2), and this action demonstrated the agreement of the officers with the revolt. Cf. S. Herrmann, *History of Israel in Old Testament Times*, 225-26.

אל גרם המעלות "on the uncovered steps" is an unknown architectural term. If the noun is derived from the verb גרם "to cut off," then dressed steps could be in mind.

ותקעו בשופר "they blew the shophar." The shophar was used to make a monotonous noise for the purposes of warning (Jer 6:17) or festivity (Ps 81:3). Here and in 1 Kgs 1:34 the latter sense is in mind. Cf. E. Werner, "Musical Instruments," *IDB* 3:469-76.

מלך יהוא "Jehu has become king." The oft-cited parallel with the Psalms (e.g., Ps 93:1; 97:1) is a false one. Jehu was king in Israel, not in Judah where such Psalms had their home. As a king Jehu was apparently not a good politician. Twice in the inscriptions from the reign of the Assyrian, Shalmaneser III (858-824 B.C.), he is mentioned (cf. *ANET*, 280; *ANEP*, 351-55). In both he is paying tribute, possibly in payment for help against Hazael. Also in both he is called "son of Omri" (DUMU-HU-UM-RI-I), which he clearly was not. However, until the reign of Sargon II (721–705 B.C.) Israel was known as the land of Omri (cf. Parpola, *Neo-Assyrian Toponyms*, 82–83). On the references to Omri in the Assyrian inscriptions cf. C. C. Smith, "Jehu and the Black Obelisk of Shalmaneser III," in *Scripture in History and Theology* (1977) 71–106.

14–15a These verses are considered by many to be an intrusion, and by Gray to be the original introduction to the reign of Jehu. They would therefore have been included here to account for the strange absence of Joram from Ramoth Gilead. See above, *Form/Structure/Setting*.

14 ויורם היה שמר "Now Joram had been keeping watch." The substitution of Jehu for Joram is favored by many, but is not necessary. Because of the obvious similarities, the relationship of this passage to 1 Kgs 22 has been raised (cf. J. M. Miller, "The Fall of the House of Ahab," *VT* 17 [1967] 307–24) and the suggestion has been made that 1 Kgs 22 is an artificial account of the death of Ahab based on 2 Kgs 9:14–15. While this would account for the absence of any record of the regaining of Ramoth Gilead after 1 Kgs 22, such an omission is not serious. From the reign of Solomon, when the town was a district capital (1 Kgs 4:13) until 1 Kgs 22, no reference is made to its capture by the Syrians, an event which must have taken place in the meantime. Ramoth Gilead was a border town, and as such was vulnerable to the fluctuating fortunes of war.

15 The repetition of 8:28–29 is again seen as evidence of literary dependency of one upon the other.

אם יש נפשכם "may this not enter your minds." Jehu is eliciting support from his fellow officers for the revolt, and the expression אל יצא פליט "let no one escape secretly" suggests that he expected some serious resistance from soldiers still loyal to the ailing king.

16–29 The approach of Jehu to Jezreel betrays a type of writing seen before. With the threefold cycle of questions and incidents it resembles the opening chapters of 2 Kings.

17 הצפה עמד "a watchman standing." This is not simply a regular watchman, but a lookout posted to warn against an anticipated danger. Cf. Job 15:22; Pss 37:32; 66:7. שפעה "commotion" is from the verb שפע "to flow abundantly." It is possible then that Jehu was accompanied by a sizeable force of men to assassinate Joram. This verse begins the cycle of three in the approach of the rebels to the royal abode.

18 עד הם "to them." Since all of the misspellings occur in reported speech, they could be uneducated colloquialisms.

20 בשגעון ינהג "he drives like a madman." Jehu's chariot driving is described with a word from the same root as משגע "crazy man" of v 11. His reputation as a reckless driver must have stayed with him all his years in the army, and was by now widespread.

21 וימצאהו בחקלת נבות "they found him at the allotment of Naboth." The concidence of the two kings' finding Jehu at Naboth's plot provides the writer with a fine twist to the plot. Ahab's family are now to "reap the whirlwind" at the symbolic site of Ahab's greed and apostasy.

22 זנוני איזבל "harlotries of Jezebel." This term must be metaphorical, since there is nothing in the preceding chapters that the queen was anything but a loyal wife to her husband. This being the case, there is here the continuation of the tradition of apostasy as adultery which is found in Judg 2:17; 8:33, and which is traced through the later prophets (Jer 2:1–13; Nah 3:4; Hosea). On the subject cf. H. D. Preuss, *Verspottung fremder Religionen im Alten Testament*, 73, 121. Not only does this imagery presuppose a "husband-wife" relationship between God and Israel (cf. Jer 2:1–13) which would provide a perfect polemic against the Baalism of the north, but it uncovers the true reasons for Jehu's revolt: a purge of Israelite worship. The avenging of Naboth is a secondary reason, albeit a convenient one. The revolt does not necessarily signify a change in the type of monarchy from an absolute to a more democratic one. That is not the point at issue here (contra Gray, *I & II Kings*, 547). Ahab's actions toward Naboth, although motivated by greed, were taken initially according to the rights of compensation (cf. Pedersen, *Israel I-II*, 81–83).

23 ויהפך . . . ידיו "then he reined about." A close parallel exists in 1 Kgs 22:34. The difference between the two texts is important. Here the king and Ahaziah are lone drivers, in their private chariots. They did not suspect any danger.

24 ויהוא מלא ידו "and Jehu took into his hand." Cf. 2 Sam 23:7. This is an idiomatic expression meaning he armed himself.

25 ויאמר אל בדקר שלשו "he then said to Bidkar, his lieutenant." That Bidkar was the "third man in the chariot" is unlikely. It would have been quicker to select another officer in another chariot to carry out this task than to stop to allow such a person to perform it, then board the chariot again. Military terms, such as שליש "third," have a tendency to lose their original meaning quickly, and become simply designations of rank. Two modern examples would be the use in English-speaking armies of the term "lieutenant" (i.e., one who stands in place of?), which is now a junior rank, and the modern Hebrew סרן for the rank of junior company commander, i.e., captain. Its original meaning was "tyrant." It is possible that a שליש commanded the kind of unit described in 11:5 (שלשית).

רכבים צמדים "rode together as a team." The term צמדים, which occurs only here and in 1 Kgs 19:19 in the plural, is used adverbially ("riding as teams" or "pairs"). No emendation of the term is needed. Not enough is known about the tactics of chariot warfare on the open field of battle during biblical times, but presumably chariots worked together in clusters to protect each other. Jehu's close relationship with Ahab is worthy of note and would place Jehu in early middle-age.

את המשא הזה "this oracle." Of a prophetic utterance the term משא is not used elsewhere in deuteronomistic literature. It occurs mainly in Isaiah 1–39, Nahum, Habakkuk, Zechariah, Malachi, and Lamentations. Cf. H. S. Gehman, "The Burden of the Prophet," *JQR* 31 (1940) 117.

26 The oracle quoted finds its closest parallel in Deut 32:43, not in prophetic literature. It might have been one of many unrecorded predictions concerning the fate of the house of Ahab. That the utterance is attributed to Elijah, not Elisha, would indicate that the resistance to Ahab's apostasy was quite broadly based.

27 Ahaziah's death was undoubtedly motivated by his relation to Ahab through his wife Athaliah. Ahaziah fled south from Jezreel, passing Beth Haggan (Jenin) toward Samaria, or Jerusalem. He was wounded at Ibleam near the "Ascent of Gur." Ibleam is identified with modern Bel 'almeh, a few kilometers south of Jenin. The "Ascent of Gur" remains unidentified. Gray's reconstruction of the geography of this incident is most confusing. If the wounded king made his way to Megiddo along the main road skirting the Plain of Jezreel (so *I & II Kings*, 548) he would have had to double back into the path of his pursuers, since that route would go northwest from Beth Haggan. A more plausible route was into the hills behind Megiddo, where a light chariot would have less difficulty that a heavy war chariot. Such weapons of war were designed for flat terrain. He eventually outdistanced them only to arrive at Megiddo to die. His destination was Ahab's great chariot city where some of his own entourage were billetted (cf. Yadin, *Hazor*, 207–32; "Megiddo," *EAEHL* 3:830–56, esp. 850–56).

29 The chronology differs from previous notes which have Ahaziah king in the twelfth year of Joram (8:25).

30–37 The details of the death of Jezebel show remarkable dramatic skill and character development. Both Jezebel and Jehu are revealed in their cynicism and callousness.

30 ותשם בפוך עיניה "and daubed paint on her eyes." The eye-paint was antimony trisulphide, which highlighted the eyes of the wearer. Cf. J. A. Thompson, "Cosmetics," *IDB* 1:701–2. An example of its effect is seen on the famous model of the head of Queen Nefertiti of Egypt, now housed at the Oriental Institute of the University of Chicago (cf. *ANEP*, 141). Jezebel's preparations to meet Jehu indicated that she wished to depart this life in style!

31 השלום זמרי "is everything well, Zimri?" The reference is to Zimri's short-lived rebellion against Baasha (1 Kgs 16:9–20), which provided a convenient parallel for Jehu's activity and reveals a wry sense of humor on the part of Jezebel. Zimri lasted only seven days in Tirzah, to be killed by Jezebel's father-in-law, Omri.

32 שנים שלשה "two or three." Cf. *Notes* above.

33–35 The report of the end of Jezebel is characterized by its complete frankness in its depiction of the absolute disdain in which Jehu held the woman (v 34). The reference to her scant remains brings to a ghoulish conclusion the prophecies against Jeroboam (1 Kgs 14:11), Baasha (1 Kgs 16:4), and Ahab (1 Kgs 21:19–24). Her husband also had dogs present at his death (1 Kgs 22:38).

37 היה "shall be" is probably an archaic form of the third feminine singular of such *lamedh-he* verbs (so Burney, *Notes*, 301). The verse is an interpretive comment since it finds no place in the original oracle of Elijah (1 Kgs 22:20–24). That it is a play on the words דמן "dung," and a component of the queen's name איזבל, which corresponds to the Arabic for the same substance (so Gray, *I & II Kings*, 551), is an entertaining possibility.

Explanation

Chapter 9 records several events which are connected chronologically and theologically. Following the command of Elisha, one of the sons of the proph-

Explanation

ets anoints Jehu, an officer in the army of Joram, as king, and thereby initiates a revolt against the house of Omri. Joram is eventually assassinated by Jehu, and this is followed by the slaying of Joram's cousin, Ahaziah. The climax of the chapter is the death of Jezebel, which is told with brilliant insight into the characters of the main actors.

The chapter presents the end of the Omride dynasty which was born in revolution (1 Kgs 16:15–20) and characterized by apostasy (1 Kgs 16:29–33) and greed (1 Kgs 21). In spite of the apostasy of the northern monarchy during this period, twice it allied itself with Jehoshaphat of Judah to embark on punitive expeditions against Syria (1 Kgs 22) and Moab (2 Kgs 3). The alliances are strange since Jehoshaphat receives abundant praise from the writer of 1 Kgs 22:41–50 as a loyal worshiper of Yahweh, and reformer of Judah's religion, abolishing many of the practices associated with the very religion which Ahab espouses (1 Kgs 22:46). The alliances, however, appear to have been initiated by Jehoshaphat himself (1 Kgs 22:44).

Ahab's activities are condemned by the biblical writer (1 Kgs 16:33), and his offspring did little to change the state of affairs in Israel. The activities of Jehu, however, are characterized by a brutality that goes beyond reason and a religious zeal which in its results has little to commend it. Jehu's character is well portrayed by this chapter. His task is clear, set out in the oracle he received at his anointing (vv 6–10). Little is gained by noting that this oracle, given by a lone member of the sons of the prophets, is an expansion upon the original oracle given him by Elisha (cf. v 3), as though this would absolve Elisha of any responsibility in the revolt. The young man is merely repeating the substance of an earlier oracle by Elijah (1 Kgs 19:15–19). Whether Elisha intended to set in motion the events which resulted in the later blood bath is not clear from the text, but he can hardly have been ignorant of the possible consequences of his action.

Jehu's slaying of the wounded king Joram and his cousin, Ahaziah, displays something of his treachery, but even these killings do not match the story of the death of Jezebel (vv 30–37) in which we see the clash of two persons well matched in their callous disregard for the life and welfare of others. There is a hint of truth in Jezebel's taunt at Jehu that he resembles Zimri, the Israelite general who killed his king, Baasha (1 Kgs 16:8–10). It is a sad pattern of history that dictatorships fall only to be replaced by regimes as brutal and as oppressive as their predecessors. Revolutions, however nobly inspired and whatever their ideology, pass through their own period of tyranny and oppression in the name of their cause. Such was the revolution of Jehu.

The writer of 2 Kings was not concerned to pass judgments of a political or sociological nature on the events he is describing. His motivations are rather found in the presentation of the history he records as the outworking of the will of Yahweh. The theology stated so forcibly by Deuteronomy is his guideline. There the possession and retention of the gift of the land of promise is so closely bound up with the nation's response to the God of the covenant. Failure to respond results in the forfeiture of the promise (Deut 4:25–31). Under this scheme of things human disasters such as those depicted in 2 Kgs 9 are not the results of historical accidents, but are expressions of the judgment of God upon unfaithfulness. To this end, the story of the end of the house of Omri confirms the accumulated prophecies of judgment upon successive apostate kings (1 Kgs 14:11; 16:4; 21:19–24), and sounds a note which runs through the material of the Former Prophets like a symphonic theme.

The Reign of Jehu (10:1–36)

Bibliography

Brand, J. "אשר על הבית." *Tarbiz* 36 (1967) 221–28. **Budde, K.** "The Nomadic Ideal in the Old Testament." *The New World* 4 (1985) 726–45. **Debus, J.** *Die Sünde Jerobeams.* FRLANT 93. Göttingen: Vandenhoeck & Ruprecht, 1967. **Frick, F. S.** *The City in Ancient Israel.* SBLDS 36. Missoula, MT: Scholars' Press, 1977. ———. "The Rechabites Reconsidered." *JBL* 90 (1971) 279–87. **Katzenstein, H. J.** "The Royal Steward." *IEJ* 10 (1960) 149–54. **Motzki, H.** "Ein Beitrag zum Problem des Stierkultes in der Religionsgeschichte Israels." *VT* 25 (1975) 470–85.

Translation

¹ *Now Ahab had seventy sons in Samaria, and Jehu wrote letters and sent them to Samaria, to the officers of Jezreel,* [a] *to the elders, and to those loyal* [b] *to Ahab, containing these words,* ² *"When this letter arrives, your master's sons are on your side; also on your side are the chariot force, the cavalry, and the fortresses* [a] *and armory.* ³ *You shall select the best and most noble of your master's sons, and you shall set him upon his father's throne, and you shall fight for your master's house."* ⁴ *But they became extremely scared* [a] *and said, "Two kings could not stand against him. How then can we?"* ⁵ *So the chief steward of the palace, the mayor of the city, the elders, and the supporters sent word to Jehu, "We are your servants, and whatever you say to us, we shall do. We shall appoint no one as king. Do what pleases you."* ⁶ *So he wrote them a second* [a] *letter containing the following words, "If you are on my side, and if you will obey my voice, take the heads of the men,* [b] *the sons* [c] *of your master, and bring* [d] *them to me this time tomorrow at Jezreel."* [e] *Now the seventy king's sons were with the great men of the city who were raising them.* ⁷ *When the letter arrived they took the king's sons, slaughtered* [a] *all seventy of them, placed their heads in baskets and sent them to him at Jezreel.* ⁸ *Then a messenger came and reported to him,* [a] *"The heads of the seventy king's sons have been brought." He said, "Put them in two piles at the city gates* [b] *until morning."* ⁹ *When morning came he went out, positioned himself and said to all the people, "You are innocent. I was the one who plotted against my master, and I killed him. But who struck down all of these?* ¹⁰ *Know then* [a] *that nothing of the word of Yahweh which he spoke concerning the house of Ahab shall fall* [b] *to the ground. Now Yahweh has accomplished what he spoke by the hand of his servant Elijah."* ¹¹ *Then Jehu proceeded to strike down all who were left of the house of Ahab in Jezreel, all his great men,* [a] *all his close associates and his priests, until there were no survivors.*

¹² Then he arose ᵃ and went to Samaria, and he came to Beth Eked ᵇ of the Shepherds. ¹³ There Jehu ᵃ found fellow soldiers of Ahaziah king of Judah, and he said to them, "Who are you?" They replied, "We are fellow officers of Ahaziah, and we are on our way down to avenge ᵇ the king's sons and the sons of the queen mother." ¹⁴ Jehu said, "Take them alive!" So they took them alive, ᵃ and they slaughtered them at the cistern ᵇ of Beth Eked, all forty-two of them. He spared ᶜ none of them.

¹⁵ Then he left there and found ᵃ Jehonadab the charioteer coming to meet him, ᵇ and he greeted him and said, "Is your heart upright, as my heart is to your heart?" ᶜ And Jehonadab replied, "It is! Yes, it is! Give me your hand." He offered him his hand, and he helped him up into his own war chariot. ¹⁶ Jehu said, "Come with me and see my zeal for Yahweh," ᵃ and he had him ride ᵇ in his chariot. ¹⁷ He then came to Samaria, and he cut down the remainder of ᵃ Ahab in Samaria, until he was completely eliminated; according to the word of Yahweh which he had spoken to ᵇ Elijah.

¹⁸ Jehu assembled all the people and said to them, "Ahab served Baal a little, but Jehu will serve ᵃ him a lot! ¹⁹ᵃ Now call to me all the prophets of Baal, all his worshipers, ᵇ all his priests. Let none be missing. I have arranged ᶜ a great sacrifice to Baal; anyone missing shall not live." But Jehu acted out of cunning, to destroy the worshipers of Baal. ²⁰ Then Jehu said, "Sanctify a solemn feast to Baal!" And they proclaimed it. ᵃ ²¹ᵃ Jehu sent word into all Israel, and the worshipers ᵇ of Baal came. Not one stayed away. They arrived at the temple of Baal, and the temple of Baal was filled from end to end. ²² He said to the wardrobe keeper, ᵃ "Bring out the vestments for all the worshipers of Baal." So he brought out vestments ᵇ for them. ²³ Then Jehu came, with Jehonadab the charioteer, to the temple of Baal, and said to the worshipers of Baal, "Search and see if there are here with you any worshipers of Yahweh in addition to worshipers of Baal." ᵃ ²⁴ They came to make the sacrifices and offerings, ᵃ and Jehu stationed eighty men ᵇ outside, and said to them, "If any man allows one of these men whom I brought here to escape, ᶜ at your hands shall I demand life for life." ²⁵ Then, when they had finished making the offering, Jehu said to the guards and the lieutenants, "Go and kill them! Let none come out!" ᵃ They cut them down with the edge of the sword. The guards and the lieutenants threw them out, ᵇ and went as far as the keep ᶜ of the temple of Baal. ²⁶ They then brought out the pillar of Baal and burned it. ²⁷ In addition to demolishing the pillar of Baal, they demolished the temple of Baal, and made it into a latrine ᵃ until this day. ²⁸ Jehu eliminated Baal ᵃ in Israel.

²⁹ But the sins of Jeroboam son of Nebat, with which he caused Israel to sin, Jehu did not turn from, namely, the golden calves which were at Bethel and at Dan. ³⁰ Yahweh said to Jehu, "Because you have done well in doing what is right in my eyes—according to all that is in my heart you have done to the house of Ahab— your four sons shall sit on your behalf on the throne of Israel." ³¹ But Jehu did not take care to walk in the law of the LORD with all his heart. He did not turn away from the sins of Jeroboam with which he caused Israel to sin.

³² In those days, Yahweh began to trim off the borders of Israel, and Hazael defeated them in all the outlying territory of Israel, ³³ from the Jordan eastward, all the land of Gilead, ᵃ the territory of Gad, Reuben, and Manasseh, from Aroer which is by the river Arnon—both Gilead and Bashan. ³⁴ Now the rest of the acts of Jehu and all he did, and all his mighty deeds, ᵃ are they not recorded in the book of the daily acts of the kings of Israel? ³⁵ Then Jehu slept with his fathers, and they buried

him in Samaria, and Jehoahaz his son reigned in his place. ³⁶ *The days which Jehu ruled over Israel amounted to twenty-eight years in Samaria.* ᵃ

Notes

1.a. The sense is strange since Jehu was already supposed to be in Jezreel. G reads προς τους ἄρχοντας Σαμαρειας "to the rulers of Samaria," and G^L offers προς τους στρατηγους της πολεως "to the commanders of the city." Most commentators (Burney, *Notes*, 302; Gray, *I & II Kings*, 552; Robinson, *Second Kings*, 91; K. D. Fricke, *Das zweite Buch von den Königen*, 128) follow this variant and suggest a Heb. original of אל שרי העיר ואל הזקנים "to the rulers of the city and to the elders," the phrase ואל העיר becoming mistaken later for יזרעאל "Jezreel."
1.b. The phrase ואל האמנים אחאב "and to those loyal to Ahab" is ungrammatical. G^L adds των υἱων, offering a possible original of ואל האמנים את בני "and to these loyal to the sons."
2.a. For the sg, G and Josephus (*Antiq.* ix.125) read pl. This is adopted by Burney and Gray, but it could indicate a collective term.
4.a. G reads σφοδρα "greatly" and on this basis BHS omits one מאד "very." This is an unnecessary emendation.
6.a. It is better with most to read שני masc "second" instead of שנית fem, although the term could be understood as a temporal adverb.
6.b. G^L omits any reference to men, reading instead λαβετω ἑκαστος την κεφαλην του υἱου του κυριου αὑτου "let each one take the head of the son of his lord." The omission is adopted by BHS.
6.c. G^A omits בני "sons" and Gray (*I & II Kings*, 552), following BHS, reads בית "house."
6.d. G reads ἐνεγκατε "bring," presupposing a hiph impv. This makes better sense and is adopted by most.
6.e. Throughout this passage G reads "Israel" for "Jezreel," and G^L follows MT.
7.a. On the basis of G's ἐσφαξαν αὐτους "they slaughtered them," most add the 3rd pl suffix to וישחטו (וישחטום).
8.a. Josephus (*Antiq.* ix.128) inserts μετα των φιλων δειπνουντι "eating with his friends." The origin of this tradition is unknown, but it is possibly an attempt at conformity with 9:34.
8.b. For פתח השער "gate entrance" G offers the longer παρα την θυραν της πυλης πολεως εἰς πρωι "beside the entrance to the city gates until morning." This seems more of an explanatory expansion than an indicator of a Heb original.
10.a. For דעו אפוא "know then" G transliterates mistakenly ἰδετε ἀφφω "see Aphō" (ראו אפוא).
10.b. For יפל "fall" G^A reads ποιησαι "to do," an error for G's πεσειται "he will fall."
11.a. G^L translates גדליו "great men" with ἀγχιστευοντας "kinsmen," possibly reading the Heb. as גאליו. Although this is accepted by some (e.g., Gray, *I & II Kings*, 553), it could well represent a harmonizing tendency of G^L with 1 Kgs 16:11.
12.a. ויבא "he came" is omitted by G.
12.b. For בית עקד "Beth Eked" 'A translates οἰκω καμψεως "house of bending," i.e., in worship? G versions offer various transliterations. The NEB adoption of "Bethakar" is surprising in view of the scant support for this reading.
13.a. ויהוא מצא "and Jehu found" is omitted by G^L, OL. Driver (*Hebrew Tenses*, 210–11) suggests והוא מצא "and he himself found." This is attractive and makes for better sense, but is no guarantee of the original.
13.b. Reading לשלם "to avenge" instead of לשלום "to greet."
14.a. ויתפשום חיים "so they took them alive" is omitted by G.
14.b. אל בור "at the cistern" is omitted by G.
14.c. For השאיר "he spared" Tg suggests נשאר "was spared."
15.a. For וימצא "he found" G reads ἐλαβεν "he took."
15.b. G^L adds ἐν τη ὁδω (בדרך) "on the road."
15.c. The language is extremely clumsy, although the intended meaning is clear. G tidies the language with Ἑι ἐστιν καρδια σου μετα καρδιας μου εὐθεια "if your heart is upright with my heart" (היש לבבך את לבבי ישר), which is attractive to some. Following Jehonadab's reply "It is!" G adds και εἰπεν Ιου "and Jehu said," thereby attributing the rest of the reply to Jehu.
16.a. G^N adds Σαβαωθ "Sabaoth."

16.b. וירכבו "he had him ride" is rendered ἐπεκάθισεν "he sat" by G, and adopted by Burney (*Notes*, 304)."

17.a. Although Syr adds לבית "to the house" before לאחאב "to Ahab," there is no reason to see this as a better reading (contra Gray, *I & II Kings*, 557).

17.b. Before אליהו "Elijah" OL adds the equivalent of ביד "by the hand."

18.a. For יהוא יעבדנו "Jehu will serve" G^L offers καὶ ἐγὼ δουλεύσω (ואני אעבדנו) "and I will serve."

19.a. 6QReg 17 offers a few fragments of vv 19b-21, but they are of little significance. Cf. Baillet, Milik, De Vaux, *DJD* 3:110.

19.b. G^L transposes כל עדיו "all his worshipers" after כהניו "his priests," and adds *waw* "and" to כל "all."

19.c. After כי זבח גדול לי "for by me a great sacrifice" G^L adds ἐγὼ ποιῶ, which presupposes עשיתי "I have arranged," and makes "sacrifice" the object, not the subject of the clause.

20.a. G reads sg.

21.a. Here G repeats parts of vv 19 and 20.

21.b. Because of this repetition G adds the words καὶ πάντες οἱ ἱερεῖς αὐτοῦ καὶ πάντες οἱ προφῆται αὐτοῦ "and all his priests and all his prophets" after עבדי הבעל "worshipers of Baal."

22.a. G inserts "house" before אשר על המלתחה "the wardrobe keeper."

22.b. For המלבוש "the vestments" G offers ὁ στολιστής (מלביש) "the robekeeper."

23.a. Some minor G MSS report the exclusion of the worshipers of Yahweh.

24.a. G^L transposes the first part of the verse to the end.

24.b. For שמנים איש "eighty men" G^L reads three thousand, which is a ridiculous enlargement of the figure. Syr compromises with three hundred and eighty.

25.a. After אל יצא "Let none come out" G adds ἐξ αὐτῶν "from them."

25.b. BHS suggests omitting the second occurrence of הרצים והשלשים "the guards and lieutenants" and reading instead אתם "them" or הַמֵּתִים "the dead." Burney (*Notes*, 350) and Gray (*I & II Kings*, 558) adopt the interpretation which locates the "missing" object of וישלכו "threw out" in the second occurrence of הרצים והשלשים and offer ארצה האשרה "on the ground of the Asherah." This is quite unnecessary. In 2 Kgs 4:41 and 6:6 the verb שלך is used without a written object. It is understood from the context, as it can be here.

25.c. On the meaning of עיר "keep" cf. *Comment* below.

27.a. לְמֹחֲרָאוֹת "latrine" is better pointed לְמַחֲרָאוֹת. G^L offers κοπρῶνα "dung heap," but G appears to have incorporated a late misinterpretation of Vg *in latrinas*, with its rendering of λυτρῶνας "ransoms."

28.a. After הבעל "Baal" G^L adds καὶ τὸν οἶκον αὐτοῦ "and his house."

33.a. After הגלעד "Gilead" G^L adds καὶ Ιαβοκ "and (the) Yabbok."

34.a. After וכל גבורתו "and all his mighty deeds" G adds τὰς συνάψεις ἃς συνῆψεν "and the plots which he made," possibly under the influence of 1 Kgs 16:20.

36.a. G^L adds considerable detail to this last verse concerning the reign of Jehu.

Form/Structure/Setting

DeVries (*Prophet against Prophet*, 119) assigns this chapter to the "Jehu accession narrative," with some editorial additions. The original accession narrative consisted of vv 1–11, 13–14, 15–17, 18–27. An unnamed redactor added vv 12, 28. Vv 29–31 comprise an addition at the hands of the deuteronomistic redactor #1, and vv 32–36 comprise a deuteronomistic "extract." The exact formal or stylistic differences between vv 29–31 and vv 32–36 are not explained.

The existence of such a "Jehu accession narrative" is taken for granted, but far from proven. The formal characteristics of such a narrative are not treated, apart from an emphasis upon the "propagandizing of certain political innovations" (ibid., ix). Propaganda, however, is not an exclusive formal characteristic of accession narratives, if it can be regarded as a formal characteristic at all. The obvious comparison between the story of the anointing of Jehu and the anointing of David in 1 Sam 16:1–3 was not made. There are similar historical circumstances in the two incidents, but no hard and fast formal similarities. There is nothing here, in fact, which would establish the genre of "accession narrative."

The "levels of interpretation" which DeVries detects in v 36 are revealing (ibid., 133). However, they are understood only from one perspective. The first level is the addition of the "word of Yahweh" in the prophetic legend, the second is the great color and detail added by the "accession historian," and the third is the reference to Elijah, added after the inclusion of the narrative in its present context. But this understanding lacks persuasion. The opposite is also possible. In fact, it is more likely that the narrative, in its present form, was placed in its present context because it suited admirably the purpose of the writer. That the figure of Elijah and not Elisha is more important in this narrative as predictor of the downfall of Ahab's house would argue against DeVries. Since it is out of keeping with the immediate context, in which Elisha plays the dominant role, the position of the chapter is dictated more by the facts of history than redactional choice.

As with many of the stories in this collection, 2 Kgs 10 is vividly told. Its form is to be detected from its present structure rather than from its supposed sources, redactional or otherwise. The chapter recounts two further stages in the downfall of the Omride dynasty with its record of the extermination of the house of Ahab (vv 1–11) and the abolition of Baalism from Israel (vv 18–28). Vv 12–17 provide an effective transition from the first to the second stage. Vv 29–36 conclude the reign of Jehu in summary.

1–11 The characteristic features of this tale of the final extermination of the remnant of Ahab's house are a close narrative style coupled with a certain repetition of form. The verses fall into four distinct stages, vv 1–6, 7, 8–9, 10–11.

After beginning with a typical subordinate clause in v 1a, the writer informs of the exchange of letters between Jehu and the officials of Joram's government. In vv 2–3 he offers them a challenge, and in v 4 they react to the challenge. They side with Jehu after the initial letter (v 5), and Jehu sends them a second letter (v 6). The ambiguous order of the letter is understood one way, and the gruesome result of this is seen in vv 7–8. The balance of the main verbs in vv 1–6 would suggest that the story opening is arranged in the form of an arch:

ויכתב "and he wrote" (v 1*b*)
וישלח "and he sent" (v 1*b*)
ויראו ויאמרו "but they were afraid and said" (v 4*a*)
וישלח "so he sent" (v 5*a*)
ויכתב "so he wrote" (v 6*a*)

The result of this sequence is expressed with the introductory clause ויהי כבא "when it arrived" (v 7). This formal characteristic is repeated in v 9 with its opening ויהי בבקר "when morning came" and Jehu's address to the people concerning the significance of what had happened. The events are justified in v 10 by an appeal to the word of God by Elijah; a summary statement is given in v 11 concerning the overall results of the action. From Ahab's house no one is left.

Form/Structure/Setting

The details of the letters correspond to the style of the diplomatic correspondence of the day. Cf. above on 5:5–7.

12–17 These verses provide the literary transition between the destruction of the house of Ahab and the subsequent attack upon Baalism. Like chapter 9, the verses also include an attack upon Ahaziah, the relative of Ahab. The verses consist of two encounters on the open road which are told in precisely the same manner. After a reference to the spread of the revolt (ויקם), Jehu journeys (וילך) and finds (מצא) a troop of men belonging to Ahaziah. He asks them a question (v 13*a*) the reply to which brings an immediate reaction on the part of Jehu which results in their complete annihilation (v 14). V 15 repeats the same cycle. Jehu journeys (וילך) then finds (וימצא) Jehonadab ben Rechab and asks him a question. Jehonadab's response to the question also results in an action, but this time it is an alliance. V 17 then repeats very closely the summary statement of v 11:

V 11	V17
ויך יהוא את כל הנשארים	ויבא שמרון
לבית-אחאב	ויך את כל הנשארים
ביזרעאל	לאחאב
וכל גדליו ומידעיו וכהניו	בשמרון
עד בלתי השאיר לו שריד	עד השמידו
"Then Jehu struck down all who were left of the house of Ahab in Jezreel all his great men, all his close associates and his priests until there were no survivors."	"He then came to Samaria and he cut down the remainder of Ahab in Samaria until he was completely eliminated."

As with the conclusion to vv 1–11, the events are justified once more with an appeal to the word of Yahweh uttered by Elijah (1 Kgs 21:20–24).

18–28 This collection of verses picks up the overtly religious purposes of Jehu which were stated in the previous section (v 16*a*) after the encounter between Jehu and Jehonadab. It is Jehonadab who provides the link between the second and the third stages of this narrative (v 23). The narrative moves swiftly to v 24. Jehu is the main actor, planning, commanding. Twice, subordinate clauses are introduced which explain the motives of Jehu (vv 19*b*, 24*b*). He is setting a trap.

By vv 25–28 the trap is sprung, and the results are the complete destruction of the Baal cult in Samaria. It cannot escape attention that the results of the plans of Jehu are introduced in typical fashion by the clause ויהי ככלתו "then when they had finished" (v 25). V 28 is to be included in this scheme as a summary statement of the same order as vv 11, 17. The complete extermination of Ahab and his apostasy has now been accomplished.

29–36 Formally these verses have echoes elsewhere in the OT. V 29 is typical of so many statements made at the end of the reigns of apostate kings, but an adaptation is made to suit the conditions of Jehu's reign. Vv 30–31 echo the promises made to Solomon by David in 1 Kgs 2:1–4 and 9:1–9, which are in turn reminiscent of Deut 4:9. Applied to Jehu, however, the promise turns to parody. The eternal throne now lasts a mere four generations, because the command to obey the law is not followed with all the heart.

The phrase בימים ההם "in those days" in v 32 is synchronistic, linking the further decline of Israel's fortunes with the sins of Jehu. (Cf. S. J. DeVries, *Yesterday, Today and Tomorrow,* 52.) The following verse has no formal structure, but coincides with numerous other geographical references in the OT (Deut 2:36; 3:12–16; 4:46; Josh 1:12–18; etc.). The concluding formula to Jehu's reign (vv 34–35) is typical of so many, except that the number of years in Jehu's reign comes at the end.

The chapter, in its present form, is understandable without recourse to redactional layers or prior sources.

Comment

1–11 Jehu begins to consolidate his position by the slaughter of the remnant of the house of Ahab. There are some interesting insights into the utterly ruthless character of Jehu in these stories.

1 שבעים בנים "seventy sons." The motif of seventy descendants is found elsewhere in Judg 8:30; 9:2–56. In view of the general nature of the term בנים "sons," there is no need to see this as a secondary insertion as some have done. The figure seventy might be a convenient round figure (cf. Jer 29:10).

אל שרי יזרעאל "to the officers of Jezreel." Although Montgomery labels this reference as "absurd" (*Kings,* 408), and although the versions change it (cf. above *Notes*) in light of Jehu's presence in the city already, the MT reading can stand. The "governors of Jezreel" could well have fled the city after the death of the king. The term שרים has military overtones, and it is often used with this meaning in the Former Prophets. It also has parallels in Assyrian documents (cf. D. D. Luckenbill, *Assyrian Records,* 2:208, 319). Cf. also 1 Kgs 22:26; 2 Kgs 23:8.

ואל האמנים אחאב "and to those loyal to Ahab." The phrase is translated "and to the guardians . . ." or a close equivalent. In Ruth 4:16 the feminine noun אמנת is translated "foster mother," and Josephus (*Antiq.* ix.125) supports this by translating האמנים as παιδαγωγοί "teachers." But such an interpretation would necessitate the insertion of the word "sons" to make sense. Cf. above *Notes.* A second meaning of the term אמנות is "support," according to the regular translation of the word in 2 Kgs 18:16. A simple change to the plural construct would accommodate our translation above.

2 ועתה "and now." On the use of this term in letters, see below. The letter is a cynical challenge to the authorities. Jehu informs them that they have a clear military advantage over him with their control of the bulk of the army units and the fortified strongholds.

3 As the letter continues, it offers a bold challenge to the authorities.

4–5 The quick capitulation of the officers was either a prudent move on their part since they felt outwitted by Jehu, an act of sheer cowardice, or an indication of a much more widespread rebellion than is portrayed in the text.

אשר על הבית lit., "he who is over the house" is a reference to the chief steward of the palace, who was a person of considerable influence in the court. Shebaniah of Isa 22:16 was such an official in the Judean court. A tomb inscription bearing a similar name and the same official designation has been found southeast of Jerusalem (cf. Gibson, *Syrian Semitic Inscriptions*, 1:23–24), and the "Gedalyahu" seal from Megiddo also refers to the same office (cf. D. W. Thomas, ed., *Documents from Old Testament Times* [New York: Harper & Bros., 1958] 230, pl. 13).

6 Jehu's second letter is ambiguous and appears to be intentionally so. The term ראשים can mean both "heads" and "leaders."

7 The speed with which the leaders acquiesce to Jehu's wishes is noteworthy. Either they wished to confirm their support of the revolt by the action, or they fell into a trap set by Jehu by overreacting. Jehu's response suggests the latter. There was no sense of outrage at such a slaughter comparable to David's reaction to the murder of Abner and Ishbosheth by Joab (cf. 2 Sam 4).

8 שימו אתם שני צברים . . . עד הבקר "put them in two piles . . . until morning." The same offhanded treatment is given the descendants of Ahab as was given Jezebel. Josephus's addition to the incident (cf. *Notes* above) enhances the utter callousness of the rebel. Once the heads had arrived they were placed in heaps as a sign of Jehu's complete control. Similar practices are noted of Esarhaddon of Assyria (Luckenbill, *Assyrian Records* 2:206) and Shalmaneser III of Assyria (Luckenbill, *Assyrian Records* 1:215).

9 אל כל העם "to all the people." The term עם can be understood one of three ways. Jehu could be addressing the army, now under his control (cf. 9:14), or he could be addressing the populace through their representatives. A further possibility is that the term designates the religious community of Israel (cf. 9:6).

צדקים אתם "you are innocent." Several meanings of the term צדקים are possible. It could mean "righteous (ones)," "innocent," or "loyal" (cf. Gray, *I & II Kings*, 555). In the light of the way Jehu continues, the second is the more likely. ומי הכה את כל אלה "but who struck down all of these?" The insinuation here is that what Jehu has done he has done at Yahweh's bidding.

10 Such a reference to a prior prophecy is typical of the "deuteronomistic history" (cf. von Rad, *Studies in Deuteronomy*, 74–91).

11 . . . וכל גדליו "all his great men. . . ." The destruction of the house of Ahab extended beyond the immediate family to his governing officials, who, according to 1 Kgs 21:11, were involved in the plot against Naboth. The dismantling of the administration of the king in such a ruthless way must have had disastrous effects upon the stability of the country. It finds echoes in many a modern coup d'etat.

12–14 In keeping with the attack upon Ahaziah of Judah recorded in chapter 9, Jehu now destroys a sizeable group of supporters of the southern king. The manner is equally ruthless.

12–13 The traditional identification of Beth Eked as modern Beit Qad, a small site near Jenin (Beth Haggan) is undoubtedly wrong unless the narrative is misplaced, or else there is more in the story than first appears. Beit Qad is about seven kilometers east northeast of Jenin, and some one hundred meters above the road which runs from Samaria through Jenin to Jezreel. It is quite off the beaten track. Also, the "kinsmen" (RSV) of Ahaziah were north of Samaria, the city where the king's descendants were (v 1). It is most unlikely that these men were completely ignorant of the events that had just taken place and were on their way, by such a devious route, to "greet" Ahaziah. The term אח "brother" can also mean fellow soldier (cf. *Comment* on 9:2 above). Further, the expression לְשָׁלוֹם is difficult to interpret as a noun. A small emendation, to point it piel infinitive construct (לְשַׁלֵּם), would offer the translation "avenge." The group intercepted by Jehu consisted of Judean soldiers on their way north, by an inconspicuous route, to avenge the death of their king and his cousins. The incident then follows well after the previous one. Jehu's "finding" of such a group might indicate that he launched a deliberate search for them or that one of his patrols chanced upon them.

14 איש ארבעים ושנים "all forty-two of them." That Jehu was able to kill forty-two men indicates that he had with him a sizable force to deal with such eventualities and increases the likelihood that his force was a regular military patrol, policing the countryside in the light of the chaos surrounding the revolt. The possibility that this incident has any thematic link with the death of the forty-two boys who taunted Elisha (2:23–24) is remote.

15 יהונדב בן רכב "Jehonadab the charioteer." The name Jehonadab is composed of two parts, the divine name יהוה "Yahweh" and the verb נדב, which means to "incite," "compel," or "be willing." The use of the verb in other names in the OT is restricted to those of persons of considerable social status. Cf. Exod 6:23; 1 Kgs 14:20; 1 Chr 2:28; 9:36. Josephus (*Antiq.* ix.132) adds considerable detail to this story, indicating that Jehonadab was a long-time friend of Jehu's, who commends Jehu for the revolt.

The designation of Jehonadab as בן רכב "son of Rechab" has caused considerable debate. Jehonadab is mentioned again in Jer 35 as the forefather of a group known as "the house of the Rechabim" (בית הרכבים). The point made by the prophet is that the group's loyalty to the command of Jehonadab is a point of comparison with the disloyalty of Judah to Yahweh. The Rechabim adhered to a strict code of conduct. However, the case that they represented the religious ideal of the desert life (so Budde, *The New World* 4 [1895] 726–45) has been overstated. If the term בן is to be taken literally as "son" then nothing at all is known of Jehonadab's father. The notion that the "house of the Rechabim" was a large group is discredited by the fact that Jeremiah could accommodate the whole group in one room of the temple complex (cf. Jer 35:4). But the term is used in a variety of ways in the OT (cf. Bergman, Ringgren, Haag, "בֵּן," *TDOT* 2:145–59), one of which is to characterize persons (1 Kgs 21:10) and another is to designate their associations (2 Kgs 4:1). F. S. Frick's suggestion (*JBL* 90 [1971] 279–87) that Jehonadab was associated with chariotry (רכב) in some way, either as a rider or as a member of the chariot-making guild (ibid., 282–83), is most attractive. It would explain

Jehu's interest in gaining the support of such a man, especially if he had access to vehicles of war. The question Jehu asks Jehonadab also echoes the establishment of military alliances (cf. 1 Kgs 22:4; 2 Kgs 3:7). Gray's objection that the association of two such persons would arouse the suspicion of the Baal worshipers (cf. *I & II Kings*, 559) is unwarranted if Jehonadab was connected with chariotry. Further, if this was Jehonadab's background, then it explains the origin of the tradition of the friendship between the two which Josephus reports. Jehu himself had already mentioned his long service in the chariot corps of Ahab (cf. 9:25).

17 כל הנשארים לאחאב "the remainder of Ahab." The remnants of the household of Ahab would have included officials, as well as the relatives of those who were already dead.

כדבר יהוה אשר דבר אל אליהו "according to the word of Yahweh which he had spoken to Elijah." Cf. above v 10. The reference is to the complete annihilation of all the males of Ahab's house mentioned in 1 Kgs 21:20–24. The text is deuteronomistic insofar as it expounds the view of history in which the prophets play such a crucial role.

18 Jehu's attempt to rid Israel of Baal worship constitutes the second thrust of his revolt, a religious purge. The episode is again characterized by its portrayal of the ruthless deceit of Jehu. אחאב עבד את הבעל מעט "Ahab served Baal a little." This might well be an accurate description of Ahab. Although he did build the Baal temple (1 Kgs 16:32), he also named his sons Aha*ziah* and *Jeho*ram, names that bear the divine name. However, the point cannot be pressed since the biblical verdict on Ahab is far from flattering (1 Kgs 16:33). Jehu's statement is born of his deceit. If the Israelites had thought that Ahab was apostate, Jehu wished them to believe that he was far worse.

19 כי זבח גדול "for a great sacrifice." This is a clever play on words on the part of Jehu. While the term זבח generally means "sacrifice," it is also used of the "slaughter" of apostates (cf. 1 Kgs 13:2; 2 Kgs 23:20). The writer's comment concerning Jehu's intention also contains a sinister pun on the homonyms עבד "to serve" and אבד "to destroy."

20 קדשו עצרה "sanctify a solemn feast" is normal language for the preparation of worship (cf. Mic 3:5; Joel 1:14; 2:15). Jeremiah uses such language in a slightly different context (cf. Jer 6:4). The term עצרה means a sacred assembly (cf. Deut 16:8; Amos 5:21).

21 ויבאו בית הבעל "they arrived at the temple of Baal." The building of this temple to Baal is mentioned in 1 Kgs 16:32. Its exact location and description are unknown, since it was never uncovered during the many excavations at Samaria-Sebaste. On the excavations cf. N. Avigad, "Samaria," *EAEHL* 4:1032–50. Whether this is due to the thoroughgoing destruction of the temple by Jehu, which is described in these verses (so Fricke, *Das zweite Buch von den Königen*, 139), or whether it still remains buried is a matter of conjecture.

פה לפה "from end to end," literally, "mouth to mouth." The expression is also found in 2 Kgs 21:16, where Jerusalem is filled with the blood of innocents.

22 המלתחה "wardrobe." The term is a *hapax legomenon*, although its meaning can be derived from the context (לבוש "vestments"). That it is related to the Akkadian *maltaktu* "proof," "testing," is unlikely (cf. W. von Soden, *Akkadisches Handwörterbuch*, 596). Jer 38:11 might provide a clue as to the origin of the word (so Gray, *I & II Kings*, 561). The wearing of special garments in worship is also attested in Exod 19:10.

23-24 Jehu's actions are hardly commendable. The deliberate way he sets up the worshipers of Baal for extermination gives a chilling view of his character.

25 הרצים והשלשים "the guards and lieutenants," lit., "runners and third men." They were undoubtedly members of an elite infantry unit whose prime task was to protect the king (cf. 1 Sam 22:7; 1 Kgs 14:27-28). The fact that this palace bodyguard now supports the rebel shows how effective the revolt had quickly become. The שלשים "lieutenants" are mid-ranking officers who were associated with the palace guard (cf. *Comment* on 9:25 and 11:4).

עד עיר בית הבעל "as far as the keep of the temple of Baal." The phrase is difficult. NEB translates עיר as "keep," but the meaning is nowhere else attested in the OT. The emendation to דביר "inner room" made by some commentators is imaginative, but unlikely. The omission of the word, suggested by *BHS*, solves nothing. The NEB translation has received some support from the study by F. S. Frick (*The City in Ancient Israel*, 27-30), who argues that some of the semitic parallels and their cognates mean "fortification."

26 את מצבות "pillars." The plural is awkward in view of the singular suffix on וישרפוה "burned it." Some versions suggest מצבת "pillar," and *BHS* suggests an emendation to אשרת "Asherah" in light of 1 Kgs 16:33. Both of these are possible, but by no means certain.

27 ויתצו את מצבת "and they demolished the pillar" is omitted by *BHS* as an unnecessary repetition of the previous verse. The repetition, however, is no guarantee of its secondary nature. וישמהו למחראות "and they made it into a latrine." This reference to the making of the Baal temple into a toilet is a parallel to the allusion to the remains of Jezebel in 9:37. The MT pointing of לְמַחֲרָאוֹת "for a latrine" with the vowels from the word מֹצָאוֹת "excrement" stresses this. עד היום "until this day." Obviously, by the time this was written, such a fate for the Baal temple was well known.

28-31 These verses consist of two summary statements concerning the reign of Jehu. The division is indicated by the closed paragraph division of MT. Both accounts contain an ambivalent attitude toward Jehu. In vv 28-29 he wipes out Baalism from Israel, but succumbs to the sins of Jeroboam son of Nebat. In vv 30-31 he is commended by Yahweh for the annihilation of the house of Ahab, but is again condemned for not keeping the Torah, following in the footsteps of Jeroboam ben Nebat. The balance between the two is discussed above in *Form/Structure/Setting*.

חטאי ירבעם בן נבט "the sins of Jeroboam son of Nebat" become the standard of apostate behavior for numerous kings of Israel. The frequent allusions to them are editorial comments by the writer on the reasons for the final destruction of the northern nation of Israel. (Cf. J. Debus, *Die Sünde*

Jerobeams.) The additional reference in v 29 to the golden calves in Bethel and Dan has probably caused the change in gender from the usual feminine חטאות to masculine חטאי.

Jehu's dynasty lasted for four generations, and included the impressive reign of Jeroboam II (786–742 B.C.) על כסא ישראל "on the throne of Israel." In former times the "throne of Israel" had a much wider application than is intended here. In the promise to David and Solomon (1 Kgs 2:4; 8:25; 9:5) it signified the complete religious community of Israel, north and south. In v 30 it covers a seriously reduced area. The allusion is deliberate, especially in light of the beginning of v 32.

31 Although this verse contains a second catalog of the sins of Jehu as in v 29, there are some slight but important differences. Here the sin of Jeroboam son of Nebat is identified as failure to keep the Torah. The deuteronomistic flavor of the verse is evident. The same interpretive tendency is seen in the repetitions of the promise made to David in 2 Sam 7, which contains a vague condition to the covenant. But in 1 Kgs 2:1–4 and again in 9:1–9 the condition is specified as keeping the law of Moses. Cf. E. W. Nicholson, *Preaching to the Exiles: A Study of the Prose Tradition in the Book of Jeremiah*, 86–87.

32 בימים ההם החל יהוה לקצות בישראל "in those days, Yahweh began to trim off the borders of Israel." The allusions of 1 Kgs 8 and 9 allow the expression "trim off." ויכם חזאל בכל גבול ישראל "and Hazael defeated them in all the outlying territory of Israel." The pressure exerted by Hazael upon Israel must have come about later in Jehu's reign (841–814 B.C.). According to the records of the Assyrian king Shalmaneser III (*ANET*, 280), in the eighteenth year of his reign (ca. 841–840 B.C.) Shalmaneser inflicted a serious defeat upon Hazael in which he confiscated 1,121 chariots, 470 cavalry horses, and all his supplies. The two were at war again in the twenty-first year (ca. 838 B.C.), and Hazael suffered a similar defeat. From this point on Shalmaneser was engaged in battles to the north and east; this would have given Hazael a respite. Hazael would have needed some time to recover such losses and then to attack Jehu. Since Jehu offered tribute to Shalmaneser, it is possible that the second attack upon Hazael was instigated by Jehu in an alliance with the Assyrians, but because the "Black Obelisk" of Shalmeneser is undated, this is not possible to determine with any degree of certainty. For a different chronology of this material cf. Gray, *I & II Kings*, 563, who argues that v 32 is a continuation of 1 Kgs 16:34. The two sections had become separated by the insertion of the Elijah-Elisha material. Cf. also on this period Herrmann, *History of Israel*, 227–42.

33 Jehu eventually lost the whole of the Transjordan to Syria. The losses extended from Aroer (modern 'Arir) five kilometers south of Diban, as far as Bashan to the north and east of the Sea of Galilee. It appears that Israel rarely had a firm hold on this area for any length of time. Mesha's revolt had sliced off a large chunk of the southern territory, including Diban, and Ramoth Gilead seems to have changed hands more than once. That Aroer is mentioned here reflects again the fluctuating fortunes of these border states.

34–36 The stereotyped ending to Jehu's reign is typical of many. Very little of the twenty-eight years is recorded in this chapter. The so-called "acts of greatness" (וכל גבורתו) might refer to his revolt and purge of Baalism, or even some military actions during his reign. Asa of Judah (1 Kgs 15:23), Baasha of Israel (1 Kgs 16:5), Omri (1 Kgs 16:27), Jehoshaphat of Judah (1 Kgs 22:45), Jehoahaz of Israel (2 Kgs 13:8), Joash (2 Kgs 13:12), Jeroboam II (2 Kgs 14:28), and Hezekiah (2 Kgs 20:20) all performed similar actions. Since few of them are known for their religious loyalty, the term probably refers to unknown military or political exploits.

Explanation

There is little to be added by way of explanation of this chapter. The narrative itself vividly portrays the progress of the revolution of Jehu and his followers, and his systematic attempts to wipe out any vestige of the house of Omri and any remnants of the cult of Baal from Israel. By all accounts he is quite successful.

Whether the chapter follows the chronological order of the revolt is not clear. It is obvious that there is a compression of history into the space of a few small comments. The complete elimination of the house of Ahab, including its officials, and anyone remotely connected with its administration (vv 1–11) is the first move of the new king. This he accomplishes with cunning and deceit. He also displays the same callous disregard for the victims of the revolt as he had shown for the corpse of Jezebel (cf. vv 7–9).

The slaying of forty-two of Ahaziah's supporters suggests a southern reaction to the revolt in the north which had taken the life of the southern king, and a serious attempt by Jehu to avoid any thwarting of his plans. The patrol accompanying Jehu had found the southern soldiers in the obscure town of Beth Eked, well off the beaten track (cf. *Comment* on vv 12–13).

The addition of Jehonadab "ben Rechab" could do nothing but strengthen the revolt, with the added access to chariotry that this alliance afforded. But again, the writer is not concerned to report, but to interpret, the events of the revolution. He consistently reminds the reader of the real motive behind the revolt, namely, the prophetic word through Elijah and Elisha of judgment upon apostasy (cf. vv 17).

Jehu's brutality reaches its lowest point with the massacre of the Baal worshipers (vv 18–28). Nothing in this story reflects favorably upon Jehu save his zeal. The brief comment at the end of this incident to the effect that "Jehu eliminated Baal in Israel" (v 28) reveals that Jehu achieved one of his intended goals, but the cost to the country in manpower must have been great.

The final verses of the chapter (vv 29–36) demonstrate the limits of even Jehu's zeal. He does not follow the LORD completely once he is king, and in spite of all the achievements of the man, judgment upon the whole of Israel for its accumulated apostasy remains inevitable. During the reign of Jehu even more territory was lost, presumably to Syria, and the fact that Jehu founded a dynasty of his own is explained on the basis of the initial motivation for the revolt.

The Revolt against Athaliah (11:1–20)

Bibliography

Borger, R. "Die Waffenträger des Königs Darius: Ein Beitrag zur alttestamentlichen Exegese und zur semitischen Lexikographie." *VT* 22 (1972) 385–98. **Falk, Z. W.** "Forms of Testimony." *VT* 11 (1961) 88–91. **Gordis, R.** "Sectional Rivalry in the Kingdom of Judah." *JQR* 25 (1935) 237–59. **Goudoever, J. van.** "A Study on the Mid-Time." *Bijdragen* 33 (1972) 262–307. **McCurley, F. R.** "'And After Six Days' (Mark 9:2): A Semitic Literary Device." *JBL* 93 (1974) 67–81. **Nicholson, E. W.** "The Meaning of the Expression עם הארץ in the Old Testament." *JSS* 10 (1965) 59–66. **Reviv, H.** "ויואש ועתליה ימי על." *BMik* 47 (1971) 541–48. **Rudolph, W.** "Die Einheitlichkeit der Erzählung vom Sturz der Atalja (2 Kön. 11)." *Festschrift für Alfred Bertholet*. Ed. W. Baumgartner. Tübingen: Mohr, 1950. 473–78. **Soggin, J. A.** "Der judäische ʿAm-Haʾarets und das Königtum in Juda: Ein Beitrag zum Studium der deuteronomistische Geschichtsschreibung." *VT* 13 (1963) 187–95. **Wernberg-Møller, P.** "Pleonastic waw in Classical Hebrew." *JSS* 3 (1958) 321–26.

Translation

¹ *When Athaliah, mother of Ahaziah, saw [a] that her son was dead, she [b] proceeded to destroy all the royal succession.* ² *But Jehosheba, King Joram's daughter and the stepsister of Ahaziah, took Joash, Ahaziah's son,[a] and kidnapped him from among the king's sons who were about to be murdered [b]—both him and his nurse in the bedchamber. She hid him from Athaliah, and he was not killed.* ³ *He remained hidden with her for six years in the temple [a] while Athaliah reigned over the country.*

⁴ *But in the seventh year Jehoiada sent word and took the centurions [a] of the Carites [b] and the palace guard, and brought them to him at the temple. He then made a pact with them and put them under oath [c] in the temple,[d] and he showed [e] to them the king's son.* ⁵ *He gave them the following orders, "This is what you will do. One of your units from those who come [a] on duty on the Sabbath shall stand guard over the palace.[b]* ⁶ *One of the units shall stand at the Gate of Sur,[a] and a unit at the city gate,[b] to the rear of the palace guard.[c] You shall stand guard over the palace.[d]* ⁷ *Two of your companies, those that go off duty on the Sabbath, shall [a] stand guard at the temple, at the [b] king's disposal.* ⁸ *You shall surround [a] the king, each man with his weapon at the ready, and anyone who approaches the ranks [b] shall die. Be [c] with the king when he goes out and when he comes in."*

⁹ *The centurions did precisely as Jehoiada the priest [a] had ordered them. Each one took his command—those who came on and those who went off duty on the Sabbath—and they came to Jehoiada the priest.* ¹⁰ *And Jehoiada the priest gave to the centurions the spears [a] and the quivers [b] which once belonged to David, and which were in the temple.[c]* ¹¹ *The palace guard stood, each man with his weapon [a] at the ready, right around from the south side of the palace to the north side, as far as the altar and the temple in support of the king.* ¹² [a]*Then he brought out the king's son, and set the badge of office [b] and dedicatory plaque upon him. They [c] made him king, anointed [d] him, applauded and said, "May the king live!"*

¹³ *When Athaliah heard the noise of the guard and the people,[a] she went toward*

the people at the temple. ¹⁴ *Then she saw the king standing by the pillar,* ᵃ *as was the rule,* ᵇ *and the singers* ᶜ *and the trumpeters* ᵈ *playing for the king while all the people of the land were rejoicing and blowing trumpets. Then Athaliah tore her garments and cried out, "Treason! Treason!"* ¹⁵ *Jehoiada the priest gave an order to the centurions, those put in command of the force, and he said to them, "Bring her out in front of the temple to the ranks. Kill with the sword anyone who follows her." For the priest had said, "She shall not die in the temple."* ᵃ ¹⁶ *So they arrested her, and she came through the horses' passage toward the palace, and there she died.*

¹⁷ *Then Jehoiada contracted a covenant between Yahweh, the king, and the people, that they should be Yahweh's people.* ᵃ ¹⁸ *Then all the people of the land went to the temple of Baal and tore it down. Its altars* ᵃ *and its images they smashed thoroughly, and Mattan, the priest of Baal, they slaughtered in front of the altars. Then the priest put specially designated persons over the temple.* ¹⁹ *The centurions, together with the Carites and the guard,* ᵃ *and all the people of the land, took the king down from the temple and brought him by way of the Guard's Gate to the Palace. He then sat down* ᵇ *on the king's throne.* ²⁰ *So all the people of the land rejoiced, and the city was at peace. Athaliah had been slain with the sword at the palace.* ᵃ

Notes

1.a. MT וראתה "and she saw" is better read ראתה "she saw."

1.b. ותקם is omitted by G^B although included by G^L. Montgomery (*Kings,* 424) is among the few commentators who retain it, offering the translation "she arose to action."

2.a. For בן אחזיה "Ahaziah's son," G reads υἱὸν ἀδελφοῦ αὐτῆς (בן אחיה) "her brother's son," and G^L conflates the two readings. The change in the Heb. is very slight; it is easy to see how such a mistake could occur.

2.b. הַמֻּמָתִים is better read הַמּוּמָתִים "who were about to be murdered" with Q. Cf. 2 Chr 22:11.

3.a. G^B omits יהוה "of Yahweh," understanding the building to be the palace. The MT reading of "temple" would explain the embellishments in 2 Chr 22:11 and Josephus (*Antiq.* ix.141) in which Jehosheba becomes the wife of the priest Jehoiada.

4.a. Here and in vv 9, 10, 15 Q suggests הַמֵּאוֹת for הַמֵּאיוֹת "centurions." Many commentators regard the *yodh* as an aid to pronunciation.

4.b. Some G MSS translate הכרי "the Carites" with τῶν παρατρεχόντων "those who chase down," the word normally reserved for הרצים "the palace guard."

4.c. וישבע "and he swore" is transposed to before וירא "and he showed" by Burney (*Notes,* 309).

4.d. בבית יהוה "in the temple" is omitted by G.

4.e. After וירא "and he showed" G^B adds Ἰωδαε "Jehoiada," and G^L adds Ἰωας "Joash." Such additions are peculiar to the G tradition.

5.a. For MT באי "those who come," G offers εἰσελθέτω "let (the third of you) come in."

5.b. After בית המלך "the palace" G adds ἐν τῷ πυλῶνι "in the gateways."

6.a. For "the Gate of Sur" G^B offers τῶν ὁδῶν "the roads," and 2 Chr 23:5 has היסוד, which can be translated "the foundation." This is followed by Montgomery (*Kings,* 424). Others suggest הסום "the horse" (cf. v 16).

6.b. For MT בשער "in the gate" G omits "in," though G^L retains it.

6.c. Here G translates הרצים "the palace guard" with τῶν παρατρεχόντων "those who chase down," in contrast to v 4, where it simply transliterates Ῥασειν.

6.d. The word מסח in MT is unknown. G omits it and G^L transliterates with μεσσαε.

7.a. For ושמרו "they shall stand guard" G reads the equivalent of שמרי "those standing guard."

7.b. The sense of אל המלך "at the king's disposal" is awkward, although preserved by G. G^L reads ἐπὶ (על) "on behalf of."

8.a. MT הקפתם "you shall surround" is rendered correctly by G^B with impv κυκλώσατε. G^L offers καταστήσατε ἑαυτούς "stand with them."

Form/Structure/Setting

8.b. Most G MSS transliterate the Heb. The Heb is related to the Akk *sidirtu* "rank of soldiers."
8.c. MT היו "be," which G^L translates correctly with γνωσθε, G^B renders ἐγένετο "he was."
9.a. G renders הכהן "the priest" as ὁ συνετός, "the clever one," although G^L and others follow MT. G^L repeats the ending of v 8.
10.a. For החנית "the spear" 2 Chr 23:9 reads pl.
10.b. G^L adds a great deal of repetitive material.
11.a. For כליו "his weapons" G reads sg.
12.a. G^L adds a long preamble in which Jehoiada summoned all the people of the land to the temple.
12.b. G^L translates הנזר "badge of office" with ἁγίασμα "holy thing" (σ' = ἅγιον "holy"), whereas G^B transliterates ιεζερ and G^A έζερ.
12.c. MT makes the first two verbs sg, attributing them to Jehoiada, but the next four are pl. G^B reads them all as sg. G^N has the easiest reading: four singulars followed by two plurals. Stay with MT.
12.d. Both G^L and Josephus (*Antiq*. ix.149) reverse the order of the verbs וימלכהו וימשחהו "they made him king and anointed him."
13.a. MT הרצין העם "the guard the people" is difficult. Burney (*Notes*, 311) and Gray (*I & II Kings*, 575) regard the *nun* ending as a gloss. G τῶν τρεχόντων τοῦ λαοῦ "the guard (lit., runners) of the people" would imply that MT should read הרצי העם, and G^L joins the two: הרצין והעם "the guard and the people."
14.a. MT עמוד could be translated "in his place," but Josephus (*Antiq*. ix.151) reads ἐπὶ τῆς σκηνῆς "on the stage." G of 2 Chr 23:13 reads ἐπὶ τῆς στάσεως "in his place."
14.b. MT כמשפט "as was the rule," which is rendered במבוא "in the entrance" in 2 Chr 23:13. Gray adopts this reading (*I & II Kings*, 575).
14.c. G renders הַשָּׂרִים as οἱ ᾠδοί "singers." This is an understandable confusion between שָׂרִים "captains" and שָׁרִים "singers." The G reading is to be preferred.
14.d. Gray suggests omitting the term, since it appears superfluous. G^L translates with the military term οἱ στρατηγοί "the generals."
15.a. The apparent ignorance of the Heb. שדרת by the G translators is seen again here (cf. *Notes* 8.b.). G^B offers τοῦ ἀσηρωθ "asherahs" and Josephus (*Antiq*. ix.151) hazards a guess with εἰς τὴν φάραγγα τὴν Κέδρον "to the ravine of Kidron." Cf. Burney, *Notes*, 311–12.
17.a. Most commentators omit this final phrase. It does appear, however, in most textual traditions. It is superfluous, adding nothing to the meaning of the sentence.
18.a. מִזְבְּחֹתָו should be pointed as מִזְבְּחֹתָיו "its altars."
19.a. G resumes its use of proper nouns for כרי (Χορρει) "Carites" and רצים (Ῥασσειμ) "guard."
19.b. MT וישב "he then sat down" but G reads καὶ ἐκάθισαν αὐτόν "and they set him," which is supported by 2 Chr 23:20 ויושיבו את המלך "and they caused the king to sit." However, G might well be an attempt at harmonization.
20.a. For בית מלך "palace" read בית המלך "the palace," adding the article.

Form/Structure/Setting

With the beginning of chap. 11 the focus of attention in 2 Kings shifts for the first time from Israel to Judah and remains there until 13:1. The abrupt change in locale and the fact that Jehoiada appears without explanation in v 4 would suggest to some a different origin for the material in this chapter from that of the previous ones (cf. W. Rudolph, *Bertholet Festschrift*, 475–76). Such an observation is correct. The royal archives of Judah would have provided the information contained in the following two chapters. The style, however, is that of the writer of 2 Kings, and the material he has used has been skillfully manipulated for his own literary purposes.

The unity of the chapter has been discussed at length by commentators. Most, since J. Wellhausen (*Die Composition des Hexateuchs*, 361) and B. Stade (*ZAW* 5 [1885] 275–97), have divided the chapter between vv 1–3, 4–12,

18*b*–20; and vv 13–18*a*. The first are seen to reflect a priestly and official account of the downfall of Athaliah, whereas vv 13–18*a* are said to reflect a more popular perspective on the coup. This opinion persists in Gray (*I & II Kings*, 570–81), Robinson (*The Second Book of Kings*, 109), and Mettinger (*King and Messiah*, 141–44). To support the argument for separate sources it is suggested that the sequence of events is disrupted at v 18 with the murder of Mattan and the destruction of the Baal temple, while Joash is still waiting in the temple (vv 12, 19). Further appeal is made to the doublet on the death of Athaliah (vv 15–16, v 20) each with slightly different details.

Whether such phenomena are sure signs of the presence of sources cannot be decided with absolute certainty, but from a methodological point of view sources cannot be presumed to exist. The division suggested above is by no means watertight. For example, Skinner (*Kings*, 337) draws attention to the distinct lack of religious motifs in the so-called priestly, official section. Further, the distinction, made on the basis of the characters who receive most attention in the narrative, between "official, priestly" and "popular" is far from satisfactory. In the "official" account the people play a prominent part (v 19), and in the "popular" account, military officials and the priest are prominent (v 15). To argue that such allusions are the results of redactional activity (so Burney, *Notes*, 308) reduces such interpretation to the absurd. For the purposes of the following formal analysis the division adopted is vv 1–3, 4–16, 17–20. The division is made on the structure of the chapter and the presentation of plot rather than on the detection of sources behind the present narrative. Although the Masoretic paragraph divisions originated at a much later time, they support this division of the structure. Vv 1–3 serve as a general introduction and provide a historical preamble to what follows. In the next two sections are two action sequences depicting the revolt against Athaliah. The sequences are parallel, but deal basically with different aspects of the coup.

1–3 In this brief but full introduction, three persons are introduced, but only two of them can be said to be actors in the dramatic sequence of events to come. The two are the women Athaliah and Jehosheba, who are contrasted vividly. Athaliah is the potential destroyer of the dynasty, Jehosheba is its savior. Throughout this narrative Joash appears as completely passive, the object of others' schemings and plans. Syntactically, the introduction begins with the common device of *waw* plus subject plus perfect (cf. 2 Kgs 3:1; 4:1, 38, 42; 5:1; 6:8; 8:1; 9:1). Such a combination of words provides a subordinate action to what follows (Williams, *Hebrew Syntax*, 96–97). Athaliah's noticing (ראתה "she saw") of the state of affairs following the death of her son spurs her quickly to action (ותקם ותאבד "she proceeded to destroy"). The events described so briefly must have taken some time, but the sense of time is lost. Athaliah's plans are thwarted by the intervention of another woman, Jehosheba, who hides the young prince for six years. After the mention of the six-year reign of Athaliah both women disappear from the narrative. Only Athaliah is to reappear again (v 13). Jehosheba is a subsidiary character, and in what follows the action shifts to the meticulous activity of the priest, Jehoiada.

4–16 This sequence of events opens with the important phrase "in the seventh year" (see *Comment*). A climax is reached in which events take a decid-

Form/Structure/Setting

edly different turn with the appearance of Jehoiada. First, Jehoiada sends for the army commanders and makes a pact with them (v 4). This agreement involves some very specific orders which must have taken some very careful planning (vv 5–8). Second, the officers respond to these orders by taking the desired action, carrying out the orders very specifically (vv 9–11). Third, this action results in the acclamation of the new king by the military (v 12). Fourth, in a highly dramatic fashion Athaliah seeks to interrupt the proceedings, but is killed by the guard at the command of the priest (vv 13–16). Within this sequence of events there is a verbal sequence which reveals a decisive shift in leadership from Athaliah to Joash, through the activity of Jehoiada:

וירא "and he showed" v 4	ותרא "then she saw" v 14
ויצום "he ordered them" v 5	ויצו "he ordered" v 15
יחי המלך "may the king live" v 12	ותומת "and she died" v 16

The result is life for Joash, death for the apostate queen.

While the scene in the temple has distinct parallels with other coronation accounts, such similarities are due more to the common events than to the existence of the formal reporting of such events. The particulars of this account must be noted. Skinner's observation on the lack of religious themes and motifs in this first section is important. What is presented here is a political and military coup d'etat, instigated by the priest and executed by the palace guard. The four stages of the sequence move the events to a decisive and desired conclusion.

17–20 This section contains a sequence of events perfectly parallel to the one found in vv 4–13. The particulars of this second report provide these verses with a more overtly religious focus. First, Jehoiada makes a "covenant" (v 17), but this time between the king and Yahweh, the people and Yahweh, and the king and the people. This is not the political agreement made in v 4 since its intention is to renew the people's status as "people of Yahweh." The sentiment is found also in Deut 4:23 and 7:6, and there the outcome of such a covenant is an attack upon false worship and the destruction of shrines and images. Second, this covenant spurs the people to action. They proceed to destroy the Baal temple and to kill the priest of Baal, Mattan (v 18). Third, this action is followed by an acclamation of the king (v 19), but with a significant addition. Here, the hitherto separate elements in the revolt are joined, as the Carites, the guards, and the people of the land acclaim Joash king (v 19). Fourth, the doublet of the killing of Athaliah (v 20) completes the sequence in parallel with vv 4–16. The whole can be depicted as follows:

Introduction (vv 1–3)

Military coup:	*Popular religious uprising:*
The covenant (v 4)	The covenant (v 17)
Action by soldiers (vv 9–11)	Action by people (v 18)
Acclamation of Joash (v 12)	Acclamation of Joash (v 19)
Death of Athaliah (vv 13–16)	Death of Athaliah (v 20)

The use of these parallel sequences need not indicate separate literary sources, although it is clear that sources of information were used by the writer. Historically, the separation of the detailed planning of the revolt and its success in the palace, because of the involvement of the army, and the popular movement is probably accurate. To be effective in such a venture, it would have been imperative to secure a solid military base. The literary presentation demonstrates the essential unity of the three important festal elements in Judean society, the priesthood, the army, and the populace, in the renewal of the Davidic dynasty under God. An obvious compression of historical data is the result.

Comment

The six-year reign of Athaliah is seen as little more than an unfortunate interlude in the progression of the Davidic dynasty. The events of the reign are passed over with little comment. What details are provided are offered indirectly, and serve only to tell the story of the downfall of Athaliah and the resumption of the Davidic line. The sense of illegitimacy of Athaliah's reign is enhanced by the absence of any formal introduction or conclusion to her reign. (Cf. 13:1–2, 10–11; 14:1–4.)

1 ועתליה "when Athaliah." The name is a combination of the verb עתל "to grow large," "to become exalted," and the divine name "Yahweh." That the daughter of Ahab and Jezebel bore such a name is a great irony since she organized the Baal cult in the Judean capital.

ותקם "and she proceeded." The most frequent use of the verb קם in a narrative sequence is with the verb הלך "to go." In some military contexts (e.g., 7:12) the verb implies preparation for action. It is this sense which is preserved here. The queen's action was decisive.

ותאבד את כל זרע הממלכה "and she destroyed all the royal succession." Athaliah's intention was to destroy all possible rivals to the throne. Undoubtedly the death of forty-two of Ahaziah's fellow officers (10:12–14) made her task easier. Josephus (*Antiq.* ix.140) makes quite explicit this opportunistic streak in Athaliah's nature.

2 יהושבע בת המלך יורם "Jehosheba, King Joram's daughter." 2 Chr 22:11 and Josephus (*Antiq.* ix.141) indicate that Jehosheba was also the wife of Jehoiada the priest. Such a detail might explain why the young prince was hidden in the temple precincts.

חדר המטות "the bedchamber." This is the priests' dormitory within the temple area.

3 שש שנים "six years." That the prince was hidden here for six years would show that Athaliah's reign and policies did not seriously affect the sanctity of the temple, even though the tradition developed that she allowed its desecration (2 Chr 24:7).

4 ובשנה השביעית "but in the seventh year." The phrase occurs elsewhere, in Lev 25:3–4, in connection with the Jubilee, but there is no need to conclude that Jehoiada planned the coup for a festal year (so Gray, *I & II Kings*, 579–81). The sequence of six, then a decisive seventh, is a device to portray a climax in a series of events (cf. F. R. McCurley, *JBL* 93 [1974] 67–81). By the same token, the mid-point in a series of seven (days, weeks,

years, etc.), is often a time of crisis (cf. J. van Goudoever, *Bijdragen* 33 [1972] 262–307). For a slightly different understanding of the same numbers see J. M. Sasson, "Generation, Seventh," *IDBSup*, 354–56.

יהוידע "Jehoiada." This name combines the divine name and the verb "to know." At this point in the narrative the occupation of Jehoiada, and thereby the reason for his intervention at this stage, are not given.

שרי המאיות "centurions." The rank mentioned here is an important one. While "centurion" sounds more Roman than Israelite, it is to be preferred over the rather clumsy "captains of units of a hundred" (NEB). The ranks above this are those of שר אלף "captain of a thousand" (2 Sam 18:1) and שר שבאה "commander in chief."

לכרי lit., "to the Carites." The syntax is unusual, and it is best to understand the prefixed preposition (ל) as an alternative to the previous noun's being in the construct state, i.e., "centurions of the Carites and the guard." For this use of the preposition cf. 1 Sam 14:16 (הצפים לשאול "the watchmen of Saul"); GKC, 129b; Williams, *Hebrew Syntax*, 48. The word כרי occurs only here and in v 19. 2 Sam 20:23 refers to הכרי, but the Qere is הכרתי, possibly a word from the root כרת "to cut." Given the context of 2 Sam 20:23, this is an appropriate military term, but cannot be equated with the כרי of the present text. The other term which occurs in 2 Sam 20:23 (הפלתי) is a *hapax legomenon*. The suggestion adopted by Gray (*I & II Kings*, 571) and Montgomery (*Kings*, 419) that the כרי were Carians in mercenary service to the Judean court, after the manner of the Carians in the Egyptian court of Psammetichus (Herodotus, Book II:154), is attractive, but unlikely. Words such as רצים and כרי are nouns derived from active verbs. It is doubtful whether they refer to the ethnic origin of such troops. Further, it is improbable that the Judean court would have entertained the notion of foreign troops so close to the seat of power. Cf. J. C. Greenfield, "Cherethites and Pelethites," *IDB* 1:557.

לרצים "of the palace guard." This term designates a special unit. The word is derived from the verb רץ "to run" (2 Sam 15:1; 1 Kgs 1:5). As with many military terms, the original term "runners" changed with time to be merely a title. The duties of the regiment are outlined in 1 Kgs 14:27. They were the elite royal bodyguard. A similar change in meaning of such designations can be seen in the regimental titles "Lancer" or "Hussar" or "Yeomanry," which were originally titles of cavalry and special foot regiments with specific duties and skills. Today they designate armored (tank) regiments. Cf. J. W. Wevers, "Guard," *IDB* 2:500–501.

ויכרת להם ברית "and he made a pact with them." The pact which Jehoiada made with these important military figures was a shrewd move. It secured for him a solid power base from which to conduct the coup and virtually guaranteed success. Modern parallels to such strategy abound. The loyalty of these palace commanders is assumed rather than stated in the story. That they had any religious reasons for joining the coup is not mentioned. Their obedience to Jehoiada, however, is absolute.

5 The precise details of the location and deployment of the troops described in the following verses are somewhat unclear. Many, such as A. B. Ehrlich (*Randglossen* 7:305) and Skinner (*Kings*, 338–39) omit v 6 either as an unnecessary doublet on v 7b (Ehrlich) or as an irreconcilable conflict with v 9 (Skinner). Our reconstruction of the verses in the translation yields the following plan. One company of Carites was to guard the palace. It was a company which normally came on duty on the Sabbath. A second company was to stand guard at the Gate of Sur, the location of which was unknown. A third company was to stand guard at the palace or city entrance and offer support to the palace guard if needed. In addition to this, two platoons were to stand guard at the temple to protect the king. These platoons were from among those who normally did not come on duty on the Sabbath.

השלישית "the unit" literally means a third of a unit. Most likely the commander of such a group was called a Shalish.

באי השבת "who come on duty on the Sabbath." This is a reference to the duty roster of the palace guards. There is no indication as to which day these arrangements were to be carried out. Since troops are designated by their sabbath duties, it could have been on such a day. That those on and off duty were organized in the coup shows that a complete mobilization of the command was involved.

ושמרי משמרת בית המלך "shall stand guard over the palace." Grammatically, the clause looks awkward, but attempts at changing it are rightly resisted. Cf. P. Wernberg-Møller, *JSS* 3 (1958) 325.

6 The inclusion of this verse, while difficult, does not present insurmountable difficulties in the flow of the narrative.

שער סור "the Gate of Sur." The location is unknown. 2 Chr 23:5 reads שער היסוד "Gate of the Foundation," but this makes little sense. סור might be a corruption of the term סוס "horse" in v 16, but there the word מבוא "passage" is used, which indicates a pathway or alleyway, not necessarily a gate.

בשער אחר הרצים "at the city gate to the rear of the palace guard." This is possibly the palace gate, since the troops stationed here had to back up the palace guard. The splitting of the force into the three units ensured mutual support if Athaliah countered the coup with a force of her own.

מסח. The meaning is lost, and attempts to understand the term have proven unsuccessful. Montgomery's suggestion (*Kings*, 420) that it is a scribal annotation is possible, but the meaning remains unknown.

7 ושתי הידות בכם "two of your companies." The suggestion that the description of these platoons as כל יצאי השבת "those who go off duty on the sabbath" forms a logical sequence to the reference to the company which came on duty on the sabbath in v 5 (so Ehrlich, *Randglossen* 7:305) is sound. But to omit all of v 6 from the original order on the basis of this seems arbitrary.

ושמרו "shall stand guard." This is a logical way to continue the order to the platoons. The change from ושמרו to a participle ושמרי is unnecessary.

אל המלך "at the king's disposal." *BHS* suggests the omission of the phrase. Ehrlich (*Randglossen* 7:305) and others suggest an emendation to על המלך "in front of the king." The phrase can stand.

8 The extremely tight security around the prince indicates something of the very careful planning that went into the revolt against Athaliah.

9 The obedience of the army commanders is expressed with simplicity, and with no attempt to explain their motivation. The military has frequently become the power tool of politicians.

10 ויתן . . . את החנית ואת השלטים "and he gave . . . the spears and the quivers." The significance of this action is puzzling. Josephus (*Antiq.* ix.148) interprets this as a distribution of weapons from the temple armory. No other reference to such an armory exists. Montgomery (*Kings*, 420) suggests that "spear and 'shield' " are honorific armor, almost badges of office stored in the temple. Gray (*I & II Kings*, 573) supplements this with his suggestion that the spear was a royal symbol. All of this is possible, and the implication would be that the ceremonial armor was intended for the young king. However, no further mention is made of these weapons in the narrative. The straightforward meaning is that the commanders were armed by the priest for the coup.

The main problem is the meaning of השלטים, often translated "shields." The parallel verse in 2 Chr 23:9 is of little help, except to add one further weapon, the המגנות to the arms of the commanders. If the root of this word is גנן, having something to do with a stringed implement (so BDB, 618), then this would indicate a bow of some kind. The term שלטים is rare in the OT, occurring in Cant 4:4, where neck adornments are likened to a warrior's שלטים; in 2 Sam 8:7 referring to the gold שלטים which David confiscated from Hadadezer's officials; in Ezek 27:11 in which they are hung on walls; in Jer 51:11 in which they are מלאו "filled" in preparation for battle. In this last reference the parallel is החצים "arrows" and the verb מלא "to fill" hardly fits with the term "shield." This would suggest a possible alternative of "quiver," i.e., something which is filled with arrows. This would certainly accord with something which can be worn (Cant 4:4) and something which can be hung in preparation for fighting (Ezek 27:11). Such a reading is supported by G^L and Vg, which offer φαρέτρα and *pharetra* "quiver." R. Borger, *VT* 22 (1972) 385–98, has linked the Hebrew term to the *saltu* "sheath" worn by Persian soldiers, and depicted in reliefs (cf. *ANEP*, 11). Skinner's suggestion that the verse is a gloss from Chronicles solves nothing.

11 With the arrangements completed the palace guard surrounded the palace on all sides, and protected the route from the palace to the temple. Burney's suggests (*Notes*, 310–11) that the word סביב "around" is misplaced in MT and that למזבח ולבית "as far as the altar and the temple" should be omitted, but these only make explicit what is already implied.

12 The subject of the verb reverts to Jehoiada, who gives the king his badges of office.

הנזר "the badge of office" is from the root נזר "to devote," and is a symbol of the king's dedication. Most versions translate it as "crown," but this is unclear. Ps 132:18 parallels the term with "clothing."

העדות "the dedicatory plaque." These are generally regarded as a form of "protocol" or list of regulations governing the conduct of kingship in Israel and Judah (see G. von Rad, "The Royal Ritual in Judah," in *The Problem of the Hexateuch*, 222–32). The verb ויתן "and they set" followed by the preposition על "upon" for the action dealing with the נזר and the עדות would suggest that the parallel cited by von Rad from Egypt (ibid., 226) is not a perfect one. T. N. D. Mettinger (*King and Messiah*, 287) suggests that it means a dedicatory inscription. See also Z. W. Falk, *VT* 11 (1961) 88–91. That the word should be emended to אצעדה "bracelets" on the basis of 2 Sam 1:10 (so Ehrlich, *Randglossen* 7:305) is unlikely.

Joash is anointed and acclaimed king by the crowd.

13 The sense of drama now conjured up by the abrupt change of subject from the young king to Athaliah is worthy of mention. This dramatic and abrupt movement in the story is by no means an indication of the composite nature of the chapter. The skillful way in which Athaliah's reaction is portrayed is to be noted.

את קול הרצין העם lit., "the noise of the guard the people." The phrase is very clumsy. The RSV "the noise of the guard and the people" is not supported by MT. Most versions, including 2 Chr 23:12, are attempts at smoothing out the difficult reading. The form of הרצין is unusual, but not a gloss (against Burney, *Notes*, 308). Ehrlich's attempt to change the word to המון "the crowd of" (*Randglossen* 7:305) has no support. The term העם "the people" can either be understood as a military designation, since to this point in the narrative only the army has been involved in the coup, or as a synonym for the later mentioned "all the people of the land" (v 14).

14 The scene of the coronation is sketched quickly and effectively by the author, and the obvious joy of the crowd stands in direct contrast to the reaction of Athaliah. That it should have been impossible for anyone, especially Athaliah, to have approached as close as she did to the proceedings, given the precautions taken earlier, seems to have escaped the author.

המלך עמד על העמוד "the king standing by the pillar." Precisely what the king was standing on or by is uncertain. The derivation of the term would suggest some kind of column, podium, or platform.

והשרים "and the singers." Since the scene was accompanied by music, the reading of הַשָּׁרִים "singers" instead of הַשָּׂרִים "officers" is preferred. The חצצרה "trumpet" is to be distinguished from the shophar.

וכל עם הארץ "and all the people of the land" has caused much discussion; various interpretations of this segment of Israelite society have been offered. From this particular narrative it is impossible to make generalizations, but it is to be noted that the "people of the land" play a secondary role in the revolt. They enter into the narrative only after the army, under the direction of Jehoiada, has made its move and anointed the new king. They lend popular support to what was essentially a palace revolt (see E. W. Nicholson, *JSS* 10 [1965] 62). Their role in the celebrations, "rejoicing and blowing of trumpets," hardly seems consistent with a dignified political power group within Israelite or Judean society. Cf. R. Gordis, *JQR* 25 (1935) 237–59.

ותקרא קשר קשר "and she cried out, 'Treason! Treason!'" Athaliah's reaction to what she saw can only help call to mind the fate of her son's cousin, Joram, at the hands of Jehu (9:23).

15 The death of Athaliah is again orchestrated by Jehoiada the priest and his military allies.

אל מבית לשדרת "in front of the temple to the ranks." The phrase is awkward. On the confusion of the G tradition cf. *Notes* above. The possible difference between the שרי המיאות "centurions" and the פקדי החיל "commanders of the force," who are regarded as holding higher rank, and the confusion of the third command with the first one in v 15a, have led Montgomery (*Kings*, 421) to see much of this verse as a gloss. Such reasons are insufficient; the very awkwardness of the verse might reflect the obvious confusion of the moment portrayed in it.

והבא אחריה המת בחרב "Kill with the sword anyone who follows her." This suggests that Athaliah did not come to the temple alone.

16 וישמו לה ידים "so they arrested her." The clause is unique, literally to be translated, "They set hands to her. . . ." From the context it is clear that Athaliah was led out of the temple area to be executed.

דרך מבוא הסוסים "the horses' passage." The place of execution is ignominious. It was the gate through which mounted riders entered the city from the east (Jer 31:40) and came to the palace. The strange location suggests a speedy end for Athaliah.

17 The ending of the chapter follows roughly the same sequence as the narrative of the military revolt against Athaliah. The emphasis of this section, however, is clearly on the religious effects of the revolt. The "covenant" referred to now is of a different order from the "pact" Jehoiada made with the soldiers in v 4.

ויכרת יהוידע את הברית "then Jehoiada contracted a covenant." The article on the term "covenant" might indicate a special procedure. The covenant has three aspects. It renewed the alliance between the king and Yahweh, it reestablished the relationship between Judah and Yahweh, and it confirmed the acceptance of Joash by the people. Both 2 Chr 23:18 and Josephus (*Antiq.* ix.153) emphasize the first aspect of the restoration of the Davidic line. The threefold covenant has a clearly "deuteronomistic" flavor to it, although this is not overplayed. The Davidic covenant with Yahweh is a consistent theme of the Former Prophets (2 Sam 7; 1 Kgs 2, 4, 9). That Judah dedicate itself as "the people of Yahweh" is an important theme in Deut 4:20; 7:6; 14:2; and 1 Sam 12:22, but this does not question the covenant's historicity in this instance (see Mettinger, *King and Messiah*, 143–44). Further, in 2 Sam 5:3 and 2 Kgs 23:3, kings enter into agreements with the people. This third feature of the covenant also serves the literary purpose of uniting the king with those participants in the revolt who had hitherto played only a minor role, the people.

18 The popular side to the revolt now follows the pattern of the purge begun by Jehu in the north six years earlier. All vestiges of the previous regime, including its religion, are now eliminated.

בית הבעל "temple of Baal." No previous mention has been made of the Baal temple in Judah. The record would show that the southern nation managed to resist Baalism more easily than did Israel. Josephus (*Antiq.* ix.154) preserves the tradition that Athaliah had built this temple, but independent corroboration of this is lacking.

מתן כהן הבעל "Mattan, the priest of Baal." The name of the priest of Baal is unusual, although not unique. With the theophoric element it was Zedekiah's name before he became king (2 Kgs 24:17). In that form it also appears in the Lachish Letters 1:5 (cf. Gibson, *Syrian Semitic Inscriptions* 1:36). Baalism is detested in the "deuteronomistic" literature of the OT, but there is no reason to doubt the historicity of this event. It is quite plausible that Baalism should make some inroads into the south, encouraged by a queen who had such close ties with the apostate house of Ahab.

וישם הכהן פקדות על בית יהוה "then the priest put specially designated persons over the temple." The appointment of special custodians over the temple of Yahweh suggests that Athaliah's reign had affected the priesthood.

How widespread this was is not clear, but it could not have been too serious. There was little resistance to the revolt, begun by a priest (contra Montgomery, *Kings*, 423).

19 At this point in the revolt the military and the populace are united in their acclamation of the new king, and the revolt is a success. The exact route from the temple to the palace is unclear, although it was probably south, to the area between the temple mount and the "City of David." That the procession went by way of the "Guards' Gate" suggests the continuing need for secrecy and care.

וכל עם הארץ "and all the people of the land." Again, that this refers to a privileged body of people within Judean society is doubtful. Gray's omission of the phrase as redactional (*I & II Kings*, 581) is groundless.

20 וישמח "so rejoiced." The rejoicing of the people is not necessarily to be taken as a contrast to the silence of the city. In Josh 11:23; 14:15; 2 Chr 13:23; 14:5 the verb שקט "to be at peace" is used in the sense of quiet after battle or war. The quiet was the cause for the rejoicing.

ואת עתליהו המית בחרב בית המלך "Athaliah had been slain with the sword at the palace." The location of Athaliah's death here is not in conflict with the statement in v 17, since both are depicted as being in the vicinity of the palace. The chapter ends the brief interlude in the Davidic dynasty.

Explanation

2 Kgs 11 changes the scene of the stories thus far in the book to the Southern Kingdom of Judah. The effects of the revolt of Jehu in the north were very widespread. Although he eliminated Baalism for a while from the nation, the events that unfolded in the south show that there was a reaction in Judah which made matters worse, not better, for the adherents to the traditional religion. Athaliah's behavior following the news of her son's death provides an insight into her character which is predictable, given her ancestry. With ruthless self-interest, she kills any possible claimant to the throne of Judah. Presumably, among them would be some of her own relatives. This action poses an immediate threat to the Davidic dynasty and thereby to the stability of the nation. Only a few sentences before (8:19) had mention been made of the mercy shown the nation of Judah because of Yahweh's promise to David.

The threat is short-lived because of the activity of Jehosheba, the daughter of Jehoram, father of Ahaziah. She hides the young prince Joash for six years (vv 1–3).

At this point the restoration of the Davidic line takes place, and many reminders of the story of David are seen here. Priest, army, and eventually people all combine to anoint Joash king, renew the covenant between themselves and Yahweh, and stamp out any religious threat posed by the activities of Athaliah during her reign. The meticulous detail with which the restoration is described is in direct contrast to the brief treatment given the actions of Athaliah. The detail regularizes the reign of Joash and gives his accession a legitimacy lacking in Athaliah's reign.

The dramatic account of the death of Athaliah (vv 13–16) reflects the brutal way in which apostates are judged elsewhere in the stories of 2 Kings. Ahab and Jezebel suffer the same fate as Athaliah does: assassination. The manner of her dispatch and its location speak to the cursory way in which the queen was dismissed. The final stage in the revolt is the acquiescence of the populace and their destruction of the shrine and officials of Baal (vv 17–20). The southern restoration followed a similar course to the revolt in the north, although some seven years later.

Athaliah's reign is but a brief interlude in the progress of the Davidic monarchy in the Southern Kingdom of Judah. The queen is never given the official trappings of monarchy by the "deuteronomist." Her reign ends as it begins, in irregularity, and no attempt is made to introduce the reign or conclude it in a formal way.

Although the reign of Athaliah is seen in this way, and although the southern monarchy is now restored, there is an emerging sense in these narratives of the postponement of the inevitable. Now the taint of Baalism has touched Judah, and although frequent attempts are made to reform the worship of the south by both Hezekiah (2 Kgs 18:1–8) and Josiah (2 Kgs 22:3–23:27), they are all frustrated. The nation eventually falls. In the scheme of the "deuteronomist," the judgment upon apostasy is a consistent feature of his presentation of history. Even the Davidic dynasty is not exempt from that judgment. Such premonitions of judgment appear in the following chapter as Joash's reign ends in ignominy.

The Reign of Joash (12:1–22 [11:21–12:21])

Bibliography

Asensio, F. "Restauración de la dinastía davídica en la persona Joás." *EstBib* 2 (1943) 475–506. **Delcor, M.** "Le trésor de la maison de Yahweh des origines a l'exil." *VT* 12 (1962) 353–77. **Falk, Z. W.** "אמנים ואמונה." *Tarbiz* 28 (1959) 251–53. **Liverani, M.** "L'histoire de Joas." *VT* 24 (1974) 438–53. **Luria, B. Z.** "בימי יואש מלך יהודה." *BMik* 52 (1972) 11–20. **McKane, W.** "A Note on 2 Kings 12:10 (Evv. 12:9)." *ZAW* 71 (1959) 260–65. **Maier, J.** "Bemerkungen zur Fachsprache und Religionspolitik im Konigreich Juda." *Judaica* 26 (1970) 89–105. **Mazar, B.** "Tell Gath." *IEJ* 6 (1956) 258–59. **Rost, L.** "Der Status des Priesters in der Konigszeit." In *Wort und Geschichte*. FS K. Elliger. AOAT 18. Neukirchen-Vluyn: Neukirchener Verlag, 1973. 151–56. Ed. H. Gese, H. P. Rüger. **Torrey, C. C.** "The Foundry of the Second Temple at Jerusalem." *JBL* 55 (1936) 247–60.

Translation

1[11:21]*Joash was seven years old when he began to reign.* a 2[1]*Joash became king in the seventh year of Jehu, and he reigned in Jerusalem for forty years. His mother's name was Zibiah, and she came from Beer Sheba.* a 3[2]*Joash did what was upright* in the eyes of Yahweh all his days,[a] as Jehoiada the priest had taught him. 4[3] The high places were not removed,[a] and the people still sacrificed and burned incense at the high places. 5[4] Now Joash said to all the priests, "Concerning the money[a] of the holy things which is brought into the temple, the money reckoned against each person currently,[b] the money reckoned for each individual,[c] and all[d] the money which the people bring voluntarily to the temple, 6[5] let each priest take from his income,[a] and let them repair the damage to the temple, wherever such damage is found." 7[6] But by the twenty-third year of King Joash the priests had not repaired any damage to the temple. 8[7] So the king Joash called together the priest Jehoiada with the other priests and said to them, "Why have you not repaired the damage to the temple? Now you shall not take any monies from your incomes, because it has been designated for the temple repairs."

9[8] Then the priests agreed not to take[a] any money from the people, nor to make repairs[b] to the temple.

10[9] And Jehoiada took a single chest[a] and bored a hole in its lid, and he placed it to the right[b] of the altar[c] as one comes into the temple. The priests appointed the keepers of the threshold to be in charge of the money brought into the temple. 11[10] Then when they saw that there was plenty of money in the chest, the king's accountant and the great priest went up, cast[a] the money found in the temple, and counted it. 12[11] Then they gave the money that was weighed into the safekeeping[a] of the workers who had been assigned[b] to the temple, and they in turn paid it out to the carpenters and builders who worked on the temple. 13[12] It went also to the wall-builders[a] and stonecutters to buy[b] timber and cut stone for the repair of the temple, and for any other outlay in repairing[c] the temple. 14[13] But silver basins, snuffers, bowls, trumpets, all the vessels of silver and gold, there were not made for the temple[a] from the money brought into the temple. 15[14] Rather, it was given specifically to the workmen[a] who labored on the temple repairs. 16[15] Nor was an accounting asked of the men into whose safekeeping they had placed the money so that they might pass it on to the workmen, because they were people who dealt honestly. 17[16] The money from the guilt offerings and money for sin offerings[a] was not brought into the temple in this way, because it belonged to the priests.

18[17] Then Hazael, King of Syria, attacked and fought against Gath and captured it, and he turned to attack Jerusalem. 19[18] But Joash, king of Judah, took all the sacred items which his predecessors Jehoshaphat, Jehoram, and Ahaziah, kings of Judah, had sanctified, together with his sacred items, and all the gold which had been found in the treasuries of both temple and palace, and sent them to Hazael, king of Syria, and he lifted[a] the siege from Jerusalem.

20[19] Now the rest of the acts of Joash, and all he did, are they not written in the book of the daily acts of the kings of Judah? 21[20] Now his servants took action and plotted against him, and they struck down Joash at Beth Millo, at the descent of Silla.[a] 22[21] It was Jozabad son of Shimeath and Jehozabad[a] son of Shomer, his officials, who struck him down, and he died and was buried with his fathers in the city of David. Then Amaziah his son reigned in his place.

Notes

1.a. In keeping with other regnal formulae for the kings of Judah, Gray (*I & II Kings*, 583) suggests that v 1 and part of v 2 be reversed. Such a change is not supported by any version.

Notes

2.a. G adds ἐκ γῆς "from the land of" before באר שבע "Beer Sheba"; G^L omits.

3.a. By analogy with Lev 13:46, Ehrlich (*Randglossen* 7:306) suggests that ימיו "his days" should be read ימי, pl constr without the suffix. This is possible, although unnecessary. G reads πασας τας ἡμερας (כל ימים) "all the days."

4.a. After סרו "they removed" G reads και εκει (ושם) "and there," omitted by G^L.

5.a. In the interests of a smoother translation, the word "Concerning" has been added.

5.b. For עובר "currently" G^BL offer συντιμησεως "estimate." This would suggest an original of ערך "order," "estimate," from the verb "to arrange in order" (so *BHS*). However, a parallel expression is given in Gen 23:16 כסף עבר לסחר "according to the weight of money current among merchants" (RSV). See Ehrlich (*Randglossen* 7:306).

5.c. The phrase כסף נפשות "money for each individual" is omitted by G, but retained by G^L. Burney (*Notes*, 313) and Gray (*I & II Kings*, 584) regard it as a "superfluous legal expression." See *Comment* for its interpretation as yet another source of income for the temple. See also M. Delcor, *VT* 12 (1962) 360–61.

5.d. With Vg it is better to read וכל "and all" instead of כל "all" (Burney, *Notes*, 314).

6.a. MT reads מַכָּרוֹ which is a hiph ptcp of נָכַר "to be a stranger," and from this is derived the usual translation of "acquaintance" (RSV). G^B with its translation of ἀπο της πρασεως αὐτου (מִכְרוֹ) "from his trade," suggests a word from the root מָכַר "to trade." Montgomery (*Kings*, 432) notes a possible Ugaritic parallel in which temple officials are designated with a similar word. Their function, however, is not explained. If the phrase is pointed מִכָּרוֹ, then it would indicate profits from trade or selling, hence the translation "income." NEB agrees with "from his own funds." See also Delcor, *VT* 12 (1962) 361–64.

9.a. One would normally expect קַחַת "to take" for the MT קְחַת. However, see GKC § 93h for other examples of the shortened first syllable in such infinitives.

9.b. G^B translates το βδελυγμα "the desolation"! Regularly in G the term is transliterated with βεδεκ.

10.a. Ehrlich (*Randglossen* 7:306) and others regard the expression אֲרוֹן אֶחָד "one chest" as un-Hebraic and suggest an emendation to אֲרוֹן אֶרֶז "chest of cedar." The parallel in Lev 24:22 (מִשְׁפָּט אֶחָד "one judgment") is regarded as "an error of the punctuators" (so Burney, *Notes*, 314).

10.b. For בימין read מימין "to the right."

10.c. For MT המזבח "the altar" G^A transliterates αμμασβη. This, together with the understanding of the location of the altar in the temple, has led some to emend the text to המצבה "pillar." On the basis of Ezek 46:19, Ehrlich (*Randglossen* 7:307) prefers המבוא "entrance," while Klostermann suggests המזוזה "doorpost." On this see *Comment* below. For support of MT see W. McKane, *ZAW* 71 (1959) 261–65.

11.a. *BHS* suggests וַיְצֻרוּ, from the root יצר "to form," "fashion." G^B certainly supports MT with its reading of ἐσφιγξαν "they bound up." On the basis of the parallel in 2 Chr 24:11, Ehrlich (*Randglossen* 7:307) and Gray *I & II Kings*, 584) prefer ויערו "and they emptied." The clause is omitted by G^L. See further Delcor, *VT* 12 (1962) 373–75. Cf. also *Comment* below.

12.a. While the Qere of יד "hand, safekeeping" reads ידי "hands," it is probably better to read the word as a sg constr (יד). This is in accord with v 16 (ידם "their hand, safekeeping"). The term "hand" is often used as a symbol of power.

12.b. Qere = המפקדים "the appointments," in keeping with 22:5. 2 Chr 24:12 substitutes עושה מלאכת עבודת "those having charge over the labor."

13.a. The immediate context of גדרים "wall-builders"suggests to *BHS* the emendation to לגזרים "cutters." See also Ehrlich (*Randglossen* 7:307). However, G supports MT.

13.b. ולקנות "to buy" is omitted by G.

13.c. MT לְחָזְקָה "for repairs." G^L, Syr, and Tg add "him," and Burney (*Notes*, 315) suggests the pointing לְחָזְקָהּ "for its repair." However, see GKC § 45d for other examples of the inf constr in this form. Cf. also Montgomery, *Kings*, 432.

14.a. The phrase בית יהוה "the temple" is omitted by G^L; Vg transfers it to after ספות "basins." However, the adverbial use of the phrase בית יהוה in this whole chapter is quite varied. Gray suggests that the text implies that no such work was carried on within the temple precincts (*I & II Kings*, 585).

15.a. MT לעשי המלאכה "to the workmen." Montgomery's objection (433) to the inclusion of this phrase as "careless," in the light of the more important rank afforded these persons in v 16, is splitting hairs. It demands of the narrative an impossible consistency. Cf. *Kings*, 433.

17.a. חטאות "sin offerings" is rendered by G as sg and, in keeping with the sg כסף "money," G, Syr, and Tg read יהיה "it belonged" for יהיו "they belonged."
19.a. In typical fashion G^L adds "Hazael" after ויעל "and he lifted."
21.a. Ehrlich's judgment on the phrase הירד סלא as "vollends unverständlich" (*Randglossen* 7:308) is sound. The phrase has become subject to much emendation. Syr understands "Silla" as a proper name, and offers the equivalent of והוא ירד סלא "as he was going down to Silla." Montgomery (*Kings*, 433) combines both and suggests והוא ירד מסלא "and he was going down the causeway," locating the causeway between the palace and the barracks. On this see *Comment* below.
22.a. For the first name G reads Ἰεζειχαρ "Jezechar" (G^L = Ἰωζαχαρ "Jōzachar") and for the second Ἰεζεβουθ "Jezebouth." For some, the similarity of the names in MT casts doubt upon their accuracy. But since the two men are distinguished by their patronyms, little confusion exists.

Form/Structure/Setting

Most commentators since Wellhausen have suggested that this chapter telling of the repairs to the temple during the reign of Joash contains a priestly record of the events (vv 5–19[4–18]) (cf. Fricke, *Das Zweite Buch von den Königen*, 154–65) which was later incorporated into a deuteronomistic framework. The priestly material is thought to have come from the Judean archives (so Gray, *I & II Kings*, 582–83, following Noth, *Überlieferungsgeschichtliche Studien*, 76). The record of the events undoubtedly has a Judean origin, but it is highly unlikely that it can be attributed to priestly circles. The Kings account of the temple repairs, compared to that found in 2 Chr 24, is decidedly critical of the priesthood. The blame for the lack of repair to the temple after Joash's original order is laid upon their shoulders (v 7[6]) and, as a result of that failure, new regulations are introduced (vv 8–9[7–8]). In the procedure outlined by those new regulations the priests play a minor role. In 2 Chr 24:4–7 it is the failure of the Levites, not the complete priesthood, which is noted.

The reform also takes place at the initiative of the king, not the priesthood, nor one of its members such as Jehoiada. The king's accountant actively participates in the reform (v 11[10]), and the priests themselves are eventually refused access to a source of income they had hitherto enjoyed (v 9[8]), because of their failure to obey the king.

The tone of the chapter then is far from "priestly," and is in fact highly critical of the priests. In its present form, the chapter falls into three clear sections: an introduction (vv 1–4[11:21–12:3]), the account of the temple repair (vv 5–17[4–16]), and a conclusion (vv 18–22[17–21]).

1–4[11:21–12:3] These verses follow the pattern of introductions to the reigns of kings of Judah found throughout the books of Kings (cf. Burney, *Notes*, x-xi). The pattern is (a) synchronization with the king of Israel, (b) age of the king at accession, (c) length of reign, (d) name of the queen mother, (e) verdict upon the character of the king. The Judean pattern differs slightly from that of Israel, a difference which might be explained on the basis of different archival techniques in each country. Elements (a) and (b) are reversed in this case. The reason for this is unknown, but it does not present cause for emendation of the text. Of the twenty Judean monarchs named in the books of Kings, including Athaliah, only five have introductory regnal formu-

Form/Structure/Setting   149

lae which fit the pattern outlined above. They are Jehoshaphat (1 Kgs 22:41–44), Amaziah (2 Kgs 14:1–4), Azariah (15:1–4), Jotham (15:32–35), and Hezekiah (18:1–3). Divergence from the complete form is not unusual, and the notion that the longest version of the form is the standard one is by no means sure. That these introductory formulae are placed here by the redactor is a truism.

5–17[4–16] The arrangement of the material dealing with the temple repairs follows nine distinct stages of the venture. First (vv 5–6[4–5]) the king, acting decisively and on his own initiative, allocates certain monies for the repair to the temple. Second, the immediate result is that nothing happens (v 7[6]). Third, the king calls together the priests, addresses them, and revises the system of collecting funds for the repairs. To this the priests acquiesce (vv 8–9[7–8]). Fourth, in reaction to this, a collection is instituted by Jehoiada (v 10[9]). Fifth, as a result of this, an adequate income is found for the repairs to the temple (v 11[10]). Sixth, the monies are redistributed to the workmen at two levels who are placed in charge of the repairs (vv 12–13[11–12]). The final three stages (vv 14–15, 16, 17 [13–14, 15, 16]) do not necessarily follow chronologically, but offer information on some of the other effects of the reform. They mention that no money was made available for the manufacture of temple utensils, the workmen were completely trustworthy, and certain monies were not allocated for the repairs.

Strong similarities exist between this account of Joash's repairs to the temple and the account of Josiah's activity in 2 Kgs 22:1–7. Both passages refer to the priest as הכהן הגדול "the great priest" (12:11[10]; 22:4). Both passages describe the temple income in precisely the same terms (הכסף המובא בית יהוה "the money brought into the temple" 12:10b[9b]; 22:4). Both passages mention that the money was placed in the safekeeping of the "keepers of the threshold" (12:10b[9b]; 22:4). V 12:12[11] is almost identical with 22:5 and 12:12b–13 [11b–12] follows 22:6. Both passages make mention of the trustworthiness of the workers, and the fact that they did not need auditing (12:16[15]; 22:7). However, the nature of the parallels is such that common historical circumstance and common authorship of the narratives would explain them. The system of collection presupposed by Josiah is that introduced by Joash. 2 Kgs 22 refers to the repairs Josiah made on the temple only as a prelude to the greater achievement of his reform, which was more widespread. It appears that Joash's only achievement worthy of comment was the program of repair. Since the order of events is slightly different in each account, the matter of the form of the narratives cannot be explained on the grounds of a rigid common genre, nor need it be explained in terms of the "dependency" of one account upon another.

The language of the account of the temple repairs in vv 5–17 [4–16] is distinctive. In contrast to many of the narratives thus far in 2 Kings the story contains a large amount of detail, and such details are given in specialized language. Also in contrast to the narratives seen thus far, there is little in the way of "drama" in this story. It is narrated in a very matter-of-fact way. No emotions are displayed and the characters on the whole are rather bland. For example, the monies collected for the repairs, and subsequent revision of the collection are described in the professional language of the accountant.

Certain specific funds are designated for the repairs. The narrow application of such terms as are found in vv 5, 6, 17[4, 5, 16] has been the cause of much debate concerning the precise meaning of the terms (cf. *Comment*). But such is the nature of language used by small circles of people.

The listing of personnel involved in the repairs (vv 12–13[11–12]) is typical of official records. The precise details of the new regulations, such as the position of the collection box and the temporary halt in the manufacture of utensils, all betray the bureaucratic flavor of the record. The reference to the lack of an audit of the workers makes sense only if such an audit were expected. The activity of the "king's secretary" in the whole affair (v 11[10]) offers further support to the notion that the record is an official one, taken from the royal archives of the southern nation. Its position and function in its present context, however, take us beyond that original setting to the literary intention of the writer.

18–22[17–21] While Montgomery (*Kings*, 433) identifies the opening particle (אז "then") as "archival," it is certainly used in other contexts (cf. 5:3). This brief note ending the reign of Joash contains other archival features. The technical use of the term עלה "attack," for the movement of an army against an objective, is characteristic of military reports. The rather dispassionate account of the attack against Jerusalem and the bribe offered by Joash to Hazael reflect archival style. The connection between vv 18–19[17–18] and the preceding story is found in the reference to the temple treasures which Joash gave away, together with money from his own treasury. The brief note provides a marked contrast to the activities of the previous story.

Vv 20–22[19–21] conclude the reign with the typical formula, with the added details of the plot and assassination. The verses bring to an abrupt end the reign of Joash; again, the contrast to what precedes is marked. The selectivity of the writer is clear. From the reasonably long reign of Joash, few incidents are picked out as worthy of mention.

Comment

In contrast to the passive role the king has played thus far in the incidents recorded from his reign, he initiates the repair of the temple in Jerusalem and introduces a new form of payment for the temple's upkeep. 2 Chr 24:17–22 contains additional historical material concerning the relationship between the king and Jehoiada the priest. Most commentators regard this additional material as being good historical tradition.

1[11:21] בן שבע שנים יהואש "Joash was seven years old." This verse is numbered 11:21 in the English versions, which follow the numbering from G. The suggestion that it should be placed after v 2 (see *Notes* above) is not to be followed. The presence of the number seven (שבע) in various forms throughout these chapters is most intriguing, but probably accidental. In 11:2 Jeho*sheba* rescues the young prince; the overthrow of Athaliah takes place in the *seventh* year of her reign (11:4); coincidentally, Joash is *seven* years old at the time (12:1[11:21]); he became king in the *seventh* year of Jehu (12:2[1]); and his mother came from Beer *Sheba*.

Comment

2[1] בשנת שבע ליהוא "in the seventh year of Jehu." Athaliah and Jehu were contemporaries, although the latter reigned for much longer. They were at opposite ends of the religious spectrum, yet the manner in which they assumed their respective thrones has much in common, the ultimate effect upon the life of their people similar.

וארבעים שנה "forty years." Although this is often used as a general figure, there is no reason to doubt its accuracy. When he died Joash would have been at the reasonable age of forty-seven. Montgomery's suggestion (*Kings*, 427) that Joash's reign should be reckoned from the death of his father, and that the forty years should include the seven of Athaliah, is attractive. It would, as pointed out by Montgomery, reduce the difference between the Israelite and Judean chronologies in their calculations of the period between Jehu and the fall of Samaria, a difference of some twenty years. However, this does not take into account the seven years of Jehu which preceded the reign of Joash. See E. R. Thiele, *The Mysterious Numbers of the Hebrew Kings*, 68–72; Shenkel, *Chronology and Recensional Development*, 78–80.

ושם אמו צביה "his mother's name was Zibiah." Such references to the king's mother are regular features of the Judean regnal formula (cf. 14:2; 15:2; etc.). The name צביה means "gazelle" and is fitting for someone from the area of Beer Sheba. A masculine form is found in Isa 13:14, and it reappears as a proper name in the Murabbaṯ Papyrus (B. 2). See Gibson, *Syrian Semitic Inscriptions* 1:31–32.

3[2] כל ימיו "all his days." See *Notes*. Some versions, in keeping with 2 Chr 24:2, suggest that the king's uprightness was of a limited duration. But 2 Kgs 12 knows of no lapses in the king's behavior, and the text should stand.

אשר הורהו יהוידע "as Jehoiada had taught him." Jehoiada's role is interesting; he emerges here as a guardian and tutor of the king. In 2 Chr 24 Jehoiada even chooses wives for Joash. That this phrase is a marginal note is suggested by Burney, *Notes*, 313. Jehoiada appears to have lost his initial influence over the king since, with minor exceptions, Jehoiada does not take a very prominent role in this incident.

4[3] רק הבמות לא סרו "the high places were not removed." Whether any wrong is implied in this statement is not clear. In spite of Robinson's assessment of this statement as expressing "partial editorial approval" of Joash (*The Second Book of Kings*, 117) there is no hint given here that these "high places" were for pagan worship. No reference is made to the "other gods" (אלהים אחרים) so common in deuteronomistic comdemnations of the monarchy. The reference is of the same order as 1 Kgs 3:2 and 15:14, and may be an observation on the state of affairs in Judah before the centralization of worship under Hezekiah and Josiah.

5–17[4–16] The narrative which follows concerning the repairs to the temple has distinct parallels with the narrative in chap. 22. The stylistic similarities can be explained by common authorship and common subject matter. This incident describes the inauguration of a new method of financing the upkeep of the temple after the failure of the priests to carry out needed repairs. The system was used until the exile, and after the return was organized on a more regular basis (Neh 10:32).

5[4] ויאמר יהואש אל הכהנים "now Joash said to the priests." An interesting feature of this whole project of repair is that it was initiated by the king himself. The same holds true for the early stages of Josiah's reform (22:3–7). In the period before the exile it appears that the king was the superior of the Jerusalem priesthood (see H. Ringgren; *Israelite Religion,* 211).

The syntax of this verse is obscure, and attempts have been made to emend it, at least by the omission of the phrase כסף נפשות ערכו "the money reckoned for each individual" which is regarded as a "gloss" (Burney, *Notes,* 313–14) or "Epexegese" (Ehrlich) on the previous phrase. The general meaning of the verse is plain and, maintaining the text as it stands, we offer the following interpretation. The king orders the priests to combine, for the purposes of the temple repair, five sources of income, four of which are mentioned in this verse. כסף הקדשים "money of the holy things" is presumably the money set aside for the manufacture and purchase of the sacred utensils of the temple. Its use for the repairs to the temple throws light on v 14. NEB's "all the silver brought as holy gifts" is not necessary. It would duplicate the latter part of the verse. The כסף עובר איש "the money reckoned against each person currently" is, literally, "the money of the crossing over of a person," an expression which has caused some debate. It has its background in the regulation which appears in Exod 30:13–14 governing the census of Israelites. That Exod 30 is generally regarded as late (cf. B. S. Childs, *The Book of Exodus,* OTL [Philadelphia: Westminster, 1974] 529) need not indicate that the regulation itself is late. In the period of the monarchy, during which time taxation, a standing army, and other reorganization were introduced, some form of enumeration would have been necessary. In Exod 30:13–14 the כסף עבר is the money taken from each person who is counted (cf. NEB). In the post-exilic period, the tax was levied annually (cf. Neh 10:32).

כסף נפשות ערכו "the money reckoned for each individual" is, literally, "the money of persons, according to his reckoning." Rather than being a gloss on the previous phrase, and therefore superfluous, it represents another source of income for the temple, namely the tax levied against persons who offered their services to the temple (cf. Lev 27:1–33). כסף אשר יעלה על לב איש "money which people voluntarily" indicates the voluntary offerings which would have been given on a less regular basis. The phrase על לב "upon a heart" is rare, elsewhere associated with the verb אמר "say" (2 Sam 19:8; Isa 40:2). That all four of these sources of income were directed to the repairs of the temple shows the sad state of the building. 2 Chr 24 places the blame for this at the feet of Athaliah and her family, but the reluctance of the Jerusalem priests to act upon the orders of the king would suggest too that they shared in the blame.

6[5] איש מאת מכרו "each from his income." The MT pointing demands the translation "acquaintance" or something similar, which Fricke (*Das Zweite Buch von den Konigen,* 160) interprets as associates of the temple personnel. But not only is it unlikely that each priest dealt only with one "friend" (cf. the remarks of Skinner, *The Books of Kings,* 344), but that each man should use a friend as a source of income is even more unlikely. Reference to the supposed Ugaritic parallel of "temple tellers" (cf. Montgomery, *Kings,* 429) is enticing, but too distant a connection to be of any real value. A simple repointing of the consonants offers the translation of "income" (cf. *Notes*). Even the priests' own personal sources of income were redirected to the repair of the temple יחזקו את בדק "let them repair the damage." Montgomery's assertion that the reference to the priests' activity at this point conflicts with the mention of the workmen in v 15*b* is unfounded. It ignores the failure of the priests and the new measures taken as a result of that failure.

7[6] בשנת עשרים ושלש שנה "by the twenty-third year." This is the year of the king's reign, therefore when Joash was thirty years old. No indication is given when the repairs were initiated, but the impression is that the priests neglected their orders for a considerable time. 2 Chr 24 omits any mention of the lapse. The verse reflects the status of the priests in the pre-exilic period compared to their increased status after the exile. Cf. L. Rost, in *Wort und Geschichte*, 151–56.

8[7] The king's strong words to both Jehoiada and the other priests again shows the authority the king had over the priests in this matter. אל תקחו כסף מאת מכריכם "you shall take no monies from your incomes" is a denial of access to the regular income of the priests and demonstrates the urgency with which the king regarded the matter of the repair of the temple.

9[8] לבלתי קחת כסף . . . ולבלתי חזק "not to take any money . . . nor to make repairs." This represents a reduction of the responsibilities of the priests. They are to be no longer responsible for the regular receipt of money offerings, presumably those listed in v 5[4], nor for the repairs of the temple.

10[9] ויקחו . . . ארון אחד "and . . . took a single chest." The general meaning of the verse is sure, but the pointing of the phrase אֲרוֹן אֶחָד is difficult (see *Notes*). The box was used as a receptacle of the silver brought into the temple, although that is not explicitly stated. To speak of coins at this time is quite anachronistic, since the earliest evidence for coinage in the Bible is Ezra 2:69. It was known earlier in the Aegean (cf. H. Hamburger, "Money," *IDB*, 3:423–35).

אצל המזבח בימין בבוא. The precise location of the box for the collection has been the cause of much debate and subsequent emendation of the text. The text reads "near the altar on the right side as one enters the temple." McKane (*ZAW* 71 [1959]260–65) has demonstrated that the text can stand in its present form and, following de Groot, identifies the מזבח as the "threshold altar" which was situated in the inner court of the temple. This understanding would be supported by the fact that the box was placed in the charge of the שמרי הסף "keepers of the threshold."

11[10] ספר המלך "the king's secretary" reappears again in chap. 22, and his presence indicates the way in which the king governed the affairs of the temple.

והכהן הגדול. Taken as "the high priest," the phrase is to be seen as an anachronism (cf. Ringgren, *Israelite Religion*, 211), notwithstanding the appeals to the Ugaritic *rb khnm* "high priest" by Montgomery (*Kings*, 429). Since the term is unique to 2 Kgs (22:4, 8; 23:4) it is not to be regarded as an indication of the man's professional status. The term גדול can be translated as "great" or "noble," and could equally well be an indication of a person's character. (Cf. the אשה גדולה "woman of substance" of 4:8.)

ויצרו וימנה את הכסף. Literally, "they bound up and counted the money," which seems to reverse the logical order (cf. the use of צרר "to bind" in 5:23). If MT is allowed to stand, then it is thought that "ring money" is involved, i.e., bracelets (so Barnes, *II Kings*, 60; Hamburger; *IDB* 3:424). A further suggestion is to change the verbal root to read וַיְצְרוּ], from יצר "to form" (see Montgomery, *Kings*, 429). The advantage of the first suggestion is that it retains MT, but the difficulty is that it presupposes a kind of currency for which there is little evidence at this time. The second suggestion owes much to C. C. Torrey (*JBL* 55 [1936]247-61), who argued for a reading of יוֹצֵר, to be translated as "temple foundry worker." The evidence gathered is late. The parallels cited are taken from Herodotus' description of an Egyptian custom (*Book* iii. 96) and the application of the evidence is to the second, not the first temple. If MT stands, then the context might aid the interpretation of the use of the term צרר. In 1 Kgs 7:15 it is stated of Hiram ויצר את שני העמודים "and he cast two pillars." There G translates the verb with ἐχώνευσεν, which is translated into English as "melted down" or "cast," and is reserved elsewhere for the usual Hebrew word נתן (2 Kgs 22:9). While in v 11[10] G offers ἐσφιγξαν "they bound tight," the previous translation suggests that in certain specific contexts the term צרר can indicate the casting of metal and may be used as a synonym for נתך. The NEB translation of "melted down" would support this. Such an interpretation would accommodate the foundry in the temple, while allowing the MT to stand.

12[11] על יד "into the safekeeping," literally, "hand." Here the hand is the symbol of power or safekeeping. The priests delegated the responsibility of the money to laypersons specially designated for the task at hand.

לחרשי העץ ולבנים "to the carpenters and builders." The list of workmen to whom the payment was made illustrates again the sad state of repair to the temple. Their skills would be applied to a wide range of damage. The only other occasions on which such an army of skilled workmen was assembled were the building of the temple (1 Kgs 5) and during the repairs under Josiah (2 Kgs 22).

14[13] אך לא יעשה בית יהוה "but there were not made for the temple." The ambiguity of this clause is indicated by the various translations: "But there was not made for the house of the LORD. . . ." (RSV); "They did not use the silver brought into the house of the LORD to make silver cups. . . ." (NEB). The difficulty is aggravated by the omission of the phrase בית יהוה "the temple" in many of the versions. Montgomery regards the phrase as an intentional gloss, but apart from the fact that the phrase is used very often in the chapter adverbially (cf. vv 5, 10, 11, 12, 13, 14, 15, 17 [4, 9, 10, 11, 12, 13, 14, 16]), to suggest that it is a gloss in this instance does not explain its function in the sentence. The context implies that the total income of the temple, with a few exceptions, was diverted toward the repair of the building (v 15[14]), including the כסף הקדשים "silver for holy things" (v 5[4]). Because of the urgency of the repairs, manufacture of the utensils used in the temple temporarily ceased. A similar list of items is found in 1 Kgs 7:20. ספות כסף "silver basins" are receptacles for use in worship (Exod 12:22). The derivation of מזמרות is unknown, although it is normally translated as "snuffers." מזרקות "bowls" is from the root זרק "to scatter" (Exod 27:3), and the חצצרות are the ceremonial trumpets.

16[15] ולא יחשבו "nor was an accounting asked." The workmen were chosen because of their obvious honesty and trustworthiness. The implication is that the priests were not as reliable as the workmen in their handling of the project.

17[16] כסף אשם וכסף חטאות "money from the guilt offerings and money for sin offerings." Two sources of income are exempt, but no reason is given other than that they belonged to the priests. The כסף אשם and the כסף חטאות are unusual terms and reference to them is omitted from 2 Chr 24. Lev 5:15–19 describes a ritual by which an offender shall (a) offer a guilt offering at a certain value, (b) make restitution to the person offended, (c) pay one-fifth of the restitution price as a tax for the priests. The possible late date for this regulation might exclude it as a precedent for the terms used in v 17[16]. Nowhere is the tax levied designated by either of these terms. Exod 30:16 refers to כסף הכפרים "the atonement money," a tax levied on the Day of Atonement. Again, the possible lateness of the regulation might rule it out of the discussion of the terms in v 17[16]. De Vaux's suggestion (*Ancient Israel* 1:429–30) that the money is either payment for faults similar to those expiated by sacrifice, a tax on sacrifice, or payments made instead of sacrifice only illustrates the confusion that surrounds the terms.

לכהנים יהיו "because it belonged to the priests." The practice of reserving some parts of offerings for priests is found in Lev 2:3; 4:13.

18–22[17–21] The end of Joash's reign is dealt with abruptly by the writer. The extensive temple repairs are to little or no avail since the kingdom is eventually saved from Syria at the expense of the temple treasures. For reasons unstated, Joash dies as ignobly as his predecessor, murdered by two of his own people.

18 [17] אז יעלה חזאל "then Hazael attacked." After two successful attacks on Damascus by Shalmaneser III in ca. 840 and 837 B.C. (cf. *ANET*, 280), Hazael was left alone by Assyria. Judging by 10:32–33 he began to expand his power in the west to protect that border of his kingdom. His expansion to the Philistine Plain represented a serious economic and military threat to Judah, since the trade routes were in danger of being lost. The expansion of Hazael is not dated, although it must have taken place after the temple repairs begun in Joash's twenty-third year (ca. 814 B.C.).

וילחם על גת "and he fought against Gath." Gath is identified with Tell es-Safi (so R.A.S. Macalister, *Excavations in Palestine During the Years 1898–1900* [London: Palestine Exploration Fund, 1902] 63–68) or as Tell Sheikh el Areini (so B. Mazar, "Tell Gath," *IEJ* 6 (1956) 258–59). Tell es-Safi (Tel Zafit) is approximately thirty kilometers west and south of Jerusalem, and Tell Sheikh el Areini (Tel Erani) is located to the north and west of modern Kiryat Gath. Biblical Gath was one of the five major Philistine cities, and played a prominent role in earlier Israelite history. See Stinespring, *IDB* 2:355–56. With the other cities nearby, it held a crucial position on the southern coastal plain. This incursion of Hazael into the south is quite possibly connected with the chaotic state of affairs in the north after the death of Jehu and the accession of his son Jehoahaz (cf. 13:1–3).

לעלות על ירושלם "to attack Jerusalem." This would have been a natural move for Hazael to have made, since it was to his advantage to remove Jerusalem as a threat from his rear, regardless of the material gains.

19[18] Without a fight, Hazael had gained much. Joash stripped the valuables from the temple to pay off the threatening Syrian.

21[20] ויקמו עבדיו "now his servants took action." The end of Joash is not explained, and even the overtly theological explanation of 2 Chr 24:24–27 does not explain the political motivation for the dissatisfaction with Joash and the plot against him.

ויכו את יואש בית מלא "and they struck down Joash at Beth Millo." The exact location of the death of Joash is a mystery. 2 Chr 24:25 has Joash wounded and helpless after a battle with the Syrians, but Kings nowhere refers to such a battle. The "Millo" is derived from the verb מלא "to fill." It has been interpreted in two ways. Either it refers to the filled terraces supporting the steep slopes of the Kidron wall of the Ophel (see K. Kenyon. *EAEHL* 2:595–96; B. Mazar, "Jerusalem in the Biblical Period," in *Jerusalem Revealed*, ed. Y. Yadin [Jerusalem: Exploration Society, 1976] 4, 6–7); or it is the district which was expanded after the death of David to the north and west of the Ophel, the city of David (see G. A. Barrois, "Millo," *IDB* 3:382–83.) In either case, what is meant by the "House of Millo" is unknown. הירד סלא "at the descent of Silla" presents another difficulty. The "descent of Silla" or any other reference to "Silla" in the OT is lacking.

22[21] ויוזבד בן שמעת ויהוזבד בן שמר "it was Jozabad son of Shimeath and Jehozabad son of Shomer." For the suggested emendations of these names see *Notes*. The name יהוזבד "Jehozabad" means "gift of Yahweh" or "endowed by Yahweh" and is common in later OT literature (cf. 2 Chr 17:18; Ezra 8:33). Similarly, Elizabad occurs in 1 Chr 12:12. The patronyms of the two men are interesting. The ending of שמעת "Shimeath" is extremely rare in the OT, although other forms such as שמע and שמעיה are found (cf. Josh 15:26; Gibson, *Syrian Semitic Inscriptions* 1:61–62). According to Noth (*Die israelitischen Personennamen*, 38), Assyrian and Arabic names commonly end with "-ath," and this might suggest a foreign origin. שֹׁמֵר "Shomer" is nowhere else found in the OT as a proper name. שֶׁמֶר (1 Kgs 16:24) and שְׁמַרְיָהוּ (1 Chr 4:37) are known, and the Samarian ostraca contain the name שמריו (cf. Gibson, *Syrian Semitic Inscriptions* 1:8). The Arad letters contain a longer form שמריהו (Gibson, ibid., 53). The difficulties with these names are illustrated by the interpretations offered by 2 Chr 24:26.

The chapter closes with the customary ending, although the final resting place for Joash differs from that mentioned in 2 Chr 24.

Excursus: The Account of Joash's Reign and the Account of Idri-mi of Alalakh

M. Liverani (*VT* 24[1974] 438–53) has suggested an ingenious inspiration for the full account of the reign of Joash contained in chaps. 11 and 12 of 2 Kings. He notes some striking parallels between the form, style, and plot of 2 Kgs 11–12, and the form, style, and plot of the self-serving account of the rise to fame of Idri-mi of Alalakh. The latter account was carved on a statue of this fifteenth-century king and first published in 1949. A new translation is to be found in *ANESTP*,

557-58, by A. L. Oppenheim. The account tells the following story. Through some misfortune Idri-mi's family was forced to flee their homeland, and he eventually left his family to settle in the land of Canaan. There he was subsequently recognized by some of his countrymen and, after sufficient time (seven years), he had built up enough forces to land near Mount Cassius on the coast of Syria. At this time his brothers joined him. For a further period of time (seven years), he was oppressed by the Hurrians, but in the seventh year he won the favor of the king of the Hurrians and entered into an alliance with him. He then was able to become king of Alalakh and embark upon a campaign of expansion. Having established himself, he introduced a series of cultic and social reforms. The account ends with the invocation of blessing and a note to the effect that the reign lasted thirty years.

Liverani identifies the style of the inscription as propaganda, and mentions several parallels in the ANE. On the basis of the similarities with the account of the reign of Joash in 2 Kgs 11-12, he concludes that the biblical account is based on such an attempt at political self-justification (propaganda), and that the original model for the biblical account was written on a statue dedicated to Joash.

There are clearly some similarities between the two accounts. Liverani's analysis of the Idri-mi inscription is as follows:

1. Crisis in the form of a revolt, and the flight of the family.
2. Sojourn for seven years in another land, while the throne was occupied by a usurper.
3. Recognition of Idri-mi by his countrymen, and the beginning of the amassing of power to return to the throne.
4. In the seventh year Idri-mi takes his throne by force of arms.
5. The people are content.
6. A covenant with god is made in the presence of the people.
7. Cultic reforms are carried out.
8. The length of the reign is given as "thirty years."

The style is theatrical and the document is clearly propaganda. Although there are some obvious similarities between the two accounts, that the account of Joash's reign is dependent in any way upon the Idri-mi inscription must be viewed with suspicion. The most telling objection concerns the temporal distance between the two documents.

There are also some marked differences in the account and, in addition to the similarities, the peculiarities of Joash material must be explained. First, the order of events is slightly different and is interrupted at 12:1-3[11:21-12:2] and 12:18-22[17-21]. In vv 1-3[11:21-12:2] the length of reign is mentioned. To be noted also is that such figures are a common feature of these editorial comments on the reigns of various kings. The Joash account contains reference to two covenants, a feature which gave rise to the doublets noted above (see *Form/Structure/Setting* for chap. 11). Further, the balance of the two accounts is far from the same. In the Idri-mi inscription the reference to the cultic changes instituted is almost in passing, obviously not an important element of the restoration to power. Furthermore, these changes are not so much reform as restoration of the old cult. Far more space is devoted to the social reforms he carried out. In the biblical account of Joash's reign the cultic changes are described in detail and are in two parts. In 11:18 the Baal temple is destroyed, but not at the initiative of the king, who is too young, but the priest. In 12:5-17[4-16] a reform in the system of financing the upkeep of the temple is inaugurated. In 2 Kgs 11-12 there is no attempt to approach the inclusive survey of beneficial acts found in the Idri-mi account.

In addition to these matters, there are many other possible parallels to the restoration of power as depicted in 2 Kgs 11-12. The general plot of each is the unjust exile of a person who is to become very important in the later history of his people, either as a leading official or as king. The restoration of that person takes place at a decisive moment in life. It involves recognition, then firm acceptance of his status. Timing is of the essence; in some cases the restoration to power begins a new phase in the ongoing history. Such a story is that of Jacob (Gen 25–50), who at one point in his life is forced to work for periods of seven years (Gen 29:15–20) before the tribal patriarchs are born. Joseph's adventures (Gen 37–50) follow a similar pattern, as does the nonbiblical story of Sinuhe (*ANET*, 18–22). But the narrative plot which has the most similarities with the story of Joash is the biblical story of David's early days and his struggle to become king of all of Israel (1 Sam 16–2 Sam 7). Although he was the designated heir to the throne, David was exiled and spends time as an outlaw. Finally, after the death of Saul, David and his men begin the process of the restoration of power and the crown to David. David becomes king at Hebron over Judah and, finally, after reigning in Hebron for "seven years and six months" (2 Sam 5:5), he takes Jerusalem and becomes king over the whole land. Important in this whole process is the making of a covenant between David and representatives of the people before Yahweh (2 Sam 5:3). Apart from the obvious changes this implied in the social structure of Israel, certain far-reaching cultic reforms were made. The Ark of the Covenant was brought to Jerusalem (2 Sam 6) and the wish is expressed for the construction of a temple (2 Sam 7), but this is postponed temporarily.

It is far more likely that a biblical narrative from the same body of material (the Former Prophets) would provide the model for subsequent biblical narratives, rather than a text such as the Idri-mi inscription which is so far removed from 2 Kgs 11–12 both geographically and temporally. Liverani's theory must be rejected. While both texts are characterized by a certain amount of "theatricality," this is a characteristic not unique to these texts; and in the case of 2 Kgs 11–12, the extent of it is rather limited.

The parallels with the rise of David are more obvious, but caution must be exercised here too lest too much be concluded. The length of the two narratives provides one of the clearest differences between the rise of David and the reign of Joash. Both accounts are "composite" in that they draw material from various traditions and that any similarity in overall plot is due more to the compiler than to any pre-existent sources. (On the David story cf. Noth, *Überlieferungsgeschichtliche Studien*, 63–66; B. C. Birch, *The Rise of the Israelite Monarchy*, SBLDS 27 [Missoula, MT: Scholars Press, 1976].) Common authorship would explain the similarities of style, and common theme—the success of the Davidic monarchy—would be sufficient motivation.

Explanation

The detail devoted to the temple repairs of Joash is noteworthy when it is compared to the absence of detail concerning the rest of his long, forty-year reign, and the cryptic way in which the events surrounding his death are reported. The reasons for the detail are to be found in the nature of the sources used for the account of the temple repairs (see *Form/Structure/Setting* on 12:5–17[4–16]), but the precise selection of such an event, to the exclusion of so many other possibilities, is motivated by the concerns of the "deuteronomist." The opening verses offer the legitimacy to the reign of Joash which was denied to Athaliah. The length of reign, the name of his mother, and the synchronization of his accession with the northern monarch (vv 1–2) are the badges of legitimacy. The dynasty is once again placed on a regular footing.

The system of temple repairs introduced by Joash (vv 5–17) is quite thorough. The king takes the responsibility of the repairs out of the hands of the priests because of their lax attitude toward their duty and places it in the hands of those who do the work. The general oversight of the fund raising is placed under the control of "the king's secretary" (v 11), who was also responsible for the allotment of funds to the workmen. The most far-reaching implication inherent in such a move by the king is the restricting of the priests' power and control, with a proportionate increase in the power and control of the king over the temple affairs. The centralizing of authority thus begun is continued by subsequent Judean kings: Hezekiah, with his abolition of worship outside the capital city (2 Kgs 18:4), and Josiah, with his purge of Judean religion (2 Kgs 22–23). The system of temple financing inaugurated by Joash was still in effect during the reform of Josiah (2 Kgs 22:3–7).

The repairs and the new system of financing were to little avail because of the attack by Hazael into the southwestern reaches of Judah. The circumstances that allowed such an attack are unknown but were probably the result of the uncertainty following the death of Jehu in Israel in 815 B.C. (see *Comment* on 12:18[17]). Hazael's designs on his western neighbors had already become apparent (cf. 10:32–33). Joash emptied the palace and temple treasury to pay the bribe to Hazael and effectively robbed the temple of any further income for repairs.

In the deuteronomistic presentation of the history of the monarchy Joash plays a minor role. He is the first king of the restored dynasty and his activities regarding the temple are worthy of mention. But nothing else is, save his untimely death. His reform was an eventual failure; his unusual death passes with little comment from the writer. Two other reformers who followed continue his work, but serious questions are raised about Hezekiah's integrity (cf. 2 Kgs 20:19) and, like Joash, Josiah dies before his time (2 Kgs 23:29–30). Their reforms do not stop the tide of judgment.

Syrian Oppression and the Death of Elisha (13:1–25)

Bibliography

Brock, S. P. "Νεφεληγερετα = rkb'rpt." *VT* 18 (1968) 395–97. **Carroll, R. P.** "Elijah and Elisha Sagas." *VT* 19 (1969) 400–415. **Conteneau, G.** *La magie chez les assyriens et les babyloniens.* Paris: Gabalda, 1932. **Cooke, S. A.** "Israel and the Neighboring States." *CAH* vol. 3. Cambridge: Cambridge University Press, 1925. 17–20. **Fohrer, G.** *Die symbolischen Handlungen der Propheten.* ATANT 54. 2d ed. Zürich: Zwingli Verlag, 1968.

Geradon, B. de "L'homme a l'image de Dieu." *NRT* 11 (1958) 683–95. **Hallo, W.** "From Qarqar to Carchemish." *BA* 23 (1962) 34–61. **Haran, M.** "The Empire of Jeroboam ben Joash." *VT* 17 (1967) 267–97. **Loretz, O.** "Neues Verständnis einiger Schriftstellen mit Hilfe des Ugaritischen." *BZ* 2 (1958) 287–91. **Malamat, A.** "The Aramaeans." *People of Old Testament Times.* Ed. D. W. Thomas. Oxford: Clarendon Press (1973) 134–55. **Mazar, B.** "The Aramean Empire and Its Relations with Israel." *BA* 25 (1962) 98–120. **McCarthy, D. J.** "2 Kings 13:4–6." *Bib* 54 (1973) 409–10. ———. *"berit* in the Old Testament History and Theology." *Bib* 53 (1972) 110–21. **Seters, J. van.** "Confessional Reformulation in the Exilic Period." *VT* 22 (1972) 448–59. ———. "The Terms 'Amorite' and 'Hittite' in the Old Testament." *VT* 22 (1972) 64–81. **Thompson, R. C.** *Semitic Magic: Its Origins and Development.* London: Hodder & Stoughton, 1936.

Translation

¹*In the twenty-third* [a] *year of Joash ben Ahaziah king of Judah, Jehoahaz ben Jehu began to reign over Israel* [b] *in Samaria for seventeen years.* ²*He behaved badly in the eyes* [a] *of Yahweh and followed after the sins* [b] *of Jeroboam ben Nebat with which he caused Israel to sin. He did not turn from it.* [c] ³*Yahweh's anger was incited against* [a] *Israel and he gave them into the power of Hazael king of Syria, and into the power of Ben Hadad, Hazael's son, for quite a while.* [b] ⁴*So Jehoahaz sought Yahweh's favor, and Yahweh listened to him because he had seen the affliction of Israel, how the king of Syria had oppressed them.* ⁵*Thus it was that Yahweh provided Israel with the deliverer, and they came* [a] *out from under the power of Syria, and the Israelites settled* [b] *again in their own dwellings as before.* ⁶*But in spite of this they did not turn aside from the sins* [a] *of the house of Jeroboam* [b] *with which he caused Israel to sin, by walking in it.* [bc] *Even the Asherah stood in Samaria.* ⁷*Jehoahaz had no army* [a] *left* [b] *to speak of save a company of mounted men, one squadron of chariots and a brigade of infantry. The king of Syria had decimated them and made them like the dust at threshing.* [c] ⁸*Now the remainder of the activities of Jehoahaz, and everything he accomplished, are they not written down in the records of the kings of Israel?* ⁹*Jehoahaz slept with his ancestors, and they buried him in Samaria, then his son Joash reigned in his place.*

¹⁰*In the thirty-seventh* [a] *year of Joash king of Judah, Joash ben Jehoahaz became king over Israel in Samaria for a period of sixteen years.* [b] ¹¹*He behaved badly in Yahweh's sight, not turning away from all the sins* [a] *of Jeroboam ben Nebat with which he caused Israel to sin, but walking in it.* [b] ¹²ᵃ*Now the rest of the activities of Joash, and all he accomplished, including his great military exploits in his war with Amaziah king of Judah, are they not written down in the records of the kings of Israel?* ¹³*Joash slept with his ancestors, and Jeroboam succeeded him to the throne. Joash was buried in Samaria with the kings of Israel.*

¹⁴*Now Elisha had become sick with the illness from which he would die, and Joash king of Israel went down to him* [a] *and wept over him* [b] *uttering the words, "My father! My father! The chariotry of Israel and its cavalry!"* ¹⁵*Elisha said to him, "Take a bow and some arrows."* [a] *So he took hold* [b] *of a bow and some arrows.* ¹⁶*Then he said to the king of Israel,* [a] *"Put your hand to the bow." And he put his hand to the bow, and Elisha placed* [b] *his own hand upon the hand of the king.* ¹⁷*Then he said, "Open the window towards the east." And he opened it.* [a] *Elisha said, "Shoot!" and he shot.* [a] *Elisha cried, "An arrow for victory from* [b] *Yahweh!*

Notes

An arrow for victory over Syria! ᶜ *You shall strike Syria at Aphek until you defeat them."* ¹⁸ *He said* ᵃ *further, "Take the arrows."* ᵇ *And he took them. He* ᶜ *then ordered the king of Israel, "Strike the ground!" He struck the ground three times, then stopped.* ¹⁹ *The man of God was furious with him and cried out, "You should have struck* ᵃ *the ground five or six times, then you would have defeated* ᵇ *Syria. Now you will only beat them three times."* ²⁰ *So it was that Elisha died and they buried him. In that year* ᵃ *raiding bands* ᵇ *from Moab were abroad.* ᶜ ²¹ *It happened that as some men were burying a corpse* ᵃ *they caught sight of a raiding band.* ᵇ *Hurriedly they threw the corpse into the tomb of Elisha and left, but the corpse* ᶜ *touched the bones of Elisha, revived and got to its feet.* ²² *Throughout the reign of Jehoahaz, Hazael king of Syria* ᵃ *had oppressed Israel,* ²³ *but* ᵃ *Yahweh was gracious and took pity on them because of his covenant with Abraham, Isaac, and Jacob. He* ᵇ *had no desire to destroy them, nor did he want to banish them from his sight until now.* ᶜ ²⁴ *Hazael king of Syria eventually died, and his son Ben Hadad reigned in his place.* ᵃ ²⁵ ᵃᵇ *Then Joash ben Jehoahaz recovered* ᶜ *the cities from the control of Ben Hadad son of Hazael, which he had taken earlier from Jehoahaz his father in battle. Three times did Joash defeat Syria, and he restored the citites of Israel.*

Notes

1.a. Josephus (*Antiq.* ix.173) reads "twenty-first."
1.b. "Over Israel" is omitted by G^B but included in G^AL Eth.
2.a. In typical and consistent fashion G^L translates בעיני "in the eyes of" with ἐνώπιον "before."
2.b. The number is confusing. The pl pointing with the sg constr consonants should be either חַטֹּאות "sins of" or חַטַּאת "sin of." To remain consistent with ממנה "from it" the latter is better. However, G reads ἁμαρτιῶν "sins of."
2.c. G^B reads ἀπ' αὐτῆς "from it," G^AN reads ἀπ' αὐτῶν "from them."
3.a. For בישראל "in Israel" G^L reads ἐπι τον (על) "against," "upon."
3.b. MT reads כל הימים lit., "all the days."
5.a. For וַיֵּצְאוּ "and they came out" G^L reads ἐξήγαγεν αὐτούς "he brought them out," and the reading of וַיֹּצְאֵם "he (Yahweh) brought them out . . . ." is accepted by Gray (*Kings*, 594).
5.b. For MT וַיֵּשְׁבוּ "and they settled" G^L reads ἀπεστράφη . . . και ἐκαθισαν "they (Israel) turned back . . . and dwelt," presupposing a dittography which the translator read from separate roots: וַיָּשֻׁבוּ . . . וַיֵּשְׁבוּ "and they returned . . . and they settled."
6.a. The same confusion of a number exists here as in v 2. For חטאות(מ) G^A reads ἁμαρτιας "sin of" and G^B reads ἁμαρτιῶν "sins of."
6.b–b. This whole phrase is omitted by G^L. MT should probably read החטיא "he caused to sin."
6.c. For MT בָּהּ "in it" G^A reads αὐταις "them," G^B reads αὐτη "it."
7.a. For עָם "people" or "army," Gray (*Kings*, 596) suggests an emendation to עֹצֶם "strength." This is quite unnecessary.
7.b. MT reads השאר "left." Montgomery (*Kings*, 434), judging the subject of the verb as Yahweh, regards vv 4–6 as an intrusion. *BHS* prefers a regular niph (נִשְׁאַר) for which there is no textual evidence. For the indefinite nature of the expression see Burney, *Notes*, 316.
7.c. G^L transposes v 23 to here. For agreement see Burney (*Notes*, 316).
10.a. For "thirty-seven" some MSS read "thirty-nine." See *Comment* below.
10.b. Syr reads "thirteen."
11.a,b. See *Notes* 6.a. and 6.c. above.
12.a. G^L transfers vv 12–13 to the end of the chapter.
14.a. G^L transposes אליו "to him" to after מלך ישראל "king of Israel."

14.b. A similar expression is found in Gen 50:1.
15.a. MT reads חצים "arrows." G^B translates βελη "darts," and G^L offers βολιδας "javelins" or "arrows."
15.b. After ויקח "and he took hold" G^L in typical fashion adds the name "Joash."
16.a. "Israel" is omitted by G^B, but included in G^AL.
16.b. See S. P. Brock, *VT* 18 (1968) 395–97, on the meaning of the verb.
17.a–a. The entire phrase is omitted by G^B, but included by G^L.
17.b. See O. Loretz, *BZ* 2 (1958) 288.
17.c. MT reads בארם "over Syria." G^L reads "in Israel," also presupposed by OL and Theod.
18.a. After ויאמר "he said further" G^L adds Ἐλισσαιε τῳ Ιωας "Elisha to Joash."
18.b. M reads חצים "arrows." G^L reads "*five* darts" or "arrows."
18.c. G^L adds "Elisha."
19.a. The MT ויאמר להכות "and he cried out, 'You should have struck'" is unusual. A. B. Davidson, *Hebrew Syntax* (1902) 59, 182–84, presupposes an "optative" sentence לוּ הִכִּיתָ "would that you had struck." So also Gray, *Kings,* 598. Burney, *Notes,* 317 accepts the text as it stands.
19.b. MT reads עד כלה, lit., "until destroyed." On this expression see Williams, *Hebrew Syntax,* 38.
20.a. The MT בא שנה "coming year" is very awkward. G^B translates ἐλθοντος του ἐνιαυτου "when the year came in." The phrase could be understood in a more general sense of a long period of time. Gray (*Kings,* 600) suggests an emendation to כבא השנה "when the year comes," but there is little to support this. On the expression see Burney, *Notes,* 317.
20.b. MT reads וגדודי "raiding bands" for which Tg reads sg, probably to conform with the appearance of the sg in v 21. Such a change is not necessary in view of the general nature of the statement. Josephus (*Antiq.* ix.183) omits any reference to Moabite raiding bands, writing instead of common robbers.
20.c. MT reads יבאו "they were coming" which is to be understood in the habitual sense.
21.a. The translation in G^B is made definite: τον ἀνδρα "the person." G^L reads ἀνθρωπον ἑνα "one man."
21.b. For the MT ראו את הגדוד "they caught sight of a raiding band," G^L offers ἠγγισε το πειρατηριον αὐτοις "the band of pirates drew near to them."
21.c. G^L reads ὁ θαπτομενος "the one being buried."
22.a. מלך ארם "king of Syria" is omitted by G^B, but included in G^AL.
23.a. See above note 7.c.
23.b. G adds the subject "Yahweh."
23.c. The phrase "until now" is omitted by G^BA, and the omission is accepted by Gray (*Kings,* 601).
24.a. G^L adds a great deal of material here, including an otherwise unknown tradition that the Syrians restricted the activities of the Philistines for a considerable time.
25.a. G^L transposes vv 12–13 to here. See Montgomery, *Kings,* 438.
25.b. G^L begins the verse with και ἐγενετο μετα το ἀποθανειν τον Ἀζαηλ "and it happened after the death of Hazael." See 1:1.
25.c. MT reads וַיָּשָׁב "and he returned," possibly to be better pointed וַיָּשֶׁב "and he restored."

Form/Structure/Setting

The chapter is a compact creation, giving a brief account of Israel during the reign of Jehoahaz, Jehu's successor (vv 1–9), and a cryptic notice of the reign of Jehoahaz's son, Joash (vv 10–13). Vv 14–21 record incidents dealing with the death of Elisha during the reign of Joash, and the chapter concludes (vv 22–25) with miscellaneous comments on incidents affecting Israelite-Syrian relations.

The precise divisions of the chapter are variously interpreted by commentators. DeVries (*Prophet against Prophet,* 119–20) assigns vv 1, 3–5, 7–10, and 12–13 to "extracts" of a deuteronomistic type. Vv 2, 6, 11, 22–25 are designated the work of RD[1] and vv 14–19 (20a), 20b–21 are found to be from the "Later Syrian War Collection." Such detailed analysis of the chapter is interesting, but not necessarily helpful; nor does it accord with the majority opinion on, for example, vv 4–6, which many commentators earlier regarded as a unit (so Montgomery, *Kings*, 433; Gray, *Kings;* and McCarthy, *Bib* 54 [1973] 409–10). If the verses are an editorial unit then they cut across two major divisions detected by DeVries.

Gray (*Kings*, 591–93) views vv 4–6 as secondary, although deuteronomistic. To what is typical Kings material have been added two tales of the collection dealing with the prophet Elisha. The collection is of two distinct types of material, the historical (vv 14–19) and the hagiographical (vv 20–21), whose origins are to be found within the "local dervish circle." No reason for the present arrangement of the material is given beyond that they "round out the tradition of Elisha" (Gray, *Kings*, 593). As a description of the present order of the stories, the statement is a truism; but as a valid motivation for it, the comment is less than adequate.

The chapter contains formal, stereotyped material in the nature of introductions and conclusions to the reigns of Jehoahaz (vv 1–2, 8–9) and Joash (vv 10–11, 12–13). The usual characteristics of such formulae are present (see Burney, *Notes* ix-xiii). The use of such formulae designates the monarch under discussion as a "legitimate" occupant of the throne.

Vv 3–7, which contain an account of the state of affairs during the reign of Jehoahaz in Samaria, are regarded by many as composite. V 7 is seen as following on directly from v 3, thus rendering vv 4–6 as secondary (see McCarthy, *Bib* 54 [1973] 409–10). Its intrusion is "the result of the meeting of deuteronomistic theology and a phrase from the style of the royal records" (p. 409), i.e., it is a deuteronomistic rationalization of the anomaly of the reference to the anger of Yahweh (v 3) and the fact that Jehoahaz was not Israel's last king. It thus explains the delay in judgment.

However, the description of events in vv 3–7 cannot be so easily fragmented. The observation that v 7 follows on logically from v 3 is not a guarantee that it did originally.

McCarthy maintains that the phrase "anger of Yahweh," while characteristic of the deuteronomist in many places, is not so here because of a parallel in the Moabite Stone (see Line 5, Gibson, *Syrian Semitic Inscriptions* 1:75–76). But it must be noted that the usage is different. The formal background to vv 3–6 is both the rhythmic summaries in the Book of Judges (deuteronomistic) (Judg 3:7–9, 12–15; 4:1–3; 6:1, 7; etc.) and the statement in Deut 26:5–9. This will be discussed more fully in the *Comment* below. In other words, the passage holds together in its present form, for which one has no need to appeal to supposed sources.

Vv 8–9 form the typical conclusion to the reign of an Israelite king and they are followed by vv 10–13, the formal opening and conclusion to a reign, with no comment between.

Vv 14–21(25) contain two final incidents associated with the prophet Elisha. The first (vv 14–19) consists of an account of symbolic actions of the prophet. Following the introduction (v 14), which is reminiscent of the departure of Elijah (see 1:10–12), the narrative is typical of many symbolic actions with its two component parts of action (vv 15–17a) and accompanying word (v

17b). The second related action follows the same pattern, although there are additional elements in the story, such as the king's apparent timidity (vv 18–19). On the form see G. Fohrer, *Die symbolischen Handlungen der Propheten, passim.*

The second incident (vv 20–21) is unusual. It is an event which took place following the death of the prophet. In the face of an external threat (Moabite raiding parties) a hasty burial of a corpse results in resuscitation and new life by contact with the remains of the prophet.

The originators of these two stories about Elisha were undoubtedly the circle of followers who were closely associated with the prophet during his ministry. That much is obvious. DeVries's allocation of the stories to the "Later Syrian War Collection" begs too many questions. Gray's observations that the two stories are typical of the two patterns of story associated with the prophet is correct. In many incidents the prophet is seen, without miracle or wonder-deed, as involved in matters of international politics, while in others he is seen as a local miracle worker. But one cannot move from such observations into a milieu such as "local dervish circles" who indulged in hagiology of such men as Elisha, with the confidence exuded by Gray.

First, his division is done on the basis of contents, not form. Second, miracles are by no means absent from the prophet's dealings with figures of international importance (see chaps. 1, 3, 5, 6). Third, such observations on the possible pre-literary origin of the stories does little to explain their present position in the narrative of 2 Kings. This latter criticism also applies to the conclusions of L. Bronner (*The Stories of Elijah and Elisha*, 106–12) that vv 20–21 were originally an anti-Baal polemic proving that Yahweh, and not Baal, was the lord of life. Further, the final paragraph of the chapter remains isolated (vv 22–25). DeVries assigns it to D[1] along with vv 2, 6, 11, but it is clearly linked thematically to vv 4–5 and v 19. It is therefore unfortunate to relegate the paragraph to the position of an editorial afterthought or a brief excerpt from the royal annals (so Gray, *Kings*, 592) appended here for no apparent reason.

As always in our discussions of the form, structure, and setting of the separate chapters in 2 Kings, our primary concern is to understand the present shape of the narrative. While a reconstruction of the history of the literature is often attempted, it is also unsatisfactory in that it often fails to understand the combination of the supposed sources into the present narrative. The art of story-telling which has been frequently displayed in these narratives must be taken seriously, and issues of "sources," "glosses," and "extracts" must not be prejudged until these more important issues are settled. See the remarks of R. Polzin in *Moses and the Deuteronomist*, 1–18.

How then does the narrative of the chapter "work"? The present form of the chapter is an exposition of the major theme of the deuteronomistic history, namely, the activity of the word of Yahweh in the history of Israel and Judah. The clever juxtaposition of incidents in this chapter further expounds this theme (note that vv 14–17 are misplaced chronologically since Joash's death had already been mentioned in vv 12–13).

Chap. 10 ended with certain expressed limitations on the achievements of Jehu, but the limitations also contained a promise that the dynasty of

Jehu would last for four generations (see 10:30). This is followed immediately by the comment on the losses to Syria suffered by Israel. Following is the interlude of Athaliah in Judah and the subsequent restoration of the Davidic dynasty under Joash of Judah. However, although the dynasty is restored, Joash's reign ends under a shadow. Not only is he assassinated (12:19–21), but he also surrenders much to Hazael of Syria (12:17–18).

Chap. 13 then opens with the rather understandable comment upon Israel's sufferings under Syria. This oppression by Syria is made all the more understandable by the comment on Joash's slipping back into the ways of Jeroboam (vv 2–3), that is, into the pre-Jehu ways of Israel. A tension is thus created with the reference to the anger of Yahweh toward Israel (v 3), which was correctly noticed by McCarthy. Contrary to McCarthy, however, the tension is not with what comes after, but with what comes before. The tension is between the justified, therefore inevitable, judgment of Yahweh upon Israel for apostasy (a well-established motif in the deuteronomistic history) and the promise to Jehu (10:30) that his dynasty would endure for four generations. With the comments in vv 6–7 and the remarkably cryptic, but uniformly negative, assessment of the reign of Joash in vv 10–13, the tension is in fact heightened.

The partial resolution of this tension now comes in both of the incidents from the end of the ministry of Elisha. The juxtaposition of vv 14–21 with the reign of Joash, which officially concludes at v 13, places it in parallel as an exposition of the reign. Through the dying prophet comes Yahweh's word that victory would be given to Israel over Syria. The limitation upon that victory is clearly seen as a result of Joash's timidity.

Vv 22–25 only make logical sense as a fitting conclusion to and a symbolic fulfillment of the word of Yahweh through the prophet. Life comes. But throughout the chapter emphasis is placed upon the initiative of Yahweh in the deliverance of Israel. It is he who gives a deliverer (v 5); it is he who announces victory (v 17); and it is he who finally provides grace and mercy to Joash (v 23)—this in spite of all the king's apostasy. In this way the present form of the chapter continues the exposition of the word of Yahweh in the adventures of Israel and Judah. Thus does it provide an explanation of the temporary delay in Israel's demise.

Comment

In chap. 13 the road to military and political recovery begins for both Israel and Judah. The recovery will be brought to its fruition under the reigns of Jeroboam II in Israel and Uzziah (Azariah) in Judah. The general historical background for chap. 13 is to be found in the decline of Syria in the latter quarter of the ninth century B.C. This decline was precipitated by attacks from Assyria in the east and the subsequent death of Hazael in 806 B.C. Hazael's son Ben Hadad II suffered further defeats at the hands of Assyria. Thus Syrian pressure upon Israel and Judah was eased. For a general survey of the events of this period see S. Herrmann, *History*, 227–42. The events described in this chapter and in chap. 14 are a prelude to the ministry of the prophet Amos of Tekoa.

1 "In the twenty-third year of Joash." Joash is thought to have become king in Judah in 840 B.C. (see *Introduction* for details). This would place Jehoahaz's accession in 815 B.C. His reign covered the eventful years at the close of the ninth century and the opening of the eighth.

2 The writer's theological concerns are always in evidence. He cannot allow any monarch of Israel or Judah to pass through the pages of history without being assessed. The apostasy of Jehoahaz, after the fashion of the archetype apostate Jeroboam son of Nebat, casts its shadow over whatever events are to follow.

3 ויחר אף יהוה בישראל "Yahweh's anger was incited against Israel." the clause echoes clearly the comments found earlier in the deuteronomistic history (Josh 7:1; Judg 2:14, 20; 3:8; 10:7). Consistent with the writer's determination to see the events of the history of Israel as the unfolding of Yahweh's will, the expression of anger on the part of Yahweh prefaces the comment about the subjugation of Israel to a foreign power. The belief in such divine action in international affairs is by no means restricted to the OT. Mesha attributes the Omride oppression of Moab to the anger of Chemosh, using very familiar language (עמרי מלך ישראל ויענו את מאב ימן רבן כי יאנף כמש בארצה "Omri, king of Israel, oppressed Moab many days because Chemosh was angry with his land"; see line 5, Gibson, *Syrian Semitic Inscriptions* 1:74–75). An unattributed "Prayer to Ishtar," lines 93–94, presupposes that misfortune is a result of the displeasure of the goddess (see *ANET*, 385). The "Cyrus Cylinder," recounting the defeat of Babylon at the hands of the Persian army, clearly attributes the Persian success to the pleasure of Marduk with his activities and, conversely, the anger of Marduk with the misdeeds of Nabonidus (see *ANET*, 315–16).

ויתנם ביד חזאל מלך ארם "and he gave them into the power of Hazael king of Syria." This becomes a stereotyped expression, used frequently in passages dealing with war, defeat, and subjugation (see von Rad, *Der heilige Krieg*, 6–8). Again, it is not restricted to the OT. "Marduk delivered into (Cyrus's) hands Nabonidus, the king who did not worship him" (*ANET*, 315–16). See also the texts cited by Albrektson, *History and the Gods*, 39–40.

כל הימים "for quite a while," lit., "all the days." The term is to be understood as a general expression of time, not that Israel was under the domination of Syria throughout the entire reign of Jehoahaz. Many commentators reject the phrase (but see Burney, *Notes*, 315, and especially 131). V 5 clearly indicates that at some time during the reign the pressure was lifted.

This verse describes the background to Amos 1:3–5 which alludes to the excesses of Hazael and Ben Hadad during their occupation of Gilead.

4 ויחל יהואחז "so Jehoahaz sought." The verb is the piel form of חלה "to be sick" and implies weakness and dependency. It is often used with the phrase "the face of the LORD" as its direct object (see Exod 32:11; 1 Sam 13:12; 1 Kgs 13:6; Jer 26:19; Ps 119:58). Here and in what follows, the verse is reminiscent of some parts of the story of Exodus. An interesting parallel is found in Jer 26:19, in which the prophet attributes to Hezekiah the same activity.

כי ראה את לחץ ישראל "because he had seen the affliction of Israel." A most striking parallel is found in both Yahweh's word to Moses in Exod 3:9 (וגם ראיתי את הלחץ אשר מצרים לחצים אתם) "also I have seen the oppression with which the Egyptians were oppressing them") and the statement in Deut 26:7 (וישמע יהוה את קלנו וירא את . . . לחצנו) "then Yahweh will hear our voice and see . . . our oppression").

5 The identity of the מושיע "deliverer" is much disputed. M. Haran (*VT* 17 [1967] 267–68) identifies him as Adad-nirari III (809–782 B.C.) whose campaign against Palestine in the fifth year of his reign (see *ANET*, 281–82) coincided with the middle of the reign of Jehoahaz (ca. 805 B.C.). See also M. Hallo, *BA* 23 (1962) 42. Herrmann's objection on the grounds of chronology (see *History*, 282) seems misplaced. Less likely is S. A. Cooke's identification of the deliverer as Zakir of Hamath (see *CAH* III [1925] 367), who was also at war with Syria. See Beyerlin, *Religious Texts*, 228–29 for translation. Zakir's activity, however, is now dated approximately 785 B.C. and is directed against a coalition of Syrians and others who attacked him. It has no direct bearing on the reign of Jehoahaz. (See Gray, *Kings*, 592–95.) Gray's own identification, following that of Noth (see *Überlieferungsgeschichtliche Studien* 84) is Elisha himself, who "acts like the charismatics in the Deuteronomistic presentation of history in the book of Judges" (p. 595). This identification is undoubtedly correct, but is made on firmer grounds than vague allusions to patterns in the book of Judges. The comment here echoes much more clearly the language and activity of the prophetic archetype, Moses. The summary of the theological significance of the Exodus, found in Deut 26:5–9 provides the pattern for the mention of the deliverer in v 5:

ונצעק אל יהוה אלהי אבתינו	ויחל יהואחז את פני יהוה
וישמע יהוה את קלנו	וישמע אליו יהוה
וירא את ענינו ואת עמלנו	כי ראה את לחץ ישראל כי
ואת לחצנו	לחץ אתם מלך ארם
	ויתן יהוה לישראל מושיע
ויוצאנו יהוה ממצרים . . .	ויצאו מתחת יד ארם
ויבאנו אל המקום הזה . . .	וישבו בני ישראל באהליהם
	כתמול שלשום

"So we cried to Yahweh the God of our fathers
and Yahweh listened to our voice
and he saw our affliction and our toil and our oppression

And Yahweh brought us out of Egypt . . .
And he brought us to this place . . . ."

(Deut. 26:7–9)

"So Jehoahaz sought Yahweh's favor
and Yahweh listened to him
because he had seen the oppression of
Israel, how the king of Syria had oppressed them.
Thus it was that Yahweh provided Israel with the deliverer
and they came out from under the power of Syria
and the Israelites settled again in their own dwellings as before."

(2 Kgs 13:4–5)

Such a direct allusion adds weight to the thesis of R. P. Carroll (*VT* 19 [1969] 400–415) that the deuteronomist(s) "had in mind a succession of prophets of which Moses was the prototype." The deliverer is a Mosaic figure, who can only be identified with Elisha and who reappears now in the story of 2 Kings after a gap of fifty years.

וישבו . . . באהליהם "and they settled in their dwellings." This is an idiomatic expression implying a land at peace. Attempts to link the phrase with the resumption of a seven-year pilgrimage to a sanctuary (so Gray, *Kings*, 59) can be ignored. It is often used by our writer (see Josh 22:4, 6, 7, 8; Judg 7:8; 1 Sam 4:10, etc.).

6 The writer interrupts the narrative with this sobering comment on the attitudes of the Israelites. The reform of Jehu, far-reaching though it was, had failed to rid Israel of this symbol of Canaanite worship. (See Reed, *IDB* 1:250–52.)

7 "Jehoahaz had no army left." On the translation see *Notes* 7.a. and 7.b. above. What was left to Israel after repeated clashes with Syria was a pitiful remnant of an army with which to defend the land. Although frequent notice is made of the 10,000 infantry that Ahab fielded in the battle of Karkar (853 B.C.), it must be remembered that his force was only a small part of a much larger coalition numbering some 78,000 men (see *ANET*, 278). There can be little meaningful comparison between the figures. This tiny force was all that was left to defend the whole country. Major battles of this period tended to be extremely costly in men. Shalmaneser III was responsible for the deaths of 16,000; 20,900; 25,000; and 20,000 enemy soldiers in successive campaigns to the west (*ANET*, 280–82). During the campaign of his fourteenth year he fielded an army of 120,000. Most significant in these figures is the drastic reduction in the number of available chariots. Ahab's force for Karkar numbered 2,000. By way of striking contrast, Shalmaneser took from Hazael a collection of 1,121 chariots. Josephus (*Antiq.* ix.174) omits any reference to a chariot force in his account.

9 The name of Jehoahaz's son was identical to that of his southern neighbor.

10 בשנת שלשים ושבע שנה "in the thirty-seventh year." According to v 1 this should read "thirty-ninth." The attempts of many of the versions to correct the number reflect the tendency to harmonize. Thiele (*Mysterious Numbers*, 75) sees the change as a return to the system of accession year dating in Israel. For fuller discussion see *Introduction*.

11–13 The concluding formula to the reign of Joash of Israel is thought by many to be an insertion, because of its repetition in 14:15–16 (see Burney, *Notes*, 316–18) and because it breaks the flow of the chapter at this point. G^L does not provide any evidence for its omission, even though the verses are missing at this precise point. They are placed at the end of the chapter, thus still duplicating 14:15–16.

"His war with Amaziah king of Judah." This anticipates the exploits related in the following chapter.

13 ישב על כסאו "he sat upon his throne." This is an unusual expression, although by no means unique in the books of Kings (see 1 Kgs 1:13, 17,

20, 24, 27, 30, 35, 46, 48; 2:12, 19, 24; 3:6; 8:20, 25; 22:10, 19; 2 Kgs 10:30; 11:19; etc.). It is a synonym for "reign" and is not of secondary origin (contra. Montgomery, *Kings*, 434).

14 Elisha has not been part of the narrative since the anointing of Jehu (9:1–10) some fifty years before. Now he is an old man at the point of death. What the prophet's activity entailed in the period since the accession of Jehu is unknown. At the same point at which Elisha was last mentioned, the "sons of the prophets" also fade from the narrative. The fact that there is such a gap in the record of the activity of the prophet demonstrates that the biographical interest in the prophet is subordinated to the main theme of the writer, namely, the history of Israel and Judah under the word of Yahweh.

וירד אליו יואש "and Joash went down to him." The verb is not to be taken literally, since it can be used of a visit to someone of lower social standing (see 3:12), as a synonym for going home (2 Sam 11:10), or a visit to the sick (2 Kgs 8:29). In this event the king visited Elisha in Samaria. The suggestion that it was Abel-meholah or Gilgal (so Gray, *Kings*, 598), while not impossible, is unlikely.

אבי אבי רכב ישראל ופרשיו "My father! My father! The chariotry of Israel and its cavalry!" The relationship between the king and prophet is nowhere else explained in 2 Kings, but in light of the king's reaction to the prophet's death, it must have been a close relationship. Unlike Elijah, Elisha is not accompanied by his supporters at the end. The similarity to the cry uttered at the departure of Elijah in 2:10–11 cannot be overlooked. Skinner's confidence (*Kings*, 350) that the expression is a metaphor of Elisha's worth is a little overdone. The precise meaning, here as in 2:10, is unclear. In the context it might well be a lament over the sad state of the Israelite military mentioned in v 7. Josephus (*Antiq.* ix.179) states, "Because of him, he said, they had never had to use arms against the foe, but through his prophecies they had overcome the enemy without battle. But now he was departing this life and leaving him unarmed before the Syrians and the enemies under them" (Marcus's translation.)

15–19 On his death-bed Elisha performs two symbolic actions. In the stories of Elisha, such symbolic actions have already been mentioned. In 4:29–31 Gehazi fails to revive the dead boy with Elisha's staff. Elisha himself replaces this symbol with his own body (4:32–37). G. Fohrer (*Die symbolischen Handlungen der Propheten*, 23–25) offers a number of parallels to the magical practices of primitive peoples. They can be supplemented by many similar actions known from ancient semitic literature (see R. C. Thompson, *Semitic Magic;* G. Conteneau, *La magie chez les assyriens et les babyloniens*). Although some have argued for a remnant of such magical practices within the prophetic tradition (so Ringgren, *Israelite Religion*, 256–57), Fohrer cautions against such judgments (see his "Gattung der Berichte," in *Symbolischen Handlungen*, 257–58). The prophetic actions are rooted in the belief in the word of Yahweh as his expression of his will for Israel. Such actions are a "miniature" of the events they depict (see H. W. Robinson, *Inspiration and Revelation*, 35–36).

16 וישם אלישע ידיו על ידי המלך "and Elisha placed his own hand upon the hands of the king." The action here is reminiscent of the action of the prophet in 4:34 where he placed certain parts of his body upon the corresponding parts of the dead boy's corpse. The hand is the symbol of the action of the will of a person (see de Geradon, *NRT* 11 [1958] 683–95) and in this act Elisha identifies himself with the actions of the king.

17 חץ תשועה ליהוה וחץ תשועה בארם "An arrow for victory from Yahweh! An arrow for victory over Syria!" The accompanying prophetic word predicts, in spite of the oppression of Israel by Syria, that Israel will prevail over her enemy. Israel will revive.

והכית את ארם באפק עד כלה "You shall strike Syria at Aphek until you defeat them." Montgomery's skepticism regarding the reference to Aphek (*Kings*, 435) is unfounded. While the possibility exists that this is a duplication of 1 Kgs 20:26–30, there is little reason to doubt its genuineness. Since Israel, now as then, was fighting Syria, the fact that the most strategic site en route to Damascus from Israel should be involved in both stories is not unusual. (See Gichon and Herzog, *Battles of the Bible*, 129.) On the basis of the narrative in 1 Kgs 20, Haran (*VT* 17 [1967] 267–97) identifies Aphek as a site on the Plain of Jezreel, an identification proposed by Eusebius in the *Onomasticon*. However, see Mazar, *BA* 25 (1962) 113.

18 In the writer's view the limitation on the number of victories over Syria is a direct result of the lack of faith of the king. Thus is the deuteronomist consistent in his purpose of depicting the close interrelationship between the fortunes of Israel and the word of Yahweh through the prophets. The three victories mentioned are not recorded, nor is it known when they took place. Pressure from the east and troubles with Zakir of Hamath in the north would have seriously weakened the Syrians (see A. Malamat, "The Aramaeans," in *People of Old Testament Times*, 145). But these political reasons are of little interest to the writer.

19 The anger of Elisha is because of the king's "lack of grit and determination" (Skinner) and his tendency to think small.

20 Elisha's death is not as dramatically portrayed as that of his master. Also in contrast to Elijah, and essential to what follows, reference is made to Elisha's burial.

וגדודי מואב יבאו בארץ "raiding bands from Moab were abroad." Montgomery's assertion (*Kings*, 435) that the reference to Moab is "an absurdity" is to be challenged. Such raiding parties would of necessity be lightly armed and relatively inconspicuous compared to a large army. They had probably taken advantage of the growing weakness of Syria and ranged far and wide.

21 The revival of the corpse is unlike anything else in the Scriptures. Since only the bones of Elisha are left, the incident clearly took place some time after the prophet's death. Josephus (*Antiq.* ix.183) rewrites the story and omits any reference to raiding parties, making the men involved robbers attempting to get rid of the body of their victim. Such color is hardly historical. The action, however, has a deeper significance. It is a foretaste of the revival of the nation recounted in the following chapter.

22 The order of events has been changed by the writer. Vv 8–9 have already formally closed the reign of Jehoahaz. What followed concerning the death of the prophet belonged to the reign of Joash, his son. This verse then is a brief recapitulation of the events described at the beginning of the chapter. Although it appears that Jehoahaz and Hazael were contemporaries, this is true only in part. The last mention of Hazael in Assyrian records is in the twenty-third year campaign of Shalmaneser III, ca. 838 B.C. (see *ANET*, 280), which is twenty years before Jehoahaz became king in 815 B.C. A campaign of Hazael into Palestine is mentioned in 12:18. In approximately 813 B.C. Adad-nirari III mentions "Mari" king of Damascus in the record of his fifth-year campaign in 806 B.C. (*ANET*, 261). This is most likely an Assyrian misunderstanding of the Aramaic title of honor, and thus confused with a proper name. But even if this is true there is no way of telling whether the Assyrian king is referring to Hazael or his son, Ben Hadad. The language of this verse recalls the official record of Mesha of the events described in 2 Kgs 3 (see line 5 of the Moabite Stone, Gibson, *Syrian Semitic Inscriptions* 1:74).

23 "But Yahweh was gracious to them." This sentiment continues that expressed in v 5. Respite was offered to Israel because of the mercy and grace of Yahweh, but the respite was temporary.

"Because of his covenant with Abraham . . . ." The reference to the covenant with the patriarchs is unusual at this point. It has long been recognized that the pre-exilic prophets tend to refrain from citing this particular covenant, but this is no reason for relegating this reference to a later period (so J. van Seters, *VT* 22 [1972] 453). Apart from the frequent mention in the book of Deuteronomy, there is one reference to this covenant in the Former Prophets (Josh 24:3). However, since it is according to the deuteronomist that the goal of the covenant with Abraham was the gift of the land (Deut 6:10), and since in Josh 24:3, when the people are finally settled, Joshua reminds them of the reasons for possession, it is not surprising that the delay in the expulsion from the land should be attributed to exactly the same cause.

24 Hazael's death is normally dated 806 B.C. The reign of his son was fraught with difficulties because of the renewed pressure from the east applied by the Assyrians under Adad-nirari III. Early in the eighth century B.C. Zakir of Hamath and Luash resisted a coalition of Syrians, Kuites, and others, thus weakening the northern borders of Syria. Adad-nirari's campaign into Syria in ca. 802 B.C. and a later one in ca. 796 B.C.—to which even Joash of Israel fell victim—served to weaken the Syrian domination of the region and end Syria's brief moment of glory (see Malamat, "The Aramaeans," in *The People of Old Testament Times*, 145).

25 It is not absolutely clear whether Joash's three victories over Syria enabled him to recapture the cities of the Transjordan. Haran (*VT* 17 [1967] 270) thinks not, but there is good reason for believing otherwise. Bright (*History of Israel*[3], 256 n.) believes Amos 1:1–2:6 allows for the possibility of some Transjordanian gains by Israel. See also M. Noth, *History*[2], 249. The fact that the victories were probably at Aphek, on the eastern side of the Jordan, would tend to support Bright's thesis. Gichon and Herzog (*Battles of the Bible*, 129) think that the towns of Lo-debar and Karnaim were retaken at this time.

Thus begins the revival of Israel under the final king of the Jehu dynasty, as promised by the prophet Elisha. The impetus received from Joash is carried further by his son Jeroboam. But before reference is made to him, Israel and Judah are found to be at war.

Explanation

With chap. 13, the second book of Kings begins the tale of the end of the dynasty of Jehu. It was a dynasty which began with such promise, but which now is seen to be already in a state of decay. The story of this end is also linked to the tale of the death of the prophet Elisha, who has not appeared in the pages of 2 Kings since chap. 9. In the present chapter the themes of death and life abound, and undoubtedly explain the surfacing of the prophet again at this point in the larger narrative. Elisha finally dies, yet his bones bring to life a corpse (v 21); the dynasty is doomed to be shortlived, and also die, yet its life is similarly extended (vv 18–19). Both these items are mentioned in the context of foreign attacks from outside. Elisha's bones offer life as Moabites are raiding the land; the Jehu dynasty is extended in the face of the increasing Syrian threat.

The theological rhythm of sin-invasion-deliverance, which is clearly seen in the chapter, is very reminiscent of the opening chapters of the book of Judges. The deuteronomist thereby continues his theme of sin and judgment. Obedience to the law is primary for him, and disobedience brings dire consequences. Yet, in this gloomy picture, he offers hope with what seems a deliberate allusion to the Exodus (v 4). Salvation (or temporary respite) comes about through Yahweh's hearing, seeing, and then acting. In keeping with another well-established biblical theme, the people reject such grace by their continuing disobedience (v 11).

The prophet in the chapter embodies the enigma of biblical prophecy: to announce deliverance and to announce judgment. The dynasty is doomed, but not yet. It will prosper, albeit temporarily. The body of the dead prophet, an unclean thing, incongruously provides life for another. In this way, not only the prophet's action of shooting the arrow and the king's action of striking the ground with the arrows symbolize the grace of God. The prophet himself embodies it. Here we anticipate the struggles of later prophecy with the inevitable judgment of God, yet the equally real salvation offered by God to his people. These struggles come to full flower in the books of Hosea and Jeremiah. To suggest, as is so commonly done, that the two words "judgment" and "hope" belong not together, but apart, is to misunderstand one of the most consistent and fundamental features of biblical prophecy. They appear invariably together.

It is interesting that the ideas present in the briefly-told incident of the revival of the corpse of the dead man (v 21) are also found in chap. 4. Not only is a corpse revived, but it is also touched in order to be revived. The action of the prophet in chap. 4, placing himself "face to face, eye to eye . . . ," is to be compared with the action of (inadvertently) throwing the corpse onto the bones of the prophet here. The actions vary in degree, but the results are identical. Out of death comes life.

However, such a revival of the sick body of Israel and the dynasty of Jehu is neither accidental nor automatic. It happens solely at the will of God. This author's comment on the incidents in this chapter make the point with admirable clarity. Even in the midst of a reign which was hardly to be noted for its piety and faithfulness to Yahweh, "Yahweh was gracious and took pity on them. . . ." (v 23). But even that is not enough. The motivation for this pity is neither the present desperate situation, nor some unintelligible shift of mood on the part of Yahweh, but rather ". . . because of his covenant with Abraham, Isaac, and Jacob" (v 23). The writer invites the reader to look back to the distant past in interpreting the recent past and the present. God has acted, but only out of his own desire, quite uninfluenced by the actions of others, kings or commoners. Thus it is that Joash restored so much territory to Israel and defeated Hazael and Ben Hadad (v 25). Such actions are firmly grounded on the prior activity of God (v 23). The pattern of complete dependence upon Yahweh is clear.

Emerging then in the second book of Kings is a theological interpretation of history which portrays history as purposive, directed by the will of God. As the inevitable invasion and deportation by Assyria approach, this is the only interpretation of history which will provide, on the one hand, a consistent picture of the past and, on the other hand, a reliable foundation for the future.

Amaziah and Jeroboam II (14:1–29)

Bibliography

Avigad, N. "Excavations in the Jewish Quarter of the Old City, 1969–1971." In *Jerusalem Revealed.* Y. Yadin, ed. Jerusalem: Israel Exploration Society (1975) 41–51. **Fowler, M. D.** "The Israelite *bama.*" *ZAW* 94 (1982) 203–13. **Hallo, W.** "From Qarqar to Carchemish." *BA* 23 (1962) 34–61. **Haran, M.** "The Empire of Jeroboam ben Joash." *VT* 17 (1967) 267–324. **Jenni, E.** "Distel und Zeder." *Studia Biblica et Semitica in Honor of Th. C. Vriezen,* 165–74. Wagenigen: Veenman & Zonen, 1966. **Kutsch, E.** "Die Wurzel עצר im Hebraischen." *VT* 2 (1952) 57–69. **Montgomery, J. A.** "Archival Data in the Book of Kings." *JBL* 53 (1934) 43–52. **Saydon, P. P.** "The meaning of עצור ועזוב." *VT* 2 (1952) 373–74. **Ussishkin, D.** *Excavations at Tel Lachish, 1973–1977: Preliminary Report.* Tel Aviv: University of Tel Aviv, 1978. **Vaughn, P. H.** *The Meaning of bama in the Old Testament.* Cambridge: Cambridge University Press, 1974. **Yeivin, S.** "To Judah in Israel (2 Kgs 14:28)." *Eretz Israel* 10 (1971) 150–51.

Translation

¹*In the second year* [a] *of Joash son of Jehoahaz, king of Israel, Amaziah son of Joash king of Judah became king.* ²*He* [a] *was twenty-five years old at his accession, and he reigned for twenty-nine years in Jerusalem,* [b] *his mother's name was Jehoaddin* [c] *from Jerusalem.* ³*He did what was right in Yahweh's eyes, but not like his ancestor*

David.[a] He did exactly as his father Joash had done. [4] The high places had not been abolished, and the people still slaughtered and offered sacrifice there. [5] When he had gained a firm hold on his kingdom he executed those of his officials who had killed the king [a] his father. [6] However, he did not kill the assassins' sons, because it is written in the book of the law of Moses, which Yahweh had commanded him, "Fathers shall not die on behalf of their sons, and sons shall not die on behalf of their fathers. Each individual shall be put to death [a] for his own sins." [7a]It was he [b] who defeated Edom in the Valley of Salt [c] and struck down ten thousand men. He captured [d] Sela [e] in battle.[f] He renamed it Joktheel, a name which it bears even to this day.

[8] Then Amaziah sent ambassadors to Joash son of Jehoahaz son of Jehu, king of Israel, with these words, "Come. Let us arrange a meeting." [a] [9] Joash, king of Israel, sent the following reply to Amaziah, king of Judah. "In Lebanon a thistle [a] sent word to a cedar, [b] 'Give me your daughter as a wife for my son.' But a wild animal passing by in Lebanon trampled on the thistle. [10] To be sure, you have defeated [a] Edom, and your ego has been boosted. [b] Be content with that honor and stay [c] at home. Why [d] should you invite disaster so that both you and Judah collapse?"

[11a]But Amaziah would not listen, so Joash [b] king of Israel prepared to fight, and both he and Amaziah, king of Judah met each other in battle at Beth Shemesh of Judah. [c] [12] The Judaeans [a] were completely put to rout by Israel, and each man fled home. [13] Joash, king of Israel captured Amaziah, king of Judah, [a] son of Joash son of Ahaziah [b] at Beth Shemesh, and he brought him [c] to Jerusalem and breached the city wall from [d] the Ephraim Gate to the Corner Gate, a distance of some four-hundred cubits. [14] He then took [a] all the gold and silver, and the vessels which were found in the temple and in the palace treasury, together with some hostages, [b] and returned to Samaria.

[15] The remainder of the activities of Joash, the things he did, his deeds of valor, and how he fought with Amaziah, king of Judah, are they not [a] written in the records of the kings of Israel? [16] So Joash slept with his fathers and was buried with the kings of Israel. Jeroboam his son reigned [a] in his place.

[17] Amaziah ben Joash, king of Judah, lived for fifteen [a] years after the death of Joash son of Jehoahaz, king of Israel. [18] Now the remainder of the activities of Amaziah, are they not written in the records of the kings of Judah? [19] Some people plotted against him [a] in Jerusalem, so he escaped to Lachish, but those same people sent after him to Lachish and murdered him there. [20] They brought his body back by horse and he was buried in Jerusalem in the city of David with his ancestors. [21] Then the Judean militia took Azariah, [a] a person of sixteen, and made him king in the place of his father Amaziah. [22] It was he who rebuilt Elath [a] and restored it to Judah after the king slept with his ancestors.

[23] In the fifteenth year of Amaziah son of Joash, king of Judah, Jeroboam son of Joash became king of Israel [a] in Samaria [b] for a period of forty-one years. [24] He behaved badly in Yahweh's eyes by not turning away from all the sins of Jeroboam son of Nebat with which he caused Israel to sin. [25] It was he who restored to Israel the territory from Lebo in Hamath to the Sea of the Arabah, according to Yahweh the God of Israel's word, which he spoke through his servant Jonah son of Amittai, the prophet [a] from Gath Hepher. [b] [26] For Yahweh had seen how extremely bitter [a] was the affliction of Israel. It seemed that there was no one left, neither bond nor free to help Israel. [27] Yahweh had not uttered a threat to blot out the name [a] of

Israel from under the heavens, so he delivered them through the might of Jeroboam son of Joash. ²⁸ The remainder of the activities of Jeroboam, all that he did, including his military exploits, how he fought, and how he restored to Israel Damascus and Hamath,ᵃ are they not written down in the records of the kings of Israel? ²⁹ So Jeroboam slept with his fathers, with the kings of Israel, ᵃᵇ and his son, Zechariah reigned in his place. ᶜ

Notes

1.a. Eth reads "third year."
2.a. G^L reads typically "Amaziah."
2.b. For "Jerusalem" G^A mistakenly reads "Israel."
2.c. Qere, supported by 2 Chr 25:1, reads יְהוֹעַדָּן "Jehoaddan."
3.a. 2 Chr 25:2 adds ". . . but not with a full heart."
5.a. Omitted by G^B.
6.a. K reads ימות "die," which should be pointed with Q יוּמָת "be put to death."
7.a. 2 Chr 25:5–13 includes a much longer account of the king's exploits.
7.b. G^L again adds the king's name.
7.c. The MT reading of בגיא המלח is variously rendered by the versions. The place is also mentioned in 2 Sam 8:13.
7.d. MT reads a perfect וְתָפַשׂ "and he captured." Gray (Kings, 604) suggests this is a mistake and offers instead an imperfect וַיִּתְפֹּשׂ]. However, see Burney, Notes, 319 for an alternative view.
7.e. MT's הסלע means "rock," hence the G rendering of τὴν πέτραν "the rock." On the location of this site see Comment below.
7.f. Ehrlich (Randglossen 7:309) argues that the word במלחמה "in battle" is a superfluous gloss, added by one who did not understand the full meaning of תפש "captured." Such hairsplitting is unnecessary.
8.a. MT reads נתראה פנים "we will look each other in the face." The context clearly indicates that the meeting was for the purpose of fighting, and that Amaziah was trying to provoke Joash into a war. See also 2 Chr 25:19.
9.a. For the MT חוח "thistle," G offers the unique ἄκαν "thorn."
9.b. Josephus (Antiq. ix.197) translates here with "cypress."
10.a. MT reads הכה הכית "to be sure, you have defeated," but see 2 Chr 25:19 (אמרת הנה הכית "you said, 'Behold you have defeated' "). G^L supports MT.
10.b. MT's ונשאך לבך means literally "your heart was lifted up."
10.c. Omitted by Theod.
10.d. MT reads ולמה "and why." Gray (Kings, 606) omits the waw, but see Burney, Notes, 319, who recognizes the sarcasm of the statement.
11.a. See 2 Chr 25:20 for additional details.
11.b. G^B omits the name "Joash."
11.c. G^B reads γῆ τοῦ Ἰούδα "land of Judah." G^{AL} agree with MT.
12.a. G^L reads here ὁ λαὸς Ἰούδα (עם יהודה) "people of Judah," possibly understanding עם in the sense of "army."
13.a. G^B omits the phrase "king of Judah."
13.b. 2 Chr 25:23 reads "Jehoahaz," an alternative spelling analogous to the use of "Jehoiachin" for "Coniah." See Jer 22:28.
13.c. On the basis of G^L ἤγαγεν αὐτόν "he brought him," Burney (Notes, 319) and others suggest a reading of וַיְבִיאֵהוּ "and he brought him," instead of the MT וַיָּבֹא "and they came."
13.d. In the light of G^L ἀπὸ τῆς πύλης "from the gate," many suggest an emendation to משער rather than MT בשער "in the gate." See also 2 Chr 25:23.
14.a. Burney (Notes, 319) regards the waw in ולקח "and he took" (perfect) as weak, but see Montgomery (Kings, 445) who suggests an emendation to ויקח (imperfect), or an omission with G.
14.b. The Hebrew התערבות "hostages" occurs only here and in 2 Chr 25:24. See BDB, 787. G reads υἱοὺς τῶν συμμίξεων "sons of mixture ("intercourse"?)," and G^L adds τῶν βδελυγμάτων (תעבות) "of abominations" neither of which makes much sense.

15.a. For חלא הם "are they not?" G^A reads ουχ ιδου (הלא הנה) "are not, behold."
16.a. For MT וימלך "and he reigned" G^L offers και εκαθισεν επι του θρονου.
17.a. For "fifteen" c₂ reads "fourteen."
19.a. In typical fashion again G^L adds the king's proper name.
21.a. G adds "and his son." On the succession see *Comment* below.
22.a. The name "Elath" is variously translated by the versions. G^L renders "Edom." See *Comment* below.
23.a. G^BL reads επι Ισραηλ (על ישראל) "over Israel."
23.b. G^L changes the order of the verse substantially.
25.a. G^B clearly understands Jonah's father to have been a prophet (Ιωνα υιου Αμαθει του προφητου "Jonah son of the prophet Amittai." MT is ambiguous.
25.b. The name Gath Hepher is spelled גתה חפר in Josh 19:13. The presence of an article is unusual. See Ehrlich, *Randglossen* 7:310.
26.a. MT's את עני ישראל מרה מאד "the affliction of Israel very rebellious" is awkward since מֹרֶה "rebellious" applies to Israel, not its "affliction" (עני). With its translation of πικραν "bitter," G understands מָרָה. But the word is feminine and עני is masculine. Burney (*Notes*, 320) and Gray (*Kings*, 616) and others suggest a transposing of the ה to give the reading אֶת עֳנִי יִשְׂרָאֵל הַמַר מְאֹד "the very bitter affliction of Israel." This is speculative, but does offer a readable text.
27.a. For שם "name" G^B reads σπερμα "seed."
28.a. MT is extremely awkward. The prepositions before the names of Israel and Judah are clumsy. In addition to this grammatical problem there are some historical questions raised by MT. See *Comment* below. Burney (*Notes*, 320–21) suggests the following emendation: ואשר נלחם את דמשק ואשר השיב את חמת יהוה מישראל "and how he fought Damascus and how he turned back the wrath of Yahweh from Israel," which is adopted by Barnes (*2 Kings*, 72), and by Gray (*Kings*, 616). However, the role then assigned to Jeroboam, as a diverter of the divine wrath against Israel, is an improbable one. See Montgomery (*Kings*, 446).
29.a. The additional phrase "with the kings of Israel," if it is understood as an explanation of "with his fathers" is clearly wrong, since not all the kings of Israel were in fact physical ancestors of Jeroboam. It can be understood as a technical reference to the royal burial place.
29.b. G^L adds "and he was buried in Samaria."
29.c. For תחתיו "after him," G^BA expands "in place of his father."

Form/Structure/Setting

This is an unusual chapter. Essentially it deals with the reigns of two kings, Amaziah of Judah (vv 1–19) and Jeroboam II of Israel (vv 23–29), but much more material is included by way of comment and description in the accounts of both reigns.

Amaziah's reign is introduced in quite typical fashion for a king of Judah in vv 1–4 (see Burney, *Notes*, ix–xiii), and the reign concludes with the standard formula (vv 18–22) with the necessary adjustments being made to take into account the manner of the king's death. Between these two points, however, there are some surprises. Vv 5–6 allows for vengeance against the murderers of the king, but the comment in v 6b betrays the writer's theological bias and agenda. He quotes directly from the book of Deuteronomy. V 7 is thought by some to be "archival" (see J. A. Montgomery, *JBL* 53 [1934] 46–52) because of its style and content. However, such a designation is one of style, and not necessarily of form. Nor does it necessarily provide any hint as to the origin of the statement.

Vv 8–14 are not in their present form "annalistic" material from Judah (contra Barnes, *2 Kings*, 68). The style does not conform to what is usually designated annalistic, and the amount of dialogue in the record gives it more

Form/Structure/Setting 177

a story-like character. More than this, however, the incident appears to have been told from a distinctively northern perspective. The reference to Beth-Shemesh "of Judah" distinguishes the site from the Beth Shemesh of Lower Galilee (Grid, 199–232). Further, stories such as these are circulated more often by the victor than the vanquished. Gray's opinion (*Kings*, 602) that the story is similar to the northern tale found in 1 Kgs 22 is helpful, though not conclusive.

Vv 15–16 present something of an anomaly. Not only are they a repetition of 13:12–13 (on these verses see above), but they also appear to have little, if anything to do with the immediate context, since they end the career of Joash rather abruptly. But they do provide explanation for the presence of the transitional statement in v 17, which clearly shifts the focus of attention in the narrative back to the south and to its king, Amaziah. V 17 in fact makes no sense outside its present context.

Vv 18–22 serve as a not unusual conclusion to the reign of the rather unfortunate Judean king. However, vv 23–29 move the center of the story back once again to Israel, with their synchronism of Amaziah and the accession of Jeroboam II, grandson of Jehu. The opening and closing formulae are quite in order (vv 23–24, 28–29), but what is of interest is the way the reign is presented in vv 25–27. The notice begins with the emphatic pronoun in v 25 in what is seen as archival style (Montgomery, *Kings*, 433), but immediately moves into the record of a prophetic word, hitherto unknown. Jeroboam's expansive policies for Israel are seen to be the direct result of the word of Yahweh through Jonah ben Amittai (v 25*b*), and vv 26–27 provide a clear echo of the comment already seen in 13:4, 23. Thus the narrative in chap. 14 reflects in part the rhythm of apostasy and deliverance found earlier in the book of Judges. The chapter concludes with the typical ending for the reign of an Israelite king, with an added reference to the exploits of Jeroboam to the north and east of Israel.

The combined effect of the various elements of this chapter is striking. In spite of the impression given by the opening comments, the main interest of the writer here is not in the fortunes of Judah, but Israel. The king of Judah becomes a cipher in the fulfillment of the word of God for Israel which promised a period of respite. This is all the more remarkable in the light of the initially favorable impression made by Amaziah at the beginning of the chapter. Within certain limitations (v 3) he behaved correctly, and even fulfilled that most important of law-codes, the deuteronomic (vv 5–6). Although they are expressed in the most cryptic way, his military exploits in the south are indeed noteworthy.

But from this point on Israel comes once again onto center stage. It is almost as though the events in Judah are a mere backdrop against which the fortunes of Israel are seen in sharp relief. Joash of Israel reluctantly fights, then defeats a Judean army on its own territory, sacks Jerusalem, and then returns home in peace (vv 8–14). The Judean king, in spite of his piety, is assassinated, and conversely, the successor to Joash, Jeroboam, reigned for a remarkably long period contrary to what one might expect from the negative assessment of the king in v 24.

An unusual tension is thus created in the chapter. The life of the pious southern king ends in calamity, and the fortunes of the impious northern kings go from strength to strength. The tension is resolved in precisely the same way as in the previous chapter. The military successes of the north, especially of Jeroboam the penultimate king of the now apostate Jehudite dynasty, are attributed solely to the word of Yahweh through the prophet Jonah (v 25), given because of Yahweh's compassion (vv 26–27).

Comment

In chap. 14 the reigns of Amaziah of Judah (ca. 796–767 B.C.) and Jeroboam of Israel (ca. 784–753 B.C.) are surveyed. As has been seen many times before, the writer selects only material from the reigns of the two kings which is relevant to the theological interpretation of the history of the two nations. The writer regularly injects his own theological judgments on the activities of the kings and the events connected with their reigns (see vv 3, 6, 24, 26, 27). From the lengthy reigns of the two kings, totaling almost seventy years, the writer has chosen some brief comments on their loyalty (or lack thereof) (vv 3, 25), on Amaziah's exploits into Edom, and on his disastrous conflict with his northern neighbor, Joash. Most surprising is the extremely small amount of space devoted to the reign of Jeroboam, whose military prowess was such that he was able to enlarge his territory once again to the old borders of the Davidic-Solomonic empire (v 25). To be noted is that Jeroboam's reign is missing from the book of Chronicles.

1 The chronological problems of the eighth and seventh centuries B.C. are notorious. The second year of Joash of Israel is 796 B.C. According to Gray (*Kings*, 604) the designation of Joash as king in the north was linked to the reversals suffered by his father at the hands of the Syrians. It is argued that Joash was appointed co-regent as a price for Jehoahaz's payment to Hazael. The evidence for such a reconstruction is lacking, but it does provide a convenient explanation. On the synchronism see E. R. Thiele, *Mysterious Numbers*, 103–24.

2 This reference to the twenty-nine-year reign of Amaziah is regarded by many, in agreement with Skinner (*Kings*, 353) as "the first of two serious errors" in the chronology of the kingdoms. (See Montgomery, *Kings*, 439, for a summary of viewpoints to date.) Montgomery's solution is to suggest a corruption of the text from either "nine" or "nineteen," but an embarrassment to this theory is the consistent witness of the versions for the present number. Various solutions are offered, but few commend themselves. The most satisfactory appears to be that of a co-regency of Amaziah and Azariah, his son, inaugurated soon after the former's disastrous battle with his northern neighbor (see Fricke, *Das Zweite Königen*, 182; Thiele, *Mysterious Numbers*, 76–89), although even this theory is not without serious difficulties.

ושם אמו יהועדין מן ירושלם "and his mother's name was Jehoaddin from Jerusalem." The reference to the mother's domicile is not unusual. The name means "Yahweh is a delight."

3 The qualified praise of Amaziah portends some future disaster.

4 It was not until Josiah's reformation that the high places were finally abolished. It is assumed that the form of worship depicted here is wrong. To be noted however is that nothing is said about worship of foreign gods

Comment

at the high places. On the use of high places in ancient Israel see Vaughn, *The Meaning of bama in the Old Testament*, and more recently, Fowler, *ZAW* 94 (1982) 203–13.

5 The verse seems to imply two things. First, that there was some form of conflict following the death of Amaziah's father (see 12:19–21). The expression חזקה הממלכה בידו, lit., "the kingdom was secure in his hand," is unique in the OT, but is similar to the comment made in 1 Kgs 2:46 following the civil war after the death of David (והממלכה נכונה ביד שלמה "and the kingdom was established in the hand of Solomon"). Second, it appears as though the plotters and assassins of Joash remained in some kind of official capacity in the court until they were dispensed with by Amaziah. That such a move was motivated by anything other than a desire for revenge and the wish to secure his hold on the kingdom is unlikely.

6 "It is written in the book of the law of Moses." The reference is to Deut 24:16, and is a modification of the law which demanded that punishment be extended to the children of criminals (see Exod 20:5; Josh 7:1–26). The quotation from Deuteronomy is hardly a "moralising addition" (Montgomery), but is fully consistent with the writer's high regard for the Mosaic law in its deuteronomic form. See G. von Rad, *Old Testament Theology*, vol. 1, 334–37.

7 הוא הכה "it was he who defeated" is unusual, though used more than once in this chapter (see v 25). Burney (*Notes*, 318) judges it an example of the "decadent" style of the deuteronomist. Montgomery, however, sees it more positively as an example of archival writing (*Kings*, 439).

בגיא המלח "in the Valley of Salt." The location can be either modern Nahal Malhata, south of Arad in the Negev, in which case the king repulsed an Edomite incursion into Judean territory (so Y. Aharoni, "Arad," *IDBSup*, 38–39), or the general area south of the Dead Sea in the southern Arabah. The absence of the article in the Qere would make the location a little more indefinite ("salty valley"). In any event either location would suffice for a battle between Judah and Edom. David fought a battle with Edom at the same site (2 Sam 8:13) and established garrisons in Edom following that battle.

Note the adverbial use of the noun phrase עשרת אלפים "ten thousand." The number slain is significant in that it is exactly the same as the total infantry force in the north during the reign of Jehoahaz (see 13:7). Such a victory would have given Amaziah enough confidence to react to Joash as he did.

ותפש "captured" is awkward; one would expect the *waw* consecutive with the imperfect (see Burney, *Notes*, 318). The identification of Sela has from antiquity been a site close to modern Petra (umm-Bayyara). See S. Cohen, *IDB* 4:262–63. G already makes this identification, but it is more recently identified with modern es-Sela, a site to the northwest of Buseir (Bozrah) overlooking Wadi Habs, and providing a fine view of the western approaches to Edom from the Arabah. See A. F. Rainey, *IDBSup*, 800. To the west, in the modern state of Israel lies Nahal Amazyahu. The name יקתאל "Joktheel" occurs earlier in Josh 15:38, but is not to be confused with the site mentioned here. The former site was near Lachish, and already part of the tribal territory of Judah.

Since the days of Joram, Edom had fought for independence from Judah (see 8:20–22), and the mention in 8:22 of the revolt against Judah lasting "to this day" indicates that this defeat of Edom at the hands of Amaziah was only a temporary setback for Edom. Edom had probably been nibbling at the southern border of Judah, taking advantage of her troubles with Hazael (12:17–18). The control of the Arabah by Edom implied in this passage effectively cut off access from Elath, and Amaziah wished to secure this once again for Judah, something which he eventually accomplished (v 22). However, by 16:16 the city was once again lost to Judah.

8 "Then Amaziah sent ambassadors to Joash." According to 2 Chr 25:6–16 there was provocation for such a move. On the Judean venture into Edom, 100,000 Israelites had been loaned to the Judean army, but were dismissed without payment. In anger, they pillaged "the cities of Judah from Samaria to Beth Horon," i.e., the border cities on the Shephelah between the two states. How accurate this incident is, is not known. It might well reflect an ongoing border dispute between the two states, and would explain the unlikely location of the battle at Beth Shemesh. לכה נתראה פנים "come, let us arrange a meeting" seems an extremely polite invitation to battle. Montgomery's allusion to the formal invitation to a duel is not appropriate since it injects a social custom into the ANE which is definitely foreign. Perhaps Amaziah initially hoped to avoid an armed conflict, but the response from the northern king precipitated it.

9 The request for meeting is met with a response which is far from flattering. The suggestion from Thiele (*Mysterious Numbers,* 37) and others that a real marriage proposal lay behind the initial request from Amaziah is unlikely. Such fables often serve to highlight differences between peoples and display a competitive spirit. See "The Dispute between the Tamarisk and the Date Palm," *ANESTP* 592–93; Judg 9:7–15. On this passage see further E. Jenni, *Studia Biblica et Semitica,* 165–74.

10 Joash's new-found strength after his victories over Syria gave him the courage to treat his neighbor to the south with such disdain.

11 בית שמש "Beth Shemesh." The location is unusual except in the light of the information provided by the account in 2 Chronicles on the troubles in this general area. It appears that Joash's strategy was sound. Jerusalem is extremely difficult to attack directly from the north, but both the Beth Horon ascent and the Valley of Sorek provide adequate entries into the central highlands of Judah. It was along the latter route that Joash chose to move. אשר ליהודה "which (is) of Judah." This note possibly reflects the northern origin of this account. It distinguishes the Judean site from the one in Lower Galilee.

12 2 Chr 25 sees Amaziah's defeat as a punishment for apostasy and idolatry, and Josephus adds further embellishment (*Antiq.* ix.199) by stating that the Judean army did not fight before they deserted the field. וינסו איש לאהלו "and each man fled home" (lit., "to his tent") is a typical expression for a defeated army (see 1 Sam 4:10; 13:2; 2 Sam 18:17; 2 Kgs 8:21). It indicates that the Judeans either gave up the fight, or were defeated and allowed to return home by the victor.

13 Amaziah's capture, however, suggests a desertion by his army, and possibly was one contributing factor in the plot against him later. Thiele and others suggest that this encounter took place in about the fifth year of the reign of Amaziah, although no precise date is given. The motivation for this suggestion is to provide a suitable context for the supposed co-regency of Amaziah and his son.

According to J. Simon (*Jerusalem in the Old Testament*, 233–34) the Corner Gate is to be placed on the site of a tower mentioned by Josephus, to the west of the Damascus Gate, and in the northwest corner of the ancient city walls. The Ephraim Gate is thought to have been situated in the middle of the northern wall, close to the modern Damascus Gate. The suggestion is certainly plausible, and would give adequate reason for the name "Ephraim Gate," i.e., it faced north towards Ephraim. The Corner Gate was later strengthened by Azariah (2 Chr 26:9) but is strangely not mentioned in Neh 12:38–43 with its description of the repaired wall. A breach in the city at this point would have given Joash access to the city from the higher ground to the northwest of the city. See further G. A. Smith, *Jerusalem*, 203–6; N. Avigad, *Jerusalem Revealed*, 41–51.

14 The plundering of the temple is reminiscent of the attack by Hazael against Joash of Judah, and is a recurring theme in 2 Kings. If the account in 2 Chr 25 is correct, then Joash of Israel might have taken what he considered his due for the nonpayment of his troops loaned to Amaziah. According to Josephus (*Antiq.* ix.202) Amaziah was released immediately after the plundering of the temple and palace. If this information rests on a sound tradition then it poses a serious problem for Thiele's reconstructed chronology. See below.

בני התערבות "hostages," lit., "sons of pledges," from the root ערב "to exchange, to give in pledge." The form appears only here and in the parallel verse, 2 Chr 25:24. G understands it as "mixture" (συμμιξεων) from an alternative meaning of the Hebrew verb.

17 If, as is thought, Joash died in 782 B.C., then Amaziah lived until 767 B.C. The problems of the dating will be dealt with below in the short *Excursus*. The suggestions that Amaziah was either in retirement (so DeVries, *IDB* 1:589–92), or still in prison (Thiele) for this period of time are without historical foundation. As it stands, the statement means no more than Amaziah outlived his former foe by fifteen years. There is nothing to indicate that he was in any way bereft of power during this time.

19 ויקשרו עליו קשר "some people plotted against him." The impersonal expression is deliberate, and lacks the precision of 12:19–21. The vagueness has allowed for considerable speculation concerning the reasons for the plot. Little information is given in the biblical account of the king's reign, except the military defeat of the king and the Israelite attack upon Jerusalem. This might provide some general hints concerning the incompetence of the king, but to be noted is the gap of fifteen years between the military defeat and sack of Jerusalem and the king's death. While memories are long in the Middle East and such a length of time is not impossible, there is no hint in the text that this was the cause for revolt. R. de Vaux, *Ancient Israel* 2:377 speculates on a priestly plot by drawing attention to the many conflicts between kings and priests within the period of the monarchy. However, while priests often fell victim to the anger of the king, regicide does not seem to be something the priests resorted to. The flight to Lachish would indicate a rather widespread threat to the king's life. Lachish (modern Tell el-Duweir) was a large garrison city to the southwest of Jerusalem, and would provide a safe hiding place for the king in the face of a rebellion in Jerusalem. In any event the flight was unsuccessful, and the king was murdered there. On Lachish see D. Ussishkin, *Excavations at Tel Lachish, 1973–1977,* especially 91–93.

20 The comments here suggest a rather cynical treatment of the king with an official burial complete with pomp after he had been murdered.

21 Unlike the assassination of Joash, Amaziah's demise came at the hands of a large segment of the population. It is possible to translate the term עם יהודה as "army of Judah," and the term is undoubtedly connected to the much disputed phrase עם הארץ, lit., "people of the land." If our interpretation is correct, then Amaziah was ousted by a military uprising and replaced by his young son. The fact that Azariah was sixteen years of age poses a problem to those who suggest that he was co-regent with his father after the defeat at the battle of Beth Shemesh. This will be discussed more fully in the short *Excursus* that follows this chapter. To assume that this verse refers to Azariah's acclamation as king at the time of Amaziah's supposed imprisonment ignores the syntax of the clause (ויקחו "then they took"), which clearly indicates an action consecutive to the death of Amaziah, not some time before it.

22 The final restoration of Elath to Judah is made under Azariah. In the light of the enormous advances made by Azariah (Uzziah) in 2 Chr 26: 6–15, the selection of only the recovery of Elath is remarkable. אחרי שכב המלך עם אבתיו "after the king slept with his ancestors." This expression would seem to lend some support to the theory of a co-regency, but the difficulties are impressive. See below.

23 On the chronology, see below.

24 Like his predecessor and namesake Jeroboam son of Nebat, Jeroboam son of Joash continued the tradition of apostasy in the north. The social effects of this king's activities are the background for the complaints in the prophecies of Amos and Hosea.

25 Josephus (*Antiq.* ix.205) attempts to tidy up the paradox of an evil, yet successful king by attributing each of the "innumerable benefits" Jeroboam's reign brought to Israel to the words of a prophet. While there is no corroborating tradition elsewhere in the OT, Josephus seems to have captured the heart of the deuteronomist's plan here.

According to M. Haran (*VT* 17 [1967] 267–97) the expansion of Jeroboam's kingdom took place only in the latter years of his reign. On this, however, see the *Comment* on 13:25 above. The translation usually given for מלבוא חמת is "Entrance to Hamath" (see e.g., RSV), and the term is found often in the OT (Num 13:21; 34:8; Josh 13:5; Judg 3:3; 1 Kgs 8:65). In the last of these references it constitutes the northern border of the kingdom of Solomon. The "Entrance to Hamath" is seen as a general area to the south of Hamath which would provide access to the Euphrates. However, a good case can be made out for a more specific location. Aharoni (*The Land of the Bible,* 72–73) identifies it as a city, Lebo-Hamath, close to the Litani River some seventy kilometers north of Damascus. The name appears in other documents from the ANE in various forms, from the city lists of Thutmoses III to the records of Tiglath Pileser III. (See D. D. Luckenbill, *Ancient Records* 1:294, § 821. Note that Aharoni mistakenly cites vol. 2.) The city is probably to be identified with modern Lebweh. In any event, the expansion to the north represents a considerable achievement by the king. Such expansion was regarded by the prophet Amos as temporary (Amos 6:14).

"According to Yahweh the God of Israel's word." This prophecy is found nowhere else in the OT and is attributed here to the main character of the book of Jonah. His home of Gath Hepher is not mentioned in the book that bears his name, but is now identified with el-Meshed, a site some five kilometers northeast of modern Nazareth where a shrine to the prophet now exists. (Grid 180–238.)

26 כי ראה יהוה את עני ישראל מרה מאד "for Yahweh had seen how extremely bitter was the affliction of Israel." The language is reminiscent of 13:5, and echoes Exod 3:7 and Deut 26:7. On the text see *Notes* above. The exact circumstances of Israel's bitter affliction are unknown. What is happening here is a compression of history, and this comment is to be seen as a reaction to the state of affairs described in 13:5–7. It is here in v 26 that the theological interpretation of the writer becomes most clear. The freedom of Yahweh is maintained by his pity on Israel in her distress. The comment is not to be seen simply as a convenient rationalization of the longevity of Jeroboam, but a serious attempt on the part of the writer to view the history of Israel consistently as *sub specie aeternitatis*. The events in the histories of both Israel and Judah are seen by him as demonstrations of the purposeful will of Yahweh. Neither the king's good deeds nor his bad ones ultimately affect this will.

ואפס עצור ואפס עזוב "neither bond nor free." The expression is a colloquial one, to denote such a universality from which not even the most miserable of people are excluded" (so P. P. Saydon, *VT* 2 [1952] 373–74; see also E. Kutsch, *VT* 2 [1952] 68).

27 "Yahweh had not uttered." This means the necessary prophetic utterance which precedes every major event in Israel's history as recorded in the deuteronomistic history. See G. von Rad, *Studies in Deuteronomy*, 74–91.

ויושיעם "so he delivered them." The term is used often of military and political deliverance in the OT. It reflects the "rhythm" of the book of Judges.

28 ואשר השיב את דמשק ואת חמת ליהודה בישראל "and how he restored to Israel Damascus and Hamath." The difficulties associated with this comment are many. The text is awkward and clumsy in its present form, and reads literally, "and how he restored Damascus and Hamath to Judah in Israel." Understandably the sentence has been the subject of constant emendation. The historical difficulties are no less acute. What does it mean that Jeroboam "restored" Hamath and Damascus to Judah in Israel, when it appears that the two cities had not been subservient to Israel since the time of David? Why are Israel and Judah paired in this way? What are the precise meanings of the prepositions? Finally, what are the circumstances in which such an expansion north and east by Israel could have taken place? Apart from the emendations suggested above (see *Notes*), and the unlikely suggestion that "Hamath" be changed to "Elath" (so Barnes, *2 Kings*, 72),

Haran reads ליהודה בישראל "to Judah in Israel" as ליהודה וישראל "to Judah and Israel," thus implying that the two nations were allies (see *VT* 17 [1967] 296), and that Israel and Judah became the overlords of tribute-paying Hamath and Damascus (see also Fricke, *Das Zweite Königen*, 190). The use of the Hiphil of שוב "restore" in such a context is seen in 3:4. However, Bright (*History*, 254) sees the control as more direct. Haran's historical reconstruction is attractive, and involves less emendation of the text than most.

The time of this expansion is also a subject of dispute. As mentioned earlier, Haran argues for a late date, suggesting that the favorable circumstances would not have been possible until the latter years of the weak Assyrian king Assur-nirari V (755–745 B.C.). However, Hallo (*BA* 23 [1960] 44) has shown that Assyria was in no position to oppose such expansion from 773 B.C. onwards. Most Assyrian campaigns were conducted to the east and south, not to the west. In any event, the gains of Jeroboam provided Israel with a certain amount of security and an increase in wealth. If the account of the reign of Jeroboam's southern contemporary, Uzziah, found in 2 Chr 26:6–15 is characteristic, then the royal coffers were replenished and the country entered a period of prosperity unequalled since the days of Solomon.

Excursus: The Chronology of 2 Kings 13–15

With the figures assigned to the various reigns of the kings of Judah and Israel, and the synchronisms offered by the writer in 2 Kgs 13–15 a most complicated problem of chronology appears. This note does not attempt a solution to the problems, since none seems readily available. Even the most persuasive theories contain serious deficiencies.

The biblical figures for the length of the reigns in these chapters are:

Israel		Judah	
Jehoahaz	17 years	Joash	40 years
Joash	16 years	Amaziah	29 years
Jeroboam	41 years	Azariah	52 years
Total:	74 years	Total:	121 years

The synchronisms offered by the writer are as follows:

Jehoahaz of Israel began to reign in the twenty-third year of Joash of Judah;
Joash of Israel began to reign in the thirty-seventh year of Joash of Judah;
Jeroboam of Israel began to reign in the fifteenth year of Amaziah of Judah;
Amaziah of Judah began to reign in the second year of Joash of Israel;
Azariah of Judah began to reign in the twenty-seventh year of Jeroboam of Israel.

Such figures, however, when calculated, leave a gap of twelve or thirteen years between the reigns of Amaziah and Azariah of Judah. About this "interregnum" the Bible is silent, but to ignore it is to destroy the synchronism established by the biblical writer.

Some of the minor differences in the figures, such as the "thirty-seventh" year of Joash of Judah (13:10), which most believe should be read as "thirty-ninth," can be satisfactorily explained by a possible change in the system of year-reckoning adopted at this time by both countries. But other major difficulties remain.

Some interpreters resort to a drastic change in the text, suggesting a reading of "nineteen" or "nine" for Amaziah's twenty-nine-year reign. Others attribute serious errors in calculation to the editor or his sources (Gray), and still others give up in despair, arguing that the problems are impossible to solve (Begrich). The supposition of a co-regency is frequently made. Gray, for example, believes that Amaziah was co-regent with his father for the last few years of the latter's reign from ca. 798 B.C. This circumstance is possible, though by no means certain. It fails to deal with other serious questions elsewhere in the text.

Thiele offers the bold solution of two sizable co-regencies for both Israel and Judah. He suggests that Jeroboam was co-regent with his father Joash from the fifth year of the latter's reign (793 B.C.) and that Azariah was co-regent with Amaziah from the fifth year of his reign (792 B.C.). The reason for this coincidence is that Amaziah appointed his son as a contingency measure before he went to war against the northern king in 793 B.C. Amaziah was captured, so his son was appointed king by the people after his father's defeat.

Such a revision of the chronology has the advantage of dispensing with the "interregnum" that the biblical figures created on their own. It also fits the figures that are given in the text. It would also accommodate the intriguing statement in 14:17 that Amaziah *lived* (not reigned) for fifteen years after the death of Joash of Israel. Similarly, the northern co-regency between Jeroboam and Joash is possibly reflected in the unusual, though significant, statement in 13:13 that Jeroboam "sat upon (Joash's) throne." A parallel is found in 1 Kgs 2:12, where it is used of Solomon, who ascended the throne after a period of co-regency with David his father.

The Amaziah-Azariah relationship is not so clear, however. If one pays close attention to the text, then it is obvious that the evidence for such a co-regency is lacking. It is here that Thiele's method of resorting to co-regencies to explain conflicting figures must be challenged. First, there is no suggestion that Amaziah was held captive for any long period of time. If the hostages taken from Jerusalem had included the king then it would have been stated. Further, the fate of Amaziah suggests that he spent the rest of his life in Jerusalem, until the plot against him forced him to flee to Lachish where he was murdered. Then his son was appointed king in his place. Second, 14:17 clearly states that Amaziah lived for fifteen years after the death of Joash, and there is no hint at all that this period was one spent in captivity. Third, comparison with other obvious co-regencies in the OT demonstrates the main difficulty of the Amaziah-Azariah theory. One such clear co-regency is that of Azariah and his son Jotham. It is stated that the son did "govern" with his father for a time before his father's death (15:5). But the language is carefully chosen. The son was not designated king, but placed "over the house and governed the people of the land." Further, the case of David and Solomon is worthy of note. The language here too is complicated, but no doubt is left in the reader's mind that Solomon did not ascend the throne, i.e., assume the full powers of kingship, until after the death of his father. No such clarity is found in the relationship of Amaziah and Azariah.

Explanation

In chap. 14 the attention of the narrator is shifted to Judah, which at this time fares poorly, contrary to what one might be led to expect. The hint at the future misfortunes of Judah comes in the damning faint praise found in v 3. This king, Amaziah, is good, but not good enough, and although he is faithful to the law (i.e., the deuteronomic law), he nevertheless leads his country into near ruin by his foolish attitudes and actions. In a fashion similar to that of his northern neighbor, Amaziah enlarges Judah's territory by his defeat of the Edomites (v 7). In keeping with the important theme of limits—physical and political—to which the writer turns frequently, such an enlargement of the borders of Judah symbolizes a renewed health for the nation.

However, there the similarity between Judah and Israel ends, and for the remainder of chap. 14 the narrative has a certain illogicality. It tells of the fortunes of Israel and the misfortunes of Judah. The decline for Judah begins with the action in v 8. Inflated by his recent successes in the south, the Judean now turns his attention toward the north, and challenges his neighbor to a fight. The motives for this are not clear. Was Amaziah overconfident, and therefore unrealistic? Did he see himself as the next David, able to unite the two nations? Note that his actions against Edom duplicate those of his ancestor. But we have been warned (v 3): he is not like David. That Jesus had Amaziah in mind when he talked of counting the cost before going to war (Luke 14:28) is a most tempting possibility. In Amaziah's case it certainly applies. Not only is he unlike David in his piety, but he is also challenging a king whose dynasty has been promised longevity for at least two more generations (see 13:23), and that promise is based on Yahweh's promise to the patriarchs. The possibility of success for Amaziah is evidently nil.

The limits of Judah are penetrated. Amaziah loses the battle because of his folly, which was so clearly brought to his attention by Joash (vv 9–10). He is captured, and the enemy reaches to the very walls of Jerusalem. Jerusalem is breached, her walls partially destroyed. Her limits are powerless to keep at bay a determined attacker, and in complete contrast to the later invasion by a much larger army (chaps. 18–19), the Israelite attack on Judah is successful. Again the temple and palace treasuries are plundered (v 14).

Subsequently, even though Amaziah outlived his enemy by some fifteen years, he was assassinated by his own people (vv 19–20), the third monarch in succession to suffer such a fate. Although the dynasty is quickly restored by the appointment of Azariah/Uzziah to the throne, the attention of the writer shifts to the fortunes of Israel under Jeroboam. Israel continues to prosper under this king (v 25), while Judah is left with an uncertain future. The reason is clearly given (vv 26–27): Yahweh willed it. Thus consistently our writer stays with his purpose.

Kings of the Eighth Century B.C. (15:1–38)

Bibliography

Aharoni, Y. "Excavations at Ramat Rachel." *BA* 24 (1961) 98–118. **Alt, A.** "Tiglath Pilesers III erste Feldzug nach Palästina." *Kleine Schriften*, vol. 2. Munich: C. H. Beck (1953) 150–62. **Avigad, N.** "The Jotham Seal from Elath." *BASOR* 163 (1961) 18–

22. **Bolsinger, G.** "Die Entwirrung." *BK* 12 (1957) 71–77. **Brin, G.** "The Formula X-יִמ and X-יוֹם." *ZAW* 93 (1981) 183–96. **Chapman, W. J.** "The Problem of Inconsequent Post-Dating in II Kings XV. 13, 17, and 23." *HUCA* II (1925) 57–61. **Cook, H. J.** "Pekah." *VT* 14 (1964) 121–35. **Donner, H.** *Israel unter den Völkern.* VTSup II. Leiden: E. J. Brill (1964) 30–38. **Douglas, M.** *Purity and Danger: An Analysis of the Concepts of Pollution and Taboo.* London: Routledge, Kegan and Paul (1966) 114–29. **Geller, M. J.** "2 Kings XV. 25." *VT* 26 (1976) 374–77. **Hallo, W. W.** "From Qarqar to Carchemish." *BA* 23 (1962) 34–61. **Haran, M.** "The Empire of Jeroboam ben Joash." *VT* 17 (1967) 267–324. **Honeyman, A. M.** "Evidence for Regnal Names among the Hebrews." *JBL* 67 (1948) 13–25. **Kaplan, J.** "The Identification of Abel beth Maacah and Janoah." *IEJ* 28 (1978) 157–60. **Levine, L. D.** "Menahem and Tiglath Pilesar: A New Synchronism." *BASOR* 206 (1972) 40–42. **Rudolph, W.** "Ussias 'Haus der Freiheit.'" *ZAW* 89 (1977) 418–20. ———. "Zum Text des Königsbuches." *ZAW* 63 (1951) 201–15. **Shea, W. H.** "The Date and Significance of the Samaritan Ostraca." *IEJ* 27 (1977) 16–27. ———. "Menahem and Tiglath Pileser III." *JNES* 37 (1978) 43–49. **Snijders, L. A.** "Het Volk des Lands in Juda." *NTT* 12 (1958) 241–58. **Tadmor, H.** "Azriyau of Yaudi." *Scripta Hierosolymitana* 8 (1961) 232–71. **Thiele, E. R.** "The Azariah and Hezekiah Synchronisms." *VT* 16 (1966) 103–7. ———. "Pekah to Hezekiah." *VT* 16 (1966) 83–102. **Weippert, M.** "Menahem von Israel und seine Zeitgenossen in einer Steleninschrift des assyrischen Königs Tiglath-Pileser III aus dem Iran." *ZDPV* 89 (1973) 26–53. **Wiseman, D. J.** "Two Historical Inscriptions from Nimrud." *Iraq* 13 (1951) 21–26. ———. "A Fragmentary Inscription of Tiglath-Pileser III from Nimrud." *Iraq* 18 (1956) 117–29.

Translation

[1] *In the twenty-seventh year of Jeroboam king of Israel, Azariah* [a] *son of Amaziah reigned as king in Jerusalem.* [2a] *He was sixteen years old when he became king and he reigned for a total of fifty-two years in Jerusalem. His mother's name was Jecoliah of Jerusalem.* [3] *He behaved well in Yahweh's eyes, just as his father Amaziah had done.* [4a] *But the high places* [b] *were not abandoned, and people still offered sacrifices and offerings at the high places.* [5] *But Yahweh afflicted the king and he became a leper until the day of his death. He lived* [a] *in quarantine* [b] *and Jotham the prince was appointed over the house and governed the people of the land.* [6] *The remainder of the activities of Azariah and all he accomplished, are they not written down in the records of the kings of Judah?* [7] *So Azariah slept with his ancestors and they buried* [a] *him with them in the city of David, and then Jotham* [b] *his son reigned in his place.*

[8] *In the thirty-eighth year* [a] *of Azariah king of Judah, Zechariah son of Jeroboam became king over Israel in Samaria* [b] *for six months.* [9] *He behaved badly in Yahweh's eyes just as his* [a] *forefathers had done. He did not abandon the sins of Jeroboam son of Nebat with which he caused Israel to sin.* [10] *Then Shallum son of Jabesh plotted against him and attacked him at Kabal-am,* [a] *killing him. Then he reigned in his place.* [11] *As for the remainder of the activities of Zechariah,* [a] *they are written down in the records of the kings of Israel.* [12] *This* [a] *was Yahweh's word which he spoke to Jehu, "Four of your sons shall sit for you upon the throne of Israel." And that is exactly how it was.*

[13] *Shallum son of Jabesh became king* [a] *in the thirty-ninth* [b] *year of Uzziah king of Judah, and he reigned for just one month* [c] *in Samaria.* [14] *Menahem son of Gadi from Tirzah took action,* [a] *came up to Samaria and struck down Shallum son of*

Jabesh in Samaria. He killed him and reigned in his place.ᵇ ¹⁵ As for the remainder of the activities of Shallum, including the plot he hatched,ᵃ they are writtenᵇ down in the records of the kings of Israel. ¹⁶ Menahem had defeated Tiphsahᵃ and all in it, and had secured all her territory from beyond Tirzah. Because it did not open up to him he attacked it, and ripped open all its pregnant women.ᵇ

¹⁷ In the thirty-ninthᵃ year of Azariah king of Judah Menahem son of Gadi began to reign over Israel, and he reigned for tenᵇ years in Samaria. ¹⁸ He behaved badly in Yahweh's eyes. For the duration of his reignᵃ he did not abandonᵇ the sins of Jeroboam son of Nebat with which he caused Israel to sin. ¹⁹ Pul the king of Assyria had come up against the land, and Menahem gave Pul a thousand talents of silver to help strengthen his hold on the kingdom.ᵃ ²⁰ Menahem exactedᵃ the silver from Israelᵇ for the payment of his soldiersᶜ to give to the king of Assyria. The amount was fifty shekels of silverᵈ for each soldier. The king of Assyria then returned home and did not stay in the land. ²¹ Now the remainder of Menahem's activities, and all he accomplished, are they notᵃ written down in the records of the kings of Israel? ²² Menahem slept with his ancestors, and Pekahiah his son reigned in his place.

²³ In the fiftiethᵃ year of Azariah king of Judah Pekahiah son of Menahem began his two-yearᵇ reign in Samaria. ²⁴ He behaved badly in Yahweh's eyes. He did not abandon the sins of Jeroboam son of Nebat with which he caused Israel to sin. ²⁵ Then Pekah son of Remaliah, his lieutenant,ᵃ plotted against him and attacked him in Samaria at the citadelᵇ of the palace.ᶜ With him in the plot were fifty men from Gilead.ᵈ Thus he killed the king and reigned in his place.ᵉ ²⁶ Now as for the rest of the activities of Pekahiah, they are writtenᵃ down in the records of the kings of Israel.

²⁷ In the fifty-second year of Azariah king of Judah, Pekah son of Remaliah began to reign over Israel, and he reigned in Samaria for twentyᵃ years. ²⁸ He behaved badly in Yahweh's eyes and did not abandon the sins of Jeroboam son of Nebat with which he caused Israel to sin. ²⁹ In Pekah king of Israel's time Tiglath Pileser king of Assyria cameᵃ and captured Iyyonᵇ and Abel beth Maacah,ᶜ together with Janoach, Kedesh, Hazor, Gilead,ᵈ Argob, and Areah,ᵉ that is, the whole of Galilee and Naphtali, and he deported the inhabitants to Assyria. ³⁰ Then Hoshea son of Elah plotted against Pekah son of Remaliah, attacked him and killed him and reigned in his place. This was the tenth year of Jotham son of Uzziah.ᵃ ³¹ As for the remainder of the activities of Pekah, and all he accomplished, they are writtenᵃ down in the records of the kings of Israel.

³² In the second year of Pekah son of Remaliah king of Israel, Jotham son of Uzziah became king of Judah.ᵃ ³³ He was twenty-five years old when he ascended the throne and he reigned in Jerusalem for sixteen years. His mother's name was Jerusha, daughter of Zadok. ³⁴ He behaved well in Yahweh's eyes as his father Uzziah had done. ³⁵ But the high places were not abandoned, for the people stillᵃ made sacrifices and offerings at the high places. It was he who built an upper gate to the temple. ³⁶ The remainder of the activities of Jotham which he did, are they not written down in the records of the kings of Judah? ³⁷ It was during this time that Yahweh began to send Rezin king of Syria and Pekah son of Remaliah into Judah.ᵃ ³⁸ Then Jotham slept with his ancestors and he was buried with themᵃ in the city of David his forefather,ᵇ and Ahaz his son reigned in his place.

Notes

1.a. The proper name is variously spelled in the versions (see Burney, *Notes*, 321).
2.a. G^L adds in typical fashion the king's proper name.
4.a. Compare with 2 Chr 26:5–30 which includes a much fuller account of the reign.
4.b. Some G^L MSS add "all."
5.a. G translates the M וַיֵּשֶׁב "and he lived" with "and he reigned."
5.b. MT reads בְּבֵית הַחָפְשִׁית, which is unintelligible. With Chronicles the reading should probably be הַחָפְשׁוּת, thus "in quarantine" G merely transliterates the latter. Both Josephus (*Antiq.* ix.227) and Tg make reference to the king's living outside the city. See *Comment* below. Burney (*Notes*, 321) regards the root meaning as "freedom" (see the KJV "several" and the RSV "separate"). Gray (*Kings*, 628) understands this as a metaphorical way of saying, "released from obligations."
7.a. For the MT impersonal plural (וַיִּקְבְּרוּ "and they buried") G^L offers instead a singular passive ἐτάφη (וַיִּקָּבֵר) "he was buried."
7.b. G^B renders "Jonathan."
8.a. G^N reads "twenty-eight."
8.b. G^L offers a minor transposition of "over Israel" to after "in Samaria."
9.a. G^L reads "all which."
10.a. Burney (*Notes*, 321) regards the MT reading of קָבָל-עָם "Kabal-am" as "senseless." The KJV translates "before the people," understanding the word קבל in its Aramaic sense of "before." As such the expression is unique, and a definite article would be needed on עם "people." The same understanding, however, is found in the G^L MS c₂ (κατεναντι του λαου "before the people"). The other G^L MSS read "Ibleam," which is accepted by most commentators. See *Comment* below.
11.a. G^L adds "and all that he did."
12.a. The MT הוא "this" is omitted by G^B.
13.a. G^L adds "in Samaria a month of days."
13.b. The G^L MS c₂ reads "twenty-eight."
13.c. MT reads ירח ימים, lit., "month of days." G^B offers a more general ἡμέρας "several days."
14.a. In military contexts the MT ויעל is better translated as something other than "to go up." See *Comment* on 3:7.
14.b. G^B omits וימלך תחתיו "and he reigned in his place."
15.a. After קשר "plot" G^L adds "against Zechariah."
15.b. For the MT הנם כתבים "they are written down" G^L offers the standard negative question οὐχ ἰδου ταυτα γεγραπται . . . "behold, are these not written . . . ."
16.a. The MT "Tiphsah," is, according to 1 Kgs 5:4 [4:24] on the Euphrates, which to many seems impossible. The variations in this word are ancient. G^B reads "Tirsah" which is meaningless. G^L offers the more local "Tappuah" which is accepted by most. See *Comment* below.
16.b. The whole verse is extremely awkward, and most suggest a change in the ending. For example, Burney (*Notes*, 322) suggests כי לא פתחו לו ויך אתה וכל ההרותיה בקע "because it did not open to him, he attacked it and ripped open all its pregnant women."
17.a. The G^L MS c₂ reads "twenty-eight."
17.b. G^B reads "ten."
18.a. The Hebrew כל ימיו, lit. "all his days," is very awkward at the end of the verse, and most suggest an emendation to בימיו "in his days" and a movement of the phrase to the beginning of v 19. However, we retain it in v 18.
18.b. MT לא סר מעל, lit., "he did not turn from upon."
19.a. להחזיק הממלכה בידו "to strengthen his hold on his kingdom" is omitted from G^B but included in G^AL.
20.a. Burney (*Notes*, 322) suggests a change to וַיְצַו "he commanded" from MT's וַיֹּצֵא "he exacted." while such a change would make sense, it is not necessary. The hiph of the verb יצא is rare in the sense of "exact," but it can be allowed to stand.
20.b. G^L adds "all."
20.c. MT reads כל גבורי החיל, lit., "all the mighty men of valor."
20.d. כסף "silver" is omitted by G^B; however, it is included in G^AL c₂.

21.a. Again G^B reads a negative rhetorical question.
23.a. The G^L MS c₂ reads "fortieth."
23.b. The variation on the number is great. G^AL read "ten," the G^L MS c₂ reads "twelfth," and G^N "twentieth."
25.a. For the MT שלישו "his lieutenant" Josephus (*Antiq.* ix.234) offers χιλιαρχος (שר אלף) "commander of a thousand."
25.b. For MT's בארמון "at the citadel" G^B reads "before the house," and G^L simply "in the house."
25.c. The MT is difficult here: את ארגב ואת האריה "Argob and Areah," which G^BL clearly understand as partners in the assassination, with their translation of μετα του 'Αργοβ και μετ' αυτου 'Αρεια "with Argob and with him Areia." The suggestion, adopted by many, that they are place names displaced from v 29, has merit. See *Comment* on v 25 below.
25.d. G^B reads "from the four hundred," which makes no sense. G^L follows MT.
25.e. The whole verse is confusing. Josephus embellishes the incident by having the king killed while at a banquet with his friends. This is a common motif in the OT.
26.a. G^L presupposes a straightforward statement, not the negative rhetorical question.
27.a. The G^L MS c₂ reads "thirty."
29.a. For the MT בא "came" G^L reads ἀνέβη (עלה) "went up."
29.b. G^A reads "Nain."
29.c. G^A reads "Kabel," see v 10.
29.d. G^L reads "and Gad."
29.e. See n. 25.c above.
30.a. G^B offers "Ahaz" here. G^L, followed by *BHS*, omits the entire phrase.
31.a. G^L again presupposes the negative rhetorical question.
32.a. G^L adds "over Jerusalem."
35.a. For the MT עוד "still" G^A reads οτι (כי) "because."
37.a. The phrase is omitted by G^B.
38.a. The second עם אבתיו "with his ancestors" is omitted by many versions.
38.b. Omitted by G^L.

Form/Structure/Setting

Of all the chapters in 2 Kings, chap. 15 is the most compact in its treatment of seven kings, two from Judah and five from Israel. In the narrative, details of historical or descriptive nature are kept to a bare minimum, and an apparently inordinate amount of space is devoted to the stereotyped introductory and concluding formulae of reigns, which gives the chapter a sense of imbalance.

Vv 1–7 cover in brief the important reign of Uzziah/Azariah of Judah, which is found in much more detail in 2 Chr 26. Vv 8–11, 13–15, 17–22, 23–26, 27–31 deal respectively with the reigns of Zechariah son of Jeroboam, Shallum, Menahem, Pekahiah, and Pekah of Israel. In vv 32–38 the narrative focus returns to Judah and offers a brief glimpse at the reign of Jotham. The rapid turnover of Israelite kings, while no doubt reflecting the unstable historical reality, is presented in such a way as to give to the narrative an impression of speed. But its speed is counterbalanced by the pedantic way in which the introductory and concluding formulae are used in the text.

The formal introductions for the kings of Judah (vv 1–4, 32–35a) and Israel (vv 8–9, 13, 17–18, 23–24, 27–28) conform to a regular pattern by now well established in the narrative of Kings. A minor exception is the absence of a comment on the behavior of Shallum son of Jabesh after v 13. The extreme brevity of his reign (one month) offers a suitable explanation for that omission. As with the introductions, the conclusions for kings of

Judah (vv 6–7, 36, 38) and Israel (vv 11, 15, 21–22, 26, 31) also follow the regular pattern (see Burney, *Notes,* ix-xii).

There is, however, a certain amount of additional material that needs comment and also provides a certain cohesion to the chapter. Vv 10, 14, 25, 30 are formal accounts of assassinations and are similar to 1 Kgs 15:27 and 16:10. Gray regards them as archival extracts (*Kings,* 617–18), but the identification is unclear. That they conform to a similar pattern is clear; that they reflect what has been detected by some as archival style is also clear, but whether they are extracts from archives, or an imitation of such style by the writer for purposes of linkage is not so easy to decide. The formal way in which the deuteronomist introduces and concludes reigns demonstrates already that such pedantic conformity to patterns is part of his technique.

V 5 provides additional information on the reign of Azariah and his son Jotham, and the information undoubtedly derives from the Judean annals (so Gray, *Kings,* 617). But such an observation is a truism, and one must investigate its present position and function. In its present form the statement is a theological judgment on the fate of the king. In contrast to his northern neighbor, who was wicked yet successful because of the grace and mercy of Yahweh, Uzziah is pious, yet afflicted by Yahweh. The same theological interests can be seen in v 37, which is a combination of historical account and theological interpretation.

V 12 finally completes the period between the prophecy to Jehu and the fulfillment of that prophecy. Classification of the verse as "an editorial comment," while popular, is again without much meaning. Its function within the narrative is to draw the reader's attention to the theme being relentlessly played upon now, namely, the power of the word of Yahweh in the fates of Israel and Judah.

The source of information in vv 16, 19–20, which provide additional data on the reign of Menahem, and v 29, which expands our knowledge of Pekah's reign, is ultimately the records of Israel's kings, but identification of the possible or even probable sources of such information is only part of our task at this stage. One must now note that the material in its present form is (i) subject to a careful process of selection, and (ii) carefully arranged in the chapter. It is incumbent upon the interpreter to follow and understand the flow of the narratives, and to examine some of the reasons for the existing form. An important methodological question is, What is accomplished by the present form of the narrative?

The high degree of selectivity apparent in this chapter indicates a deliberate choice on the part of the writer to use some information and an equally deliberate choice to ignore other information. By his repeated references to the records of the kings of Judah and Israel, it is clear that he had access to far more information than he eventually employed. Through his skillful juxtaposition of elements from various sources his agenda becomes clear. However, the brevity of the writer's statement that Uzziah's otherwise "good" reign (it was judged so, and he reigned for a remarkable fifty-two years) was blighted by Yahweh's having afflicted him so that he lived in quarantine for some time is puzzling. No time is given for this affliction; exactly how long the king lived in this condition is not stated. That the seemingly successful reign is blighted by sickness is the only information available to the reader from those fifty-two years. Montgomery (*Kings*, 448) cites a supposed parallel concerning the king of Elam, who suffered a stroke during his reign. The similarities are to be noted, but so also are the differences. The fact that this is the only information from Uzziah's long reign and that the incident is chosen for theological interpretation, makes it stand out.

V 8 returns the narrative to Israel, but v 12 places the events there in context. The violent death of the king, Zechariah, great-grandson of Jehu, is not seen as a mere historical accident, but entirely in keeping with the earlier word of Yahweh concerning the Jehudite dynasty.

Although Menahem's reign is "legitimized" by its formal literary presentation (i.e., it has a formal introduction and conclusion), it serves to introduce a hitherto unknown element into the political, and social life of Israel, namely, the armies of the king of Assyria, Tiglath Pileser III (vv 19–20). The Assyrians came to Menahem's aid, but in effect had laid claim to the land, a claim that is collected in part in v 29. The formal similarity of this statement with the conclusion of the reign of Jehu (10:32–33) is marked. Not only had large portions of Israel's holdings in the Transjordan been lost, but substantial territories in the north, Galilee and Naphtali, fell victim to the designs of Menahem's new-found "ally." The pattern will repeat itself for Judah with the initial involvement of Babylon in the affairs of the south during Hezekiah's reign (see below 20:12–19). So quickly does the fortune of Israel change. A short while before (i.e. in terms of the narrative) Israel enjoyed prosperity under Jeroboam; now she is quickly disintegrating into chaos, her period of respite over. The cryptic nature of the narrative, demonstrating the high degree of selectivity by the writer, create this impression of fast decay.

Although vv 32–38 return to Judah not all there is at peace. Brief reference is made—in anticipation of chap. 16—to the activities of Pekah and Rezin, which will throw a shadow over the south.

Comment

2 Kgs 15, which describes Israel and Judah in the closing years of the eighth century B.C., is fraught with difficulties for the interpreter. Although there is a wealth of material from Assyrian sources for this period of great Assyrian expansion into the west, this material serves at times only to confuse the picture. Much of the comparative data is fragmentary, readings are in dispute, and at the point where it could prove most helpful—that of chronology—it becomes less so. Many of the Assyrian texts are undated, and the problems of Hebrew chronology are compounded by the equally problematic chronology of the Assyrian sources.

This last half of the century began with renewed Assyrian expansion under an aggressive and victorious king, Tiglath Pileser III (745–727 B.C.), who left records of his achievements engraved upon his palace at Nimrud (see D. D. Luckenbill, *Ancient Records* 1:269–95; and the less complete collection in *ANET*, 282–84). Tiglath Pileser was succeded by kings no less aggressive than himself, such as Shalmaneser V (727–722 B.C.), Sargon II (721–705 B.C.), and Sennacherib (704–681 B.C.), all of whom had a profound effect upon the fortunes of both Israel and Judah.

Politically, the determined goal of the Assyrians to expand into the west towards Egypt seriously harmed the shrinking kingdoms of Israel and Judah. Judah was apparently able to resist longer, but the kingdom of Israel was plagued by internal strife, and soon after the long and prosperous reign of Jeroboam II, the country was plunged into decades of uncertainty and instability. For a general survey of the second half of the eighth century B.C. see Bright, *History*, 267–71 and Herrmann, *History*, 243–54.

Our writer of course was concerned to interpret these events in the light of the will and purpose of Yahweh. Therefore he passes judgment, not so much upon the individual achievements of the kings, but upon their faithfulness or lack thereof, and at certain points in the narrative his theological presuppositions become very evident (e.g., vv 12, 37). In the short space of the chapter he covers the fifty-two years of Uzziah of Judah (vv 1–7), and the rapid succession of kings in Israel, including Zechariah, Shallum, Menahem, Pekahiah, and Pekah. The chapter ends with a brief mention of the reign of Jotham of Judah (vv 32–38).

1 The chronological difficulties of this dating have been touched on above. Many date the twenty-seventh year from the beginning of Jeroboam's supposed co-regency with his father Joash in either 793 B.C. (so Thiele) or 791 B.C. (so Gray).

עזריה "Azariah." The name is spelled variously in the Bible. In vv 13 and 30 it appears as עזיה "Uzziah," and in vv 32 and 34 as עזיהו "Uzziahu." In 21:18 a shortened form, עזא "Uza," is found. On the relationship between the names Azariah/Uzziah see A. M. Honeyman, *JBL* 67 (1948) 13–25. The name עזריהו has also been found on a jar handle from Gibeon (see Gibson, *Syrian Semitic Inscriptions* 1:56) and on a Hebrew seal. The variant of עזריה has been found on a seal (see Gibson, 63). The name is a combination of "Yahweh" and the verb "to help."

2 A co-regency is also suggested for Azariah and his father from approximately 792–767 B.C. (see Thiele, *Mysterious Numbers*, 205). See the *Excursus on chronology* above. Again, the place of origin, not the father's name, is given for the queen mother, "Jecoliah of Jerusalem." The name means "Yahweh is able."

3 The comment is brief and damns with faint praise. The true standard of piety in the south was of course David, but such a favorable comparison with David is reserved for only Hezekiah (18:3) and Josiah (22:2). Azariah's father, Amaziah, had received a similar backhanded compliment (14:3).

4 The comment has become a standard one for the period. No hint is given, though, that such cultic activity at the high places was apostate.

5 "But Yahweh afflicted the king and he became a leper." This cryptic comment is unexplained by the writer. There is no reason to assume, however, that there is a lacuna in the text (so Montgomery, *Kings*, 448); this high degree of selectivity by the writer is an established characteristic of his style. 2 Chr 26:5–21 offers an explanation of two things, the king's longevity and his leprosy. Josephus (*Antiq.* ix.222–25) naturally follows the Chronicler's account, which appears to add considerable detail from reliable sources. With Yahweh as the initiator of the affliction some form of judgment is intended by the leprosy. The tradition contained in the book of Chronicles, which has the king trying to usurp priestly powers, might have been well enough known to have been presupposed by the writer of Kings. Naaman's leprosy did not necessitate a withdrawal from public life, yet Azariah's did. This could reflect the degree of severity of Azariah's illness, but it probably has more to do with the social role of the king in society. A monarch whose skin (i.e., outer limits) was thus affected would have been a very inadequate symbol of the Davidic ideology. (For the importance of such symbolism of the body see M. Douglas, *Purity and Danger*, 114–29.)

בבית החפשית "in the house of quarantine." The phrase is very unusual and is frequently paraphrased by commentators. See W. Rudolph, *ZAW* 89 (1977) 418. The term has been compared to a similar one in Ugaritic which signifies some kind of degradation (see Gray, *Kings*, 619; Y. Aharoni, *BA* 89 [1961] 116–17). Aharoni also suggests that a structure he excavated at Ramat Rachel, five kilometers south of Jerusalem and dating from this period, would serve well the needs of the king at this stage of his life. The co-regency with Jotham, precipitated by the king's condition, is one of the few clearly described arrangements of this nature. Jotham's status as על הבית "over the house" indicates his control over the affairs of the palace and state as is evident from the explanatory note which follows. שפט את עם הארץ "he governed the people of the land." In this context it is unlikely that the phrase עם הארץ means anything other than the general populace (see Exod 18:22).

6 "All he accomplished." Judging by the parallel account in 2 Chr 26, the activities of the king were considerable. The selectivity of the writer of Kings then becomes more marked. Azariah's long and apparently profitable reign takes up no more lines than his description of the reigns of Zechariah or Shallum of Israel who reigned for a fraction of the time. The brevity of the account, comparable with the earlier treatment of Jeroboam, Azariah's contemporary in the north (see 14:23–29), serves the literary purpose of moving the narrative swiftly along to the final stages of the disintegration of the northern country of Israel.

According to the campaign account of Tiglath Pileser's third year (743–742 B.C.), the Assyrian monarch extracted tribute from one "Azaryau of Iauda" (see Luckenbill, *Ancient Records* 1:274). The frequent identification of this character with Azariah of Judah (see Thiele, *Mysterious Numbers*, 93–94; Cogan, *Imperialism and Religion*, 65) while it might seem obvious is problematic. See the helpful discussion in Montgomery, *Kings*, 446–47. The Bible knows of no subjugation of the Judean king to Assyria during his long reign, and the military exploits of Azariah were directed toward the south and west of Judah (2 Chr 26:6–15), not to the north, where he would not have come into contact with the Assyrians. Thiele's reason for the identification is clear. He wishes to date many of the records of Tiglath Pileser earlier than is generally accepted, to 743 B.C. rather than 737 B.C. (see the discussion by W. H. Shea, *JNES* 37 [1978] 43–49; L. D. Levine, *BASOR* 206 [1972] 40–42). The now commonly accepted identification of the character as one Azariau of Iauda in northern Syria (see Herrmann, *History*, 246) seems much more plausible, though even this identification must be treated with caution (see Bright, *History*, 268).

7 "So Azariah slept with his ancestors." The importance of this date for the OT is that it pinpoints the year of the call of Isaiah the prophet (see Isa 6:1). Chronicles contains a slightly different tradition on the burial of Azariah, stating that he was buried "in the burial field which belongs to the kings," which might be an alternative to "buried with his fathers." Josephus (*Antiq.* ix.227) diverges even further, stating that Azariah was buried alone in his own garden. While the two accounts seem contradictory, there is evidence that at a much later date the bones of the king were moved to an alternative site. A Second Temple inscription in Aramaic records the transfer of these bones (see Y. Yadin, ed., *Jerusalem Revealed* [New Haven: Yale U.P., 1976] 8, for illustration). וימלך יותם "and then Jotham reigned." An interesting difference is to be noted here between the verb used for the activity of Jotham during the co-regency (שפט "govern") and the verb used after he had become king in his own right (מלך "reign"). Such a distinction tends to be ignored in the frequent appeals to co-regencies to solve some of the difficult problems of chronology in 2 Kings.

8 The thirty-eighth year of Azariah is reckoned to be 754 B.C., counting from 791 B.C., at which time Azariah began a co-regency with his father. The solution, however, is not without problems (see the *Excursus* below). The name זכריהו "Zechariah" also appears in 2 Chr 26:5, but it is not the same person. There is the name given to one who instructed the king in the fear of God. The brief reign of six months was a direct result of the reversals suffered by Jeroboam, which are implied in 14:26–27 (see T. Ishida, *Royal Dynasties in Israel*, 173). The reckoning of the reign as six months is also interesting in its implications for chronology. It implies that fragments of years were counted as such, not as full years.

9 This standard is used with regularity and provides a monotonous indictment against successive kings of the north.

10 The name שלם "Shallum," a derivative of the verb שלם, appears in the Lachish Letters (iii.20; see Gibson, *Syrian Semitic Inscriptions* 1:41). The verb was also incorporated into the names of two of David's sons, Absalom and Solomon.

בן יבש "son of Jabesh" is most likely a reference to Shallum's place of origin, and Jabesh is to be identified with Jabesh-Gilead. This indicates that Shallum came from the eastern side of the Jordan. Ishida's thesis (*Royal Dynasties*, 173–76) that many of the revolts in the north at this time reflect a rivalry between the Transjordan and Cis-jordan tribes finds support here. See also Thiele, *Mysterious Numbers*, 118–27. This would help as well to explain the enigmatic role of the Gileadites in a subsequent coup (v 25), and the reference to Menahem "from Tirzah" (v 16). However, if "Menahem son of Gadi" is meant to indicate that Menahem was the son of a Gadite, or himself a Gadite, then the theory is not so well-founded. But the possibility does exist, and it highlights the rapid disintegration of the northern state after the long reign of Jeroboam. Josephus (*Antiq.* ix.228) adds color to the story of Shallum's revolt by having him be a close friend of Zechariah. Gray's identification of Jabesh with modern Yasuf (*Kings*, 623) is unlikely.

קבל עם "Kabal-am." While the vast majority of commentators follow G and adopt the reading of "Ibleam" (see n. 10.a above), there are problems with this emendation. The term קבל עם is a *hapax legomenon*, and is virtually untranslatable in its present form. Refuge is often taken in the Aramaic term *qublu,* meaning "what is in front," but without additional evidence from Hebrew sources that this was the meaning of a related word such comparisons are not very useful. If the term is to be translated as an adverbial phrase "at Kabal-am," then the syntax is unusual, though by no means impossible. The use of a noun in this adverbial sense is known elsewhere in the book (see the use of בית in 12:11–12). Using the principle of "the most difficult reading," it is much easier to see a smoothing out of an apparently unintelligible text "Kabal-am" to a known "Ibleam," especially under the influence of the memory of 9:27 in which the assassination of a former king takes place at Ibleam, than it is to see the move in the other direction toward obfuscation. One is forced to conclude that the present location of "Kabal-am" is unknown, but the text should stand.

12 The reference is to 10:28–31 in which the prophecy was originally given; it is in keeping with the writer's view of Yahweh's control over the history of Israel and Judah. The prophet by whom this word came remains anonymous.

13 Shallum's short reign reflects the degree of instability in the Northern Kingdom. Of his predecessors only Zimri (1 Kgs 16:15–20) reigned for a shorter period, seven days. This too was in a time of uncertainty.

14 The name מנחם "Menahem" means "Comforter" and is the piel participle of the root נחם. Its form is analogous to Manasseh (מנשה). בן גדי "son of Gadi" is probably a reference to his father, not his homeland, since it is stated that Menahem originated from Tirzah. The patronym is a shortened form of the longer Gaddiyahu, a version of which is found in the Samarian Ostraca (ii.2) from approximately the same period. For the text see Gibson, *Syrian Semitic Inscriptions* 1:11, and for the date see W. H. Shea, *IEJ* 27 (1977) 16–27.

Menahem's quick reaction to Shallum's coup is remarkable. His place of origin, Tirzah, suggests he was a Manassite, and this in turn lends credence to the theory of intertribal rivalry. Josephus (*Antiq.* ix.228) preserves an independent tradition of Menahem's vengeance and a civil war which followed the coup. This tradition also implies that Menahem was a general in Zechariah's army.

15 The formal conclusion to the reign of Shallum legitimizes his reign, although it certainly did not amount to much.

16 Grammatically, the verse is clumsy. The phrase ואת גבוליה מתרצה "and her territory from beyond Tirzah" is awkward, though not devoid of meaning. The masculine פתח "open" clashes with the feminine designation for Tiphsah, and the order of the sentence כי לא פתח ויך "because it did not open up he attacked," while not completely impossible, is better reversed with the clause ויך "he attacked" at the beginning. The final part of the sentence should be preceded by the conjunction, but even then the clumsiness remains. The particle אז "then" followed by the simple imperfect is thought to betray the archival origins of the statement, and explains the catalogue of the result of Menahem's fighting (see Burney, *Notes,* 322). From the brief account contained here, it is not clear where in Menahem's reign the events described should be placed. Josephus (*Antiq.* ix.230–31) clearly places the events immediately after Menahem's accession; these deliberate atrocities were designed to punish the stubbornness of "Thapsa." It is more likely that the general, Menahem, was already on a punitive mission when he was called away to deal with the coup of Shallum. This would also provide a perfect setting for such a coup. The clause אז יכה allows for either an action contemporary with the preceding sentence, or prior to it (see Josh 10:33; Judg 5:11, 13; 19:22; 2 Sam 21:18).

תפסח "Tiphsah." The identification of this site is much disputed. Almost all commentators have adopted the emendation to Tappuah provided by G^L (see n. 16.a. above). The only Tiphsah known is on the Euphrates (see 1 Kgs 5:4), and it is thought that the likelihood of Menahem's being involved in fighting this far north on behalf of his king is very remote. But neither is it impossible (see M. Haran, *VT* 17 [1967] 284–90). The emendation to Tappuah would locate the battle at a site mentioned in Josh 16:8 on the northern border of Ephraim. The statement ". . . its border from Tirzah" is then also illuminated, since Tirzah would not be far away. However, that this small Ephraimite city was so important as to have such an extensive territory under its control is most unlikely. Its supposed location, near modern Iskaka (Grid 172–168), would offer no apparent reason for such an attack upon a neighboring town by Menahem. It is a remote village, of no strategic significance, and away from the main highway. On the other hand, the likelihood of Menahem's being involved in a campaign as far north as the Euphrates is not as far-fetched. This was, after all, the northeastern limit of the expansion under Jeroboam (14:28), and such an expedition by Menahem on behalf of Zechariah, Jeroboam's son, would have been to either regain or strengthen those outer limits. The evidence one way or the other is not completely convincing, but Tiphsah cannot be lightly dismissed. Gray's theory (*Kings,* 622), that the turn of events is evidence for the tribes asserting their rights to a choice of a king over the principle of a hereditary monarchy, is an interesting piece of western idealism. Such democratic ideals are hardly part of the scene in the period of the monarchy. To be noted is that Menahem himself was followed by his son, Pekahiah, thus establishing a short-lived dynasty. See Ishida, *Royal Dynasties,* 173–76.

The brutality of Menahem's actions was, sadly enough, a very common feature of warfare in the ancient Near East. Such deeds were regarded as the right of the victor, and ought not to be judged by modern philosophies of international conflict. See *Comment* on 8:12. Siege warfare, perfected by the Assyrians at this time, was a particularly horrible form of conflict. Slaughter of civilians of towns under siege was something the Assyrians had added to their repertoire of warfare.

17 The problems of chronology now become specially complicated, and even more so when the attempt is made to link the biblical data with the data made available by the Assyrian records. The problem is discussed more fully at vv 19–20.

18 The comment by now is typical, and occurs with increasing regularity in connection with the kings of Israel. The persistence with which this judgment is made keeps the corruption of the Northern Kingdom ever before the reader. The phrase כל ימיו, lit., "all his days" is strange as an appendage to a verse, and many regard it as the beginning of v 19, with the emendation to בימיו "in his days" (see *BHS*). This would certainly bring it into accord with v 29, but the emendation remains a conjecture. The phrase in its present form designates a general length of time (see Gen 5:5; Brin, *ZAW* 93 [1981] 183–96).

19 The problems associated with vv 18–19 are connected by most commentators with the problems of the chronology of the period. Concentration has generally been upon the date of the invasion of Israel by Assyria, which is thought to correspond to a reference in Tiglath Pileser's own annals. However, on reading the Hebrew text the question must be raised whether the verses do in fact refer to an armed invasion, and also whether the verses do shed any light at all on the complicated chronology of the period. A careful reading of the text suggests that these verses do neither. Evidence from the Babylonian King List (*ANET*, 272) makes clear that Tiglath Pileser and Pul are the same person, the latter name being given to him after he seized the throne of Babylon. The older separation between the two (see I. Benzinger, *Die Bucher der Könige*, 168–69) is no longer possible. The date of the Assyrian lordship over Israel, which undoubtedly took place during the reign of Tiglath-Pileser (745–727 B.C.), is a disputed one. More than once the Assyrian records mention tribute from Menahem of Samaria. These inscriptions, translated in Luckenbill's collection (*Ancient Records* 1:269–96), are extremely difficult to interpret, in spite of the detail they provide for the reign of the Assyrian king. In the order found in Luckenbill, it would appear that tribute was exacted from Menahem during the third-year campaign to the west (ca. 743 B.C.). This is a position adopted by Thiele (*Mysterious Numbers*, 94–117), who puts forward a strong case for understanding certain sections of inscription (numbered according to Luckenbill: 769, 770, 772, 785, 796, 797, 813, 814, 821) as referring to the same series of events in the third year of the king. On the other hand, Levine (*BASOR* 206 [1972] 40–42) has drawn attention to an additional inscription, hitherto unpublished, in which evidence is found for tribute from Menahem being exacted in the ninth-year campaign in the west (i.e., 737 B.C.) Almost by way of compromise, Shea (*JNES* 37 [1978] 43–49) revised the chronology on the basis of the same evidence to suggest that Menahem paid tribute to Tiglath Pileser while the Assyrian was using Arpad as his western campaign headquarters. Since, according to Shea, Arpad was secured only in 741 B.C., a date of 740 B.C. for Menahem's subservience is offered. Each of the above theories and chronological reconstructions has several points in its favor, and at this stage the evidence has to be regarded as inconclusive. A more important question is whether the solution to the problem is in any way connected with the information offered in 15:19–20. This can be decided only after a careful study of the verses.

The translation of vv 19–20 is extremely difficult, and the one offered above differs in many ways from others given by commentators. The language and the syntax of the verses are not easy, but cannot support the translation given, for example, by NEB, which captures the sense adopted by other commentators. That translation implies, first, that an invasion of Israel by Assyria is recorded in these verses, and second, that the wealthy classes were taxed to pay off the invader, who withdrew after the receipt of one thousand talents of silver. In fact, neither of these points can find support in what the sentences say.

בא פול מלך אשור "Pul the king of Assyria had come" is not the regular language used to describe an invasion. The normal word for such a venture is עלה "go up," which is found, for example, in 6:25; 12:18; 17:3, 5, 9, etc. V 29 is no exception to this pattern since the use of the verb בא "come" is further qualified by other activities of the king. If Tiglath Pileser then did not come in this incident as an invader, in what capacity did he come? ויתן מנחם לפול אלף ככר כסף להיות ידיו אתו להחזיק הממלכה בידו "and Menahem gave Pul a thousand talents of silver to help strengthen his hold on the kingdom" provides the clue. The language is reminiscent of a military alliance (see 10:15). It would be meaningless to suggest that Menahem paid an invader tribute so that he (Menahem) could have a stronger hold on a land which he had already effectively lost to that invader! The sum of money paid, one thousand talents, while a considerable sum, is mentioned without reference to anything else. Such a sum compares well with other sums extracted from vassals by the Assyrian, as is evident from his records. However, such payment of tribute is invariably associated with devastation of cities and land, destruction of property, slaughter of soldiers, and deportation of the inhabitants. In connection with this particular payment of tribute, none of these is mentioned. This is all the more important since precisely those sections of Tiglath Pileser's annals that are appealed to as background for this payment (772 and 815 according to Luckenbill) go into great detail on such actions. In comparison, vv 19–20 and sections 772 and 815 bear little or no resemblance. As an alternative, we suggest that Menahem paid Tiglath Pileser for military aid at a time when his kingdom was threatened by a third party. The circumstances were repeated in Judah during the reign of Ahaz.

The background to such aid is easy to sketch. The twenty-year reign of Pekah during this period of confused chronology has been a particularly difficult problem. It can be easily accommodated by positing a rival kingdom contemporary with that of Menahem, probably to the east of the Jordan (see below on vv 27–28). If this suggestion is correct, then the two kingdoms, or claimants, would have been bitter rivals. Menahem's payment to Tiglath Pileser would then have been an attempt to rid himself of the eastern threat. By all accounts it was not completely successful.

Such an interpretation throws light on the unusual words used in v 20. The translation of the hiphil of יצא as "tax" or "levy a tax" is not correct; in fact, it is impossible. The normal word for the verb "tax" is the hiphil of ערך and it occurs in 23:35 in circumstances of obvious tribute-paying. The hiphil of יצא means "to send out" or "to bring out." With a direct object of הכסף את the translation best suited is "Menahem paid out the silver." The preposition על is also accommodated by this understanding with its sense of "because of. . . ." גבורי החיל is often translated to indicate wealthy people. RSV offers "all the wealthy men," which is close to Montgomery's "magnates of wealth" (an extremely clumsy English rendering—see *Kings,* 450) or Herrmann's "free landowners liable to the levy" (*History,* 245). See also Cogan, *Imperialism and Religion,* 97–98. While this rendering offers attractive possibilities for the tables to be turned upon the wealthy against whom Amos preached (so Herrmann), the translation cannot be sustained. There is no justification for the translation "wealthy men," as the apologetic way in which this version is offered by many commentators illustrates. The phrase is a most common one for "soldiers," and can be sustained here. The mercenaries offered by Assyria were paid fifty shekels per person for their duties in aid of Menahem, then allowed to return home. Whatever the circumstances for the payment of tribute mentioned in Tiglath Pileser's own records, it is unlikely that the Bible makes mention of them here. Such selectivity on the part of the writer is by no means unusual. The verses therefore bring us no closer to solving the problem of this period, or of fixing the date of Assyria's attack on Menahem in 743 B.C., 740 B.C., or 737 B.C. This has to be settled in the light of other, as yet unavailable, evidence. In these historical discussions, however, sight must not be lost of the writer's thematic program, which repeats itself later (see *Comments* on 16:5–9).

23 The name פקחיה "Pekahiah," related to the verb פקח "to open," is combined with the theophoric element and means "Yahweh opens (the eyes)," or "Yahweh illumines." On the chronology see above. The two years of Pekahiah's brief reign again illustrate the unstable political situation in the Northern Kingdom at this time.

25 The name פקח "Pekah" is derived from the same root as that of his predecessor. Another occurrence of the name was found on a jar at Hazor, Stratum V (late eighth century B.C.). The inscription reads לפקח סמדר ("belonging to Pekah Samdar"). See Y. Yadin, *EAEHL* 2:474–95, esp. 489. The origin of the name "Remaliah" is unknown although BDB, 942, suggests it is related to an Arabic word for "adorn." Isa 7:4, 5, 9; 8:6 use the patronym only, and are contemptuous of the northern king. The term שליש has been discussed above (see *Comment* on 9:25) and is best translated "lieutenant," i.e., close military associate. The expression here indicates that, before his break from Menahem, Pekah was an important military officer, involved possibly in Menahem's attack on Tiphsah (v 16).

The death of the king at the ארמון "citadel," that is, the protective fortress of the palace, means that the plot against him was either a palace coup, or a surprise attack on the palace. It is the latter possibility that Josephus exploits (*Antiq.* ix.233–34) with his reconstruction of a meal between Pekahiah and his friends during which he was murdered by Pekah. The account is reminiscent of, and influenced by, 1 Kgs 16:8–10, 15–20.

את ארגב ואת האריה "Argob and Areah." This expression is omitted by most (see n. 25.c above). The suggestion is that they are misplaced from v 29. This is probably correct, but takes us no closer to the meaning of the terms. Deut 3:4, 14 suggest that the district of Argob was located in the upper Transjordan in biblical Bashan, but the reference to "lion" is confusing. The form in which the terms appear in this verse is awkward, one being a definite noun, the other, indefinite. In addition, syntactically they appear as direct objects of a nonexistent verb. In 6:5 above the occurrence of a supposed direct object marker was interpreted as a demonstrative, but it is unlikely that the same holds true here. M. J. Geller's theory (*VT* 26 [1976] 374–77) that the ארגב and the אריה represent the decorative sphinxlike statues symbolically guarding the royal palace is most interesting. It has no support, however, other than a remote Ugaritic example (*CTA* 19:121), and the sphinx motif which was found on the Samarian ivories. The possible parallel between this incident and the death of Sennacherib "between the colossi" (Luckenbill, *Ancient Records* 2:304) is pure concidence.

The presence of a company of Gileadites in the plot and assassination of the king certainly strengthens the theory of the intertribal rivalry at this time (see Ishida, *Royal Dynasties*, 177). The participants in the plot are designated by a military unit (חמשים "fifty").

27–28 Some adjustment has to be made in the figure of twenty years for the reign of Pekah. If Menahem is mentioned in the inscription of Tiglath Pileser that refers to events that took place in 738 B.C. (see above on vv 19–20), and the Assyrian was also active in the overthrow of Pekah in 732 B.C., then the twenty years of Pekah and the two years of Pekahiah cannot be accommodated. The number 20 is seen by many as "improbable" (Herrmann, *History*, 246) and quickly changed for a shorter span of years. Begrich, for example, reduces it arbitrarily to 2 (see *Die Chronologie der Könige*, 103, 155). Even if Thiele's date of 743 B.C. is adopted for the incursion of Assyria into Israel during the reign of Menahem, this still leaves insufficient room for the twenty-two years needed to cover the reigns of Pekah and Pekahiah. F. Hommel (*HDB* 1:176–90) offered the ingenious but unsatisfactory solution of regarding Pekahiah as pure fiction. This, however, seems more a gesture of despair than the fruit of careful analysis.

Many are prone to follow Thiele's suggestion (*Mysterious Numbers*, 124) that the twenty-year reign of Pekah is dated not from his accession to the throne of the whole kingdom, but from the initial establishment of a separate kingdom on the east side of the Jordan. The case is most persuasively argued by H. J. Cook, *VT* 14 (1964) 121–35. Thus the twenty-year dating is seen as partisan, offering the (false) impression that Pekah was king over all Israel throughout his reign, when in actual fact he was in such a position for a much shorter time (so Gray, *Kings*, 626). While such a possibility does retain the biblical numbers, it is clearly not without its own problems. It is to be noted that the verse has a slight change in the normal order of expressions. Here the figure follows the reference to Samaria, giving the very distinct impression that Pekah reigned for twenty years in the capital city, and that his accession coincided with the fifty-second year of Azariah of Judah. This theory simply creates a greater problem. In the interests of calculation of the figures of reigns it hardly seems good method to ignore what the text itself states. Further, on Thiele's understanding of the figures, a reason needs to be found why such a "partisan" dating found its way into the records used by the deuteronomic historian. In any event, having established himself as king, Pekah proved to be no better than his predecessor.

29 בימי פקח "in Pekah's time." The vagueness of the expression contrasts markedly with the precision found in 17:6; 25:1. It is a general expression indicating a rather informal use of time (see G. Brin, *ZAW* 93 [1981] 183–96).

The writer reverts to תגלת פלסר "Tiglath Pileser," the normal name for the Assyrian king, in contrast to v 19. The incident referred to in this and the following verse is to be identified in all probability with the undated campaign report found in Luckenbill, *Ancient Records* 1:815–16, and *ANET*,

283–84. Most would now date this campaign in 733 B.C. The campaign report mentions an expedition into the area around Gebail (Byblos) and other cities "on the shore of the upper sea," then a swing to the south to include "... nite, Gal'za, Abilakka which are adjacent to Bit Hu-umria (Israel) ... the land of ... li, in its entire extent, I united with Assyria. Officers of mine I installed as governors over them" (so *ANET*, 283). The campaign ended in Gaza where a similar fate awaited the inhabitants. In the Assyrian inscription the reference to Menahem in the following lines is unclear, therefore the date cannot be fixed with certainty. Similarly, the much-quoted reference to "Naphtali" (*ANET*, 283) is now regarded as wrong. In the inscription only the final syllable is legible (see D. J. Wiseman, *Iraq* 18 [1956] 117–29). A more likely reading is Haza'ili, i.e., Syria. The Assyrian references to Gal'za and Abilakka are possible Assyrian versions of Gilead and Abel beth Maacah.

The place-names in the list have been variously interpreted, but they can be seen as forming a distinct geographical pattern in the north, a fact that demonstrates the Assyrian plan and strategy. עיון "Iyyon" is a site on the River Iyyon (Grid 204–311) some fifteen kilometers north of אבל בית מעכה "Abel beth Maacah." The latter site is identified with the large Tel Abil, situated to the north of modern Qiryat Shemona (Grid 204–296). ינוח "Janoach" is difficult to identify. The modern sites of Khirbet Yanum near Nablus, Janua, ten kilometers southeast of Megiddo, and Janoah, sixteen kilometers east of Acco, are all candidates. The last-mentioned is the most favored, although the first-mentioned has its strong supporters (see Aharoni, *Land of the Bible*, 111). The likelihood of its being any of these three is remote. None of these sites fits the pattern developed in the list of towns and fortresses in northern Galilee. Recently, J. Kaplan (*IEJ* 28 [1978] 157–60) argued persuasively for the location of the site at Khirbet Niha (Grid 202–295), one kilometer south of modern Kefar Giladi, on the main road south from Abel beth Maacah. קדש "Kedesh" is to be identified with Tell el Majunna (Tel Kedesh) approximately halfway between Abel beth Maacah and Hazor (Grid 200–279), governing the access westwards into the Galilean hills. חצור "Hazor" (Tell el-Qedah) is the well-known large site found eight kilometers south of the ancient Lake Huleh (Grid 203–269). The site was excavated in the 1950s by Yadin, and much has been made known of the findings (see Y. Yadin, *Hazor* [1972]; *EAEHL* 2:474–95). On the Upper City at Stratum V extensive conflagration damage was found. The fire destroyed many of the magnificent buildings erected by Ahab a century before. It is this level of destruction that is identified with the capture of the city by Tiglath Pileser III.

"Gilead, the whole of Galilee and Naphtali." These names are more general than the sites mentioned above, and constitute a picture of the widespread effect of the capture of the cities from Iyyon to Hazor. (For "Argob and Areah" see above on v 25.) By the capture the Assyrian accomplished many things. First, he held firmly the northern limits of the great trunk road in Israel (the *"Via Maris"*). Second, with the rather limited scope for travel in the surrounding countryside he gained control of the northern access to Israel. Third, with the capture of Kedesh he controlled the access westwards into Galilee. Fourth, with his control of Hazor he guarded the eastern branch of the *Via Maris* to Damascus. Fifth, by slicing into the country along this road he effectively isolated Gilead from the rest of the country. The strategy was masterful and effective. ויגלם אשורה "and he deported them to Assyria." The Assyrian records are littered with references to such mass deportations. On the Assyrian policies toward vassal states see M. Cogan, *Imperialism and Religion*, 97–103, and the literature there cited.

30 This further revolt against the throne is yet another very graphic illustration of the political disintegration of the Northern Kingdom. Hoshea son of Elah is given no other description, but it is possible that he was an important figure in the north. Assyrian sources provide us with additional information, namely, that the revolt took place under the auspices of the Assyrian king. Tiglath Pileser's own account states "They overthrew Pekah their king, and I placed Hoshea as king over them" (*ANET*, 284). Presumably Hoshea functioned as a puppet ruler for the Assyrians, in a manner similar to Gedaliah in the south after the deportation of Judah.

The name "Hoshea" contains an ironic twist. It is derived from the root ישע "to save" and contrasts vividly with the activities of the promised מושיע "savior" mentioned in 13:5. Hoshea's patronym appears in Gen 36:41–42 as an Edomite name, although in 1 Kgs 16:8 it reappears as the name of a former Israelite king, son of Baasha, who was assassinated by Zimri.

The reference to Pekah's death in the tenth year of Jotham is an embarrassment. Pekah is known to have been active in the so-called Syro-Ephraimite alliance against Ahaz, Jotham's successor (see Isa 7:1–8:8). This evidence is found again in 2 Kgs 16:5. Thiele's solution (*Mysterious Numbers*, 118–40) is to posit a co-regency between Jotham and his successor Ahaz which began in Pekah's seventeenth year (16:1). To allow for this, Ahaz "deposed" Jotham, who lived for four years more. This accommodates the numbers, but creates a fiction for which there is no evidence at all in the text. The absence of any evidence of a co-regency between Jotham and Ahaz is all the more remarkable in the light of the clear evidence for a co-regency between Jotham and his father, Azariah (15:5). Begrich's theory (*Die Chronologie der Könige*, 155), in which the reigns of Jotham (758/7–743/2 B.C.) and Pekah (734/3–733/2 B.C.) are separated by a decade, is even more problematic. The deletion of the figures suggested by *BHS*, on the basis of G^L (see n. 30.a. above), only serves to highlight the problem, not solve it.

31 In spite of the irregular beginning, the reign of Pekah is legitimized by this concluding formula.

32 The formal beginning to Jotham's reign is necessary at this point in the narrative since most of the information related in this chapter applies to Israel. The name יותם is probably a shortened form. An analogy exists in the abbreviated form of "Jehoiakim" found in a seal impression (see Gibson, *Syrian Semitic Inscriptions* 1:61, 63). In this case the name would mean "Yahweh makes perfect" from the verb תמם, or "Yahweh is perfect" (so Gray, *Kings*, 629). The possible parallel found in a seal at Ezion Geber, is in fact no parallel at all (see Gibson, *Syrian Semitic Inscriptions*, 63).

33 שש עשרה "sixteen." Gray, with others, emends the length of the reign to six years, although there is no textual evidence for such a change. The form of the mother's name, ירושא "Jerusha," is unusual. It is pointed as a feminine passive participle, but no verbal root רשא is known to exist in Hebrew. An emendation to ירושאל (so Gray) is possible, but conjectural. If Zadok was a priest, as seems likely from his name, then Jotham had noble parentage and represents a mixture of the royal line and the priestly line in Jerusalem. But he receives only cautious praise (v 34) and his activities were neither worse nor better than those of his father. He is denied a comparison with David.

35 "It was he who built an upper gate to the temple." 2 Chr 27 goes into far greater detail on the building program of Jotham. It is clear from that evidence that his construction projects added considerably to the defenses of the country. Such a move was undoubtedly necessary in the very disturbed times which characterized his reign. On the location of the "Upper Gate" see G. A. Smith, *Jerusalem* 2:125.

37 The attacks by Rezin of Damascus and Pekah of Israel form the background for Isa 7:1–8:8. 2 Chr 27 refers to considerable military activity directed against the Ammonites, but Kings is silent on such ventures. In connection with this verse the relevant passages in Isaiah ought to be read. It is apparent that the allies united against Judah and sought to place one of their own, the son of Tabeel, upon the throne. The name is Aramaic. The attempt was unsuccessful, and the prophet treats both attackers with complete contempt (Isa 7:7–9). Out of this historical context came the "Immanuel sign" (Isa 7:10–14). The concluding remarks of chap. 15 now prepare the way for a fuller account of these events from the perspective of Judea in the following chapter.

Excursus: Additional Note on the Chronology

The vexing problems of the chronology of the last days of Israel continue in chap. 15, again partly because there is such an abundance of comparative Assyrian material. The problem is twofold: (1) how to reconcile the data within the Hebrew text of 2 Kgs 15, and (2) how to reconcile the data of the Hebrew text with the data found within the Assyrian sources (the records of Tiglath Pileser III).

Uzziah's long reign of fifty-two years (v 2) witnessed the end of the dynasty of Jehu in the north with the death of Jeroboam and the accession of Zechariah in Uzziah's thirty-eighth year (v 8). Zechariah's reign is short, six months, and he dies at the hand of Shallum. Shallum reigned for an even shorter period, one month (v 13). Zechariah was avenged by Menahem, who reigned for ten years (v 17) and who was succeeded by his son, Pekahiah, in the fiftieth year of Uzziah (v 23). Following Pekahiah's two-year reign came the reign of his assassin Pekah. It is at this point that the Hebrew chronology becomes very confused, and confusing. Pekah is said to have reigned for twenty years (v 27). During his reign Uzziah died and was succeeded by his son, Jotham, who reigned for sixteen years (v 32). But a serious problem now arises since this took place in the second year of Pekah, who is said to have died in the tenth year of Jotham (v 30). Not only does this cut short Pekah's twenty years, but the sequence would suggest that Pekah in fact outlived Jotham by some two years at least. Thus it is the reference to the twenty-year reign of Pekah that has been the cause of considerable debate.

To add to this confusion is the record of Tiglath Pileser III, who became actively involved in Syria and Palestine during his reign. The Assyrian reigned for eighteen years ca. 745–727 B.C.) and a number of accounts of his various campaigns exist (see Luckenbill, *Ancient Records* 1:269–95). In his third-year campaign, Tiglath Pileser mentions that he exacted tribute from Menahem. This, as was seen above, is not related to the events described in 2 Kgs 15:19–20. The Assyrian also claims that he was responsible for the overthrow of Pekah and the accession of Hoshea. The inscription is undated, but it accords well with the information found in 15:29. The problem is again the twenty-year reign of Pekah, since it does not fit even into the Assyrian information which mentions Menahem and Hoshea within a space of eighteen years. The shortest time between these two figures according to the biblical data that includes the twenty years of Pekah is twenty-two years. At the present time, it is best to leave out of the discussion the enigmatic reference in Assyrian sources to "Azaryau of Iauda," which we have argued is not a reference to the Judean king (see *Comment* on v 6 above).

However, the problem is further complicated by the data given in the following biblical chapters. In 17:1 Hoshea's reign is synchronized with the twelfth year of Ahaz. Finally, Jotham, who is said to have become king in the second year of Pekah (15:32–33), would have ascended the throne of Judah two years after his father's death. Thus are created an interregnum for which the biblical texts offers no additional evidence. For much of this period, Assyrian records are extant and include not only the records of Tiglath Pileser, but also those of Shalmaneser V and his son Sargon, plus Sennacherib's account of his attack on Jerusalem. This latter event can be dated with some precision in 701 B.C.

Two elements emerge as crucial in arriving at a solution to the problems of chronology. The first is the date of Menahem's tribute to the Assyrian invader, and the second is the nature of the twenty-year reign of Pekah. On the first, opinion is divided between 743 B.C. and 737 B.C. (see *Comment* on v 19). Since "Azaryau of Iauda" is not to be identified with the Judean king, and since 15:19–20 do not refer to a payment of tribute, the dating is unknown.

On the second issue, the suggestion is attractive and certainly plausible that the twenty years of Pekah be dated, not from the death of Menahem, but from the establishment of a rival kingdom on the eastern bank of the Jordan. The enigmatic references to eastern tribal groups, such as the company of Gileadites, support this theory, and are dealt with in the *Comment* above. If Pekah's "reign" is reckoned by the writer beginning from his accession to an independent "kingdom" in the east, then his twenty-year reign presents no problem, and the accession of Jotham in Pekah's second year is also accommodated. This dating allows for the co-regency mentioned in 15:5 and does not leave a gap between Azariah and Jotham. Nevertheless, it does contain serious difficulties. The text (v 27) clearly states that the twenty-year reign took place "in Samaria," and the slight change in word order emphasizes this point (see *Comment* on v 27). Also, the synchronization of the beginning of Pekah's reign with the last year of Azariah is a problem. Added to this is that Ahaz's succession in 16:1 must be pushed back three years before the death of Jotham (15:38), whom he deposed, to synchronize with the threatened attacks of Pekah and Rezin in 735/4 B.C. Such a solution, offered by Thiele, while solving some of the serious chronological difficulties of the text (or rather difficulties of reckoning), sacrifices too much.

Explanation

Chap. 15 presents the final chaotic years of the life of Israel with a succession of kings and assassinations, coups d'état, and foreign intervention (vv 8–31). But these events are sandwiched between the accounts of the reigns of two kings of Judah, Azariah (vv 1–7) and Jotham (vv 32–38). A major theme links it all together.

A brief glance at the account of the reign of Azariah reveals some glaring features. Here it seems the principle of selectivity that guides our writer has dominated to the point of excluding much of the detail of his reign. Azariah reigned for fifty-two years (v 2), yet of all the incidents deemed worthy of mention from that long, and presumably prosperous, reign, the writer chooses only the fact of the king's leprosy and quarantine (vv 4–5). Nothing more of his reign is known. Assumptions can be made on the data found in the book of Isaiah about the nature of Judean society inherited by Jotham from his father, but they are tenuous at best. To search for a motive for this selection one does not have to wander far beyond the immediate context. Azariah's predecessor had suffered an invasion by Joash of Israel, and the walls of the capital city were breached. Broken borders or limits and their symbolic significance emerge. The matter is brought up again with the reference in v 19 to the presence of Pul, the Assyrian, in Israel. We have argued in the *Comment* that this presence is not to be seen as an invasion, but an offer of help to Menahem in return for payment. Pul (Tiglath Pileser III) here plays the same anticipatory role as does Merodach Baladan in chap. 20. The anticipated threat arrives in force by v 29 with the major invasion of the Assyrian into northern Israel and with the occupation of major sections of the country. Finally, the theme is played again with the incursions of Syria and Israel (Rezin and Pekah) into Judah during Jotham's reign (v 37). The verse begins with a generalizing temporal reference, which we have argued elsewhere is a characterization of a period of time (see *Introduction*). The whole era—Jotham's reign and the state of affairs in the north—is characterized as one of incursion, the breaking of limits, and invasion. Biblical leprosy provides a perfect symbol for this. The health of both Judah and Israel is in jeopardy.

It is Israel who suffers first. The description of events in vv 8–31 is characterized by a quick succession of anecdotes on the last of the kings of Israel. The overall impression is one of increasing disintegration of the northern society. Zechariah, the last of the dynasty of Jehu, is assassinated by Shallum, who in turn is killed by Menahem. Menahem's son, Pekahiah, is assassinated by Pekah, who in turn is killed by Hoshea. Although, from contemporary sources, some of the historical reasons become plain—Tiglath Pileser was active in the deposing of Pekah (see above on vv 29–30)—the writer wishes to keep in mind the theological rationale for this rapid disintegration. He accomplishes that aim in two ways. First, the prophecy concerning the limited duration of the dynasty of Jehu is fulfilled in the death of Zechariah (v 12). Yahweh is in control of the declining fortunes of Israel. Second, in this chapter and the preceding one, the specter of the sins of Jeroboam ben Nebat is raised again. In these two chapters the references to those sins outnumber all others in the books of Kings, and in this way the writer reminds the reader of the inevitable judgment which must now take place as a result of those actions of Israel's first king. The nation is doomed. The time of prosperity for Israel is ended; the delay in judgment is exhausted.

The Apostasy of Ahaz (16:1–20)

Bibliography

Ackroyd, P. R. "Historians and Prophets." *SEÅ* 33 (1968) 18–54. **Childs, B. S.** "The Formula 'Until This Day.'" *JBL* 82 (1963) 279–92. **Derchain, P.** "Le plus anciens témoinage de sacrifice d'enfants chez les semites occidenteaux." *VT* 20 (1970) 351–55. **Hallo, W.** "From Qarqar to Carchemish." *BA* 23 (1962) 34–61. **Haran, M.** *Temples and Temple-service in Ancient Israel.* Oxford: Clarendon Press (1978) 130–45. **Luria, B. Z.** "The Siege of Jerusalem in the Time of Ahaz." *BMik* 45 (1971) 139–45. **McCarthy, D. J.** "The Symbolism of Blood and Sacrifice." *JBL* 88 (1969) 166–76. **McHugh, J.** "The Date of Hezekiah's Birth." *VT* 14 (1964) 446–53. **Myers, J. M.** "Edom and Judah in the Sixth-Fifth Centuries B.C." In *Near Eastern Studies in Honor of William Foxwell Albright,* H. Goedicke, ed., 377–92. Baltimore: Johns Hopkins Press, 1971. **Rudolph, W.** "Zum Text des Königsbuches." *ZAW* 63 (1951) 201–15. **Sales, R. H.** "Human Sacrifice in Biblical Thought." *JBR* 25 (1957) 112–17. **Tadmor, H., and Cogan, M.** "Ahaz and Tiglath Pileser." *Bib* 60 (1979) 491–508. **Vaux, R. de.** *Studies in Old Testament Sacrifice.* Tr. J. Burke and R. Potter. Cardiff: University of Wales Press (1964) 27–90.

Translation

¹*In the seventeenth* [a] *year of the reign of Pekah son of Remaliah, Ahaz son of Jotham became king in Judah.* ²*Ahaz was twenty years old when he became king and he reigned for sixteen years in Jerusalem. He did not behave well in Yahweh his God's eyes* [a] *as David his ancestor had done.* ³*In fact he walked* [a] *in the ways of the kings of Israel,* [b] *even to the extent of making his son "pass through fire" after the sordid fashion* [c] *of the nations* [d] *whom Yahweh had driven out before the people of Israel.* ⁴*He sacrificed and burned incense on the high places and on the high hills and under every green tree.*

⁵*But then Rezin king of Syria and Pekah son of Remaliah, king of Israel, marched against Jerusalem to do battle. They besieged Ahaz but were unable to defeat him.* [a] ⁶*At that time Rezin* [a] *king of Syria* [b] *restored Elath to Syria, and expelled the Judeans from Elath. Then Syrians* [c] *came to Elath and live there even to this day.* ⁷*Ahaz reacted by sending messengers to Tiglath Pileser the king of Assyria with these words,* [a]*"I am your servant and your son. Come up and rescue me* [b] *from the clutches of the king of Syria and the clutches of the king of Israel, who have both risen up* [c] *against me."* ⁸*Ahaz took the silver and gold which was found in the* [a] *temple and in the palace treasury, and sent it as a payment to the king of Assyria.* [b] ⁹*The king of Assyria listened to his plea, and launched a campaign against Damascus and took it.* [a] *He sent its inhabitants into exile toward Kir. He killed Rezin.*

¹⁰*Now when Ahaz went to meet Tiglath Pileser king of Assyria at Damascus,* [a] *he saw the altar which was in Damascus. So Ahaz the king sent Uriah the priest a model of the altar and its design in all its detail.* ¹¹*Uriah the priest built a copy of the altar following all the plans sent to him from Damascus by Ahaz the king.* [a]*Uriah the priest was thus occupied until Ahaz the king returned from Damascus.* ¹²*The king returned from Damascus* [a] *and inspected the altar. He then approached* [b] *it and*

climbed up to it, **13** *and he offered his holocaust* **a** *and his cereal offering, and poured out his drink offering, and cast the blood of his peace offerings upon the altar.* **14** *As for the bronze* **a** *altar which stood before Yahweh, he removed it from the front of the temple,* **b** *that is from between the altar and the temple, and set it* **c** *on the north side of his altar.* **15** *Then King Ahaz gave Uriah the priest the following instructions, "Upon the great altar burn the morning burnt offering, and the evening cereal offering, that is, the king's burnt offering and cereal offering, together with the burnt offerings of all the people of the land,* **a** *and their cereal offerings and their drink offerings. Throw upon it all the blood of the burnt offerings and the blood of the sacrifice. The bronze altar shall be for me to pray at."* **b** **16** *Uriah the priest followed the instructions of Ahaz to the letter.*

17 *King Ahaz cut off the frames* **a** *of the carriages and took away the laver from them, and took down the sea from the bronze oxen* **b** *which were underneath it. Then he set it on a stone platform.* **18** *The structure for the sabbath* **a** *which* **b** *had been built in the palace, and the outer entrance for the king, he removed* **c** *from the temple in deference to the king of Assyria.* **19** *As for the remainder of the activities of Ahaz* **a** *which he did, are they not* **b** *written down in the records of the kings of Judah?* **20** *So Ahaz slept with his ancestors, and was buried with them* **a** *in the city of David, and Hezekiah his son reigned in his place.*

Notes

1.a. For "seventeenth" the G MS c₂ and Eth read "eighteenth."
2.a. After "his God" G^B adds πιστως "faithfully."
3.a. G^L adds the proper name "Ahaz."
3.b. G^AN read "Jeroboam, king of Israel."
3.c. MT reads כתעבות, lit., "like the abominations." G^AN correctly render κατα βδελυγματα. G^B mistakenly reads και τα βδελυγματα "and the abominations."
3.d. G^L precedes with των Θεων "of the gods."
5.a. MT reads ולא יכלו להלחם "but were unable to defeat him," to which G^L offers ηδυνηθησαν του λαβειν την Ιερ. "they were unable to take Jerusalem." This is also the understanding of Josephus (*Antiq.* ix.244). Ehrlich (*Randglossen* 7:311) suggests an unnecessary ולא יכל לחם "but he was not able to fight."
6.a. *BHS* suggests that the proper name is an addition.
6.b. *BHS* offers an alternative of אֱדוֹם "Edom."
6.c. K reads ארמים "Syrians" followed by Josephus (*Antiq.* ix.245). Q אֲדֹמִים and G read "Idumeans." On this see *Comment* below.
7.a. The G MS e₂ omits the words עבדך ובנך אני "I am your servant and your son."
7.b. MT reads הושעני "rescue me," G^L translates with ρυσαι "drag away."
7.c. The participial form of הַקּוֹמִים "who have risen up" is highly unusual, the more normal form being הַקָּמִים, which is suggested by *BHS*. GKC § 72p attempts to regularize MT, but with little success. Either the term is spelled wrongly, or, since it is in direct speech, it is a colloquial form of the ptcp. Ehrlich's emendation to הַחוֹגִים "those who encircle" is entirely speculative (see *Randglossen* 7:311).
8.a. G^B reads "the treasury of the temple," which is understandable but unnecessary expansion of the text.
8.b. Omitted by G^B.
9.a. After "he sent into exile" G^L adds την πολιν "the city" which might reflect an understanding of קָרְיָה "city" instead of קִירָה "toward Kir." G^B omits.
10.a. The form דּוּמֶּשֶׂק for "Damascus" is very unusual. Chronicles often reads דַּרְמֶשֶׂק.
11.a.–12.a. Omitted by G^B as a result of homoioteleuton.
12.b. Omitted by G^B. Ehrlich (*Randglossen* 7:312), following Tg, suggests וַיַּקְרֵב "and he brought near" and וַיַּעַל "and he offered up" (hiph) rather than the qal indicatives.

Form/Structure/Setting   209

13.a. MT reads עלתו "his holocaust." G^L presupposes עלה "a holocaust."
14.a. MT reads המזבח הנחשת "the bronze altar." Burney (*Notes*, 326) suggests that the second word is a gl from v 15b. G omits.
14.b. G^B adds κυριου "of the Lord."
14.c. MT reads ויתן "and he set," or "gave"; G^B reads ἔδειξεν "he displayed," which is a misreading of the correct rendering in Greek of ἔδωκεν "he gave," retained in G^L.
15.a. G^B reads simply "of the people." See Burney, *Notes*, 327.
15.b. M reads לְבַקֵּר, which is the cause of much debate. The only other forms of the infinitive of this verb are found in Prov 20:25 where the verb is translated "reflect" (rsv) and in Ps 27:4 "to inquire." Burney (*Notes*, 327) suggests that the investigation of an oracle is in mind, thus making the verb בקר a synonym for דרש "to seek." Our translation above is little more than a guess, since the correct meaning of the verb is unknown. G^B offers εἰς τὸ πρωι, thus reading לְבַקֶּר as לַבֹּקֶר "for the morning." Ehrlich (*Randglossen* 7:312) is also guessing when he suggests a paraphrase "That it may show me the difference. . . ."
17.a. The MT המסגרות המכנות, lit., "the rims, the bases," is impossible. Most suggest that the article be omitted from the first word. Many of the versions transliterate the phrase.
17.b. Some MSS read "twelve." Burney (*Notes*, 328) suggests that "bronze" is an addition.
18.a. MT is awkward here reading מיסך השבת (Q השבת מוּסַךְ) "the structure for the sabbath." The term מוסך is a *hapax legomenon*, possibly from the root סכך "to weave together," i.e., make a screen (see BDB, 697). G^B reads τον θεμελιον της καθεδρας (תָּ) מוּסַד הַמּוּשָׁב "the foundation of the throne").
18.b. G^B omits the relative pronoun, thus changing the meaning somewhat.
18.c. MT reads הֵסֵב "he removed," translated by G^B with ἐπέστρεψεν "he turned," which is rare, but not unknown (see 1 Kgs 8:14; 2 Kgs 20:2).
19.a. G^L adds και παντα "and all."
19.b. G^L reads οὐχὶ ἰδού "behold, are they not."
20.a. Omitted by G^B, but included in G^A, Syr.

Form/Structure/Setting

The presentation of the sixteen-year reign of King Ahaz of Judah in this chapter is short compared to the chapters that precede and follow it. However, the space devoted to the reign of one king is noteworthy by comparison with the extremely brief descriptions of the reigns of both Azariah and Jeroboam II. Nevertheless, the material in the chapter is limited by a clear principle of selectivity. What appear to be important political events are overshadowed by what is in the writer's mind a much more important event.

The formal introduction (vv 1–4) and conclusion to the reign of Ahaz (vv 19–20) are by now easily recognizable as standard formulae providing a framework of "legitimation" within which the activities of the king are placed. To be noted, however, is the annotation in v 3 that expands on the information of v 2 in typical deuteronomistic fashion. Also within this section there is a rare element of style, that is, the comparison of the Judean king with "the kings of Israel." Approaching the end of the northern kingdom, such a comparison becomes very severe.

Vv 5–9, which purport to be a summary of one aspect of Ahaz's reign, are phrased in the most cryptic fashion, with a great economy of words. Little information beyond the "bare bones" of the confrontation between Ahaz, Pekah, and Rezin is found here. Israel and Syria attack. They are repulsed with Assyrian aid. During this period of turmoil Syria regains Elath. The origin of such information is clearly the court records of Judah. But such a judgment is far from satisfying. Baldly stated, it is a truism, and although some detect still the residue of archival style in the verses (see Montgomery,

Kings, 457–58) such as the אָז "then" of v 5, the בָּעֵת הַהִיא "at that time" of v 6, and the עַד הַיּוֹם הַזֶּה "even to this day" of the same verse, more needs to be stated. V 7b, although brief, contains language characteristic of diplomatic correspondence of the period (see *Comment* on 5:5) and thus appears to be a quotation from an original, or a deliberate attempt to reflect convention. What is most remarkable about the opening section to the chapter is the compactness of presentation, which is made all the more clear by comparison with the remainder of the chapter (vv 10–18) in which details seem quite overdone.

The information contained in vv 10–18, because of the subject matter and the attention to detail, is most likely taken from the temple records in Jerusalem. The same was seen to be the case in the reform of Joash (see 12:10–19). The precise stages by which Ahaz was first attracted by the altar and then brought its plans to Jerusalem, the repeated reference to careful attention to orders, and the details of the installation of the new altar, together with the careful adjustments made in the existing temple furniture, all reflect the product of careful record-keeping and betray the bureaucrats' love for such detail.

But whatever the original source of the information here, the present shape of the chapter is more important, and it is imperative that the interpreter ask after the effect of the present arrangement in the ongoing narrative of the histories of the kingdoms.

Apart from the introduction and the conclusion (vv 1–4, 19–20) the imbalance of the chapter is to be noted. A serious military and political threat to the city of Jerusalem, the coalition of Syria and Israel, and the lifting of that threat are dealt with very briefly. Of course the information that is lacking can be found elsewhere (e.g., Isa 7–9), but such a fact only serves to emphasize the paucity of this account as a historical source. This incident is supplemented by a reference, almost as an aside, to the loss of Elath to Syria. Ahaz's way of relieving the pressure upon Jerusalem and Judah is to appeal to Tiglath Pileser, and to invite the Assyrian king to be more deeply involved in the unfolding drama. Note that no allusion is made here to the role of Isaiah the prophet (on the two accounts see P. R. Ackroyd, *SEÅ* 33 [1968] 18–54). For the immediate purpose Isaiah is unimportant. On its own, as an isolated incident, the invitation to Assyria would appear as a very questionable political move, fraught with danger, and most likely to court national disaster. In the narrative context, such a gesture on Ahaz's part becomes even more foolhardy. Ahaz's actions mirror the action of Menahem of Israel in 15:19–20, and the eventual sequel to that incident is seen in 15:29–30. In the case of Ahaz, the sequence of events is adjusted, no doubt to accommodate historical fact, but the dramatic effect is quite clear. Assyria, once involved, is difficult to dislodge. The theme will repeat itself at the end of the reign of Hezekiah with his gestures toward Babylon (see 20:14–19).

As if to stress the point more forcefully, an addition to the standard introduction is made. Ahaz was "like the kings of Israel" (v 3), an unflattering but also uncommon assessment of a Judean king. Ahaz is one of only two kings of Judah to be so judged.

V 6, which appears to disrupt the flow of the account of the reign of

Ahaz with its mention of the loss of Elath, also has a place within this scheme. Already in 2 Kings it has been seen that the loss of land is a theme of judgment (see on 1:1; 3:4–5; 10:32–33; 12:17–18; 13:3–4).

Vv 10–18 confirm the general direction of thought in the chapter. The detailed information, as indicated above, is undoubtedly from the temple records, but the deliberate way in which the story is presented is worthy of note. The visit to Damascus, in response presumably to an invitation from the Assyrian king, is merely the backdrop, the "setup" for what follows. There the king begins a series of actions that take the reader through the rest of the chapter. With the exception of v 11 (ויבן "and he built," עשה "he did") all the action verbs, *waw* consecutives, and following perfects have the king as the subject. He sees (וירא) the altar, sends (וישלח) word to Uriah, who builds according to the king's instructions. The king returns (ויבא), sees (וירא), approaches (ויקרב), offers sacrifice (ויקטר), and rearranges the cultic celebrations and the temple furnishings. Uriah carries out his instructions to the letter, but all of this is done under the shadow of the king of Assyria (מפני מלך אשור, v 18). The deliberate, and in the writer's mind, dangerous, behavior of the king could not have been more clearly portrayed.

The writer is thus drawing a parallel between the activities of the kings in the northern nation, which by now seem to have sealed the impending fate of Israel, and the activities of the southern kings. The similarities are not absolute, no doubt because of the differing historical circumstances, but echoes of one now continually reappear in the actions of the other. Thus the drama intensifies.

Comment

Additional material on the period covered by this chapter can be found in Isa 7 and 2 Chr 28. In the case of the latter material, there is information that is difficult to reconcile with the account in the present chapter (see 2 Chr 28:5–8), but the effect on Judah of the tumultuous years between 738 and 732 B.C. can be clearly seen. During this time Judah was invaded from the north by Israel and Syria, from the southeast by Edom, and from the southwest by Philistia (2 Chr 28:18).

According to contemporary Assyrian sources, from 743 B.C. Tiglath Pileser moved westwards and by 738 B.C. had conquered several regions of Syria, coming to a halt in the deserts east of Damascus. From here successive campaigns were launched between the years 734 and 732 B.C., eventually resulting in an Assyrian presence along the eastern Mediterranean coast as far south as Gaza, the severing of Galilee from the rest of Israel, and the fall of Damascus. Although the chronology of these years is not absolutely certain, it is accepted by most historians that the coastal campaign took place in 734 B.C., the Galilean campaign in 733 B.C., and the fall of Damascus in 732 B.C. (see *MBA*, map 147; H. Tadmor & M. Cogan, *Bib* 60 [1979] 491–508). The occupied land was organized into several administrative districts under Assyrian control.

This chapter concentrates in part on the fortunes of Judah during those tumultuous years, although it becomes very clear that the interests of the writer are far from an annalistic record of events (see above in *Form/Structure/ Setting*). Jotham died to be succeeded by his son Ahaz (v 1), whose apostasy draws critical comment from the author (vv 2–4). Under pressure from Israel and Syria, Ahaz appealed to Assyria and during a visit to Tiglath Pileser in his new headquarters at Damascus became enamored with an altar, a copy of which he established in Jerusalem. After a reign of sixteen years Ahaz died, to be succeeded by his son Hezekiah.

1 Few commentators doubt the figure "seventeen," and the change to "nineteen" by some MSS is not significant. McHugh's attempt to change the accession year to "seven" (*VT* 14 [1964] 446–53), while it opens up some interesting possibilities for adjustment in the chronology of the period, is pure conjecture and can appeal to no textual support. See below on 18:9–12.

The king's name, אחז "Ahaz," appears in a fuller form in the annals of Tiglath Pileser as Yauhazi (Jehoahaz; see Luckenbill, *Ancient Records* 1:287). The absence of any reference to the queen mother is very unusual. Of all the kings of Judah listed in the books of Kings only Ahaz and Jehoram (2 Kgs 8:16–17) receive no mention of their mothers. For the standard form see Burney, *Notes*, ix.

2 No variant exists for either the length of Ahaz's reign or his age at accession. Nevertheless, the chronological reference provided here is confusing. According to 2 Kgs 18:2, Hezekiah succeeded his father when he (Hezekiah) was twenty-five years old. However, according to the information here, Ahaz would have been only thirty-six when he died, making him a father at the age of eleven. Several adjustments are suggested. Bright (*History*, 274n) accepts Albright's dating of the reign of Ahaz from 735 B.C. to 715 B.C., arguing that the fourteenth year of Hezekiah (701 B.C.), the year in which Sennacherib invaded Judah, indicates that Ahaz must have died in 715 B.C. Thiele (*Mysterious Numbers*, 121), van der Meer (*Chronology*, 75), and Gray (*Kings*, 631) all posit a co-regency between Ahaz and his father, Jotham. Van der Meer alludes to the Israelite-Syrian attack on Jerusalem in 734 B.C. as indication of Ahaz's complete control over the country. Therefore he was co-regent. Alternatively, Gray proposes that 734 B.C. is the beginning of the co-regency with Jotham when Ahaz was twenty years of age, and that his sixteen-year reign began in 730 B.C. proper. At the time of his accession as sole ruler Ahaz would have been twenty-four, and when he died, forty. In this case he would have fathered Hezekiah at the more realistic age of sixteen, not eleven. While such theories are extremely attractive, and go a long way toward solving some of the difficulties of chronology of this confusing period, the text contains no direct support for the co-regency between Jotham and Ahaz. The necessary vocabulary, which was present in the case of David and Solomon, and of Jotham and his father Azariah, is not found here.

"He did not behave well . . . as David his ancestor had done." Such a comparison with David, either favorable or unfavorable, is rare in the judgments made upon the kings of Judah. Only Solomon and Rehoboam receive similar unfavorable assessments (1 Kgs 11:4; 15:3), while Asa (1 Kgs 15:11) and Josiah (2 Kgs 22:1–2) are viewed much more positively in such a comparison. Amaziah receives qualified praise (2 Kgs 14:1–5).

Comment   213

3 "He walked in the ways of the kings of Israel" is a very rare condemnation for kings of Judah. Only Jehoram is similarly judged (8:18). The "ways of the kings of Israel" are those encouraged by both Jeroboam son of Nebat and the arch-apostate, Ahab. כתעבות הגוים "after the sordid fashion of the nations" is quite in keeping with the previous comment, since such syncretism was openly encouraged by Ahab. The comment is in direct contrast with the warning in Deut 5:33, and deliberately so. The writer clearly sees the activities of the reign of Ahaz as a return to the Canaanitish practices which flourished before the conquest. On this see M. Cogan, *Imperialism and Religion*, 72–73.

That this particular activity, "making his son 'pass through fire,' " should have been chosen as an example of behavior "after the sordid fashion of the nations," and also as an illustration of the "ways of the kings of Israel," is strange. Not only was no Israelite king ever accused of such practices, but the evidence outside the OT for such activity is very scant. Josephus (*Antiq.* ix.243) reflects a polemical view when he states that the children of the king were sacrificed upon the altars erected in Jerusalem. On the evidence for the practice outside Israel, see P. Derchain, *VT* 20 (1970) 351–55; R. de Vaux, *Studies in Old Testament Sacrifice*, 60–63; Cogan, *Imperialism and Religion*, 77–79. A common critical assumption is that Lev 18:21 and 20:1–5 legislate against such practices as are in mind here (see Sales, *JBR* 25 [1957] 112–17), but these passages are unclear about their subject, and they do not mention fire. Deut 18:10 reflects the language of the present text, as is to be expected, and links the practice together with other "non-Israelite" passages. Exactly what is meant by העביר באש "passing through fire" is unclear. The term becomes a symbol of deuteronomistic thought for the apostasy of the monarchy. It is possible that Mic 6:7; Jer 7:31; 19:5; 32:35, which speak clearly of "burning" children in fire, refer to this same practice. In any event the inspiration for the writer's standard of behavior, the book of Deuteronomy, clearly sets the deed in a context of exclusivity to Yahweh. Being "like the nations" is a derogatory comparison (see Deut 8:20).

4 ועל הגבעות ותחת כל עץ רענן "and on the high hills and under every green tree." The expression is found frequently in deuteronomistic material. See Deut 12:2; 1 Kgs 14:23; 2 Kgs 17:10 and frequently in Jeremiah. Weinfeld's thesis (*Deuteronomy and the Deuteronomic School*, 322) that the phrase was inspired by Hos 4:13 is attractive, although the practice itself, if widespread, would be enough to bring criticism from the deuteronomist. For the first time in the book "pouring out and sacrificing on the high places" is linked clearly with apostate behavior.

5 אז "but then" is normally seen as a relic of archival sources. The parallel between this account and Isa 7:1 is clear, but the Kings account contains less information than do Isa 7 and 2 Chr 28, which include Isaiah's advice to the king and the account of the Philistine invasion of parts of the Shephelah (2 Chr 28:18). The omissions in Kings represent an abbreviation of the sources in the interests of the narrative style. See above *Form/Structure/Setting*.

6 The phrase בעת ההיא "at that time" is not to be taken as indicating contemporaneous events, nor events in close sequence. The capture of Elath was not the result of Aramaic involvement in the war of Judah with Edom.

See Tadmor and Cogan, *Bib* 60 (1979) 497–98. In historiographic writing the expression is common. אילת . . . לארם הֹשיב "he restored . . . Elath to Syria." See nn. 6.b and 6.c above for the emendations suggested. The earlier reference to Elath in 14:22, when it was taken from Edom after Amaziah's battle with the southern neighbor, would lend support to the emendation from "Aram" to "Edom." "Restored" would mean then that the city reverted back to Edom, not to Aram. The archaeological evidence of Edomite occupation of Elath is inconclusive (see Gray, *Kings*, 633). On Edom in the Bible see J. M. Myers, *Albright Festschrift*, 377–92; Y. Hoffman, *The Bible and Jewish History*, 76–89.

Childs (*JBL* 82 [1963] 286) identifies the expression "even to this day" as part of an "ethnic ideology," reflecting an ongoing state of affairs that persisted until the time of writing. It could also be classified under his heading of "political etiology" (p. 289) after the fashion of 2 Kgs 17:23, reflecting a political situation which persisted. The distinction is made by Childs primarily on the basis of content rather than any distinguishing form. The "day" referred to is the exilic period when Edom took advantage of Judah's weakness to attack in the south (for background see Y. Aharoni, *Arad Inscriptions*, 149–51). That Syrians were active this far south is not impossible, but unlikely. The present state of the text clearly understands this to be so, but is influenced by the context of the Syrian and Israelite attack on Jerusalem.

7 "Ahaz reacted by sending messengers to Tiglath Pileser the king of Assyria." Now begins the process by which Assyria became actively involved in the political life of Judah. עבדך ובנך אני "I am your servant and your son" is by no means an unusual self-designation for a person of Ahaz's position. He was dependent upon Assyria and used language befitting his status. It is in standard form denoting respect and submission (see Loewenstamm, *Leš* 34 [1969] 148). Cogan's translation as "vassal" (*Imperialism and Religion*, 66) is strong and not necessary. In the light of the deuteronomistic ideal of the state, the action is wrongly motivated and potentially disastrous.

8 Ahaz's action is similar to that of Menahem in 15:20. The taking of "bribes" was forbidden in Deut 10:17; 16:19; and 27:25 and was a sin for which the sons of Samuel were blamed in 1 Sam 8:3. The effect was to distort judgment and to confuse motive for action. It is in this light that the term is to be seen here. Its use implies an action on the part of both Ahaz and Tiglath Pileser that meets with the disapproval of the writer. For the ANE background to such usage see Tadmor and Cogan, *Bib* 60 (1979) 491–508. The use of the term here implies a telling criticism of Ahaz's actions. The expression "in the temple and in the palace treasury" is found elsewhere, in 1 Kgs 7:1; 14:27; 15:18; 2 Kgs 12:19; 14:18; 24:13. Since such storehouses would contain funds for the running of the affairs of state, they would be the primary source of tribute and "bribery" mentioned here.

9 In this account the invasion of Syria by Tiglath Pileser is seen as a direct response to Judah's request for help. No record of such motivation is found in the Assyrian sources, which is to be expected. The precise date is unknown, but the most persuasive argument, for 734 B.C., is put forward by Tadmor, that is, before the attack on Samaria, which probably took place a year later (see Cogan, *Imperialism and Religion*, 65–67). The possibility is that Ahaz's request was precipitated by the presence of some Assyrian troops on his west flank. During his campaign to Gaza, Tiglath Pileser came close to Jerusalem with his capture of Gezer (see W. Hallo, *BAR* 2:173). In any event the capture of Damascus and the death of Rezin, which were the culmination of the third campaign of Assyria, signaled the end of the local threat to Judah. Since the "middle campaign" against northern Israel had already been dealt with in 15:29–30, mention of it is not made here.

The phrase קירה "toward Kir," omitted by G, has raised some questions concerning the authenticity of the comment. G^L sees it clearly as the direct object of the verb (see n. 9.a above), which should be more consistently read as ויגל. Gray (*Kings*, 633) sees the expression as a misunderstanding of the term קיר "city," i.e., Nineveh, under the influence of Amos 1:5. The connection is striking, but while the Assyrians might have referred to Nineveh in this way, there is no hint that such code was used by Israel or Judah at the time of writing. The location of Kir is unknown, but Amos 9:7 identifies it as the Syrians' original home, to which they were forcibly returned (Amos 1:5; see Gordon, "Kir," *IDB* 3:36, but compare Astour, "Kir," *IDBSup*, 524).

10 Everything in the chapter up to this point has been a preface for what follows. There is no evidence for such a journey in Assyrian sources, but the practice was certainly not unknown and is reminiscent of Manassah's journey to Nineveh (see 2 Chr 33:10–13).

וירא "and he saw." The close connection between "seeing" and then "acting" which often carries with it the sense of misdeed or sin, runs throughout the OT (see Gen 3:6; 6:2; 12:15; 34:2; 38:2; 2 Sam 11:2). But further it runs deep in the OT understanding of the human being. Sight opens the persons to judgments of the will, which are then acted upon. Frequently in the OT, and indeed in the whole Bible, parts of the body such as eyes, heart, ears, mouth, hands, feet are used together in descriptions of human activity. On this topic, see the excellent article by B. de Geradon, "L'homme à l'image de Dieu," *NRT* 11 (1958) 681–95.

The critical notion that the altar seen by Ahaz was of Assyrian design and that it was adopted by the king "as an expression of subservience to Assyria" (Gray, *Kings*, 635) must be put to rest. It is strongly disputed, and on good grounds (see J. W. McKay, *Religion in Judah*, 6–10; M. Haran, *Temples*, 135n; M. Cogan, *Imperialism and Religion*, 72–77). 2 Chr 28:23 indicates that the altar was built in honor of "the gods of Syria," and further, that the known Assyrian altars were not designed for the uses to which this one later was put in Jerusalem. Precise reasons for the introduction of such an altar into the cultus in Jerusalem are unclear, but since it would have been used for a reorganized Yahwistic cult in Jerusalem, there is no need to see it as being involved in Ahaz's status as an Assyrian vassal.

אוריה הכהן "Uriah the priest." The name occurs elsewhere in the OT in its shorter form אורי (Exod 31:2) and its longer form אוריה, notably the ill-fated husband of Bathsheba. An alternative form also appears in the Samarian Ostraca (ארי) (see Gibson, *Syrian Semitic Inscriptions* 1:10). Isa 8:2 undoubtedly refers to the same person, and note should be taken of Isaiah's estimate of the man as a "trustworthy witness."

11 The very factual nature of the following paragraph is noteworthy.

Ahaz is neither praised nor condemned. The syntax of the account clearly shows that it was under the king's direction that the altar was built, with the complete agreement of the priesthood. No hint is given in the account that the altar was to be used for anything other than Yahwistic worship. The detail is comparable to that in 2 Kgs 11–12 and comes from the same source.

12 The omission of the first clause (see *BHS*) adds nothing to the verses and is quite unnecessary. וירא המלך "and the king inspected." The parallel with v 10 is clear, and deliberate. Again, sight precedes action. The expression ויעל עליו "and he climbed up to it" is very awkward. NEB translates "mounted the steps." Gray (*Kings*, 636) reads ויעל as hiphil, which makes good sense. Thus עליו is understood as "on its behalf," i.e., at its dedication (see KJV). But the hiphil of the verb used this way when speaking of sacrifice is nowhere else used with a following adverbial phrase, but with a direct object, such as עולה "holocaust." The translation above should stand. It provides the impression of a deliberate action.

13 וַיַּקְטֵר "and he offered." This hiphil is a common priestly expression for the burning of an offering, as distinct from the piel, which is used for the burning of incense. The fact that the piel is more common in the deuteronomistic material betrays the priestly origin of this account (see Haran, *Temples*, 142). The trio עלה מנחה נסך "holocaust, cereal offering, drink offering" is a common one in the literature on sacrifice in the OT. For a good summary see R. de Vaux, *Studies in Old Testament Sacrifice*, 27–90; *Ancient Israel*, 415–24; T. H. Gaster, "Sacrifices and Offerings, OT," *IDB* 4:147–59. The עלה was consumed upon the altar, the מנחה was a bloodless offering of produce, hence the translation of "cereal offering." The נסך was a libation of liquids such as wine and oil, and the שלמים "peace offerings" were consumed by worshipers. The term is also frequently translated as "communion offering." (See Lev 1–3.) A full description of the composition of offerings and the standards set for offerings is found in Num 28. Note the use of the 3rd person masculine suffix to distinguish the king's offering from that of the common people. Such individual distinctions are common in the literature of sacrifice (see Lev 16:24; Num 6:16, etc.). The sense of the king officiating at the ceremony as did Solomon (1 Kgs 8:63) is not to be found here (contra Gray, *Kings*, 636). ויזרק דם "and he cast the blood." On the significance of the symbolism of blood in general in the OT, see D. J. McCarthy, *JBL* 88 (1969) 166–76 and H. Christ, *Blutvergiessung im Alten Testament*; M. Kopfstein et al., *TDOT* 3:234–50. The background to this practice is found in legislation that appears in a later form in Lev 2. The action of sprinkling was an act of consecration.

14 The detail into which the writer now goes reflects the source of the information contained in the following sentences. It also presupposes a detailed understanding of the temple plans and ceremonies by both the writer and his original readers.

On "the bronze altar," see Ezek 9:2. G omits the adjective "bronze" (see n. 14.a. above), and it is suggested that its inclusion here is editorial, correctly distinguishing the old altar from the newer one installed by Ahaz (see Burney, *Notes*, 326). 1 Kgs 8:64 mentions the inadequacies of the bronze altar referred to here. Burney's suggestion, however, is not necessary. G's change itself might be secondary, avoiding duplication with v 15b. In any event the verse describes a significant innovation by Ahaz. לפני יהוה "before Yahweh" is an important phrase indicating respect and worship (see Mic 6:6). The reference is again to 1 Kgs 8:22, 54, 64. The bronze work Hiram completed for the temple did not include the original bronze altar. See the helpful remarks on the relationship of temple and altar in M. Haran, *Temples*, 15–17.

מבין המזבח "from between the altar." The altar referred to here must be the new one installed by Ahaz, which was placed directly in front of the sanctuary entrance. The old bronze altar was then placed to one side (the north).

15 The purpose to which the new altar was put appears to solve the problem already recognized in the inadequacy of the bronze altar mentioned in 1 Kgs 8:64. From this account the motivation of Ahaz was clearly not apostasy, since the organization of the sacrifice that follows is consistent with the other legislation on sacrifice in the OT. This is so in spite of the Syrian style altar that was used. The four types of sacrifice mentioned are עלת הבקר "the morning burnt offering," מנחת הערב "the evening sacrifice," עלת המלך "the king's burnt offering," and עלת כל עם הארץ "the burnt offering of all the people of the land." There appears to be a progression in the organization of such sacrifices. Consistent with the reference here, Ezek 46:13–16 thinks of the burnt offering as a morning ritual (see also 2 Kgs 3:20). However, by the time of the finished priestly legislation in Exod 29:38–42 and Num 28:2–8, the same offering was made in the morning and evening (see de Vaux, *Studies in Old Testament Sacrifice*, 36).

The word לבקר "to pray at" is puzzling. Some interpret it as the examination of animal entrails (so Gray, *Kings*, 637), but the evidence for this is slight. Haruspicy was certainly known in the cultures surrounding Israel, as is seen in the clay models of livers found at Hazor (see *ANEP*, pl. 844). But this evidence is from the sixteenth century B.C., and there is no evidence to link the practice with the use of the Hebrew verb בקר. In the Hebrew Bible the verb is used in a variety of contexts. In Lev 13:27, 33 it means the ritual examination of the skin of a diseased person. In Ps 27:4 it is a synonym for prayer. In Prov 20:25 it means careful reflection upon one's actions, and in Ezek 34:11, 12 it is used in the context of looking for something lost. The term then certainly contains the meaning of "seek," and can be used as a synonym for prayer. In the deuteronomistic literature "seeking God" (בקש) is a common expression, and involves prayer.

The distinction made here between the king's offering and the people's offering reflects an attempt at reorganization in the interests of regulating the practice of sacrifice. Such a distinction can be inferred from 1 Kgs 8:62–64, although the text is not too clear on this point. Certainly such a distinction is presupposed by Ezekiel when he describes the future temple in his eschatological vision (see Ezek 46:2).

16 The involvement of the priest Uriah is important here, especially in the light of Isaiah's assessment of him (Isa 8:2). The acquiescence of the priest is a reflection of Jehoiada in chap. 12, and Hilkiah in chap. 23. The division of responsibilities between king and priest seems clear. The king would have had the role of "chief executive officer" of palace, city, and temple, and the priest would have been the immediate subordinate in charge of the temple and one who took orders from the king in matters of temple management. To be noted is that Uriah obeys the king to the letter.

17 After the reorganization of the sacrifice with the installation of the new altar, other minor reforms are made in the temple furnishings. The first of these was a rearrangement of the laver and the "sea," which were placed upon a stone platform rather than their original bronze one. The מסגרות "frames" are described in detail in 1 Kgs 7:27–37. The term is a cognate of the verb "to close," and the construction held panels on which were depicted various forms. The "carriages" (not "supports," RSV) enabled the laver and the "sea" to be moved around. For a diagram see P. L. Garber, "Laver," *IDB* 3:76. That they were קצץ "cut off" would be quite in order for bronze fittings, and there is no hint here that they were then given to the Assyrian king. The rearrangement is simply part of a larger reorganization undertaken by Ahaz, presumably for the smoother running of the temple.

18 מיסך השבת "the structure for the sabbath." See *Notes* on the difficulty of this expression, which is highlighted by the various English versions' attempts to render a satisfactory translation (NEB, "structure"; RSV, "covered way"; KJV, "covert") none of which is more than an inspired guess. The same is true of Fricke's "Sabbathalle" (*Die Zweite Könige*, 212). What exactly happened to this structure is unclear. The hiphil of סבב (הסב), which is used here, means "to cause to turn," i.e., "reverse" (2 Chr 35:22; Ezra 6:22; 1 Kgs 18:37; Jer 21:4; Ezek 7:22).

מפני מלך אשור "in deference to the king of Assyria." The likelihood that this indicates that the bronze thus removed from the temple was given to the king of Assyria in tribute (so Montgomery, *Kings*, 462) is very remote. The expression comes at the wrong point in the narrative, and refers to whatever was done to the "sabbath-structure" and the "outer entrance for the king." Presumably something about each of these items offended the Assyrian, and they were therefore removed. The expression indicates an attitude of subservience, or even fear, but cannot bear the weight of "paying tribute."

19–20 The chapter ends abruptly with the standard concluding formula for the reign of a king in Judah.

Explanation

Having left Israel in a state of chaos and Judah being threatened by the outsiders Rezin and Pekah, our writer turns a closer attention to Judah, and for a moment the fortunes of Israel are held in abeyance, although their final outcome can hardly be in doubt. Chap. 16 devotes its entire attention to the activities of Ahaz, king of Judah. The initial introduction of Ahaz (v 2b) does not bode well for what follows. This is confirmed by the writer's assessment of him in v 3. It is a serious one indeed. The sins of Jeroboam have been reintroduced into the narrative in the preceding two chapters as the cause of Israel's downfall, and in 16:3 Ahaz behaves like successive kings of Israel. The judgment is a harsh one. By the end of the reign of Ahaz, evil is lodged within, and attacks come from outside.

The historical issue of the nature of the altar, along with the kind of reforms initiated by Ahaz, is an important one. It is now evident that he did not introduce into the temple any worship of Assyrian astral deities but developed the temple cultus in a distinctively west Semitic way. However, it is also clear that the writer does not look upon this as any better than the introduction of overt Assyrian-style cultic activity. The final comment on the reforms is that many were carried out in deference to the king of Assyria (v 18b). This is to be understood as a clear alternative to regular Judean temple worship and certainly does not conform with the standards of the book of Deuteronomy.

The political actions of Ahaz might engender a little sympathy, given the nature of his situation. He had inherited from his father a threatened state that was under attack from both Israel and Syria. The Syria with which he is dealing is one that had experienced recent success in the south with the expansion of its borders to Elath (v 6). In that expansion Syria had encroached upon Judean territory. To appeal to a larger force, namely, that of Tiglath Pileser, made sense in the short term. It could and, in fact, did, relieve Judah of pressure from the north and east. What seems to be of concern for our writer, however, are the long-term effects. Indeed, this is the concern of the prophet Isaiah. Although the attack by Syria and Israel upon Jerusalem proved unsuccessful (v 5), Ahaz, by inviting aid from Tiglath Pileser, created circumstances that had virtually the same outcome. To pay for the aid, he had to raid the palace and temple treasury (v 8).

The picture of Ahaz, when viewed from a distance, is of one who has now abandoned the ideal standards of the deuteronomist. He has corrupted the temple worship in Jerusalem with the introduction of an altar of foreign design, he has made alterations to the temple to please the king of Assyria, and he has invited as his helper the very king who has ravaged the northern nation. Ahaz lives now by the standards of others; hence the judgment in v 3.

In the broader context of the book of Kings, this chapter is important, for in the midst of the rapid decline of Israel in the north, the king of Judah invites precisely the same fate upon the southern kingdom.

The Fall and Resettlement of Samaria (17:1-41)

Bibliography

Aharoni, Y. "Arad: Its Inscriptions and Temple." *BA* 31 (1968) 2–33. **Ahuvya, A.** "שב Meaning Sometimes שבי Sat, Rested, Was Tranquil." *Leš* 39 (1975) 21–36. **Al-**

bright, W. F. "The Elimination of King 'So.' " *BASOR* 171 (1963) 66. ———. "The Original Account of the Fall of Samaria." *BASOR* 174 (1964) 66–67. **Baena, G.** "Pss. el vocabulario de 2 Reges 17.7–23, 35–39." *EstBib* 32 (1973) 357–84. ———. "Caracter literario de 2 Reges 17.7–23." *EstBib* 33 (1974) 5–29. **Carroll, R. P.** "Elijah and Elisha Sagas." *VT* 19 (1969) 400–415. **Celada, B.** "Al rey 'So' (2 Reyes 17.4)." *CB* 25 (1968) 376–77. **Childs, B. S.** "The Formula 'Until this day.' " *JBL* 82 (1963) 279–92. **Coggins, R. J.** "The OT and Samaritan Origins." *ASTI* 6 (1967–1968) 35–48. **Deller, K.** "Review of *Les Sacrifices de l'Ancien Testament* by R. de Vaux." *Or* 34 (1965) 382–86. **Dever, W. G.** "Excavations at Shechem and Mt. Gerizim." *Eretz Shomeron. The Thirtieth Archaeological Convention, September, 1972.* Jerusalem: Israel Exploration Society (1973) 8–9. (Heb.). **Driver, G. R.** "Geographical Notes." *Eretz Israel* 5 (1958) 10–15. **Ebach, J.** "ADRMLK, Moloch, und BA'ALADR." *UF* 11 (1979) 211–26. **Ephal, I.** "Israel, Fall and Exile." *World History of the Jewish People. Age of the Monarchies: Political History.* Vol. 4. Ed. A. Malamat. Jerusalem: Massada Press (1979) 180–92. **Goedicke, H.** "The End of King So of Egypt." *BASOR* 171 (1963) 64–66. **Gray, J.** "The Desert God 'Attar." *JNES* 8 (1949) 78–80. **Hallo, W.** "From Qarqar to Carchemish." *BA* 23 (1962) 34–61. **Hobbs, T. R.** "Amos 3.1b, and 2.10." *ZAW* 81 (1969) 384–87. **Huffmon, H. B.** "The Covenant Lawsuit in the Prophets." *JBL* 78 (1959) 285–95. **Krauss, R.** "So—König von Aegypten—ein Deutungsvorschlag." *BN* 11 (1980) 29–31. **Krige, J. D.** "The Social Function of Witchcraft." *Witchcraft and Sorcery.* Ed. M. Marwick. 2d ed. Harmondsworth: Penguin Books, 1982. 263–75. **Levine, L. D.** *Two Neo-Assyrian Stelae from Iran.* Toronto: Royal Ontario Museum, 1972. **Moran, W. L.** "The Scandal of the 'Great Sin' in Ugarit." *JNES* 18 (1959) 280–81. **Nicholson, E. W.** *Preaching to the Exiles: A Study of the Prose Tradition in the Book of Jeremiah.* Oxford: Blackwell, 1970. 33–34. **Oded, B.** *Mass Deportations in the Neo-Assyrian Empire.* Wiesbaden: Harrasowitz, n. d. **Parker, E. A.** "The Chronology of 2 Kgs 17:1." *AUSS* 6 (1968) 129–33. **Rabinowitz, J. J.** "The 'Great Sin' in Ancient Egyptian Marriage Contracts." *JNES* 8 (1959) 73. **Rudolph, W.** "Zum Text des Königsbuches." *ZAW* 63 (1951) 201–15. **Sayed, R.** "Tefnakht ou Horus SI3-JB." *VT* 20 (1970) 116–18. **Shea, W. H.** "The Date and Significance of the Samaritan Ostraca." *IEJ* 27 (1977) 16–27. **Tadmor, H.** "The Campaigns of Sargon II of Asshur." *JCS* 12 (1958) 22–40, 77–100. **Talmon, S.** "Biblical Traditions on the Early History of the Samaritans." *Eretz Shomeron. The Thirtieth Archaeological Convention, September, 1972.* Jerusalem: Israel Exploration Society, 1973. 19–33. (Heb.). **Vattioni, F.** "Il 'grande peccato' nei contratti matrimoniali egiziani." *RevistB* 7 (1959) 68–69. **Vogt, E.** "Samaria a 722 et 720 ab Assyriis capta." *Bib* 39 (1958) 535–41. **Welten, P.** "Kult Höhe und Jahwe Tempel." *ZDPV* 88 (1972) 19–37. **Yeivin, S.** "Who Was So, the King of Egypt?" *VT* 2 (1952) 131–36.

Translation

¹ *In the twelfth [a] year of Ahaz king of Judah, Hoshea son of Elah became king in Samaria over Israel for the next nine years.* ² *He behaved badly in Yahweh's eyes, but not quite like the kings of Israel who preceded him.* [a] ³ *It was against him that Shalmaneser king of Assyria had come, because Hoshea had once become his vassal and used to send him tribute.* [a] ⁴ *But the king of Assyria had discovered Hoshea's treachery* [a] *in that he had sent ambassadors to So,* [b] *to the king of Egypt, and he no longer sent the annual* [c] *tribute to the king of Assyria. So the king of Assyria had arrested him* [d] *and put him in prison.* ⁵ *Then the king of Assyria had attacked the whole country including Samaria, and had besieged it for three years.* ⁶ *In the ninth year* [a] *of Hoshea, the king of Assyria sacked Samaria and exiled* [b] *Israel to Assyria.*

He resettled them at Halah and at the Habor, the River of Gozan, and in the cities ^c *of the Medes.* ^d
⁷ *This happened* ^a *because the people of Israel had sinned against Yahweh their God who brought* ^b *them up from the land of Egypt, from the grip of Pharaoh king of Egypt, and had worshiped other gods.* ^c ⁸ *They walked in the manner of the nations whom Yahweh had expelled before the people of Israel, and followed the example of the kings of Israel.* ^a ⁹ *The people of Israel did things in secret* ^a *against Yahweh their God which they ought not to have done. They built for themselves high places in all their cities, from watchtower to fortified keep.* ¹⁰ *They erected for themselves pillars and asherahs upon every high hill and under every green tree.* ¹¹ *They burned incense on all the high places like the nations which Yahweh had driven into exile before them had done. They did evil things* ^a *and angered Yahweh.* ¹² *They worshiped idols of which Yahweh had expressly said, "You shall not make such a thing!"* ^a
¹³ *Yahweh had warned both Israel and Judah through the agency of every prophet and seer* ^a *with these words, "Repent of your evil ways, and keep the commandments* ^b *and the statutes and all the law* ^c *which I commanded your ancestors, and which I conveyed to you through my servants the prophets."* ¹⁴ *But they simply did not listen. They became as stubborn as their predecessors had been* ^a*who did not remain faithful to Yahweh their God.* ^a ^{15 a}*They rejected his statutes and his covenant which he had made with their predecessors,* ^a *and they rejected the warnings he had given them. They went after useless things and themselves became as useless. They deliberately copied the nations* ^b *which surrounded them, which Yahweh had ordered them not to do.* ¹⁶ *They abandoned all the commandments of Yahweh their God and made for themselves two molten images of calves. They also made an asherah, and bowed and scraped before all the hosts of heaven and adored Baal.* ¹⁷ *They even made their sons and daughters "pass through fire." They performed sorceries and practiced divination.* ^a *They sold themselves into wickedness in the eyes of Yahweh their God to anger him.*
¹⁸ *Yahweh's wrath was inflamed against Israel, and he removed them out of his sight. Nothing was left except the tribe of Judah.* ¹⁹ *But not even Judah kept the commandments of Yahweh their God.* ^a *They copied exactly what Israel* ^b *had done.* ²⁰ *Thus it was that Yahweh rejected* ^a *all the descendants of Israel. He hurt them by handing them over to spoilers,* ^b *then* ^c*he cast them out of his sight.*
²¹ *When he had torn* ^a *Israel from the house of David, they made Jeroboam son of Nebat king,* ^b *and Jeroboam allured* ^c *Israel away from Yahweh and made them commit the great sin.* ²² *So from then on the people of Israel deliberately walked in the sins* ^a *of Jeroboam* ^b *which he committed. They did not turn from it.* ^c ²³ *The moment came when Yahweh removed them from his presence, precisely as he had declared through his servants the prophets, and he exiled them to Assyria where they remain to this day.*
²⁴ *Then the king of Assyria brought people from Babylon, from Cuthah,* ^a *from Avva, from Hamath, and from Sepharvayim, and resettled them* ^b *in the cities of Samaria thus displacing the people of Israel. They took possession of Samaria and settled in her cities.* ²⁵ *When they first settled there* ^a *they did not revere Yahweh so Yahweh sent lions* ^b *among them which killed a few of them.* ²⁶ *It was eventually reported* ^a *to the king of Assyria in this way, "The people whom you exiled and resettled in the cities of Samaria do not know the religious customs* ^b *of the country. Now the god has sent lions among them and they are killing them because of their*

ignorance of the religious customs of the place." ²⁷ *So the king of Assyria gave this order, "Get one of the priests* ᵃ *who were exiled* ᵇᶜ *from there to return* ᵈᵉ *and let him teach* ᶠ *the religious custom of the country."* ²⁸ *So one of the priests who were exiled from Samaria went back and settled at Bethel, and he became their instructor in how to worship Yahweh.*

²⁹ *But nation after nation* ᵃ *was still making its own gods and placing them in the shrines* ᵇ *at the high places which the Samarians* ᶜ *had made, nation after nation in their cities where they had resettled.* ³⁰ *For example,* ᵃ *the men of Babylon made Succoth-benoth,* ᵇ *the men of Cuth made Nergal, and the men of Hamath made Ashima.* ³¹ *The Avviyites made Nibchaz and Tartak and the Sepharvayim burned their children in fire for Adramalek and Anamelek, the gods of the Sepharvayim.* ᵃ ³²ᵃ *So they worshiped Yahweh, but also appointed for themselves their own priests at the high places who performed rituals for them at the shrines of the high places.* ³³ *On the other hand, they worshiped Yahweh, but they also served their own gods after the fashion of the nations whom they displaced.* ³⁴ *To this day they behave in this manner.* ᵃ *There were no people* ᵇ *who feared Yahweh exclusively, and there were none* ᵇ *who behaved according to the ordinance or statutes, law, or commandment which Yahweh stipulated for the descendants of Jacob, to whom he gave the name Israel.*

³⁵ *Yahweh had once made a covenant with them and given them this order, "You shall never worship other gods; you shall not bow down to them; you shall not serve them nor shall you offer sacrifice to them!* ³⁶ *Instead you shall worship Yahweh* ᵃ *who brought you up from the land of Egypt with a great display of strength and with an outstretched right arm. To him you shall bow, and to him you shall offer sacrifice.* ³⁷ *As for the statutes, the ordinances, the law, and the commandment which he wrote for you, you shall take care to do* ᵃ *them every day.* ᵇ *But you shall not worship other gods!* ³⁸ *As for the covenant which he made* ᵃ *with you, you shall not forget it. You shall not worship other gods.* ³⁹ *Instead you shall worship Yahweh your God exclusively. It is he who has delivered you from the grip* ᵃ *of all your enemies."* ⁴⁰ *But they would not listen. Instead they behaved in the manner just described.* ᵃ

⁴¹ *Thus these people were worshipers* ᵃ *of both Yahweh and their graven images. It was the same with the children and grandchildren. They copied their predecessors, and do so even to the present time.*

Notes

1.a. MT reads בשנת שתים עשרה "in the twelfth year." The G MS c₂ translated "fourteenth" and Gray (*Kings*, 641) conjectures "second."

2.a. Gᴸ reads here παρα παντας τους γενομενους "beyond all who were" (before him).

3.a. Gᴮᴬ transliterate with μαναχ, μαναα respectively. Gᴸ has the correct δωρα "gifts" or "tribute."

4.a. For MT קֶשֶׁר "treason," Gᴮ reads αδικιαν "a wrong" which presupposes an original שֶׁקֶר "falsehood," although this is not supported by Gᴸ, which follows MT. Gᴮ is favored by Burney (*Notes*, 329) among others. But שקר is not normally found in Hebrew as the direct object of מצא "discover." For a parallel expression to the existing MT text see Jer 11:9.

4.b. All the versions interpret "So" as the name of a king. Here it is interpreted as the name of a city. See *Comment* below.

4.c. MT reads כשנה בשנה "as a year in a year."

4.d. MT reads ויעצרהו "so he arrested him," which Gᴮ reads as from the root יצר "to form, fashion." See v 5.

6.a. Reading a more grammatical בשנה "in the year" (absolute) for the existing MT בשנת (construct).

6.b. Gᴸ adds the phrase "the king of Assyria."

6.c. MT reads וְעָרֵי מָדַי "and the cities of the Medes," which G^B transliterates as Ὄρη Μήδων. G^L offers ἐν ὁρίοις Μήδων "on the frontiers of the Medes," on the basis of which Ehrlich (*Randglossen* 7:313) suggests an original וְהָרֵי מָדַי "and the hill-country of the Medes."

6.d. G^L adds the equivalent of עַד הַיּוֹם הַזֶּה "to this day."

7.a. G^L after וַיְהִי "this happened" adds "the wrath of the Lord against Israel," which Burney (*Notes*, 331) regards as "superior." This is an opinion shared by Montgomery (*Kings*, 478), but with the corrective that it is not therefore necessarily original. We follow MT.

7.b. MT reads הַמַּעֲלֶה "who brought up." Eth, however, offers ἐξαγαγόντι "who led out," which presupposes הַמּוֹצִיא. The two verbs are standard in statements about the Exodus, but the latter is more characteristic of the deuteronomistic writings than the former. See T. R. Hobbs, *ZAW* 81 (1969) 384–87.

7.c. G^L adds "from those days until the present," which is an unnecessary duplication of the frequently expressed sentiment of the chapter.

8.a. The last clause of the verse is clumsy, although the evidence for omitting it is very weak (see *BHS*). Burney (*Notes*, 332) regards it as a senseless gloss, and Ehrlich (*Randglossen* 7:313) as an exclamation. Neither of these opinions is satisfying. Josephus (*Antiq.* ix.282) is probably closer to the meaning of the statement when he sees it as an allusion to Jeroboam son of Nebat.

9.a. MT reads וַיְחַפְּאוּ "and they did in secret." Most of the versions, ancient and modern, follow G by translating the verb as a synonym for חָפָה "to cover" (see BDB, 341). An analogy for the interchange of *lamedh he* and *lamedh aleph* verbs is found in 2:19–22. The *lamedh aleph* form of this verb, however, is unique, and many, together with Tg and Syr which read "to utter," see the verb as a Hebrew version of the Akkadian *khapu*, "to utter." See G. R. Driver, *The People and the Book*, 73–120 and Gray, *Kings*, 646.

11.a. G^B reads κοινωνούς for דְּבָרִים "things," probably misunderstanding the Hebrew as חֲבֵרִים "companions." There is little merit to the emendation suggested by Ehrlich (*Randglossen* 7:313) for דְּבָרִים רַבִּים "many things."

12.a. G^B adds κυρίῳ.

13.a. MT reads נְבִיאוֹ, which could be read with Q as כָּל נְבִיאֵי כָל חֹזֶה "all the prophets of every seer" or as נְבִיאָיו "his prophets" (so G) or as a singular נָבִיא "prophet." Burney (*Notes*, 332) accepts G, regarding the reference to seers as a later insertion. Montgomery (*Kings*, 478) accepts the consonantal text and offers a plausible theory that the pointing was later made to avoid reference to "seer" as a noun. However, since the double phrase beginning with the adjective "all" cannot be removed, we suggest with *BHS* that it is regularized with the shifting of the *waw* to the second adjective, and the reading of each noun as singular: "every prophet and every seer." The term "seer" is not foreign to the OT prophetic tradition (see Amos 1:1) and can stand as original.

13.b. G^L adds the phrase "my ways."

13.c. G^L adds "my."

14.a–a. The line is omitted by G^B.

15.a–a. Omitted by G^B

15.b. G^L reads τῶν θεῶν "the gods."

17.a. G^L adds ". . . and made an ephod."

19.a. G^B reads simply τοῦ θεοῦ "of God."

19.b. G^L adds παντός "all."

20.a. G^L reverses the subject and the object of the opening clause, which is favored by Burney (*Notes*, 333). The change is not necessary in the light of the tenor of the chapter and the indictment against Israel. Yahweh is seen repeatedly as the subject of verbs of punishment against Israel. The change is gratuitous.

20.b. G^L precedes with "all."

20.c. In the light of the change at the beginning of the verse, G^L adds Κύριος "the Lord" at this point.

21.a. G^B and others avoid making God the subject of this action, but such a motivation is no reason to emend the text. See 1 Kgs 11:32.

21.b. G^L adds ἐφ' ἑαυτοῖς (עֲלֵיהֶם) "over them."

21.c. MT וַיִּדַּח is better read with Q as וַיַּדַּח, lit., "and he forced." The verb is used of seduction in Prov 7:21.

22.a. G^B reads singular here.

22.b. G^L in typical fashion adds "son of Nebat."
22.c. G^B reads the singular.
24.a. The word has no accent in MT. See *Comment* below.
24.b. G^L reads κατωκισεν αὐτοὺς "and he settled them" for the MT וישב "and settling."
25.a. G^L reads the equivalent of "After these nations settled there in the beginning. . . ." G^B omits שם "there."
25.b. Josephus (*Antiq.* ix.289) reads λοιμον "pestilence."
26.a. Reading the third person masculine plural as an impersonal.
26.b. MT has משפט "custom, judgment." G^L τον νομον presupposes התורה "law."
27.a. MT reads אחד מהכהנים "one of the priests." Gray (*Kings*, 650) argues for a change to אחדים מהכהנים "a few of the priests," the first plural ending being lost through haplography.
27.b. The whole expression is omitted by G^B.
27.c. MT reads הגליתם "you exiled them," but it is better read as הגליתים "I exiled them."
27.d. MT is awkward and שם "there" is omitted in the translation.
27.e. MT's וילכו וישבו "and let them go and let them return" is better read as a singular. In the interests of English style the translation here is a paraphrase.
27.f. Gray (*Kings*, 651) suggests a plural (וירום "and let them teach them") for MT וירם "and let him teach them."
29.a. MT contains the idiomatic expression גוי גוי "nation nation."
29.b. MT reads בבית "in the shrine." G^L reads the plural.
29.c. MT reads שמרנים "Samarians" (G^B Σαμαρειται "Samaritans"), which is the first occurrence of the word in the Bible. See *Comment* below.
30.a. See Ehrlich (*Randglossen* 7:314). The conjunction here introduces an example.
30.b. The versions contain many variants of the name.
31.a. K's אלה ספרים "god of the Sepharîm" is better read with Q as אֱלֹהֵי סְפַרְוָיִם "gods of the Sepharvayim."
32.a. G^B contains a much larger sentence at this point in the narrative, and only its second part corresponds to MT. Burney's suggestion (*Notes*, 337) that the Gr. is to be favored over the Heb. is suspect. Expansion of the text is a more likely phenomenon than abbreviation.
34.a. Omitted by G^B but retained by G^L.
34.b. The negative expression אינם "nobody" is omitted by G both times, giving quite a different understanding in the Gr. tradition of the condition of the new settlers.
36.a. G^L reads κυριῳ τῳ θεῳ ὑμων "Lord your God."
37.a. G^B reverses the order of the verbs.
37.b. G^L reverses the nouns.
38.a. With G^B we read כרת "he made" for MT's "I made."
39.a. MT מיד "from the grip" is omitted by G^B.
40.a. MT's הראשון, lit., "the former" is omitted by G^B.
41.a. MT reads היו עבדים "they were worshipers." G^L makes it into a finite verb עבדו "they worshiped."

Form/Structure/Setting

This lengthy and difficult chapter purports to be an account of the fall of Samaria to the Assyrians in 722 B.C., but it is clear from a survey of its contents that it is more nearly a theological commentary upon the incident, and as such an exposition of deuteronomistic theology of history. A typical introduction for a king of Israel (the last) begins the chapter (vv 1–2), and is followed by a brief account of the siege of Samaria by Shalmaneser V (vv 3–6). Vv 7–23 are a lengthy "homily" (Montgomery) on the fall of the city, providing the reasons for the event. This is followed by a description of the resettlement of Samaria (vv 24–34*a*) and its effects upon the life in the north. A final section of the chapter (vv 34*b*–41) provides further commentary upon the situation in Samaria in the style of vv 7–23.

Typical of the source-analyses of the chapter is Gray's (*Kings*, 638–40).

He regards vv 3–6, which bear a strong resemblance to 18:9–12 and vv 24–28, as part of a historical source which owes its origins to the annals of the two nations Israel and Judah. Deuteronomistic redactional comments are found in vv 1–2, 18, 21–23; and vv 7–17, 19–20, 34b–41 are seen as a "sermon" on the fall of Samaria, also in deuteronomistic style. Because of their overt interests, vv 29–34a are seen as a local priestly fragment, with vv 24–28 from an independent historical source. V 41 is redactional, a comment from a period earlier than vv 29–34a. This analysis is shared by Robinson (*2 Kings*, 157). Montgomery's analysis is similar.

At other places in this commentary such a tendency to fragment an existing narrative has been criticized. Here again some important issues need to be raised. The method is somewhat less than satisfactory when seen as an interpretation of a passage of the OT (or any other literature for that matter) since it analyzes, but does not reconstruct. First, it confuses detailed analysis of a piece of literature with historical reconstruction of the supposed stages of its growth. The two are not the same. Second, the composition techniques understood by this kind of analysis defy description, except to be judged clumsy in the extreme. Third, the overall result is an apparent lack of cohesion in a given narrative, with the various individual units serving often to emend and even contradict what previously existed (see Robinson, *2 Kings*, 157, on vv 20, 27). Fourth, any sense of and appreciation for the narrative qualities of the material under discussion are lost. In 2 Kgs 17, in which the material reaches a historical and narrative climax with the final destruction of the nation of Israel, such techniques demonstrate most clearly their obvious shortcomings. There is a growing reaction to such methods (see J. Licht, *Storytelling in the Bible;* R. Alter, *The Art of Biblical Narrative;* R. D. Miscall, *The Workings of Old Testament Narrative*).

Vv 1–2, as noted above, comprise a typical introduction to the reign of a king of Israel (see Burney, *Notes,* ix–xiii). But it offers only a modified criticism of Hoshea (v 2b).

Vv 3–6 open with an unusual word order of preposition (עליו "against him"), verb (עלה "had come"), and subject (שלמנאסר "Shalmaneser"). The effect is to draw attention to the event so described, "It was against *him* that Shalmaneser had come. . . ." At first, the following paragraph reads as though this were the order of events:

1. Shalmaneser invaded Samaria	v 3
a. Hoshea became his vassal	
b. Hoshea paid tribute	
2. Hoshea rebelled	v 4
a. Hoshea sends to Egypt	
b. He stopped paying tribute	
3. Hoshea is arrested and imprisoned	
4. Shalmaneser invaded Samaria (7th year)	v 5
a. The land is sacked	
b. Samaria is besieged three years	
5. Samaria falls (9th year)	v 6
a. The city is invested	
b. The population is exiled	

Thus it appears that there were two sequential invasions of Samaria by Shalmaneser. A lack of Assyrian sources at this point confuses the issue. Snaith (*IB* 3:278–79) raises the literary relationship of the two verse pairs and argues that vv 3–4, which appear to have Hoshea as a vassal of Shalmaneser after his invasion, ignore 15:30–31 in which Hoshea is seen as a vassal from his accession. Thus, according to Snaith, vv 5–6 are a corrective of vv 3–4. Snaith appeals to the impression in v 4 that Hoshea was arrested and imprisoned before the second invasion. If Snaith's reconstruction of events is correct, then the course of events must be extended to include some gesture of contrition on Hoshea's part, perhaps a journey to Shalmaneser by the Israelite king to assure his overlord of his loyalty. (See Skinner, *Kings,* 372–74). There exists no corroborating evidence for such a reconstruction of the events, and this route leads only further and further into speculation. In fact, by taking into account the narrative syntax of the chapter, there is little need to read the paragraph in the way commonly done.

The emphatic opening to v 3, עליו עלה "against him he had come," contains a considerable amount of irony, contrasting the fact of the invasion of Israel by Assyria (the final judgment of God upon Israel) and the reign of Hoshea. Hoshea is described as one of the best of the kings of Israel (v 2*b*). In the translation above we have stressed the pluperfect sense of עלה and the consecutive ויהי "because he had become" (see A. B. Davidson, *Hebrew Syntax,* 72). V 3 recounts an event which would already have been engraved in the memories of the original readers, hence the pluperfects. V 4 announces the reason for the attack which saw the end of Israel. Her king had rebelled (from his original vassal status) with the aid of Egypt, and the verse ends with the effect of the invasion upon Hoshea himself—arrest and imprisonment. Vv 5–6, rather than recounting a different series of events which followed those in vv 3–4, go over the same events, but this time with the effect of the invasion of the Assyrians upon the land of Samaria and the city and her population. Together the two verse pairs provide a summary of the main result of Hoshea's reign and then provide the historical circumstances (the "backdrop") for the commentary in vv 7–23 and the historical description in vv 24–41.

The deuteronomistic flavor of vv 7–23 is quite unmistakable. (For a detailed listing of the vocabulary, see M. Weinfeld, *Deuteronomy and the Deuteronomic School,* 320–65). The whole commentary is introduced by a general statement giving the main reasons for the destruction of the north. The statement is straightforward and simple. The people had sinned by worshiping foreign gods (v 7) and by adopting the religious practices of their neighbors (v 8). V 9 then begins a more detailed catalog of the misdeeds of the people, which are mainly religious in nature. This detailed listing continues until v 12. V 13 is almost an aside, making reference to the prophetic tradition, which appears here as a firm supporter of the deuteronomistic viewpoint. V 14 again begins a catalog of the nation's acts of disobedience, which are given form in the people's deliberate rejection of the laws of Yahweh. Vv 17*b*–18 mention the reaction of Yahweh to this state of affairs, which is anger, and the result of that anger, which is to remove Israel from his presence.

In the following paragraph, v 19 picks up the theme of v 18*b* and notes that Judah, the remaining tribe, had behaved no better than Israel in spite of the obvious warning the fate of Israel held for the south. The conclusion to this section (vv 20–23) is a recapitulation of the major theme. Yahweh had rejected Israel because, since her beginning as a nation independent from Judah (v 21), her people had persisted in their apostasy (v 22) to the point where Yahweh had sent them into exile. The whole section is more than a deuteronomistic "homily." It has balance and form. Each part of the section begins with a general statement (vv 7–9a, 14), which is followed by a specific catalog of misdeeds (vv 9b–12, 15–18), which is in turn followed by a warning. In the first case the prophets had warned Israel (v 13), and in the second, Israel stands as a warning to Judah (v 19). The clear balance between the two is certainly no accident. Each part approximates the typical structure of a deuteronomistic "sermon," a form created by the deuteronomist (see E. W. Nicholson, *Preaching to the Exiles*, 33–34, 51). It is found, for example, in Deut 6, 7, 8; Josh 1, 23; and Judg 2. The recapitulation is added in vv 20–23. Of special importance is the theme that is played in this section, namely, the equation of the prophetic warning to Israel with the warning to Judah contained in the fate of Israel. As the narrative of 2 Kings unfolds, this becomes an important motif.

The remainder of the chapter, vv 24–41, follows essentially the same pattern as vv 1–23. A historical summary of a certain state of affairs (vv 23–33) is then followed by a theological commentary (vv 34–41) couched in distinctive deuteronomistic terminology. A number of commentators have detected a variety of sources here for varying reasons (see above), with divisions at vv 24–28 (a late historical source—Gray), vv 29–34 (a priestly source from Bethel), vv 34b–40 (a deuteronomistic commentary). Such divisions are too exact, since many of the differences in style and vocabulary that have been detected result in large measure from the variety of subject matter under discussion. Vv 24–28 recount an attempt to alleviate the lot of the new settlers in Samaria by sending them a priest to teach them the local religious customs. The story is etiological, seeking to explain the strange mixture of Yahwism and syncretism that existed in the north after the exile, exemplified by the Yahwistic shrine at Bethel. But the narrative is extended beyond v 28 and reaches a climax in vv 33–34a.

Vv 34b–41 present an indirect theological comment on this state of affairs with their comparison of what obtained in the north after the exile and what should have existed in Israel before the exile. Note that v 35 is translated again as a pluperfect. This general narrative structure is a common deuteronomistic form, brimming with typically deuteronomistic vocabulary (see Nicholson, *Preaching to the Exiles*, 36; Weinfeld, *Deuteronomy and the Deuteronomic School*, 320–65).

Seen in this light, chap. 17, which contains something of a climax in the narrative of 2 Kings, is by no means a haphazard collection of random historical comments and observations and homily, but a purposefully constructed commentary on the fate of Israel—a commentary that is formally consistent with deuteronomistic writing. Contained within the chapter is a clear warning to Judah that her fate could be similar. Chap. 18, which follows and which narrates events in the reign of Hezekiah, is to be seen in this light.

Comment

This is undoubtedly an important chapter in the narrative of 2 Kings, due in no small measure to its subject matter. The chapter records the final destruction of the northern nation of Israel by the Assyrians and the deportation of large segments of the Israelite population to various parts of the Assyrian empire (vv 1–6). This is a climax to the story of the kings thus far. In addition to this record the writer takes the opportunity to develop his theme of accountability in the history of Israel (vv 7–23). This is followed by a description of the community which was resettled in Samaria (vv 23–33) and an assessment of that community (vv 34–41). Throughout the chapter deuteronomistic phrases and vocabulary abound.

1 The problems of chronology of the latter period of the history of Israel already noted in previous discussions are now aggravated by the information supplied in the present chapter. It is generally assumed that Ahaz became king in 734 B.C., therefore his twelfth year would be 722 B.C. for the accession of Hoshea. However, 15:30 shows that Hoshea was established as king in the north by Tiglath Pileser in the place of Pekah in 732 B.C. Some adjustments are therefore made, usually in the form of textual emendation. Gray, for example (*Kings*, 641), suggests "two" for "twelve" in 17:1, thus bringing the later figures into line. Thiele (*Mysterious Numbers*, 135) suggests that the reigns of Ahaz and Jotham be moved back some years and that a co-regency be posited between the two. In neither case does evidence exist to support the changes, and the arguments are more in the nature of counsel of despair than adequate explanations for the difficulties. We have already discussed the weaknesses in the multiple co-regencies seen by Thiele as a convenient way of dealing with numerical discrepancies.

Another important chronological difficulty concerns the available records of the destruction of Samaria. Sargon II (722–705 B.C.), successor to Shalmaneser V, himself claims responsibility for the capture of the city early in his reign (*ANET*, 284). It is suggested therefore that Shalmaneser died during the siege, and the action was completed by his successor. The Hebrew text is vague on the identity of the king of Assyria who completed the sack of the city, although it mentions Shalmaneser as launching the original attack. The fact that Sargon refers to "Samarians" in his inscription would lend some support to the theory in which the king is deported before the final attack on the city (so Hallo, *BA* 23 [1960] 51).

2 "But not quite like the kings of Israel who preceded him" adds an ironic note to the chapter. There is a hint here of a slight improvement in the state of religious affairs in Israel under this king. By this comment Hoshea is also compared quite favorably with his southern contemporary Ahaz, who copied the actions of "all the kings of Israel" (16:3). However, the writer implies here, and later expands upon the theme, that the cumulative effect of the sins of the Israelite monarchy is not to be diverted by a slight improvement at the end. See vv 7–23.

3 עליו עלה שלמנאסר "it was against him that Shalmaneser had come." The word order is important and implies a change for the sake of emphasis (see above in *Form/Structure/Setting*). All the judgment on the northern kingdom is to be focused on the unfortunate moderate Hoshea. The perfect form of the Hebrew verb עלה is best translated into English as a pluperfect for the reasons given above in *Form/Structure/Setting*. If the verb is understood in this way, then the need for drastic rearranging of the paragraph disappears. Vv 3–6 are no longer to be seen as sequential, as though they describe two invasions of Samaria. Rather the paragraph contains a brief sketch of well-known events, then provides the reasons for those events, concluding with the attack on the city. Although it might be feasible, there is no need to posit a conciliatory journey of Hoshea to Shalmaneser after the failure of an Egyptian venture (so Skinner, *Kings*, 373–76), nor, on the same grounds, is it necessary to posit two separate campaigns of Shalmaneser.

Shalmaneser V reigned for a brief period, from 727 to 722 B.C., and was the son of Tiglath Pileser III. His throne name was Ululai. He died either during or shortly after the siege of Samaria under unknown circumstances. His brother and successor, Sargon II, claims credit for the capture of the city (see *ANET*, 284). However, the Babylonian Chronicle suggests that Shalmaneser is to be credited with the victory (see K. Grayson, *Texts from Cuneiform Sources* 5:73; H. Tadmor, *JCS* 12 [1958] 22–40; 77–100).

וישב לו מנחה "and he used to send him tribute." Note the use of the same form of the same verb in 3:4. The noun מנחה is most commonly used of sacrificial offerings, but in Judg 3:15, 17, 18; 2 Sam 8:2; and 1 Kgs 5:1 it is also used of payment of tribute to an occupying power.

4 וימצא קשר "but he discovered the treachery." See n. 4.a. on the variants. The noun is frequently used of conspiracy (see 2 Sam 15:12; 1 Kgs 16:20; 2 Kgs 11:14; 12:2; 14:19, etc.). The root, קשר "to bind," is used on occasion for the ornamental bindings on a young girl's clothing.

שלח מלאכים is a standard expression for the sending of ambassadors or emissaries (see Gen 24:7; 1 Sam 16:19). However, the action has already received a negative connotation in 2 Kgs 12. Hosea the prophet strongly criticized such activity (see Hos 5:13; 7:8–16; 8:9) since it is opposed to the ideology of Holy War which demanded trust in Yahweh as the norm and trust in numbers or allies as a sign of unfaithfulness. For a fine exposition of this ideology see M. Lind, *Yahweh Is a Warrior* (1980). Implicitly this is an ideology shared by our writer.

אל סוא מלך מצרים "to So (to) the king of Egypt." The present syntax appears to regard the two as appositional phrases, and has resulted in a long search for the identity of "So," king of Egypt. He has been identified with Pharaoh Shabaka, with the Sibe of the reports of Sargon (see *ANET*, 284–85), and even with an unknown Arabian on the reading of "Mizrayim" as "Musri," which is seen at times as the Akkadian designation for Arabia. In the first case the dates are wrong. Shabaka reigned from 710 to 696 B.C. In the second case, Sibe is never designated as "king of Egypt." Third, the designation of the Hebrew "Mizrayim" as the equivalent of the Akkadian "Musri" is problematic. Such transferences of meaning from one language to another are very difficult to prove, and it is also doubtful whether in fact "Musri" denotes anything other than Egypt in Mesopotamian sources. Most now regard "So" as the name of a city, possibly the capital of Tefnakhte in the Delta region. Syntactically, the phrase "king of Egypt" is then to be read as an adverbial phrase.

ולא העלה מנחה "and he no longer sent tribute." That the Egyptian king "persuaded" Hoshea to stop paying tribute to Assyria is reading too much into the simple conjunction (contra J. A. Wilson, "So," *IDB* 4:394). It appears from the language that Hoshea's appeal to Egypt and his refusal to pay tribute were both part of a single act of rebellion. From all accounts the appeal to Egypt was quite unsuccessful. It was indeed suicidal (Bright, *History*, 273) but also part of a much longer process of decline. L. D. Levine (*Two Neo-Assyrian Stelae from Iran*, 39–41) draws attention to a parallel incident in which the Harharites withhold tribute from Assyria. It was four years before the reaction came. When it did it was swift and deadly.

כשנה בשנה lit., "as a year in a year." The revolt would have taken some time to organize, and reaction from Assyria would not have been immediate. Whether Hoshea was arrested in Samaria or was deported to Assyria is not clear. Sargon's reference to Samarians with no mention of a king suggests to some commentators that the king was deported before the final invasion. But it is difficult to envisage such an arrest and deportation without an invasion.

5 The Assyrian record simply states "he ravaged Samaria" (see Grayson, *Texts from Cuneiform Sources* 5:73), which is probably a reference to the land of Samaria, even though it is an unusual name for the land. The normal Assyrian designation is "house of Omri" (*bît Huumri*) (see *ANET*, 281–83). Some archaeological evidence for destruction in *ca.* 724 B.C. has been found at Shechem (see W. G. Dever, *The Land of Samaria*, 8–9 [Heb.]). The strategy of the Assyrian invasion was to paralyze the country, then to circumscribe the capital city after its military and economic support had been taken away. The same strategy is seen in the later invasions of Judah's Shephelah by both Sennacherib and Nebuchadrezzar. The economic support for the capital is reflected in the Samarian Ostraca, listing receipts for goods and produce from outlying regions in Israel. For the text see Gibson, *Syrian Semitic Inscriptions* 1:5–13; and for commentary on their date see W. H. Shea, *IEJ* 27 (1977) 16–27. A three-year siege of a city is by no means unusual. Although the Assyrians perfected the art of siege warfare to a very high degree (see R. Humble, *Warfare in the Ancient World*, 13–36), the main ingredient of success was an inordinate amount of patience. The horrors of such warfare are clearly depicted in 2 Kgs 6.

6 A date of 722 B.C. is normally given for this year. The events are not in sequence here if by "Israel" is meant that part of the population beyond the immediate inhabitants of the capital city of Samaria. Presumably, during the time the capital was under siege, the rest of the country was being deported. The evidence from Shechem would certainly illustrate this. (See v 5 above.) The precise sociological unit described by the term "Israel" is never clearly defined in the narrative. The deportation policies of the Assyrians are well illustrated in the Assyrian records (see *ANET*, 281–85) and are repeated here. For a full description see B. Oded, *Mass Deportations and Deportees in the Neo-Assyrian Empire*. Sargon's record states that he deported a total of 27,290 people (presumably men) from Samaria, but whether land or city is in mind is unclear even from the Assyrian sources. The number is large for deportees from one city. Sargon's hostages from Rafia numbered one-third of this total (see *ANET*, 28). Our suggestion is that the number is of the

male population as a whole, and would constitute the male inhabitants of ten large centers of population. The size of the number should be compared with 4,600 which Sennacherib took from Jerusalem (Jer 52:30). Sargon's boast that he took enough men from Israel to form a regiment of fifty chariots indicates that one of his aims was to build up his army.

וישב אתם "and he resettled them." Do we detect here an echo of the comment in v 3 (וישב מנחה) "and he used to send tribute")? The verbal roots are different, but the assonance is striking. בחלח ובחבור "in Halah and in Habor." These are unknown places in the Assyrian empire. Gray (*Kings*, 645) identifies one with Ptolemy's Chalchitis. Gozan is probably *tel Halaf*, and Habor is unknown. I. Ephal, *World History of the Jewish People* 4:189–90 identifies Halah as *kurHallahhu*, to the northeast of Nineveh. ערי מדי "cities of the Medes" is a reference so vague as to be beyond challenge. See n. 6.c. for alternative suggestions.

7 With this verse begins the theological commentary on the events described in vv 1–6 which continues until v 23. The section is full of the vocabulary and style long identified as "deuteronomistic." See M. Weinfeld, *Deuteronomy and the Deuteronomic School*, 320–65.

Although the expression ויהי כי "this happened because" is extremely rare, it introduces the following explanation, and makes it dependent upon the preceding recitation of the events of the fall of Samaria. חטאו ל "they sinned against" is a standard expression in biblical Hebrew (see K. Koch, "חטאה chatah," *TDOT* 4:309–19). ליהוה אלהיהם "against Yahweh their God" is an expression that echoes a covenant relationship between Israel and Yahweh (see Deut 5:6). המעלה אתם מארץ מצרים "who brought them up from the land of Egypt" is a common epithet for Yahweh (see Jer 2:6), but the use of the verb עלה "to bring up" is not common in deuteronomistic material (see Hobbs, *ZAW* 81 [1969] 384–87). "From the grip of Pharaoh king of Egypt" offers an ironic twist to the completion of the appositional clause. Now Israel is handed over to the Assyrians. This repeats the pattern established in the book of Judges, later to be repeated in Jer 34. The deliverance from Egypt is now reversed.

ויראו "and they worshiped," lit., "feared." There is no need to psychologize this term as does Snaith ("Kings," *IB* 3:280). It is possible that the use of the term originated in a sense of the numinous expounded by R. Otto in his important work *The Idea of the Holy*. It is clear, however, that in the deuteronomistic vocabulary that the term is a synonym for "worship" (עבד), or more specifically, to obey the laws and customs of a particular god. In Deut 4:10 "fearing Yahweh" is listening to his word; in Deut 5:29 it is keeping his ordinances; and in Deut 6:24 it is doing all his statutes. The results of "not fearing Yahweh" are clearly described in Deut 28:58–68.

8 "Walking in the manner of the nations" is specifically prohibited in Lev 18:3; 20:23 and by implication throughout the book of Deuteronomy. מלכי ישראל אשר עשו, lit., "the kings of Israel what they did" is syntactically very clumsy. See n. 8.a. for the suggested emendations, and the obvious difficulties encountered by the translations. The implication is that the kings of Israel set the pattern of behavior, which was copied by the people as a whole. The very difficulty of the sentence would argue against its omission (contra, e.g., Snaith, *IB* 3:280 and Burney, *Notes*, 332). The emendation suggested by Burney, מלפני ישראל "from before Israel," solves nothing.

9 ויחפאו "they did in secret" is a difficult word to translate. The popular rendering of "to utter" for the root is attractive, but this is no guarantee of its accuracy. It must be established that there was a conscious (i.e., consistent) borrowing of such a word and meaning from the Akkadian. Evidence is lacking. Whatever the translation, the impression of the comment is clear. Israel's activity, inspired by its rulers, is far removed from what was demanded of the nation by Yahweh.

In many of the references to במות "high places" thus far in the book of Kings there is no stigma attached to the construction or use of them. The high places are found without negative comment in stories pertaining to the period before the monarchy such as 1 Sam 9:16–24 and 1 Kgs 3:4 (see K. D. Schunck, "במה bamah," *TDOT* 2:139–45). In the present context, in which they are connected to the worship of "other gods," the danger to the religious integrity of Israel is apparent. For the deuteronomist the high places eventually become symbols for apostasy and later fall victim to the extensive reform under Josiah. ממגדל . . . עד עיר "from tower to keep." Here, as in 18:8, the expression is an idiom referring to small fortified structures and to large garrison cities. Two extremes are in mind, and the expression finds a human parallel in the frequent use of מקטון עד גדול "from small to large."

10 Literally, מצבות ואשרים means "pillars and asherahs." The word translated "pillar" can have a purely architectural significance, but in this context it is clearly seen as a cultic object which had a place of importance in worship. In the mind of the deuteronomist pillars are frequently associated with Canaanite religious practices, seen as a symbol of idolatry, and therefore condemned. This was not always the case, and some ancient stories retain the significance of the pillars in the context of traditional Yahwism (see Gen 35:14). The two pillars of Jachin and Boaz erected in the temple might reflect ancient Canaanite usage of such structures, as does the presence of two such pillars in the temple at Arad (see Aharoni, *BA* 31 [1968] 2–33). But the pillars condemned by the deuteronomist seem to have a different function. An Asherah is undoubtedly related to the worship of the ANE goddess Asherah (see De Moor, "אשרה Asherah," *TDOT* 1:438–44), but the precise nature of an "asherah" as a cult object is not known. Deut 16:21 clearly connects it with a tree planted alongside an altar, and the connection with a pillar in v 22 is clear. The pairing of the two is common throughout the OT. It is clearly something that stands erect, hence the verbs נצב "be stationed," עמד "stand" (2 Chr 33:19), and קום "arise" (Isa 27:9). Destruction of an asherah is "uprooting" it (Mic 5:14) or cutting it down (Deut 7:5). But it could also be manufactured (2 Kgs 17:16) and placed in a grove of trees (1 Kgs 14:23). The OT attitude toward the structures is consistently antagonistic because they symbolize apostasy.

On "every high hill and under every green tree," see *Comment* on 16:4 and the literature there. The expression is characteristically deuteronomistic and also found elsewhere as a stereotyped description of behavior

Comment

associated with pagan worship. See Weinfeld, *Deuteronomy and the Deuteronomic School*, 320–65.

11 The litany of apostate activities continues with this reference to "sacrificing on the high places like the nations." Some forms of the verb, such as the hiphil, are often used of legitimate sacrifice and other cultic activity of Israelite priests (see Lev 1:9, 13, 15, 17; 2:2, 9, 16 etc.). But the piel is used consistently in deuteronomistic material referring to pagan worship (see Jer 7:9; 11:13, 17; 2 Kgs 16:4, etc.). The expression כגוים "like the nations" is a standard deuteronomistic expression for apostasy. See Deut 18:9; 1 Sam 8:20. Especially in 2 Kings this kind of behavior is censured (see 2 Kgs 16:3; 17:26; 21:2,9). להכעיס "to anger" is an almost exclusively deuteronomistic expression in the Hiphil.

12 The derivation and precise meaning of הגללים are unclear. The common translation in Ezek 6:4, 5, 6 is "idols." See also 1 Kgs 15:12. In 2 Kgs 23:24 it is placed in parallel with a common derogatory term, שקצים "detested things," although not necessarily in apposition. The latter term is more a slanderous epithet than a descriptive term. The same is true of תעבות "disgusting things" in 2 Kgs 21:11. From Ezek 4:12 it is possible to link the term with "ball of dung," used probably for fuel. But whether the operative term in Ezekiel's mind is circle (גל) or dung (צאת) is unclear. In the present text it could be used metaphorically and in the light of Deut 26:16 it might mean a round idol or pillar. But so much is uncertain. Even more confusing, a specific prohibition against the worship of גללים is not found in the OT.

13 In both style and vocabulary the verb "he warned" stands well within the deuteronomistic tradition. On the awkward syntax, see n. 13.a. above.

שבו מדרכיכם "repent of your ways." Prophets who are recorded as having said words like this are Jeremiah (Jer 7:3, 5; 18:11) and Ezekiel (Ezek 33:11). Therefore this statement is an anachronism since both prophets postdate the events described here. But there is no need to see this as representative of the views of post-exilic Judaism (so Gray, *Kings*, 647). The presentation of a prophet who proclaims the keeping of the commandments (מצות), statutes (חקום), and law (תורה) is reminiscent of Moses in Deuteronomy and therefore thoroughly typical of the deuteronomistic understanding of prophecy. The inspiration of this ideal prophetic model is Deut 18:18. For an exposition of this view of the prophetic tradition, see M. Buber, *The Prophetic Faith*, and R. P. Carroll, *VT* 19 (1969) 400–415.

אשר שלחתי "which I sent." The language is typical of the prophetic tradition and an important element of the vocabulary of prophetic consciousness (see S. H. Blank, *Of a Truth the Lord Hath Sent Me*). עבדי הנביאים "my servants the prophets" is an expression first found in Amos (3:7) and then becomes a common one in the deuteronomistic tradition of prophecy (2 Kgs 9:7; 17:23; 21:10; 24:2; Jer 7:25; 25:4; 26:6; 29:19; 35:15; 44:4). It unifies the diversity of the prophets, giving them a common interest and a common task.

14 The view of history presented here can only be described as tragic. Yahweh, the deliverer from Egypt, is treated with disdain and disobeyed. Though repeated warnings are given, the nations refuse to listen. The term ערף refers to the back of the skull, which is turned to the person rejected (see 2 Sam 22:41; Jer 18:17). The neck or back of the head is the very antithesis of the face. In the ANE culture respect was symbolized by "lifting up the face" (see 5:1).

האמינו "they remained faithful" is not a characteristically deuteronomistic word, since it is found more in the poetic sections of the OT. The word is often translated "to believe in . . ." in the NT sense, but this is too restrictive. "Confidence," "reliability," and "trust" are all English terms that one can connect with the OT usage of the verb. For an excellent survey see A. Jepsen, "אמן ʾaman," *TDOT* 1:292–23. In the present context it reveals that Yahweh was reckoned as unreliable, i.e., not worthy of the trust of his people.

15 וימאסו "and they rejected," an unusually strong term, is also found in the prophets of Yahweh's attitude to his people (see Jer 6:30). את בריתו "his covenant" is the first reference to covenant in this passage, and the first reference to the Sinai covenant in 2 Kings. In 2 Kgs 11:4, 17 the term is used of the pact made to reinstate Jehoash, and in 13:23 of the covenant with Abraham. Implicit in this reference is that everything thus far discussed in the chapter belongs in the context of the covenant relationship between Yahweh and his people.

עדותיו אשר העיד "his warnings which he warned." The combination of these words is unusual. The term עדות is not to be taken as written documents, although it probably has that meaning elsewhere (see 11:12). In Deut 4:26; 30:19; 31:28 the hiphil form of the verb is used in the sense of calling of witnesses to the activity of Yahweh, and to guarantee the faithfulness of the people. The context is again the covenant between Yahweh and Israel. See H. B. Huffmon, *JBL* 78 (1959) 285–95, for survey of ideas connected with the theme. However, in Deut 8:19 and 32:46 the verb is used in the sense of warning. The RSV translates "I solemnly warn you this day. . . ." In the present context the implication is that the prophetic warnings have been rejected together with the law and statutes of Yahweh. This is thoroughly consistent with the deuteronomistic understanding of the prophetic tradition and Moses' place therein. A faint undertone is also heard here. Israel's fate is to be seen as a warning for Judah.

ההבל ויהבלו "useless things and themselves became as useless" is a very common expression in Jeremiah and deuteronomistic literature, and is part of the deuteronomistic polemic against foreign worship. Etymologically the word הבל is connected to "wind," "mist," and signifies something of no value whatsoever. See K. Seybold, "הבל hebel," *TDOT* 3:313–20. The present context gives some substance to the statement with the addition of the phrase . . . ואחרי הגוים "they deliberately copied the nations . . . ," which is an important theme of the section. See also Deut 8:20.

16 More specific misdeeds are not cataloged to indicate the extent of the apostasy of the northern nation. "Two molten images of calves" are also mentioned in Exod 32 and 1 Kgs 12. This act was archetypical of the sins of Israel and characterized as the "sin of Jeroboam." See K. Debus, *Die Sünde Jerobeams*. On the Asherah see above. This was the sin of which the next major Israelite apostate, Ahab, was accused.

צבא השמים "the hosts of heaven." Although the OT clearly regards the heavens and the earth as creations of God, it is also conscious of the real danger of the illegitimate worship of the creation. Deut 4:19 and 17:3 warn against such activity, and in the context of the ANE such prohibitions are to be seen as directed towards syncretism and polytheism. In many of the surrounding countries such items of nature were deified and worshiped. In 2 Kgs 21:3 Manasseh is accused of the same acts of apostasy as are listed here, though it is impossible that he introduced them into Israel and Judah. Amos 5:26 already provides evidence for the worship of astral deities in the mid eighth century B.C. "And they adored Baal" is an inevitable and predictable addition to the list of apostasies of the northern nation. Among Israel's kings, Ahab is most clearly linked with this particular activity, although the tendency to such apostasy is already found in the story of Gideon (Judg 6).

17 On this expression and practice "pass through fire" see *Comment* on 16:3. This verse begins what has been called ". . . an epitome of the Deuteronomistic understanding of the action of Yahweh in the history of his people" (so R. J. Coggins, *ASTI* 6 [1967–1968] 37).

ויקסמו קסמים וינחשו "they performed sorceries and practiced divination." On these expressions see S. R. Driver, *Deuteronomy*, 221–27; B. O. Long, "Divination," *IDBSup* 241–43, and the literature cited there. The terms are widely used in the OT, but there is a striking resemblance here to the vocabulary of Deut 18:10. To be noted is that Deut 18:10 is in the context of a discussion on the truth of prophecy. Gray's point (*Kings*, 648) that a resort to divination is a result of the "perplexity" of the people in the face of adversity is a popular one, and to a certain extent true. It overlooks the role that "sorcery," "witchcraft," and "divination" played in the life of so-called primitive societies. To modern ears the terms convey negative meanings, as indeed they do in the OT, but the reasons are different. Whereas to the modern ear such terms often conjure up the "spooky" and the abnormal, the OT advises avoidance of them because of their inherent tendency toward apostasy. Such activities are "intelligent responses to man's fundamental needs in the context of the society in which they are found" (so J. D. Krige, *Witchcraft and Sorcery*, 275). The OT criticism against such activity is that its center of focus is the manipulation of forces beyond the human by the human. The OT's alternative is trust in the God of creation. For the standard study of witchcraft, see E. E. Evans-Pritchard, *Witchcraft, Oracles and Magic among the Azande* (Oxford: Clarendon, 1937), and for a convenient summary see I. M. Lewis, *Social Anthropology in Perspective* (Harmondsworth: Penguin Books, 1976) 68–91.

The hithpael of מכר "to sell" is used only four times in the OT. In Deut 28:68 it is used literally of selling oneself into slavery, and in 1 Kgs 21:20, 25 it is used metaphorically of the activities of Ahab under the inspiration of his wife Jezebel.

18 The anger of God is understood throughout the OT as the motivation for actions such as this. It is also common outside the OT. Mesha of Moab regards the Israelite occupation of Moab under Omri and after as the result of the anger of the god Chemosh. See Gibson, *Syrian Semitic Inscriptions* 1:74; B. Albrektson, *History and the Gods*, 24–41.

"Nothing was left except the tribe of Judah." And then there was one! As with the popular tale, the remaining ones were meant to take the warning from the fate of the unfortunate others. The motif is a common one in the prophets and an important aspect of the OT understanding of history. Mic 1 views the destruction of Samaria as a warning for Jerusalem. The same is implied in Jer 2–3 and Ezek 16.

19 Snaith (*IB* 3:282), Robinson (*2 Kings*, 158), and Burney (*Notes*, 330) regard this verse as an unnecessary insertion because it repeats much of the vocabulary of the previous section. The syntax is indeed awkward, but there are other considerations. Methodologically it seems grossly unfair to expect conformity of style in one author, then when it appears, to excise the offending passage as secondary. Moreover, the principle of typology which is developing here is an important motif of the OT presentation of history, and in fact fundamental to the OT theology of history. (For an exposition of this "paradigmatic" view of history, see R. Smend, *Elemente alttestamentlicher Geschichtsdenkens.*) To state as many do that the perspective of this verse is post-587 B.C. is a mere truism.

20 וימאס יהוה "thus Yahweh rejected." With Yahweh as the subject the clause is not a common one. Yahweh rejected Saul in 1 Sam 15, Jerusalem in 2 Kgs 23:27, and the people in Jer 2:37; 6:30. Yahweh's attitude to his people recalls their attitude to his laws, statutes, and ordinances (see v 15). Their fate becomes Israel's fate. It is a type of *ius talionis*.

The verb שסים "spoilers" is either *lamedh he* (שסה) or a double *ayin* (שסס), and not very common in the OT. It does occur in Judg 2:14, 16 and 1 Sam 14:48, but this time there is no deliverer to rescue them.

21 קרע "he had torn" is a clear reference to 1 Kgs 11 and the prophecy of Ahijah which was given to Jeroboam. The prophecy is appropriately echoed here with the use of the verb קרע. See the parallel in 2 Kgs 10:32. On וידא "and he allured," see n. 21.c. above. There is an obvious link here with Deut 13:6. חטאה גדולה "the great sin" is a covering expression for apostasy.

22 The verse contains an expression which is standard throughout the book of 2 Kings. The repetition of such action now finds a tragic conclusion.

23 The same pattern is found here as with the verb "reject" in vv 15, 20. Israel did not turn from sin, so she is removed (lit., "caused to turn") from the presence of Yahweh. The historical manifestation for this is the removal of the people from their land into exile in Assyria. On the expression עד היום הזה "to this day" see Childs, *JBL* 82 (1963) 279–92. The expression betrays the didactic intention of the writer.

24 This verse begins a new descriptive section of the chapter, following the theological commentary in vv 7–23. The many historical issues raised by this section have given rise to several attempts to detect the various redactional layers of the account. (See above in *Form/Structure/Setting.*) The repopulation policy of the Assyrians is well documented from their own records, and the picture here is quite consistent with what is known from those sources. Both Esarhaddon and Asshurbanipal carried out similar policies of displacement. Such a program, however, would have taken careful planning and equally careful execution, and would have been completed a long time after the initial deportations. See the parallel in Sargon's record (*ANET*, 284).

בבל "Babylon" at this time was under Assyrian control. The exact location of כותה "Cuthah" is not completely certain, but is identified by many with Tel Ibrahim, some twenty kilometers northeast of Babylon. In Akkadian sources it is Kutu. עוא "Avva" is unknown. חמת "Hamath" is most likely a reference to Hamath on the Orontes, which at this time was an enemy and a vassal of Sargon II (see *ANET*, 284). Such a mixing of both populations would have fitted in well with the Assyrians' overall plan. The dual form of ספרוים "Sepharvayim" might well refer to the two known Sippars on the Euphrates. Alternatively, it might refer to the ancient site of Shabarain in Syria, which was captured by Shalmaneser. Again, such a mixing of two populations like this would fit well into the Assyrian policy.

בני ישראל "the people of Israel." The exact social unit referred to here is unclear. The term has a wide range of meaning, from the small religious community addressed by the prophets, to the army. It most probably refers to the male population of the towns and cities of the country.

The term וירשו "they took possession" is a favorite of the deuteronomist for the occupation of the promised land by the Israelites, and the irony is that now the tables are completely turned, and the people of Yahweh are themselves dispossessed. For an excellent study of this general theme, see W. Brueggemann, *The Land*.

את שמרון "of Samaria." Here the city and the country are in mind, although this is an unusual meaning for the term. Of the forty-eight occurrences of the term in Kings most are restricted to the city.

25 "So Yahweh sent lions." This action is consistent in a writer whose world-view regards God as the "prime mover" in all historical activities. This is a position he shares with the rest of the OT writers. The plague of lions can be rationalized since lions are not uncommon in the OT; however, it is the interconnectedness of events and the drawing out of a sense of purpose that is the motivation behind the narrative here.

26 Although the sentiment of this verse might appear at first to be crude, it does have a very important point to make. The appeal for help (by whom it is not stated, but apparently the new settlers) and the interpretation placed on the events of misfortune in Samaria, were precisely those things which Israel had failed to do (see vv 10–17). The newly settled nations behave more correctly than did their predecessors in the land. There is no need to see this account as unhistorical since such a belief in the relationship between the correct worship of a local god and the fortunes of the local inhabitants is a widespread belief in the ANE. For the general use of the term משפט "custom" see *Comment* on 1:7, where the word is used in a nonlegal sense. See also on the relationship between "custom" and "law," S. Roberts, *Order and Dispute: An Introduction to Legal Anthropology* (Harmondsworth: Penguin Books, 1979). For whatever reasons, the new inhabitants sought to worship the local god Yahweh in the correct manner, something the Israelites had completely failed to do.

27 No Assyrian parallels exist for this kind of activity, although it was certainly within the power of the Assyrian king to allow such an exile to return home. אשר הגליתם "whom you exiled." The change in persons and number is abrupt and awkward, and is even more so with the plural jussives וילכו וישבו "and let them go and let them return" (see *Notes*). This is, however, a superb piece of irony which has a priest exiled for his apostasy now returning to teach the customs of his God to those who replaced him.

28 The reference to בית אל "Bethel" has led many to separate this paragraph (vv 25–28) from the preceding one. On the use of the verse for information on the origins of the Samaritan sect, see below.

29 A new paragraph now begins and the narrative moves in a different direction. Many scholars have taken vv 29–41 to be a later addition to the chapter and a deliberate polemic against post-exilic Samaritanism (so Montgomery; Coggins, *ASTI* 6 [1967–68] 35–48; Talmon, *Eretz Shomeron* 19–33; etc.). This will be discussed below.

ויהיו "but they were" begins with a contrastive *waw*. The new settlers in fact did not attempt to learn the local religious customs to the exclusion of the worship of other gods. Instead each group brought with them their own local deities. It is clear from the earliest interpretations (see the translations of the Vg, G[B]) that שמרנים "Samarians" was taken to mean the Samaritans, the sectarians referred to in John 4. They still exist today on Mt. Gerizim near modern Nablus (Shechem). The original meaning, however, must have been something different. To be noted is that in the whole section there is neither a reference to Samaria nor to Shechem, where the group has its center. In Hebrew the term is ambiguous. Sargon's inscription refers to "Samarians," that is, local inhabitants. Samaritans developed into an extremely conservative religious group, and the image here of undisciplined syncretism hardly matches with the historical picture.

It is wise, however, to make a distinction between the religious group of the Samaritans, whose origins are lost to us, and the community in the north as a whole. The latter, because of its mixed background, would have been avoided by the pious who eventually returned from exile. The term שמרנים "Samaritans" does not refer to the religious sect and is probably a parody on the word שמרים "guardians, keepers." There is nothing here that needs to be questioned historically. The passage describes the state of affairs in the north during the next several generations, and its causes are a direct result of well-established Assyrian policy. How widespread such admixture and syncretism was is not clear. The impression given here is that it was characteristic of the whole northern territory. This was an impression which remained embedded in Jewish memory (see H. L. Ginzberg, *Legends of the Jews* 1:412; 4:265–66; R. J. Coggins, *ASTI* 6 (1967–68) 35–48.

30 The list of deities worshiped by the new settlers is confusing because of our lack of detailed information on them. Since many of them are localized gods, they do not find their way into the stories of the gods of the ANE and are thus obscure.

סכות בנות, lit. "booths for daughters," which *BHS*, followed by many, emends to מרדך וזרבנית "Marduk-Zarbanit," is a combination of the name of the god of Babylon and the name of a consort. Burney (*Notes*, 336) links the term בנות "daughters" with the verb בין "to judge," a tenuous link at best. The term is probably to be read in light of Amos 5:26.

נרגל "Nergal" is the god of the underworld in Mesopotamia (see H. Ringgren, *Religions of the Ancient Near East,* 63). אשימא "Ashima" is very difficult. Gray ("Ashima," *IDB* 1:252) and Snaith (*IB* 3:284) link it with Amos 8:14, the "ashima" of Samaria. The deity reappears in the Elephantine papyri as "ashim-bethel," apparently a consort of Yahweh (see B. Porten, *Archives from Elephantine*, 171–72, 175–76).

31 Nibchaz is an unknown god. Tartak has been tentatively identified with Attargatis (see Gray, "Tartak," *IDB* 4:519; Ringgren, *Religions of the Ancient Near East*, 156–57), a form of the west Semitic great goddess. This is certainly possible, and the names are similar. How likely it was for exiles from Assyria to bring a west Semitic god into captivity is not clear. Their tendency for syncretism, though, makes such a move quite feasible. The two other gods mentioned here also resemble known Mesopotamian deities. With Albright (*Archeology and the Religion of Israel*, 162–64) we can read Adramelek as Adadmelek, or, if left, it can be seen as a Hebrew version of Attar-melek (so Gray, *JNES* 8 [1949] 78–80). Attar was another version of the name Ishtar/Astarte. Anamelek is a reference to the Mesopotamian sun-god Anu. Human sacrifice was not normally associated with the worship of this deity. It appears that the state of affairs in the north is being presented in as bad a light as possible. Such a position is inspired by Deut 4:6–18 and coupled with a desire to belittle and ridicule. This certainly happened in later Jewish tradition. Sanhedrin 63b likened Succoth-benoth to a hen, Nergal to a cock, Ashima to a ram, Nibchaz to a dog, Adramelek to a mule, and Anamelek to a horse!

32 ויהיו יראים את יהוה "So they worshiped (feared) Yahweh." Many commentators see a contradiction between this statement and that in v 25, which seems to say exactly the opposite. But surely a clear progression is implied here in vv 29–32. Such a settlement and the establishment of such practices of organized religious activity would have taken considerable time. Further, the term "to fear Yahweh" is a common synonym in the deuteronomistic literature for "worship," and does not always signify the ideal of exclusive worship of Yahweh. Here this is certainly the case. In the present description there is more than a little sarcasm with the new settlers covering as many religious options as possible in their new, perilous situation. The Elephantine documents betray a similar situation among the exiles in Egypt. The final comment in v 33 effectively drives home this very point.

The chapter concludes with what many regard as a repetitive and therefore secondary homiletic expansion on the description of life in the north after the Assyrian deportations. But the language is thoroughly deuteronomistic, and therefore not to be dismissed so lightly. Repetition is not uncommon in biblical narratives (see R. Alter, *The Art of Biblical Narrative*, 88–113). If something is said twice, then the usual intention of the speaker is to emphasize a point. The repetitiveness can therefore be misleading, but, as we have seen above (see *Form/Structure/Setting*), the final paragraph follows a clever structure.

34 "To this day" is a comment confirming existing conditions at the time of writing. See Childs, *JBL* 82 (1963) 279–92.

כמשפטים הראשנים "in this manner," lit., "according to the former customs," draws attention to the state of affairs formerly described in the narrative of chap. 17. The term יראם "they feared" is expounded in what follows, namely, the obedience to the statutes, ordinances, laws, and commandments—

a typically deuteronomistic quartet—given to the "sons of Jacob." The latter is a very uncommon designation for the people of Israel, but used previously in 1 Kgs 18:31. It might reflect prophetic language since "Jacob" is a common term used of the northern tribes in the prophetic tradition. (See Isa 2:5; Jer 5:29; Amos 3:13; Mic 3:1, etc.)

35 On ברית "covenant" see v 15. The covenant involved exclusive worship of Yahweh. The whole section, reminiscent of Deut 4, clearly betrays the writer's standards of judgment in his survey of the history of Israel and Judah. The climax to this final paragraph comes in v 40 with its tragic comment on the people's refusal to listen to the commands of God. The effect is loss of religious exclusivity and hence loss of identity for Israel.

Explanation

Chap. 17 offers a brief account of the final collapse of the northern nation, Israel, but the chapter is more than a simple retelling of the past. The deuteronomistic tendency to interpret and to theologize appears here in its most blatant form. A brief historical account (far too brief for the weight of historical incident it has to bear) is followed by a lengthy and somewhat repetitive commentary (vv 1–6, 7–23). The outline is then repeated. Vv 24–31 provide a historical description of the state of affairs in Samaria following the deportation, and another commentary follows in vv 32–41.

In the account of the end of Israel there is a clear note of tragedy and irony. The final king of the north, Hoshea, who surprisingly enough was not like the other kings of Israel (v 2), is the monarch who has to witness the loss of his land and people. This character stands in contrast to his counterpart Ahaz in Judah, who enthusiastically followed the ways of the kings of Israel (16:3). An added ironic touch is seen in the final episode of the deportation. A priest who was deported because of his apostasy and unfaithfulness to Yahweh is called back from exile to instruct the new settlers in the religious customs of the north (vv 26–33). The newcomer apparently had no lasting effect upon the immigrants in the north.

The length of editorial comment found in this chapter betrays the writer's interest in interpreting the past. The collapse of the north has already begun in chap. 15 with the rapid succession of kings and assassinations, but in the present chapter, after a brief detour into the fortunes of the southern nation, the writer returns to make sense of the end of the nation of Israel. He does this by listing again the actions of the people which stand in stark contrast to the standards of behavior and worship expected of them. Throughout the interpretive commentaries, deuteronomistic language abounds, and there one finds clear echoes of the exclusivity demanded by the deuteronomic law (see *Comment* above). Time and again the people reject these demands and walk a different way. Apart from the record of the reform of Josiah, no other passage in the books of Kings so strongly reflects the reliance upon deuteronomistic ideas and phraseology as does this commentary.

The chapter is more than a mere recitation of event and interpretation written in a distinctive style, however. The writer makes some important theological points. In the first instance he portrays a complete and absolute breakdown of the society in the north. The population was exiled, not as a group, but in smaller sections, to various parts of the Assyrian empire. The historical reason is clearly the Assyrian reaction to the revolt of Hoshea (v 4). The effect of the invasion is to destroy whatever cohesiveness existed in the north, and to use the exiles for Assyria's own military ends (see above on v 6). The nation does not survive, but loses its identity, along with its territory. In addition, the writer is at pains to point out the nature of the society which replaced the deported Israelites. It was one that bore no resemblance at all to what existed previously. Various groups were imported, and no central religious system prevailed. Each worshiped in its own way. The return of the Yahwistic priest to teach the new inhabitants the ways of Yahweh does nothing to clear up this chaotic situation since Yahweh is thence worshiped as one of many gods of the north. With the destruction of the north, any vestige of the deuteronomic ideal of one people, one God, and one covenant is lost.

In recording and commenting upon this, the writer attempts to make sense of it. Change is a fundamental part of human experience, and indeed provides opportunities for reflection (see L. Gilkey, *Reaping the Whirlwind* [New York: Seabury Press, 1976] 3–35). In a time in which change does not normally take place rapidly, such violent change as was experienced by the people of God with the loss of the north and the subsequent exile of the south, forces a complete reassessment of the past. The reassessment is all the more urgent when one important ingredient of that past is seen as stability—a stability focused on the nature of God and his actions. How can this fundamental breaking of order and stability be integrated into one's knowledge and understanding of the past? This, it seems, is the question addressed by our writer.

The events of the recent past are understood in terms of the breaking of covenant (vv 15, 35). The social and religious organization that grows out of the notion of covenant is destroyed because the covenant is broken. The senior partner of that agreement reacts to the loss of fidelity on the part of the junior partner. But there is hope in this. The destruction of the north now has meaning. It is not an isolated, irrational, or capricious event. It is purposed. The same God is active in judgment. Reconstruction is therefore possible.

Hezekiah and the Siege of Jerusalem (18:1–37)

Bibliography

Ackroyd, P. R. "Historians and Prophets." *SEÅ* 33 (1968) 18–54. **Aharoni, Y.** "Arad: Its Inscriptions and Temple." *BA* 31 (1968) 1–32. ———. "Tell Beersheba." *RB* 82 (1975) 92–95. **Ahlstrom, G. W.** "Is Tell el-Duweir ancient Lachish?" *PEQ* 112 (1980) 7–9. **Alt, A.** "Die territorialgeschichtliche Bedeutung von Sanheribs Eingriff in

Palästina." *Kleine Schriften*, vol. 2. Munich: C. H. Beck, 1953. 242–49. **Avigad, N.** "Baruch the Scribe and Jerahmeel the King's Son." *BA* 42 (1979) 114–22. **Barnett, R. D.** "The Siege of Lachish." *IEJ* 8 (1958) 161–64. **Barr, J.** "Story and History in Biblical Theology." *JR* 56 (1976) 1–17. **Boecker, H. J.** "Erwägungen zum Amt des Mazkir." *TZ* 17 (1961) 212–16. **Bright, J.** "Le probleme des campaignes de Sénnacherib en Palestine. Un nouvel examin." *Maqqel Shaqqedh. Homage à W. Vischer.* Neuchâtel: Delachaux, 1960. 20–31. **Childs, B. S.** *Isaiah and the Assyrian Crisis.* London: SCM Press, 1967. **Clements, R. E.** *Isaiah and the Deliverance of Jerusalem.* Sheffield: JSOT Press, 1980. **Crown, A. D.** Messengers and Scribes." *VT* 24 (1974) 366–70. **Davies, G. I.** "Tell el-Duweir = Ancient Lachish." *PEQ* 114 (1982) 25–28. **Eissfeldt, O.** "Ezechiel als Zeugnis für Sanheribs Eingriff in Palästina." *Kleine Schriften*, vol. 1. Tübingen: Mohr, 1962. 239–46. **Elat, M.** "The Political Status of Judah after Sennacherib's Conquest of Lachish." *Yediot* 31 (1967) 140–56. **Elliger, K.** "Die Heimat des Propheten Micha." *ZDPV* 57 (1934) 81–152. **Geyer, J. B.** "2 Kings XVIII 14–16 and the Annals of Sennacherib." *VT* 21 (1971) 604–6. **Gorg, M.** "Zur Decoration der Tempelsäulen." *BN* 13 (1980) 17–21. **Haag, H.** "La compagine de Sennacherib contre Jérusalem en 701." *RB* 58 (1951) 348–59. **Hestrin, R.** and **Dayagi, M.** "A Seal Impression of a Servant of King Hezekiah." *IEJ* 24 (1974) 27–29. **Hobbs, T. R.** "The Land: A Neglected Feature of Old Testament Study." *Theodolite* 6 (1982) 5–20. **Horn, S. H.** "Did Sennacherib Campaign Once or Twice against Hezekiah?" *AUSS* 4 (1966) 1–28. **Jenkins, A. K.** "Hezekiah's Fourteenth Year." *VT* 26 (1976) 284–98. **Joines, K. R.** "The Bronze Serpent in Israel." *JBL* 87 (1968) 245–56. **Kitchen, K. A.** *The Third Intermediate Period in Egypt (1100–650 B.C.).* Warminster: Aris & Phillips, 1973. **Leeuwen, C. van.** "Sennachérib devant Jerusalem." *OTS* 14 (1965) 245–72. **Millard, A. R.** "In Praise of Ancient Scribes." *BA* 45 (1982) 143–53. **Montgomery, J. A.** "Archival Data in the Book of Kings." *JBL* 56 (1934) 46–52. **Moriarty, F. L.** "The Chronicler's Account of Hezekiah's Reform." *CBQ* 27 (1965) 399–406. **Naaman, A.** "Sennacherib's Campaign to Judah and the Date of the *lmlk* Stamps." *VT* 29 (1979) 61–86. ———. "Sennacherib's Letter to God." *BASOR* 214 (1974) 25–39. **Nicholson, E. W.** "The Centralization of the Cult in Deuteronomy." *VT* 13 (1963) 380–89. ———. *Preaching to the Exiles.* Oxford: Blackwell, 1970. **Reventlow, H. von.** "Das Amt der Mazkir." *TZ* 15 (1959) 161–75. **Rowley, H. H.** "Hezekiah's Reform and Rebellion." *Men of God.* London: Thomas Nelson, 1963. 98–132. ———. "Zadok and Nehushtan." *JBL* 58 (1939) 113–41. **Rudolph, W.** "Sanherib in Palestina." *PJ* 25 (1929) 59–80. ———. "Zum Text des Königsbuches." *ZAW* 63 (1951) 201–15. **Stade, B.** "Anmerkungen zu 2 Kö 10–14." *ZAW* 5 (1885) 275–97. ———. "Anmerkungen zu 2 Kö 15–21." *ZAW* 6 (1886) 156–89. **Tadmor, H.** "The Chronology of the Last Kings of Judah." *JNES* 15 (1956) 226–30. ——— and **Cogan, M.** "Ahaz and Tiglath-Pileser." *Bib* 60 (1979) 491–508. **Todd, E. W.** "The Reforms of Hezekiah and Josiah." *SJT* 9 (1956) 288–93. **Ungnad, A.** "Die Zahl der von Sanherib deportierten Judaer." *ZAW* 59 (1942–1943) 199–213. **Ussishkin, D.** "The 'Camp of the Assyrians' in Jerusalem." *IEJ* 29 (1979) 137–42. **Vogt, E.** "Samaria a 722 et 720 ab Assyriis capta." *Bib* 39 (1958) 535–41. ———. "Sennacherib und die letzte Tatigkeit Jesajas." *Bib* 47 (1966) 427–37. **Weinberg, W.** "Language Consciousness in the OT." *ZAW* 92 (1980) 185–204. **Weinfeld, M.** "Cult Centralization in Israel in Light of a Neo-Babylonian Analogy." *JNES* 23 (1964) 202–11.

Translation

1a*In the third* b *year of Hoshea son of Elah king of Israel, Hezekiah son of Ahaz became king of Judah.* 2 *He was twenty-five* a *years of age when he began to reign and he reigned for twenty-nine years in Jerusalem. His mother's name was Abi* b *daughter of Zechariah.* ³ *He behaved well in Yahweh's eyes as David his ancestor had done.* ⁴ *It was he who removed the high places, smashed the pillar and cut down the Asherah. He also crushed the bronze serpent which Moses had made, because up to that time the people of Israel had burned incense to it, and it was nicknamed* ᵃ *"The Brass Thing."* ᵇ ⁵ *He trusted* ᵃ *in Yahweh the God of Israel, and compared* ᵇ *to all* ᶜ *the kings of Judah who preceded him,* ᵈ *and followed him, there was none like him.* ⁶ *He was completely faithful to Yahweh, and did not stray from Him. He kept the commandments which Yahweh had commanded Moses.* ⁷ *Yahweh was with him, and wherever he went out he prospered. He even rebelled against the king of Assyria and would not serve him.* ⁸ *He defeated the Philistines to as far south as Gaza and its regions, striking both watchtower and fortified keep.*

⁹ *Now it happened in the fourth year of Hezekiah, which was also the seventh year of Hoshea son of Elah, that Shalmaneser, king of Assyria, attacked Samaria and besieged it.* ¹⁰ *He took it at the end of the third* ᵃ *year, the sixth year* ᵇ *of Hezekiah.* ᶜ *It was the ninth year of Hoshea king of Israel when Samaria was taken.* ¹¹ *The king of Assyria exiled Israel to Assyria, and set* ᵃ *them down at Halath and Habor, the River of Gozan, and in the cities* ᵇ *of the Medes.* ¹² *It was all because they* ᵃ *did not obey the voice of Yahweh their God, and they broke the covenant which he commanded Moses the servant of Yahweh. They neither listened nor obeyed.*

¹³ *Then in the fourteenth year of Hezekiah, Sennacherib king of Assyria attacked all the cities of Judah, that is, the fortresses, and took them.* ¹⁴ *Hezekiah sent word* ᵃ *to the king of Assyria at Lachish, "I have acted wrongly. Withdraw from me and I will raise whatever penalty you impose upon me." So the king of Assyria imposed a fine on Hezekiah king of Judah of three hundred talents of silver and thirty talents of gold.* ᵇ ¹⁵ *Hezekiah handed over all the silver which was found in the temple, and in the palace treasury.* ¹⁶ *It was then that he stripped the doors of Yahweh's sanctuary and the supports* ᵃ *which he had previously overlaid, and gave them to the Assyrian king.*

¹⁷ *Following this, the king of Assyria sent the Tartan, the Rab-saris, and the Rab-shakeh from Lachish with a sizable force to king Hezekiah at Jerusalem. After ascending, they arrived at Jerusalem,* ᵃ *and they halted at the aqueduct of the Upper Pool which is on the highway of the Fuller's Field.* ¹⁸ *They summoned the king,* ᵃ *but Eliakim son of Hilkiah, the minister of state,* ᵇ *came out together with Shebna the scribe and Joah son of Asaph,* ᶜ *the archivist.*

¹⁹ *The Rab-shakeh declared to them, "Tell Hezekiah, Thus has the great king of Assyria said, 'What is this confidence* ᵃ *with which you trust?* ²⁰ *You seem to say that mere words are counsel and strength enough for battle.* ᵃ *Now in whom can you trust after rebelling against me?* ²¹ *Look, are you entrusting yourself to that broken reed of a staff, Egypt? It will pierce the hand of anyone who leans upon it for support!* ²² *And if you dare to say,* ᵃ *"We will trust in Yahweh our God," is he not the one whose high places and altars Hezekiah has removed, declaring to both Judah and Jerusalem* ᵇ *that on the surface of this altar they shall sacrifice in Jerusalem?' "* ²³ *Now make a bet with my master, the king of Assyria. I will give to you two thousand horses if you are able to place riders upon them.* ²⁴ *How can you even repulse the strength of one of my master's most junior officers* ᵃ *if you rely on Egypt for chariots and cavalry?* ²⁵ *Furthermore,* ᵃ *is it without Yahweh that I have attacked this place* ᵇ *to destroy it? Yahweh himself said to me 'Attack this country and destroy it.' "*

²⁶ Then Eliakim ᵃson of Hilkiah, ᵃ Shebna, and Joah responded to the Rab-shakeh, "Please speak to your servants in Aramaic, so that we understand. Please do not speak in Judean with us within earshot of the soldiers on the ramparts."ᵇ ²⁷ But the Rab-shakeh replied, "Is it only to ᵃ your master and to you that my master sent me to speak all these words? Is it not also to the men who are stationed along the walls,ᵇ who are destined to eat ᶜ their own excrement ᵈ and drink their own urine ᵉ along with you?"
²⁸ So the Rab-shakeh stood and called loudly in Judean, "Hear the word of the great king of Assyria. ²⁹ Thus has the king declared, 'Do not let Hezekiah ᵃ deceive you. He is not able to deliver you from my grasp.'ᵇ ³⁰ Neither let him make you trust in Yahweh with the promise 'Yahweh will surely save us and not hand the city over to the king of Assyria.' ³¹ Do not listen to Hezekiah, for thus has the king of Assyria declared, 'Make peace with me,ᵃ and surrender to me. Then each man will eat of his own vine and fig tree, and drink from his own well, ³² until I come and take you to a land similar to your own land, a land of grain and wine, a land of bread and vineyards, ᵃa land of olive trees and honey. You shall live and not die. So do not listen to Hezekiah ᵃ when he states that Yahweh will deliver you. ³³ Has any of the gods of the nations been able to deliver his land from the grip of the king of Assyria? ³⁴ Where are the gods of Hamath and Arpad? Where are the gods of the Sepharvayyim, Hena, and Ivvah? ᵃ When did they deliver Samaria from my grip? ᵇ ³⁵ Which of any of the national gods delivered their country from my grasp? How then can Yahweh deliver Jerusalem from my grasp?'"
³⁶ But the people kept silence,ᵃ and offered no response, for the king's order had been, "Do not reply to him." ³⁷ So Eliakim the minister of state, together with Shebna the scribe and Joah son of Asaph the archivist returned to Hezekiah with their clothes torn,ᵃ and reported to him the words of the Rab-shakeh.

Notes

1.a. The opening וַיְהִי֙, lit., "and it was" is unusual in such a context, though not impossible. Ehrlich's suggestion (*Randglossen* 7:315) that it be omitted is quite unnecessary.
1.b. The G MS c₂ reads "fourth."
2.a. In typical fashion G^L adds "Hezekiah."
2.b. In the versions the name of the mother is variously spelled.
4.a. G^L reads the plural.
4.b. The name "Nehushtan" is spelled many different ways in the versions. See *Comment* below.
5.a. G^L again adds the proper name.
5.b. The punctuation of MT is awkward. Burney (*Notes*, 338) suggests that the word be excised.
5.c. בכל "to all" is omitted by G.
5.d. The clause "which were before him" is regarded by many as a gloss. See *BHS* and Montgomery, (*Kings*, 510).
10.a. Ehrlich (*Randglossen* 7:315) suggests that the punctuation is clumsy and remedies this by placing the *athnah* under the word שָׁנִים "year."
10.b. For "sixth" the G Ms c₂ reads "tenth."
10.c. For "Hezekiah" the G Ms c₂ reads "Ahaz."
11.a. Read וַיַּנִּחֵם "and he set them" (so *BHS*) for the awkward וַיַּנְחֵם.
11.b. See n. 17:6.c.
12.a. G^L adds "children of Israel."
14.a. G supplies an object, "messengers."
14.b. Vv 14–16 are omitted by Isa 36.

Form/Structure/Setting 245

16.a. MT reads האמנות "the supports," which is variously rendered by the versions, and even transliterated by some. See the *Comment* above on 10:5. Ehrlich's suggestion (*Randglossen* 7:315) that the word be emended to הַמָּגִנּוֹת "shields" need not be followed. It is quite conjectural.

17.a. ויעלו ויבאו "after ascending they arrived" is repeated in MT, but not in G^BL. Isa 36:2 omits both as well as both references to "Jerusalem." Burney (*Notes*, 341) agrees with the omission.

18.a. The opening words are omitted by Isa 36:3.

18.b. The Heb. is literally "Who was over the house." On the function of this official see below.

18.c. The proper name is variously spelled in the versions.

19.a. G^L adds "you and the whole of Judah."

20.a. G^L omits אמרת "you say."

22.a. MT reads תאמרון "you (pl) say." *BHS* with G offers a reading of תאמר "you (sg) say" which is supported by MT of Isa 36:7. However, the oldest MS, 1QIsa^a, reads the plural. The Hebrew text of Isaiah appears to have been corrected under the influence of the G tradition.

22.b. The phrase "in Jerusalem" is omitted by Isa 36:7, but the change is of no significance for 2 Kings.

24.a. The sentence is extremely awkward, and the general sense of the Heb. is sought in the translation. Burney (*Notes*, 342) suggests that the word פחת "officer" has been attracted into the state of the following adjective. Montgomery (*Kings*, 502) omits it.

25.a. MT reads עתה "furthermore." G^B renders και νυν "and now" and G^A offers νυν ουν "now therefore."

25.b. For המקום "the place" Isa 36:10 reads הארץ "the land."

26.a–a. The phrase is omitted by Isa 36:11.

26.b. G renders the MT החמה על אשר העם באזני "within earshot of the soldiers on the ramparts" in a different form: και ινα τι λαλεις εν τοις ωσιν του λαου του επι του τειχους "and why do you speak in the ears of the people on the wall?"

27.a. MT reads העל, lit., "upon," for which *BHS* suggests a more normal האל "to." However, the prepositions are often interchangeable.

27.b. For MT החמה "the wall" Rudolph (*ZAW* 63 [1951] 214) suggests a reading of לחם מה "what food," but without foundation.

27.c. The infinitive construct with the *lamedh* is awkward with the preceding subject הישבים "who are stationed."

27.d. See Q's euphemism צוֹאָתָם "their filth."

27.e. See Q's euphemism מֵימֵי רַגְלֵיהֶם "water of their feet."

29.a. G precedes with "the words. . . ."

29.b. MT reads מידו "from his grasp," which Isa 36:14 omits. G^B supports MT, but other versions read "from my grasp."

31.a. MT reads עשו אתי ברכה "make peace with me" which is an unusual, though not impossible, use of the word ברכה "blessing."

32.a–a. Omitted by Isa 36:17.

34.a. The names Hena and Ivvah are omitted by G^B and Isa 36:19, although included in some versions.

34.b. G^L adds the equivalent of the Heb. ואיה אלהי ארץ שמרון "and where are the gods of the land of Samaria?" which Burney (*Notes*, 342) regards as an "indispensable insertion" [sic!].

36.a. MT reads וְהֶחֱרִישׁוּ "but they kept silence" (perfect), although Isa 36:21 and G favor וַיַּחֲרִישׁוּ (imperfect). 1QIsa^a agrees with the MT of 2 Kings.

37.a. MT reads קרועי בגדים "their clothes torn," the noun being used adverbially.

Form/Structure/Setting

In all fairness to the writer of 2 Kings, chaps. 18 and 19 ought to be treated together as a single narrative unit. The almost universal disapproval of the chapter division in its present position would lend support to that wish. However, in spite of the fact that the two chapters together tell a continuous story, we have to treat them separately because of the sheer bulk of material in each.

By way of summary of the chapter we note the following. In terms of the narrative sequence chap. 18 shifts the focus of attention from Samaria, which has now been judged because of its apostasy, to Judah, where it appears at first glance as though a similar fate awaits the nation. The narrative continues without a major break to 19:37. 18:1–3 constitute a typical introduction to the reign of a Judean king and are followed by an extended comment on the achievements of the king in vv 4–8. Vv 9–12 recapitulate briefly the events already described in chap. 17, and in so doing set the historical stage for the events which take place in the rest of this chapter. To be noted, however, is that the chapter moves quickly beyond the fall of Samaria to the encounter between Hezekiah and Sennacherib some twenty years later.

Vv 13–16 offer a short account of the Assyrian invasion of Judah and the humiliation of Hezekiah and his country. Both become vassals of Assyria. 18:17–19:9 recount the "diplomatic discussions" which took place between the Assyrian envoys and the representatives of Hezekiah's court. The Assyrians had come from Lachish to Jerusalem with the intention of forcing the final surrender of Judah. The Assyrian overtures are rejected, and a second attempt is made in 19:9–37. This second attempt is all the more urgent for the Assyrians because a threat is developing on their southern flank (19:9). This overture too is rejected. The Assyrians then withdraw because of a disaster in their own camp and eventually Sennacherib dies in rather ignominious circumstances in his own country (19:36–37).

The account of the reign of Hezekiah, which assumes an important theological dimension for the deuteronomist, continues beyond into chaps. 20 and 21. Throughout, events are carefully orchestrated by Yahweh, often through the agency of his prophets. This theological perspective is found elsewhere in the deuteronomistic history and is also consistent with the vocabulary and style found elsewhere in these chapters.

Since B. Stade's article on the narrative (*ZAW* 6 [1886] 156–89), most commentators detect more than one literary source in the chapters. 18:13–16, which are viewed as an "annalistic tract," are one account. 18:17–19:9*a* (19:36–37?) also form a continuous account with the introduction of the prophet Isaiah into the story. For some, this second account owes its origins to the "memoirs of Isaiah" (so Montgomery, *Kings*, 486). Yet a third account is found in 19:9*b*–35. For the sake of convenience these accounts are called A, B[1], B[2]. For a useful summary of these discussions see B. S. Childs, *Isaiah and the Assyrian Crisis*, 78–100. While separate sources might be detected in the narrative, our concern, as always, is the interpretation of the existing text and the literary relationships which are evident in a given narrative. This matter will be now examined in more detail.

Vv 1–8 begin with the typical synchronization and an introductory formula for a king from Judah (see Burney, *Notes*, ix–xii). This introduction includes a very positive assessment of Hezekiah. This is followed by a summary of some important events from his reign. An important stylistic and formal feature of this brief summary is seen by comparing it with 17:7–23. Hezekiah removed the cultic aberrations (v 4), whereas Israel became completely absorbed in them. Hezekiah followed Yahweh and kept his commandments (vv 5–6), whereas Israel deliberately disobeyed and rejected them (17:14–

18). Hezekiah initially prospered in everything because of Yahweh's help (vv 7–8), whereas Israel was sent into exile rejected by Yahweh (17:20–23). In other words, the Judean king epitomizes exactly the opposite of the attitudes and actions of Israel, hence the glowing commendation of v 3. The narrative dealing with Judah then begins on a very positive note.

Vv 9–12 are regarded by many as a quotation from the Judean annalistic account of the fall of Samaria (see Gray, *Kings*, 658; Snaith, *IB* 3:291). This is possible, but it is also a brief summary of the events, and hence a reminder of the events in chap. 17. There are two reasons for its position here. One, it provides a synchronization of the fall of Samaria with the reign of Hezekiah, and, two, it sets the historical stage for the subsequent events narrated from the reign of Hezekiah.

The style of the opening to vv 13–16 is noteworthy because it provides a counterpoint to the previous paragraph. Both begin in virtually the same way:

V 13	V 9
ובארבע עשרה שנה למלך חזקיה	ויהי בשנה הרביעית למלך חזקיהו
עלה סנחריב מלך אשור	. . עלה שלמנאסר מלך אשור
על כל ערי יהודה . . .	על שמרון
ויתפשם	ויצר עליה
"Then in the fourteenth year of King Hezekiah Sennacherib king of Assyria attacked all the cities of Judah . . . and took them."	"Now it happened in the fourth year of King Hezekiah . . . that Shalmaneser king of Assyria attacked Samaria and besieged it."

While the style of each is designated by many as "annalistic" because of the similarities of language and syntax, the juxtaposition of two such similar statements in such a short space is eye-catching and important. Its importance is seen most clearly when the immediate context is noted. Already in chap. 17 an inherent comparison between Israel and Judah was noted, and the same theme is at work here. The possibility of Judah now suffering the same fate as Israel at the hands of the Assyrians looms large.

The composition of vv 13–16 is much discussed by commentators. V 13 is thought by many to be "secondary." 2 Chr 32 contains a much more lengthy account, as befits its style and agenda, but both the Chronicler and Isa 36 omit the equivalent of vv 14–16, suggesting that the paragraph in 2 Kgs 18 is secondary. (For a summary of viewpoints see B. S. Childs, *Isaiah and the Assyrian Crisis*, 69–71.) However, that v 14 and v 17 begin in the same way suggests that the omission in Isaiah is due to haplography. The designation of the paragraph as "annalistic" is also a very popular one (see e.g. Snaith, *IB* 3:292; Gray, *Kings*, 660), but one must beware of too promiscuous a use of the term lest it become a meaningless epithet. It is often not clear whether the term implies a direct quotation from the official records, or a rather free adaptation of the information available from such sources. If the former is in mind then it appears that the evidence is rather arbitrarily interpreted, since the evidence collected by Montgomery (*JBL* 53 [1934]

46–52) for such annalistic records is very slight. If the latter is intended then the label is a truism, since this is what one would expect from a reasonably competent writer or interpreter of history.

The impending sense of doom for Judah is stressed by the closing statements of the paragraph in vv 15–16. So frequent is this kind of statement in the deuteronomistic history that it takes on the character of a literary convention. Its antecedents are to be found in 1 Kgs 14:25–28 (Rehoboam's tribute to Shishak), 2 Kgs 12:17–18 (Joash's tribute to Hazael), 2 Kgs 14:14 (Amaziah's tribute to Joash), and 2 Kgs 16:8–9 (Ahaz's tribute to Damascus). Common to all are similar language, and the fact that such plundering of the temple and palace treasures is accompanied by some act of cultic reform or innovation. The action of giving tribute takes the force out of whatever positive results might have come from the reforms. Hezekiah's reform (vv 4–8) falls into exactly the same pattern. Its effect is countered by his indebtedness to Sennacherib (vv 15–16). The impression of the short distance in time between the reform and the capitulation to Assyria, which involved a staggering amount of money (see Solomon's GNP in 1 Kgs 10:14 for comparison), sets an awesome historical stage for what follows. King, prophet, and Yahweh are now presented with a seemingly impossible task, especially in the light of the additional advances Sennacherib makes on Jerusalem.

18:17–19:9a constitute a continuous narrative of the first diplomatic mission of Sennacherib's forces to gain the prize of Jerusalem, and the whole section should be treated together. The second mission is recorded in 19:9b–35. Many commentators accept them as two separate accounts of the same incident, bonded together by a common subject matter and complementing the brief account of reform and rebellion in vv 13–16.

There is substantial agreement with the parallel passage in Isa 36. Where variants occur they are usually minor and the tendency of the Isaiah passage is towards abbreviation. There is no reason to emend the text of 2 Kings on the basis of the Isaiah text, unless it is assumed that the Isaiah text was the source for 2 Kings (see Montgomery's argument that the Isaiah text is from the "memoirs" of the prophet [*Kings*, 486–87]). The nature and purpose of the supposed additions in 2 Kings would still demand further explanation, since they would not have been entirely fortuitous. (For the relationship between prophetic texts and the text of 2 Kings, see Ackroyd, *SEÅ* 33 [1968] 18–54.) The question of the category of "history" implied by Gray's comment that the nature of the literary themes of 18:17–19:9 remove it from the realm of historical account (*Kings*, 661–62) needs some comment, however brief. Suffice it to say that the categories used are too vague, yet as tools of interpretation are applied too rigidly. It is highly unlikely that the modern divisions between "literature" and "history" can be imposed upon the ancient writer in such a way. (See the helpful comments in R. Polzin, *Moses and the Deuteronomist*, 16–18; J. Barr, *JR* 56 [1976] 1–17.)

What then is the literary relationship between 18:1–16 and 18:17–19:9? How does it encourage the progression of the narrative which is now caught between the obvious tension created by the positive assessment of Hezekiah (18:3) and the clear sense of impending disaster (18:13–16)? Initially the narrative serves to deepen that crisis in which Hezekiah and Jerusalem find

Form/Structure/Setting 249

themselves, and thus forms a fitting prelude to the so-called B² narrative (19:9b–35) which offers a dénouement.

18:17–19:9a are a narrative of action and movement. The opening two verses introduce all its main characters. How they act is very important. The King of Assyria begins the main action by sending his ministers (the Rabshakeh and the Rab-saris with the Tartan) to Hezekiah, who at this stage remains quite passive (v 17a). The Assyrian delegation continues the movement of the narrative by approaching the city (v 17b) and summoning Hezekiah, who still remains inactive (v 18a). Instead, three of his ministers, Eliakim, Shebna, and Joah, approach to talk with the Assyrians (v 18b). In vv 19–25 the Assyrians taunt the three Judean ministers and their king, but again Hezekiah, who is the main object of attack, remains passive (v 19). The response of the Judeans is fearful and weak (v 26), so the taunt continues, this time within the hearing of part of the Judean army. The object of the taunt is still Hezekiah, who continues to be in the background and remains silent (vv 27, 29). Whether this is through fear or confidence is not yet stated. Nor do the people respond (v 36). When the three Judeans return to their king to inform him of the events (v 37), he has yet to make his first move!

In 19:1–9a Hezekiah "comes to life." Thus far he has been standing in the wings as the Assyrian king, the Assyrian officials and the Judean officials perform the actions of the story. Finally, the Judean king acts, but his action only serves to deepen the shadow over Judah. He tears his clothes in an attitude of mourning (19:1), then enters the temple. He again lapses into inactivity, but not before sending messengers to Isaiah the prophet (v 2). This action now introduces an additional actor into the drama, and one who has not been seen or heard of before. It is clear that this almost casual introduction of the prophet presupposes a familiarity with his role in the story of Sennacherib's invasion. A similar conclusion can be drawn from the abrupt introduction of the prophet Elijah in 1 Kgs 17:1. In vv 3–4 the message from Hezekiah to Isaiah (so formally expressed!) does nothing to lighten the load now imposed upon Judah and Jerusalem. Hezekiah is tentative and uncertain about his ability to do anything (note the many "perhapses") and is prepared for the worst (v 4).

The marked hesitation and pessimism of Hezekiah is in sharp contrast to the confident word of Yahweh which comes through his prophet. The divine message is a direct command not to be afraid (v 6b) and a confident promise that the Assyrians will withdraw from the city (v 7). As with the opening of chap. 7, the prophetic word of hope is completely contrary to the existing circumstances, and demands belief. The final comment of this section (vv 8–9) is at first puzzling and contributes much to the theory of the two invasions of Sennacherib (see *Comment* below). Within the formal structure of the story, its effect is to suspend the fulfillment of the prophetic word, which is for the deuteronomist the climax of so many of his stories. For a while Sennacherib withdraws, but only to fight against an Egyptian threat, not to return home. At this stage the dramatic tension thus created between the dismal circumstances of Jerusalem and Judah and the prophetic promise of deliverance is almost at breaking point. One is thereby drawn to the second narrative for the dénouement.

Comment

Here, no less than elsewhere in the narrative of 2 Kings, questions of chronology are raised, and the discussions, though lengthy, are no more conclusive than others. In most reckonings, Hezekiah's reign begins at the death of his father in 715 B.C. (see Bright, *History*, 278; Herrmann, *History*, 249; Thiele, *Mysterious Numbers*, 209). Direct synchronization of the reign of Hezekiah with the fall of Samaria in 722 B.C. is therefore out of the question. Various emendations and alternative interpretations of vv 1, 9 are suggested (see below) but none can claim complete confidence.

As with the various campaigns of Shalmaneser V and Tiglath Pileser III into the west, Sennacherib's invasion is well-documented from Assyrian sources. Although there are some striking similarities between the biblical and the Assyrian sources, there are enough inconsistencies to warrant a fuller discussion of the issue below. From the historian's point of view, the crux of the matter is whether, in the interests of harmonization of the available sources, it is wise to posit one or two invasions of Judah by Sennacherib.

1 According to the generally accepted chronology for the reign of Hoshea, his third year was 729/728 B.C., but this date does not accord with that given in v 9. The invasion referred to there took place in 701 B.C. The discrepancy is dealt with in various ways. Gray (*Kings*, 669) suggests that the verb מלך in v 1 be best rendered "was designated king," i.e., he had not yet become king officially. The suggestion is ingenious but does not bear the weight of careful scrutiny. There are cases in the OT record of the monarchy of Israel, the united monarchy, and Judah, in which regular succession is interrupted and a different heir is named. Solomon, Jehoram of Israel, and Zechariah would be cases in point. But on the other hand there is no ambiguity in the use of the term מלך (see 1 Kgs 1:11; 2 Kgs 1:17 and 2 Kgs 24:17). The narrative contexts explain the unusual circumstances in which such new heirs were named. In the case of Hezekiah there is nothing in the story to indicate that his succession was in any way irregular.

Rowley (*Men of God*, 98–112) suggests a variant in v 13 from "fourteen" to "twenty-four." This has the advantage of bringing the variant chronologies virtually into line. 728/729 B.C. would be the accession of Hezekiah and 704/703 B.C. would be the beginning of the revolt of Hezekiah, which coincided with Sennacherib's own accession. This would have been a time of uncertainty in Assyria, and it appears that Hezekiah then took advantage of it. Attractive though the suggestion is, it is completely without manuscript evidence, and remains a conjecture. Thiele's suggestion (*Mysterious Numbers*, 132–33) that the synchronizations here are off by twelve years is also not without its difficulties, but the adjustment he suggests and the reasons are quite plausible. They do explain the error, and have the advantage of offering a satisfactory explanation for other features of the text as well.

2 ועשרים ותשע "and twenty-nine." Gray (*Kings*, 670) is shown to be inconsistent at this point. If 715 B.C. is taken as the beginning of his regular reign, then Hezekiah died in 686 B.C. Note that 2 Chr 29:1 adds the divine name to the name of the king's mother. This is not inconsistent, and was apparently a common practice. An alternative spelling of the name of Baruch

(ברוך), the friend of Jeremiah, has been found as "Berechiah" (ברכיהו); (see N. Avigad, *BA* 42 [1979] 114–21).

3 The comment is entirely favorable, and therefore a rare accolade. It contrasts very sharply with the many negative comments on the kings of the northern nation in the previous chapter.

4 This verse is a *locus classicus* for the theory of the "reform and rebellion" of Hezekiah. In brief, the thesis argues that the cultic reform depicted here was double-sided because "repudiation of the Assyrian gods amount[s] virtually to an announcement of rebellion. . . . The likelihood is that Hezekiah's policy was at first pushed tentatively with an eye open for possible Assyrian reaction, and then intensified and broadened as the independence movement gained momentum" (Bright, *History*, 282). On closer examination this thesis is found to be sadly wanting. At best it is an overinterpretation of the available data. As v 4 describes it, the cultic reform had four main objectives, (i) removal of the high places, (ii) destruction of altars, (iii) cutting down of the Asheroth, (iv) removal of Nehushtan, "The Brass Thing." None of these activities points to anti-Assyrian motivation for the reform, but to a radical reorganization of the native Judean cultus.

High places, altars, and Asherahs outside Jerusalem were a consistent feature of religion in the united and divided monarchy up to this time. Repeated references to them in the introductions to the reigns of various kings demonstrate this point. Also to be noted is that the use of such cultic objects is not automatically condemned, nor are they necessarily to be seen as evil. High places and altars existed in the reign of Solomon as precursors to the temple (1 Kgs 3:2, 3). They persisted during the reigns of Jehoshaphat (1 Kgs 22:43), Joash (2 Kgs 12:4), Amaziah (2 Kgs 14:4), Azariah (2 Kgs 15:4), and Jotham (2 Kgs 15:35). What is important about these references is that each of the above-named kings is praised for "doing well in Yahweh's eyes." Only in places like 1 Kgs 12:31; 13:2, 32; 2 Kgs 17:11 where the context is most explicit are activities on the altars, etc., condemned. But the activities condemned there are not pro-Assyrian.

Although the idea has long persisted, there is no reference here to the abolition of Assyrian cults as an act of rebellion, and to maintain so is to read too much into the text. Snaith's comment (*IB* 3:290) is typical of many, "If the reform of Hezekiah was primarily a reaction against Assyrian cults, the reference to the abolition of local shrines may be due to an editor who read into Hezekiah's time policies which belonged to a later generation." This is surely a most unusual exercise in logic. Snaith thus includes in the text what is not there, and explains away what is! Bright's rejoinder notwithstanding (*History*, 376), the arguments of Cogan (*Imperialism and Religion*), and McKay (*Religion in Judah under the Assyrians*) have put the idea to rest for good.

There is no denying, however, that Hezekiah's moves were quite political. But the object had more to do with internal political strength, perhaps in preparation for the rebellion, than anything else. Religious and local political power is now located in Jerusalem. The destruction of local shrines (even Yahwistic ones) has received remarkable confirmation in the findings at Tel Arad. The Iron Age Temple found at the site was during this time devoid of sacrifice. A late eighth century B.C. wall renders the sanctuary wall obsolete. (See Y. Aharoni, *BA* 31 [1968] 2–33.) For an interesting parallel to such centralization of religious and political power, see M. Weinfeld, *JNES* 23 (1964) 202–11.

Although it is correct to see the royal records of Judah as the source for the information here (so Montgomery, *Kings*, 481), the language reflects the style of the deuteronomist.

The expression "he also crushed the bronze serpent" is awkward, especially without the necessary direct object marker (see *BHS*). The verb כתת implies beating the metal into something else (see Isa 2:4). For a good discussion see McKay, *Religion in Judah*, 84–85. נחש הנחשת "bronze serpent" alludes to the tradition found in Num 21:6–9, and the link testifies to the antiquity of the use of the bronze serpent figure. The serpent might well have been an ancient Jerusalem cult symbol (so Rowley, *JBL* 58 [1939] 113–41). But in view of its widespread use, attested in literature and archaeology, as a fertility symbol in Canaanite religion, it is understandable that it should be banned from the temple by a reformer like Hezekiah. In our writer's mind the legitimation for the banning is found in Deut 4:5–18. Regardless of its early associations with Moses, it is possible that by the time of Hezekiah the symbol had become associated with Canaanite worship (see K. R. Joines, *JBL* 87 [1968] 245–56).

ויקרא לו נחשתן "and it was nicknamed 'The Brass Thing.'" See n. 4.a. for the variants suggested. The singular has much to commend it. Frequently, when the phrase ויקרא "and he called" is used in the OT it indicates the presence of a new reality, such as the naming of a new city, or the giving of a new name to a person. So it is that in creation things are "called" by their names (Gen 1:5, etc.). Places of special significance are also given new names (Gen 26:20, etc.). Newly occupied cities are renamed (Judg 1:17; 2 Sam 5:9). The term נחשתן Nehushtan "The Brass Thing" is a clever combination of the similar words נחש "snake" and נחשת "bronze," and outside this passage the word does not exist. It is not a regular word for the deity, but rather a pun on the name and the symbol. In other words, it is a nickname.

5 The sweeping and generous commendation of Hezekiah is most unusual. In light of the comment made later about Josiah (23:25), many scholars detect here a different editorial hand at work. It is argued that Dtr[2] who re-edited the historical work at the time of Josiah would never have agreed with this judgment upon Hezekiah. The argument has some obvious and serious weaknesses. (See the *Introduction*.) Even less likely is the suggestion that by the time the writer recorded his assessment of Josiah he had already forgotten what he had written about Hezekiah (so Barnes, *2 Kings*, 95)!

בטח "he trusted" is a key word in the chapter, and one that is fully exploited by the writer as the narrative unfolds. On the word, see A. Jepsen, "בטח *batach*," *TDOT* 2:88–94. Note the change of word order in Hebrew to emphasize ביהוה "in Yahweh." ואשר היו לפניו "who preceded him" is not a later addition that ignored the figure of David (so Gray, *Kings*, 671) but a comment entirely in keeping with the writer's previous statements. The kings of Judah alone are mentioned here.

6 The inspiration for this judgment is Deut 4:4. The chapter from Deuteronomy is reflected throughout this present narrative. The vocabulary of the complete sentence is quite deuteronomistic (see Weinfeld, *Deuteronomy and the Deuteronomic School*, 336; on the use of דבק "be faithful to, cling to" in the deuteronomistic history see G. Wallis, "דבק *dābaq,*" *TDOT* 3:79–84).

7 "Yahweh was with him" is reminiscent of many OT incidents (see Gen 21:22; 28:15; Deut 20:1, etc.) and it echoes the experience of David in 2 Sam 8:14. That this comment is the "beginning of the legend of good king Hezekiah" which was used by later writers (so Gray, *Kings*, 671) is unfair to the narrative. The comment reciprocates Hezekiah's "clinging to" Yahweh and trusting in Yahweh. That such piety be rejected as fiction is a position which seems quite unreasonable.

There is no hint at all as to when Hezekiah's rebellion took place. A punitive campaign of Sennacherib was launched in 701 B.C., but exactly how long before Hezekiah had declared his independence from Assyria is not clear. Some months would have passed before the news reached Assyria, and then the preparation to launch such a large campaign in the west would have taken considerable time, in some cases at least a year. Another difficulty is that we are not sure whether the events listed in this chapter are in chronological or thematic order.

8 According to Assyrian sources, Sargon II (721–705 B.C.) had conquered Hammo of Gaza and an Egyptian force at Raphia. During this campaign Ashdod also surrendered (see *ANET*, 284–85). Apparently Assyrian control over the area was fairly firm as is supposed by the account of Sennacherib's later invasions. When an opportunity to launch an attack upon Philistia would present itself is impossible to pinpoint. The purpose of the attack would have been to weaken the alliance of Philistia with Assyria, and to open up a clear line of communication with Egypt. Philistia sat astride the main route into Egypt. For precisely the same reasons a strong alliance with Philistia was essential for Assyria, but extremely difficult to maintain. But from Sennacherib's account it was clearly the Assyrian intention not to maintain a large occupying force in the region, but to install pro-Assyrian governors in Philistia. It is this state of affairs which probably emboldened Hezekiah to make such an expedition into the south-west. Following the death of Sargon II in 705 B.C., there was a period of uncertainty before Sennacherib consolidated his grip on the empire. This would have provided a perfect opportunity for such a campaign. See A. Naaman, *VT* 29 (1979) 67 and *BASOR* 214 (1974) 25–39.

ממגדל נוצרים עד עיר מבצר "from watchtower to fortified keep" is an idiomatic expression. See *Comment* on 17:9.

9 All of the following paragraph is identified by many as a quotation from the royal records of Judah concerning the fall of Samaria. It is rather a summary of the events given in more detail in chap. 17, especially from vv 5–6. Its position here serves to set the stage for what follows, and to provide a brief recapitulation of events in the north.

ויהי "now it happened" opens a new paragraph and a new thought. בשנת הרביעית "in the fourth year." Hezekiah's reign, which began in 715 B.C., could not have coincided with the fall of Samaria in 722–720 B.C. Even the revised chronology of 729 as the date of the designation of Hezekiah as king does not fit, and most attempts at revision of the figures (e.g., Snaith to "second") are quite speculative.

עלה "to go up," when used in a military context, is best translated "to launch an attack." שמרון "Samaria" is the capital city. Note the use of the verb ויצר "he besieged."

10 The chronology relative to Hoshea is identical to that in 17:5.

11 See 17:6.

12 The verse is a summary of the extended commentary on the fall of Samaria found in 17:7–23. The verse reflects both the language and thought of the deuteronomist, and forms the conclusion to the historical summary from v 9.

13 This following paragraph (to v 16) provides an interesting counterpoint to the preceding paragraph (vv 9–12). As we have seen above (in *Form/Structure/Setting*) both begin in the same way. The composition of the paragraph is much discussed by commentators and most regard v 13 as secondary. 2 Chr 32 contains a much lengthier account and Isa 36 omits vv 14–16. On this see above. The paragraph offers a very cryptic account of the invasion of Sennacherib in 701 B.C., which is also covered more fully in the Assyrian's own records (*ANET*, 287–89). It offers a date for the invasion and for the loss of the fortified cities of Judah. Hezekiah sends a letter to Sennacherib offering him money for withdrawal. The tribute is imposed and the payment is taken from the palace and temple treasury.

ובארבע עשרה שנה "then in the fourteenth year." Dating back from 701 B.C., the date calculated from Assyrian sources for the invasion, Hezekiah would have become king in 715 B.C. Many prefer an emendation to "twenty-fourth," but this is conjectural.

"All the cities of Judah, that is the fortresses." The strategy of Sennacherib was clearly to regain control over the Philistine territory originally captured by Sargon, and to remove any threat from Judah to the east of the Philistine plain by destroying the garrison towns along the Shephelah still under Judah's control. This is one of the striking points of contact between the biblical account and Sennacherib's own account of the invasion to the west (see *ANET*, 287–89). According to Sennacherib, he captured forty-six of the fortified cities of Judah, plus walled forts and many villages before Hezekiah finally submitted. Many of the cities given over to Assyria were on the coastal plain and included Beth-dagon (Grid 134–156), Joppa (Grid 126–162), Bene-berak (Grid 134–166), Azor (Grid 131–159), Ekron (Grid 136–131), Eltekeh (Grid 128–144?), Timnah (Grid 141–132), Lachish (Grid 135–108), and Libnah (Grid 145–116?). Mentioned in a separate document in the form of a prayer are Azekah and Gath, taken in response to Hezekiah's attacks on the Philistines (see A. Naaman, *BASOR* 214 [1974] 26–28). Additional data on the invasion is probably reflected in Mic 1:10–16 with its list of towns and cities on the Shephelah which suffered attack during the reign of Hezekiah. (However, see A. Naaman, *VT* 29 [1979] 68 for a different interpretation.) Isa 10:27b–32 also contains a reference to an invasion against Jerusalem from the north. However, since most of the other more factual data contains names of cities on the coastal plain and the Shephelah, the reference in Isaiah is probably a figurative representation of a threat to the city. An invasion from the north would not only have been more difficult but seems to detract from Sennacherib's main purpose of strengthening his place on the coastal plain and in Philistia. Again, however, see Naaman, *VT* 29 (1979) 72–74, for a different viewpoint. Much is implied in the simple statement that Sennacherib took the cities of Judah. Such a move would have made Jerusalem completely vulnerable. Strategically the campaign was correct. It was duplicated by Nebuchadrezzar, and even covers some of the same ground as the conquest represented in the book of Joshua (see T. R. Hobbs, *Theodolite* 6 [1982] 5–20).

14 וישלח "and he sent" is a term denoting diplomatic channels of communication, probably by letter (see 19:14). The last line of Sennacherib's account hints at this. Dramatic confirmation of Sennacherib's siege and capture of Lachish (Tell el-Duweir) has been provided by the palace relief in which the city is depicted under attack (see R. D. Barnett, *IEJ* 8 [1958] 161–64). Recent excavations have also confirmed the late eighth century fall of the city (see D. Ussishkin, *Excavations at Tel Lachish 1973–1977*, 67–73). G. W. Ahlstrom's recent attempt to relocate Lachish (see *PEQ* 112 [1980] 7–9) is not well-founded. For a response see G. I. Davies, *PEQ* 114 (1982) 25–28.

חטאתי "I have acted wrongly." The root is normally reserved for "sin" in the OT, but the political use of this term finds a parallel in the use of פשע "transgress" for the rebellion of Mesha of Moab in 1:1 and 3:5.

"Three hundred talents of silver and thirty talents of gold." Sennacherib himself lists eighty talents of gold, eight hundred talents of silver, and other booty taken from Hezekiah during his campaign. The discrepancy is not serious. It can be explained on the basis of different measurements for the metals in the two countries, or a doctoring of the accounts. Compared to other amounts of tribute taken in the various campaigns the amount is not excessive.

15 The language is stereotyped. It is found in descriptions of similar incidents in the books of Kings (1 Kgs 14:25–28; 2 Kgs 12:17–18; 14:14; 16:8–9) thus establishing a clear pattern. Dipping into the temple treasury in this way would have undoubtedly affected the running of the temple affairs.

16 בעת ההיא "it was then." See Montgomery, *JBL* 53 (1934) 49–50, for the idea that this is an "archival expression." It is too vague to be such and represents a more informal use of time. See Tadmor and Cogan, *Bib* 60 (1979) 497–98. It is more typical of historiographic writing of the ANE.

"He stripped the doors." An apparent parallel in 2 Chr 29:3–6 concerning the doors of the temple is, on closer examination, no parallel at all. The Chronicler, who is most interested in cultic matters, mentions the "opening" of the temple doors in either a factual or metaphorical manner, during the reform in the first year of the king's reign. This action possibly remedied some ill done by Ahaz. See McKay, *Religion in Judah*, 16–17. ואת האמנות "and the supports" is a difficult expression, and a *hapax legomenon*. It is normally translated "pillars," with a meaning derived from the root אמן "to trust, to have confidence in." But the meaning is not absolutely clear (see *BDB*, 52–54). The term can be omitted without loss to the sense of the text, but this is not recommended.

17 This verse begins a section of the narrative which continues through 19:9a. On וישלח "he sent," see *Comment* on v 14. The duplication of the beginning of v 14 here has led to an omission by haplography in Isa 36.

תרתן "Tartan." The earliest known reference to the "tartan" is found in the records of Adad-nirari (911–891 B.C.) in which he is clearly an official connected to the Assyrian army (see Luckenbill, *Ancient Records*, vol. 1, § 368). It appears that, befitting his status, he was also involved in administrative duties. רב סריס "Rab-saris" is literally "chief eunuch," but not to be taken in this sense. As with the former, evidence suggests an officer with high rank in the army, and with some administrative powers. רב שקה "Rab-shakeh." If the term שקה is related to the verbal root שקה "to drink," from which the Hebrew משקה "cupbearer" is derived (see Gen 40:5), then the official was connected with the maintenance of the court of the king at home and away. Again, the term need not be taken literally. Many official bureaucratic titles tend to retain their original designation while at the same time the specific function of the official so designated has changed. A comparable phenomenon is seen in the western political titles of "Secretary" (Secretary of State for . . .) or the British government office of Lord Chamberlain.

בחיל כבד "with a sizable force." The mission to Jerusalem was clearly a show of force to intimidate Hezekiah into surrender. The fact that such a force advanced on Jerusalem is confirmed by the record of Sennacherib who states that Jerusalem itself was besieged with the full force of a siege like that at Lachish. If Isa 1:7–8 reflects conditions during the invasion, then it appears as though Sennacherib's description is accurate. The repetition of the clause ויעלו ויבאו "after ascending they arrived" is awkward, and most would favor its omission. It adds nothing to the sense of the passage. The precise location of "the aqueduct of the Upper Pool," where the Assyrian delegation stopped to deliver their ultimatum, is the subject of an *Excursus* below.

18 אליקים "Eliakim" is also mentioned in Isa 20:22, where he is described as replacing Shebna as minister of state. The names were fairly common at this time. Eliakim was Jehoiakim's name before he became king, and nonbiblical references are also known (see Gibson, *Syrian Semitic Inscriptions* 1:24, 65), in which case the persons need not be the same. However, the likelihood of four persons with the same names sharing the same two offices within such a short period of time is very remote. אשר על הבית, lit., "who was over the palace," is not to be translated "royal steward." His role here clearly presupposes a major administrative responsibility, and he was an important member of the king's inner circle of advisers.

הספר "the scribe." Scribal activity was a skilled enough art to require special training. See A. R. Millard, *BA* 45 (1982) 143–53. The function would have been a necessity in any court at this time. המזכיר "the archivist" is clearly connected with the root זכר "to remember," and the context clearly identifies some court official. If, as the etymology of his title suggests, he "remembered" or better "brought to memory" events of national importance, then it is perhaps to Joah ben Asaph that we owe the substance of the record of the meeting between the Assyrian delegation and the Judean officials. On the title see H. J. Boecker, *TZ* 17 (1961) 212–16, and H. Graf von Reventlow *TZ* 15 (1959) 161–75.

19 The stereotyped language with which the Rab-shakeh begins his speech reflects the conventions of diplomacy. In the present context such language provides an effective contrast to the much more direct language of the prophet. The juxtaposition of the word of "the great king" and the word of Yahweh now becomes a deliberate feature of the narrative, and reminiscent of the encounter between Elijah and the messengers of Ahaziah in chap. 1. In this verse we are introduced to the theological use of the term בטח "to trust," which is a motif running through the rest of the narrative. This usage does not support Childs's contention (*Isaiah and the Assyrian Crisis*, 78) that this section is a younger element of deuteronomistic origin. The use of the term in this way is not characteristic of the deuteronomist.

20 על מי בטחת "in whom can you trust?" The irony of the official's question is that indeed "mere words" and trust in Yahweh are sufficient counsel and strength for war. The whole of the early Holy War tradition is predicated upon this assumption (see recently M. Lind, *Yahweh Is a Warrior*, esp. 24–35). The command of Moses at the Sea of Reeds (Exod 14:13–14) is typical of this ideology. Of course, implied in the Assyrian's comment is that Hezekiah's army had been seriously depleted by the campaign.

21 Although not stated in the earlier narrative, it is implied here that Hezekiah had opened negotiations with Egypt. It is a move criticized by Isaiah (Isa 30:2–4; 31:3). Although by this time Egypt had regained some of her former strength and had become a formidable power, her army was no match for the Assyrians. הקנה הרצוץ "broken reed." See the use of this image in Ezek 29:6 and Isa 42:3. It is a telling image of an unreliable ally who will not only fail at the crucial moment, but harm those who rely on her.

22 This comment by the Rab-shakeh is extremely shrewd. Not only has he demolished the political basis for the revolt against Assyria in v 21, but now seeks to show that the religious basis (trust in Yahweh) is equally without foundation. He demonstrates a remarkable knowledge of the internal affairs of Judah, but this is not unexpected, since the campaign would have been carefully prepared and information from agents and deserters would have been used to good advantage. In any event, by this time in the campaign the Assyrians would have collected enough evidence of the centralizing reform of Hezekiah from their observation of the towns already taken. In light of this situation, it is quite unnecessary to see the reference to centralization as deuteronomistic and therefore secondary (so Childs, *Isaiah and the Assyrian Crisis*, 78–79). "We will trust in Yahweh our God" contains an ironic twist since this is precisely what Hezekiah is later advised to do by the prophet.

23 As with the comment above on the centralization of the cult under Hezekiah, this comment reveals a sound intelligence of the military state of affairs in Judah. Sennacherib's own account speaks of the large numbers of desertions from Hezekiah's ranks (*ANET*, 288) indicating a decimation of the Judean army. Judah and Israel rarely used cavalry in their battles, and the Assyrians frequently did. The taunt might then be an invitation to match forces and fight, in which case the Judeans would still lose. In defensive warfare, cavalry, which is ideally suited for the surprise attack, would be less than useful. From records such as 2 Chr 32:1–8 it is clear that most of Hezekiah's preparations were for defensive war with Assyria.

24 איך תשיב את פני פחת "how can you repulse the strength of the officer?" The construction is very awkward and many suggest various emendations (see n. 24.a. above, and Burney, *Notes*, 341–42), but note the parallel construction in Deut 21:11, which would caution against too hasty an emendation of the existing text. Rab-shakeh again tries to disparage the aid provided by Egypt which he clearly, and rightly, regarded as no match for the Assyrians.

25 As a final gesture in this introductory speech, the Rab-shakeh appeals to what was a common ANE belief (see Albrektson, *History and the Gods*, 24–41) namely, that events were directed by the gods, even the gods of those who were defeated. Mesha acknowledges Chemosh's anger with Moab as the reason behind Omri's occupation, and later Cyrus acknowledges the help of Marduk in the taking of Babylon (*ANET*, 315). This apparent sudden shift in the argument of the Rab-shakeh has been interpreted as a "logical inconsistency" by many (see Childs, *Isaiah and the Assyrian Crisis*, 79), but such a judgment is hardly fair. Precise adherence to literary convention in such circumstances can hardly be expected, nor can perfectly consistent logic. In all, the Rab-shakeh has used three important arguments to press home his case: (i) Egypt is not a reliable ally, (ii) Hezekiah has offended Yahweh, and (iii) Yahweh is therefore the initiator of the attack against Judah and Jerusalem. Any of these three arguments would have sufficed, but together they provide an insurmountable logic, which, it appears, is precisely the intention of the writer.

26 This verse provides a transition between the two parts of the Rab-shakeh's initial speech. ארמית "Aramaic" had become a major language of diplomacy. This explains the court officials' knowledge of the language. By the time of the Persians it had become the official language of the Persian Empire. יהודית "Judean" is the west-semitic dialect spoken in Judah at the time. On this point see W. Weinberg, *ZAW* 92 (1980) 186–87. העם אשר על החמה "the soldiers on the ramparts" is a reference to the remaining and discouraged soldiers, who manned their positions on the city walls of Jerusalem, and who witnessed much of the discussion between the Judean and Assyrian officials.

27 In response to the Judeans' request, the Assyrians continue to speak in Hebrew (Judean), and they now press home their appeal for the surrender of Jerusalem. The initial response is dramatic, but not designed as an insult to those standing by (contra Snaith, *IB* 3:295). It is a rather vivid description of the fate of those condemned to a long seige when the will for self-preservation is all that is left to the victims. Already in chap. 6 we have seen the lengths to which victims of such warfare will go. In the annals of warfare such incidents are unfortunately not uncommon.

28 Here again there is a dramatic juxtaposition of the king's word and the prophet's word (see 19:6).

29 In the first section of this renewed verbal attack, the Rab-shakeh turns his attention to the impotence of the Judean monarch. It coincides with the point made in vv 23–24 that the Judean soldiers are no match in their present condition for the fighting power of the Assyrians.

30 הצל יצילנו יהוה ולא תנתן "Yahweh will surely save us and not hand over." Note the emphatic construction. This is standard terminology from the tradition of Holy War (see G. von Rad, *Der heilige Krieg im alten Israel*, 7). Within the OT this promise is normally connected with the victories of

Yahweh's and Israel's army. In the context of the present passage it is an anticipation of the outcome of chap. 19. Through language such as this the arrogance of Sennacherib becomes a major element of the story (see Childs, *Isaiah and the Assyrian Crisis*, 88–90). The argument of the Rab-shakeh now shifts ground, presumably against what he considers the intransigence of the Judeans. He depicts Yahweh's role now not as participant or as initiator of the invasion, but a helpless bystander who can do nothing against the Assyrian designs. Again, to impose upon this the standards of western logic is quite unfair and those commentators who see this section as a secondary insertion on those grounds are to be disregarded.

31 In a final gesture the Rab-shakeh appeals for surrender. עשו אתי ברכה is an unusual use of the term ברכה "blessing," which is normally related to the gift of something. Most translators offer "Make peace with me. . . ." It might be connected with the gift of a token of peace, or the restoration of tribute. See J. Scharbert, "ברך *barak*," *TDOT* 2:279–308, esp. 298–99.

"Each man will eat of his own vine" is a tempting contrast with the threat of v 27, and promises the Judeans security and peace. Wartime propaganda of this kind is very common in the history of warfare, and hardly to be taken at its face value. "And drink from his own well" is a counterpart to the first comment. The book of Proverbs uses this notion as a metaphor of marital faithfulness (Prov 5:15–20), and this might be a double entendre here. Often after a siege the fate of women was to be raped, then taken as hostages to the victor's country (see Amos 7:17). The promise then is that the soldiers will be able to remain with their wives and families. The appeal is clever, if typical propaganda. Discussions in commentaries on the precise location of such good things are out of place and miss the tenor of the speech. The possibility of these promises ever being fulfilled even if the inhabitants of Jerusalem were to surrender is extremely remote.

32 This delay of Sennacherib at Lachish is regarded as temporary. In spite of the promises, forcible transmigrations of peoples are never pleasant, certainly not as depicted here. In the writer's mind the comments of Rab-shakeh are a parody of Deut 8:7–9. The threefold repetition in the description of the land is also found of the wilderness in Jer 2:6, and might reflect a popular form of speech.

ואל שמעו "so do not listen." The theme introduced in v 29 (thought by many to be a contradiction of v 25) is now resurrected. Yahweh is unable to save. By having the Rab-shakeh repeat this assertion, our writer sets a trap to be sprung later. The whole incident now turns on this point.

33 Deut 4:34 is echoed here in an interesting contrast between Yahweh and the gods of the nations. In the mouth of Rab-shakeh, with the support of his arguments, it is mockery of Yahweh. In the context of the deuteronomistic history it is the supreme irony. This is the very theological core of the deuteronomistic history. 2 Kings began with this contrast and established the premise that the gods of the nations were inferior.

But given the immediate historical context, the Rab-shakeh's argument is a telling one, and it involves one view of history and the lessons to be drawn from it. Most of the nations listed here were already mentioned in 17:30–

31. The addition is Arpad (possibly Tell Arfid) north of Aleppo, a Syrian town whose inhabitants were also apparently transferred to Samaria after the fall of the northern kingdom.

34 Implied here, although not mentioned explicitly in either Assyrian or biblical sources, is the information that Sennacherib attacked and subjugated Samaria on this campaign. However, given the circumstances of the north after the deportation of 722 B.C., this hardly seems possible. Here in fact is a reference to the events in chap. 17. The fall of Samaria, as we have seen, was the backdrop against which the invasion of Sennacherib and the threat against Judah is to be viewed. This is the reason for the brief recapitulation of the events of 722 B.C. at the beginning of the present chapter.

35 A useful, but false analogy. In the view of the Rab-shakeh it is a useful argument, but in the complete view of the deuteronomist the emptiness of the comparison is evident. See Deut 4:34.

36 With this verse the narrative undergoes another transition in the form of a "scene change." The action now moves to Hezekiah. "But the people kept silence." In the face of this powerful, if erratic, speech of the Rab-shakeh no answer is forthcoming.

37 See *Comment* on v 18. The scene closes, *exeunt* Judeans. קרועי בגדים is literally "torn of garments." This was a common gesture of despair or remorse, even for Ahab (1 Kgs 21:27). In 2 Kgs 5:7–8 it comes close to the present usage, and to 6:30; 11:14; 22:11, 19. Within the scope of the whole work of the deuteronomist an interesting comparison is to be made between the tearing of clothes as an act of remorse and the act of Jehoiakim in Jer 36:24 (see Nicholson, *Preaching to the Exiles*, 43).

"The words of Rab-shakeh." Again, note the link with 1:5–8 and the similar juxtaposition of the word of the "great king" and the word of Yahweh through his prophet. That the chapter should thus end heightens the drama considerably. By this time the nadir of the fortunes of Hezekiah and Judah has been reached. The crisis is at its worst, and the king has yet to act.

Excursus: 2 Kings 18:17

Amiran, R. "The Water Supply of Israelite Jerusalem." In *Jerusalem Revealed.* Ed. Y. Yadin. Jerusalem: Israel Exploration Society, 1976. 75–78. **Avigad, N.** "Excavations in the Jewish Quarter of the Old City, 1969-1971." In *Jerusalem Revealed.* 41–51. **Broshi, M.** "The Expansion of Jerusalem in the Reigns of Hezekiah and Manasseh." *IEJ* 24 (1974) 21–26. **Burrows, M.** "The Conduit of the Upper Pool." *ZAW* 70 (1958) 221–27. **Simons, J.** *Jerusalem in the Old Testament.* Leiden: E. J. Brill, 1957. **Smith, G. A.** *Jerusalem.* Vol. 1. London: Hodder & Stoughton, 1907. **Wilkinson, J.** "The Pool of Siloam." *Levant* 10 (1978) 116–25.

The precise location of the meeting place of the delegation from Sennacherib and the Judean officials mentioned in 18:17 is a mystery, and an intriguing problem of historical geography. Several items need to be discussed to gain a clear picture of the precise nature of the difficulties involved.

The first concerns the translation of the terms used in the description. The term תעלת is translated by most as "conduit." It is clearly related etymologically

Comment

to the verb עלה "to go up." It is rare in the OT, occurring in 1 Kgs 18:32, 35, 38; 2 Kgs 18:17 (Isa 7:3; 36:2); 20:20; Ezek 31:4; and Job 38:25. In 1 Kgs 18, Ezekiel and Job the word can well be translated as "channel," i.e., a water-channel, cut by hand to direct the flow of water from one place to another. The context clearly shows this. In spite of the etymology, water would normally travel *down!*
מסלת translated "highway," which it literally is. It is related to the verb סלל "to lift up" and is often used of the building of roads through rough terrain, which would involve banking the sides of the path (see Isa 57:14; 62:10; Jer 18:15). Another cognate, סללה, is used of siege-works that are thrown up around a city (2 Kgs 19:32; Jer 6:6; etc.).

שדה כבס is literally "field of the fuller." The verb כבס in the qal form is rare, occurring only here and in related passages. The other translation of "fuller" in Mal 3:2 uses the piel participle, masculine plural (מכבסים). The piel normally means "to wash." There are many occurrences of this form of the verb, especially in the Priestly Code, where it is used of the preparation of sacrifices. The term שדה, although mostly translated "field," means the "open country," and can be used adjectively for "wild" (see discussion on 4:39). In 1 Sam 6:1 in a similar construction it means the country controlled by someone.

The second problem concerns the location of the "Upper Pool." From the available sources it appears that the meeting between the Assyrians and the Judeans took place outside the city, but within earshot of the walls. Isaiah is told to "go out" to meet Ahaz (Isa 7:3), and this is certainly the impression gained from 2 Kgs 18. The impression is reinforced by the proximity of the מסלה "highway," a term never used of city streets (רחבות), and the use of שדה "field," a clear reference to uncultivated land, open country. Bearing this in mind, the theories that place the encounter at the Pool of Siloam, inside the city limits since Hezekiah's reorganization of the city's water supply, are in serious jeopardy. Gray, for example (*Kings,* 678–80), places the encounter at the point where the Tyropoeon and Kidron Valleys meet, at the southern tip of the city of David, that is, at the Pool of Siloam. The term מסלה is understood not as a "highway" but an embankment that separated the Lower (Old) Pool (modern Birket al Hamra and possibly the original Shiloah– Isa 8:6) from the Upper (and presumably the New) Pool which caught water from Hezekiah's tunnel. This pool, it is thought, could have been used by the "fullers."

The problems with this are obvious. The translation of מסלה is unique, the more normal term for such structures being סללה. Gray does not discuss the "conduit." There is also a problem of dating. Isaiah is depicted as going to precisely the same spot (Isa 7:3), but according to Gray the Upper Pool was built by Hezekiah some time later. If the activity of Hezekiah is depicted in Isa 22:9–11, then most of his construction was inside the city, and does not therefore correspond with the meeting place's being in the open country. The identification of the various pools is also to be questioned. R. Amiran (*Jerusalem Revealed,* 75–78) identifies the Lower Pool as that built by Hezekiah. Finally, there is a serious problem of strategy. The route of the Assyrians to Jerusalem would have been quite circuitous if it ended up at the junction of the Tyropoeon and Kidron Valleys. That would have put them in one of the lowest points in the city region, hardly a place, it seems, from which to make the kind of boast recorded in the story. A higher piece of ground is surely called for.

George Adam Smith, *Jerusalem* 1:105, argued for one of the most popular theories, namely, that the Lower Pool was Shiloah and the Upper Pool was the "basin of the Virgin's Fountain," i.e., the Spring of Gihon. The canal connecting the two was the one built by Solomon. This has the advantage of solving five of the problems raised by Gray's theory, but the ones remaining are important. These are the presence of a "highway" in the vicinity, and the strategic problem of the location. This viewpoint is shared by many including M. Burrows, *ZAW* 70 (1958) 221–27. Interestingly enough, Smith abandons this theory in vol. 2 of his work on Jerusalem, but offers no reasons as to why he did so. Smith anticipates the strategic problem by stating that this was a place of abundant water. But it appears that the presence of water at the meeting place was purely incidental. That there was a road going through the Kidron was certainly true, but it was never a major highway, nor could it have been banked up. Incidentally, there is no evidence that the Gihon Spring was anything but a spring. Its location and nature make its use as a reservoir or pool impossible.

A third option (there are in fact others which can be discounted, such as the location of the site near the late Mamilla Pool) is to find the source of the water to the northwest of the city. The demands of this site are that it be outside the city, be a reliable source of water, be near a highway, have a channel running from it, and be a suitable place from the Assyrian point of view for such a meeting. In other words, it had to be on high ground. Since the land rises to the north and west of the city the location is ideal from that point of view. It would also be near a highway, in fact, the main one running north-south through Judea and Samaria. J. Simons (*Jerusalem in the Old Testament*, 334–37) locates to the north of the city an Upper Pool which was constructed by Hezekiah in response to the increase in population the city experienced during his reign. In light of the supposed location the theory has great merit. It is in the catchment area north of the present Damascus Gate and would be just outside the wall constructed by Hezekiah during his rebuilding program (see N. Avigad, *Jerusalem Revealed*, 41–50). The increase in population which necessitated such a building program has now been carefully depicted (see M. Broshi, *IEJ* 24 [1974] 21–26).

The greatest difficulty with Simons's theory is that at present it is impossible to prove archaeologically. The supposed location is in the heart of a modern built-up area. It does have the advantage, however, of locating the canal near the "Mishneh" or second quarter (i.e., enlarged section) of the city. According to Josephus (*Wars*, v. 331) and Zeph 1:11, this was the region in which many craftsmen and artisans had their dwellings.

In the final analysis, none of the theories is completely convincing, but the most plausible is the third.

Explanation

The preceding chapter ended with a view of the near-complete annihilation of the north. The only remnant of Yahwism left is the returned priest who tried, unsuccessfully, to educate the new immigrants in the ways of Yahweh. The effort was a failure. The theological comment, however, left open the distinct possibility of reconstruction since the writer stressed that the God of the deportation was also the God of Israel's past. Initially, in contrast to what precedes, chap. 18 begins with a bright ray of hope. The apostate Ahaz is now followed by Hezekiah, who begins his reign in a very promising way.

Vv 1–8 present a wholesome picture of Hezekiah. He is well-behaved in Yahweh's eyes, he is like David (an important accolade), he purifies the nation from within, and he enlarges the borders of Judah by defeating the Philistines as far south as Gath. In his adherence to the model of David as the ideal king, the writer has fashioned the initial impression of Hezekiah according to the image of David at the outset of his reign (cf. v 7*a* and 2 Sam 8:14).

Explanation 263

The judgment upon this king in v 5 is matched only by that given to Josiah later. With the clear attempt to place Hezekiah's reign within the historical context of the collapse of Israel in vv 9–12, the presentation of Hezekiah exudes hope. The southern nation and its king are healthy.

By vv 13–15 the situation has dramatically changed. Here Judah's borders are broken, and a foreign army has reached the very gates of Jerusalem. From this follows the dramatic confrontation between Hezekiah and Sennacherib, in the persons of their respective envoys. It is a wounded Judah that Hezekiah now represents. Her borders are breached and, reminiscent of chaps. 14 and 16, her temple treasures have been plundered to pay off the invader. The dramatic setting for the conversation that follows is the end of the north, and the serious threat now facing Judah. The survival or death of the south is the issue, and the partners in the struggle are unequally matched. It does not take much reading beyond this to see that the setting is a device for a far more important confrontation, between Assyria as the boastful manipulator of people and events, and Yahweh as the Lord of History.

With v 19 the struggle between these two is joined, and from this point on the narrative moves back and forth between the boastful utterances of Sennacherib, through the Rab-shakeh ("Thus has the great king of Assyria said . . .") and the word of the prophet that appears in chap. 19. The clash is one of appearance and promise. In the strong verbal attack the Rab-shakeh delivers to the guardians of Jerusalem, there is little that can be contradicted. Egypt cannot be relied upon for help (v 21), the army of Judah is now no match for the much larger Assyrian force (vv 23–24), and he has destroyed the northern nation of Samaria and the collection of small nations whose people he has moved into the north (vv 33–34). Sennacherib thus oscillates between boasting of his defeat of Yahweh (vv 22, 30, 35) and claiming that Yahweh is on his side (v 25). But his argument is well-founded and can be supported by recent evidence. His great mistake, however, is in claiming to be himself the architect of history. He believes his power alone is the source of his victory.

In the light of the testimony of the Scriptures and with the advantage of hindsight, the claim is ludicrous. However, even within the context of the recent chapters, the claim is equally ill-founded. In the preceding chapter the writer interpreted the downfall of Samaria, not as the unhappy result of historical accident, but as the deliberate action of a God who had seen his people break covenant. Even though the action resulted in the near-annihilation of his people, God had acted in judgment. Sennacherib is little more than a victim of these circumstances, a point brought out well in the poem that appears in chap. 19. It is also the same insight offered by Isa 10:5–19.

But this is the broader viewpoint of the prophet. In the light of Rab-shakeh's boasting, the people remain silent, almost convinced of the truth of his claims. As yet, God has remained silent. He has not spoken, and he has not responded to the boast. Only later, when the prophet is brought into the story, does it begin to come to any satisfactory conclusion.

The chapter concludes with Hezekiah and Judah in a desperate position. Wounded, they now stand before sheer political and military power. They are battered by the words of a boast which has to it a ring of truth. However, the truth of Sennacherib's claim is dependent upon the vision of the listener. It is only when that boast is brought before the prophet and Yahweh that the focus is correctly adjusted, and that the Assyrian claims are seen for what they really are, bombast.

Isaiah's Prophecy and the Assyrian Retreat (19:1-37)

Bibliography

Note: The bibliography for chap. 18 contains much material relevant to the story in chap. 19. The following lists items in addition to those of the previous chapter.

Albright, W. F. "What are the Cherubim?" *BA* 1 (1938) 1-2. ———. "New Light from Egypt on the Chronology of Israel and Judah." *BASOR* 130 (1953) 4-11. **Ellul, J.** *The Politics of God and the Politics of Man.* Grand Rapids: Eerdmans, 1977. 143-89. **Fichtner, J.** "Jahwes Plan in der Botschaft des Jesajas." *Gottes Weisheit.* Ed. K. D. Fricke. Stuttgart: Calwer Verlag, 1965. 27-43. **Fohrer, G.** "Zion-Jerusalem im Alten Testament." *Studien zur alttestamentliche Theologie und Geschichte (1949-1966).* BZAW 115. Berlin: De Gruyter, 1969. 195-241. **Fullerton, K.** "Isaiah's Attitude in the Sennacherib Campaign." *AJSL* 42 (1925-1926) 1-25. **Gilula, M.** "An Egyptian Parallel to Jer 1:4-5." *VT* 17 (1967) 114. **Hallo, W.** "A Sumerian Prototype for the Prayer of Hezekiah." *AOAT* 25 (1976) 209-24. **Hasel, G. F.** *The Remnant: The History and Theology of the Remnant Idea from Genesis to Isaiah.* AUM 5. Berrien Springs, MI: Andrews University Press, 1972. **Holladay, W. L.** "The Background of Jeremiah's Self-Understanding." *JBL* 83 (1964) 153-64. **Horn, S. H.** "The Chronology of King Hezekiah's Reign." *AUSS* 2 (1964) 40-52. **Janssen, J. M. A.** "Que sait-on actuellement du Pharaon Tirhaqa?" *Bib* 34 (1953) 23-43. **Lambert, W. G.** "Destiny and Divine Intervention in Babylon and Israel." *OTS* 17 (1972) 65-72. **Lettinga, J. P.** "2 Kings xix.37." *VT* 7 (1957) 105-6. **MacDonald, J.** "The Status and Role of the *Naar* in Israelite Society." *JNES* 35 (1976) 147-70. **Mendenhall, G. E.** "The Census Lists of Numbers 1 and 26." *JBL* 77 (1958) 52-67. **Mitchell, H. G.** "Isaiah on the Fate of his People and the Capital." *JBL* 37 (1918) 149-62. **Muilenburg, J.** "The Intercession of the Covenant Mediator." In *Words and Meanings: Essays Presented to David Winton Thomas,* ed. P. R. Ackroyd and B. Lindars, 159-81. Cambridge: Cambridge University Press, 1968. **Orlinsky, H. M.** "The Kings-Isaiah Recensions of the Hezekiah Story." *JQR* 30 (1939-1940) 33-49. **Roberts, J. J. M.** "The Davidic Origin of the Zion Tradition." *JBL* 92 (1973) 329-44. **Stuhlmueller, C.** "The Theology of Creation in Second Isaiah." *CBQ* 21 (1959) 429-67. **Tawil, H.** "The Historicity of 2 Kings 19:24 (Isaiah 37:35): The Problem of YE'ÔRÊ MASÔR." *JNES* 41 (1982) 195-206. **Wevers, J. W.** "Double Readings in the Books of Kings." *JBL* 65 (1946) 307-10. **Wiener, H. M.** "Isaiah and the Siege of Jerusalem." *JSR* 11 (1927) 195-209.

Translation

¹*After Hezekiah the king had listened he tore his clothes, covered himself with sackcloth and entered the Temple.* ²*Then he dispatched* ᵃ *Eliakim his minister, Shebna*

the scribe ᵇ together with the senior priests to Isaiah son of Amoz, the prophet, ᶜ covered in sackcloth. ³ They told him, "Thus has Hezekiah said, 'This is a day of distress, of rebuke and disgrace because children are at the point of birth, ᵃ but the strength to bear them is lacking. ⁴ Perhaps Yahweh your God heard all ᵃ the words of the Rab-shakeh, whom his master the king of Assyria sent to pour scorn on the living God, and perhaps he will rebuke ᵇ the words which Yahweh your God has heard. Now offer a prayer for the few who are left.'" ⁵ Thus did the servants of Hezekiah come to Isaiah, ⁶ and Isaiah said to them, ᵃ "Thus shall you say to your master, 'Thus has Yahweh declared, "Do not be afraid because of the words which you have heard, and with which the attendants of the king of Assyria have blasphemed me. ᵇ ⁷ See, I am about to place a spirit ᵃ in him, and he shall hear a rumor ᵇ and return to his own land. ᶜ I shall make him fall by the sword in his own land."'"

⁸ In the meantime the Rab-shakeh had returned to find the king of Assyria fighting at Libnah, for he had heard that the king had left Lachish. ⁹ Someone had told the king ᵃ that Tirhakah king of Cush had advanced to fight him. ᵇ So ᶜ again he sent messengers to Hezekiah with the following instructions, ¹⁰ᵃ "Thus you shall say to Hezekiah king of Judah, ᵃ 'Do not let your god on whom you depend deceive you with the promise that he will not hand over Jerusalem to the king of Assyria. ¹¹ You yourself have heard what ᵃ the kings of Assyria have done to all their lands, ᵇ completely destroying them, ᶜ so how shall you be delivered? ¹² Have the gods of the nations which my predecessors destroyed ᵃ delivered them, ᵇ such as Gozan, Haran, Reseph, and the people of Eden who were in Tel-assar? ᶜ ¹³ Where ᵃ is the king of Hamath, or the king of Arpad or the king of the city of the Sepharvayyim, Hena, or Ivvah?'"

¹⁴ Hezekiah received the letters ᵃ by the messengers and he read them. ᵇ He then went up to the temple and spread them out before Yahweh. ¹⁵ᵃ Hezekiah ᵇ prayed before ᶜ Yahweh ᵃ and said, "O Yahweh, ᵈ the God of Israel, who dwells among the cherubim, ᵉ you are truly God among all the kingdoms of the earth. It was you who made the heavens and the earth. ¹⁶ Incline your ear and hear Yahweh. Open your eyes ᵃ and see Yahweh. Listen to the words ᵇ of Sennacherib which he has sent ᶜ to mock the living God. ¹⁷ To be sure Yahweh, the kings of Assyria have put nations ᵃ and their lands ᵇ to the sword. ᶜ ¹⁸ They have put ᵃ their gods to the torch, even though they are no gods, but the product of someone's craftsmanship, pieces of wood and stone. But they have destroyed them. ¹⁹ And now Yahweh our God ᵃ save us ᵇ from his clutches. May all the kingdoms of the earth know that you alone are God."

²⁰ Isaiah son of Amoz then sent word to Hezekiah, "Thus has Yahweh the God of Israel ᵃ declared, the one to whom you have prayed in the face of Sennacherib king of Assyria, 'I have heard you.' ᵇ ²¹ This is the word Yahweh has declared concerning him:

'She despises you, she scorns you,	4+2
the virgin daughter of Zion;	
to your back she wags her head,	3+2
the daughter of Jerusalem.	
²² On whom have you poured such scorn, and reviled?	3+3+3
Against whom have you raised your voice, ᵃ	
or lifted your eyes in mockery?	
Against ᵇ the Holy One of Israel!	2
²³ By your messengers ᵃ you have poured scorn on Yahweh,	4+4
and you have said, 'With my force of chariots ᵇ	

I have ascended the heights of the mountains,	3+2
the farthest reaches of Lebanon.	
I have felled [c] *its tallest cedars,*	3+2
its best cypresses. [d]	
I have entered its fullest limits, [e]	3+2
its most fruitful forests.	
24 *I have dug wells,*	2+3
I have drunk foreign [a] *water,*	
with the sole of my foot I have dried up	2+3
all the streams of Egypt. [b]	
25 *Have* [a] *you not heard?*	2+3
In the distant past I planned it,	
in ancient times I devised	3+2
what I am now causing [b] *to happen,*	
that you should turn	2+2+2
fortified cities	
into heaps of ruins	
26 *so that their inhabitants, divested of power,*	2+2
are dismayed and confounded,	
and have become like wild foliage,	3+2+2
like fresh green grass,	
like grass on the rooftops,	
scorched [a] *before it had chance to rise.* [b]	3
27 *I know your sitting down, your going out, your coming in,*	4+3
and your ranting against me.	
28 *It is because you have ranted against me,* [a]	3+3
and your arrogance has come to my attention	
that I will place my hook in your nose,	3+2
my bit in your mouth	
and I will spin you around in the way you came.'	2+2

29 This shall be a sign for you. This year eat what grows without cultivation. In the second year the same.[a] However, in the third year sow, harvest, plant vineyards and eat their fruit. 30 What is left of the house of Judah shall sink roots and bear fruit upwards, 31 because from Jerusalem a remnant shall go out, and from Zion a band of escapees. The zeal of Yahweh[a] will do this. 32 Therefore,[a] thus has Yahweh declared concerning the king of Assyria, he shall not come to this city, nor shall he fire a single arrow at it, nor shall he face it with a shield, nor erect siege works against it. 33 He will go back the way he came. He will not come to this city, says Yahweh. 34 I will protect this city and deliver it[a] but for my sake, and for the sake of David my servant."

35 So it happened that very night[a] that the angel of Yahweh went out and struck down one hundred and eighty-five thousand men of the Assyrian camp. By morning when they were to get up all these were dead. 36 Then[a] Sennacherib king of Assyria retreated and withdrew to live in Nineveh. 37 As he was worshiping in the temple of Nisrock his god (and Adramelek and Sareser)[a] some people attacked him with the sword, then escaped to the land of Ararat. Then Esarhaddon became king in his place.

Notes

2.a. After the verb G^L adds the name Hezekiah.
2.b. The list of names is expanded by G^L. See Burney, *Notes*, 343 for an acceptable explanation.
2.c. The MT order ישעיהו הנביא בן אמוץ "Isaiah the prophet son of Amoz" is quite unusual. G^A changes the text.
3.a. G understands the pointing as לְיֹלֵדָה "to the one in travail," which is accepted by *BHS*. However, the existing form לְלֵדָה can be an infinitive constr; see GKC § 69c.
4.a. כל "all" is omitted by G^L.
4.b. MT reads וְהוֹכִיחַ "and he will rebuke," which is acceptable. G understands וּלְהוֹכִיחַ "and to rebuke."
6.a. Isa 37:6 reads אליהם "unto them." Such changes of prepositions are quite common in the two versions and do not necessitate a change in either version.
6.b. MT אתי "me" is omitted by G^B.
7.a. The word order is changed slightly by G^L to רוח בו "spirit in him."
7.b. G^L adds רעה "evil," reminiscent of 1 Kgs 22:22.
7.c. Isa 37:7 reads אל ארצו "unto his land."
9.a. G^L adds "the king of Assyria."
9.b. הנה "behold" is omitted by Isa 37:9.
9.c. MT reads וישב "so again." Isa 37:9 reads וישמע "and he heard." G of Isaiah and 1QIsa^a incorporate both readings.
10.a-a. Omitted by G^B, although included in most other G MSS.
11.a. MT reads את אשר "what" which is omitted by Isa 37:11. G^B adds כל "all."
11.b. MT reads הארצות "the lands." G^A reads γενεας "generations," a corruption of γαις "lands."
11.c. MT reads להחרימם "completely destroying them," from the root חרם "to ban." Montgomery (*Kings*, 502) suggests a change to להחריב "to kill with a sword," along the lines of v 17. The change is conjectural. Burney's suggestion (*Notes*, 345) would have exactly the opposite effect from the text.
12.a. MT reads שִׁחֲתוּ "they destroyed." Isa 37:12 offers the hiph הִשְׁחִיתוּ.
12.b. אתם "them" is omitted by G^L.
12.c. Spelled בתלשר in Isa 37:12.
13.a. Isa 37:13 offers the simple interrogative איה "where" for the interrogative combined with the 3 masc. sg. suffix as here. See Mic 7:10 for a similar construction.
14.a. G^L reads the sg.
14.b. For ויקראם "and he read them," Isa 37:14 reads ויקראהו "and he read it," although retains a pl noun throughout. See the RSV and NEB translations.
15.a-a. Omitted by G^B.
15.b. 2 Chr 32:20 adds "the king."
15.c. For לפני "before," Isa 37:15 reads אל "unto."
15.d. G^L adds παντοκρατωρ "almighty."
15.e. The phrase is awkward in MT without the preposition, though not unique. See 1 Sam 4:4; 2 Sam 6:2.
16.a. Isa 37:17 reads sg.
16.b. Isa 37:17 precedes this with "all," which some regard as original. (See Gray, *Kings*, 687.)
16.c. Reading the more convenient sg with G.
17.a. Isa 37:18 reads כל הארצות "all the lands," which is redundant.
17.b. The phrase את הארצם "their land" is omitted by G^B. G^L follows Isa 37:18 with the fuller expression πασαν την γην αυτων "all their land."
17.c. See n. 11.c.
18.a. MT reads וְנָתוֹן "they have put," which is irregular and awkward. Montgomery (*Kings*, 504) and Gray (*Kings*, 687), among others, suggest a change to the qal inf abs נָתֹן, which makes good sense of the text.
19.a. The word אלהים "God" is omitted from Isa 37:20.
19.b. MT reads הושיענו "save us." G^L translates with ρυσαι "draw out (of danger)."

20.a. MT reads יהוה אלהי ישראל "Yahweh God of Israel," which is rendered as κυριος ὁ θεος δυναμεων θεος Ισραηλ "the Lord God of Hosts God of Israel" by G^B, and κυριος δυναμεων θεος Ισραηλ "the Lord of Hosts God of Israel" by G^L.
20.b. שמעתי "I have heard" is omitted by Isa 37:21.
22.a. MT reads קול "voice," which is read as קולך "your voice" by G^L.
22.b. For על "against" Isa 37:23 reads אל "unto."
23.a. Isa 37:24 reads עבדיך "your servants."
23.b. Most accept the Qere בְּרֹב "with abundance." See Isa 37:24 and Burney, *Notes,* 345; Gray, *Kings,* 688.
23.c. MT reads וְאֶכְרֹת "let me cut"; G^BL presuppose וָאֶכְרֹת "I have cut."
23.d. MT reads מבחור ברשיו "its best cypresses"; Isa 37:24 reads מִבְחַר "best."
23.e. קצה מלון, lit., "lodging of its end." Gray (*Kings,* 689) suggests מרם קצו "farthest height." The meaning is clear without such an emendation.
24.a. Isa 37:25 omits זרים "foreign."
24.b. On the basis of some references to Egypt in ANE literature, many interpret the Hebrew word מצור as Egypt. See the full discussion in Burney (*Notes,* 346) and Montgomery (*Kings,* 504). G^B's rendering of περιοχης "blockade" and G^L's συνεχεις "unceasing" suggest a word from the root צור "to besiege, fortify." The use of this word with יארים "streams" is unusual. The pl constr of the noun makes it even more so. We translate the term מצור as a poetic form of מצרים "Egypt."
25.a. The first half of the verse is omitted by G^L.
25.b. MT reads וּתְהִי, which is read by most as וַתְּהִי.
26.a. MT reads וּשְׁדֵפָה "scorched," which is rendered by Isa 37:27 as וּשְׁדֵמָה "field." Burney (*Notes,* 346) suggests a passive הַשְּׁדוּף "the scorched one," which is supported in part by 1QIsa^a which reads the Niphal נִשְׁדָף "being scorched."
26.b. MT reads לפני קמה "before rising." Many have adopted Wellhausen's emendation to לפני קמך "before your rising" (see v 27). Others have favored a reading of לפני קדים "before the east wind." See Gray, *Kings,* 689; Montgomery, *Kings,* 505. The latter reading is supported now by 1QIsa^a.
28.a. The first pl is omitted by 1QIsa^a (37:29).
29.a. The term סחיש is unknown. Isa 37:30 reads שחיס, not שחים as implied by BHS. The word implies random growth.
31.a. Isaiah and others join Q in adding צבאות "of Hosts."
32.a. G begins the verse with οὐχ οὕτως "is it not so?"
34.a. Omitted by G.
35.a. MT reads בלילה ההוא "that very night," which is omitted by Isa 37:36. G^BL reads νυκτος "at night."
36.a. The order is different in G^L. The verbs וישב "retreated" and וילך "withdrew" are omitted.
37.a. Qere בָּנָיו "his sons" is supported by G^B. The king was therefore assassinated by his sons according to this tradition.

Form/Structure/Setting

Most commentators have regarded 19:9b–37 as an account parallel to that in 18:17–19:9a. The judgment is made upon the basis of the general similarities between the two passages. The differences that are also obvious are appealed to as signs of different literary origins. For example, R. E. Clements (*Isaiah and the Deliverance of Jerusalem,* 54) notes that in the supposed second account there is "an awkward sense of duplication in the way in which the story of the negotiations is recounted." Gray (*Kings,* 668) states the point much more forcibly. "The difference in emphasis . . . in the sections 18:13–19:7 and 19:9b–35 is undoubtedly owing to the fact that in the first passage the deuteronomic compiler has elaborated on historical tradition and the redactor in the latter on an edifying legend and cult-tradition." Gray distinguishes further between the "literary genre of history" applicable to the first, and "popular anecdotal tradition centering on the prophet Isaiah and the good king Hezekiah."

Our consistent position on matters of this kind has been to interpret a continuous narrative in 2 Kings, unless forced to do otherwise. The case for this is made in the *Introduction*. At this point several reactions are in order. "Awkwardness" in literature of this kind is, like beauty, often in the eye of the beholder. It depends a great deal on the predisposition of the critic, and is an unreliable tool for interpretation. If the duplication noted by Clements were in fact removed, the resulting analysis of the passage would not have been much different. The detection of "awkwardness" is in fact an irrelevant pastime.

Regarding Gray's strong point, it is extremely doubtful whether "history" can be classified as a distinct literary genre as he suggests, and certainly "popular anecdotal tradition" cannot be excluded from the concept of history. The ancient writer would not make such a nice distinction between the two, nor would the modern historian recognize "history" as a literary genre.

The chapter opens, as was noted in the discussion on chap. 18, with the conclusion of the series of events which began in the previous chapter. The chapter division here ranks among the most unfortunate in the Hebrew Bible. Hezekiah mourns his predicament and sends word to Isaiah the prophet. In return, Isaiah offers a word of assurance that Sennacherib's siege would be lifted. Up to this point in the narrative this is the only shaft of light on the dark fortunes of Hezekiah and Judah.

V 10 opens the "second movement" of the biblical account of Sennacherib's siege of Jerusalem, and it is one which eventually ends in complete vindication of the word of Yahweh through the prophet. However, the transition from the first to second paragraph, the bulk of which is carried by v 9, is not an easy one, and many regard the apparent clumsiness of the verse as the remnant of a very ugly seam left by the joining of two separate narratives. The MT version of v 9 reads:

וישמע אל תרהקה מלך כוש	And he heard concerning Tirhakah king of Cush
לאמר הנה יצא להלחם אתך	"Behold he is advancing to fight you,"
וישב וישלח מלאכים אל חזקיהו לאמר	so again he sent messengers to Hezekiah saying:

The parallel account in Isa 37 reads the same except for the verb וישב "so again"; it reads וישמע "so he heard." The Greek text of Isa 37 and the corresponding verse in 1QIsa[a] have a double reading of וישב and וישמע. Burney (*Notes*, 343) regards the reading of וישמע in Isa 37 as a corruption of the original וישב, which appears in MT of 2 Kings. However, in the light of the reading now apparent in 1QIsa[a], which clearly supports the double reading of G, many are of a different opinion. The Hebrew of 2 Kgs 19:9 translates:

"and he heard . . . so again he sent."
The Hebrew of Isa 37 translates:
"and he heard . . . and when he had heard he sent."
G and 1QIsa[a] translate:
"and he heard . . . so again when he had heard then he sent."
Gray favors the G and 1QIsa[a] reading proposing that the וישב be seen as the conclusion of the preceding section. But, in spite of the early date for 1QIsa[a], the G version of Isaiah is a clear example of conflation by a "double reading" of two alternative readings (see J. W. Wevers, *JBL* 65 [1946] 307–10). The MT version of 2 Kgs 19:9 stands.

Structurally, v 9 is to be seen as the beginning of a new section in the narrative. The transition is not easy, but neither is it an impossible one. That the existing awkwardness is the result of a clumsy attempt to bond two originally separate accounts of the same incident begs the question. A parallel exists to the combination of the verbs וישב and וישלח "and he sent" in 1:10, 13. That וישב reappears in v 36 is hardly reason to detach it, and to suggest further that the present version is an abbreviation of a longer account is speculation (see Childs, *Isaiah and the Assyrian Crisis*, 74–75, 96).

Additional literary critical problems arise in this chapter. Vv 21–28 (31) (or vv 22–32) are regarded by many as an interpolation (see O. Kaiser, *Isaiah 1–39*, in loc; Clements, *Isaiah and the Deliverance of Jerusalem*, 57; Childs, *Isaiah and the Assyrian Crisis*, 96–97) which has expanded, but not substantially altered the message of Isaiah. Without this section, it is argued, the text reads smoothly. But this implied superfluity is hardly reason for the section's omission. That the text does read smoothly without the poem is no reason to believe that it originally did so. As will be seen in the *Comment* below, the poem is quite consistent with the thoughts of Isaiah expressed elsewhere on the subject of Assyria.

Since many regard vv 32–34 as the "most original" of the prophecies of Isaiah (see Clements, *Isaiah and the Deliverance of Jerusalem*, 57) v 35 is seen as the climax for the second part of the narrative ("B[2]"), therefore an addition. The process by which this came to be so defies description.

Vv 9b–14, rather than being an awkward duplication of what had already been reported in chap. 18, concentrate on a second, and new, element of the encounter between the Assyrian envoys and the Judean delegation, namely, the written word. Mention is made for the first time of a letter. Not only that but, as most commentators acknowledge, the object of Sennacherib's ridicule is now not Hezekiah, but Yahweh. In the light of the word of Yahweh through the prophet which is spoken in vv 6–7, a confrontation has now developed between the Assyrian and Yahweh, the God of Israel. An important dynamic in this confrontation is the words that each speak. The initiation of this new level of the drama is Hezekiah's visit to the temple, and his spreading out the written words of the Assyrian king before Yahweh (v 14).

Vv 15–19 contain the prayer of appeal to Yahweh, and follow the traditional pattern of invocation (v 15), complaint (vv 16–18), and supplication (v 19), which is only to be expected. The prayer contains many affirmations similar to those found in Deutero-Isaiah, but the traditional structure of the prayer and its language betray nothing necessarily later than the eighth century B.C. To be noted is that the prayer ends with an appeal for the widespread understanding and acknowledgement of the uniqueness of Yahweh (v 19*b*). The appeal is reminiscent of the prayer of Elijah in 1 Kgs 18:36.

In the remainder of the narrative (vv 20–37) the climax of the story is reached in three stages, corresponding to the three aspects of the second response of Isaiah to the appeal of Hezekiah. Many commentators have noted that this response does not contain one straightforward answer, but three, addressed to different audiences, and have made this a reason for further fragmentation of the story (see Clements, *Isaiah and the Deliverance of Jerusalem*, 56–57). The three elements are a taunt-song (vv 20–28), an assurance concerning the remnant of Jerusalem (vv 29–31) and a general announcement of the protection of the city of Jerusalem (vv 32–34). The temptation to use this division as an excuse to search for sources or as an occasion for the classification of each paragraph in terms of degrees of originality is to be avoided, although it is a popular critical endeavor (see Gray, *Kings*, 692; Clements, *Isaiah and the Deliverance of Jerusalem*, 57). The threefold pattern is one detected elsewhere in 2 Kings (see chaps. 1 and 9) and one long recognized by interpreters of the Bible (see J. Licht, *Storytelling in the Bible*, 75–95).

Vv 20–28 constitute the first response to Hezekiah's prayer, and are in the form of a poem. The poem has a clear structure:
  a. Statement (v 21)
  b. Question and answer (v 22)
  c. Boast (vv 23–24)
  d. Question and counter-boast (vv 25–26)
  e. Statement (v 27)
  f. Threat (v 28)
Not only the vocabulary, but the form appears twice in the second part of the book of Isaiah in the context of affirming the greatness of Yahweh in the face of human challenge (Isa 40:18–24, 27–31). The effect of the use of each of these patterns is to stress the power of Yahweh, and in 2 Kgs 19:20–28 the human challenge to that power is Sennacherib's boast of his own greatness (vv 23–24). To counter this boast Yahweh affirms his control of history (vv 25–27) and then threatens judgment (v 28). The poem therefore places the incident of Sennacherib's invasion in its proper perspective. It is to be seen not as a power-struggle between two nations, Assyria and Judah, but as a profoundly theological issue. In this it is quite within the parameters of the OT prophetic tradition (see A. Heschel, *The Prophets* 1:xiii, xiv).

Vv 29–31 constitute a second oracle in this part of Isaiah's response. In keeping with his advice to Ahaz (Isa 7:14) the king is offered a sign by the prophet. The sign does not promise immediate relief from the siege, but it confirms that the prediction concerning Sennacherib is quite reliable. Few, if any, would deny this as an original Isaianic oracle (see G. F. Hasel, *The Remnant*, 332), although many detect here a disjointed passage and regard either vv 29–31 or 30–31 as an interpolation into the whole narrative (see Gray, *Kings*, 692; Clements, *Isaiah and the Deliverance of Jerusalem*, 57). Hasel's own solution is to read the oracle against the background of the supposed second invasion of Sennacherib, a theory which he enthusiastically espouses. The theory is discussed below in *Comment.* As part of the ongoing narrative of chap. 19 the giving of this sign does not intrude or interrupt, but is syntactically sound and consistent with what is known of Isaiah's prophetic activity.

Vv 32–34, the third and final response in this section, is undoubtedly the most controversial of them all. In view of the historical information given in the oracle, most believe that some adjustments need to be made for its background. Clements (*Isaiah and the Deliverance of Jerusalem,* 57) reflects the majority opinion that of the three vv 32–34 is the "most original." Therefore, that it belongs to a later editorial hand is out of the question. Three new historical contexts for the giving of the oracle are suggested: (i) it belongs to an early period of the revolt against Assyria, and was therefore a prophetic encouragement for rebellion; (ii) it belongs to a later Assyrian invasion by either Esarhaddon or Asshurbanipal which bypassed Jerusalem; (iii) it belongs to a second invasion by Sennacherib shortly before his death.

Questions of degrees of originality or authenticity raised by Clements above are without meaning. The verses obviously echo other sentiments of the prophet Isaiah, but can one automatically assume that the lack of such agreement would preclude authenticity? The fundamental question here is whether the oracle agrees with other known facts about the period, and then the function of the oracle in the present context. To answer the first we must digress into a brief historical analysis.

Sennacherib's own account of the invasion is quite specific concerning Jerusalem:

(Hezekiah) I made a prisoner in Jerusalem, his royal residence, like a bird in a cage. I surrounded him with earthwork in order to molest those who were leaving Jerusalem (*ANET,* 288).

Later, Sennacherib mentions the many elite troops who had deserted Hezekiah during this time. Obviously, Sennacherib claims to have erected siegeworks against the city, and held it in siege until a tribute was paid. The problem is to reconcile this with Isaiah's prophecy here, which appears to deny that a siege will in fact take place (see D. Ussishkin, *IEJ* 29 [1979] 137–42).

For the "historicist" two possible alternatives exist: (i) Sennacherib lied; (ii) Isaiah lied. Both are possible. But Sennacherib after all did exact tribute from Hezekiah and therefore some considerable pressure was brought to bear upon the Judean to that end. Exaggeration in the Assyrian sources was indeed common, but there is no reason to doubt his account once the biblical text is carefully examined.

Rab-shakeh and his colleagues were sent to Jerusalem with a "large force" (חיל כבד) to force the surrender of the city, not just for personal protection. On their return from Jerusalem to Libnah, the large force is not mentioned, presumably because it remained at the walls of the city as a reminder of the threat to Jerusalem and its king. Second, the recovery that Isaiah speaks of following the taunt of Sennacherib will take three years, indicating that the devastation of the land and the stranglehold upon the capital city was very real indeed. This again accords with Sennacherib's account of the devastation of forty-six cities of Judah. Third, Isaiah's own description of the siege (Isa 1:7–9; 29:1–4) confirms the sad state of affairs for Judah. Fourth, archeological evidence would suggest a widespread destruction of Judah during this period (see A. Naaman, *VT* 29 [1979] 61–86). There is, therefore, enough corroboration with the biblical record for Sennacherib's account. The oracle in vv 32–34, if viewed from a strict historicist perspective, not only contradicts Sennacherib's record but the biblical one as well.

Any editor or writer composing such a narrative as this would have been well aware of such "contradictions." This must be allowed for, and part of the process of interpretation of the form and structure of the passage is to ascertain why this oracle is included at this particular place in the narrative. In answering this question there is no need to resort to a change in the historical background for the oracle. Instead, we turn to a consistent feature of prophetic proclamation.

The oracle is introduced with the typical prophetic introductory formula לכן כה אמר יהוה "therefore thus has Yahweh declared," and the word which follows appears to be quite contradictory to the current state of affairs. But such a pattern is very common in the prophets, and an essential characteristic of OT prophecy as well as a most fundamental feature of the genre of prophetic literature. Contradictory statements are set out side by side. Amos, for example, offers oracles of condemnation which fly in the face of the material prosperity common in the days of Jeroboam II. In the book of Micah, the juxtaposition of oracles of doom and hope reflects a similar pattern but with opposite effect. This feature of Micah is the most consistently discussed critical issue of the book. The fact that oracles of doom and hope exist side by side within most prophetic books of the OT demonstrates that it is a basic characteristic of the genre of prophetic literature, and that resort to different historical circumstances does not always address the issues of interpretation. Such effort only highlights the problem of the juxtaposition of two opposites; it does not solve it.

In terms of the prophetic tradition, such a "contradiction" is therefore not unusual. In fact, we have seen already in 2 Kgs 7:1–2 that it is a feature of prophecy in the understanding of the deuteronomist. Any interpretation of 2 Kgs 19:32–34 must surely bear these features in mind.

How then does the oracle function? In the light of the historical evidence that the siege had taken and indeed was taking place, to state that it is not happening would be quite ludicrous. In the context the oracle must mean (as in 7:1–2) that the state of affairs that now exists would cease. That it is expressed in such definite language is not surprising since this is a common feature of prophetic style (see for example Jer 4:23–26).

The final paragraph (vv 35–37) is regarded by many as the climax to B², added during the Josianic recension of the deuteronomic history (see *Introduction*). In terms of the narrative, however, it provides not only a fitting but necessary conclusion to what has gone before, especially in vv 21–34. The pattern is typical of the deuteronomist (for example, see 14:6; 17:7–18, etc.). In the final form of the narrative the position is advanced that the attack on Jerusalem is to be seen in its proper perspective as a clash between Assyria and Yahweh. As such, it is doomed to failure; hence the prophetic words to that effect. The character in the story who draws attention to this dimension of the narrative is the prophet Isaiah.

Comment

1 Although v 4 introduces what many have labeled a "prophetic fast liturgy" (see Amos 7:1–6), the tearing of clothes by Hezekiah did not necessarily take place on a public fast day (contra Gray, *Kings*, 684). The Assyrians were hardly likely to be so accommodating as to allow for the coincidence. The activity, like that of putting on sackcloth, was a common way of expressing repentance, remorse, or despair. In this case it duplicates the actions of the king's envoys at the end of the previous chapter, thus heightening the general sense of despair that pervades this part of the narrative. A similar chain reaction is to be seen in chap. 5. ויבא בית יהוה "and he entered the Temple." The absence of the preposition is normal in deuteronomistic literature. Hezekiah's attitude in the face of the Assyrian threat and taunting is to be contrasted with that of other kings, who in similar circumstances took a different course of action (see Ahaz, Zedekiah, and Jehoiakim).

2 After his initial approach to Yahweh, Hezekiah now involves Yahweh's prophet in the sequence of events. Up to this point Isaiah had been very much in the background. The addition of זקני הכהנים "the senior priests" in the party that was sent to Isaiah is important insofar as it implies a concerted effort on the part of the Jerusalem establishment to seek a way out of their dilemma.

ישעיהו בן אמץ "Isaiah son of Amoz" is the first reference to the prophet in the narrative, and he is introduced quite suddenly. Of all the Latter Prophets, with the possible exception of Jonah (see 14:25), Isaiah is the only one mentioned by name in the deuteronomistic history. However, the silence, if it is that, is not to be overinterpreted. The abruptness with which Isaiah is introduced here, and the way in which Elijah is introduced in 1 Kgs 17:1, would imply that they were well-known figures to the original readers. Deuteronomistic versions of the books of the prophets, most clearly exemplified by the book of Jeremiah (see most recently R. P. Carroll, *From Chaos to Covenant, passim*), link the historical and prophetic literature closely. The headings to the final books of the prophets make the clear connection between prophet and history. (On this further see Ackroyd, *SEÅ* 33 (1968) 18–54.) In the present context the abrupt arrival of Isaiah on the scene is dramatic, and one additional step in the series of events begun in chap. 18. The ministry of Micah, a contemporary of Isaiah, is not mentioned in this context, but ought not to be ignored.

3 יום צרה "day of distress" is a concept much used in the deuteronomistic history, and often linked to promises of deliverance and salvation (see Judg 10:14; 1 Sam 10:19; 26:24; 2 Sam 4:9; 1 Kgs 1:29). Hezekiah establishes his dependence upon Yahweh at such a time. The way in which the complaint is expressed involves the use of what must be a popular proverb of the time. Ironically, it also portrays the conditions of siege in which lack of good nourishment would have been commonplace.

4 "Perhaps Yahweh heard." The despair of the king is evident here. Yahweh is depicted as "hearing" and thereby being affected by the words of the Rab-shakeh, and acting upon them even though the mission of the Assyrian was to mock the living God. The theme of mockery (לחרף "to pour scorn") is now introduced into the narrative. As many have pointed out, the second section of the complete story of the siege, B², will shift to a confrontation between Yahweh and the one who mocks Him. השארית הנמצאה "the few who are left." Not only does this phrase anticipate the words of Isaiah later in the chapter, but it correctly describes the sorry situation of Judah after the invasion and siege. The role of the prophet as intercessor is indeed an ancient one and has its roots in the presentation of Moses as the archetypical prophet. On this see J. Muilenburg in *Words and Meanings,* 159–81. Jer 15:1 is an excellent illustration of this role.

5 In this literature, commands are often carried out to the letter. This convention is not only a literary one but adds an air of careful deliberation to the story.

6 The response of the prophet is immediate and the question of the king is met with a word from Yahweh. אל תירא "do not be afraid." The first statement of the prophet is one of reassurance, one which echoes throughout the pages of the OT, not only in the stories of Abraham (Gen 15:1), but also in the tradition of Holy War (Josh 8:1; 10:1; 11:6), which is quite appropriate for the present situation. The word גדפו "they blasphemed" is here intended as a clumsy synonym for חרף "to scorn." Its etymology is uncertain (see G. Wallis, "גדף *gadaph,*" *TDOT* 2:416). נערי is used here of attendants of noble birth, and is an accurate description of the rank of the Rab-shakeh and company. It is not a derogatory term, and the NEB translation of "lackeys" is quite unjustified. See J. MacDonald, *JNES* 35 (1976) 147–70.

7 הנני נתן "I am about to place." The construction is a common one in the deuteronomistic literature, and indicates an immediate future action. It is quite appropriate to the situation. The action involving רוח "a spirit" is reminiscent of both 1 Kgs 22:22 and 2 Kgs 7:6. In the former the prime mover of even the false prophets is a lying spirit under the control of Yahweh, and in the latter the effect of a rumor on an unsuspecting army is devastating. לארצו "to his land" is ambiguous. It can mean one's own territory, i.e., that occupied by Sennacherib, or his homeland. On the death of Sennacherib see *Comment* below on vv 35–37. The initial response of Isaiah to the crisis according to 2 Kgs 18–19 is brief and to the point. Hezekiah is not to fear because Sennacherib's mission will be aborted. There is no mention at this point of any detail of the withdrawal, neither is there any reaction to the boasting and arrogance of the Assyrian. The response is curt. The contrast with the later poetic response in vv 21–28 is marked, in terms of both contents and style. However, this is not to be interpreted automatically as an indicator of separate sources.

8 The initial withdrawal of the Assyrian forces at this stage seems inexplicable, since it was clearly not in response to any show of force by Hezekiah. Such a gesture was quite out of the question. One must assume that the Rab-shakeh returned to Sennacherib to report on the state of the discussions, leaving behind the bulk of his large force to press home the siege. The verse is regarded as awkward by many, and v 8*b* is seen as an editorial addition to combine two originally separate accounts. On this see *Form/Structure/Setting* above. Gray's identification of Libnah as Tel es-Safi (Grid 135–123) at the western end of the Valley of Elah is most unlikely (see *Kings*, 663). If such an identification is granted, the strategic problems connected with such a move and noted by Gray are valid. However, Tel es-Safi is now identified by most with biblical Gath, and Libnah is better identified with Khirbet Tell el-Beida (Grid 145–116) to the east of Lachish. This makes very good sense in terms of the narrative. Sennacherib with his main force is pressing his mission closer to Jerusalem. Such a line of advance rests on a sound historical basis. Gath and Azekah were besieged in sequence during the campaign (see Naaman, *BASOR* 214 [1974] 25–39), and the second identification for Libnah would be in the path of an eastward advance from Gath and Lachish. Both Sennacherib's own account and Mic 1:10–16 attest to extensive military activity over the whole area.

9 אל תרהקה "concerning Tirhakah." The use of אל "unto" and על "upon" as interchangeable is not without precedent in 2 Kings. A more serious problem is the mention of the name Tirhakah, King of the Sudan (Cush). The latter phrase, although not accurate in 701 B.C., is certainly admissable since Tirhakah did become king in *ca.* 698 B.C. Believing him to have been born in 709 B.C., many thought it impossible that he would have been old enough to fulfill the role assigned to him in 2 Kgs 19:9 in 701 B.C., let alone as "king." But this second objection can now be laid aside. As regards his birth, no date has been agreed upon, but there is a growing body of opinion that he was born earlier than was originally suggested, and that he would have been in his late teens, and old enough to have assisted Shabataka in the Delta region at the beginning of the latter's reign. See S. Horn, *AUSS* 4 (1966) 1–28 for details. Although he became a Pharaoh in the Twenty-fifth Dynasty, the reference to him as king of Sudan (Cush) does accurately reflect his origins. See further H. Reviv, *World History of the Jewish People* 4:197.

10 The diplomatic dialogue continues. Childs (*Isaiah and the Assyrian Crisis*, 98) is quite correct in noting a distinct shift in focus from what is normally designated as B¹ to B². "Everything has been subordinated to one theological concern." In contrast to 18:29 the attention has now shifted to the God of Judah and the argumentation has changed accordingly. But this shift in argument and indeed style is to be expected. According to the initial reaction of Hezekiah and the Judeans, the first approach was singularly ineffective. It drove Hezekiah to seek out Yahweh and his prophet. The Assyrians' strategy changes accordingly, and the shift need not be ascribed to the use of different sources. לא תנתן "it will not be handed over" is the language of the Holy War (see von Rad, *Der heilige Krieg im alten Israel*, 7–9). The traditional (Judean) associations of such language and the traditions surrounding Jerusalem-Zion are now challenged by the Assyrians. The confrontation becomes more intense.

11 Historical analogy is a well-worn, but not always safe, way of understanding history in the OT. It does not allow for the "new thing," so well expounded in the prophets before and after the Exile. Here Sennacherib appears to have fallen into a trap of his own making, and the trap is to be sprung later. Among the "kings of Assyria" are undoubtedly Tiglath Pileser, conqueror of northern Israel, and Shalmaneser and Sargon, destroyers of Samaria. The term להחרימם "completely destroying them" is connected to the חרם, the sacred "ban" of the Holy War. Mesha used the term (line 17, see Gibson, *Syrian Semitic Inscriptions* 1:76–77) as Nebo was "devoted" to Ashtar Chemosh. Placing such a city under the ban was to destroy it completely. But that such a claim is made here by Sennacherib does not seem entirely consistent with known Assyrian policy. That policy was to take prisoners and loot from the captured towns and cities. Of course, massive numbers of dead would result from their campaigns, but this was not the primary aim. However, putting the destruction of so many cities in this light would certainly make good propaganda for the Assyrians. It is an effective use of hyperbole.

12 The rhetorical question answers itself, but thereby the drama of the narrative is heightened. As yet, no claim made by Sennacherib can be disputed. For "my predecessors," see above, v 11. All of the cities and regions mentioned here are to be located in northwest Mesopotamia. On Gozan see 17:6. Haran was an important town on the trade route linking Mesopotamia with the territory of the Hittites. Resef is modern Rusafa, and Beth Eden is the Bit Adini conquered by Asshur-nasirpal II in 856 B.C. (*ANET*, 275). Tell Eser is unidentified. All places mentioned reflect the early expansion westwards of Assyria in the ninth century B.C.

13 On these locations, see 17:24 and 18:34. Sennacherib ends a brief historical survey of Assyrian conquests by bringing it up to date with the activities of his recent predecessors at the end of the eighth century B.C. One must assume that the events depicted in chap. 17, which form the literary background to this incident, would also have been in the memory of many who witnessed Sennacherib's attack.

14 This is the first mention of letters in the diplomatic activity of this and the previous chapter. While one must agree that this is "not wholly consistent" (Childs, *Isaiah and the Assyrian Crisis*, 97), not too much should be made of it. A letter would be the normal means of such discourse, and it would certainly reinforce the spoken words of the Assyrian delegation. A parallel exists in chap. 5. Hezekiah's attitude is quite consistent. Having sought out the prophet and requested prayer, he is faced with an additional setback, so he enters the temple himself to pray. Josephus (*Antiq.* x.16) adds what is probably an unhistorical note, but one quite in keeping with the spirit of the complete story. According to him, Hezekiah ridicules the letters, folds them, and then stores them in the temple.

15 Hezekiah's prayer follows the traditional pattern (see *Form/Structure/ Setting* above). In the face of the Assyrian threat, the prayer opens with an ascription of praise (invocation) to Yahweh the God of Israel "who dwells among the cherubim." In the OT the cherubim are winged, nonhuman creatures who have a number of functions. They guard the tree of life (Gen 3:24), are closely associated with the Ark of the covenant (Exod 25:18–20), and accompany Yahweh on his majestic journeys through the heavens (Ps 18:11). In ANE mythology they are intercessors (*karibu*). The temple of Jerusalem was symbolically decorated with them in the great hall and inner sanctuary (1 Kgs 6:19–36). Such was the inspiration of Hezekiah's prayer.

אתה הוא האלהים לבדך "you are truly God." With language anticipating the frequent refrain of Deutero-Isaiah (Isa 42:8; 43:13, 25; 44:6; 45:18; etc.) Hezekiah addresses God, and establishes a major countertheme to the boasting of Sennacherib. Yahweh is beyond comparison "in all the kingdoms of the earth." He is not like those gods defeated by Sennacherib. This refrain occurs frequently in the Latter Prophets (Isa 23:17; Jer 15:4; 24:9; 25:26; 29:18). "It was you who made heaven and earth." Establishing Yahweh's superiority is confirmed by this reference to creation. Beyond the creator no greater power exists, and Hezekiah's faith rests in this confidence. A clear line of thought is seen between these affirmations and the many in Deutero-Isaiah (see C. Stuhlmueller, *CBQ* 21 [1959] 429–67). Generalizations about the "late" theology represented here are not particularly helpful (see Childs, *Isaiah and the Assyrian Crisis*, 99).

16 הטה יהוה אזנך "incline your ear, Yahweh." The plea is typical of so many prayers of lament and complaint (Ps 17:6; 71:2; 86:1; 102:13; 116:2; etc.). פקח עיניך "open your eyes." Such anthropomorphisms are quaint to modern ears, but quite consistent with the general outlook of the OT, and in fact contain a profound insight into the human personality (see B. de Geradon, "L'homme à l'image de Dieu," *NRT* 11 [1958] 683–95). The appeal is for Yahweh to grasp fully the significance of what was happening. לחרף "to mock." The key theme of confrontation is again repeated. Sennacherib the scoffer now stands as the antithesis of God and his people. The theme has already been played by the deuteronomist (see 1 Sam 17:10, 36, 45).

17 Here Hezekiah admits the basic premise of Sennacherib's boast. The kings of Assyria have indeed put nation after nation to the sword. In terms of the story, such an admission only serves to weaken the position of Hezekiah and Judah outwardly.

18 The downfall of a nation in the ANE world-view meant that its god was defeated and discredited. Assyrian records do not mention the burning of idols, but rather their capture and use as booty (see Sargon's treatment of the idols of Gath and Ashdod, *ANET* 286). The comment here in fact reflects typical Israelite treatment of such idols and symbols of apostasy (see Deut 7:5; 2 Kgs 23:11). כי לא אלהים המה "even though they are no gods." Although this comment sounds like a precursor of Isa 44, it does have affinities with Jer 2:13, and is not to be regarded as "late" theology.

מעשה ידי אדם "the product of someone's craftsmanship" is a typical deuteronomistic epithet, and quite derogatory when applied to gods (see Deut 4:28; Weinfeld, *Deuteronomy and the Deuteronomic School*, 324). Yahweh is distinguished from the gods thus far destroyed. They are עץ ואבן "wood and stone," he is אלהים חי "the living God" (v 16).

19 ועתה "and now." This is an important juncture in the prayer, but not at all common in other such prayers (Ps 39:8 being one of the few examples). With this call for deliverance an appeal is made for Yahweh's reputation to be defended. Twice before in the deuteronomistic history, during confrontations between champions of Yahweh and foreign threats, similar appeals have been made. One was David's fight with Goliath (1 Sam 17:46) and the other was Elijah's struggle with the prophets of Baal on Carmel (1 Kgs 18:37). It is perhaps at this point in the prayer and indeed the narrative that the fortunes of Judah begin to change.

Comment

20 With this verse begins the series of three answers to the prayer of Hezekiah. The response to Hezekiah's plea for a hearing is immediately positive. Yahweh has heard, and now speaks his will against Sennacherib. The combination of hearing, seeing, and acting is a common one in the OT (see de Geradon, *NRT* 11 [1958] 683–91). It is also found in the story of the Exodus (Exod 3:7–8). The narrative now turns against Sennacherib, and this verse is the antithesis of 18:17–19. The prophecy of Isaiah which follows also appears in an almost identical form in Isa 37:21–35. The major difference between the two is that Isaiah rarely uses the *matres lectionis* (vowel letters).

21 Sennacherib's word is now opposed by the word of Yahweh. As we have seen, this theme is not new in the book (see chap. 1). On the authenticity of the oracle see above *Form/Structure/Setting*, and G. F. Hasel, *The Remnant*, 332–33. Gray's ambiguous designation of the oracle as "on the periphery of the Isaianic tradition" (*Kings*, 688) is less than helpful. On analysis, there is little in the oracle that cannot be confidently attributed to Isaiah. לעגה
. . . בזה "she despises . . . she scorns" are synonyms. In Num 15:31 the language is descriptive of breaking the law, by willful sinning and "holding the word of God in contempt." The term לעג figures as a gesture of contempt in one of Jeremiah's "Confessions" (Jer 20:7). Of great interest is the use of the term in 1 Sam 17:42, almost as though the confrontation between David and Goliath served as a model for the present one. "She wags her head" is a typical gesture of derision (Ps 22:8). Note that the verse is in perfect parallelism.

22 Mocking and abusing Jerusalem is here equated with mocking and abusing Yahweh. This is established by the use of the questions in the verse, and is a classic element of the religious motifs associated with the tradition of Jerusalem-Zion (e.g., Ps 2). (At this stage, discussion of the origins of the Jerusalem-Zion tradition as a pre-Israelite motif, or a later development of the David tradition, is irrelevant. See the helpful discussion in Clements, *Isaiah and the Deliverance of Jerusalem*, 72–89.) "Scorn" is now a constant theme of the story. קדוש ישראל "the Holy One of Israel" is the most Isaianic of all the epithets of Yahweh in the OT. Gray's suggestion (*Kings*, 688–90) that the *kinah* meter demands the omission of one phrase, such as ועל מי "against whom" or קול "voice," begs the question.

23 All ideas of the poem as an interpolation are seriously challenged by this verse. The introduction to the verse embeds the poem in the current context. ביד מלאכיך "by the hand of your messengers." The term יד "hand" is understood here as "agency." The hand is a symbol of the action of the will in OT anthropology (see de Geradon, *NRT* 11 [1958] 683–95). The link with the previous narrative is clear, but the poem now rehearses not only the activities of the Rab-shakeh and company, but also the previous conquests of the western lands. Any conquest with chariotry in mountainous regions is slightly ludicrous. Ideal terrain for such a war vehicle is the flat open plain with good drainage. Hills and mountains are highly unsuitable. Therefore, such feats as are mentioned here quickly go into records as events of importance. Luckenbill, *Ancient Records* 2:236, offers an example of such a case after Assyrian wars with tribes to the east.

ירכתי לבנון "the farthest reaches of Lebanon" is an expression similar to ירכתי צפון "the farthest north" in Isa 14:13. In a similar context (Isa

6:22) the term יַרְכְּה "flank, side" is used poetically of "limits" or "edges." The expression here is in apposition to מְרוֹם הָרִים, the high mountainous region of inland Lebanon. The boast continues with its retelling of Sennacherib's conquest of Lebanon, and the verse ends with a parallel construction:

ואכרת קומת ארזיו מבחור ברשיו   I have felled its tallest cedars,
                                                         its best cypresses.
ואבואה מלון קצה יער כרמלו   I have entered its fullest limits,
                                                  its most fruitful forests.

The translation of מלון קצה is difficult. Isa 1:8 uses the first noun as "lodge," i.e., a temporary shelter in a vegetable field. NEB's "farthest corners" is a good paraphrase.

24 קרתי "I have dug wells" occurs only here and in Isa 37:25, but the context provides a clue to its meaning. The exact significance of the action is not clear. Jewish tradition has taken this comment and incorporated it into the narrative of Sennacherib's invasion. According to the tradition, so large was Sennacherib's army that it drank the Jordan dry! (See L. Ginzberg, *Legends of the Jews* 4:267.)

זרים "foreign" is omitted by Isa 37:25, but it forms a parallel to the term מצור "Egypt." "With the sole of my foot I have dried up" is again picked up by Jewish legend. Destruction of streams by stepping on them, which seems to be what is implied here, is an unusual feat, unless it refers to either natural springs which are blocked up in this way, or to canals (perhaps a better reading of יארי), the banks of which are broken down by treading on them. מצור is properly translated as "fortress," which might support the idea of blocking up water supplies in time of siege. Most, however, read it as a poetic form of the word for Egypt (מצרים). The Akkadian expression is *musur*. That Sennacherib never reached Egypt does not necessarily matter at this point. His activities on the Philistine coastal plain demonstrated that he had cleared the way for such a move. According to Josephus (*Antiq.* x. 18–20) an Egyptian campaign was tried but repulsed.

25 In language closely resembling the common refrain of Deutero-Isaiah the prophet puts the boasting of Sennacherib in proper perspective. His movements are nothing more than actions done under the direction of the one, sovereign God. The affinities with Isa 10 cannot escape attention. After the opening question, the verse resorts to parallelism:

למרחוק אתה עשיתי   In the distant past I planned it,
למימי קדם ויצרתיה   in ancient times I devised it.

The notion of "creation" and "forming" of persons is connected with election for service in the OT (see W. L. Holladay, *JBL* 83 [1964] 153–64), but the terms are more widespread. An Egyptian parallel to Jer 1:4–10 has been found, which places the concept firmly within some royal ideologies of the ANE (see M. Gilula, *VT* 17 [1967] 114). The possibility exists here that Yahweh is parodying the claims of Sennacherib as a divinely appointed king. However, this claim that Sennacherib is appointed by Yahweh to destroy fortified cities is consistent with the sentiment in Isa 10:5–11. Amos had previously expounded the theme of Yahweh's involvement in the affairs of nations (Amos 9:7). It is a theme fully exploited by Deutero-Isaiah (Isa 41:2; 55:1).

26 Now follows a general, but accurate, picture of people under siege; confused, they are as vulnerable as fresh wild grass. קצרי יד "divested of power" is literally "short-handed," i.e., unable to act. The imagery of grass carries great meaning in the Near East. Its greenery is short-lived, especially under the hot winds of spring (see Isa 40:6–8). "Grass on the rooftops" refers to a phenomenon still seen today in some of the rural villages of the West Bank. Grass grows out of the roofs of some of the smaller mud houses, but for only a short while. Unable to put down long roots, it withers, then dies.

לפני קמה "before it had a chance to rise." The *Translation* follows MT. The sentence, however, is complete with the term ושדפה "scorched," and the link with what follows has intrigued commentators since Wellhausen. On the variants see n. 26.b. As it stands, the text makes sense, especially given the imagery it is trying to evoke.

27 Ps 139:2 portrays in similar fashion the all-encompassing knowledge of Yahweh. Nothing the Assyrian can do is beyond the knowledge of Yahweh, least of all his ranting. The root of התרגזך "your ranting" is רגז "tremble," and the image is humorous, with a double entendre. It can be used of "standing in fear" of Yahweh (Ps 4:5), and, as here, of trembling with rage.

28 At this point the climax of the poem is reached. Now Yahweh utters his word of condemnation and judgment against the Assyrian. The use of יען "because" makes it clear that the judgment is in direct response to the arrogance of Sennacherib. Yahweh's attention has been drawn to Sennacherib's ravings. שמתי חחי באפך "I will place my hook in your nose." This is a copy of what appears to have been an Assyrian practice. See also Amos 4:2. Ashurbanipal's treatment of Uateʾ is an illustration of the practice: "Upon an oracle command of Asshur and Ninlil I pierced his cheeks with the sharp-edged tool, my personal weapon . . . I put the ring in his jaw" (*ANET*, 300). והשבתיך בדרך "and I will spin you around." The poem ends on the note sounded by the initial response of the prophet in v 7.

29 This verse begins the second oracular response of this series, and promises that in spite of some privations from the invasion, Jerusalem will retain her inhabitants, albeit reduced in number, because Yahweh is her champion. The gift of a אות "sign" is typically Isaianic (see Isa 7:10; 8:1) and indicates a special interpretation of some ordinary natural phenomenon. ספיח from the root ספח "pour out" indicates that which had spilled from the sower's basket, or that which had dropped its own seeds to grow without cultivation. סחיש is a *hapax legomenon*, taken by most as a synonym for ספיח.

31 Hasel's study has distinguished between the notion of the future eschatological remnant and the survivors of the historical misfortune, and sees this as a reference to the latter. The oracle promises simply enough that survivors will continue life in the city. However, it is unlikely that such a watertight division can be made between the two notions, since in Isaiah's thought historical analogy frequently becomes part of the stuff of his eschatology (see Isa 9:1–11). קנאת יהוה תעשה זאת "the zeal of Yahweh will do this." See Isa 9:6. The action is initiated solely by the will of Yahweh, and brought to its conclusion through Him.

32 The text from here to the end of the chapter forms a fitting conclusion to all that has been said thus far. On the difficult historical problem of the two-invasion theory see above on *Form/Structure/Setting*.

34 להושיעה "and deliver it." The use of this verb is quite consistent with our interpretation of the historical background for this chapter. Although it has religious content, it is also used for deliverance from enemies in the deuteronomistic literature. The motivation for the deliverance "for the sake of David" (cf. 1 Kgs 11:36; 2 Kgs 8:19; 20:6) lends strong support to the close connection found between the Jerusalem-Zion tradition and the Davidic covenant. (see J. J. M. Roberts, *JBL* 92 [1973] 329–44). It also makes clear that, in spite of his piety and his prayer, Hezekiah played a minor role in the deliverance. Yahweh acted because of his promise to David.

35 The final section of the chapter climaxes the narrative with its fulfillment of the prophetic word. That the disaster which befell the Assyrian army is not mentioned in Assyrian sources is to be expected. What appears as an independent tradition of Herodotus (bk. 2.141) and quoted by Josephus (*Antiq.* x.17–23) attests to some violent disaster which caused Sennacherib to withdraw from Judah. "The angel of Yahweh went out." The description is reminiscent of the final plague of the Exodus (see Exod 12). The number מאה שמונים וחמשה אלף "one hundred and eighty-five thousand" seems large compared with contemporary figures of armies. It is particularly large when it is presented as only part of Sennacherib's total army. By comparison, the allied force, including Ahab, at the battle of Karkar totaled only fifty thousand (*ANET*, 278), and Shalmaneser III's expedition to the west was made with a total army of one hundred and twenty thousand men (*ANET*, 280). The military term אלף can be reinterpreted as a smaller unit of fighting men (see G. E. Mendenhall, *JBL* 77 [1958] 52–67) but this is generally reserved for the premonarchic times. During the monarchy the term means one thousand.

36 ויסע וילך וישב "and he retreated and he went and he lived." This sequence reverses the sequence of verbs in 18:17 describing Sennacherib's approach to Jerusalem. Supporters of the two-invasion theory argue that the verse implies that Sennacherib died very shortly after returning to his homeland, but nothing in the verse states that. The term וישב "and he lived" implies in fact that he was there over a period of time before his death. Compressing history in this manner is typical of biblical narrative.

37 ויהי "and it was" is not unusual in OT history writing (contra Clements, *Isaiah and the Deliverance of Jerusalem*, 11). See 1:17 and v. 35. The deity נסרך "Nisrock" is unknown but possibly is to be identified with Nusku (see Ringgren, *Religions of the Ancient Near East*, 63, for a description of this god). אדרמלך "Adramelek" is better rendered as Adad-melek (see *Comment* on 17:31), which is an easy transition to make. שראצר "Sareser" is the god Nergal-shar-eser.

The circumstances surrounding Sennacherib's death in approximately 680 B.C. are shrouded in mystery. Asshurbanipal, grandson of Sennacherib, left a brief description of the punishment meted out to the assassins (*ANET*, 288), but details of his demise are not given. Esarhaddon (*ANET*, 289–90) provides evidence of a struggle for the succession after Sennacherib's death, but few details are given. Part of the army was involved in the fight against Esarhaddon, and the fact that Esarhaddon was Sennacherib's youngest son strengthens the impression that Sennacherib was killed by others of his sons (see the variants, n. 37.a.). This is indeed confirmed by the Babylonian Chronicle, which states simply, "on the 20th day of the month Tebet Sennacherib, king of Assyria, was killed by his son in rebellion" (see A. K. Grayson, *Texts from Cuneiform Sources* 4:81). אררט "Ararat" is Armenia where they were eventually captured and punished by Esarhaddon.

Explanation

The desperate situation with which the reader was left at the end of the previous chapter is now resolved in a grand manner, with an enlarged cast of characters now in the drama. From the very one-sided debate between the envoys of two opposing kings, the action moves to the palace and to the reaction of the king. Also brought into the story are the prophet Isaiah, the true interpreter of history, and Yahweh, its architect.

In reaction to the words of Sennacherib, Hezekiah enters a symbolic state of despair (v 1b), and then makes the move that begins the course of recovery. He approaches the prophet Isaiah with the situation (vv 3–4). Up to this point the prophet has been standing in the wings waiting for his cue. His first words seem inadequate in response to the desperate state of affairs, "Do not be afraid . . ." (v 6), but in the sentence that follows, the prophet places the struggle in its correct perspective. Not simply his claim about the weakness of Yahweh, but all his words, especially his claims to absolute power, are seen for what they are—blasphemy against Yahweh. Sennacherib had erected an idol of his own invincibility and paraded this before the inhabitants of Judah and Jerusalem. This now is the subject of attack, since nothing can claim this kind of authority or allegiance. Ellul's insight is welcome at this point. The Judeans were invited to accept this authority by surrendering and following Sennacherib into exile (see Ellul, *The Politics of God and the Politics of Man*, 158–59). For the faithful Yahwist nothing other than Yahweh can claim allegiance. Even to consider that an alternative authority is possible is blasphemy. The word of God is straightforward in its reaction to this claim: Sennacherib would fail in his attempt to take Jerusalem (vv 6–7).

This word of Yahweh is met in the story with another, delayed attempt by Sennacherib to press home his claim (vv 10–13). He repeats the comment about the inadequacy of Yahweh and the superiority of Sennacherib's own power over against the power of Yahweh or any other god. Hezekiah's reaction is to pray, and the substance of his prayer brings the real issue to the fore: Yahweh is the incomparable, unequalled creator, and it is on this basis that Hezekiah appeals for deliverance (vv 15–19). The response of Yahweh through the prophet is direct and overpowering. In tones reminiscent of Job's confrontation with God, the poetic oracle of the prophet establishes the true nature of the current struggle. It is a struggle between the claims of Sennacherib to be the powerful ruler and conqueror of the world, and Yahweh as creator of heaven and earth and lord of history. The outcome is never in doubt when the struggle is seen in these terms. Yahweh alone must prevail.

The response of Sennacherib to this claim is never made. He is a silent actor in the rest of the drama, retreating to his homeland, where he eventually dies in simple fulfillment of the word of Yahweh (vv 35–38).

The perspective of this chapter is grand. Against the most powerful nation on earth, Yahweh prevails easily. Yet concessions are made to Sennacherib. There is no contradiction of the series of events which led up to the fall of Samaria. The historical survey of attacks on Lebanon and the coast, and even the approach to the borders of Egypt, are acknowledged. The answer to why they had happened is found in the poem's forceful statement of the complete control of Yahweh over events—events that mean both good or evil. Yahweh is a God who exists, yet his very existence means more. He is creator, and controler of history.

As stated previously, the notion of an angry God punishing or allowing others to punish his disobedient people, is one that sits very uneasily with the modern mind. The alternative, however, is even less attractive. The choice is one between an aroused or an apathetic God, a random or a purposive world, a just or a capricious universe. The exile of the north, the attack and subsequent exile of the south have meaning within this context. Outside it, they lose all meaning.

Hezekiah and Isaiah (20:1–21)

Bibliography

Ackroyd, P. R. "An Interpretation of the Babylonian Exile: 2 Kings 20, Isaiah 38–39." *SJT* 27 (1974) 329–52. **Allen, L. C.** "Cuckoos in the Textual Nest at 2 Kings xx. 13, Isa xlii. 10, xlix. 24, Ps xxii. 17, and 2 Chron. 9. *JTS* 22 (1971) 143–50. **Childs, B. S.** *Memory and Tradition in Israel.* SBT 37. London: SCM Press, 1962. **Cornfeld, G.**, and **Freedman, D. N.** *The Archaeology of the Bible Book by Book.* San Francisco: Harper & Row, 1980. 156. **Halpern, B.** *The Constitution of the Monarchy in Israel.* HSM 25. Chico, CA: Scholars Press, 1981. 1–12. **Illman, K. J.** *Old Testament Formulas about Death.* Åbo: Research Institute of Åbo Academic Foundation, 1979. 24–25. **Landy, D.**, ed. *Culture, Disease and Healing: Studies in Medical Anthropology.* New York: Macmillan, 1978. 278–85. **Millard, A. R.** "Baladan, the Father of Merodach Baladan." *TynB* 22 (1971) 125–26. **Munch, P. A.** *The Expression Bayyom Hahhu: Is It an Eschatological Terminus Technicus?* Oslo: J. Dybwad, 1936. **Pilch, J. J.** "Biblical Leprosy and Body Symbolism." *BTB* 11 (1981) 108–13. **Warren, C.**, and **Conder, C. R.** *The Survey of Western Palestine: Jerusalem.* London: The Committee of the Palestine Exploration Fund, 1884. 353–56. **Wilkinson, J.** "The Pool of Siloam." *Levant* 10 (1978) 116–25. **Zakowitz, J.** "2 Kings 20:7—Isaiah 38:21–22" (Heb. with Eng. summary). *BMik* 50 (1972) 302–5.

Translation

¹ *In those days Hezekiah became deathly sick, and Isaiah son of Amoz the prophet visited him and said, "Thus has Yahweh declared, 'Put your house in order, because you shall die and not recover.'"* ² *Then Hezekiah* ᵃ *turned to face* ᵇ *the wall and prayed to Yahweh with these words,* ³ *"O Yahweh, I pray remember how I conducted myself before you truthfully, and with sound intentions, and I did what was right in your eyes." And Hezekiah cried bitterly.* ⁴ *Now Isaiah had not yet gone out as far as the middle court* ᵃ *when the word of Yahweh came to him,* ⁵ *"Turn around* ᵃ *and say to Hezekiah the prince of my people,* ᵇ *'Thus has Yahweh the God of David your father declared, "I have heard your prayer, and I have seen your tears.* ᶜ *I am about to heal you, and on the third day you shall go up to the temple.* ᶜ ⁶ *I will add fifteen years to your life. I will deliver this city from the grip of the king of Assyria, and I will protect this city* ᵃ *for my own sake, and for the sake of my servant David."'"* ᵃ ⁷ *Isaiah then said, "Fetch a cake of figs!" So they brought it and placed it on the sore so that he would recover.* ᵃ ⁸ *Hezekiah asked Isaiah, "What sign shall there be that Yahweh will heal me, and that I shall go up to the temple on the third day?"* ⁹ *Isaiah replied, "This shall be the sign* ᵃ *from Yahweh himself that he will do the thing he promised. Shall* ᵇ *the shadow go forward or back ten paces?"* ¹⁰ *Hezekiah said, "It is easier for the shadow to lengthen by ten paces than for it to go back ten paces."* ¹¹ *But Isaiah the prophet prayed to Yahweh and he brought back the shadow the same distance it had already descended* ᵃ *on the steps of Ahaz,* ᵇ *by ten paces.* ¹² *At that time Merodach* ᵃ *Baladan son of Baladan king of Babylon sent letters* ᵇ *and a gift* ᶜ *to Hezekiah, because he had heard that Hezekiah was sick.* ¹³ *Hezekiah heard* ᵃ *of them, and showed the delegation all his treasure house,* ᵇ *the silver and the gold, the spices and the fine oil, his armory and everything that was to be found in his treasuries. There was nothing in his palace or his realm* ᶜ *that he did not show them.* ¹⁴ *Isaiah the prophet then came to Hezekiah the king and asked him, "What did these men have to say? Where did they come from?"* ᵃ *Hezekiah replied, "They came* ᵇ *from a distant country, from Babylon."* ¹⁵ *He then asked, "What did they see in your palace?" To which Hezekiah replied, "They saw everything in the palace. There was nothing in my land* ᵃ *they did not see."* ᵇ ¹⁶ *Isaiah said to Hezekiah, "Hear Yahweh's* ᵃ *word.* ¹⁷ *'The days are soon to come when everything in your palace, all that your predecessors have kept until this day will be carried off to Babylon. Not a thing shall be left,' says Yahweh.* ¹⁸ *'Some of your sons which are born to you* ᵃ *shall be taken, and they shall become officials* ᵇ *in the palace of the king of Babylon.'"* ¹⁹ *Hezekiah responded to Isaiah with the words, "Yahweh's word is good." But to himself he said, "Why not? Since there will be peace and prosperity in my time!"* ᵃ ²⁰ *Now the remainder of the activities of Hezekiah, all his great deeds, and how* ᵃ *he constructed the pool and the aqueduct and brought water into the city, are they not written in the records of the kings of Judah?* ²¹ *Hezekiah slept with his fathers,* ᵃ *and Manasseh his son became king in his place.*

Notes

2.a. The proper name is omitted here, but supplied by Isa 38:2.
2.b. The phrase פניו "his face" is omitted by Gᴮ, but included in Gᴺ.

4.a. The sentence ישעיהו לא יצא העיר התיכנה "Isaiah had not yet gone out as far as the middle city" is awkward and omitted by Isa 38:4. Qere suggests הָצֵר "court, village" which most accept.

5.a. For שוּב "turn around" Isa 38:5 reads הָלוֹךְ "go," a normal use of the infinitive absolute.

5.b. The phrase נגיד עמי "prince of my people" is omitted by Isa 38:5.

5.c–c. Omitted by Isa 38:5.

6.a–a. Omitted by Isa 38:6.

7.a. MT reads וַיֶּחִי "and he recovered," which is pointed as וִיחִי "so that he would recover" in Isa 38:21. Opinion is divided on this reading. Both are grammatically acceptable, although the latter introduces an element of modality into the sentence. MT as it stands makes the healing definite.

9.a. לְךָ "to you" is omitted by G^B.

9.b. MT reads הָלַךְ "it went." Burney (*Notes*, 349) suggests הֲיֵלֵךְ "shall it go" which is in keeping with the context. But see Montgomery, *Kings*, 512.

11.a. The subject of ירדה "it had descended" (fem) is not הַצֵּל (masc) "the shadow." Burney (*Notes*, 349) suggests the addition of הַשֶּׁמֶשׁ "the sun."

11.b. G^B omits any mention of the "steps of Ahaz."

12.a. With Isa 39:1, G and others read מרדך "Merodach" for MT's בראדך "Berodach."

12.b. For ספרים "letters" Burney (*Notes*, 351) suggests סריסים "eunuchs," which is an ingenious but conjectural change.

12.c. MT reads מנחה "a gift," G^B offers μαναων "tribute," but G^L reads the more correct δωρα "gifts."

13.a. MT reads וישמע "he heard"; Isa 39:2 and G^B read וישמח "he rejoiced," which is adopted by both Montgomery (*Kings*, 513) and Gray (*Kings*, 701).

13.b. MT reads בית נכתה "treasure house," which is simply transliterated by G. It is thought to be related to the Akkadian *bit nakamti* "treasure house."

13.c. For בכל ממשלתו "in all his realm" G^L reads παντι θησαυρω "all his treasury."

14.a. This is a more polite form of the question.

14.b. G adds אלי "to me."

15.a. G reads ἐν τῷ οἴκῳ μου "in my palace."

15.b. G adds ἀλλα και τα ἐν τοις θησαυροις μου "but also the things which are in my treasuries."

16.a. Isa 39:5 adds צבאות "of Hosts"; G^L adds παντοκρατορος "Almighty."

18.a. Gray (*Kings*, 701) following 1QIsa^a reads ממעיך "from your loins." This is a possible, though unnecessary, emendation.

18.b. G^L translates with σπαδοντας "eunuchs."

19.a. The latter part of this verse is omitted by G^B, and included in a slightly different form in G^L.

20.a. G^L adds "all."

21.a. G^L adds "and was buried with his fathers in David's city."

Form/Structure/Setting

The chapter consists of two major parts, vv 1–11 and vv 12–19, each of which begins with a temporal phrase. The first of these sections deals with Hezekiah's sickness and recovery, and the second with Hezekiah's initial involvement with Babylon. The chapter concludes in vv 20–21 with a typical ending and the addition of some incidental information. It becomes obvious in the chapter that through subtle use of concepts and the juxtaposition of established themes the deuteronomist has woven a narrative of considerable art and effect. The tendency of many commentators to break up the chapter into constituent sources clouds this impression, and is therefore to be resisted.

Vv 1–11 tells of an initial confirmation by Yahweh of the terminal nature of Hezekiah's undisclosed sickness (v 1) and the reaction of Hezekiah to the news. It appears to be one of dependence upon Yahweh (vv 2–3). This is then followed by a further word, and the promise of recovery for the king.

Form/Structure/Setting

The king's reign is extended by fifteen years as a result (vv 4–6). This word is in turn accompanied by a gesture of healing on the part of the prophet (v 7). The paragraph concludes with an additional sign, given at Hezekiah's request. It symbolizes the rolling back of time (vv 8–11). The outline of the section is:
a. The situation (v 1a)
b. Yahweh's word (vv 1b, 4–7)
c. The king's reaction (vv 2–3, 8)
d. Additional sign (vv 9–11)

V 1a thus establishes the setting for the first prophetic word (v 1b), to which the king reacts with a gesture of repentance. The second word, accompanied by a symbolic action, also evokes a reaction from the king, which in turn gives rise to another sign. This general outline is supported by the syntax. V 1 begins with a perfect (חלה "became sick") and each main verb that follows is consecutive (ויבא "he came," ויאמר "he said," ויסב "he turned," ויתפלל "he prayed," ויבך "he cried"). V 4 breaks the sequence with a pluperfect (לא יצא "he had not gone out") and a clause denoting synchronicity (ודבר יהוה היה "and the word of Yahweh came").

The second word from the prophet (vv 4–7), while initially appearing to be a reversal of the first, contains much more than that. The king will in fact be healed, but also he will visit the temple, his reign will be extended by fifteen years, and Jerusalem will be protected. The reasons for this change are clearly given: Yahweh has seen Hezekiah's tears and heard his prayer. He will answer for his own sake and for David's. This last point is emphasized by the use of the self-designation of Yahweh as אלהי דוד אביך "the God of David your father."

Finally, Isaiah adopts an ancient medical practice, healing a sore on the body, as a symbolic action anticipating the fulfillment of the prophetic word. To be noted in the reaction of the king is that it concentrates only on one aspect of the positive word to the king, namely, that which concerns the king alone. Excluded from his reaction are any mention of the extension of the reign and the deliverance of the city. The sign which follows, concerning the shadow, deals with the complete prophetic word (את הדבר אשר דבר "the thing he promised" v 9a) and is almost a rebuke for Hezekiah's self-centeredness.

This structure, however, needs to be seen in the light of numerous allusions also found in the chapter. Many have pointed out that Isaiah is behaving here not so much like an eighth-century B.C. "classical" prophet, but rather like Elijah or Elisha. The observation is quite sound, although by no means an excuse for designating this image as "secondary." But this allusion is not alone. Sickness is a common motif in 2 Kings. Ahaziah is deathly ill (1:1), Ben Hadad likewise suffers (chap. 8) and even Elisha himself eventually succumbs (chap. 13). But alongside this motif is that of recovery. In chap. 1 the king dies, but in chap. 2 the waters are "healed." Elisha has not only raised a dead boy (chap. 4) but in chap. 13 his bones bring to life a corpse. But the motif has more than one, obvious application; it is often symbolic of the fate of the nation. This is especially true of chap. 1 (see T. R. Hobbs, "2 Kings 1 and 2: Unity and Purpose," *Studies in Religion/Sciences religieuses*

13 [1984] 327–34) and of chap. 13. It cannot escape attention that the language of chap. 13 and the present description are virtually the same. The two kings pray and are heard by Yahweh, who responds with deliverance. A nice touch is seen in the use of two homonyms for the actions of the kings. The antecedents are to be found in Exod 3:9 and Deut 26:5–9. As the judgment is delayed in chap. 13 through the intervention of a deliverer, so also the death of Hezekiah and the fate of Jerusalem is postponed. What more appropriate sign to convey this than the one which depicts the rolling back of time (vv 8–11)? See also 13:22; 14:26–27.

Vv 12–19 concern the visit to Hezekiah of a delegation from Merodach Baladan, erstwhile king of Babylon. The incident is seen clearly as temporarily connected with the preceding one (v 12 בעת ההיא "at that time"). The whole is a continuous narrative from v 12 to v 19, as is seen by the series of consecutive verbs. A close examination also reveals that the structure of this second part of the chapter is identical to the first. An historical setting is established against which a prophetic word is given. The king then reacts to that word:

Setting: The king is sick.   The visitors from Babylon.
Word: You shall die/recover.   Exile will take place.
Reaction: Prayer—delay.   Shrugs it off—delay.

The balance reveals that as the king's life will be extended, so will the lifetime of the nation of Judah. The king's cynical comment in v 19 clearly demonstrates this, although it is not explicitly stated in the prophecy other than the reference to "the coming days" (v 17).

Again, however, other motifs and allusions are to be seen. Babylon appears here for the first time in 2 Kings, except for the merely incidental reference in 17:24. But from this point on Babylon is an element in the narrative to be reckoned with. But its role ought to be compared to the role of the nations which is assigned in 1 and 2 Kings. We have already seen that in chaps. 1–3 Moab emerges in rebellion as a symbol of the decay in Israel. Loss of territory is seen throughout the book as a sign of judgment (10:32; 12:17–18; 15:29). The appearance of Babylon at the time of Hezekiah's blatant self-interest is an example of the blindness of the king to historical reality, and a foretaste of a threatening future. This is reinforced by the use made in the chapter of the verb ראה "to see." Before Yahweh delivers, he sees (v 5) and Babylon's "seeing" the complete stock of the treasuries and kingdom prefigures the opposite. This in fact is the point of the oracle of the prophet in response to the visit (vv 17–18). Nor can it be missed, finally, that the treasures of the temple and the palace have already suffered at the hands of foreign invaders (1 Kgs 14:25–28; 2 Kgs 12:17–18; 14:14; 16:8–9; 18:3–6). With such a strong theme already established the intention of the writer is clear. Yet Hezekiah gladly uncovers the complete treasure of the kingdom for the Babylonians' acquisitive gaze.

Comment

In contrast to the incidents in chaps. 18 and 19 those in chap. 20 are vaguely dated. Hezekiah's sickness is בימים ההם "in those days" (v 1), but it is clear from the narrative that this is around the time of the invasion. The fifteen years added to his life plus the fourteen years before the invasion complete the twenty-nine for the full reign (18:2). The visit of Merodach Baladan's delegation is also imprecisely dated (בעת ההיא "at that time" v 12). Synchronizing this information with other data known of the Babylonian is not easy, and estimates for the date of the visit vary from 714 B.C. to 703 B.C. According to the Babylonian Chronicle (Grayson, *Texts from Cuneiform Sources* 5:75–77), Merodach Baladan was king of Babylon from 720 to 709 B.C., during which time hostilities persisted between him and Sargon II of Assyria. The Babylonian was then deposed and fled to Elam. For a brief spell in 703 B.C. he was once again king, but was defeated by Sennacherib in battle and withdrew. His exile is not located, but is again probably Elam. He was replaced by Bel-ibni who reigned for three years (702–700 B.C.) and was followed by Sennacherib's own son, Asshurnadin-shumi for the next six years (699–694 B.C.). A constant feature of this period was war between Assyria and Elam in which Babylon figured prominently. The question is, does this chronology provide a suitable framework for Merodach Baladan's visit to Hezekiah? Since Hezekiah was sick during the visit, and since his sickness was shortlived, the biblical dating for the visit is during the Assyrian attack on Judah (i.e., in or shortly after 701 B.C.). Strictly speaking, Merodach Baladan was not "king of Babylon" in 701 B.C., so most place his visit earlier (see Fricke, *Zweite Konigen,* 295—between 714–711 B.C.; Gray, *Kings,* 701— between 711–703 B.C.; see also H. Reviv, *World History of the Jewish People* 4:196). The main argument for an early dating is the chronological problem of Merodach Baladan's erratic career as king of Babylon. A secondary argument concerns the amount of temple treasure still in the Judean treasury. Since much was taken for payment to Sennacherib, it is argued that there would have been little left to show the Babylonian.

The chronology, however, does not preclude a visit from the Babylonian in or around 701 B.C. The fact that he was called "king" is unimportant. Deposed monarchs tend more than ever to hold on to such titles, and since the Babylonian was involved in fighting against Assyria from Elam during much of the time he was in exile, such a title would have been even more important to him. The lack of treasure in the treasury (see 18:13–15) needs to be seen in the light of Hezekiah's complete reign. Hezekiah's resourcefulness is seen in the account of his reign in 2 Chr 32:27–31. The achievements listed there took place for the most part after the Assyrian invasion and throw some light on the ability of the Judeans to recover from material loss. There is much to be said for the suggestion that the visit of Merodach Baladan to Hezekiah was to discuss issues of mutual significance, and in the case of the former to seek aid to make a final grab at his throne (so Thiele, *Mysterious Numbers,* 159).

1 The use of the plural ימים "days" is deliberately vague and imprecise (see G. Brin, "The Formulas X-ימי and X-יום," *ZAW* 93 [1981] 183–96). The phrase is used both for past events (Gen 6:4; Exod 2:11, 23; Deut 17:9; 19:17; 26:3; etc.) and for future events (Jer 3:16; 3:18). See further P. A. Munch, *The Expression Bayyom Hahhu*; S. J. de Vries, *Yesterday, Today and Tomorrow.* Even though the incident is vaguely dated, the fact that Hezekiah is given fifteen more years to live (out of twenty-nine) means that the sickness afflicted him during or shortly after the invasion of the Assyrians. חלה למות "he became deathly sick." See the similar comment on Elisha in 13:14. On the expression "sickness unto death" see K. J. Illman, *Old Testament Formulas about Death*, 24–25.

ישעיהו בן אמוץ הנביא "Isaiah son of Amoz the prophet." This new introduction can be taken as indication of a separate origin for the following verses; however, the repetition of the detail is best understood as a device to emphasize the prophet's role in the events. In 19:2 and 19:20 the prophet has already been introduced in the same way. Here the prophet functions as a royal adviser to ensure a proper and orderly succession. Such "putting the house in order" would avoid any unnecessary strife after the death of the reigning king. David's indecision over these matters led to a bloody conflict. כי מת אתה "because you shall die": this is an immediate future construction as in Gen 50:5. Often such announcements of impending death are seen as judgment (1 Sam 2:31–34; 1 Kgs 14:10; 2 Kgs 1:2–4), but here there is no hint that the king is being punished for any misdeeds. Gray's suggestion (*Kings*, 697) that this incident took place in 695 B.C. is unlikely in view of the fifteen years added to the king's life. ולא תחיה "and not recover." See Ahaziah's request in 1:1–4.

2 "Then Hezekiah turned to face the wall." That this gesture of the king's is to be interpreted as a "renunciation of the world and a turning to God alone" (so Gray, *Kings*, 696) is too fanciful and overworks the image of Hezekiah as a pious king. The face has great symbolic significance in the ancient world, and gestures to do with the face are extremely important. Hence "lifting the face" is a synonym for showing respect and indicates that a person is thus treated as an equal. "Turning the face" either toward or away is to either pay attention or to disregard something or somebody (see 1 Kgs 21:4; Ezek 7:22). In spite of his piety and faithfulness thus far, the news of his impending death (he was only thirty-nine) sent Hezekiah into a sulk! The gesture is finally accompanied by a prayer as in 19:15; but there are some marked differences in tone. Whereas the first prayer of the king concentrated on the greatness and majesty of Yahweh, the second prayer concentrates on Hezekiah's own piety.

3 The prayer is rather self-serving, and provides a sharp contrast to the image of the king presented thus far in the account of his reign. On the use of זכר "remember" with God as the subject, see B. S. Childs, *Memory and Tradition in Israel*, 31–34; and Eising, "זָכַר zakhar," *TDOT* 4:69–72.

התהלכתי באמת ובלבב שלם "I conducted myself truthfully and with sound intentions" is a metaphorical use of the hithp form of the verb "to go." The claim, while no doubt quite well-founded, is to be contrasted with 19:34, where Yahweh delivers the city "for my sake and for the sake of David my servant." Jewish tradition expands upon Hezekiah's piety and love for the Torah (see Ginzberg, *Legends of the Jews* 4:273–77). However, the contrast between the two attitudes, the king's and Yahweh's, is taken further by Hezekiah's weeping—presumably for himself! The phrase is deuteronomistic and used most significantly as a demand upon the people at the inauguration of the monarchy (1 Sam 12:24) and of the successor to David (1 Kgs 2:4; 3:6).

4 For העיר התיכנה "the middle city," see n. 4.a above. The temple had an upper, a middle, and an outer court (see G. A. Smith, *Jerusalem* 2:256). But, since this incident would have taken place in the palace and not the temple, one of the courts of the king's residence was clearly in mind.

5 With this verse some "Davidic" concepts are introduced into the story. In v 3 Hezekiah has identified himself with the ideal king and is now addressed in similar fashion by the phrase נגיד עמי "prince of my people." Although this is omitted from Isa 38:5, it is consistent with the flavor of the section. If it is true that the term "prince" atrophied in the later monarchy (so B. Halpern, *The Constitution of the Monarchy in Israel*, 1–12), then its use here recalls an earlier ideal. אלהי דוד אביך "God of David your father." The connection is thus finally established. Note the use of דוד אבי "David my father" in Solomon's prayer in 1 Kgs 8. שמעתי . . . ראיתי "I have heard . . . I have seen." Note the combination of verbs again; see *Comment* on 19:20.

6 "I will add to your days." The only commandment with a promise attached grants length of days for honoring parents. Such an allusion is consistent with the Davidic theme running through this section. David, the "father" of Hezekiah, was referred to in the previous verse.

The latter part of this verse is almost a repetition of 19:34. This, together with the substantial differences from Isa 38:6, has caused a number of commentators to omit the end of the verse (see Montgomery, *Kings*, 507). But left in place, the half-verse links the current incident with the attack on Jerusalem by Sennacherib and preserves the thematic link between Jerusalem and David. The repetition, in fact, stresses an important point. Yahweh, for his own sake and for the sake of David, is committed to the preservation of the city. This is a correction to Hezekiah's prayer which is centered on his own achievements.

7 In this incident Isaiah functions less like the character of Isaiah of Jerusalem as has been developed thus far in the OT, and more like Elisha (especially in 2:20–22), who also had to deal with issues of life and death. Many commentators have consistently failed to understand the significance of this story because of this difference and have therefore denied it to be an authentic narrative of Isaiah, deeming it out of place in 2 Kgs 20. The statement "After the high sounding oracle of Isaiah this prescription sounds ludicrous" (Gray, *Kings*, 698) is typical. The verse is relegated to the dubious status of "editorial gloss."

The nature of Hezekiah's sickness is not exactly clear from this incident, but it obviously involved some kind of skin disorder. The term used to describe it, שחין "sore," is most probably related to a root meaning "to be hot," "to be inflamed," and is used of the plague against Egypt (Exod 9), the skin maladies in Lev 13, and the affliction of Job in Job 2. In Deut 28, it is a judgment for the breaking of covenant. Note that in this last reference the judgment is translated as "boils of Egypt," linking it with Exod 9. What is overlooked by many commentators is that the treatment prescribed for such an ailment in this verse has many parallels in the ancient Mediterranean world. See briefly R. K. Harrison, "Medicine," *IDB* 3:331–34. Pliny refers to something very similar (*Natural History* 23.63) and it is clear that in Ugarit raisins were used medicinally for similar ailments in animals (*UT* 55.28; 56.33). The first point to be made, then, is that in the light of these parallels the cure cannot be regarded as ludicrous, but something which ancient Mediterranean society took for granted. This fact alone demands some considerable measure of adjustment on the part of western commentators.

Neither is the cure of Hezekiah's skin malady to be seen strictly in the category of miracle, that is, a supernatural and unexplainable act, but rather within the realm of folk medicine. Later Jewish tradition (*Berakot* 10b, *Pesahim* 56a, *Tg. Yerushalmi* 9.36c–36d) connects Hezekiah with books of medical remedies. If this is the case, the clinical medicinal properties of dates judged according to modern western medical standards are really beside the point, since the judgments are made on the basis of standards of health and science that were quite out of reach for the ancient practitioner of such medical arts. A less kind description of this approach is "medical materialism." Diagnoses and remedies of afflictions like this one abound in folk medicine from many different parts of the world (see D. Landy, ed., *Culture, Disease and Healing: Studies in Medical Anthropology,* 278–85).

The action of the prophet has in fact as much social as medical significance. Mary Douglas's excellent study of the social significance of the symbol of the body (*Natural Symbols,* New York: Pantheon, 1970) has demonstrated that the treatment of the body and the afflictions of the body, especially in certain older societies, mirror the view of the community and the social order held by the larger group. This has been further developed in her book *Purity and Danger: An Analysis of the Concepts of Pollution and Taboo,* in which the special emphasis is on the social significance of body limits, exits, and entrances (see Leviticus), such as the skin, mouth, anus, etc.

The act of healing has social meaning for the king. It symbolizes the "provision of personal and social meaning for the life problems created by the sickness/disease" (J. J. Pilch, *BTB* 11 [1981] 108–13); in other words, it represents for the ailing king a form of "rehabilitation" back into society. But within the context of the narrative, through the repeated allusions to the ancestor of Hezekiah, David, we have noticed that the king is himself representative of the dynasty. Further, the link between the Davidic dynasty and Jerusalem is reinforced by the deliberate literary link between the two in the oracle of the prophet to the dying king. Not only will he be healed, but the city will be delivered also (see vv 5–6). The fact that the skin of the king is affected by the sickness clearly reflects the attack on the limits of the society carried out by the Assyrians which reached the very gates of Jerusalem, but stopped there.

One further point to be noted is that the healing is limited. The king will live for fifteen years (v 6), not forever. As regards the rest, to be noted is that once the Assyrian threat is removed another reappears in the form of Merodach Baladan, for whom Hezekiah drops all the guards (vv 12–19).

8 The incident that now follows from v 8 to v 12 is a strange one, again the occasion for much discussion among commentators. The discussion revolves frequently around the question of its "authenticity." Considered to be marks against its originality are the different versions in Isa 38 and 2 Chr 32, the implied *non sequitur* (why does Hezekiah need a sign when he is already recovered?), and the additional role of Isaiah as miracle-worker and astronomer, which again contrasts sharply with his role as a judgment prophet (so Fricke, *Zweite Königen*, 290). The contrasts are clear and correctly observed. That they have been correctly interpreted is something we challenge.

"What sign?" The question of this king at this point, especially in the light of the preceding incident, throws his character into sharp relief. A sign has in fact already been given, yet he is unable to interpret it, and is unsure enough to ask for another more immediate one. The sequence reflects the healing of the paralytic in the Synoptic Gospels (Mark 2:1–12) in which the original word of Jesus is followed up, because of the cynicism of the onlookers, with a "which is easier . . ." riddle.

9 זה לך האות "this shall be the sign for you." The same words were addressed to Moses at his call (Exod 3:12) and to Eli at the announcement of his family's downfall (1 Sam 2:34), and previously to Hezekiah himself after the lifting of the siege of Jerusalem (19:29). Although the term אות "sign" is often translated with the idea of miracle in mind, it is not always to be so understood. See J. Helfmeyer, "אות 'oth," *TDOT* 1:167–88. "That Yahweh will do the thing he promised" is a promise fraught with meaning. The issue between the king and the prophet is that of obedience to the word of God, a theme very common in the prophetic tradition.

הלך הצל "the shadow went." The past tense is very awkward, which is reflected in the desire to emend the verb and add an interrogative. The suggestion certainly tidies up the grammar and syntax. מעלות "paces" is from the root עלה and is often translated "degrees" on the understanding that a timepiece (a sundial) is in mind here. Normally the term means "steps," and is so understood here. The question is straightforward, and involves the turning back of time, indicated by the length of a shadow measured in steps or paces. The presentation of a second, more difficult option is, as we have seen, reflected elsewhere in the Bible.

10 יחזקיהו "Yehezekiah." The different form of the name is unimportant. It appears as a proper name in the Ophel Inscription (see Gibson, *Syrian Semitic Inscriptions* 1:24–25). Such alternative spellings are common throughout the books of Kings. לנטות "to lengthen" means literally "to stretch out." That this is presented as the easier of the two options indicates that the incident took place during the afternoon when shadows would normally lengthen. The response of Hezekiah is significant. Here, he insists that the sun cannot alter its course by retreating, yet in 19:15–20 he had extolled Yahweh's creative powers! The deterioration in the character of Hezekiah is marked.

11 וישב "and he brought back." In this hiphil with the direct object marker the implied subject must be Yahweh. MT of the present text has a confusion of genders (see n. 11.a.), and Isa 38:8 accommodates this with the addition of השמש "the sun." Many (e.g., Montgomery, *Kings*, 512) would argue that the clause אשר ירדה במעלות אחז "which it had descended on the steps of Ahaz" is a gloss from Isa 38.

Exactly what is meant by "the steps of Ahaz" is difficult to say. Earlier scholarship interpreted the term as reference to a timepiece, a sundial (see Burney, *Notes*, 349–50; Montgomery, *Kings*, 508–9 and the literature cited there). A clue in Herodotus (bk. 2.109) leads many to suggest that it was brought from a foreign country (Babylon?) and was therefore a pagan symbol.

However, on the basis of 1QIsa^a of Isa 38:8, which reads עלית "upper chamber" for מעלות "steps," the notion of a sundial has been abandoned. The "upper chamber" is thought by Gray to have been a "shrine for astral worship" (*Kings,* 619). The observation is very imaginative, however, since such a structure would not have been left standing in the reform of Hezekiah with which the account of his reign begins.

There is nothing in the text to indicate such a structure, and little to indicate a sundial. Y. Yadin has suggested the most common-sense approach, namely, that the "steps of Ahaz" were precisely that—steps built up to a roof or higher structure, upon which shadows were cast at certain times of the day. Whether the device was used as a means of telling the time is unlikely, since it is not stated. (For a diagram of Yadin's reconstruction see Cornfeld and Freedman, *Archaeology of the Bible,* 156.) Although the precise details are vague, the intention of the illustration is clear. The incident implies, as do the previous ones, that there will be a delay. Hezekiah is reprieved, Jerusalem is saved, time is stretched, for the sake of David.

12 בעת ההיא "at that time" is a precise linking of the following incident with the preceding one, and not to be dismissed as an editorial gloss (so Gray, *Kings,* 696). Similar use of the phrase is seen in Gen 21:22; 38:1. בראדך בלאדן "Berodach Baladan." His Babylonian name, Marduk-apal-iddina, is better rendered in Hebrew as מראדך "Merodach." In Babylonian sources his patronym is Son of Yakin, which is probably a dynastic title, since his kingdom is frequently referred to as Bit-Yakin. "Because he had heard that Hezekiah was sick": note the parallel with 8:7, 29. A courtesy visit, it was also designed to secure from Hezekiah some help in regaining his kingdom from the Assyrians before Hezekiah died.

13 את כל בית נכתה "all the treasure house." The descriptive noun must here be used of the contents of the building. Qere reads it as נכתו "his treasure" but the term is still unique and variously understood. The suggestion that it is connected to the Akkadian *nakamti* "treasure" is ingenious. The term נכאת "spices" might have been misprinted here, since הבשמים "the spices" is mentioned in the next phrase. Although most see the phrase הטוב "the fine" as adjectival, the absence of a corresponding article on שמן "oil" is ungrammatical.

The inclusion of the royal armory on the tour was hardly a discreet move on the part of the king. ואת כל אשר נמצא באוצרתיו "and everything that was to be found in his treasuries" (see 18:15). This was presumably some time after the withdrawal of Sennacherib, and Hezekiah had time to replenish his coffers. The expression הראם "he showed them," however, has sinister significance (see above, *Form/Structure/Setting*). The incident appears as a portent for 24:13. The presence of so many personal suffixes on the buildings and contents of the various storehouses is significant in representing hubris on the part of Hezekiah. The model king is in fact one who will not set out to accumulate for himself such things (Deut 17:17). On this see Halpern, *The Constitution of the Monarchy in Israel,* 175–250. Hezekiah now falls short of the Davidic ideal.

14 Isaiah reacts with suspicion, which is quite consistent with his insistence on reliance upon Yahweh alone for help and with his utter distrust of foreign alliances (see Isa 30:1–7; 31:1–3). These suspicions are confirmed by Hezekiah's response. Babylon is called a ארץ רחוקה "distant land." Foreigners from such distant lands are to be viewed with suspicion and are often agents of judgment (see Deut 29:21; Josh 9:6, 9; 1 Kgs 8:46).

16 Out of this third incident comes a further word from Yahweh which forms a climax to the chapter. The word, however, casts a dark shadow over all the positive incidents that precede.

17 הנה ימים באים "the days are soon to come." This is a general announcement about some future event. The expression that follows confirms the suspicions about the contents of the palace and temple and anticipates 25:13. עד היום הזה "until this day" is not an etiological expression here but simply a confirmation of the terminus ad quem of the temporal sequence (see Childs, "The Formula, 'Until This Day'," *JBL* 82 [1963] 279–92). "Not a thing shall be left." Note the contrast with 19:31.

18 ומבניך "some of your sons" means direct descendants, among whom could be considered Jehoiachin and Zedekiah. On סריסים "officials," see the discussion on 9:32. This verse has suffered at the hands of commentators. For Montgomery (*Kings*, 510) it is "an apocryphal prediction" from post–597 B.C. For Gray it represents "editorial retouching" (*Kings*, 702), and for Burney it is exilic or post-exilic (*Notes*, 351–52). Barnes (*2 Kings*, 115–16) argues that since Babylon was not a major power at this time, and since only the royal treasures and a few of the king's sons are affected, it then refers not to the exile but to Manasseh's enforced travel to the Assyrian king (2 Chr 33:11). This latter suggestion is clever, but overlooks the representative nature of the treasures and the sons in this narrative, and also overlooks the important allusions to 2 Kgs 24 and 25. It is interesting to note that on precisely the same grounds, namely, that the oracle does not fully accord with history, it is declared genuine by Fricke (*Die Zweite Königen*, 294).

19 טוב דבר יהוה "Yahweh's word is good." This is a clear public attitude of resignation to the word of God on the part of the king. From the earliest tradition הלוא אם שלום ואמת יהיה בימי "Why not? Since there will be peace and prosperity in my time!" has been interpreted as a very impious response of the king to the word of God and thus is omitted by G^B. It does appear inconsistent with the initial response of the king, and so it is. The clay feet of Hezekiah are now apparent.

20 The conventional formula for closing the reign of Hezekiah is tantalizingly brief and cryptic. 2 Chr 32:27–33 contains much more to provide a glimpse of his social and economic measures. Since most of these would have taken place after 701 B.C., it is clear that Hezekiah spent the remainder of his reign (fifteen years) in prosperity and in peace.

"The pool and the aqueduct" were constructed either in anticipation of the Assyrian invasion, or in reaction to it. 2 Chr 32:2–8 does not include the famous "Hezekiah Tunnel" in the preparations for the invasion. At this time the water supply outside Jerusalem was blocked up to deny access to the invader. 2 Chr 32:30 provides more detail on the digging of the tunnel. It went from the Gihon spring (now blocked) "down [to] the west side of the city of David." This is correct. The water was taken underneath the city from one side to the other. Other more specific information is found in Sir

48:17, and the description offered there can only apply to what is today identified as Hezekiah's Tunnel.

The tunnel is approximately 580 meters long and was begun from both ends. Edwin Robinson, the father of historical geography of Israel, was the first modern individual to travel its entire length (see his *Biblical Researches* 1:338) in 1838. The British Survey of Western Palestine repeated the act thirty years later (see Warren's account in *Survey of Western Palestine* 3:353–56). The work is undoubtedly a remarkable feat of engineering. How it was directed is still something of a mystery. An inscription from the tunnel offers a brief account of the digging. See Gibson, *Syrian Semitic Inscriptions* 1:21–23. For a survey of the system see R. Amiran in *Jerusalem Revealed*, 75–78; J. Wilkinson, *Levant* 10 (1978) 116–25; N. Shaheen, "The Siloam End of Hezekiah's Tunnel," *PEQ* 109 (1977) 107–12.

Another reason for such an expansion of the water supply to the city was the increase in population which Judea experienced after the fall of Samaria. See M. Broshi, "The Expansion of Jerusalem," *IEJ* 24 (1974) 20–26.

21 עִם אֲבֹתָיו . . . וַיִּשְׁכַּב "and he slept with his fathers." 2 Chr 32:33 makes mention of "the ascent to the graves of the sons of David," and later Jewish tradition states that Hezekiah was buried next to David and Solomon (see Ginzberg, *Legends of the Jews* 4:277). If the tombs discovered by Raymond Weill in the city of David are those of the kings, then we have a location of the burial. However, the tombs are so badly damaged that certain identification is impossible.

The rather ambivalent attitude toward Hezekiah displayed in this chapter now gives way to the transparent dislike of Manasseh.

Explanation

The writer's final judgment on Hezekiah is that he cuts a negative figure on the stage of Judah's history. The reign, which clearly began with promise and which received a demonstration of Yahweh's grace and deliverance, now ends on a note of potential disaster. A large gap stands between the Hezekiah of chaps. 18–19, who sought Yahweh in time of trouble and who turned to the prophet to seek guidance and help in complete contrast to Ahaziah of chap. 1, and the Hezekiah who is portrayed in this chapter. The situations are similar. The land has suffered an intrusion; Hezekiah suffers from a skin malady. The prayer of Hezekiah in the second circumstance is characterized by its self-centeredness, not its faith. When he receives the promise of a longer reign, out of his unbelief he demands more proof. Finally, he parades his wealth before a potential invader and, when he is criticized for it, reacts with an offhand remark that demonstrates his complete lack of responsibility.

The prophet, however, speaks on behalf of Yahweh. His words stand in judgment upon Hezekiah's attitudes. God still acts, not out of reaction to circumstance, but out of freedom. Hezekiah parades his piety before God (v 3), but Yahweh responds for his own sake and for the sake of his servant David (v 6). Even when faced with unbelief, Yahweh heals and extends the reign of the king by some fifteen years (v 6a).

If in any way the king stands as a symbol for the nation, then the lesson of history had not been learned. Israel had fallen because of her apostasy. Judah's life had been graciously extended. Jerusalem itself had been attacked, but miraculously delivered, and yet the threat of impending judgment had never been taken seriously by the king. He appeals instead, almost out of self-pity, to his piety and God's grace, never fully facing the deep moral and religious issues that were at the heart of the life of the nation. The prophetic cry of a hurt and abandoned God who had given so much, yet received so little loving response in return (Hos 11) can be heard here. Even if the great acts of God are recalled and seen by the people, they still do not offer repentance. With so much from recent history to learn from, the people still turn away.

The final note left in the chapter is one of impending doom. Tiglath Pileser had set foot in Israel, had offered help, had taken money for that help, then later came back to ravage the land. His successors returned to destroy the land. So now Merodach Baladan too has set his claim on Judah, Jerusalem, and the nation's treasures. Tragedy beckons. Yet the alternative is so easy (vv 9–11). Time can be delayed by God's free action. Judgment can be averted. Nothing in Hezekiah's actions allows for these hopeful possibilities, so the reign that began with so much promise ends with no progress having been made. Judah too is threatened.

The Reigns of Manasseh and Amon (21:1–26)

Bibliography

Bach, R. *Die Erwählung Israels in der Wüste.* Dissertation, University of Heidelberg, 1956. **Barnett, R. D.** "Bringing in the God to the Temple: Parallels in the Assyrian and Israelite Traditions." *Temples and High Places in Biblical Times.* Jerusalem: Hebrew Union College and the Israel Exploration Society, 1977. 2–3. **Clements, R. E.** "Deuteronomy and the Jerusalem Cult Tradition." *VT* 15 (1965) 300–312. **Malamat, A.** "The Historical Background of the Assassination of Amon." *IEJ* 3 (1953) 82–102. ———. "Josiah's Bid for Armageddon." *JANESCU* 5 (1973) 268–78. ———. "The Twilight of Judah in the Egyptian-Babylonian Maelstrom." *Congress Volume: Edinburgh.* VTSup 28. Leiden: E. J. Brill, 1974. 123–45. **Nicholson, E. W.** "The Centralization of the Cult in Deuteronomy." *VT* 13 (1963) 380–89. **Nikolsky, N. M.** "Pasche im Kulte des jerusalemischen Tempels." *ZAW* 45 (1927) 171–90, 241–53. **Oded, B.** "The Reigns of Manasseh and Amon." *Israelite and Judaean History.* Ed. J. H. Hayes and J. M. Miller. Philadelphia: Westminster, 1977. 452–58. **Porteous, N. W.** "Jerusalem-Zion, the Growth of a Symbol." *Living the Mystery: Collected Essays.* Oxford: Blackwells, 1967. 93–112. **Roche, M. de.** *The Wilderness Motif in Jeremiah: A Rhetorical Analysis.* M. A. thesis: McMaster University, 1979. **Rudolph, W.** "Zum Text des Königsbuches." *ZAW* 63 (1951) 201–15. **Seters, J. van.** "The Terms 'Amorite' and 'Hittite' in the OT." *VT* 22 (1972) 64–81. **Talmon, S.** "The Desert Motif in the Bible and in Qumran Literature." *Biblical Motifs—Origins and Transformations.* Ed. A. Altmann. Cambridge, MA: Harvard U.P. 1966. 31–66. **Wenham, G. J.** "Deuteronomy and the Central Sanctuary." *TynB* 22 (1971) 103–118. **Zakovitz, J.** "To Cause His Name to Dwell There" (Heb.). *Tarbiz* 41 (1972) 338–40.

Translation

¹*Manasseh was twelve years old when he began to reign, and he reigned for fifty-five years in Jerusalem.* ªHis mother's name was Hephzibah.ª ²*He behaved badly* ª *in Yahweh's eyes, according to the disgusting actions* ᵇ *of the nations whom Yahweh had driven out before the Israelites.* ³*He rebuilt* ª *the high places* ᵇ *which Hezekiah his father had destroyed. He even erected altars* ᶜ *to Baal* ᵈ *and constructed an Asherah as Ahab king of Israel had done,* ᵉ *and he bowed down to all the hosts of heaven and worshiped them.* ⁴*He also built* ª *altars in the temple of Yahweh, of which Yahweh had declared, "In Jerusalem I will set down my name."* ᵇ ⁵*In fact, he built altars to all the host of heaven in the two courts of the temple.* ⁶*He even made his son* ª *pass through fire, and indulged in soothsaying and divination,* ᵇ *and practiced* ᶜ *necromancy and wizardry. He did sufficient evil in Yahweh's eyes to provoke him to anger.* ⁷*The carved image of the Asherah* ª *he had made he set up in the temple* ᵇ *of which Yahweh had declared to David and his son Solomon, "In this temple and in Jerusalem,* ᶜ *which I have chosen out of all the tribes of Judah, I will set my name forever.* ⁸*I will no longer allow Israel's feet to wander* ª *out of the land I gave to their fathers on the condition that they take care* ᵇ *to carry out* ᶜ *all the commandments and law* ᵈ *which Moses my servant commanded them."* ᵉ ⁹*But they did not listen* ª *and Manasseh beguiled them into committing more evil* ᵇ *than the nations whom Yahweh had destroyed before Israel.*
¹⁰*So Yahweh said through his servants the prophets,* ¹¹*"Because Manasseh has done more of these disgusting things* ª *than all* ᵇ *the Amorites before him,* ᶜ *and has forced Israel to sin with idols,* ¹²*therefore thus has Yahweh the God of Israel* ª *declared, 'See, I am about to bring upon Judah and Jerusalem such calamity that the ears of those who hear it* ᵇ *will tingle.* ¹³*I will measure Jerusalem with the standard of Samaria, and the norm of the dynasty of Ahab, and I will wipe Jerusalem like someone wiping out a bowl, wiping it and turning it upside down.* ¹⁴*I will throw away the remainder of my inheritance, and hand them over to the control of their enemies. They shall become common prey and loot for their enemies.* ¹⁵*This is because they* ª *have become practitioners of evil in my eyes, and have provoked me, from the day I brought their ancestors out of Egypt until now.'"*
¹⁶*In addition, Manasseh spilled a great deal of innocent blood so that Jerusalem was filled with it from end to end. This was beyond the sin with which he made Judah to sin and commit such evil in Yahweh's eyes.* ¹⁷*Now the remainder of Manasseh's activities and all he did, including the sins* ª *he committed, are they not* ᵇ *written in the records of the kings of Judah?* ¹⁸*So Manasseh slept with his fathers and was buried in the garden of his own palace,* ª *that is in the Garden of Uzza, and Amon* ᵇ *his son reigned in his place.*
¹⁹*Amon was twenty-two years of age when he began to reign, and he reigned for two years in Jerusalem. His mother's name was Meshulemeth* ª *daughter of Harutz from Jotbah.* ²⁰*He behaved* ª *badly in Yahweh's eyes as his father Manasseh had done.* ²¹*He behaved in every way like his father. He worshiped the idols his father*

had worshiped and bowed down to them. ²² *He abandoned Yahweh the God of his ancestors and did not walk in Yahweh's way.*ᵃ ²³ *Amon's own servants plotted against him and killed him* ᵃ *in his palace.* ²⁴ *But the people of the land executed* ᵃ *those who had plotted against King Amon, and the people of the land made Josiah his son king in his place.* ²⁵ *As for the remainder of the activities of Amon which he did, are they* ᵃ *not written in the records of the kings of Judah?* ²⁶ *He was buried* ᵃᵇ *in his tomb in the Garden of Uzza,* ᶜ *and Josiah his son reigned in his place.*

Notes

1.a–a. Omitted by 2 Chr 33:1.
2.a. G^L adds the proper name of the king.
2.b. G^L adds "all."
3.a. MT reads וישב ובן "and he returned and built," which is a way of expressing an action repeated (see *Comment*). G^L adds the proper name again to the sentence.
3.b. The G MSS oc₂ read "altars."
3.c. 2 Chr 33:3 (G) reads στήλας "monuments."
3.d. In Chronicles this word is in the pl.
3.e. Omitted by Chronicles.
4.a. MT reads וּבָנָה "he also built." The syntax is clumsy. Ehrlich (*Randglossen* 7:316) suggests וּבְנֹה, using the infinitive absolute in sequence (see R. J. Williams, *Hebrew Syntax*, 39). However, Burney (*Notes*, 353), Montgomery (*Kings*, 522), and Gray (*Kings*, 705) argue that the present text is an archival style, and can remain intact.
4.b. 2 Chr 33:4 adds "forever," and G^A reads "throne" for "name."
6.a. 2 Chr 33:6 and G^B read pl.
6.b. G^B reverses the order of these words.
6.c. MT reads ועשה "he even made," which Burney (*Notes*, 354) translates as "instituted," and Ehrlich (*Randglossen* 7:316) as "und bediente sich. . . ."
7.a. 2 Chr 33:7 reads הסמל "the idol" for האשרה "the Asherah."
7.b. G^L adds "of Yahweh."
7.c. The conjunction is omitted by G^B.
8.a. MT reads להניד "to wander." Ehrlich (*Randglossen* 7:316) suggests a reading of להניע, one meaning of which is "to cause to wander" (see BDB, 631). The emendation is quite unnecessary.
8.b. G^L presupposes וישמעו "that they hear," or "obey."
8.c. לעשות "to carry out" is omitted by G^B.
8.d. For תורה "law" G^B offers ἐντολήν "commandment."
8.e. For אתם "them" is omitted by G^B.
9.a. MT reads לא שמעו "they did not listen." Ehrlich (*Randglossen* 7:316) suggests a singular, making Manasseh the subject.
9.b. G^B adds "in the eyes of Yahweh."
11.a. MT's הֵרַע "he did evil" is ungrammatical. G^BL's πονηρα suggests the adjective הָרַע "evil."
11.b. For מכל אשר "than all who" G^L reads κατα παντα οσα "according to all those."
11.c. For אשר לפניו "who were before him" G^L reads ὅς ἦν ἐν τῇ γῇ "who were in the land."
12.a. אלהי ישראל "the God of Israel" is omitted by the G MS e₂.
12.b. Q reads שמעה "who hear it" with a fem suffix to agree with רעה "calamity." K reads a masc: שמעיו.
15.a. G^L adds ἀπερρίφησαν ἀπο ὀπισθεν μου και "they have departed from behind me and."
17.a. G^B reads singular.
17.b. G^L translates οὐχ ἰδου "behold are they not."
18.a. Omitted by G^L.
18.b. There are many variants on this proper name in the versions.
19.a. In the versions the mother's name is variously rendered, but no change in the text is necessitated by this.
20.a. Characteristically, G^L adds "Amon."

22.a. The G MS e₂ adds καὶ ἐπορεύθη ἐν ὁδῷ τῶν ἐθνῶν "and walked in the way of the nations."
23.a. MT reads "the king," but G^L has "they killed him."
24.a. For MT's ירו "execute," G^L translates ἀπέκτειναν "they killed."
25.a. See above 17.b.
26.a. The MT reading of ויקבר אתו "he buried him" needs paraphrasing. It is a way of expressing passive action which is not acceptable in English. Ehrlich (*Randglossen* 7:317) accepts G's reading of a passive. The Gr., however, is caught with the same limitations as English at this point.
26.b. G^L again reads the king's proper name.
26.c. G^L adds "of his father."

Form/Structure/Setting

The flow of the narrative of chap. 21 is quite straightforward. After the typical opening formula for the reign of a king of Judah (vv 1–2) which emphatically states Manasseh's sinfulness, the first full paragraph offers a catalogue of the cultic abuses patronized by the king (vv 3–9). The writer's model for this kind of activity is Ahab (v 3). Within this paragraph is a quotation, prophetic in style, of Yahweh's original plan for Israel and Judah.

Vv 10–15 repeat a general prophetic indictment of the reign of Manasseh which cannot be linked to any specific prophet. The main point of the indictment is to compare current Judah with apostate Israel, and thereby to raise the prospect of a similar fate for the Southern Kingdom (v 13). V 16 continues the catalogue of sins with its reference to the shedding of innocent blood in Jerusalem. The account ends abruptly with the characteristic concluding formula (vv 17–18).

Vv 19–26 contain a brief account of the reign of Manasseh's son, Amon. It is a typical and stereotyped account, with an opening formula (vv 19–22) making a judgment upon the king; a brief comment on events of his reign—the most notable of which was his assassination (vv 23–24); a succession notice and a typical concluding formula. These latter end the reign of Amon and legitimize the reign of his successor, Josiah.

Many have questioned the unity of the chapter (see Gray, *Kings*, 704–5; Robinson, *Second Kings*, 203; and Snaith, *IB* 3:312). A detailed account of the analysis of the chapter is presented in R. D. Nelson, *The Double-Redaction of the Deuteronomistic History*, 65–70. Nelson summarizes, "It seems most likely that the exilic editor found before him 1–3*b* and 16–18, with the annalistic notices 4*a*, 6*a*, and perhaps 7*a*, floating somewhere in between. In his revision of the history, he expanded Manasseh's sins and sermonized upon them in 3*c*–15, utilizing in the process some fragments of the historian's comments upon the evil of this king, which probably consisted of quoted annalistic sources" (p. 67). This is a majority opinion with which Nelson concurs.

Some initial reactions are in order. The model of literature in mind is difficult to understand. The multiplicity of layer upon layer of sources, endless redactional glosses, and other accretions is limited, it seems, only by the imagination of the interpreter using such methods of analysis. Second, the sheer impracticability of such a repeated production of the document every time one or another of such additions is made needs to be taken into account. The prohibitive cost of such ventures, while not impossible, is certainly improbable. Third, many of the phenomena noticed by this kind of analysis lend themselves to alternative explanations. "Annalistic" is a designation of style, not necessarily of contents or source. The appearance of distinctive vocabulary and theological themes at this point in the larger narrative of 2 Kings, if interpreted solely as signs of sources and redactional activity, denies to the writer any stylistic or ideological development in his story.

On closer examination, the six major items of "literary critical evidence" that Nelson marshals in support of his analysis are less than convincing. Of the six, four are primarily stylistic, and two are theological. Nelson draws attention to the clause "I have set my name . . . ." (vv 4, 7), which has a finite verb in it. This is unique, and is certainly "a clear-cut divergence from the practice of the historian" (p. 67). However, one must ask whether any other form of the expression would have been in order at this point. In the statements using the infinitive (לשׂים), which is the "standard" practice (1 Kgs 9:3; 11:36; 14:21), the form is inevitable, given the point to be made. The same is surely true of 21:4, 7.

An additional point is the absolute use of the term הכעיס "anger" (v 6), as well as the combination of Judah and Jerusalem in v 12. But these, together with the observation that the people are referred to as the inheritance of Yahweh (v 14), are hardly weighty arguments for sources. This is a concession that Nelson makes (p. 68). This leaves two important theological indicators of sources—the combination of the election of the temple and the election of the city of Jerusalem (vv 4, 7) and the expression "to bring evil upon" (v 12) as a harbinger of the final fall of Judah.

That these hitherto unknown phenomena now appear in the narrative of 2 Kings is granted. But the proper question is "Why?" The expression "to bring evil upon" (v 12) is used of a specific judgment only twice previously (1 Kgs 14:10; 2 Kgs 10:24). In the sense of an unspecified judgment upon Judah and Jerusalem the expression is used eight times (2 Kgs 21:12[?], 16, 20; Jer 4:6; 5:15; 6:19; 11:11; 19:3). If "normal" is connected to frequency of use, then the general judgment on Judah and Jerusalem is a normal application of the expression. Further, if the subtlety of the theological point is admitted, then an alternative interpretation to that of Nelson is certainly possible. The idea of enlarging the scope of the judgment of God on the monarchy from individual kings to the whole nation is not beyond the writer. It is certainly in keeping with the idea of a cumulative judgment upon a nation, already seen in chap. 17. That the writer sees the judgment after the fact is not a problem, since that is the general perspective of our writer.

Why this shift comes just here in the narrative is very important. First, it continues the theme of Israel as the paradigm for what is happening to Judah and as a warning for what might happen. Not only is this a strong point in the deuteronomistic history, but also in the prophets. It also casts a shadow over the reign of Josiah which is to follow. In effect, judgment has now been pronounced and set in motion. The reign of Josiah which begins with such promise eventually falls into the pattern of the presentations of reigns of earlier reformer-kings, that of unfulfilled promise.

The other theological point of the connection between the election of the city of Jerusalem and the temple also deserves some attention. "One must say that the historian viewed the choice of the city as part of the royal election, whereas the exilic editor saw it as the corollary of the Deuteronomistic theology of the election of the temple" (Nelson, *Double Redaction*, 68). According to Nelson, the exilic editor is responsible for 1 Kgs 8:44, 48; 2 Kgs 21:4, 7; and 23:27. The deuteronomistic link with David is seen in 1 Kgs 11:13, 32, 34; 14:21, in which the deuteronomist has overlaid a prior (prophetic) source. In Deut 31:11; Josh 9:27; 2 Sam 7:13; 1 Kgs 3:2; 5:5; 8:17-20, 29, 43; 9:3 the temple alone is chosen.

The argument hinges on the discussion of the fifth petition of the prayer of Solomon (1 Kgs 8:44-51), which is different from the previous four for the following reasons:

1. It contains reference to the temple and city.
2. It contains unnecessary (*ipso facto* inadmissible) repetition (vv 33-34, 46-56).
3. "Israel" is not present.
4. It alone contains the concept of פשע "sin."
5. V 50 is more ominous than anything prior to it.

The argument for a secondary source, it will be noticed, does not concentrate on questions of style, but rather on contents. The whole, in fact, is thoroughly deuteronomistic, and the main argument hinges on the first point made. But the burden of proof is on Nelson. The second observation is a value judgment and the conclusion does not necessarily follow from the observation. Although the expression "Israel" is missing, what else would be understood by the expression עמך "your people"? The fourth and fifth observations are quite inconclusive.

One must delve deeper regarding the first point, the identification of city and temple. If it can be demonstrated that at an early stage of OT religion the link between city and temple is established, then the argument that the link is a sign of later editorial activity is seriously weakened. In the ANE such a link is widespread. Solomon's dedicatory prayer in 1 Kgs 8 has many ANE parallels (see R. D. Barnett, *Temples and High Places in Biblical Times*, 2; also R. E. Clements, *God and Temple*, 74-82). Therefore, the association of king-temple-city is common and ancient (see also T. Jakobsen, *Treasures of Darkness*, 76-91, and the symbolism associated with the metaphor of the god as ruler). Within the OT itself there is adequate testimony for the link between city and temple in the ideology of Jerusalem-Zion (see N. W. Porteous, *Living the Mystery*, 93-112; N. Poulssen, *König und Tempel im Glaubenszeugnis des Alten Testaments*). Mic 4:1-4 and Isa 2:1-4, clearly an ancient hymn, presuppose the connection, and Ps 48 with its combination of the "divine mountain" theme and love for Jerusalem reflects the same. In the absence of solid stylistic criteria for identifying this link as from a different hand, such an examination of the ideological background is essential, albeit absent from Nelson's discussion.

The final effect of the completed account of the reign of Manasseh is intriguing not only for its individual design, but also for its contribution to the context. It follows hard upon the reign of Hezekiah (with its shadowy lining to the silver clouds of reform) and, with the brief necessary interval of the inauspicious reign of Amon, precedes the reign of the important king, Josiah. After an examination of the shaping of this link between the two reformers, one must inquire as to its contribution to the progression of the plot of 2 Kings.

The chapter is characterized by constant repetition of themes and vocabulary, but these repetitions are employed more for the sake of emphasis than as indicators of secondary sources. The theological point to be made in the chapter is radical, no less than the divinely willed destruction of Jerusalem and Judah. Several important topics are stressed in the chapter. First, the sins of Manasseh are worse than those of the other nations dispossessed by Israel (vv 2, 9, 11). Second, Manasseh is compared unfavorably with Ahab of Samaria (vv 3, 13). Third, Yahweh is thereby provoked into anger (vv 6, 15). Fourth, like Samaria, Jerusalem and its temple will be destroyed (vv 4, 13). This collection of themes is buttressed by language typical of the deuteronomist, but it also contains some strong prophetic elements. Comparisons between the sins of Judah and Israel are found in prophets like Micah, Jeremiah, and Ezekiel. That the fate of each should be the same is almost a foregone conclusion, a theme also stressed by the prophets. A literary device found frequently in prophetic literature, the reversal of important theological traditions, is reflected in the reversal of the tradition of the settlement (vv 7, 8, 14) and the tradition of Jerusalem-Zion (vv 4, 7, 12, 13).

The point made by this chapter is that the fulfillment of the word of judgment from Yahweh through the prophets now begins with the reign of Manasseh. Vv 10–15 contain a general prophetic reaction to the reign of Manasseh. The statement is not for the most part couched in formal prophetic speech patterns. But it does have a pattern. It picks up the themes of the opening description of Manasseh's reign and deals with the items listed in reverse order. Such historicizing of prophetic theological themes is typical of deuteronomistic writing.

Within the broader context of the ongoing tale of the nation of Judah this reign plays a very important role. It takes up hints already made concerning the possible fate of Judah (8:16–24; 12:17–18; 14:1–15; 17:13, 19–20; 20:12–19) and makes them certain. Judah, now under her "Ahab," is in a state of terminal decline. As a preface to the initially promising reign of the third, and most thorough, of the Judean reformer kings, Josiah, the chapter casts a shadow over the future.

Comment

Few accounts of reigns in the books of Kings betray the selectivity of the writer more than does 2 Kgs 21. The material contained within the chapter and the comparison of it with what is known of Manasseh from other sources shows that we are dealing here not so much with historiography to be judged according to modern standards, but rather with an overt theological interpretation of history. Although the account here mentions "the remainder of the activities of Manasseh" (v 17), there is no hint whatsoever in the chapter of doing anything other than to show the most determined apostasy as characteristic of his reign. Nothing else from Manasseh's long and presumably prosperous reign can be reconstructed from the information offered to us in 2 Kgs 21.

It is clear from Assyrian sources that throughout this long reign, which overlapped those of Esarhaddon (681–669 B.C.) and Ashurbanipal (668–627 B.C.), Manasseh was for the most part a vassal of Assyria. That is, he paid tribute regularly into the Assyrian treasury. Further, his aid was enlisted, together with that of eleven "kings of the seacoast," in the rebuilding of Esarhaddon's palace and in the construction of the coastal town of Sidon after its capture by Esarhaddon (*ANET*, 291). This took place in ca. 671 B.C. A decade later Ashurbanipal used Judean troops, among others, to invade Egypt in order to subdue the revolt of Tirhaka (*ANET*, 294). The records of Esarhaddon and Ashurbanipal reveal that military traffic along the eastern Mediterranean coast between Assyria and Egypt was very heavy up to 651 B.C. Judah would therefore have been under considerable pressure to conform to the wishes of her Assyrian overlord. Nothing of these political realities can be detected from 2 Kgs 21.

Another intriguing omission is the account of Manasseh's enforced visit to the Assyrian king at Babylon, recorded in 2 Chr 33. Apparently Manasseh was called to account by the Assyrian king and scared into further submission. While reference to any such visit is also lacking in the Assyrian sources, it was quite in keeping with Assyrian practice toward its vassals, particularly those in the western part of the empire. That 2 Kgs 21 chose to omit the incident serves to throw into sharper relief the material contained in the chapter.

That material is quite provincial in its outlook. It comprises a polemical indictment of the local apostasy of Manasseh, in the tradition of the earlier polemic against Ahab. According to the writer, Manasseh's legacy to Judah was wholesale and unrelieved apostasy and disobedience to the Mosaic law, the undoing of all the good done by Hezekiah, and the reintroduction of foreign cults into the temple. As a prelude to the reign and reformation of Josiah, Manasseh's reign is perfect.

1 The chronology here is again difficult. A fifty-five-year reign is regarded by most as far too long, and is therefore reduced by a decade to accommodate the period of time from the death of Hezekiah to the fall of Jerusalem. If the figures are taken at their face value, then Manasseh was born after 701 B.C., since at least fifteen years had elapsed between the Assyrian invasion and the death of Hezekiah. Manasseh's birth would be 698 B.C., and he would have become king in 686 B.C. But allowing for a reign of fifty-five years places the death of Manasseh in 633 B.C., which is far too late. Gray (*Kings*, 706) and others, following Thiele (*Mysterious Numbers*, 155–61), move Manasseh's reign back, and argue for a co-regency of approximately ten years between Manasseh and his father. 696 B.C. is then the designation of Manasseh as heir-apparent at the age of twelve. His reign as sole monarch was then forty-five years, and not fifty-five. The details and the problems associated with this kind of adjustment have been discussed elsewhere in this commentary. The argument put forward is basically one of accommodation, and therefore theoretical. That such arguments, particularly the rather promiscuous use of the theory of a co-regency, provide plausible explanations of the notorious chronological difficulties in the text of the books of Kings cannot be disputed. But that is not evidence. Thiele's solution does not adequately deal with the problem of the date of Manasseh's birth, nor does it explain the meaning of the statement מלך בירושלם, which is normally translated "He became king in Jerusalem. . . ." The lack of any linguistic or historical information on the co-regency of Manasseh with his father should be taken very seriously. חפציבה "Hephzibah." The mother's name is "In whom I delight."

2 כתועבות הגוים "according to the disgusting actions of the nations." In keeping with the implied standard of behavior of the kings, the phrase is deuteronomistic. It is used in 2 Kgs 20:18, but more important in the light of the way in which the narrative develops, it is used also in Deut 18:9–14. This is clearly the ideal from which the writer works.

3 וישב ויבן is correctly translated as a repetition of an action: "he rebuilt." The verb וישב is not to be regarded as a distinct verb in the sequence with the meaning of "return." Note the similar use in 1:11, 13; 19:9. את הבמות "the high places" is a clear reference to Manasseh's attempt to undo the reforms of Hezekiah, and a reversal of the process of centralization undertaken by the new king. מזבחת לבעל "altars to Baal." Manasseh allowed localized Baal worship in the south, something of an innovation not seen in Judah since the reign of Athaliah (see chap. 11).

כאשר אחאב "like Ahab." Manasseh is the only Judean king so described. The sins of Ahab have replaced the criterion of the sins of Jeroboam son of Nebat. The model sketched is that of 1 Kgs 16:31–34, and Manasseh duplicates the activity of Ahab. The long-held view, still current in some quarters (see Bright, *History* 312–13), that the activity described here implied the installation of an Assyrian astral cult in the temple has now been seriously, and successfully, challenged by Cogan (*Imperialism and Religion*) and McKay (*Religion in Judah under the Assyrians*). Such a view is lacking in evidence and the text describes distinctively west Semitic religious activity. לכל צבא השמים "to all the hosts of heaven." The practice referred to here is also found in Zeph 1:6 and Jer 8:2 and was in vogue during the pre-Josianic period in Jerusalem. It was a practice also common in the north, no doubt introduced by Ahab, one for which Samaria was eventually punished (2 Kgs 17:6). The direct prohibition against such practices is, as one might expect, found in Deut 4:9; 17:3. In all references to such apostate behavior the origin of the cult is understood to be pre-Israelite and Canaanite, not Assyrian.

4 These are altars to Baal. Such activity offered a direct challenge to the superiority of Yahweh and his exclusive worship, which is affirmed by the events of the reign of Hezekiah. אשים את שמי "I will set down my name" is a synonym for the centralization of worship, an action clearly supported by the present form of Deuteronomy (see R. E. Clements, *God's Chosen People*, 74–82; Nicholson, *Deuteronomy and Tradition*, 94–106). It is not our purpose at this point to argue for or against the dating of the book of Deuteronomy in the seventh century B.C. (see Nicholson, *Deuteronomy and Tradition*, chap. 1, for details, and P. C. Craigie, *Deuteronomy*, for an opposing view). We note, however, the consistent dependence of the writer of 2 Kings upon the regulations and ideals found in Deuteronomy (see Deut 12:5–6; 1 Kgs 8:15; 11:36; 14:21).

5 This verse has a more complete description of the altars mentioned in vv 3–4. On the identification of the altars as dedicated to the Assyrian astral cult see below on v 7. בשתי חצרות בית יהוה "in the two courts of the temple." According to 1 Kgs 6:36, the temple proper possessed only one court, the inner court. Ezek 40:17–19 implies that there were two courts, but this might reflect a post-exilic ideal. In pre-exilic times the complete complex of temple and palace had three courts (upper, middle, and outer), and this is reflected in the activities of Manasseh (see Smith, *Jerusalem* 2:256). But this does not solve the problem entirely, since the Hebrew here is best translated as "both courts." It is entirely possible that the writer understood that only two of the three courts were used for worship, either of Yahweh, or as is the case here, of Baal.

6 On this practice of "passing through fire" see *Comment* on 16:3. The background for this description of Manasseh's activity is clearly Deut 18:9–14, where the prohibition is quite specific, "Yahweh your God will not permit you to do this . . ." (Deut 18:14). Although the list of apostate activities is shorter here than in Deuteronomy, it is in the same order, demonstrating the obvious link. The exact etymology of עונן "he indulged in soothsaying" is uncertain. A root ענן is unknown, and some attempts to link it to the practice of divination are nothing less than fanciful. The practice is a non-Israelite activity of Israel's neighbors, as is clear from Isa 2:6. The *locus classicus* for "necromancy and wizardry" is 1 Sam 28:3. להכעיס "to provoke (him) to anger" is a typically deuteronomistic word (see Weinfeld, *Deuteronomy and the Deuteronomic School*, 340).

7 וישם את פסל האשרה "he set up the image of the Asherah." The parallel in 2 Chr 33:7 reads פסל הסמל "image of the idol," which is a Phoenician word for image. It is on grounds such as this and others that McKay strongly argues for the introduction of Canaanite, rather than Assyrian, religious practices into Judah (see *Religion in Judah under the Assyrians*, 21–27). Thus is the model of Ahab which is the inspiration for the portrait of Manasseh here preserved. The style is deuteronomistic, and Manasseh's activities are to be seen as a direct challenge to the exclusive worship of Yahweh. Snaith (*IB* 3:312) suggests that vv 7–15 are from a later deuteronomic redactor in exile, but such distinctions within material that so consistently reflects the deuteronomistic style are hard to maintain.

8 The allusion to the often-repeated promise of rest from enemies round about (Deut 3:20; 12:10; Josh 21:44) is dependent upon obedience to the Torah. Such is the foundation of the imperatives of the book of Deuteronomy. On this theme see W. Brueggemann, *The Land*, 45–70.

9 The deliberate nature of the policy to apostasy is exposed with the use of the word ויתעם "he beguiled them." The nation was seduced by its king into apostasy, and the people's subsequent actions are judged to be more horrendous than those of the nations whom they replaced. The prophets make much of the theme that Israel should have behaved better than the neighbors who worshiped "no-gods" (see Amos 9:7; Jer 2:9–13). That theme even finds its way in a different form into the teaching of Jesus (Matt 11:21). The portrait of Manasseh is now in sharp contrast to that of his father. The Hezekiah/David comparison has been replaced by one of Manasseh/Ahab.

10 The reference to the prophetic tradition contrasts initially with the absence of any known prophetic figure during the reign of Manasseh. Isaiah and Micah had ceased their activities before the death of Hezekiah, and Jere-

Comment

miah and Zephaniah began their ministries during the reign of Josiah. None of the canonical prophets impinge on Manasseh's fifty-five years. The reign is characterized by a "famine of the word of God." But the initial contrast is not serious. There is nothing in vv 11–15 to suggest that the quoted prophets were active during the reign of Manasseh. Jer 15:1–4 is evidence that the sins of Manasseh were burned into the memory of the prophetic tradition long after he had left the scene, and that they provide a counterpart to the example of Jeroboam son of Nebat.

11 The oracle that follows cannot be traced to any single prophet, nor should it be. The inclusive expression עבדיו הנביאים "his servants the prophets" (v 10) precludes that possibility. Although some of the oracle's phrases are found also in Ezekiel and Jeremiah, there are others not common to them. What is given here is a deuteronomistic summary of the prophetic preaching from before the exile as the deuteronomists understood it. The introduction of an oracle with יען "because" should be compared to the promise of deliverance for Jerusalem in 19:34 which is "for my sake (למעני) and the sake of my servant David." האמרי "the Amorites" is not a word used often by the prophets, but the group becomes a paradigm of Baal worshipers in the OT who are therefore driven out of the land by Yahweh. On the use of the term in the OT see H. B. Huffmon, "The Amorites," *IDBSup* 20–21; J. van Seters, *VT* 22 (1972) 64–81. On גלולים "idols" see *Comment* on 17:12.

12 הנני מביא "see, I am about to bring." The expression is an immediate future, and the style is typically deuteronomistic. See 1 Kgs 14:10 and 2 Kgs 22:16. תצלנה "will tingle" is not a common term but is found on occasion in deuteronomistic material (see Nicholson, *Deuteronomy and Tradition*, 29). It has the sound of the popular proverb akin to the one on sour grapes (Jer 31:27–30) and is very descriptive. The fame of Judah and her God, recognized by "all the kingdoms of the earth" (19:15), is now replaced by her shame because of the activities of Manasseh.

13 Amos's vision of the plumbline is brought to mind here (Amos 7:7–8). The line (קו) and the measure (משקלת) are to be seen as metaphors of the standards by which Samaria was judged (see similar use in Isa 28:17) and therefore bring to mind the sermonic material in 17:7–24. So much of the current chapter implies a link between Manasseh and Ahab that such a comment is in keeping with the intention of the chapter. The rhetorical point, which is clear and well made, echoes the prophetic theme comparing the current addressee with an obviously sinful group (see Mic 1:1–9; Jer 2–3; Ezek 16).

צלחת "bowl." The word is rare. In 2:20 a different spelling is used (צלחית). The idea of wiping out a bowl again sounds like a popular proverb or aphorism, akin to the English "wiping the slate clean," but with the opposite effect! מָחָה וְהָפַךְ "he wiped and turned." *BHS* suggests in the interests of smoother grammar that the perfects be changed to infinitive absolutes (מָחֹה וְהָפֹךְ). But if the sentence is a popular proverb and therefore a quotation, then the perfect forms can remain.

14 The judgment against Judah because of the sins of Manasseh is, according to the summary of prophetic preaching, to be complete. As if the image of the clean bowl were not vivid enough, the writer reverses the cherished notion of the inheritance of Yahweh. It is to be uprooted and thrown away. Coming after the generally optimistic tone of the account of the reign of Hezekiah, such a judgment is stark.

נטשתי "I will throw away." This vocabulary is taken up by Jeremiah (Jer 12:7). שארית נחלתי "the remainder of my inheritance." The good done in the reform of Hezekiah is now undone by the actions of Manasseh. The roots sunk by the פליטת "escape" of Judah following the crisis of 701 B.C. are now to be torn up and thrown away. Micah's vision of the future is that this state of affairs will be reversed (Mic 7:18). "Hand them over to the control of their enemies" is reminiscent of the rhythmic movement of the book of Judges. Unlike the earlier statements, however, there is an air of finality to the present statement. The special relationship between Yahweh and his people is to be abandoned. Judah, once Yahweh's possession, is now the property of looters. See also Jer 2:14–19.

15 The comment in this verse—that the fathers continually provoked Yahweh to anger from the time of the Exodus on—is surely hyperbole. It corresponds neither to the pentateuchal traditions of the wilderness wanderings, nor to some of the later prophetic interpretations in which the wilderness period is seen as a time of closeness and intimacy between Yahweh and his people (see e.g., Jer 2:1–8). Whether there existed in Israel a "wilderness election tradition" (see R. Bach, *Die Erwählung Israels in der Wüste*) is a moot point, although Bach has drawn together evidence of a strand of thought quite opposed to that expounded in the present verse. The period of the wandering is viewed a number of different ways in the OT (see S. Talmon, "Wilderness," *IDBSup*, 946–48). The notion that there was a clearly defined "desert motif" in which the desert itself represented an ideal of purity, is now discounted (see S. Talmon, *Biblical Motifs*, 31–63; M. de Roche, *The Wilderness Motif in Jeremiah*, 2–40). It should come as no surprise that our writer should present such a tendentious view of the former history of the nation. Two such different views of that history are not confined to material such as this but are found in the hymnic summaries of the past (see Pss 105 and 106). Our writer's treatment of Manasseh is quite as selective, and to saddle him with the restraints of modern history-writing is hardly fair.

16 To the idolatrous sins listed thus far in the account of Manasseh's reign is added widespread murder sanctioned by the king. The expression "to shed innocent blood" is quite deuteronomistic (Deut 19:10, 13; 21:8, 9; 27:25; 1 Sam 19:5; Jer 7:6; 19:4; 22:3, 17; 26:15). Jewish tradition has linked this statement with the dramatic silence of the prophets during the reign of Manasseh, and developed the image of the king as a persecutor and murderer of the prophets (see Ginzberg, *Legends of the Jews* 4:277–81; Josephus, *Antiq.* x.37–39; *Ascension of Isaiah* 11:41) and the NT echoes this tradition in Heb 11:37. However, if such an activity were intended by the statement, then one could expect it to be more specific. דם נקי "innocent blood" is the life of one who does not deserve to die, and in ancient Israelite law such a one was protected. The term נקי "innocent" is not to be seen as a judgment on the status of the victim in a court of law, and the verb שפך "spilled" with the phrase can be paraphrased as "murder" (see H. Christ,

Die Blutvergiessung im Alten Testament, 34-36). Reviv's suggestion that Manasseh brutally suppressed any dissent against his pro-Assyrian activities (*World History of the Jewish People* 4:199) removes the action of the king out of the realm of persecution of prophets and into politics. Of course, in such a program of suppression many prophets might fall victim, but silencing the prophets would not necessarily have been the main aim of the king. The suggestion is attractive, but without proof. The point the author is making is that such an activity encompassed by the expression is directly prohibited by deuteronomic law and, as such, is quite in character. The shedding of innocent blood in such large quantities demonstrates the complete disregard for the deuteronomic law under the sponsorship of the king. פה לפה "end to end" is literally, "mouth to mouth." In this expression the mouth symbolizes the extremity of the city (the gate?); hyperbole is again at work here. The report is reminiscent of the descriptions of the crusader attack on Jerusalem in the twelfth century A.D. with the attackers said to be wading knee-deep in the blood of their victims. Within the OT tradition of Jerusalem, the city of justice (משפט) had become indeed a city of bloodshed (משפחה) (see Isa 5:7). In the eyes of the deuteronomist the behavior of Manasseh is without any redeeming feature.

17 The incident of 2 Chr 33:11-17 is omitted by the deuteronomist, but the historicity of the account in Chronicles cannot be doubted. Such an action on the part of the Assyrian is quite in keeping with known Assyrian policies (see McKay, *Religion in Judah under the Assyrians,* 25-26), and the confused state of affairs in Assyria following the revolt of Shamash-shum-ukin (652-648 B.C.) would provide an adequate historical background for Manasseh's visit to Babylon (see Bright, *History,* 311-14). The reference to Babylon and not Assyria is no difficulty, although it appears to have misled Josephus (see *Antiq.* x.40-41). At this time Babylon was under Assyria's control.

Why 2 Kgs 21 chose to omit any reference to this incident must remain a matter of speculation. The writer repeatedly refers to the records of the Judean court, so he is unlikely to have been unaware of it. However, his principle of selectivity has become clear, and in his account of the reign of Manasseh he includes nothing that would soften the harsh tones with which he paints the apostate king. The results of such a policy are easy to see. Manasseh in 2 Kgs 21 not only provides a complete opposite of the image and role of Hezekiah as a reformer, but also a perfect foil for Josiah, who follows him after the brief interlude of the reign of Amon.

18 בגן עזא "the Garden of Uzza," understood by many to be a garden built by Uzziah, can also be understood differently. Gray (*Kings,* 710) and, more recently, McKay (*Religion in Judah under the Assyrians,* 24-25), suggest that it is an enclosure constructed in honor of a Canaanite astral deity, Attarmelek. In the light of Manasseh's other activities this is a strong possibility; however, such an enclosure is hardly likely to have remained intact during the reign of Josiah, and there is no reference to its abolition during the latter's reform. The location was no doubt a well-known site close to the royal tombs. The exact site is unknown, but it was probably near the southern end of the city of David (the Ophel). אמון "Amon" is an unusual name for a Judean, and some have noted its Egyptian sound. The name does appear in 1 Kgs 22 as that of the governor of Samaria, and it is a fairly common ANE name related to the root אמן "to have confidence in" (hiph), "to be faithful." The name contains a touch of irony.

19 The brief and apparently inauspicious reign of Amon is dealt with in a few sentences. His most notable achievement was to continue the policy of his father, and the most significant event of his reign was his untimely assassination. משלמת "Meshulemeth," a feminine form of שלמה "Solomon," is related to the root שלם "to recompense." Derivatives of the root are common in Hebrew names (Shallum, Meshullam, Absalom, Solomon, etc.), and it appears in Lachish 3:20 and 9:7. The only other occurrence of this particular name is found in the later Elephantine Papyri (see B. Porten, *The Archives from Elephantine*, 139–40). McKay's suggestion that it is an Arabic name (*Religion in Judah under the Assyrians*, 24) is not necessary. בת חרוץ "daughter of Harutz." In Hebrew the name is a poetic one for gold (see Ps 68:14), possibly derived from a root meaning "to be yellow" (BDB, 359). A similar name appears in an Arabic inscription from Sinai (see H. Lidzbarski, *Handbuch der neue Epigraphik*, 280), so the possibility of the queen mother's having some southern (deep southern!) connections is real. Her place of origin also hints at this. Jotbah is unknown, although Num 33:33 and Deut 10:7 mention a site with the same name which has been identified with a place some thirty kilometers north of Elat. Its modern Arabic name is el Taba. However, the Yotapata of the revolt against Rome (Josephus, Wars, iii.158), now identified with the Hebrew Yodefat (Grid 176–248), is also a candidate for the site. This site is in the opposite direction, in Galilee. In neither case, though, is a Judean site named, which might suggest a non-Judean influence on the king. If this is so, then the parallel between Ahab and Manasseh is even more clearly drawn.

23 Amon's ignominious end is the only event of his short reign deemed worthy of comment by the writer. Since the assassination took place within the palace, it has all the marks of a palace coup, but the reasons are nowhere stated. A. Malamat (VTSup 28 [1974] 126) suggests that the assassination was instigated by Egypt. Implied in the account is that Amon's death at such an untimely moment (he was thirty-two years old) was a judgment for apostasy, but other political reasons were undoubtedly present. Malamat (VTSup 28 [1974] 126; *IEJ* 3 [1953] 82–102; *JANESCU* 5 [1973] 268–78) suggests that the murder was for his pro-Assyrian policies, and at the instigation of Egypt (so also Reviv, *World History of the Jewish People* 4:207). Nikolsky (*ZAW* 45 [1927] 171–90, 241–53) suggests exactly the opposite. The former seems more likely, but such motivations are obviously of no concern to our writer. If Amon continued the policies of his father, which included indiscriminate and unjustified murder, that would be sufficient reason for the assassination.

24 On the role of עם הארץ "the people of the land" see *Comment* above on 11:14–18. The idea that they were a wealthy, privileged group within society is unfounded. In 11:14–18 they lend enthusiastic support to the restoration of the Davidic dynasty. Here they execute those responsible for the death of the rightful king, albeit an apostate one. In his place they install his son and heir, an eight-year-old boy, with no guarantee, therefore, that things will change for the better. High notions of democracy (so Montgomery) have no place in the narrative at all, any more than they do in chap. 14. Monarchic society in ancient Israel was anything but democratic. The people of the land function as supporters of the Davidic monarchy.

Explanation

As if to complete the picture of decline begun at the end of the reign of Hezekiah, the writer offers us a portrait of Manasseh of Judah in which we find no redeeming features at all. Manasseh is judged simply as the worst king ever to have reigned over Judah. His actions left an indelible impression upon the character of Judah that even the reform of Josiah was unable to erase (see 23:26–27). As we have argued elsewhere, Manasseh assumes the role of Judah's Ahab, the king who precipitated the southern nation into the judgment of exile. To suggest that Manasseh behaved as badly as those nations whom Yahweh had driven out from before Israel (v 2), and further to suggest that Manasseh acted as Ahab had acted (v 3) is damnation indeed. In the first instance Manasseh wipes out centuries of growth in understanding of Yahweh by the people. Time is reversed, and it is as though the promise to David (2 Sam 7), the establishment of Zion (2 Sam 5–6), had never been made. Manasseh chose instead what was before. He must therefore be judged in that light. No longer can appeal be made by Yahweh to the promise to David, nor even to his own name, since the king has ruled that inadmissible. Manasseh lives now before the time of that promise, and hence beyond it.

To stress this point even further, the writer takes pains to show that the very places in which Yahweh had chosen to set his name, namely, Judah, Jerusalem, and the temple, had been desecrated by this arch-apostate. Strange altars were established there (vv 3–5). Idols were erected in place of worship of Yahweh (v 6). The conditions of faithfulness and trust in Yahweh were now absent (v 7). Therefore, Judah would wander again and would be rejected (vv 7–9). So Manasseh affected Judah more than leading her into the sins of Ahab and Jeroboam, which he undoubtedly did. He led Judah back before the time when Yahweh had given the people "rest from their enemies round about," before the voice of the prophets, before the settlement.

Yahweh then is free to withdraw his inheritance. He is free to measure Judah according to the measure her king had chosen, the standards of an apostate, pro-Canaanite Israel (vv 13–14), and he will wipe clean the past and return Judah to days of wandering (v 14). The depth of apostasy is matched only by the awful depth of the judgment. A Jerusalem where innocent blood is spilt from "end to end" (v 16) is no place where Yahweh can allow his name to dwell.

Little reason is offered for Manasseh's actions. Hezekiah, it appears, foolishly acts out of pride and self-centeredness, but Manasseh simply acts. He has no motivation other than to be apostate. He appears here, contrary to his image in Chronicles, as a king bent on self-destruction who will drag his people with him into judgment. The picture is stark and horrible. Judah chooses to live like the nations before the settlement, so she suffers the consequences and becomes common prey and booty (v 14), no longer able to appeal to the promises of Yahweh, but now dependent upon the shifting fortunes of life without Yahweh. It is undoubtedly one of the most tragic pictures in 2 Kings.

Manasseh's son is stamped with the image of his father. He does no worse, but can certainly do no better than his father (v 21). His dispatch in v 23 is not so much a judgment for this apostasy as an indication of the sickness that has now pervaded the royal palace, although the two can never be completely separated. His removal inadvertently brings to the throne the king who attempts to stem the tide of apostasy. The succession of Josiah is inadvertent because the effort to bring him to the throne is in the interest of preserving the Davidic line. At eight years of age, the young king is hardly in a position to manage the affairs of state on his own. However, in his reign Judah makes one last attempt to reform. But the reform and reign ends in tragedy. The die is now irretrievably cast.

The Reign of Josiah (22:1-20)

Bibliography

Ackroyd, P. R. "The Theology of the Chronicler." *LTQ* 8 (1973) 103-16. **Aharoni, Y.** "Arad: Its Inscriptions and Temple." *BA* 31 (1968) 1-32. **Alt, A.** "Judas Gaue unter Josias." *Kleine Schriften,* 2:276-88. Munich: C. H. Beck, 1953. **Asmussen, J. P.** "Sacralen Prostitution im AT." *ST* 11 (1957) 167-92. **Avigad, N.** "Two Newly-found Hebrew Seals." *IEJ* 13 (1963) 322-24. **Barrick, W. B.** "What Do We Really Know about High Places?" *SEÅ* 45 (1980) 50-57. **Berry, G. R.** "The Code Found in the Temple." *JBL* 39 (1920) 44-51. **Boyd, W. J. P.** "The Secondary Meaning of אחר." *JTS* 12 (1961) 54-56. **Budde, K.** "Das Deuteronium und die Reform König Josias." *ZAW* 44 (1926) 177-224. **Claburn, W. E.** "The Fiscal Basis of Josiah's Reform." *JBL* 92 (1973) 11-22. **Croatto, J. S.,** and **Soggin, J. A.** "Die Bedeutung von שדמות im Alten Testament." *ZAW* 74 (1962) 44-50. **Cross, F. M.,** and **Wright, G. E.** "The Boundary Lists of the Kingdom of Judah." *JBL* 75 (1956) 202-26. ——— and **Freedman, D. N.** "Josiah's Revolt against Assyria." *JNES* 12 (1953) 56-58. **Diaz, J. A.** "Le muerto de Josias en la redacion deuteronomic de libre de los Reges como anticipación de la teologia de libro de Job." *Homenaje a Juan Padro,* 167-77. Madrid: Inst. B. A. Montano, 1975. **Dietrich, W.** "Josia und das Gesetzbuch (2 Reg. 22)." *VT* 27 (1977) 13-35. **Freed, A.** "The Code Spoken of in 2 Kings 22-23." *JBL* 40 (1921) 76-80. **Frost, S. B.** "The Death of Josiah: A Conspiracy of Silence." *JBL* 87 (1968) 369-82. **Granild, S.** "Einige Voraussetzungen des Gesetzbuches in 2 Kön. 22:8." *DTT* 19 (1956) 199-210. **Gressmann, H.** "Josia und das Deuteronium." *ZAW* 42 (1924) 313-37. **Har-el, M.** "Orientation in Biblical Lands." *BA* 44 (1981) 19-20. **Hoppe, L.** *The Origins of Deuteronomy.* Dissertation, Northwestern University, 1978. **Horst, F.** "Die Kultusreform des Königs Josias." *ZDMG* 77 (1923) 220-38. **Jepsen, A.** "Die Reform des Josias." In *Festschrift für A. Baumgartel,* 97-108. Berlin: A Topelmann, 1959. **Lauha, A.** "Vastaan vai aucksi?" *TAik* 68 (1963) 143-51. **Lehman, M. R.** "The term שדמות." *VT* 3 (1953) 361-71. **Lohfink, N.** "Die Bundesurkunde des Königs Josias." *Bib* 44 (1963) 261-88. ———. "Die Gattung 'Historischen Kurzgeschichte'." *ZAW* 93 (1978) 319-47. **Lundbom, J. R.** "The Lawbook of the Josianic Reform." *CBQ* 38 (1976) 293-302. **Malamat, A.** "Josiah's Bid for Armageddon." *JANESCU* 5 (1973) 268-78. ———. "Megiddo, 609 B.C.: the Conflict Reexamined." *AcAnt* 22 (1974) 445-49. ———. "The Organs of Statecraft in the Israelite Monarchy." *BA* 28 (1965) 34-65. **Margalit, O.** "The Death of Josiah." *BMik* 12 (1966-67) 111-15. (Heb.) **Mayes, A. D. H.** "King and Covenant: A Study of 2 Kings 22-23." *Hermathena* 125 (1978) 34-47. **McKay, J. W.** "The Horses and Chariot of the Sun in the Jerusalem Temple." *PEQ* 105 (1973) 167-69. **Milgrom, J.** "Did Josiah Subdue Megiddo?" *BMik* 44 (1970) 23-27. (Heb.) **Nicholson, E. W.** "Josiah's Reformation and Deuteronomy." *GUOST* 20 (1963-64) 77-84. **North, C. R.** "The Religious Aspects of Hebrew Kingship." *ZAW* 50 (1932) 8-38. **North, R.** "Bamot arte factae temporis Josiae?" *Bib* 35 (1954) 272-73. **Oden, R. A.** "The Persistence of Canaanite Religion." *BA* 39 (1976) 31-36. **Ogden, G.** "The Northern Extent of Josiah's Reforms." *AusBr* 26 (1978) 26-34. **Paton, L. B.** "The Case for the Post-exilic Dating of Deuteronomy." *JBL* 47 (1928) 322-57. **Platarotti, D.** "Zum Gebrauch des Wortes *mlk* im Alten Testament." *VT* 28 (1978) 286-300. **Priest, J. B.** "Huldah's Oracle." *VT* 30 (1980) 366-68. **Rose, M.** "Bemerkungen zum historischen Fundament des Josiabildes in II Reg. 22 ff." *ZAW* 89 (1977) 50-63. **Rost, L.** "Josias Passa." In *Theologie in Geschichte und Kunst*, Festschrift für K. Elliger, ed. S. Hermann, 169-75. Wittenburg: Luther Verlag, 1968. **Sekine, M.** "Beobachtungen zu der josianischen Reform." *VT* 22 (1972) 361-68. **Snaith, N. H.** "The meaning of שערים." *VT* 25 (1975) 115-18. **Stern, E.** "Israel at the Close of the Period of the Monarchy: An Archaeological Survey." *BA* 38 (1975) 26-53. **Uffenheimer, B.** "The Question of the Centralization of Worship in Ancient Israel" (Heb.). *Tarbiz* 28 (1959) 138-53. **Weinfeld, M.** "The Worship of Molech and the Queen of Heaven and Its Background." *UF* 4 (1972) 133-54. **Würthwein, E.** "Die josianische Reform und das Deuteronium." *ZTK* 73 (1976) 395-423. **Yadin, Y.** "Beer Sheba: The High Place Destroyed by King Josiah." *BASOR* 222 (1976) 5-17.

Translation

¹ *Josiah was eight years* [a] *old when he began his reign, and he reigned in Jerusalem for thirty-one years. His mother's name was Jedidah daughter of Adiyah from Bozkath.* ² *He behaved* [a] *well in Yahweh's eyes and he conducted himself as David his ancestor had. He did not stray to the right or to the left.* ³ *It was in King Josiah's eighteenth year* [a] *that the king sent Shaphan son of Azalyah, son of Meshullam, the scribe, to the temple* [b] *with this command,* ⁴ *"Go up to Hilkiah the Great Priest* [a] *and count* [b] *the silver of the temple income which the Keepers of the Threshold have collected from the people.* ⁵ *Let it then* [a] *be entrusted* [b] *to the workmen who have been appointed over the temple,* [c] *and then let it be* [d] *distributed to the laborers who are in the temple to make repairs on the sanctuary,* ⁶ *namely, the carpenters, the builders, the masons* [a] *for the purchase of timber and dressed stone for the temple repair.* ⁷ *But no accounting shall be made of the money handed over to them because they are reliable workmen."*

⁸ *Then Hilkiah the Great Priest said to Shaphan the scribe, "I have found the Law Book in the temple."* *He handed the book to Shaphan who read it.* ⁹ *Shaphan the scribe* [a] *went* [b] *to the king* [c] *and reported this to the king, "Your servants have emptied out the silver found in the temple and have handed it over to the designated workmen of the temple."* ¹⁰ *Shaphan then reported* [a] *to the king,* [b] *"Hilkiah the priest gave me a book."* [c] *Shaphan then read it in the presence of the king.*

11 *When the king heard the contents of the book he tore his clothes* **12** *and gave the following order to Hilkiah the priest, Ahikam son of Shaphan, Achbor son of Micayah, Shaphan the scribe and Asayah the civil servant,* **13** *"Go and inquire of Yahweh on my behalf and on behalf of the people and for the whole of Judah* [a] *concerning the contents* [b] *of this newly discovered book, for the anger of Yahweh which has flared up against us is great. Our ancestors did not listen to the words of this book to do all that is written concerning us."* [c]
14 *So Hilkiah the priest went together with Ahikam, Achbor, Shaphan, and Asayah to Huldah the prophetess, wife* [a] *of Shallum son of Tokvah, son of Harhas, Keeper of the Vestments (now she lived in the Mishneh* [b] *in Jerusalem) and they spoke to her.* [c] **15** *She responded to them,* [a] *"Thus has Yahweh the God of Israel declared, 'Say to the man who sent you all to me,* **16** *"Thus has Yahweh declared, 'See, I am about to bring evil upon this place and upon all its inhabitants—all the contents of the book which the king of Judah has read.* **17** *This is because they have abandoned me and offered incense to other gods, to provoke me to anger with all* [a] *their handiwork. Therefore my anger is kindled against this place, and it will not be doused.'"* **18** *To the king of Judah who sent you to inquire of Yahweh, say this, "Thus has Yahweh the God of Israel declared concerning the things you have heard,* [a] **19** *Because your heart was repentant, and you have humbled yourself before* [a] *Yahweh when you heard what I had spoken about this place and its inhabitants (that they should become a symbol of devastation and a curse), and have torn your clothes and wept before me, I have listened," says Yahweh.* **20** *"Therefore, I will gather you to your ancestors, and you shall be gathered to your family grave* [a] *in peace.* [b] *Your eyes shall not see all the evil I am about to bring upon this place."'"* [c] *They brought this word back to the king.*

Notes

1.a. MT reads שמנה שנה "eight year" (see 8:17). Ehrlich (*Randglossen* 7:317) and many others suggest a reading of שמנה שנים. However, see Montgomery, *Kings*, 526.

2.a. Characteristically G^L adds the proper name of the king.

3.a. G^LB adds here ". . . in the eighth month."

3.b. MT reads הספר בית יהוה "the scribe the temple." G^BA and others suggest an understanding of the phrase as "the scribe of the house of Yahweh." But the Hebrew הַסֹּפֵר "the scribe" is not in the construct state and will not allow this translation. The phrase בית יהוה "temple" is best understood as an adverbial expression, qualifying וישלח "he sent."

4.a. The designation "Great Priest" is regarded by some (e.g., Gray, *Kings*, 723) as an exilic gloss. However, the pre-exilic priesthood would have had some form of organization and hierarchy; therefore the term need not be seen as late.

4.b. MT reads וְיַתֵּם "may he count," lit., "may he bring to end." G translates σφραγισον impv "seal" suggesting an original of וְחֹתֵם. Tg, followed by NEB, offers "melt down." See the discussion above on 12:11.

5.a. K's וְיִתְּנָה "and let him give it" is better pointed with Q וְיִתְּנֻהוּ "and let them give it."

5.b. MT reads ויתנה על יד "and let him (or them) give into the hand."

5.c. G^B understands as בבית "in the temple," but Q drops the preposition.

5.d. G^L adds ". . . as the king had spoken."

6.a. MT reads ולגדרים "wall-builders." G^L offers the general τεχνιταις "laborers."

9.a. שפן הספר is omitted by G^B.

9.b. For וַיָּבֹא "he went" G^L presupposes וַיָּבֵא שָׁפָן הַסֹּפֵר אֶל הַמֶּלֶךְ "he brought Shaphan the scribe to the king."

9.c. Before the phrase אל המלך "to the king" G^B adds ἐν οἴκῳ Κυρίου "in the house of the Lord."

Form/Structure/Setting 315

10.a. Gᴮ reads καὶ εἶπεν (ויאמר) "and he said."
10.b. Gᴸ adds ". . . Josiah concerning the book."
10.c. Gᴺ adds ". . . of the law."
13.a. The phrase ובעד כל יהודה is regarded by many as superfluous (so *BHS;* Ehrlich, *Randglossen* 7:318; Montgomery, *Kings,* 527).
13.b. MT reads על דברי "concerning the contents of." The preposition is offered as περί (Gᴮ) or ὑπέρ (Gᴸ).
13.c. MT reads עלינו "concerning us." Burney (*Notes,* 356) reads the singular עליו "concerning him."
14.a. For אשה "wife" Gᴮ reads "mother." Gᴬᴺ reads γυναικα "wife."
14.b. The Hebrew משנה "copy" or "second part" is transliterated by G as ἐν τῇ μασενα. See *Comment* below.
14.c. Gᴺ adds κατα ταυτα "in this same way."
15.a. Omitted by Gᴮ.
17.a. Omitted by Gᴮ.
18.a. Gᴸ contains a much shorter verse and links the end to v 19.
19.a. MT's מפני יהוה "before Yahweh" is understood as מפני "before me" by Gᴸ.
20.a. MT reads קברתיך "your family grave," which is correctly rendered as τον ταφον (Gᴮ). An interesting mistake within the G tradition is seen by Gᴬ's reading of τον τοπον "the place."
20.b. MT reads בשלום "in peace." Gᴬ offers "Jerusalem," a corruption of either the Heb. or the Gr. ἐν εἰρήνῃ "in peace."
20.c. Gray (*Kings,* 727) adds ועל ישביו "and upon its inhabitants" (see Gᴸ).

Form/Structure/Setting

As with the account of the reign of Hezekiah (chaps. 18–20), the reign of Josiah involves more than one chapter of the present book of Kings (chaps. 22–23). Although there is a natural pause in the narrative at 22:20 with the announcement of the king's death before the judgment is brought upon Judah, the pause is nothing more than the break between two paragraphs. The beginning of chap. 23 continues the narrative, and the verb וישלח "he then sent" (v 1) provides a direct continuation of the story line begun in chap. 22. Accordingly, the remarks on form and structure at this point will include both chapters in their range of vision. In the present English versions the chapter division is unfortunate and offers a distorted picture of the story of the reign of Josiah. In the books of Chronicles the same pause in the story is not aggravated by the insertion of a chapter division (see 2 Chr 34:28–29).

The account of the reign of Josiah in 2 Kgs 22–23 contains many critical issues and has become one of the most discussed passages in the OT. Not only is it important for an understanding of the story of the monarchy in the books of Kings, but it is also regarded as a crucial passage for the dating of the Pentateuch. Some of the details of the international background to the reign are not difficult to sketch, although the precise sequence of events within the reign is. The presence in the OT of a second account of the reign (2 Chr 34–35) rather than lessening these difficulties increases them. Harmonization of the two accounts in every detail is impossible.

OT introductions appeal frequently to this section of 2 Kings for evidence on the dating of the book of Deuteronomy. (See, for example, O. Eissfeldt, *Introduction to the Old Testament,* 171–76; A. Soggin, *Introduction to the Old Testament,* 114–19). And some express a confidence in one interpretation of the evidence that is not shared by all (see H. H. Rowley, *The Growth of the Old*

Testament, 29–31). For a good treatment of the issues, see E. W. Nicholson, *Deuteronomy and Tradition*, 1–17, and B. S. Childs, *Introduction to the Old Testament as Scripture*, 201–25. The identification of the "lawbook" found in the temple as part or all of the book of Deuteronomy is an ancient one and a very important component in the argument. However, the identification has not gone unchallenged, and the earlier certainty that this passage provides a cornerstone for the dating of Deuteronomy is now somewhat eroded. Newer questions are being raised about the validity of such a course of inquiry (see R. Polzin, *Moses and the Deuteronomist*, 1–72).

Initially the two chapters appear to contain a number of inconsistencies and changes of style, which are used as evidence of their composite nature. The conceptual basis for such judgments has been dealt with at many places throughout the commentary and need not be repeated here. However, some of the issues raised do need comment since they affect one's understanding of the form and structure of the chapters. Plotting the exact course of the reform of Josiah is dependent upon one's assessment of the relationship between the two accounts of the reform in 2 Kgs 22–23 and 2 Chr 34–35, and of the important differences between them. Numerous minor differences, such as the inclusion and omission of phrases, alternate spellings of names, and extra details added by the Chronicler will not be discussed here. For a thorough comparison, see the relevant sections in P. Vanutelli, *Libri synoptici Veteris Testamenti*, 620–75, and for a preliminary discussion, see Nicholson, *Deuteronomy and Tradition*, 8–13. The following chart will serve as a guide:

a.	2 Kgs 22:1–2	2 Chr 34:1–2
b.	———	2 Chr 34:3–7
c.	2 Kgs 22:3–23:3	2 Chr 34:8–31
d.	2 Kgs 23:4–20	2 Chr 34:32–33
e.	———	2 Chr 35:1–17
f.	2 Kgs 23:21–23	2 Chr 35:18–19
g.	2 Kgs 23:24–27	———
h.	2 Kgs 23:28–30	2 Chr 35:20–27

It is evident that some passages have no exact parallel in the alternative account. 2 Chr 34:3–7 (b) is placed after the introduction to the reign, and although 2 Chr 34:32–33 (d) is a summary of the parallel account of the reform in 2 Kgs 23:4–20, there are sufficient similarities in (b) and (d) to show that the same event is in mind. 2 Chr 35:1–17 (e), which details the type of Passover celebration inaugurated by Josiah, has no equal in 2 Kings, but both accounts more or less coincide at (f), which offers two brief summaries of the Passover and a comment on its significance. 2 Kgs 23:24–27 (g) has no parallel in 2 Chronicles, nor does the latter contain a summary statement. The final parallel (h) deals with the same series of events, but it contains a number of significant differences that warrant comment.

Some of the differences in the accounts of the reign can be harmonized, but it must be noted that the harmonization takes place where there are no alternative versions of the incident. The unique material in 2 Chr 35:1–17 (e) and in 2 Kgs 23:24–27 (g) reflects the interests of each writer. The same kind of detailed attention to cultic practices is found elsewhere in the Chronicler and is therefore consistent with his emphases and purposes (for comment, see J. M. Myers, *I Chronicles*, AB 12:lxiv–lxxxiii, and P. R. Ackroyd, *LTQ* 8 [1973] 103–16). Similarly, the abolition of wizardry and sorcery from Judah and Jerusalem not only has deuteronomic justification (Deut 18), but is also a common theme of the deuteronomistic historian and features prominently in the reform of Hezekiah. Its presence here then is not unusual.

Minor details, such as alternate spellings (see 2 Chr 34:20 and 2 Kgs 22:21), the addition by the Chronicler of various characters (see 2 Chr 34:12 and 2 Kgs 22:7–8), and the omission or addition of certain words and phrases (see 2 Chr 34:30 and 2 Kgs 23:2) are understandable and are of little importance beyond establishing stylistic preferences.

In (b) and (h) a serious problem arises. The Chronicler clearly offers a different order of the events of the reign from that of the deuteronomist. Not only does the initial purge of the cult of Judah and Jerusalem precede the finding of the "lawbook" in Chronicles, but it does so by six years (2 Chr 34:3 and 2 Kgs 23:4). Further, 2 Kings restricts the reform to Judah, Jerusalem, and within the territory from Beer Sheba in the south to Geba and Bethel in the north (22:8; 23:15). The Chronicles account widens the effects of the reform to "Manasseh, Ephraim, and Simeon, and as far as Naphtali" (2 Chr 34:6).

The details of the death of the king differ in each account. 2 Kgs 23:29–30 has Josiah moved north to "meet" (לקראת) Pharaoh Necho. He is slain in his chariot at Megiddo and then brought back to Jerusalem for burial in his family tomb. In Chronicles this outline is considerably expanded. The ambiguous journey of Necho is made clear. He went north to fight at Carchemish and Josiah went "against him." There follows a dialogue between the two, reminiscent of that between Amaziah and Joash in 2 Kgs 14. During the ensuing battle Josiah is mortally wounded and is taken to Jerusalem where he dies of his wounds. Following his death the whole community goes into mourning.

Not all of the different details of this second parallel are beyond reconciliation, but some of them are. Josiah died either at Megiddo or Jerusalem, but not both. Presumably the author of Chronicles had at his disposal the version found in Kings (so Myers, *I Chronicles*, AB 12:xlix–lxiii, following M. Noth, *Überlieferungsgeschichtliche Studien*, 131–55), so the information he offers represents an independent tradition of the death of Josiah. Certain details of that tradition, such as the reference to Carchemish, show that it was well informed and therefore cannot be dismissed out of hand.

The details of the sequence of events during the reform raise an issue that is very complicated. There is a marked difference between the order found in 2 Kgs 22–23 and that found in 2 Chr 34–35. A diagrammatic listing will prove helpful:

2 Kings	2 Chronicles
a. Josiah born in 648 B.C.	Josiah born in 648 B.C.
b. Began to reign at 8 years (22:1–2)	Began to reign at 8 years (34:1–29)

c.   Began to seek the God of David in 8th year of reign (632) (34:3)
d.   In 12th year (628) he began to purge Jerusalem, Judah, and Naphtali (34:3)
e. Lawbook found in 18th year (622) (22:3–23:3)   Lawbook found in 18th year (622) (34:8–31)
f. Covenant in same year (622) (23:1–3)   Covenant in same year (622) (34:29–31)
g. Widespread reform (622) (23:4–20)   Widespread reform (622) (34:32–33)
h. Passover (622) (23:21–25)   Passover (622) (35:1–17)
i. Additional reform (622) (23:24–27)
j. Death in 31st year   Death in 31st year

To attempt a historical reconstruction from the data available, as many have done, is perhaps the wrong approach to the text. It is here especially that the selectivity and tendentious approach to source material of both the writer of Kings and the writer of Chronicles is evident, and this should offer a caution to those seeking a complete historical picture. Indeed both writers offer to their readers reference to their major source for supplementary data on the reign of Josiah, namely, the records of the Judean court. Unfortunately this source is no longer extant, but the historian is thereby warned that neither of these writers is concerned with reconstructing the chronological sequence of events. Apart from the scanty additional data in Chronicles, nothing is known of the reign of Josiah in Kings besides his reform and some of the circumstances of his death. It is to be noted that the reform is presented as though it took place in one year, the eighteenth, out of a total of thirty-one. The description of the death of the king is extremely cryptic. Like so many of the accounts of the reigns of kings in the OT, the information offered here is selected according to narrow principles that do not help the cause of the dedicated historian. This is a fact of life with which interpreters of the Scriptures must learn to live.

This does not mean, of course, that nothing can be said about the reign and reform of Josiah. It does mean, however, that what can be said is quite limited in scope. Harmonization of the accounts in Kings and Chronicles is possible to a limited degree, such as that offered by Nicholson (*Deuteronomy and Tradition*, 13). But what must be borne in mind is that it is a reconstruction from a limited set of data, and by its very nature it goes beyond the individual account of either Kings or Chronicles. For our purposes such a reconstruction is of limited use since it is a revision of the data from Kings.

Many commentators have detected numerous sources and redactional layers in 2 Kgs 22–23. Würthwein (*ZTK* 73 [1976] 395–423) proposes an editorial combination of a "discovery-covenant report" (22:3–23:3) and a "reform-report" (23:4–15), neither of which is an original unity. 23:16–20 is regarded as late and nonhistorical. He argues that the completed combination of all these elements is a tool in the attempt by the deuteronomist to place the deuteronomistic view of life and religion in the center of the Judean community. The argument is based on form-critical presuppositions but, as such, is at its base false. The so-called forms that are detected ("discovery-covenant report" and "reform-report") are unique, having no parallel in contemporary literature. Therefore they break the primary rule of form criticism. There is no pattern to which they conform.

By way of contrast, Gray (*Kings*, 714–15) suggests that 22:3–23:3, 21–25 is a composition of the deuteronomist himself, and that 23:4–20 is borrowed from the annals of Judah. The whole "is in the mainstream of the deuteronomistic tradition" (p. 715). Dietrich (*VT* 27 [1977] 13–35) maintains that fragments of a pre-deuteronomistic source can be found in 22:3, 8, 10, 12, 13, 14, 20*b* to which the deuteronomist added vv 4–7, and to which a later redactor added v 2. Additional analysis can be found in R. D. Nelson, *The Double Redaction of the Deuteronomistic History*, 76–85.

While the differences in results of these analyses do not invalidate the basic arguments of the method, they do question the importance of such analyses for the understanding of the final portrait of Josiah and his reform in 2 Kgs 22–23. All the above analyses have one point in common, that the whole is the product, from whatever sources, of the deuteronomist. Our main concern will be, as always, with the structure and effect of the deuteronomist's narrative (see N. Lohfink, *ZAW* 93 [1978] 319–47). From this perspective the parallels with Chronicles, the origin of the supposed sources, and a historical reconstruction (however well meant) are only marginally useful.

The outline of 2 Kgs 22–23 is straightforward. 22:1–2 open the reign of Josiah with the conventional introductory formula for the reign of a king from Judah. 22:3–7 recount the incident of the redistribution of the temple collection to facilitate the repairs to the temple. 22:8–23:3 contain the king's reaction to the finding of the lawbook and the inauguration of a covenant with the people. 23:4–20 give an account of the purging of the cult in Jerusalem and Judah of Canaanite practices. 23:21–23 provide a brief reference to the inauguration of a new kind of Passover celebration in Jerusalem at the king's initiative. 23:24–27 allude to further reforms and contains an editorial comment on the piety of the king. However, included in this is a note of impending judgment, which even Josiah's actions are unable to divert. The same point is made in 22:15–20. 23:28, which appears out of place, is a typical closing formula for the reign, and vv 29–30 comprise a brief account of the death of Josiah at Megiddo.

Two stylistic points intimately connected to the narrative development should be mentioned at this point. In an extremely clever way the writer maintains an air of mystery about the contents of the book until late in the story. The book of the Torah first appears in v 8, when Hilkiah mentions that it has been found during the repairs to the temple. It is read to the court officials; they immediately return to the king with the book, and it is read again (v 10). Yet still no contents of the book are disclosed. The king's reaction in v 11 hints at the serious nature of the contents, but the reader is kept in suspense. V 13 hints in the same direction since the punishment is due because the ancestors had not listened to the words of the book. At this point the king seeks the true interpreter of the book, the prophet of Yahweh (vv 13–14). Finally, in the speech of the prophet (v 16) the contents are disclosed. "All the words of the book which the king of Judah had read . . ." are words of judgment. From this point on the king reacts by initiating a serious reform of the cult in Judah and Jerusalem. This same motif of the "hidden contents" of a written document is to be found in Jer 36, where the contents of the prophet's scroll are not disclosed until very late in the story of Jeremiah's confrontation with Jehoiakim.

Another item of plot development, which has been seen earlier in 2 Kings but which is also a characteristic of Jer 36, is the development of the circle of those involved in the action. In 22:3 the king is the first actor and sends Shaphan to the temple. Shaphan meets the priest Hilkiah and returns to the king with the book. The next mission of Shaphan involves not only himself, but also Hilkiah, Ahikam, Achbor, and Asayah (v 14). The circle is extended from one, to two, to three, and now to five. A sixth person is involved in the figure of Huldah the prophetess. This step-by-step enlargement of the actors in the drama gives to the narrative an increasing sense of business, and therefore urgency. It has been seen before in Joash's reform in chap. 12 and, to a certain extent, in Hezekiah's. It is most marked in the progression of the story in Jer 36 and also in the account of the arrest of the prophet in Jer 26.

Apart from these features of the narrative, which demonstrate good style and make for a good story, some other important formal features of the story need attention. It is more sound, methodologically, to look for formal and structural parallels within the complete literary work of 2 Kings than it is to look for them outside, or to create unique forms that cannot be verified. It is with the recognition of important themes and patterns within the book that the results are more fruitful and helpful. Setting the passage under discussion in its literary context and comparing it with known parallels seem eminently more sensible than creating otherwise unknown forms, or comparing the text with supposed but unproven parallels.

Josiah's reign as presented in 2 Kgs 22–23 is dominated by the reform of the king. A preliminary step ought to be the comparison of this account of the reform with other similar accounts in the book. Earlier the writer has presented accounts of the reforms of two Judean and one Samarian king, Joash (2 Kgs 12), Hezekiah (2 Kgs 18), and Jehu (2 Kgs 9–10), respectively. An examination of all of them reveals several common features. First, all of the previous reformers succeed a predecessor who was characterized by his or her worship of Canaanite deities. With the Omride dynasty that preceded Jehu this is taken for granted. But it is also true of the predecessor of Joash, Queen Athaliah, who not only introduced Baal worship into Judah, but is also noted as a relative of Ahab (8:26). Ahaz of Judah receives a judgment reserved for him alone among the kings of Judah. He did what the Israelite kings had done, including making his son "pass through fire" (16:3–4). Whatever the origin of this practice, it is clearly seen by our writer as a practice connected with the worship of Canaanite deities.

Second, it follows that the reforms of each were specifically anti-Canaanite and were directed against all those practices that were abhorrent to the deuteronomist. Again, with Jehu this is most clear. One of the results of the reforms of Joash was the slaying of the priests of Baal (11:17–20), and Hezekiah set about deliberately to reverse the policies of Ahaz his father (18:1–8). The long-held view that these reforms were anti-Assyrian has been successfully challenged (see *Comment* on 2 Kgs 8–10; 12; 18).

Third, in the south the reforms also involved some form of temple repair and reorganization of the running of the temple. Joash devised a new system of collecting money for the temple repair which involved a lesser role for the priests. Hezekiah's purge is preceded by some extensive repairs on the temple which involved the system established by Joash.

Fourth, none of the reforms concludes with a completely positive note. Even the most enthusiastic northern reformer, Jehu, is finally condemned for his apostasy (10:28–33) and his dynasty cut short therefore. The end of his reign is also accompanied by loss of territory on the eastern side of the Jordan. Joash is attacked by Hazael of Syria and forced to buy off the invader with the very gold and silver he had collected with his reorganization of the temple treasury. He is then assassinated by some of his close associates. In spite of his reform, and in spite of Sennacherib's abortive attack on Jerusalem, Hezekiah finally invites potential disaster by showing off all those same temple and palace treasures to the Babylonian ambassadors. It is at this point in the history of Judah that the real threat of exile is finally made explicit in the prophetic word to the king (20:12–19). Up to this point such a danger had only been hinted at (see 8:19).

On examination it is clear that the account of the reform of Josiah follows the same pattern. Manasseh, his most important predecessor, is explicitly compared to Ahab and is seen by the writer as the southern version of that northern embodiment of apostasy. Like the reforms of Joash and Hezekiah, Josiah's reform was primarily anti-Canaanite. The items that are so important to the reform are those which the deuteronomist has consistently found so abhorrent (see *Comment* below). The reform is also accompanied by some form of temple reorganization. It began in the context of temple repair and ends with the inauguration of a new Passover celebration in Jerusalem. But like those reformers who preceded him, his reign is not without its shadows. In the midst of the reform Huldah repeats again the word of judgment (22:15–20) against the nation uttered by Isaiah, and Josiah dies an untimely death at Megiddo. In spite of everything, his reign ends with Judah under foreign domination—that of Egypt.

It is clear to see that if any form or pattern is followed in the narrative it is the writer's previously established one. The climax of the reign of each reformer, however good the beginning, is a shadow cast over the country. Two out of three reformers in the south die before their time; the third comes close to death with sickness. We have seen many times in the narrative of 2 Kings how the fate of the king mirrors the fate of the nation. The judgment on both Israel and Judah is delayed only through the intervention of Yahweh. The narrative of Josiah's reign and reform takes its place among the others as finally pointing toward the inevitable fate of Judah. According to 22:18–20 and 23:26–27, judgment is not averted by anything done by Josiah.

Comment

Josiah became king at a young age and inherited the policies of his father and grandfather, both of whom were subjects of Assyria. The once strong Assyrian empire was already showing signs of weakness in the latter part of the seventh century B.C., and following the death of Asshurbanipal in 626 B.C., serious flaws began to develop in the structure of the empire. Nabopolassar, the so-called "architect" of the neo-Babylonian empire (626–605 B.C.), allied himself with the Medes, inhabitants of the territory in modern northwestern Iran. According to Herodotus (bk. 1.95–104), they too were uniting and expanding. Together this alliance posed a very serious threat to the ailing Assyria. At the other end of the empire, the Egyptians, who had won independence from Assyria in 655 B.C., made significant inroads into Palestine under Psammetichus I, father of the Necho of 2 Kgs 23:29–31. To add to the woes of Assyria, bands of Cimmerians and Scythians harassed her northern borders.

Josiah's reign witnessed the final demise of Assyria. In 612 B.C. Nineveh fell to the neo-Babylonians, just two years after Asshur had fallen to the Medes. In 610 B.C. the third and final capital, Haran, fell, and in the following year the combined pressure of Babylon, Media, and Egypt effectively saw the end of Assyria as a world power. (See Bright, *History*, 313–16; B. Oded, *Israelite and Jewish History*, 458–68, and H. F. W. Saggs, *The Greatness that was Babylon*, 141–45, for convenient summaries of these events.)

By any reckoning the reform described in 2 Kgs 22–23 began in 622/621 B.C., but a much debated issue is the precise motivation for the reform. While it is often customary to see the reform of Josiah in the context of the rapid disintegration of the Assyrian empire outlined above, it is going far beyond the evidence to interpret it as a grand gesture of independence on the part of the Judean king. Many interpreters still persist in referring to Josiah's expulsion of Assyrian astral deities from the Jerusalem temple (see Nicholson, *Deuteronomy and Tradition*, 1–17; Bright, *History*, 317–21), whereas evidence for this is completely lacking (see McKay, *Religion in Judah under the Assyrians*, 97–108). The available data and the extant record of the reform clearly portray it as the purging of the cultic practices of Judah and Jerusalem of those elements encouraged by Manasseh and his son Amon. As we have seen, the two previous kings introduced not Assyrian, but Canaanite practices into Judah. It is these practices which the deuteronomistic writer sees as the cause of the downfall of the northern kingdom. The battle against these practices is an ancient one and an important theme in the theological schema of Deuteronomy and the deuteronomistic history. In the account in 2 Kgs 22–23, nothing more is stated by way of reason for the reform.

Two phases of the reform can be traced in the extant record: first, the purification of Judean religion as an action dependent upon a covenant between king and people (23:1–20, 24–27) and second, an attempt at the centralization of worship in Jerusalem, inferred from the destruction of local shrines outside the city and the celebration of the royal passover in Jerusalem. This latter action is regarded as somehow unique in the history of the monarchy.

Claburn has offered an interesting interpretation of the reform from the point of view of economic and social change (see *JBL* 92 [1973] 11–22). He states, "Under a banner proclaiming the purification of Yahwistic worship, all Yahwistic shrines in Judah are desecrated and destroyed except the one having the greatest propensity of all towards pagan syncretism—the temple in Jerusalem. . . . And in the name of sacred national unity against foreign influence major traditional religious practices of a sizable segment of the indigenous population were vigorously attacked . . ." (p. 11). Claburn goes on to argue persuasively for a fiscal motivation for the so-called reform. Whatever the merits of his thesis—the pros and cons cannot be argued here—Claburn's shrewd observation does point out that modern notions of "nationalism," "national unity," and "independence," which many interpreters use in their search for understanding the actions of Josiah, are foreign to the text and to the stated motivation for the reform. Josiah's activities are presented as having more in common with the prophetic ideal and enthusiasm that inspired the coup d'état of Jehu. The measures undoubtedly had political overtones and results, but it is the religious motivation that is the target of attention for our writer.

1 The introduction to the reign of Josiah is the standard one for kings of Judah. בן שמנה שנה "eight years old." See Montgomery, *Kings*, 523, for some questions concerning the grammar. Amon dies at the age of twenty-three and was thus a father at fourteen. Josiah, dying at the age of thirty-eight with two sons of twenty-three and twenty-five, became a father at thirteen/fourteen and fifteen/sixteen. The name of Josiah's mother, ידידה "Jedidah," means "beloved" and is a feminine form of Solomon's first name. The name also occurs in 2 Sam 12:25. בת עדיה "daughter of Adiyah." The name is from the root "ornament" and is a very common one especially in the post-exilic period. בצקת "Bozkath": According to Josh 15:39 the site is on the Shephelah between Lachish and Eglon. Lachish is almost universally identified with Tel ed-Duweir (but see G. Ahlstrom, "Is Tell ed-Duweir Ancient Lachish?" *PEQ* 112 [1980] 7–9, and the response by G. I. Davies, "Tell ed-Duweir = Ancient Lachish" *PEQ* 114 [1982] 23–28). Eglon is either Tell el-Hesi (so Albright) or Tell Eton (so Aharoni). If the former is correct, then Tell Nagila is a good candidate for Bozkath, but the identification is uncertain.

2 Josiah equals Hezekiah in his piety and matches the standard of royal piety for the deuteronomist, King David. לא סר ימין ושמאול "he did not stray to the right or to the left" is a deuteronomistic expression (see Deut 5:32; 17:11, 20; 28:14). Hezekiah and Josiah are matched here. However, as the narrative unfolds it is clear that neither can avert the final judgment on Judah.

3 The account of the first visit to the temple (vv 3–7) is very reminiscent of the visit in 12:10–16 [9–15]. This is understandable because of the nature of the common subject matter and the probable source for the information contained here, namely, the temple archives (see Burney, *Notes*, 355). However, the formal similarities between this and chap. 12 and other narratives of reform should be noted. The present story betrays no sense that the move on the part of the king was an innovation. It appears to be a continuation of the policy for financing temple projects initiated by Joash in 2 Kgs 12. However, in the light of the state of affairs during the reigns of Ahaz and Manasseh, this might be a return to older policies. בשמנה עשרה שנה למלך "in the king's eighteenth year." In view of the problems of harmonization with Chronicles noted above, it is tempting to read the phrase למלך, lit., "to the king," as a reference to the king's age. This would then be in the tenth year of his reign, which is not too far removed from the twelfth year of Chronicles. But this is merely juggling with the figures. The term למלך is used consistently elsewhere of the reign of a king (12:7; 18:9, 13). The eighteenth year of the reign would have been 622/621 B.C. Whether this move on the part of the king was in reaction to the chaos in Assyria following the death of Asshurbanipal is not stated in the text and is in fact unlikely. The temple repairs would have been part of the day-to-day (or year-to-year) responsibilities of the king and not necessarily a symbol of reform. In the narrative the reform begins with the discovery of the lawbook.

The name שפן "Shaphan" means "rock badger" and is one of many animal names in this narrative. Such names were popular at this time. Shaphan also figures prominently in other narratives from this period. In Jer 26:24 his son Ahikam aids Jeremiah the prophet; and his other son, Gemariah, was a noble in Jerusalem during the reign of Jehoiakim (Jer 36:12, 25). A grandson, the ill-fated Gedaliah (Jer 40:5–41:10), was an important-enough figure to be named governor of Judah after the fall of Jerusalem to the Babylonians The name אצליהו "Azalyah" is from a semitic root indicating nobility (see Exod 24:11). That Shaphan, הספר "the scribe," was involved in this venture is only natural. The system of temple accounting which involved the palace bureaucracy is seen in 12:11 [10] and the reason for their involvement is also seen in chap. 12, namely, the lax attitude of the priesthood. It is quite possible too that the detailed record of the events in chap. 12 and here owe their origin to such people. Note the adverbial use of the noun phrase בית יהוה "(to) the temple," as in 12:17 [16]. This is common deuteronomistic style.

4 Montgomery's judgment (*Kings*, 524) that the whole passage, especially v 4, is secondary because of its clumsy arrangement is unjustified. The language is more pedantic than clumsy and supports our suggestion that it owes its origin to the palace bureaucrats. Further, nothing in the actions of the king thus far has given the slightest hint that he was in open revolt against Assyria (see Nicholson, *Deuteronomy and Tradition*, 12). Shaphan's ascent to the temple is presented as nothing more than part of his regular responsibilities. Even during an Assyrian overlordship the temple would have to be maintained.

It is unlikely that חלקיהו "Hilkiah" is to be identified with the father of the prophet Jeremiah, who was presumably also a priest (Jer 1:1–2). Jeremiah's family was not from Jerusalem, but from Anathoth, and therefore of Levitic stock, not Zadokite. Nothing in the book of Jeremiah favors the identification, and the prophet's deep antipathy to Jerusalem (Jer 24) would speak against it. On the office of הכהן הגדול "the Great Priest," see 12:11 [10] and the comments there. ויתם. See n. 4.b. for the variants. A change is tempting but not necessary. Gen 47:15 uses the same verb with כסף "silver," and the RSV translates it there as "spend." According to the account in chap. 12, Shaphan's duties would have involved the supervision of the distribution of the money in the interests of the repairs to the temple. הכסף המובא "the silver of income." See 12:10–17 [9–16] and the comments there. There had been serious periodic drains on the resources of the temple and palace. Not only had Joash been forced to use the money to pay off an invader, so had Hezekiah. Josiah used it here for the purposes for which it was originally intended. שמרי הסף "Keepers of the Threshold." See 12:10 [9] and the comments there.

5 The verse is almost a duplicate of 12:12 [11] but cannot be taken as a simple copy. The most probable source for the information contained here— the palace and temple archives—would account for the measure of homogeneity. Note that everything is done "by the book" following long-established procedures for the management of the temple.

6 See 12:12–13 [11–12] for a similar list of persons, and 1 Kgs 5:17– 18.

7 As with the workmen in 12:15, no accounting was made of the money once it was distributed to the workmen. The latter clearly worked well and honestly.

8 The finding of the lawbook has generated a considerable amount of discussion among commentators. The contents of the book and its precise relationship to the reform are the main items of discussion. The date of Deuteronomy has also been calculated from this incident. However, such historical conclusions from what is so clearly a theologically determined picture are less than certain. It is clear in the deuteronomistic history that the ideal standards of Israel's behavior are enshrined in the deuteronomic law code. It is our belief, argued in the *Introduction,* that the final form of the book of Deuteronomy is late, and the book forms a preface to the greater work of the deuteronomistic history. The laws within the book, however, have ancient roots. That the incentive for reform should come from a document that offers the ideals found in Deuteronomy is thoroughly consistent with what one might expect from our writer.

The term ספר designates not a book in the modern sense of the term, a codex, but a written document probably scrolled and written in columns. The earliest examples of such documents are the extant Dead Sea scrolls. ספר התורה "the lawbook" is a very common term in the deuteronomistic writings (Deut 17:18; 28:58, 61; 29:20, 21, 27; 30:10; 31:24, 26; Josh 1:8; 8:31, 34; 23:6; 24:6) and is also a term in vogue in the post-exilic period, as reflected in its use in the books of Ezra-Nehemiah. The scroll is found by accident in the story, and the contents of it are not revealed until quite late. The writer's intention to echo the ideals of Deuteronomy becomes clear. However, this close identification of the lawbook with Deuteronomy has recently been challenged (see J. R. Lundbom, *CBQ* 38[1976] 293–302). To be noted is that the repairs on the temple had already begun before the book was found; therefore to link them to the deuteronomic reform is a mistake. Rather, the reform is directed more to the purging of shrines of Canaanite religious practices. ויקראהו "and he read it." This is an important step in the narrative. Certain actors are now aware of the contents of the scroll, and their subsequent actions show that the contents are of a very serious nature. The reader is not yet aware of what the scroll contains.

9 Shaphan functions as a go-between for some of the main actors in the story. וַיָּשֶׁב is an awkward construction, though not impossible. The pointing is hiphil, "he caused to return." (See the use in 3:4.) התיכו "they have emptied out." The root is נתך, literally, "pour out," and is often associated with the melting of metals. It could be used here in a metaphorical way, "doled out." (See *Comment* on 12:11.)

10 ספר נתן "he gave me a book." Shaphan's comment to the king contains an interesting shift in emphasis. The affairs of the temple repair have been taken care of, but the next comment stresses the importance of the book which Hilkiah gave him. Note the change in the word order from the normal Hebrew sentence of verb-subject-object. ויקראהו "and he read it." This is the second occurrence of this verb in the narrative. Still the reader does not know what the contents of the scroll are, but the circle of those who do know is now extended to include the king.

11 In 5:7 the king of Israel tore his clothes as a gesture of despair and anger, but here Josiah, like Hezekiah, acts out of repentance. The numerous parallels with Jer 36 have been noted above in *Form/Structure/Setting*. An additional contrast is the reaction of each king to the written word. One heeds it, another cuts it up and deposits it in the fire. An underlying theme of the chapter is the relationship of king to the word of Yahweh. It is interesting that the prophet who is most critical of the kings of Judah, Jeremiah, should fail to make any statement directly to Josiah (for a development of the theme in the Book of Jeremiah, see R. P. Carroll, *From Chaos to Covenant*, 136–57).

12 With this verse the king now takes the center-stage, and the events that follow revolve around the king, his actions, and his fate. אחיקם "Ahikam" is the father of the ill-fated Gedaliah (25:22), and the family was obviously an important one in Jerusalem at this time. The name means "my kinsman rises (up)" and is not found outside the OT, although both elements of the name are found in other names. Ahikam's later aid to Jeremiah (Jer 26:24) saved the prophet from death. עכבור "Achbor" means "field mouse," another of the animal names of the passage. His son Elnathan also figures in Jeremiah's arrest, trial, and eventual release (Jer 26:22). עשיה עבד המלך "Asayah the servant of the king." The name means "Yahweh makes," and his rank is that of senior civil servant. The phrase is not a proper name. (For occurrences of the name outside the Bible, see Gibson, *Syrian Semitic Inscriptions* 1:62.)

13 Another king, Ahaziah, "sought" a deity in 2 Kings chap. 1. Whether the contrast is deliberate or not, it does bear reflection. The breadth of Josiah's concern is noteworthy, especially when compared with Hezekiah's attitude toward the end of his reign. The earlier king was basically self-centered. The inclusion of העם "the people" and כל יהודה "the whole of Judah" is cause for the omission of the second by many commentators (see *BHS*). The two terms, however, are not necessarily synonymous, and there is no textual evidence for the omission of the latter. על דברי הספר "concerning the contents of the book." This is the first hint in the narrative of the seriousness of the contents of the lawbook, and it reminds the reader of the warnings given to Solomon (see 1 Kgs 2:1–4; 9:1–9). The warnings are now being brought to fruition. כי גדולה חמת "for the anger is great" is a reference to immediate judgment, not to something past. Both Deuteronomy and Jeremiah modify the law concerning family complicity in the sins of an individual (see Jer 31:29–30; Deut 24:16). This makes the thought expressed by Josiah unusual. The point to be made, however, is the cumulative effect of the repeated apostasies of the kings of Judah, which will inevitably end in judgment. **14** וילך אל חלדה הנביאה "so he went to Huldah the prophetess." Nothing is known about this woman apart from the information offered here, and little is known about the tradition of female prophets in the society of ancient Israel. Huldah joins the ranks of Miriam, Deborah, the wife of Isaiah, and Noadiah. Two other prophets are known to have been active at this time, Jeremiah and Zephaniah, but they are not mentioned nor even involved in the reform. Huldah was related by marriage to a court official, the keeper of the royal wardrobe (see 10:22), and she is, in Wilson's borrowed terminology, a "central prophet." (See R. R. Wilson, *Prophet and Society in Ancient Israel*, 219–23; for an exposition of the meaning of "central" and "peripheral" to describe social roles, see the foundational article by E. Shils, *Center and Periphery: Essays in Macrosociology*, 2–16, first published in 1961.) Huldah was part of the "structure of activities, roles and persons" at the center of society. Hence she is quickly consulted by the king and his servants. In the light of Jeremiah's vicious attacks on Jerusalem and Judean society in general and his origin from the levitic town of Anathoth, his absence from these incidents is not unusual.

במשנה "in the Mishneh" is generally taken to be the northern part of the city—the part extended during the monarchy—hence the name "The Second Quarter." Evidence has shown that during the late monarchy the city expanded considerably (see M. Broshi, "The Expansion of Jerusalem" *IEJ* 24 [1974] 21–26). For the location of the Mishneh, see G. A. Smith, *Jerusalem* 1:201–2. Another area of the extended city was the "Maktesh," the "depression," possibly the area in the central valley (the Tyropean). In postexilic times the Mishneh became an official administrative division of the city (see Zech 1:10; Neh 11:9, 17).

15 Huldah speaks in the style of the classic prophetic tradition of the OT. אמרו לאיש אשר שלח אתכם אלי "say to the man who sent you all to me" echoes the words of the prophet Elijah (chap. 1) to those sent by Ahaziah to Ekron. Many divide the oracle into two sections (vv 15–17, 18–20), and the impression is that they are two separate ones, addressed to "the man who sent you" and to "the king of Judah." But both abound in deuteronomistic terminology. J. Priest (*VT* 30 [1980] 366–68) regards Huldah as a cult-prophetess, but such an activity would be difficult to carry out in the Mishneh.

16 הנני מביא רעה "see, I am about to bring evil." See the link with an oracle given in the reign of Manasseh (21:12). Outside these stories the style is not common. המקום הזה "this place." Jerusalem is clearly intended. את כל דברי . . . "all the contents . . ." The style is that of the covenant curse and has the material of Deut 27–28 in mind.

17 The catalogue of apostasy which is the reason for the impending judgment is deuteronomistic and reminiscent of numerous similar summaries. ולא תכבה "and it will not be doused" (see Jer 7:20). The delay of judgment against Judah, which began in 8:19, is now fast running its course, and the inevitability of the judgment is stressed.

19 The delay in judgment here results from the repentance of the "second David" and reflects Yahweh's response to Hezekiah. The echo is heard again with the comment אנכי שמעתי "I have listened" (see 19:20).

20 In the light of what follows concerning the death of Josiah, the promise is somewhat enigmatic. The expression אספך על אבתיך "I will gather you to your ancestors" is a standard one for death in the OT, usually implying a nonviolent death (see Gen 25:8). The enigma is highlighted by the use of the adverbial phrase בשלום "in peace." The events that follow imply the opposite. That the term applies to the nation and not the king (so Nicholson, *Deuteronomy and Tradition*, 15) is possible but unlikely, since a nation at war with Egypt can hardly be said to be בשלום. The only possibility is that the term refers to the period before the exile under Babylon and is therefore relative. See the use of the idiom ולא תראינה עיניך "your eyes shall not see" in Gen 21:16 and 44:34. Like Hezekiah, Josiah will be spared the agony of his nation's destruction. וישיבו את המלך דבר "they brought this word back to the king." With this comment the first "movement" of the story of the reign of Josiah is ended.

The Reign of Josiah, Continued (23:1-37)

Bibliography

See Chap. 22.

Translation

¹ *The king then sent word and all the elders of Judah and Jerusalem were gathered* [a] *to him.* ² *The king went up* [a] *to the temple, and with him went each man of Judah and all the inhabitants of Jerusalem, together with the priests and the prophets* [b] *everybody went up, from the least to the greatest. In their hearing* [c] *he read all the words of the book of the covenant which had been discovered in the temple.* ³ *The king then took his position by the column and made a pact with Yahweh to follow Yahweh and to keep his commandments, his testimonies, and his statutes with his heart and soul,* [a] *to establish* [b] *the words of this covenant written in this book, and all the people joined in* [c] *the covenant.*
⁴ *The king ordered Hilkiah the Great Priest, the deputy priests,* [a] *and the keepers of the threshhold to bring out from Yahweh's sanctuary all the vessels made for Baal, Asherah, and all the host of heaven, and to burn them outside Jerusalem in the open country* [b] *near Kidron. Then they carried* [c] *their ashes to Bethel.* ⁵ *He deposed the idol-priests* [a] *whom the kings of Judah had installed to burn incense* [b] *in the high places in the Judean cities and in the environs of Jerusalem, together with those who burned incense to Baal, to the sun, to the moon, to the constellations* [c] *and all the host of the heavens.* ⁶ *He brought out the Asherah from the temple to the Valley of Kidron outside Jerusalem and ground it to dust. Then he scattered its ashes on the public cemetery.* ⁷ *He demolished the quarters of the (male) prostitutes which were in the temple, where women used to weave tent coverings* [a] *for the Asherah.*

⁸ *He brought out all the priests of the cities of Judah and defiled the high places where the priests had offered incense, from Geba* ᵃ *to Beer Sheba. He demolished the high places of the gates* ᵇ *which were at the entrance to the Gate of Joshua the city governor. They were on the left as one entered the city gate.* ⁹ *But the priests of the high places did not come up to the altar in Jerusalem; instead they ate unleavened bread* ᵃ *among their fellow-priests.* ¹⁰ *He desecrated Topheth, which is in the Valley of the Sons* ᵃ *of Hinnom, so that no man might force* ᵇ *his son or daughter to pass through fire for Molech.* ᶜ ¹¹ *He put an end* ᵃ *to the horses which the king of Judah had dedicated to the sun near the entrance* ᵇ *to the temple by the quarters of Nathanmelek,* ᶜ *the eunuch who was in the area.* ᵈ *He burned the chariots of the sun with fire.* ¹² *The altars* ᵃ *on the roof of the upper room of Ahaz* ᵃ *which the kings of Judah had made, and the altars which Manasseh had constructed in the two temple courts, the king demolished. He crushed them* ᵇ *and scattered their dust into the Valley of Kidron.* ¹³ *As for the high places* ᵃ *facing Jerusalem to the south of the Mount of Spoiling* ᵇ *which Solomon king of Israel had built for Ashtoreth, the detested thing of the Sidonians, and for Chemosh, the detested thing of Moab, and for Milcom, the abomination of the Ammonites, the king desecrated them.* ¹⁴ *He smashed the pillars and cut down* ᵃ *the Asherim and filled their locations with human bones.*

¹⁵ *The altar at Bethel, the high place Jeroboam son of Nebat had constructed and with which he caused Israel to sin, that same altar and high place he demolished. He burned* ᵃ *the high place* ᵇ *and crushed it, and he burned the Asherah.* ¹⁶ *Josiah turned and saw the graves which were upon the hill,* ᵃ *and he sent someone to take the bones from the graves and burn them upon the altar, thus desecrating it, according to Yahweh's word which the man of God* ᵇ *had announced, the one who had declared these things.* ¹⁷ *He then said, "What is that* ᵃ *monument* ᵇ *which I see?" Then the men of the city replied, "It is the grave* ᶜ *of the man of God who came from Judah and announced all these things which you have just done to the altar at Bethel."* ¹⁸ *He said, "Let him rest. Let no one disturb his bones." So they let his bones alone with the bones of the prophet* ᵃ *who had come from Samaria.* ¹⁹ *All the shrines of the high places which were in the Samarian cities made by the kings of Israel as a provocation, Josiah removed. He did to them exactly as he had done in Bethel.* ²⁰ *He slaughtered on the altars all the priests of the high places who were there and burned human bones upon them; then he returned to Jerusalem.*

²¹ *The King ordered all the people, "Perform the Passover to Yahweh your God, as it is written in this book of the covenant."* ²²ᵃ *For such a Passover* ᵇ *had not been performed from the days of the judges who governed Israel, through all the days of the kings of Israel and Judah,* ²³ *except in the eighteenth year of King Josiah; this* ᵃ *Passover was performed to Yahweh in Jerusalem.* ²⁴ *In addition, all the mediums, the wizards, the teraphim, the idols, and all such despicable things which were to be seen in the country of Judah and in Jerusalem, Josiah exterminated so that he might affirm the words of the law written in the book which Hilkiah the priest found in the temple.* ᵃ ²⁵ *There was no king like him who returned to Yahweh body and soul* ᵃ *in keeping with the law of Moses. Neither did one ever appear after him.*

²⁶ *But still Yahweh did not revert from the ferocity of his great anger which was aroused against Judah because of all the provocations of Manasseh.* ²⁷ *Yahweh had declared, "I will remove Judah from before me* ᵃ *as I have removed Israel. I will reject this city I have chosen, the same Jerusalem and temple of which I declared, 'My name shall be there.'"*

330   2 KINGS 23:1-37

²⁸ Now the remainder of the activities of Josiah, are they [a] not written in the record of the kings of Judah? ²⁹ In his days Pharaoh Necho, king of Egypt, came up to fight on behalf of the king of Assyria at the River Euphrates. King Josiah went to engage him in a battle, but Pharaoh Necho killed him at the battle of Megiddo. ³⁰ His servants carried his body from Megiddo and brought it to Jerusalem and buried him in his grave. [a] The people of the land then took Jehoahaz, anointed him and set him up as king in the place of his father.

³¹ Jehoahaz was twenty-three years old when he began his reign, and he reigned for three months in Jerusalem. His mother's name was Hamutal of Libnah. ³² He behaved badly in Yahweh's eyes, as all his ancestors had done. ³³ Pharaoh Necho imprisoned him at Riblah in the land of Hamath during his reign [a] in Jerusalem, then he imposed a penalty upon the land [b] of one hundred talents of silver and one talent of gold. ³⁴ Pharaoh made Eliakim son of Josiah king in place of his father, and he changed his name to Jehoiakim. He took Jehoahaz away and brought [a] him to Egypt, but there he died. ³⁵ Jehoiakim handed over the silver and the gold to Pharaoh, and he taxed the land to give the money into Pharaoh's coffers. With the help of [a] the people of the land, he exacted the silver and the gold according to each person's assessment to give to Pharaoh Necho.

³⁶ Jehoiakim was twenty-five years old when he began to reign, and he reigned eleven years in Jerusalem. His mother's name was Zebidah daughter of Pedayah from Rumah. ³⁷ He behaved badly in Yahweh's eyes, as his ancestors had done.

Notes

1.a. MT reads וַיַּאַסְפוּ "and they gathered." G^BL has a sg. The verbal form is awkward since it is usually transitive. Montgomery (Kings, 538) suggests it be read as pointed niph.
2.a. G^L again adds the king's proper name.
2.b. For "prophets" 2 Chr 34:30 reads "Levites," which Ehrlich (Randglossen 7:357) readily accepts. However, see Burney's sound caution (Notes, 357).
2.c. For באזניהם "in their hearing," G^B offers an unusual ἐνώπιον αὐτῶν "in their presence."
3.a. The Heb. expression בכל לב ובכל נפש, lit., "with all heart and with all soul" is an idiom and is therefore translated by an English idiom signifying total commitment.
3.b. MT reads להקים "to establish." G^L presupposes לעשות "to do."
3.c. For ויעמד "joined in" some versions read ויעבר "entered into."
4.a. Tg reads the sg. See Ehrlich, Randglossen 7:319.
4.b. MT reads בשדמות "in the fields." But the topography of Kidron hardly lends itself to this description. The term could also be translated "open country," but even this is a very generous description of the area. G^B offers a near-transliteration with ἐν σαλημωθ "in Salemoth." G^L, however, reads ἐν τῷ ἐμπυρισμῷ τοῦ Χειμάρρου "in the furnace by the streambed (of Kidron)," which appears to have been influenced by the MT of Jer 31:40. The precise nature of the activity in the Kidron which resulted in the burning is not clear. Gray therefore suggests a translation of "limekilns" (see Kings, 730). For a helpful discussion see Montgomery, Kings, 538.
4.c. MT reads ונשא "then he carried."
5.a. MT reads כמרים "idol-priests," but G transliterates.
5.b. G reads the pl, and G^L suggests לקטר "to burn incense" for MT's "and he burnt incense."
5.c. MT reads מזלות, lit., "heavenly stations"; see Comment below.
7.a. The Heb. בתים "houses" is awkward. G offers χεττιεω, which might be a transliteration of כתנים "tunics." G^L translates στολας "robes." Montgomery (Kings, 539), following an early suggestion of G. R. Driver ("Supposed Arabisms in the OT," JBL 55 [1936] 101-20), thinks the Heb. might be related to an Arabic batt. The word means garment.
8.a. For MT גבע "Geba" G^B offers Γαβαλ "Byblos."
8.b. MT reads הַשְּׁעָרִים "the gates." Gray (Kings, 7) suggests a pointing of הַשְּׂעָרִים "the gatekeepers." Burney (Notes, 359) suggests בֵּית הַשְּׂעִירִים "house of the satyrs."

Notes 331

9.a. Many accept the emendation of מַצּוֹת "unleavened bread" to מִצְוֹת "commandments" used adverbially: "They ate according to custom . . ." (so Gray, *Kings*, 730; Ehrlich, *Randglossen* 7:320).
10.a. Qere suggests בֵּן "son." See Josh 15:8.
10.b. MT reads לְבִלְתִּי הַעֲבִיר "so that he might not force to pass through." G^B omits לְבִלְתִּי "so that not."
10.c. The pointing of מֹלֶךְ "Molech" is taken to be a reflection of the pointing of בֹּשֶׁת "shame."
11.a. MT reads וַיַּשְׁבֵּת "he put an end"; G^B reads κατεκαυσεν "he burned."
11.b. מָבֹא "entrance" is better pointed מָבוֹא or בְּמָבוֹא.
11.c. G^L reads the phrase as "Nathan, the king's eunuch."
11.d. G transliterates בפרורים "in the area."
12.a–a. G^L changes the opening of the sentence somewhat with ἃ ἦν ἐπι των δωματων των ὑπερωων ἀχαξ βασιλεως Ἰουδα "which were upon the upper chambers of Ahaz, king of Judah."
12.b. MT reads נתץ המלך וירץ משם lit., "the king demolished and he crushed from there." G^L expands this considerably. As it stands the Heb. is difficult. וירץ (from the root רצץ) "and he crushed" is awkward with the double preposition משם. Gray (*Kings*, 731) suggests וידקם (from the root דקק) "and he crushed them there." Although the primitive Heb. consonants might look similar to what is found in MT, the change is still a large one. Rudolph's suggestion (*ZAW* 63 [1951] 201–15) that we read וַיָּרֶץ משם "and he banished from there," or וַיְרִצֵם שׁם "and he banished them there," from the root רוץ "to banish," is an attractive possibility, but uncertain.
13.a. G^B reads בֵּית "house."
13.b. MT reads הַמַּשְׁחִית "the Spoiling." G treats this as a proper name, comparable to "The Hill of Shemer" purchased by Omri (1 Kgs 16:24). Ehrlich (*Randglossen* 7:321) identifies the hill as the Mount of Olives (הַר הַזֵּיתִים). Most, in fact, regard the MT reading as a corruption (deliberate) of the term הַר הַמִּשְׁחָה "Mount of Oil," an earlier name for the Mount of Olives.
14.a. For וַיִּכְרֹת "and he cut down" G reads ἐξωλεθρευσεν "he utterly destroyed," but G^L follows MT.
15.a. For וַיִּשְׂרֹף "and he burned" G reads συνετριψεν (וַיְשַׁבֵּר) "he broke in pieces."
15.b. MT = אֶת הַבָּמָה "the high place." G^BL suggests a reading of אֶת אֲבָנָיו "his stones," adopted by Burney, *Notes*, 361.
16.a. MT = בָּהָר "upon the hill." G^B reads εν τη πολει (בָּעִיר) "in the city," which is accepted by some. However, the evidence suggests that only the royal tombs were inside the city.
16.b. Following אִישׁ הָאֱלֹהִים "the man of God," G adds much which Burney considers original (see *Notes*, 361).
17.a. The MT הַלָּז "that" reflects a northern dialect (cf. *Comment* on 4:25).
17.b. MT reads הַצִּיּוּן "monument." See Ezek 39:15.
17.c. MT = הַקֶּבֶר אִישׁ הָאֱלֹהִים "the grave of the man of God." The syntax is clumsy and הַקֶּבֶר "the grave" would be expected without the article. The word is omitted by G^B. There are occurrences of such constructions elsewhere in the OT (see GKC § 127g).
18.a. G^L adds the equivalent of הַנָּבִיא הַזָּקֵן הַיֹּשֵׁב בְּבֵית אֵל "the senior prophet who lived in Bethel," which is adopted by Burney, *Notes*, 362.
22.a. G^L adds και ἐποιησαν οὕτως "and they did this."
22.b. MT = כַּפֶּסַח הַזֶּה "such a Passover." Ehrlich (*Randglossen* 7:322) favors an emendation to פֶּסַח לַיהוה "Passover for Yahweh." Such a move is unnecessary.
23.a. הַזֶּה "this" is omitted by G^B.
24.a. G reads ἐν οἴκῳ "in the house of," which does not necessitate a preposition on the Heb. noun. In deuteronomistic literature nouns like this often function adverbially without prepositions.
25.a. In G^B the words נֶפֶשׁ "soul" and מְאֹד "might" are reversed. G^ALN and the G text of 2 Chr 35:19*b* all agree with MT.
27.a. G^B presupposes פָּנָיו "his face."
28.a. G^L translates οὐκ ἰδου "behold, are they not."
30.a. G^N adds ". . . in the city of David," a gloss to standardize the burial formula.
33.a. MT = בְּמָלְכוֹ "during his reign" but Qere reads מִמָּלְכוֹ "from his reign," which is supported by G^B (του μη βασιλευειν). The emendation would provide the translation ". . . to prevent him from reigning." This makes better sense, but it is still clumsy.

33.b. The phrase עֹנֶשׁ עַל הָאָרֶץ "a penalty upon the land" is omitted by G^B.
34.a. MT = וַיָּבֹא "and he came." Vg G^BL presupposes וַיָּבֵא "and he brought."
35.a. MT reads אֶת עַם הָאָרֶץ "(with) the people of the land"; either the direct object or the preposition "with" is intended. G reads the latter with μετα του λαου της γης.

Comment

Chap. 23 continues the narrative of the reign of Josiah which was begun in chap. 22, but it moves into the reform proper. Vv 1–3 depict the king's reaction to the contents of the lawbook. He called together an assembly of the people and entered into a pact with them before Yahweh. All partners in the covenant, king and people, promised to obey the stipulations of the lawbook (now called a covenant–book). The action is reminiscent of Josh 24, and the style throughout is deuteronomistic. Some would argue that vv 4–5 constitute an ancient tradition used and expanded by the deuteronomist and that vv 16–20 are part of an independent tradition incorporated into the chapter by the writer (see G. S. Ogden, *AusBR* 26 [1978] 26–34). On the supposed sources of the chapter, see chap. 22, *Form/Structure/Setting*.

1 Now the king begins to act decisively and takes "center stage" in the narrative. The elders, the old family heads, are often portrayed as holders of limited political power in the period of the monarchy. Although they retained some political role, their real power was probably nonexistent, usurped by the new stratification of society which became inevitable with the introduction of the centralized monarchy. (For a full description of this process, see S. N. Eisenstadt, *The Political Systems of Empires*.) In terms of narrative development, the circle of those involved in the reaction to the contents of the lawbook now widens even further. (See also G. Henton Davies, "Elder in the OT," *IDB* 2:72–73; and A. Malamat, *BA* 28 [1965] 34–65.)

2 The inclusion of the whole list of civil and religious officials in this verse widens the circle of those privy to the contents of the lawbook. Now all the religious and civil representatives of the people are involved in the narrative. For similar groupings, see Jer 13:13; 26:7. סֵפֶר הַבְּרִית "book of the covenant." Now a different term is used for the book found in the temple. Although the terms בְּרִית "covenant" and תּוֹרָה "law" are not to be equated, in Deuteronomy they are closely related. The English translation of תּוֹרָה as "law" often confuses the issue.

3 The people, led by the king, now take decisive action. The king stands at a spot עַל הָעַמּוּד "by the column" in the temple signifying his authority. See the similar narrative in 11:14. וַיִּכְרֹת אֶת הַבְּרִית "and he made a pact." This action is not necessarily a repetition of the pact thought to be drawn between the king and people at the accession of the king (see Malamat, *BA* 28 [1965] 34–65). The literary echoes here are more prominent. Josiah functions as did Moses and Joshua, and the deuteronomist understands this action as a renewal of the Sinai covenant. The language of the verse is thoroughly deuteronomistic. See Deut 6:17; 1 Kgs 2:3; 4:29. That the people יַעֲמֹד "stand" in the covenant is unusual though by no means impossible.

4 On the dissection of vv 4–14, see chap. 22, *Form/Structure/Setting*. See 25:18 where one man, Zephaniah, is given the rank of "deputy priest." לַבַּעַל וְלָאֲשֵׁרָה "for Baal and Asherah." If Josiah is reacting against the activities of his father and grandfather, then this is clear evidence in support of the thesis of Cogan and McKay that in Judah under Assyrian overlordship Canaanite religion flourished. ולכל צבא השמים "and for all the host of heaven." See Deut 4:19 and the specific prohibitions there. The deuteronomic law clearly regards this activity as Canaanite. Burning is the customary fate of such trappings of apostasy. The action was as much symbolic as physical since stone and metal would be difficult to burn.

בשדמות "in the open country" is the poetic form for "pasture land," which hardly suits the terrain of the Kidron. Emendations range from משרפות "fires" to שדי מות "death fields." But neither is necessarily more appropriate or correct. The land east of Jerusalem was certainly suitable for grazing sheep and goats, as it is today. The difficulties of understanding come more from a cultural barrier. "Pasture lands" in the eastern Mediterranean are far from the image of rural England or Europe, which some commentators seem to have in mind. קדרון "Kidron" is the valley to the east of the city of David. Eventually emptying into the Dead Sea, it is already steep by the time it reaches the Ophel ridge. It is right below the temple area and would provide a convenient dumping ground for the items thrown out of the temple. ונשא is literally "and he will bear," which makes little sense in the context; one would expect a *waw* consecutive with an imperfect. בית אל "Bethel" anticipates the action in vv 15–18.

5 The reform is now broadened to include not only the trappings of idolatry, but also those who took part in idolatrous worship. On כמרים "idol priests," see Hos 10:5; Zeph 1:4. The term has many ANE parallels (see BDB, 485), but is not restricted to Assyrian priests (see McKay, *Religion in Judah under the Assyrians*, 36–38). "Whom the kings of Judah had installed" refers no doubt to the activities of Amon and Manasseh.

ויקטר, lit., "and he burned incense" is better understood as an infinitive construct or a plural (see n. 5.b.). ולמזלות "and to the constellations" is a common semitic astrological term. It is literally "mansions" or "stations" of the heavenly bodies. Later Heb. connected the term with the zodiac, but this is not so here (see Amos 5:26). The astral deities are found also in the Stele of Zakkir of Hamath, 1.24–26 (see Beyerlin, *Religious Texts*, 229–32).

6 Together with the other items used in Baal worship, the Asherah is destroyed. The Kidron area was used as a necropolis from at least the time of the First Temple. Archeological remains still stand as testimony. The graveyard was a suitable symbolic place for the dumping of these objects. The grinding to dust is a gesture of absolute destruction, of turning something from its form into chaos. על קבר בני עם "on the public cemetery." Barnes suggests changing the phrase to ב הנם "son of Hinnom" (*2 Kings*, 129), but this is hardly necessary. "Common grave" is a perfectly good rendering of the Heb. Such gestures as this were not to defile the graves; it is contact with dead bodies which defiles. Rather, the Asherah, now ground to dust, was placed where it belonged in the outlook of the reformers—with the dead.

7 ויתץ את־בתי הקשדים "He demolished the quarters of the (male) prostitutes." These quarters were set aside for the practice of cultic prostitution in the temple. Little is known of the practice except that it is roundly condemned by the OT, especially Deuteronomy (see 23:18–19). The next phrase is

an extremely puzzling comment. Even if the words are translated accurately, what they convey is still confusing. The quarters of the male prostitutes are unlikely places for the activity of weaving (ארג), and what was woven is obscure. Barnes (*2 Kings*, 130) following the RV margin, and others have suggested "tents" or "vestments." (See n. 7.a. for variants.)

8 The reform moves beyond Jerusalem now to include places of sacrifice in the whole of Judah. In view of the move, some regard vv 8–9 as dislocated (see Nicholson, *Deuteronomy and Tradition*, 14; Montgomery, *Kings*, 538). "The priests of the cities of Judah" presupposes a flourishing localized cult throughout Judah up to this point, and Josiah's expulsion of these local priests highlights the motivation of centralization which is clear in the record of the reform. "Defiling" made the high places no longer fit for any kind of worship.

Geba is to be identified with modern Jaba, a small village a few miles north of Jerusalem in the ancient territory of Benjamin (Grid 175–140). It is not far from Bethel and would have performed the same function as Bethel during the period of the monarchy, namely, that of a border shrine. During the excavations at Beer Sheba in the 1970s Aharoni discovered a dismantled horned altar which probably went out of use during the reform of Josiah (see Y. Yadin, *BASOR* 222 [1976] 5–17).

במות השערים "high places of the gates" is difficult to understand. It presupposes the location of several high places at one gate of the city. Such a location would not be out of the ordinary because of the symbolic nature of the city gate, but the plural is unusual. Gray's suggestion (*Kings*, 73) that the term be reread as שעירים "satyrs" is ingenious. שער יהושע "the Gate of Joshua" is a gate of the city not mentioned anywhere else in the OT, and its precise location is unknown to the modern reader. Yet it is obvious that it was known to the original readers and might have been an alternative name for a long established gate to Jerusalem. On שר העיר "the city governor," see *Comment* on 10:1. With this act of destruction the move for centralization is obvious.

9 The comment in this verse is an unusual and enigmatic one. If לא יעלו "they did not come up" is understood as frequentative, then it could imply that the priests did not come to sacrifice at Jerusalem either before or after the reform. Both are possible. It seems that they were allowed, or chose, to eat unleavened bread but not to participate in the sacrifice to Yahweh. In view of the tone of the record of the reform (and Deut 18:6–8), it appears that this was a result of the reform, and one which reduced the status of the country priests.

10 The verse is poorly preserved textually. It continues the saga of the reform in the vicinity of Jerusalem and concentrates on the other major valley bordering the city, the Valley of the Sons of Hinnom, which lies to the south and west of the old city. The term "Topheth" is thought to be connected to the Aramaic term for "furnace" or "fireplace," a plausible suggestion in view of the context. However, see M. Weinfeld *UF* 4 (1972) 133–54. Nonbiblical evidence for the practice of "burning" one's offspring is nonexistent. The act is possibly to be interpreted as one of dedication.

11 הסוסים "the horses" were statues or figurines dedicated to the worship of the sun. Barnes's earlier suggestion (*2 Kings*, 130) that they were live horses used in processions to pull "sun chariots" has recently received some support from McKay (see *PEQ* 105 [1973] 167–69). But the evidence cited there is late—third century A.D.—and hardly applicable. Kathleen Kenyon did discover in the city of David small figurines of horses with disks on their heads and necks, but the significance of the figurines is unknown. (For an illustration, see McKay, *Religion in Judah under the Assyrians*, 126.)

אשר בפרורים "who was in the area" (?). The location of Nathan-melech's quarters is precisely given. The word is Persian, suggesting colonnades (see 1 Chr 26:18). רכבות השמש "the chariots of the sun." The use of such vehicles remains a mystery, although their connection with the worship of the sun (Shamash) is obvious. (See Deut 4:29.)

12 The reform now includes additional altars made and installed in the temple by previous rulers, including Ahaz and Manasseh. The two had already been noted for their characteristic apostasy. The expression על הגג עלית אחז "on the roof of the upper room of Ahaz" is awkward, and one would expect no article on the noun גג. Gray thus describes it as a gloss (*Kings*, 737). However, the term עלית אחז could be either adverbial or appositional (see the similar expressions in Zeph 1:3; Jer 19:13). Many, of course, link the structure to the "steps" of Ahaz in 20:11. Ahaz alone was not responsible for the construction. The altars had long been in use by the Judean monarchy. Thus Josiah is turning over a long-established practice of the kings and cult in Jerusalem in the interests of the demands of the lawbook. On the two courts of the temple, see 21:5. The altar rubble eventually suffered the same fate as the other trappings of apostasy, being dumped into the Kidron Valley.

13 Still within the environs of Jerusalem, Josiah removes the high place built by Solomon. הר המשחית "the mountain of offense" is today identified with that which rises above the modern Arab village of Silwan. The location of the high place was to the south (מימין) of the hill. On the use of such geographical terms, see M. Har-el, *BA* 44 (1981) 19–20. Montgomery's suggestion (*Kings*, 533) that the term is a play on words and sarcastic has merit. The historical allusion is to the events described in 1 Kgs 11:5, 7, 33, in which Solomon allowed apostasy into the land through his many alliances by marriage with other nations. In this he plays the role of an erstwhile Ahab; see M. Buber, *The Prophetic Faith*, 76–77. On לעשתרת "for Ashtoreth," see R. A. Oden, *BA* 39 (1976) 31–36. On Milcom and Chemosh, see Ringgren, *Religions of the Ancient Near East*, 139. The term used to describe these deities, שקוץ "detested thing," is a derogatory one, reminiscent of the polemics of the prophets (see Hos 9:10; Jer 7:30; etc.).

14 The pillars and the Asherim are forbidden in Deut 7:5; 12:3; 16:21–22, and they are now abolished in accordance with that directive. The existence of these items in Jerusalem prior to the purge is presupposed but nowhere mentioned. Num 19:16–19 reveals the attitude to the touching of dead bodies. For an interesting insight into the social meaning of such action, see M. Douglas, *Purity and Danger*, 35–36.

15 The reform once again moves north to the territory of Benjamin, to Bethel. Benjamin had at various times belonged to Judah (see 2 Chr 11:12) so there is nothing unusual about this move on Josiah's part. Bethel was a border shrine when the northern nation was first established. For the high place built by Jeroboam, see 1 Kgs 12:25–33.

Many regard the second part of the verse as secondary (see Montgomery,

Kings, 534) on the grounds that a high place cannot be burned. That such apparent illogicalities are indicators of secondary glosses is itself illogical. Additions are made for the sake of clarification, rarely obfuscation. In any event, the burning of such installations, which would have included more than a simple stone platform, would have been as much symbolic as anything else. The asyndetic verb הדק "he crushed" here is also regarded by some as a sign of an addition (Montgomery, *Kings*, 534).

16 The whole of this section to v 20, because of "its generalities dependent upon the midrash of 1:13," is seen as an addition. Ogden, for example, suggests that the image of Jehu, which appears to lie behind the picture of Josiah, is sufficient indicator of its secondary nature. But such a model of Jehu for the presentation of Josiah, which becomes clearest in vv 19–20, is what one might expect. Josiah is correcting the excesses of the southern Ahab, Manasseh, and the picture is entirely in keeping with the deuteronomist's literary scheme.

Graves of prominent religious leaders are still to be found on hills throughout the West Bank even today. The grave lies among a clump of trees. Seemingly, the practice is an ancient one.

17 The verse brings to fulfillment the prophecy first given in 1 Kgs 13:2–3. The link is abundantly clear and consistent with the deuteronomist's understanding of history. On this see G. von Rad, *Studies in Deuteronomy*, 74–91. The noun הציון "the monument" is found only here and in Jer 31:21 and Ezek 39:15. The root is probably צוה, and the term indicates a very prominent landmark. לז "that" is a rare demonstrative, also found in Judg 6:20 and 2 Kgs 4:5. In Gen 24:65 it appears in a slightly different form. It seems to reflect a northern dialect of the language since it is found in direct speech and in two of the cases is used in incidents that take place in the north. הקבר איש האלהים "the grave of the man of God." In 1 Kgs 13 it is the man of God who comes from Bethel and the prophet who comes from Judah, thus indicating that the two terms are interchangeable. The article on הקבר is unusual on what would normally be perceived as a construct. Burney, however, suggests that the phrase איש האלהים might be used adjectivally here (see *Notes*, 361–62). Burney's parallel המזבח בית אל "the altar of Bethel" is not quite a parallel since in the latter the second phrase is used adverbially.

18 The gesture of the king to the bones of the man of God is one of respect for the man and his initial action. הנביא אשר בא משמרון "the prophet who had come from Samaria" refers to the second of the two characters in 1 Kgs 13. The prophet from Judah was buried in the family tomb of the Bethel holy man. משמרון must refer to the broader country of Samaria, although it is still an anachronism. Samaria was not built until the time of Omri, and the city eventually gave its name to the whole of the northern country.

19 The antecedent of this action is the oracle in 1 Kgs 13:2 and the reinforcement it receives from the northern prophet in 1 Kgs 13:32. The kings of Israel no doubt took their cue from Jeroboam. Their actions then become the characteristic of the northern monarchy.

20 The final gesture of the purge in the north was the killing of the cultic officials at Bethel. The action is reminiscent of that of Jehu in chap. 10 and of Jehoiada in 11:17–19 when the latter annihilated the priests of Baal. It is presumed from the narrative that the priests killed at Bethel were priests of Baal, although that is not stated. 2 Chr 34:6 suggests that Josiah's reform reached much farther north than Bethel—to Manasseh, Ephraim, Simeon (sic), and Naphtali. The references there are anachronistic since these tribal areas ceased to exist at the fall of Samaria. One possible understanding is that these terms refer to towns occupied by refugees from the north after the fall of Samaria, but this is uncertain. That the south did experience a sizable increase in population after 722 B.C. is evident from archeological studies (see E. Stern, *BA* 38 [1975] 35).

21 Comparison of vv 21–25 with the parallel account in 2 Chr 35:1–19 reveals the importance of the event of the new Passover for the chronicler. It does not have the same significance for the deuteronomist. For the latter it is important that the event is in accordance with the demands of the book found in the temple. No other motivation is given in the narrative. Therefore the common search for political motives for the move (see the works cited by Montgomery, *Kings*, 535–36) is finally fruitless and often speculative. If, as seems likely, the inspiration for the Passover is what is now contained in Deut 16, then the element of centralization of worship is prominent. However, the original act of worship was also an expression of loyalty to Yahweh, as it brings to mind the Exodus from Egypt. In spite of the suggestion of some scholars that the celebration of the Passover and Unleavened Bread were originally independent of each other (so H.-J. Kraus, "Gilgal—ein Beitrag zur Kultusgeschichte Israels," *VT* 1 [1951] 181–99; "Des Passah-Mazzot Festes im AT," *EvT* 18 [1958] 47–67), the omission of the reference to the Unleavened Bread here is not important. At this date the joint practice can be presupposed.

22 The evidence from Kings could be interpreted to say that there was no celebration of the Passover in Jerusalem during the monarchy. But although this would constitute an interesting indictment of the monarchy, the evidence does not support this. 2 Chr 30 reveals that Hezekiah celebrated the Passover. There Hezekiah's case is singled out for the uniqueness of its appointed time and the numbers of people involved. It is interesting too that one could argue from silence and conclude that there were no celebrations of the Passover during the period of the Judges, but such was not the case. Josephus (*Antiq.* x.72) adds the comment οὕτως "in such a manner," which interprets the Hebrew correctly. The significance of Josiah's Passover lies not in the fact that it was a "circus" for the entertainment of the peasants bringing their surplus to Jerusalem (so Claburn, *JBL* 92 [1973] 17), but is found in the text itself. It was "as is written in the book of the covenant" (v 21). Exod 12:1–13:16 places the celebration of the Passover in a domestic setting, showing it as a family celebration over which the father of the house presides. It is therefore a local celebration. In contrast, Josiah's celebration offers several new aspects. First, it is a national festival; second, it takes place exclusively in Jerusalem; third, according to 2 Chronicles, it allows a prominent role for official cultic functionaries who replace the father. It was an innovation in the monarchy. (See R. de Vaux, *Ancient Israel*, 484–86.)

24 This verse concludes the account of the reform with its reference to other wide-ranging and important moves in Jerusalem. Various alternative religious practices were banned from the city. That they in fact existed provides substance for the prophetic comparison at this time of Judah with Israel, and the expulsion of them is in keeping with the commands of Deuteronomy (see 18:9–12) and in direct contradiction to the activities of Manasseh (21:5). התרפים "teraphim" were used in the practice of divination. See Gen 31:19–35; Judg 17:5; 18:14–20; 1 Sam 19:13, 16; Hos 3:4–5; C. H. Gordon, "Teraphim," *IDB* 4:574.

25 The praise heaped on Josiah in this verse is great, and because of it the verse has become a *locus classicus* for the theory of the "double redaction" of the deuteronomistic history, promulgated by Cross (*Canaanite Myth and Hebrew Epic*, 274–90) and reinforced recently by R. D. Nelson (*The Double Redaction of the Deuteronomistic History*). Since the issue is dealt with fully in the *Introduction*, the details need not be repeated here.

The statement "there was no king like him" is in tension—some would argue outright contradiction—with the assessment of Hezekiah in 18:5. Such (repeated) praise of important figures in the OT is not uncommon, although at times it is an enigma. Moses is supremely meek (Num 12:3) and no prophet arose like him (Deut 34:10–12)—in spite of the promise in Deut 18:15–20. David is given similar praise to that of Hezekiah and Josiah (1 Kgs 9:4)—in spite of the picture of David in 2 Sam 12–24. The language is hyperbolical but conventional praise of such important figures. בכל לבבו, lit., "with all his heart" reflects the epitome of piety as depicted in the "shema" (Deut 6:5). ככל תורת משה "in keeping with all the law of Moses." See 1 Kgs 2:1–2; 6:11–13; 8:25–26; 9:1–9. Josiah lived up to the standard of piety passed on by David to his son Solomon. No greater praise can be found in the deuteronomistic history than this.

26 The verse ". . . strikes a note strangely alien to the enthusiasm of the . . . author in view of Josiah's reformation" (so Burney, *Notes*, 356) and is therefore relegated to the exilic redactor (RD²). However, it is perhaps more correct to say that the verse provides a sharp contrast to the presentation of the reform of Josiah. It does not necessarily come from another source, but rather suits the pattern already established of reforms and their consequences (see chap. 22, *Form/Structure/Setting*). All of the reformers in Judean history have their accomplishments somewhat reversed in the final analysis. מחרון אפו הגדול "from the ferocity of his great anger." Terms such as these sit heavily on modern sensibilities, but they were common expressions of the activity of God or the gods in the ANE. Mesha attributed the occupation of Moab by the Israelites to the anger of Chemosh (Moabite Stone, line 5; see Gibson, *Syrian Semitic Inscriptions* 1:74–76). (For an excellent discussion, see B. Albrektson, *History and the Gods;* and for an outstanding theological treatment, see A. Heschel, *The Prophets* 2:59–86.) אשר הכעיסו מנשה "with which Manasseh provoked him." The language betrays the deuteronomistic flavor of the section (see Weinfeld, *Deuteronomy and the Deuteronomic School,* 340). Manasseh's sins, which were in flagrant violation of the deuteronomic code of law, now occasion the downfall of Judah. The judgment is delayed, as it was after the reign of Hezekiah, but it is nevertheless inevitable. The fall of Israel stands as awful testimony to this fact.

27 The word of Yahweh spoken of here most certainly came through one or more of the prophets. There is no direct quotation here, but in keeping with the established pattern, there is a summary of prophetic indictments and announcements of judgment. Again the analogy is drawn between what is to happen to Judah and what has already happened to Israel. This is a theme common to both the preaching of the prophets and the books of Kings. ומאסתי "I will reject." See the comparable statement in Jer 6:30. The comment is astonishing in the light of the history of the people of God, but it demonstrates the seriousness of the situation shortly before the exile. That this statement is made in the context of the reign of Josiah is a striking indictment of the effect of the monarchy on the life and faith of Judah and Israel. "This city which I have chosen" is in keeping with the previous statement and reveals a reversal of the theme which permeates not only the Book of Deuteronomy but also the deuteronomistic history. The very dwelling place of God, where his character is to be recognized, is now rejected. Compare with the comments in 19:34 and 21:7.

28 The description of the conclusion of the reign of Josiah is noted for its extreme brevity. As mentioned above, the incident is recorded more fully and with additional information in 2 Chr 35:20–27. The outline is basically the same, although the details are different. Barnes (*2 Kings*, 134) overstates the differences. V 28 is a standard concluding reference to the reign of a king of Judah, with slight change. It omits reference to the "great acts" (גבורתו) of Josiah, which is very unusual. That the brevity is judged "deplorable" by Gray (*Kings*, 746) reflects more on the commentator's expectations than the literary agenda of the biblical writer.

29 The historical background of this venture of Pharaoh Necho is made all the more clear since the publication of the *Chronicles of the Babylonian Kings* by Gadd and Wiseman. Soon after becoming king in 609 B.C., Necho moved north to fight with Babylon over what remained of the Assyrian empire. It was three years after the fall of Nineveh. A battle between the two was indecisive, and Necho moved back south, assuming control over the small territory of Judah. Four years later he attempted a similar move against Nabopolassar. The son of the Babylonian king, Nebuchadrezzar, bettered the Egyptian at Carchemish and brought to an end the power of Assyria and Egypt. See Jer 46:2 (W. Rudolph, *Jeremia*, HAT 12 [Tübingen: J. C. B. Mohr, 1968²] 268–69).

An additional historical issue raised by this account is the extent of Josiah's control in the north. Oded (*Israelite and Judean History*, 463–65) takes 2 Chr 34:6–7 at its face value and adds 2 Kgs 23:4 to it to suggest that Josiah's control extended north into Galilee. This seems unlikely, although Judah had undoubtedly extended her power to the west, as is seen in the Mesad Hashavyahu inscription (see Gibson, *Syrian Semitic Inscriptions* 1:26–29), and had been strengthened in the south during the reign of Josiah. As stated elsewhere, it is possible that the names in 2 Chr 34:6–7 refer to sites occupied by refugees from the north. Most agree that Megiddo was not in Judean hands at this time (see A. Malamat, *JANESCU* 5 [1973] 267–79; *AcAnt* 22 [1974] 445–49).

In any event, the action of Josiah, disastrous as it turned out to be, presupposes a large army under his command at the time. At Arad reference was made in the military correspondence that circulated among the southern fortresses to the "Kittim," which either suggests Greek mercenaries in the Judean army (so A. Lemaire, *Inscriptions hebraiques* 1:229–31) or Greek traders moving through southern Judah at the time (so Y. Aharoni, *Arad Inscriptions*, 12–13).

The term בימיו "in his days" is a general one, although it is evident from the context that the incident to be recorded took place at the end of the reign of Josiah. (See Brin, *ZAW* 93 (1981) 182–96.)

See the *Comment* on 3:7 for the use of עלה "go up" in military contexts throughout the OT. על מלך אשור "on behalf of the king of Assyria." The preposition is problematic since on first reading it implies that Necho's attack was against the Assyrians (see 6:24; 12:18, 19). But it also appears that the prepositions על and אל are interchangeable (see 16:9).

The Pharaoh נכה "Necho" was the son of Psammetichus I, founder of the Twenty-sixth Dynasty. With an army he moved north along the coastal plain to link up with the fragments of the Assyrian army near the Euphrates. The situation is probably reflected in Jer 47:1, 5. וילך המלך יאשיהו לקראתו "King Josiah went to meet him" (see Josh 11:20; 2 Kgs 14:8, 11). The meeting was one between enemies on the field of battle. וימיתהו literally means "put him to death," which might imply a formal execution. However, 2 Chr 35:20–27 indicates that there was a battle before Josiah's death.

מגדו "Megiddo" is identified with Tell el Mutsellin, a site that stands at the exit of the Iron Valley to the Plain of Jezreel. Along it ran the ancient trunk road (*Via Maris*) from Egypt to Mesopotamia, a route that has seen many expeditions going either way. For a vivid description of the dangers of this particular stretch of the road, see the record of the campaign of Thutmoses III in *ANET*, 22–23, 234–43, and the satirical letter written during the reign of Ramses II in *ANET*, 476–78. The tradition in the Book of Chronicles that tells of negotiations prior to the battle is probably correct. Necho's goal was something other than the subjugation of Judah, and the attack by Josiah was no more than an irritant. Necho would not have wished to have been delayed by such battles. Josiah's choice of ground was clearly not in his favor, and he lost the battle.

30 According to this account, Josiah's dead body was transported back to Jerusalem for burial, whereas 2 Chr 35:20–27 has the wounded Josiah being taken back to Jerusalem to die. The conflict is obvious and irreconcilable. The role of the עם הארץ "people of the land" is prominent in the political affairs of Judah, especially those dealing with the selection of a Judean king in the line of David. We have discussed elsewhere the various theories concerning the identity of this group, and the facts as presented here are consistent with our interpretation of them as the popular militia leaders who held considerable political power. The name יהואחז "Jehoahaz" means "Yahweh has taken hold" and is an alternative spelling for "Ahaziah." In Jer 22:10–11 he is referred to by "Shallum," his other name. The anointing of the king appears to be a uniquely Israelite action. On its significance, see C. R. North, *ZAW* 50 (1934) 8–38.

31 The very brief reign of Jehoahaz/Shallum is a reflection of the confusing state of affairs which followed immediately after the death of Josiah. שם אמו חמוטל "his mother's name was Hamutal." In keeping with the formula for the reigns of Judean kings, the name of the queen mother is given. The name is a combination of חם "kinsman, relative" and טל "mist (?)." For a similar compound name, see 2 Sam 3:4. מלבנה "from Libnah." For Oded (*Israelite and Judean History*, 464) this is a symbol of the expansion of Judah under Josiah. But this need not be so. Libnah is identified with Tell el Beide (Grid 145–116) and not Tell es Safi, which is now normally identified with Gath. It was a Shephelah border town and as such probably changed its allegiance often. Hamutal's parents, however, could have been among the many refugees in and around Jerusalem during the period under discussion.

32 In light of the glowing commendation of Josiah, this judgment is a strange one, but it does make sense in the light of vv 26–27. Jehoahaz managed to do much wrong in brief reign. It is hardly fair to accuse the "people of the land" of making an error in judgment because of this indictment (so Gray, *Kings*, 750). It is always easier to make such observations from the vantage point of time. The "people of the land" were concerned primarily with the preservation of the integrity of the Davidic dynasty. The hope that the kings they appointed would be loyal supporters of the deuteronomic way of life is clearly secondary. Jehoash, whom they appointed, was only seven years old at the time, and Josiah only eight, and the religious expectations of such children would have been minimal. Their motives are much more political than pious.

33 Riblah was an important town near Kadesh on the Orontes, some thirty kilometers south of Hama. It seems strange to deport the king north since Necho would eventually return to the south, but one must bear in mind that much has been left out of the narrative. That the king was deported is clear from Jer 22:10–12. במלך בירושלם "in his reign in Jerusalem" is an awkward phrase. See n. 33.a. for possible variations. Most understand it as a negative statement, "so that he would not reign in Jerusalem. . . ," hence RSV's adoption of the variant ממלך "from his reign." However, as it stands the text can indicate an interruption of the brief reign, ". . . as he reigned . . ." and is so translated. On ענש "a penalty," see Exod 21:22; Deut 22:19; Amos 2:8. One hundred talents was not an exorbitant figure when compared to other payments, such as that to Sennacherib. This might reflect on the "accidental" nature of Necho's occupation of Judah and is probably little more than a token.

34 The appointment of Eliakim, the second son of Josiah, says much about the position of Jehoahaz. The inference is that Jehoahaz continued the anti-Egyptian policy of his father, but that Eliakim was willing at first to "toe the line." The name אליקים "Eliakim" is ironic—"God establishes." The change to יהויקים "Jehoiakim" is a minor one, substituting the name יהוה "Yahweh" for אל "God." The grammar and syntax of the verse are clumsy. לְקַח is better read as לָקַח "he took," and וַיָּבֹא "and he came" is better pointed as a hiphil (see n. 34.a. and 2 Chr 36:4). The word מצרים "Egypt" is used adverbially. The implication is that Jehoahaz died of natural causes. No clue is given as to when this happened.

35 Jehoiakim willingly paid over the annual tribute to Necho, but at some cost to his own country. For איש כערכו נגש "he exacted according to each person's assessment," see 12:5 and Lev 5:15, 18, 25. This is a standard bureaucratic term for taxation. The verb, however, implies excessive force. In other contexts it is translated as "drive" (Deut 15:2, 3; Isa 58:3) and "oppress" (1 Sam 13:6; Exod 5:6). The participial form is translated as "tyrant" (Isa 14:2; 60:17). את הכסף ואת הזהב את עם הארץ "the silver and the gold with the people of the land." These terms are awkward. *BHS* suggests the deletion of the first pair and the addition of מאת "from" before עם הארץ "the people of the land." The sentence is thus smoothed out. However, the sense of the words is clear even if clumsy.

36 The chapter ends with the typical opening formula for the reign of a Judean king. Jehoiakim reigned for eleven of the most crucial years of the southern kingdom (609–598 B.C.) It was a time which saw the rise of Babylon, and by the end of his reign the Babylonian presence in Judah was forcefully real.

שם אמו זבידה "his mother's name was Zebidah." The form of the mother's name is questionable. Qere reads זְבוּדָה which some MSS follow. The root is זבד, which means "to bestow a gift." A feminine passive participle is then appropriate. פדיה "Pedayah" is a common name (see 1 Chr 3:18, 19; Neh 3:25; 8:4; 11:7; 13:13). The root means "to ransom." מן רומה "from Rumah." Oded's suggestion (*Israelite and Judean History*, 464) that the mention of this Galilean town shows the extent of Josiah's northern influence is questionable.

37 The customary evaluation of Jehoiakim is substantiated by the record of his activities in Jer 19:3–5; 27:13–19; 26:20–23; 36:9–26. The shift of loyalties that occurred from Josiah's time to Jehoiakim's is noticeable and tragic.

Explanation

As with the treatment of *Form/Structure/Setting*, the *Explanation* of chaps. 22–23 will deal with both chapters together. It is clear from the sweep of the reign and reform of Josiah that the narrative is to be read without a break between these two chapters. The construction in 23:1 (וישלח "and he sent") continues the story begun in chap. 22. The present chapter division is artificial.

Inherent in the account of the reign and reform of Josiah is a contradiction. The contradiction is highlighted when the reign is seen in the context of the story of the last decades of Judah. Undoubtedly, the reign and reform of Josiah were important for our writer, as the amount of detail presented and the amount of space devoted to the record of the reign testify. The reform, which for the writer is the most important event of the reign, could well have taken only a matter of weeks, or at most, months. It is not begun until halfway through the reign (22:3), so the first eighteen years are left unaccounted for in 2 Kings. The contradiction lies in the effect of the reform. It is amazing that the reform is so short-lived. The four successors of Josiah— Jehoahaz, Jehoiakim, Jehoiachin, and Zedekiah—demonstrate no willingness at all to emulate their predecessor. In fact all of them are condemned as "behaving badly in Yahweh's eyes" (23:32, 36; 24:9, 19). They show none of the reforming zeal of Josiah, and their reigns are characterized by a singular lack of any vestige of the reform. The contrast is truly remarkable.

Traditional explanations have resorted to theories of a multiple redaction of the books of Kings or the deuteronomistic history. We have found these theories to be less than satisfying. Another explanation must and can be found by noting the pattern already established by our writer in presenting reforms. In the case of Josiah, there is a clear echo of the reforms of Hezekiah and of the character of David. This is a point that has long been recognized. The efforts to purge Jerusalem of foreign worship are common to all three characters. Similarly, all three are responsible for ventures that widen the borders of Judah. David establishes the outer limits of an empire, Hezekiah enlarges the southern border as far as Gath, and Josiah ventures into the north for conquest and reform. The link is also made by the comment that the writer adds to the reign of Hezekiah and to the reign of Josiah (see 18:5; 22:2; 23:24–25). These comments have been a constant source of speculation on the multiple redactions of the book since they appear to contradict each other. However, repetition also establishes order in a narrative, and we prefer to regard the echo as deliberate. Josiah's reign and reform are meant to be seen in the light of Hezekiah's. If this is true, it is hardly surprising that Josiah's reign ends as it does. Hezekiah's reign has continued a pattern already established in chaps. 14 and 16. Reforms end finally in loss or, as in the case of Hezekiah, potential loss of the temple and palace treasures.

Such is the case with Josiah; the reign and reform fit the pattern, only this time with more disastrous consequences. Judah is reduced to the status of vassal of a relatively minor power for a short while, but she is never free again until after the exile. A major link in this chain is the reign of Manasseh which has recently preceded that of Josiah. The stamp of that reign can never be eliminated, even by the attempt of Josiah to regain Jerusalem and the nation for Yahweh. It is in connection with the reign of Manasseh that the first clear pronouncement of judgment against Judah is given (21:26–28). Judgment is already implied in the imitation of Israel's behavior by Judah.

In the view of the writer, there is a most serious lesson to be learned from the reign and reform of Josiah. Not even the deliberate imitation of David, so clear in the narrative of Josiah's reign, can restrain the hand of judgment. Yahweh acts again out of his freedom. If any hope is to be found in exile, it must be firmly anchored in this truth. The promise of deliverance and restoration must come from the same freedom to offer grace which is dependent upon nothing.

Attack and Deportation (24:1–20)

Bibliography

Aharoni, Y. "Arad: Its Inscriptions and Temple." *BA* 31 (1968) 2–33. **Albright, W. F.** "The Seal of Eliakim and the latest Pre-exilic History of Judah." *JBL* 51 (1932) 77–106. **Baltzer, K.** "Das Ende des Staates Juda und die Messias-Frage." In *Studien* zur Theologie der alttestamentliche Überlieferungen. Neukirchen: Verlag das Erziehungsvereins, 1961. 33–43. **Freedy, K. S.** and **Redford, D. B.** "The Dates in Ezekiel in Relation to Biblical, Babylonian, and Egyptian Sources." *JAOS* 90 (1970) 462–85. **Greenberg, M.** "Ezekiel 17 and the Policy of Psammeticus II." *JBL* 76 (1957) 304–9. **Kutsch, E.** "Das Jahr der Katastrophe, 587 v. Chr." *Bib* 55 (1974) 520–45. **Larsson, G.** "When Did the Babylonian Captivity Begin?" *JTS* 18 (1967) 417–23. **Malamat, A.** "The Twilight of Judah in the Egyptian-Babylonian Maelstrom." *Congress Volume: Edinburgh.* VTSup 28. Leiden: E. J. Brill, 1974. 123–45. **Meek, T. J.** "Translation Problems in the OT." *JQR* 50 (1959) 45–54. **Noth, M.** "Die Einnahme von Jerusalem in Jahre 597 v. Chr." *ZDPV* 74 (1958) 133–57. **Oded, B.** "When Did the Kingdom of Judah Become Subjected to Babylonian Rule?" *Tarbiz* 25 (1965) 103–7. **Selms, A. van.** "The Name Nebuchadnezzar." In *Travels in the World of the Old Testament: Studies Presented to M. A. Beek,* ed. Herma van Voss, 223–29. Assen: Van Gorcum, 1974. **Tadmor, H.** "Chronology of the Last Kings of Judah." *JNES* 15 (1956) 226–30. **Talmon, S.** "Divergencies in Calendar Reckoning in Ephraim and Judah." *VT* 8 (1958) 48–74. **Wevers, J. W.** "Double Readings in the Books of Kings." *JBL* 65 (1946) 307–10. **Wiseman, D. J.** *Chronicles of the Chaldaean Kings (626–556 B.C.) in the British Museum.* London: The Trustees of the British Museum, 1956.

Translation

¹*In his days Nebuchadrezzar king of Babylon attacked,* [a] *and Jehoiakim became his vassal for three years. Then he turned against him in rebellion.* ²*Yahweh* [a] *sent against him* [b] *raiding bands of Chaldeans, Syrians,* [c] *Moabites, and Ammonites. He sent them into Judah* [d] *to destroy him, according to Yahweh's word which he uttered through his servants the prophets.* ³*This indeed happened to Judah at the command* [a] *of Yahweh to remove* [b] *them from his sight for the sins* [c] *of Manasseh and all he had done and* ⁴[a] *for the innocent blood he had shed;* [b] *for Jerusalem had been filled with innocent blood, and Yahweh would not forgive this.* ⁵*As for the remainder of the activities of Jehoiakim and all he accomplished, are they not* [a] *written into the records of the kings of Judah?* ⁶*Jehoiakim slept with his fathers,* [a] *and Jehoiachin his son became king in his place.* ⁷*No more did the king of Egypt come out from his own land,* [a] *because the king of Babylon had seized all the land under the control of the king of Egypt from the River of Egypt to the River Euphrates.*

⁸*Jehoiachin was eighteen years old when he became king, and he reigned in Jerusalem for three months. His mother's name was Nehushta daughter of Elnathan of Jerusalem.* ⁹*He* [a] *behaved badly in Yahweh's eyes, just as his father had done.*

¹⁰*At that time the generals* [a] *of Nebuchadrezzar attacked Jerusalem, and the city came under siege.* ¹¹*While his generals were besieging the city, Nebuchadrezzar arrived;* [a] ¹²*and Jehoiachin king of Judah, together with his mother, his servants,* [a] *his generals, and his officials, came out to the king of Babylon;* [b] *and the king of Babylon accepted his surrender in the eighth year of his reign.* ¹³[a]*He then brought out all the treasures of the temple and the treasures of the palace and cut up all the gold vessels which Solomon king of Israel had made for Yahweh's sanctuary, exactly as Yahweh had declared.* ¹⁴*He exiled all of Jerusalem—all the high officials, all the important military officials—ten* [a] *thousand captives,* [b] *together with the carpenters and the sappers.* [c] *No one was left except the less important of the population.* ¹⁵*He exiled to Babylon Jehoiachin, his mother, the king's wives, his high officials, and the elite* [a] *of the land. He transported them from Jerusalem to Babylon.* ¹⁶*All the fighting men, seven thousand,* [a]

the carpenters and the sappers, all those in fact who would be useful in war, the king of Babylon brought them in exile to Babylon. ¹⁷ *Then the king of Babylon made Mathaniah, his uncle,*ᵃ *king in place of Jehoiachin and changed his name to Zedekiah.* ¹⁸ *Zedekiah was twenty-one years old when he began to reign, and he reigned for eleven years in Jerusalem. His mother's name was Hamital*ᵃ *a daughter of Jeremiah of Libnah.*ᵇ ¹⁹ *He behaved badly in Yahweh's eyes,*ᵃ *as had Jehoiakim.* ²⁰ *Yahweh had cast Jerusalem and Judah out of his presence because his anger was directed against them. Yet Zedekiah rebelled against the king of Babylon.*

Notes

1.a. Gᴸ adds "upon the land."
2.a. MT reads יהוה "Yahweh." On the basis of Gᴮ *BHS* regards the word as a gloss and recommends omitting it. Nebuchadrezzar then becomes the subject of the verb. This is certainly possible, but having Yahweh as the subject of the verb is entirely in keeping with the idea expressed elsewhere that Yahweh is the controller of history (see 5:1–2).
2.b. Gᴸ adds "upon Jehoiakim."
2.c. Most suggest that "Edom" be read here, but such a change is not necessary. See *Comment* below.
2.d. MT reads ביהודה "in Judah." Gᴮ offers ἐν τῇ γῇ Ἰουδα "in the land of Judah."
3.a. MT reads על פי, lit., "at the mouth," which G renders as ἐπὶ τὸν θυμόν "at the will." This same Gr. word is used in v 20 to translate אף "anger."
3.b. Gᴮ adds αὐτόν "him."
3.c. Gᴸ translates with διὰ πάσας ἁμαρτίας "for all sins."
4.a. MT reads וגם דם, lit., "and also the blood." The force of the preposition is carried over from the prior בחטאות "for the sins." See Burney, *Notes*, 365.
4.b. Gray (*Kings*, 757) regards the parenthetical statement as a gloss, but there is no textual evidence for this judgment.
5.a. Gᴮ translates οὐκ ἰδού "behold, are they not?"
6.a. Gᴸ adds "and he was buried in the garden of Oza (Uzzah) with his fathers."
7.a. Ehrlich's judgment (*Randglossen* 7:323) that the phrase ארצו "his land" is a gloss is entirely speculative.
9.a. Characteristically Gᴸ adds the proper name.
10.a. The Heb. עלה עבדי נבכדנאצר "the generals (pl) of Nebuchadrezzar attacked (sg)" is awkward. Gᴮ does not translate עבדי "generals." Some suggest changing the verb to עלו "they attacked."
11.a. Gᴸ adds "and he set down (i.e., encamped) against the city. . . ."
12.a. Gᴮ reverses "mother" and "servants."
12.b. MT reads על מלך בבל "upon the king of Babylon."
13.a. Gᴸ begins the verse, "and the king of Babylon entered the city . . ." This is to smooth out the sense which is a little rough in the Heb. with no direct antecedent for מִשָּׁם "from there."
14.a. K reads עשרה "ten." Q constructs it עשרת.
14.b. Changing the pointing from the ungrammatical גֹּלָה to גּוֹלָה "captives," a collective noun.
14.c. The root is סגר "to shut," "to close." The word is often associated with prisons (BDB, 688–89). See *Comment* below.
15.a. K reads אולי, Q אֱיָלֵי, which G translates as τοὺς ἰσχυρούς "the mighty." Ehrlich (*Randglossen* 7:323) suggests an emendation to גְּדֹלֵי, but this is unnecessary. Most regard the word as derived from a verbal root אול "to be foremost." See BDB, 17–18.
16.a. Gᴸ changes the order to ". . . powerful men, strong men for war, seven thousand."
17.a. MT = דֹּד, lit., "his beloved one" (see Isa 5:1). In Lev 10:4 the word is translated "uncle," and that is the meaning adopted by Gᴸ. Gᴮ translates "his son."
18.a. Q = חֲמוּטַל "Hamutal."
18.b. Omitted by Gᴮ.
19.a. MT = בעיני "in the eyes of," which both Gᴮ and Gᴸ translate with ἐνώπιον "before," a term normally exclusive to Gᴸ.

Form/Structure/Setting

2 Kgs 24 compresses material from the reign of three kings: Jehoiakim (vv 1-7), whose reign had already begun in the previous chapter, Jehoiachin (vv 8-17), and Zedekiah (vv 18-20), whose reign continues into the next. The accounts of the reigns, leaving aside the necessary limitations, follow the formal pattern of records of previous reigns. Nevertheless, several commentators see signs of composite authorship in the chapter.

R. D. Nelson (*Double Redaction*, 85-90) offers a comprehensive and typical analysis of the chapter. According to him vv 1, 7 are "annalistic," whereas vv 2-4 and v 20 are "theologizing, editorializing," betrayed by the substitution of the name Yahweh for an original Nebudchadrezzar at the beginning of v 2. Vv 3, 20, although in the style of the deuteronomist, are not from his hand. Further, vv 8-9, 18-19 (together with 23:31-32, 36-37) represent a "rigidification" of the original regnal formula. Finally, vv 13-14 are a "post-redactional insertion" which are dependent upon a prophetic viewpoint and are therefore secondary. However, on closer analysis the chapter offers little in the way of such clues to its composite nature.

"Annalistic," as we have already noted, is a comment on style, not form. Few clear criteria have been established by form-critics to allow the reader to identify quotations from annals. In fact, the term בימיו "in his days" is far too general to be an annalistic comment. It does appear to be a rather constant feature of history writing in the OT (see Brin, *ZAW* 93 [1981] 195). In v 7 the kind of detail offered is certainly not beyond the capabilities of a good historiographer.

As far as vv 2-4 are concerned, little *formal* distinction can be made between "theologizing, editorializing," "theological editorializing" and simple theological comment. Nothing in vv 2-4 is inconsistent with the theological and historical outlook of the writer (see 10:32-33). As for "Yahweh" being a substitute for "Nebuchadrezzar" in v 2, this is wishful thinking. No textual evidence for this claim can be found, and that it suits Nelson to change it in this way is hardly sufficient evidence for its truth. Vv 3, 20 are also quite consistent with deuteronomistic theology and style.

Further comment ought to be made concerning vv 8-9, 18-19 as representing a "rigidification" of the normal regnal formula. The observation is unsound. No evidence for such a judgment is in fact brought by Nelson. It is merely stated. An analysis of the regnal formulae is to be found in Burney's *Notes*, ix-xiii. Those for Judean kings follow a five-part pattern:
1. Synchronization with Israelite kings (where possible).
2. The age of the king.
3. The length of reign.
4. The name of the queen mother.
5. The verdict on the reign.

Apart from (1), which one would expect to be omitted after the fall of Samaria, vv 8-9 and vv 18-19 follow the form precisely. If "rigidification" is meant to convey that the writer has followed the form too closely and has therefore betrayed his hand, then the comparison is meaningless.

The constant search for sources that has characterized studies on 2 Kings,

Form/Structure/Setting 347

intriguing though it is, has its limitations. First, it is subjective and intuitive, protestations to the contrary notwithstanding. Second, it is often speculative. Third, the results for interpretation as opposed to analysis are minimal. Our pattern of approach, which will be continued in chap. 24, has been to view sections of the narrative of 2 Kings primarily in the context of the completed text itself.

The structure of 24:1–7, the reign of Jehoiakim, is most intriguing. V 1 mentions the king's subjugation to the Babylonian Nebuchadrezzar following the invasion, and the king's rebellion after three years. Two things are of note here. The sentence begins with the general comment "in his days" (בימיו). The phrase is used in 8:20; 15:29; 23:29, and here. Although the term is vague, not offering any specific point at which the events described in association with it take place (see J. R. Wilch, *Time and Event*, 55), it does carry with it some specific associations in the way it is used by our writer. In the case of Pekah (15:29) it precedes the notice of the invasion of Tiglath Pileser III. In the case of Joram (8:20) it precedes the mention of the declaration of independence from Judah by Edom, and in the case of Josiah (23:29) it introduces the campaign of Necho and the battle of Megiddo at which Josiah died. In other words, it is used as a prelude to invasion. In keeping with this usage it is found here. In the days of Jehoiakim, Nebuchadrezzar invaded Judah. The "days" of these kings are therefore characterized by the attacks of foreigners. This puts the rebellion of Jehoiakim, therefore, in an ambiguous light. Such a rebellion against an invader would normally have been viewed favorably, as a gesture of independence, but now through the use of this simple item of historiography, the rebellion is cast in shadow.

The ambiguity is quickly removed with the word and subject which begin v 2. It is Yahweh himself who now moves against his king by sending marauders from neighboring countries against Judah. The inevitability and the justification for this now become clear. It is the beginning of the final dénouement of the drama of the word of Yahweh in the history of Judah. In reaction to the activities of Manasseh, Yahweh now moves against his people. He "rejects" them. The tone is thoroughly prophetic and consistent with deuteronomistic theology. It also provides an advance upon the sentiments found in 8:19.

The incomplete nature of vv 5–6, noticed by many, with its lack of reference to the burial of the king, raises questions of form, but they are not serious. Either the omission is accidental and can be restored by reference to G^L (so Nelson), or the reference to "sleeping with the fathers" includes burial. The latter is preferred (see 20:21).

V 7 is ironic. The king of Egypt, the patron of Jehoiakim and the overlord of Judah, is no longer powerful enough to keep hold of his vassal. He is replaced, however, not by an independent Judah but by a greater power—Babylon. Judah at this stage is passed around by the powerful nations of the ANE—Assyria, Babylon, and Egypt—and has become indeed the property of all and sundry (see Jer 2:18).

Vv 8–9 constitute the typical formula for the beginning of the reign of a Judean king and offer a characteristically negative assessment of Jehoiachin. V 10 begins with a much more specific temporal reference. The changeover in kings has clearly coincided with the attack of Nebuchadrezzar's army on

Jerusalem. A glance at the verb sequence in the paragraph which conveys the sense of movement in the narrative demonstrates a notable shift in action. Jehoiachin is the subject of only one verb (v 12). He leaves the city in surrender. Dominating the action in the rest of the paragraph is Nebuchadrezzar, who together with his officers is the subject of the other verbs (see עלה "he attacked," ויבא "he arrived," ויקח "he accepted," ויוצא "he brought out," ויקצץ "he cut up," והגלה "he exiled," ויגל "he exiled," ויביאם "he brought them," וימלך "he made king"). The action is now entirely Babylon's; it is no longer Judah's. At the center of this activity is the brief but telling comment, כאשר דבר יהוה "exactly as Yahweh had declared" (v 13b). The theme continues.

Zedekiah's reign opens formally in v 18 and receives the same assessment as his predecessor (v 19). The awkward final verse of the chapter (v 20) reinforces an important theme: Yahweh's anger is at work in the events surrounding the reign of Zedekiah. Yet in spite of this, the king rebels against Nebuchadrezzar. A feeble gesture, it is doomed to failure as was the rebellion of Jehoiakim (v 1).

Comment

The Babylonian Chronicle (see Wiseman, *Chronicles*, 43–77, and Grayson, *Texts from Cuneiform Sources* 5:99–102) provides an outline of the international events that led up to the Babylonian invasion and the sacking of Jerusalem. To be noted is that from 609 B.C. onward the Babylonian interests under Nabopolassar are decidedly towards the west. In mid-609 B.C. Nabopolassar's army attacked Harran (BM 29101:66–75). In the following year they fought against Beit Hanunya and returned home in the month of Tebet (BM 22047:1–4). Early in 607 B.C. Nebuchadrezzar, the son of Nabopolassar, was engaged against various enemies on the banks of the Euphrates (BM 22407:5–15), and in the latter part of 606 B.C. Nabopolassar fought against Egyptian and Syrian armies in the northwest of his territory.

In 605 B.C. Nebuchadrezzar fought at the head of the Babylonian army at Carchemish (BM 21946:1–10) and returned home to assume the throne on the death of his father. Then followed a series of campaigns into "Hatti" (Palestine), after which he returned home in 605/604 B.C. in the eleventh month. In his first year (604/603 B.C.) he marched into Palestine, and by the ninth month (Kislev) he had sacked Ashkelon. In the second month (Iyyar) of the following year (603/602 B.C.) he again ventured into Palestine, as he did again in the third month (Siwan) of his third year (602/601 B.C.). Late in his fourth year (601/600 B.C.) he marched against the borders of Egypt but was met with a serious setback and consequently spent his fifth year recuperating and refitting his army. In 599/598 B.C., in the ninth month (Kislev), he again moved west and plundered several Arab towns to the east of Palestine. The following year he attacked Palestine, again in the ninth month. The account offers very specific details of his capture of Jerusalem on the second day of Adar (the twelfth month), i.e., February 16, 597 B.C.

This sketch of international affairs, to which can be added the activities of Psammetichus II of Egypt, provides the background for the events found in 2 Kgs 24 and 25. Sometime after the defeat of the Egyptian army at Carchemish in 605 B.C., Judah became subject to Babylon. Exactly when is not known. The campaign to Ashkelon in 604/603 B.C. would provide a suitable context for this (see A. Malamat, VTSup 28:129–31, for the possibilities).

1 With this verse compare 2 Chr 36:6–7, which is not a complete parallel. Chronicles adds the note about the confiscation of the temple vessels and their installation in Nebuchadrezzar's temple in Babylon, a statement challenged by Jer 27:18. On the use of עלה "attack," see 3:21; 6:24; 16:5, etc. The expression בימיו "in his days" is not helpful in dating the invasion of Nebuchadrezzar. It must have been sufficiently early in the reign of Jehoiakim to allow him three years' servitude. The campaign records in the Babylonian Chronicle are imprecise enough to be of little use. The most likely context is the Babylonian attack on Ashkelon in Kislev of 604/603 B.C. (so Malamat, VTSup 28:131–32, and Albright, *JBL* 51 [1932] 90–91). Josephus (*Antiq.* x. 87) mistakenly places the first invasion of Nebuchadrezzar in his fourth year (i.e., 601/600 B.C.), but the Babylonian Chronicle proves this to be false. Larsson (*JTS* 18 [1967] 417–23) seeks to harmonize this material with Chronicles and comes up with a date of 605 B.C. for Jehoiakim's subjugation. But this is unlikely.

The name נבוכדנצר, lit., "Nebuchadnezzar," is more properly written "Nebuchadrezzar," as in Jeremiah and Ezekiel, and this is the practice in translation here. Like his father he bore the name of the Babylonian god Nebo, and his Akkadian name is "Nabu-kudduriusur," the English translation of which is "May Nebo protect my boundary stone." (See A. van Selms, *Beek Festschrift*, 223–29.) וימרד "then he turned in rebellion" is a synonym for פשע (see 1:1; 3:3); G translates both with ἐθήτησεν. The rebellion could well have taken place within the period between Kislev 601/600 B.C. and Kislev 599/598 B.C. The first of these dates corresponds to Nebuchadrezzar's abortive attack on Egypt; the second is the date of his attack on Hatti and the neighboring Arabs. In the year between, no military activity took place. Instead, Nebuchadrezzar stayed at home to refit.

2 The rebellion, while it first appeared to provide some respite from Babylon, eventually proved to do otherwise, and Jehoiakim and Judah found themselves under even more military pressure. וישלח יהוה "Yahweh sent." *BHS* et al. suggest the omission of the subject written (see n. 2.a. above). The comment is in keeping with the sentiments of our writer and suits the theological point to be made here (see above *Form/Structure/Setting*). For him, nothing happens outside the will of Yahweh.

גדודים "raiding bands." These marauders, lightly armed troops best suited for hit-and-run tactics, were taking advantage of the relatively weak position of Judah at this time. The nature of the coalition suggests that Nebuchadrezzar hired mercenaries from the east of the Jordan to act on his behalf, presumably until he was strong enough himself to launch a full-scale attack on Palestine. This attack did not come until Kislev of 598/597 B.C. (see BM 21946:11–13). The subjugation of the Arabs the year before would have provided the Babylonians with sufficient power east of the Jordan to encourage such mercenary raids on Judah. That these raids netted Nebuchadrezzar some Jewish prisoners (so Malamat, VTSup 28:131) is an attractive possibility. It is unlikely that such raids were just for fun. It might also help solve some of the confusing problems over the final number of prisoners taken into exile. The situation is reflected in Jer 35:11.

ארם "Syria." A number of scholars suggest an emendation to "Edom," which is a slight change in Hebrew. Aharoni's interpretation of the corpus of Arad Letters suggests that Edomite incursions were taking place during the late monarchy (see *Arad Inscriptions*, 149–51; *BA* 31 [1968] 17–18). But this late date for the circumstances described in the Arad correspondence is not shared by all interpreters (see A. Lemaire, *Inscriptions hebraiques* 1:207–9, 234–35). Textually there is nothing to support the change, and in the light of the repeated activity of Edom in the south it is difficult to put any single date on their incursions.

"According to Yahweh's word which he uttered through his servants the prophets." A comparison with other statements on the fulfillment of prophecy throughout the books of Kings is invited. The theological thrust of the deuteronomistic history is the importance of the prophetic word in interpreting history (see von Rad, *Studies in Deuteronomy*, 75–91; W. Dietrich, *Prophetie und Geschichte*, passim). In mind here of course is a summary of prophetic teaching, not specific oracles of individual prophets.

3 The theme continues in this editorial statement. On the translation, see T. J. Meek, *JQR* 50 (1959) 45–54. On להסיר "to remove," see 17:23; 23:27 for similar statements of God's intention.

4 The first part of the verse echoes 21:16, and the comment "and Yahweh would not forgive this" now demonstrates that in the mind of our writer the state of affairs had reached the point of no return. Nothing could now avert the inevitable judgment which had been building up in the history of the kings. The dénouement approaches.

5 Compare with 2 Chr 36:5–8 and note the minor additions. No mention is made in Kings of Jehoiakim's death, whereas the account in Chronicles states that the Babylonian king had him bound and dragged off to Babylon. Josephus (*Antiq.* x.97–98) adopts a similar understanding of events, although in his account Jehoiakim is subsequently executed. Josephus's chronology has recently been revived by Larsson (*JTS* 18 [1967] 417–23), and Oded (*Israelite and Judean History*, 471) attempts a synchronization. However, the expression "he slept with his fathers" would suggest burial of some form in Jerusalem, not beyond Judah. This point is made by G[B], which adds "in the garden of Uzzah." There is nothing here to throw light on Jeremiah's comment (Jer 22:19; 36:30) on the death of the king. The suggestion that the king was assassinated (so Bright, *History*, 327) is certainly possible, but one would have expected a reference to it in the text. The king was replaced by his son who carried on the same policies, at least for a short while. The name יהויכין "Jehoiachin" means "Yahweh founds" and is remarkably like that of his father. The name appears on two seals from the period found at Lachish and Tell Beit Mirsim (see Gibson, *Syrian Semitic Inscriptions* 1:40, 65–66, and Albright, *JBL* 51 [1932] 77–106).

7 The repeated incursions of the Babylonians into Palestine provide the background for this comment. Necho, the same Egyptian king who killed Josiah at Megiddo, had been seriously weakened by Babylon in 601/600 B.C.

Although the Babylonian army was also dealt a severe blow, it did have the reserve strength to recover, whereas the Egyptians did not. It was left to Necho's successor, Psammetichus II (594–588 B.C.), to correct this situation. At this time, however, Egypt was simply not strong enough to exert any influence in Palestine.

8 The record of the reign of Jehoiachin begins with the typical formulaic introduction. בן שמנה עשרה "eighteen years old." 2 Chr 36:9 reads "eight," but this is unlikely. An eight-year-old boy who reigned for three months is hardly likely to have merited the criticism offered in v 9. שם אמו נחשתא "his mother's name was Nehushta." The queen mother's name is related to the verb "to divine" or the noun "bronze." But the association is vague. אלנתן "Elnathan." The name, or others similar, occurs with great frequency in the OT. Jehoiachin's uncle and successor, Mathaniah, has a name made of the same compound.

9 Although no details of the reign are given, this condemnation presupposes the kind of apostasy seen in the records of Jehoiakim.

10 The Babylonian army attacked Jerusalem in response to the rebellion. According to the Babylonian Chronicle the attack began in the month of Kislev (Nov.–Dec.) 598/597 B.C. and ended three months later on the second day of Adar (Feb.–Mar. 597 B.C.). On the dating, see E. Kutsch, *Bib* 55 (1974) 520–45. The three-month period corresponds neatly with the length of the reign of Jehoiachin.

The siege of the city was entrusted to the generals of Nebuchadrezzar. Such a move would not be unusual, although in the royal annals Nebuchadrezzar himself takes credit for the campaign. Noting that line 10 of the reverse of BM 21946 refers to the king alone returning home after his campaign against the Arabs in his sixth year, Malamat (VTSup 28:134) concludes that the Babylonian army remained in the region to carry out the campaign against Judah while the king was home in Babylon. The late arrival of Nebuchadrezzar could then be explained by reference to his lengthy journey from Babylon to Judah to join his main force. The suggestion is interesting, but it overlooks the fact that the king is often referred to in the Chronicle alone, although the full army is also included. Tactically, the siege of Jerusalem would have been begun by an advance guard, as Sennacherib's siege had begun a century before.

The terrifying aspects of siege warfare have already been mentioned in the comments on chap. 6. This slow form of torture was one in which the Assyrians and the Babylonians excelled. At the time of the year that the siege took place (November to February), water would not have been scarce, but with the notable increase in the size of the city's population and with the harvest still some months off, food would have been. The relatively swift capitulation of the city would have been motivated by this factor.

12 Jehoiachin's willing surrender of the city anticipates the advice given later by Jeremiah to Zedekiah. The quick surrender has been rightfully interpreted as reason for the Babylonians' remarkably lenient treatment of the king and his officials (see Oded, *Israelite and Judean History*, 471). Jehoiachin surrendered with his closest political advisers: "his mother, his servants, his generals, and his officials."

בשנת שמנה למלכו "in the eighth year of his reign." The date is according to Nebuchadrezzar's reign. The perspective is therefore now that of one who was familiar with the Babylonian method of reckoning, or familiar with the date of Nebuchadrezzar's accession. It corresponds well with the date in the Babylonian Chronicle. To build too much on this in terms of the redaction history of the book (see Gray, *Kings*, 753) is a mistake. Jer 52:28, universally regarded as a later edition of the fall of Jerusalem, reads "seventh," which ignores the Babylonian reckoning by not taking into account the accession year of the king. According to the Chronicle, the city fell on the second of Adar (Feb. 16) in the seventh year of the king. The exile of prisoners would have taken some weeks to organize and would therefore have taken place in the early months of the following year, the eighth.

13 Following the fall of the city, the Babylonians help themselves to the spoils of war. As one might expect, the temple and palace treasures are a primary target, as had happened many times before. Not only is the pattern followed, but also the prophecy of 20:16–19 is now being fulfilled. אשר עשה שלמה "which Solomon had made." See 1 Kgs 7:51, some of which had been removed once before (1 Kgs 14:26). Montgomery (*Kings*, 556) and Gray (*Kings*, 752) regard the passage as secondary, partly because of its similarity with the preceding accounts of the sacking of the treasures and partly because it anticipates the later destruction of the temple. It is argued that Jer 27:19–22 is a contradiction because it refers to vessels still in the temple during the reign of Zedekiah. There is no contradiction here. In neither account, Babylonian or Judean, is it stated that everything was looted. Nebuchadrezzar clearly made provision for the continuation of the economic and political life of Judah after the first deportation, albeit in a much reduced form, by the appointment of Zedekiah as king.

14 In keeping with the nature of the document (i.e., propaganda), the Babylonian Chronicle speaks of the vast tribute taken from Jerusalem. The tribute would have included personnel who would have been of some use in Babylon. Here, in addition to those listed in v 12, is an accounting of such people. From what follows it is clear that the deportees at this stage were part of the Jerusalem establishment. No reference is made in the Babylonian Chronicle to any other part of Judah, and Albright (*JBL* 51 [1932] 77–106) has shown that for the most part the south and the Negeb were unaffected by this first invasion.

שרים "high officials" is often translated "princes," but depending on the context, the designation can be varied. In a military context, followed by a number, it means commander. גבורי החיל "the important military officials." RSV and others translate the phrase literally, "mighty men of valor." They would be soldiers of repute who could be drafted into the Babylonian army. Gray's translation of "men of property" is untenable.

עשרה אלפים "ten thousand." In the light of v 16, this number has raised several questions in the minds of interpreters. The later figure of seven thousand is difficult to reconcile with this, as is the figure given in Jer 52:28 of 3,023 for the first year of exile (597 B.C.). No corroborating figures are available from Babylonian sources, and the different numbers could account for different groupings of those taken into exile. This point will be discussed more fully below.

החרש והמסגר "the carpenters and the sappers." *RSV* reads "craftsmen and smiths," which is an inspired guess. The terms are collective ones for skilled men, who are contrasted with the דלים "less important." Montgomery (*Kings*, 557) suggests some form of trade guilds. חרש is from a root whose precise meaning is unclear, but it is perhaps related to work with wood (see Exod 28:11; 2 Kgs 12:12). BDB suggests "locksmith" for המסגר, a word derived from the root סגר "to close." These terms are discussed more fully below in the *Comment* on vv 15–17. דלה is often translated "poor," but the word has a broad range of meaning in the English translations. (For an excellent discussion see the comprehensive article by Fabry, "דל dal," *TDOT* 3:208–30.) The term often, though not exclusively, indicates the lower strata of society. Gray's translation of עם הארץ as "peasantry" (*Kings*, 761) is to be rejected. This specific deportation is confined to members of the Jerusalem establishment. Such an elite would not include peasantry.

15 This verse and the next appear to repeat the information found already in v 14, and because of this and the different numbers found in Jer 52:28, one or the other passage is regarded as secondary by many commentators. Montgomery (*Kings*, 556) offers a good summary of opinion on the matter. Usually the more detailed vv 15–16 are favored over the sketchy v 14, the detail being seen as evidence of reliable archival sources. But the addition to this of a different counting which would appear to be contradictory is difficult to conceive. When compared, the two passages betray a different interest. V 14 is concerned mainly with the removal of specifically military personnel from the Jerusalem establishment. Vv 15–16 are more widely based. Malamat's suggestion (VTSup 28:133–35) that the addition of 3,023 (Jer 52:28) and 7,000 (v 16) is approximately 10,000 (v 14), and that there were therefore two initial deportations in the seventh and eighth years of Nebuchadrezzar is most tempting. The initial 3,023 referred to the "Jews," i.e., those from outside Jerusalem who were deported before the fall of the city by the army Nebuchadrezzar had left in Palestine when he returned home after the Arab campaign in his sixth year. It is here, however, that the theory falters. That Nebuchadrezzar left such an army behind is unlikely and is not supported by the Babylonian Chronicle.

V 14 refers, as we have stated, to exclusively military personnel who were exiled from Jerusalem. שרים "high officials" is certainly a word common in military contexts, and it is found in that context here, as evidenced in the reference to גבורי החיל "important military officials." In v 14 the total of military personnel, including the המסגר and the החרש, was ten thousand. The second list in vv 15–16 includes personnel specifically from the royal household—the queen mother, the king's wives, his advisers, and some leading citizens, plus some soldiers. This group totaled seven thousand and was swelled by an additional thousand החרש and המסגר. What follows (הכל גבורים עשי מלחמה "all those in fact who would be useful in war") is clumsy, with two terms in absolute states. The term הכל is to be separated from what follows and is to be regarded as the final summary expression of what precedes—"all of them" or "the whole number" (so Montgomery). What follows is then superfluous, but it should not necessarily be excised since it might have come from an incomplete listing of those exiled.

In this context, who then are the החרש and the המסגר? They are clearly skilled workmen, and the terms are collective. They are also used in warfare, especially siege warfare. In modern terms they would be engineers. The החרש would have been involved in constructions of wood and stone, staple elements of siegeworks, and the מסגר would have been involved in "enclosures," i.e., siegeworks, either their construction or destruction, or both. Malamat's suggestion of "sappers" (VTSup 28:133) has considerable merit.

17 וימלך "and he made king." Nebuchadrezzar's own records confirm this, and the new king was "after his heart," well disposed towards Babylon. Ironically, מתניה "Mathaniah" means "Gift of Yahweh," and appears on Lachish I (see Gibson, *Syrian Semitic Inscriptions* 1:36–38). For דד "his uncle," 2 Chr 36:10 reads אחיו, which is not to be taken literally as "brother" but in the more general sense of kinsman or relative. The vocabulary for the various possible family relationships is limited in biblical Hebrew. The Davidic line is thus not brought to an end, but it is under a considerable strain. צדקיהו "Zedekiah," the throne name of Mathaniah means "Yahweh is righteous." Although this might indicate a degree of respect for Jewish traditions on the part of Nebuchadrezzar (so Gray, *Kings*, 762), the use of a non-Judean name would have been most unlikely. Jer 23:5–6 makes an ironic play on the word.

19 This verse's judgment on Zedekiah is confirmed by the incidents from his reign found in Jer 27–39. From these stories Zedekiah emerges as a weak, indecisive figure, easily swayed by the weight of circumstance. The reason for his similarity to Jehoiakim is not stated here, but in the mind of the writer both of them are probably connected in their refusal to heed the prophetic word.

20 The concluding editorial comment is quite in keeping with the statement in v 3. כי על אף is variously translated. "Because on account of the anger" is a literal translation. Meek (*JQR* 50 [1959] 45–54) translates, "It was actually because the Lord was angry enough." The sense is clear. On Meek's understanding the clause וימרד should be translated in a purposive way, "that he rebelled." Our translation offers a slightly different understanding. The point to be made is that even though the disasters which had befallen Judah, of which Zedekiah was fully aware, had happened by the will of Yahweh, Zedekiah still chose to rebel against Babylon. During his reign Jeremiah's repeated advice was surrender to Babylon (Jer 21:1–10; 34:1–3; 37:6–10; 38:17–23), partly because the odds were so clearly against Judah and Jerusalem, but, more important, because the prophet perceived that nothing could stand in the way of the will of Yahweh. Zedekiah is being true to form here.

The occasion for the revolt against Babylon can only remain the subject of speculation. The Babylonian Chronicle for Nebuchadrezzar ends in the king's eleventh year (594/593 B.C.) with a brief reference to an additional campaign into Palestine. This seems to be far too early a response to the revolt of Zedekiah, which took place towards the end of the Judean's reign. However, 594 B.C. was a year of ferment (see M. Greenberg, *JBL* 76 [1957] 304–9). War against the Elamites and the inability of the Babylonians to wage campaigns in the years 596 and 595 B.C. tell their own story. The campaign in the west mentioned in the Chronicle was accompanied by a visit of Zedekiah or some ambassadors from Judah (see Jer 51:59). Following this, an anti-Babylonian conspiracy was hatched in Jerusalem and involved the strange mixture of Judah, Edom, Moab, Ammon, and Tyre (see Jer 27-28). On the dating of this event, see Rudolph, *Jeremia*, 174-76; Malamat, VTSup 28:135-36; and Oded, *Israelite and Judean History*, 472.

Tadmor (*JNES* 15 [1956] 230) links the revolt to the resurgence of Egyptian interests in Palestine following the accession of Psammetichus II (594-588 B.C.), who carried out what had become an established foreign policy (see Freedy and Redford, *JAOS* 90 [1970] 480-85). If, as Albright (*JBL* 51 [1932] 77-106) and Bright (*History*, 329) suggest, the revolt came out into the open in 589 B.C., then the setting is perfect. Egypt had been involved for some years in the eastern Mediterranean, and after the initial attack on Palestine, Babylon appeared to have lost interest or the strength to keep her vassals in order that far from home. The kind of restructuring of conquered lands that made such control possible came into its own under the Persians some years later. The false sense of security this gave Zedekiah was encouraged by the Egyptians and is clearly reflected in some passages from the book of Jeremiah. Such a date also suits Ezek 20:1 where the prophet is asked to provide an interpretation of current events to the elders in exile. That the revolt seriously misfired becomes evident from the unfolding narrative.

Explanation

Jehoiakim's reign begins ignominiously. He not only carries out the same domestic policy as his deposed father, Jehoahaz, but he suffers the same fate: invasion and vassal status. A rebellion against the Babylonians who now controlled the region is greeted with neither favor nor enthusiasm by the writer (v 1). Instead it is countered with the statement that Yahweh himself is now working against his people by siding with the Babylonians (v 2). The reason offered is very clear. It is consistent with the threats long uttered by the prophets that are now coming to fruition (v 3), and the reason offered is the effect of the apostasy of Manasseh (v 3b). This comment and justification for what is about to take place can hardly come as a surprise to the reader. Already in 1:1 and the initial chapters of the book the point had been made. In the context of a narrative, the point of which is the succession of Elijah in the person of Elisha, both nation and king suffer loss. The Moabites rebel against Israel after long years of submission (1:1), and Israel's borders shrink. The king too is sick to the point of death. From this point on the prophetic word is not merely to challenge and to bring to repentance, but also to condemn and to pronounce judgment. Through the words he utters "The prophet who is in Israel" also brings about the end of the nation of Judah.

As Israel had suffered attack and deportation for her sins, so now Judah suffers for traveling in "the ways of the kings of Israel." The Babylonians attack while Jehoiakim is king and take Jerusalem early in the reign of his successor, Jehoiachin (vv 9-10). The Babylonians begin systematically to dismantle the machinery of government in Judah; but more than this, they begin to whittle away at the symbols of order and stability by deporting the king and his court and by plundering the temple (vv 9-16). In the king's place, the Babylonians appoint one who is not in direct line for succession, Zedekiah (v 17).

Zedekiah's reign is characterized in typical fashion. Like so many other rulers, he behaved badly (v 19). Yet, while the historical context of his reign is the collapse of the south piece by piece, and the theological context of his reign is that this is happening because of the rejection of Judah and Jerusalem by Yahweh (v 20a), the king makes a last desperate attempt to stem the tide of collapse by rebelling against the might of Babylonia.

The attempt is futile, but not so much because of the might and power of the Babylonian army. Israel's history is littered with battles fought under odds equally as unbalanced, yet which resulted in victory for the faithful Israelite force. A century before, Isaiah had recommended resistance to the Assyrian invaders on the basis of this past and its lessons. Now the situation is different. A new element is expressed. Yahweh himself is fighting against his people, as the prophets have repeatedly warned. The foregoing history of the nation has culminated in this point. To resist is useless. Herein lies the futility. It is a fight against Yahweh himself. The frightening truth of the story of Judah's fall is that it is willed by Yahweh. There is here no contradiction with the past but a sound integration of the recent past with those same historical traditions. Were Yahweh to be absent from the exile, then it would lose any meaning.

Jerusalem Destroyed and Second Deportation (25:1-30)

Bibliography

Ackroyd, P. R. "Historians and Prophets." *SEÅ* 33 (1968) 18–54. ———. "The Temple Vessels—a Continuity Theme." *Studies in the Religion of Ancient Israel.* VTSup 23. Leiden: E. J. Brill, 1972. 66–81. **Albright, W. F.** "King Jehoiachin in Exile." *BAR* 1:106–12. ———. "The Site of Mizpah in Benjamin." *JPOS* 3 (1923) 110–21. **Auerbach, E.** "Wann eroberte Nebukadnezzar Jerusalem?" *VT* 11 (1961) 128–36. **Bade, W. F.** "The Seal of Jaazaniah." *ZAW* 51 (1933) 150–56. **Brunet, G.** "La prise de Jérusalem sous Sedecias." *RHR* 167 (1965) 156–76. **David, M.** "Manumission of Slaves under Zedekiah." *OTS* 5 (1948) 63–79. **Gorg, M.** "Zur Decoration der Tempelsäulen." *BN* 13 (1980) 17–21. **Hobbs, T. R.** "Composition and Structure of the Book of Jeremiah." *CBQ* 34 (1972) 257–75. **Horn, S. H.** "The Babylonian Chronicle and the Ancient Calendar of the Kingdom of Judah." *AUSS* 5 (1967) 12–27. **Hyatt, J. P.** "New Light on Nebuchadressar and Judean History." *JBL* 75 (1956) 277–84. **Malamat, A.** "The Last Kings of Judah and the Fall of Jerusalem." *IEJ* 18 (1968) 137–56. **Meyers, C. L.** "The Elusive Temple." *BA* 45 (1981) 33–41. **Myers, J. M.** "Edom and Judah in the Sixth-Fifth Centuries B.C." In *Near Eastern Studies.* Ed. H. Goedicke. Baltimore: Johns Hopkins Press, 1971. 377–92. **Rudolph, W,** "Zum Text des Königsbuches." *ZAW* 63 (1951) 201–15. **Schedl, C.** "Nachmals das Jahr der Zerstörung Jerusalems."

ZAW 74 (1962) 209–13. **Scott, R. B. Y.** "The Hebrew Cubit." *JBL* 77 (1958) 205–15. **Stern, E.** "Israel at the Close of the Period of the Monarchy: An Archaeological Survey." *BA* 38 (1975) 26–54. **Tsevat, M.** "The Neo-Assyrian and Neo-Babylonian Vassal Oaths and the Prophet Ezekiel." *JBL* 78 (1959) 199–204. **Vogt, E.** "Neubabylonische Chronik über die Schlacht bei Carchemisch und die Einnahme von Jerusalem." *Congress Volume: Strasbourg.* VTSup 4. Leiden: E. J. Brill, 1957. 67–96. **Weidner, E. F.** "Jojachin König von Juda in babylonischen Keilinschriften." In *Mélanges syriens offertes à M. Réné Dussaud*, 933–35. Paris: Gabalda, 1939. **Weinberg, S. S.** "Post-exilic Palestine: An Archaeological Report." *IASHP* 4 (1971) 78–97. **Wilkinson, J.** "The Road from Jerusalem to Jericho." *BA* 38 (1975) 10–24. **Zenger, E.** "Die deuteronomistische Interpretation der Rehabilitierung Jojachins." *BZ* 12 (1968) 16–30.

Translation

¹ It was in the ninth year [a] of his reign, in the tenth month and on the tenth day of the month that Nebuchadrezzar [b] king of Babylon came in person with all his army against Jerusalem. He set up his camp near it and erected siegeworks against the city. ² The city came under siege until the eleventh year of King Zedekiah. ³ By the ninth day of the month [a] the famine was so severe in the city that there was no bread for the people of the land. ⁴ [a] Then the city was broken into by night by soldiers at the road between the two walls near the king's garden. While the Chaldeans surrounded the city the king fled along the Arabah road. ⁵ A Chaldean force pursued the king and caught up with him at the Jericho Flats; then all his men deserted him. ⁶ The Chaldeans captured the king and brought him up to the king of Babylon at Riblah, [a] and they passed sentence [b] upon him. ⁷ They butchered [a] the sons of Zedekiah before his eyes, then they blinded Zedekiah, bound him in chains, and brought him to Babylon.

⁸ In the fifth month, on the seventh [a] day of the month—that was in the nineteenth year of King Nebuchadrezzar, king of Babylon—Nebuzaradan, the commander of the guards and official of the king of Babylon, [b] came to Jerusalem. ⁹ He put the temple and the palace to the torch with many buildings of Jerusalem. Every house of note [a] he set alight. ¹⁰ The guard commander with [a] all the army of the Chaldeans broke down the walls surrounding Jerusalem. ¹¹ The remainder of the people who were left in the city, the deserters who had gone over to the king of Babylon and the rest of the mob, [a] Nebuzaradan the guard commander sent into exile. ¹² The guard commander left a few of the lower classes to be vinedressers and plowers. [a]

¹³ The Chaldeans broke up the bronze pillars which were in the temple [a] together with the stands [b] and the sea of bronze; then they shipped the bronze off to Babylon. ¹⁴ The pans, the trowels, the snuffers, the incense bowls—all the bronze utensils which were of service there they took away. ¹⁵ This included the censers and the bowls. What was gold the guard commander took for gold; what was silver, for silver. [a] ¹⁶ As for the two pillars and the one sea and the stands which Solomon had made for the temple, the bronze of these items was beyond measurement. ¹⁷ A single pillar was eighteen cubits, topped by a bronze capital, the height of which was three [a] cubits, with a cluster of pomegranates on top, all of bronze. The second with the cluster [b] was exactly the same.

¹⁸ The guard commander took Seraiah the head priest and Zephaniah the deputy priest [a] and the three keepers of the threshold. ¹⁹ From the city he took an official who had been in charge of the soldiers, together with five men of the king's privy council ᵃ who were discovered in the city. In addition he took the scribe, the "commander-in-chief" who was responsible for mustering the militia, plus sixty of the militia who were also discovered in the city. ²⁰ Nebuzaradan the guard commander took them and led them to the king of Babylon at Riblah. ²¹ The king of Babylon executed them at Riblah in the land of Hamath. Thus was Judah exiled from her own land.

²² Over the remaining people in the land of Judah, whom Nebuchadrezzar king of Babylon had left, he appointed Gedaliah son of Ahikam, son of Shaphan. ²³ When the troop commanders and their men heard that the king of Babylon had appointed Gedaliah, they came to Gedaliah at Mizpah. They were Ishmael son of Nethaniah, Jochanan son of Kareach, Seraiah son of Tanchumeth the Netophathite, and Jaazaniah the son of the Maacathite, they together with their troops. ᵃ ²⁴ Gedaliah promised them and their troops, "Do not be afraid of the Chaldean officials. ᵃ Return to the land and serve the king of Babylon, and it will be well with you." ²⁵ But in the seventh month Ishamael son of Nethaniah, son of Elishama of the royal line, came with ten ᵃ men and attacked Gedaliah, and he died ᵇ along with the Judeans and Chaldeans who were with him at Mizpah. ²⁶ Then all the people, small and great, and the army officers fled to Egypt because they were afraid of the Chaldeans.

²⁷ In the thirty-seventh ᵃ year of the exile of King Jehoiachin, king of Judah, in the twelfth month on the twenty-seventh day of the month, in the very year he began his reign, Evil-Merodach king of Babylon showed clemency ᵇ to Jehoiachin king of Judah and released him from prison. ²⁸ He treated him well ᵃ and offered him the seat of seats ᵇ among all the kings who were in Babylon. ²⁹ He changed his prison garb and ate bread continually in his company for the rest of his life. ³⁰ For his allowance a continual supply was given him each day by the king for as long as he lived.

Notes

1.a. MT reads בשנת (constr), which should be read more correctly as absolute, בשנה "in the year" (see Jer 39:1).

1.b. The proper spelling for the name of the king of Babylon is Nebuchadrezzar, as in the book of Jeremiah. The practice throughout the commentary is to use this spelling even when the Heb. substitutes an "n" for the "r."

3.a. MT reads בתשעה לחדש "by the ninth day of the month." Jer 52:6 adds בחדש הרביעי "in the fourth month," which is needed in the sentence. RSV offers a double reading.

4.a. MT reads ותבקע העיר "then the city was broken into." No subject is indicated in the sentence for the verb וילך "and he fled," so it must be supplied from the context. The most obvious subject is Zedekiah. G supplies the subject at the beginning of the verse, thus implying that the Judean king is the subject throughout the verse. Gray (*Kings*, 763) follows this lead. Ehrlich (*Randglossen* 7:324) adopts a similar interpretation but with a sizable insertion. Rudolph (*ZAW* 63 [1951] 215) does the same. Our interpretation is slightly different.

6.a. The Heb. term רבלתה "at Riblah" is variously interpreted by the versions.

6.b. MT reads וידברו "and they passed (sentence)." With Gᴮ many accept the sg verb and make the king of Babylon (so Gᴸ) the subject. This is not necessary.

7.a. In keeping with the preceding change Gᴸ reads sg.

8.a. Jer 52:12 reads "tenth" and Gᴸ reads "ninth." (See Gray, *Kings*, 766.)

8.b. MT reads עבד מלך בבל "official of the king of Babylon." G presupposes "the one standing before the king of Babylon," which is supported by Jer 52:12.

9.a. The Heb. is literally translated as "each house (of) a great one." Jer 52:13 reads בית הגדול "house of the great one." Gᴮ with the MT of Jer 39:8 omit גדול "great." Gray (*Kings*, 766) and Burney (*Notes*, 368) also omit the word as superfluous. Its inclusion does make a difference, however. It seems that the Babylonian policy was to destroy the section of the

Form/Structure/Setting 359

city where the elite (political, military, religious) lived. The recent discovery of eighth century B.C. houses in the lower part of the city of David would support the present MT reading. The houses are small residences and not part of the quarter where the elite would have lived. (See Y. Shiloh, "The City of David Archaeological Project: The Third Season." *BA* 44 [1981] 161–70.)

10.a. MT reads אשר רב טבחים "which the guard commander." Jer 52:14 reads את אשר רב טבחים "which was with the guard commander." See *Comment*.

11.a. Gray (*Kings*, 766) regards the word ההמון "the mob" as "tautological and excessive," which is no reason for its omission, however. Jer 52:15 offers האמון "artificers," but the word is rarely used of people in this way.

12.a. Some MSS read ולגבים, which might be connected to the word for "ditches" (see 3:16). This is supported by G^B (ταβειν), although MT reads ולגבים "husbandmen."

13.a. To the typical phrase אשר בית יהוה "which were in the temple" G adds an unnecessary preposition. G^L presupposes an additional verb וַיָּבֵא "and he brought in."

13.b. Most versions transliterate המכנות "the stands."

15.a. G omits the second occurrence of the nouns from the Heb. idiom.

17.a. The Jeremiah parallel reads "five."

17.b. The Heb. is שבכה "cluster" (see 1:2). G transliterates.

18.a. MT reads צפניהו כהן משנה "Zephaniah the deputy priest," to which G adds unnecessarily "son of. . . ."

19.a. For the phrase מראי פני המלך "those seeing the face of the king," see Exod 33:11; Esth 1:14.

19.b. G^L expands the list somewhat.

23.a. The Heb. המה ואנשיהם "they and their men" at the end of the verse is possibly a dittography.

24.a. The word מֵעַבְדֵי "of the officials" is omitted by G^B. The MT of Jer 40:9 reads מֵעֲבוֹד "of the official."

25.a. The word ועשרה "with ten" is omitted by G^B.

25.b. MT reads a simple active, whereas G^L presupposes a hiph plus the 3d person sg suffix. Rudolph (*ZAW* 63 [1951] 201–15) suggests וימיתו אתו "and they killed him."

27.a. Jer 52:31 reads "eighth," and the G of Jer 52:31 reads "fourth."

27.b. The Heb. idiom is נשא את פניו "he lifted his face," a gesture of respect (see *Comment* on 5:1).

28.a. The Heb. reads, lit., "He spoke to him good things."

28.b. MT reads מעל כסא "from upon a seat," which is better read as ממעל לכסא "above the seat," as in Jer 52:32.

Form/Structure/Setting

Every paragraph of 2 Kgs 25 is found in the same or similar form in the book of Jeremiah:

2 Kgs 25	Jeremiah
vv 1–12	52:4–16
	(39:1–10)
vv 13–17	52:17–23
vv 18–21	52:24–27
vv 22–26	⎡40:5–9
	⎣41:1–18
vv 27–30	52:31–34

Jer 52 follows the same outline as 2 Kgs 25, except that it omits any reference to the incident surrounding the figure of Gedaliah (see Jer 52:28–30). The prophetic book, however, contains material elsewhere on Gedaliah which is much longer, so the omission is not significant. What the book of Jeremiah also does is to offer some additional information and interpretation of the events in 2 Kgs 25 (see, for example, the figures of deportees in Jer 52:28–30). This latter phenomenon raises a number of questions for the interpretation of the book of Jeremiah. For a recent interpretation see R. P. Carroll, *From Chaos to Covenant*, 226–48.

The precise significance of these parallels and near-parallels has been sought through a number of means. Strict historical reconstruction, which is often interpreted as a reconstruction of the correct chronological sequence of events, is a path many have taken, but in the final analysis it is one that proves fruitless. The presuppositions in the interests of historical harmony which dominate the approach often produce judgments about the text which tend to obscure individual insights rather than expound them. So, for example, Nelson (*Double Redaction*, 89–90) regards 25:21*b* as an exilic editorial link to chap. 17, and Gray (*Kings*, 768) sees it as the original ending of the book. Vv 22–26 are thereby relegated to an inferior status when compared to the "better informed" parallel in Jeremiah (so Gray, *Kings*, 770). It is argued that the information in 2 Kgs 25 has come to the deuteronomist "second hand" and that he passes it on in summary and inferior form. A similar judgment is made on vv 13–17, which are seen as "an intruded antiquarian, but historical note" (so Montgomery, *Kings*, 567); it is independent of, though not as good as, its more complete parallel in Jer 52:17–23.

It can be assumed, though with extreme caution, that 2 Kgs 25 is a summary of the longer passages in the book of Jeremiah. It must be noted that arguments for priority based on length are often double-edged and inconclusive. In the final analysis it is questionable whether such comparisons are all that helpful. Ackroyd (*SEÅ* 33 [1968] 18–54; VTSup 23:166–81) recommends a much more balanced approach to the consideration of such varied accounts of events within the Scriptures. Each offers, regardless of source and comparative length, its distinct contribution to the development of themes within the OT. If this is to be taken as methodologically sound—and it is a point we have argued for throughout the commentary—then it offers a point of departure for our interpretation which will be able to uncover the meaning of 2 Kgs 25 in a more fruitful way.

The final chapter of 2 Kings is a composition of six vignettes about the end of the state of Judah. In a systematic way the chapter records the fate of several elements of city life following the collapse of the city of Jerusalem. First, the king's fate is recorded (vv 4–7). After a failed attempt to escape from Babylonian custody, he is blinded and then dragged off into exile. Second, the city is systematically burned (vv 8–12). Third, the temple suffers as it too is burned and its treasures taken into exile (vv 13–17). Fourth, the religious, military, and civil personnel who remained in Jerusalem are captured and then summarily executed (vv 18–21). Fifth, the remainder of the inhabitants suffer further setbacks as their appointed governor is assassinated, and they flee to Egypt in fear of the Babylonians (vv 22–26). Sixth, and finally, the king, who was exiled prior to all this, is released from prison and treated well in Babylon (vv 27–20).

The effect of this series of incidents is twofold. First, it destroys decisively any symbol of religious, civil, or military life remaining in Judah. Sacred and symbolic buildings are destroyed, sacred vessels are taken away, and the remaining king is maimed and exiled. Even the puppet administration of Gedaliah fails, and those responsible flee to Egypt. Second, all the symbols that remain intact—the temple vessels and the king, Jehoiachin—are not in Judah, but in Babylon.

Ackroyd's exposition of this phenomenon (VTSup 23:166–81) is accurate up to a point. The symbolic significance of the temple vessels in exile is one of continuity in a time of radical discontinuity. However, one must question whether 2 Kgs 25 disallows the possibility that there is room for restoration. The opposite seems to be the case, at least in the perspective of the deuteronomist. His record of the destruction of the temple vessels includes only the bronze pillars, not the smaller utensils. Jer 27–29 can be used as evidence to show that the presence of some of the vessels in exile was a source of hope for some of those who remained in Jerusalem after the first deportation.

In its final form then, the chapter presents a picture of destruction of Judah—widespread destruction—but the continuity of certain symbols of faith, and indeed hope, outside of Judah in Babylon. "It is correct to say that the deuteronomist's view is 'Only in exile and among the exiles is there hope for the future,' but that principle needs to be made more precise so as to reflect the proper nuances of the [writer]. 'Only in the Babylonian exile and only among the Babylonian exiles is that hope to be found'" (Carroll, *From Chaos to Covenant*, 248). With this assessment this commentary fully concurs.

Comment

The chapter summarizes the effects upon Judah of the Babylonian reaction to the Judean revolt. On the circumstances of the revolt, see *Comment* on the previous chapter. The unstable year of 594 B.C., which would have provided a perfect context for the Judean revolt, is far removed from the final Babylonian reaction in 589/588 B.C., although by no means impossible. Babylon had enough to deal with during these years (see Malamat, VTSup 28:123–45). In any event, the effect upon Judah was devastating. A systematic campaign to cripple the nation had begun, and the final result was the end of a phase of Judean history, the monarchy, and the collapse of a way of life.

1 The ninth year is that of Zedekiah, 589/588 B.C., and the precise dating of day and month, the tenth of the tenth, places the invasion and attack against Jerusalem on December 26, 589 B.C. Montgomery's comment (*Kings*, 560) that the presence of Nebuchadrezzar at Jerusalem is "incorrect" is splitting hairs. Although v 6 places him in his headquarters at Riblah in Syria, and Jer 38:17 mentions the surrender of Jerusalem to the generals of Nebuchadrezzar (שרים), the language of v 1 must be understood properly. Such expressions are not to be taken literally. Nebuchadrezzar was undoubtedly the mastermind behind the campaign into Palestine. His army represented his power and his will, and one can therefore speak of Nebuchadrezzar as being at Jerusalem, in the same way one speaks of supreme commanders in the same breath with battles of the Second World War, although generals of lower rank were responsible for the conduct of the battles.

The exact route by which Nebuchadrezzar's army approached Jerusalem is not known, but it can be reconstructed with a fair degree of accuracy. It certainly included the Shephelah. Jer 34:7 mentions the siege of Lachish and Azekah as the last in a series, and this is supported by Lachish IV (see Gibson, *Syrian Semitic Inscriptions* 1:41–43). Nebuchadrezzar's grand strategy was to remove any military threat by systematically destroying the various fortress systems in Judah. The Shephelah is noted for such fortresses. This swing round to the southwest might also have been motivated by the threat of Egyptian interference, a threat which was realized according to Jer 37:5.

The RV translates דיק with "built forts," but the context alone determines the meaning. G offers περιτειχος "circumvallation." Josephus's description (*Antiq.* x.131) owes much to methods of siege perfected by the Romans, which he undoubtedly witnessed. So his picture is not entirely accurate, although the roots of such warfare had been sunk deep by the Babylonians and the Assyrians before them. The purpose of the structures mentioned here was to provide a platform higher than the walls of the city under attack so that archers and others could rain down missiles on the defenders.

2 The duration of the siege was approximately two years. Josephus (*Antiq.* x.116) estimates it more precisely at eighteen months. Jer 52:6, which ends the siege in the fourth month and ninth day, allows sixteen months. This period of time is noteworthy since the location of monarchical Jerusalem makes it an easy city to attack. The hills surrounding the city are all higher than the city itself. The one feature that made Jerusalem a desirable place to live—its water supply from the Gihon Spring—was situated at one of the lowest points in the area. Because of the nature of the terrain to the north and west of the city, at the beginning of the rain shadow, the city was especially vulnerable from this direction. (See the excellent illustration in R. Humble, *Warfare in the Ancient World,* 223.) The length of time could have resulted from the sheer size of the Babylonian venture, which included not only the destruction of the capital, but also the fortresses of Judah.

3 On "the famine was so severe," see *Comment* on 6:25 and the remarkable parallel found in Assyrian sources (*ANET,* 299–300). Famine, not thirst, is the particular curse of the city under siege. Hezekiah had ensured that the city had a suitable water supply, but food supplies would have been quite limited; the opportunity to grow more to supplement what had been gathered from the previous harvest was almost nonexistent within the immediate environs of the city. לעם הארץ "for the people of the land." The translation "common people" (NEB) does not convey what is intended here.

4 This verse is confusing. Literally it reads: "The city was broken, and all the men of war that night, the way of the gate between the twin walls which were by the king's garden, while the Chaldeans were surrounding the city, and he went by the Arabah road." Such a translation is pedantic, but it does demonstrate the ambiguities of the Hebrew. The issues of interpretation are syntactical and topographical. In the present text the expression וכל אנשי המלחמה "and all the men of war" is very awkward. Assigning it to the status of an "intrusion" from Jer 52:7 (so Montgomery, *Kings,* 561) solves nothing, and the versions are characterized by various attempts to smooth out the difficulties. Context allows that the king, originally accompanied by a bodyguard, escaped to the east. Thus, the "men of war" probably refers to those who broke into the walls of the city, an action that precipitated the king's flight.

The wall was probably breached in the north of the city, although there is no evidence to substantiate this; it makes strategic sense to attack the city from this direction.

The escape would have been made from the southern end of the city of David, at the confluence of the Kidron and Hinnom Valleys, and the continuation of the Kidron to the southeast would have provided access to the route to Jericho. דרך הערבה "the Arabah road" is also mentioned in 2 Sam 4:7 and according to Aharoni (*Land of the Bible*, 59–60) is the road from Jerusalem down to Jericho. (See also J. Wilkinson, *BA* 38 [1975] 10–24.) One can only guess at the final destination of Zedekiah. It was away from the Babylonians, who were occupied on the northern and western sides of the city. Since both Moab and Ammon lay in the general direction of his flight, and since both had been involved in the original revolt against Babylon (Jer 27:4), it is likely that he was going to seek refuge there.

5 The king's attempt at escape failed because of the swift and efficient reaction of the Babylonians. In view of the location where they finally caught up with him, the capture probably took place on the following day. ערבות ירחו "the Jericho flats" are the stretches of flat dry ground to the east of Jericho. The area, which is exposed and devoid of any substantial vegetation, would not have been easy for the fugitive king to cross unseen. נפצו "they deserted": the same verb in Judg 7:19 is translated "shatter." The image thus conjured is of a wholesale and panic-ridden desertion at the appearance of the Babylonians by the troops who had accompanied the king.

6 The king is arrested and taken before Nebuchadrezzar to offer an account of himself. רבלה "Riblah" (see Num 34:11) is a city in northern Syria where Nebuchadrezzar made his headquarters. (See A. Haldar, "Riblah," *IDB* 4:78.) וידברו אתו משפט, lit., "and they spoke to him judgment," is a technical phrase for a trial and the passing of sentence (see Jer 21:1). The tradition preserved by Josephus (*Antiq.* x.138–39) that Zedekiah was accused of breaking his covenant with Nebuchadrezzar has a ring of truth. This is undoubtedly a factor in the harsh punishment meted out to the Judeans.

7 The punishment of Zedekiah seems inordinately cruel, though it was by no means unusual in warfare in the ancient world. If, however, Zedekiah had broken faith with Babylon and contravened treaty regulations, the punishment is understandable, though no less cruel. The verb שחטו "they butchered" is often used in the killing of sacrifices (Lev 6:25) and in this context implies a brutal slaughter of the sons of Zedekiah. The rabbis saw in the blinding of Zedekiah a fulfillment of Ezek 12:13. Blinding of prisoners was a common Assyrian practice, but little evidence is found for the practice by the Babylonians. The symbolic significance of such an act is obvious. The eyes are important as gateways to the intellect and will (see the frequent "in the eyes of"), and without them a person is rendered powerless. (See especially M. Douglas, *Natural Symbols*, 96–113.) בנחשתים "in chains," in this dual form is a *hapax legomenon*, but the context provides the meaning. As a relatively young man of thirty-two years of age, Zedekiah had little to look forward to but the dark misery of exile.

8 Following the breach of the city walls and the collapse of resistance in the city, which was accomplished by the fighting troops of the Babylonian army, other officials now moved in to take stock of the situation, catalog the loot, and set up an administration under occupation. This was done by rendering ineffective important centers of influence and by destroying any possible source of resistance in the city.

"The fifth month on the seventh day of the month" is approximately one month after the fall of the city and would be in July of 586 B.C. נבוזראדן "Nebuzaradan." The role of this official is slightly different here from that depicted in Jer 39. His title רב טבחים is an interesting one. In 1 Sam 9:23 it is translated as "cook." The verb can certainly be used of a domestic servant, like "butcher," but in the present bureaucratic context it has a slightly different nuance. In Gen 40:3 the expression is used of one into whose custody Joseph was placed. While we have followed the RSV translation of "guard commander," the role was not an exclusively military one.

9 The first task of this official was to destroy all the important symbolic centers in the city, including the temple and other structures, including "every house of note."

10 He then destroyed the protective walls of the city, thus rendering it vulnerable to further attack. The expression אשר רב טבחים "which the guard commander" is awkward; a preposition ל "belonging to" before רב would smooth out the sentence.

11 Three remaining groups of people are now added to those already taken from the city. They constitute a ragtag assortment of what was left in the city after its fall. הנפלים "the deserters" (see 7:4) had sided with the group that advocated surrender to the Babylonians (see Jer 38:19). During the siege there was clearly no unanimity on what ought to be done in the face of the attack by Babylon. Caught in the middle of the struggle was the indecisive king, Zedekiah. The "mob" (see n. 11.a.) that remained during the siege would by this time have been completely exhausted and probably have no will left to resist.

12 On ומדלת "a few of the lower classes," see *Comment* on 24:14. See n. 12.a. for the variants on ליגבים "plowers." The verb from which the noun is derived is thought to be "husband" (BDB, 387), but such a translation is dependent entirely on the associations in this context. G translates γεωργοις "farmers, plowers," and the general understanding of the expression is "ditch-diggers" (ולגבים). The impression here is that the Babylonians left such behind to work as laborers in Judah, in which case the Babylonian policy was to ensure that some form of agricultural life continued in the land. It is clear from what follows (vv 22–30) that life did not come to an abrupt end at the exile.

13 In this paragraph (through v 17) is an inventory of the utensils taken from the temple. The list should be compared with 1 Kgs 17:15–50 where the original manufacture of the items is recorded. The style and contents of the paragraph betray the source of the information—the official records. The details are found elsewhere in matters dealing with the temple (see e.g.,

12:14). For עמודי הנחשת "bronze pillars," see 1 Kgs 17:15–22. These are the large pillars "Jachin" and "Boaz" which stood at the entrance to the sanctuary. For המכנות "the stands" see 1 Kgs 17:27–37.

16 In 1 Kgs 7:15–20 the dimensions of the pillars, but not the volume of the bronze, are described.

17 שלש אמה "three cubits"; Jer 52:22 reads "five cubits." (On the cubit see R. B. Y. Scott, *JBL* 77 [1958] 205–15.)

18 The third part of the activity of Nebuzaradan concerned the elimination of certain key figures who did not fit into the overall strategy of the Babylonians. שריה "Seraiah" is a name not known outside the Bible, although it is common within it. The person referred to here might be the Seraiah of Jer 36:26. כהן הראש "the head priest" is the first such designation in the OT; it probably should be identified with the office of כהן הגדול "the great priest" of chap. 12. צפניהו "Zephaniah" was Zedekiah's agent against the prophet Jeremiah (see Jer 21:1; 29:25; etc.). כהן משנה "the deputy priest" was second in rank to Seraiah.

19 After the taking of these religious officials, the Babylonian turned his attention to others who held a mixture of civil and military offices, no doubt due to the rather unstable circumstances within the city in the later months of Zedekiah's reign. סריס אשר פקיד על אנשי המלחמה "an official who had been in charge of the soldiers." The man probably warrants an official title such as "minister of the army." That such a role persisted after the deportation of Jehoiachin does not contradict the record of that original deportation. It shows that in the meantime the resistance to Babylon was organized. מראי פני המלך "those seeing the face of the king." This expression is reminiscent of the description of Naaman in 5:1–2. (See also Esth 1:14.) The designation indicates an intimate involvement with the king, hence the translation "privy council." As it stands, the two parts of the expression הספר שר הצבא are in apposition, "The scribe, that is, the commander-in-chief." Although it is awkward, it is certainly not impossible. His duties are described in the following comment המצבא את עם הארץ "the commander-in-chief with the people of the land," i.e., the one who mustered the militia for action to deal with the siege. His title, "scribe," suggests that either he was a civil servant responsible for the job or that his role as army commander was a temporary one, perhaps one for which he was not formally trained.

20–21 These men too are taken to Nebuchadrezzar's headquarters in Syria and executed; they are not taken into exile. Their elimination effectively robs Judah of any firm leadership. ויגל יהודה מעל אדמתו "thus was Judah exiled from her own land." For many this signifies the end of the book (see Montgomery, *Kings*, 564). That it has a thematic parallel with 17:23*b* is clear. The implicit warning that Judah would suffer the same fate as Israel is now realized. By "Judah" is meant the ruling elite. It is clear from what follows that some form of life and administration continued in the land after the fall of Jerusalem. (For the extent of the destruction, see E. Stern, *BA* 38 [1975] 26–54.)

22 Following the invasion and deportation, the new masters of Judah attempted to establish some form of administration in the conquered land. Unlike the Assyrians, the Babylonians made no attempt to repopulate the land with people from other parts of the empire. The new administration, while characterized by a strong Babylonian presence (v 25), was headed by local Judeans of some standing. But within a very short time dissatisfaction had grown among those who had survived the invasion, and an attempt was made to overthrow the puppet regime of Gedaliah and to reinstate a Judean one, allied perhaps with Ammon. The attempt was a failure and was crushed. Babylonian control over Judah continued for another fifty years.

"The remaining people": Babylonian deportation policy appeared to have been directed towards those who were skilled and who could prove their usefulness to the Babylonians. The name גדליהו "Gedaliah" means "Yahweh is great." According to Jer 40:10, which is a much fuller account, Gedaliah also had some fiscal responsibilities. His name is found on a seal of the period from Lachish (see Gibson, *Syrian Semitic Inscriptions* 1:62) and also on one of the ostraca from Arad (see Aharoni, *Arad Inscriptions*, 42–43). The name is a common one. בן אחיקם "son of Ahikum": this name is also found at Arad (see Aharoni, *Arad Inscriptions*, 56–58). The same person is mentioned in 2 Kgs 22:12 and Jer 26:24, where he appears as a moderate member of the court. בן שפן "son of Shaphan." See 22:3 and Jer 26:24. Gedaliah is then associated with some members of the Jerusalem establishment and represents the pro-Babylonian group in Jerusalem.

23 Gedaliah provided a rallying point for many of the military and civil officials who still remained in the land, no doubt in hiding after the defeat of their army and the collapse of their capital city. המצפה "Mizpah" is to be identified with the modern Tell en Nasbeh (see M. Broshi, *EAEHL* 3:912–18), a site admirably suited to its name of "watchtower." It lies a few miles north of Jerusalem on the small plain near Bethel (Grid 170–143). It reveals no destruction level for this period and was spared the fate of many Judean towns and cities. As in Judg 20:1 and 1 Sam 7:16, it proved to be an important center to which Israel could go in times of trouble.

ישמעאל בן נתניה "Ishmael son of Nathaniah." The name and patronym of Gedaliah's assassin are common, either in this form or one slightly different (see Gibson, *Syrian Semitic Inscriptions* 1:32, 45, 63, and Lemaire, *Inscriptions hebraiques*, 213–14). יוחנן בן קרח "Jochanan son of Kareach." The man is unknown apart from this incident. שריה "Seraiah" is not to be confused with the man of the same name in v 18. תנחמת "Tanchumeth" is an unusual name for a man since it has a feminine ending. The root is נחם "to comfort." It does appear in the Arad correspondence (see Aharoni, *Arad Inscriptions*, 68–69) without the ending. הנטפתי "the Netophatite" possibly refers to modern Khirbet Bedd Falu (Grid 171–119; see F. M. Abel, *La geographie de la Palestine* 2:399). יאזניהו "Jaazaniah" is a common name and means "Yahweh gives ear." It appears in Ezek 8:11 and in many nonbiblical sources such as Lachish I:2–3, a seal found at Tell en Nasbeh, and in Arad 39.9. (See Gibson, *Syrian Semitic Inscriptions* 1:63, 67; Lemaire, *Inscriptions hebraiques*, 206–7; and Broshi, *EAEHL* 3:918.) בן המעכתי "son of the Maacathite." The site of Abel-beth-Maacah is well in the north, but perhaps this is what distinguishes the man in this context.

24 Gedaliah's advice to the gathered officials is similar to that of Jeremiah (Jer 27:8). It also provides a clear picture of Babylonian policy in Judah during the exile. They were clearly not interested in the complete devastation of the country. ולאנשיהם "and to their men" is a clear indication of the presence of bands of troops wandering around the country after the war had finished. The plan of Gedaliah was, in part, to organize and then demobilize these troops and put them to a more productive way of life. There is no need to read into the expression מעבדי "officials" the idea of foreign mercenaries (see Barnes, *2 Kings*, 146–47).

25 The new administration is short-lived, and its demise at the hands of Ishmael and his men created an intolerable situation in Judah. This took place two months after the inauguration of Gedaliah's administration (cf. v 8). מזרע המלוכה "of the royal line" is a hint at Ishmael's background. How close he was to being a legitimate heir to the throne is unclear. His pedigree provides no hint. His actions, however, place him squarely within the camp of those opposed to collaboration with Babylon.

עשרה אנשים "ten men." The precise number suggests a military formation. It is the smallest unit within the army. ואת היהודים ואת הכשדים "along with the Judeans and Chaldeans" reflects the make-up of the administration of Gedaliah at Mizpah, with both Judean and Chaldean advisers. Josephus (*Antiq.* x.168–70) adds considerable color to the incident, reminiscent of 1 Kgs 20:16–22, although he does follow in outline the version found in Jer 41:1–3.

26 All of those with the slightest connection with the administration at Mizpah fled in fear of reprisal by the Babylonians. Their destination, Egypt, was probably chosen because of the anti-Babylonian activities of Hophra (see Jer 37:5). The fact that all fled possibly indicates the widespread nature of the conspiracy against Gedaliah. In another account (Jer 41) a minor civil war breaks out, and Ishmael flees in the direction of Ammon, a possible source of support for the rebellion.

27 In almost complete contrast to the sordid end to the inhabitants of Judah, the concluding paragraph of the chapter turns to the relative tranquility of the exiles some years later. Before we are allowed to leave the history of the monarchy, the writer provides us with a glimpse of hope. Jehoiachin, whose exile had been recorded some time before, is now seen cared for. The thirty-seventh year of his exile takes us to 560 B.C., and the precise date is the twelfth of March.

אויל מרדך "Evil Merodach" was the son of Nebuchadrezzar; he reigned for a brief time from 562–560 B.C., when he was assassinated by his successor, Neriglissar. נשא . . . את ראש, lit., "he lifted . . . the head." The body symbolism of the language is again obvious here. (See *Comment* on 3:14 and 5:1–2.) The head is the symbol of power and respect. "Lifting" the head is a gesture of rehabilitation. Conversely, "subduing" the head, or crown, is a gesture of humiliation. (See Jer 2:16.) No motivation is given for this gesture on the part of Evil Merodach. No record of his reign remains extant. According to rabbinic sources, the release from prison was a reward for continence (see Ginzberg, *Legends of the Jews* 4:281). Albright (*BAR* 1:109) suggests that Jehoiachin was imprisoned by Nebuchadrezzar only after the disturbances in Judah which gave rise to the rebellion of Zedekiah. However, the release from prison is presented as though it represents a new policy inaugurated with the advent of a new ruler.

28 "He treated him well." The contrast with v 6*b* is marked and deliberate.

מעל כסא כסאו "the seat of seats" presupposes a hierarchy of royal prisoners in the Babylonian jails. The chair was a symbol of important social status; that Evil Merodach was prepared to offer the Judean king this symbol demonstrates his amazing liberality.

29 The treatment afforded Jehoiachin echoes that offered to Joseph (Gen 41:14), but more closely, Daniel. Under Evil Merodach apparently Jehoiachin and numerous other captives were well treated (see Albright, *BAR* 1:106–12). The records of provisions for these captives also demonstrates that the exiles were still regarded as kings of their homelands, although to all intents and purposes that status was ineffective. The position of Jehoiachin stands in sharp contrast to the treatment dealt Zedekiah.

כל ימי חיו "for as long as he lived." The parallel in Jer 52:34 adds the reference to the day of Jehoiachin's death, possibly indicating that its perspective is a later one than the present text (see T. R. Hobbs, *CBQ* 34 [1972] 272–73). It is fair to conclude that Jehoiachin was still alive when 2 Kgs 25 was written. It thus presents some form of hope after the debacle of the revolt against Babylon and the subsequent sack of Jerusalem.

Explanation

The final chapter of the deuteronomistic history begins with a surprising note of precision. The events of the final collapse of Judah and Jerusalem are set within history in a more careful way than before. The years of reigns now give way to year, month, and day, a pattern that is continued in the book of Ezekiel and to a certain extent in the book of Jeremiah. The general dating of invasions and attacks by foreigners into Judah and against Jerusalem, such as "In his days . . . ," now gives way to an unusual exactness not seen before in Kings. The events are in "the ninth year . . . the tenth month . . . the tenth day" (v 1), to be concluded in the "fifth month . . . the seventh day . . . the nineteenth year" (v 8). Possible adaptation of a different system of time reckoning is granted, but why does it occur only at this point? The possibility for such dating existed earlier in the narrative, yet it was not used. The answer is that general characterizations of reigns with the phrase "in his days" (e.g., 24:1) are no longer needed. There is now no time left to be so characterized. The end has come. Judah is attacked, plundered, and exiled.

In the narrative that follows a similar precision is to be noted in the systematic elimination of any vestige of order and symbol. Sacred place (land, city, temple) is violated. Sacred persons (king, priests, officials) are killed, maimed, or exiled. The actions are deliberate, without comment, and have an air of finality about them. Here is dénouement. This is the point to which the narrative of 2 Kings, and indeed the deuteronomistic history, has been moving. It is a point at which Judah, its land, its people, and its symbols of order and society ceased to exist in their former state. As Manasseh, in his worship of the gods of Canaan, sought to reestablish the time before settlement, the time after settlement and monarchy has abruptly come.

In the so-called postscript of 2 Kings (25:27–30) many have sought for signals of the writer's orientation toward the future. Is it for him a time of hope, or a time of despair? The question must be dealt with on a much broader footing than the implications of these last few verses of the book. Hope in the survival and even return of the king can be inferred from the final verses, in spite of the obvious lack of detail. The fact that the royal line is still alive is important in this regard. However, in the light of the prophetic warnings against such hopes in Jer 27–29, it is unlikely that this implied hope forms the basis of our writer's view of the future.

Following the precise end of Judah (vv 1–21) is the Gedaliah incident. The version here is much shorter than that in the book of Jeremiah (see *Form/Structure/Setting* above). While it is tempting to look for signs of historical priority in a comparison of the two, we must look at the incident in a different light if we are to discover its significance at this point in the deuteronomist's narrative. The account is brief and describes the failure to bring about a semblance of order and cohesion to the remainder of Judeans in the land. The attempt is quite unsuccessful, and many of the important people who are left flee the country. Following the end there is no life for Judah in the land. All trace of order, stability, and religion is exterminated. For hope, if there be any, the search must be made elsewhere.

The Gedaliah incident is followed by the release of Jehoiachin from prison, which is introduced with the same precision as the fall of Judah (see v 27). It would not be possible on the basis of that formal similarity alone to argue for the arrival of a new age. But the argument is nevertheless possible. The only remaining symbols of Yahweh's presence with his people—the temple vessels, the king, the leaders, including the priests—are newly located in Babylon. They are to be found in the new place to which they have gone, not because of some historical accident, but rather because of the will of Yahweh expressed in judgment. Hope can be found in Yahweh, who for the sake of his name and for the sake of David, saves. The ability to hope is to be found among those in exile in Babylon. The hope is not completely dependent upon the survival of any institution alone, whether it be king or temple, as the Gedaliah incident illustrates. Hope is rather to be found among those whose trust is in the God who has brought them out of Egypt, given them the land, judged them, and taken them into exile.

Index of Authors Cited

Abel, F. xlvi, 76, 366
Ackroyd, P. R. xxxiii, xxxiv, 207, 210, 241, 248, 274, 284, 312, 317, 356, 360, 361
Aharoni, Y. xlvi, 35, 40, 100, 103, 104, 179, 182, 183, 186, 194, 202, 211, 214, 219, 241, 252, 312, 323, 340, 343, 350, 363, 366
Aharoni, Y. and M. Avi-Yonah 50
Ahlstrom, G. W. 241, 255, 323
Ahuvya, A. 219
Albrektson, B. xlvi, 166, 235, 258, 338
Albright, W. F. xxxviii, xliv, xlv, xlvi, 67, 93, 102, 219, 220, 239, 264, 323, 343, 349, 350, 352, 355, 356, 367, 368
Allen, L. C. 284
Alt, A. xxii, 186, 241, 312
Alter, R. xxvi, xxvii, xxx, xxxi, 225, 239
Amiran, R. 260, 261, 296
Andersen, K. T. xxxviii
Asensio, F. 145
Asmussen, J. P. 312
Astour, M. 90, 215
Auerbach, E. 356
Avigad, N. 129, 173, 181, 186, 242, 251, 260, 262, 312
Avi-Yonah, M. and E. Stern xiii

Bach, R. xlvi, 297, 308
Bade, W. F. 356
Baena, G. 220
Baillet, M., J. T. Milik, and R. de Vaux xlvi, 58, 85, 95, 123
Baltzer, K. 343
Baly, D. 76
Barnes, W. E. xlvi, 52, 84, 154, 176, 183, 252, 295, 333, 334, 339, 367
Barnett, R. D. 242, 255, 297, 302
Barr, J. 242, 248
Barrick, W. B. 312
Barrois, G. A. 50, 156
Beek, M. A. 13, 22
Begrich, J. xxxviii, xliv, 185, 201, 203
Benzinger, I. xlvi
Bernhardt, K. H. 28, 114
Berry, G. R. 312
Beyerlin, W. xlvi, 8, 9, 39, 52, 167, 333
Bin-Nun, S. R. 93
Birch, B. C. 158
Blake, I. M. 13, 23
Blank, S. H. xlvi, 233
Bloch, M. xxx
Boecker, H. J. 242, 256
Bolsinger, G. 187
Borger, R. 133, 141
Botterweck, G. J. and H. Ringgren xiv
Bowman, R. A. 79
Boyd, W. J. P. 312
Brand, J. 120
Bratsiotis, N. P. 11
Bright, J. xxii, xxx, xxxi, xl, 171, 184, 193, 194, 212, 230, 242, 250, 251, 305, 309, 322, 350, 355
Brin, G. 187, 201, 289, 340, 346
Brock, S. P. 159, 162
Bronner, L. xlvi, 164

Brooke, A. E., N. MacLean, and H. St. J. Thackeray xliv, xlv
Broshi, M. 260, 261, 296, 327, 366
Brown, F., S. R. Driver, and C. A. Briggs xii, 51, 66, 89, 104, 141, 175, 200, 209, 223, 255, 299, 310, 333, 345, 353, 364
Brueggemann, W. xxii, xlvi, 237, 306
Brunet, G. 356
Buber, M. 233, 335
Buchholz, W. 1, 9
Budde, K. 120, 128, 312
Burney, C. F. xliv, 4, 11, 20, 23, 30, 31, 37, 44, 57, 58, 71, 72, 84, 85, 95, 96, 99, 104, 109, 118, 122, 134, 135, 136, 141, 142, 147, 148, 151, 152, 161, 162, 163, 166, 168, 175, 176, 179, 189, 191, 196, 209, 212, 216, 222, 223, 225, 232, 236, 238, 244, 245, 258, 267, 268, 269, 293, 295, 299, 315, 323, 330, 331, 336, 338, 345, 346, 358
Burrows, M. 260, 262
Butler, T. C. xxii, xlvi

Campbell, E. F. and D. N. Freedman xxxviii
Canosa, A. C. xlvii
Carroll, R. P. xxxiii, xxxiv, xxxviii, 13, 159, 168, 220, 233, 274, 326, 360, 361
Celada, B. 220
Chapman, W. J. 187
Childs, B. S. 152, 207, 214, 220, 236, 239, 242, 246, 247, 257, 259, 270, 276, 277, 278, 284, 290, 295
Christ, H. 216, 308
Claburn, W. E. 312, 322, 323, 337
Clements, R. E. 242, 268, 269, 270, 271, 272, 279, 282, 297, 302, 305
Cochrane, R. G. 63
Cochrane, R. G. and T. F. Davey 63
Cogan, M. 194, 199, 203, 213, 214, 215, 251, 305, 333
Coggins, R. J. 220, 235, 238
Conteneau, G. 159, 169
Cook, H. J. 187, 201
Cooke, S. A. 159, 167
Cornfeld, G. and D. N. Freedman 284, 294
Couroyer, B. xlvii
Craigie, P. C. xlvi, 78, 305
Croatto, J. S. and J. A. Soggin xlvii, 312
Cross, F. M. xxii, xxiii, xxiv, xxv, xxviii, xliv, xlv, xlvii, 338
——, and G. E. Wright 312
——, and D. N. Freedman 312
Crown, A. D. 242
Crusemann, F. xlvii
Culley, R. C. xxvi, 45, 61, 73
Cummings, J. T. 69, 76

David, M. 356
Davidson, A. B. 162, 226
Davies, G. H. 332
Davies, G. I. 242, 255, 323
Debus, J. 120, 130, 234

Delcor, M. 145, 147
Deller, K. 220
Deltombe, L. F. xlvii
Dentan, R. C. xxx
Derchain, P. 28, 207
Dever, W. G. 220, 230
—— and S. M. Paul xlvi
DeVries, S. J. xxii, xlvi, 4, 6, 15, 16, 31, 32, 34, 45, 50, 58, 61, 72, 73, 85, 86, 88, 92, 98, 99, 100, 101, 110, 111, 112, 113, 123, 124, 126, 162, 163, 164, 181, 289
Diaz, J. A. 312
Dietrich, W. xxii, xxiii, xlvii, 4, 11, 312, 319, 350
Donner, H. xxx, 187
Douglas, M. xxxiii, xxxiv, xxxv, xxxvi, xxxvii, 187, 194, 292, 335, 363
Driver, G. R. xlviii, 8, 220, 223, 330
Driver, S. R. xxii, xlvi, 62, 71, 100, 112, 122, 235

Eakin, F. E. xlviii
Ebach, J. 220
Ehrlich, A. B. xliv, 10, 20, 22, 139, 140, 141, 142, 147, 148, 152, 175, 208, 209, 223, 244, 299, 300, 314, 315, 330, 331, 345, 358
Eisenstadt, S. N. xlvi, 332
Eising, H. 290
Eissfeldt, O. xiii, xlvi, 45, 58, 61, 72, 96, 98, 242, 315
Elat, M. 106, 242
Elliger, K. 242
Ellis, P. F. xlvi
Ellul, J. 264, 283
Engle, J. xlvi
Ephal, I. xlvii, xlviii, 220, 231
Evans-Pritchard, E. E. 235

Fabry, E. 353
Falk, Z. W. 133, 141, 145
Fensham, F. C. 1, 8
Fichtner, J. 264
Field, F. xliv
Finegan, J. xxxviii
Fitzmyer, J. A. 55, 62, 64
Fohrer, G. xlvi, xlviii, 52, 159, 164, 169, 264
Fokkelman, J. P. xlvii
Fowler, M. D. xlviii, 173, 179
Freed, A. 313
Freedy, K. S. and D. B. Redford 344, 355
Frick, F. S. xlvii, 67, 120, 128, 130
Fricke, K. D. xlvi, 122, 129, 148, 152, 178, 184, 218, 289, 293, 295
Frost, S. B. 106, 312
Fullerton, K. 264

Galling, K. 13, 19, 20
Garber, P. L. 218
Gaster, T. H. 8, 22, 216
Gay, P. xxx, xxxii
Gehman, H. S. 106, 117
Gelb, I. J. 90
Geller, M. J. 187, 200

Index of Authors Cited

Geradon, B. de 160, 170, 215, 278
Gese, H. xlviii
Gesenius, W., E. Kautzsch, and A. E. Cowley 8, 15, 20, 23, 50, 71, 72, 84, 139, 147, 208, 267, 321
Geus, C. H. J. de 28
Geva, H. xlviii
Geyer, J. B. 242
Gibson, J. C. L. xxxviii, xxxix, xliii, 20, 35, 39, 51, 67, 102, 127, 143, 151, 156, 163, 166, 171, 193, 195, 196, 203, 215, 230, 235, 256, 277, 293, 296, 326, 338, 339, 350, 362, 366
Gichon, M. and C. Herzog xlvii, 82, 91, 104, 105, 170, 171
Gilead, C. 1
Gilkey, L. 241
Gilula, M. 264, 280
Ginzberg, L. xlvii, 9, 10, 36, 50, 51, 238, 280, 290, 296, 308, 367
Glueck, J. J. 9
Goedicke, H. 220
Gordis, R. 133, 142
Gordon, C. H. xiv, 338
Gorg, M. 242, 356
Goshen-Gottstein, M. xliv, xlv
Goudoever, J. van 133, 139
Granild, S. 313
Gray, J. xlvi, 11, 19, 21, 23, 24, 25, 26, 31, 32, 34, 43, 44, 45, 51, 52, 53, 62, 64, 71, 72, 76, 79, 80, 84, 92, 100, 101, 102, 103, 114, 115, 116, 117, 118, 122, 123, 127, 129, 131, 135, 136, 138, 139, 141, 144, 146, 147, 148, 161, 162, 163, 164, 167, 168, 169, 175, 177, 178, 185, 189, 191, 193, 194, 195, 197, 201, 203, 204, 212, 214, 215, 216, 220, 222, 224, 227, 228, 231, 235, 238, 239, 247, 248, 250, 253, 261, 267, 268, 269, 270, 271, 274, 276, 279, 286, 289, 290, 291, 294, 295, 299, 300, 304, 309, 314, 315, 319, 330, 331, 334, 335, 339, 341, 345, 352, 353, 354, 358, 359, 360
Grayson, K. xxxviii, xxxix, 229, 230, 289, 348
Greenberg, M. 344, 354
Greenfield, J. C. 139
Greenwood, D. 17
Gressmann, H. 313
Grill, S. and E. Haag 13
Gurney, O. R. 82, 89, 90

Haag, H. 104, 128, 242
Haldar, A. 65, 363
Hall, E. T. xxxviii, xl
Haller, E. 41
Hallo, W. 160, 167, 173, 184, 187, 215, 220, 228, 264
Halpern, B. 284, 291, 294
Hamburger, H. 153, 154
Haran, M. 160, 167, 170, 171, 173, 182, 184, 187, 197, 207, 215, 216, 217
Har-el, M. 312, 335
Harrison, R. K. 291
Harvey, V. A. xxx
Hasel, G. F. 264, 271, 279, 281
Helfmeyer, J. 293
Heller, J. 41, 55
Herdner, A. xii, 201
Herrmann, S. xxx, 79, 115, 131, 165, 167, 193, 194, 199, 200, 201, 250
Heschel, A. xxxiii, xxxviii, 271, 338

Hestrin, R. and M. Dayagi 242
Hobbs, T. R. 220, 223, 231, 242, 255, 287, 356, 368
Hoffman, Y. 214
Holladay, W. L. 264, 280
Hommel, F. 201
Honeyman, A. M. 187, 193
Hoppe, L. 312
Horn, S. H. 242, 264, 276, 356
Horst, F. 312
Huffmon, H. B. 220, 234, 307
Humble, K. 230, 362
Hyatt, J. P. xxii, 356

Illman, K. J. 284, 290
Ishida, T. 106, 195, 197, 201

Jagersma, H. xxx
Jakobsen, T. 302
Janssen, J. M. A. 264
Jellicoe, S. xliv, xlv
Jenkins, A. K. 242
Jenni, E. 173, 180
Jepsen, A. xxii, xxiii, xxxix, 234, 252, 312
Jeremias, J. 21
Jobling, D. 46
Joines, K. R. 242, 252
Juon, P. 1

Kahle, P. xliv, xlv
Kaiser, O. xlvi, 270
Kaplan, J. 187, 202
Katzenstein, H. J. 93, 120
Kawin, B. F. xxvi, xxvii
Khanolkar, V. R. 68
Kenyon, K. 156, 335
Kilian, R. 41
Kipfstein, M. 216
Kitchen, K. A. xxxix, 242
Kittel, R. xlvi
Klein, R. W. xxxiii, xxxiv, xxxvii, xxxix, xlviii
Knott, J. B. xlvii
Koch, K. xlvii, 4, 9, 17, 85, 86, 231
Kraus, H.-J. xlviii, 13, 19, 337
Krauss, R. 220
Krige, J. D. 220, 235
Kutsch, E. xxxix, xlviii, 173, 183, 344, 351

Lambdin, T. O. 90
Lambert, W. G. 264
Lance, H. D. xlviii
Landy, D. 284, 292
Larsson, G. xxxix, 344, 349, 350
Lauha, A. 312
Leeuwen, C. van 242
Lehman, M. R. 312
Lemaire, A. xlvii, xlviii, 41, 340, 350, 366
Lettinga, J. P. 264
Levine, L. D. 187, 194, 198, 220, 230
Lewis, I. M. 235
Licht, J. xxvi, xxvii, xxviii, xxx, 225, 271
Lidzbarski, H. xlvii, 310
Lind, M. xlvii, 229, 257
Lindars, B. xlviii
Lindblom, J. 25, 36, 102
Lipinski, E. xlviii
Liver, J. 28
Liverani, M. 145, 156, 157, 158
Loewenstamm, S. E. 214
Lohfink, N. 312, 319

Long, B. O. xxxii, xlvii, 28, 31, 32, 36, 37, 98, 99, 235
Loretz, O. 160, 162
Luckenbill, D. D. xxxix, 126, 127, 183, 192, 194, 198, 199, 201, 205, 212, 256, 279
Lundbom, J. R. 1, 11, 13, 18, 19, 20, 22, 313, 325
Luria, B. Z. 145, 207

Macalister, R. A. S. 155
McCarthy, D. J. 160, 163, 165, 207, 216
McCurley, F. R. 133, 138
MacDonald, J. 264, 275
McHugh, J. 207, 212
McKane, W. 145, 147, 153
McKay, J. W. xlvi, 215, 251, 252, 255, 305, 306, 309, 310, 313, 322, 333, 335
Maier, J. 145
Malamat, A. xlviii, 160, 170, 171, 297, 310, 313, 332, 339, 344, 349, 351, 353, 354, 355, 356, 361
March, W. E. 82, 85
Marcus, R. xlvii, 109, 169
Margalit, O. 313
Martin-Achard, R. xlvii
Mastin, B. A. xlviii
Mauchline, J. A. xlvi
Mayes, A. D. H. 313
Mazar, B. 145, 155, 156, 160, 170
Meek, T. J. 344, 350, 354
Meer, P. van der xxxix, 212
Mendenhall, G. E. 264, 282
Messner, R. G. 13
Mettinger, T. N. D. xlvii, 103, 136, 141, 143
Meyers, C. L. 356
Milgrom, J. 313
Millard, A. R. 242, 256, 284
Miller, J. M. xxxix, xlviii, 106, 116
Miller, P. D. xlvii, 21, 69
Miscall, R. D. xxvi, xxx, 225
Mitchell, H. G. xlviii, 264
Mol, H. xxxiii, xxxiv
Montgomery, J. A. xlvi, 24, 38, 59, 76, 84, 92, 103, 114, 115, 126, 134, 139, 140, 141, 142, 144, 147, 148, 150, 151, 152, 153, 161, 162, 163, 169, 170, 173, 175, 176, 177, 178, 180, 192, 193, 199, 209, 223, 224, 225, 238, 242, 244, 245, 246, 247, 248, 252, 255, 267, 286, 291, 293, 295, 299, 310, 314, 315, 323, 324, 330, 334, 335, 336, 337, 352, 353, 360, 361, 362, 365
Moran, W. L. 220
Moriarty, F. L. 242
Motzki, H. 120
Mowinckel, S. xlviii
Muilenburg, J. 19, 264, 275
Munch, P. A. 284, 289
Myers, J. M. xlvi, 207, 214, 317, 356

Naaman, A. 242, 253, 254, 255, 273, 276
Napier, B. D. 106
Nelson, R. D. xxii, xxiii, xxiv, xxv, 300, 301, 302, 319, 338, 346, 360
Nicholson, E. W. xxii, xxxiii, xxxviii, 131, 133, 142, 220, 227, 242, 260, 297, 305, 307, 313, 315, 318, 322, 324, 334
Nikolsky, N. M. 297, 310
North, C. R. 313, 340

Index of Authors Cited

North, R. 313
Noth, M. xxii, xxiii, xxxiii, xxxviii, xlviii, 9, 33, 103, 148, 156, 158, 167, 171, 317, 344

Oates, J. xxxix
Oded, B. xlviii, 220, 230, 297, 322, 339, 341, 342, 344, 350, 351, 355
Oden R. A. 313, 335
Ogden, G. 313, 332, 336
Orlinsky, H. M. 264
Orni, E. and E. Efrat 76, 100
Otto, R. 231

Pardee, D. 62
Parker, E. A. 220
Parker, S. B. 106
Parpola, S. 84, 116
Parzen, H. 106
Paton, L. B. 313
Pedersen, J. 52, 100, 117
Phillips, A. 21
Pilch, J. J. 284
Platarotti, D. 313
Polzin, R. xxii, 164, 248, 316
Porten, B. 239, 310
Porteous, N. W. 297, 302
Poulssen, N. 302
Preuss, H. D. 117
Priest, J. B. 313, 327
Pritchard, J. B. xii, xl, 50, 67, 78, 80, 90, 99, 101, 102, 115, 118, 131, 141, 155, 156, 166, 167, 168, 171, 180, 198, 201, 202, 217, 228, 229, 230, 236, 237, 253, 254, 257, 258, 272, 277, 278, 281, 282, 340

Rabinowitz, J. J. 220
Rad, G. von xxxiii, xxxvii, 11, 21, 25, 36, 55, 77, 78, 102, 106, 112, 127, 141, 166, 179, 183, 258, 276, 336, 350
Radday, Y. T. 88
Rahlfs, A. xliv, 2
Rainey, A. F. 179
Raitt, T. M. xxxiii, xxxiv
Reed, W. L. 168
Reiser, W. 13
Rendtorff, R. 106, 114
Renier, G. J. xxx
Reventlow, H. G. von 242, 256
Reviv, H. 133, 276, 289, 309, 310
Ringgren, A. xlvii, 8, 22, 66, 114, 152, 153, 169, 238, 239, 282, 335
Roberts, J. J. M. 264, 282
Roberts, S. 237
Robinson, E. xlvii, 296
Robinson, H. W. xlvi, xlvii, 22, 122, 136, 151, 169, 225, 236
Roche, M. de 297, 308
Rofé, A. 1, 16, 17, 21, 25, 46
Rogerson, J. W. xliv
Rose, M. 313
Rost, L. 28, 145, 153, 313
Rowley, H. H. xlvii, 242, 250, 252, 315

Rudolph, W. xlvi, 1, 20, 31, 133, 135, 187, 194, 207, 220, 242, 297, 331, 339, 355, 356, 358, 359

Saggs, H. W. F. xlvii, 10, 322
Sales, R. H. 28, 207, 213
Sanda, A. xlvi, 44
Sasson, J. M. 139
Sawyer, J. F. A. 8
Saydon, P. P. 173, 183
Sayed, R. 220
Scharbert, J. 52, 259
Schedl, C. 356
Schmitt, A. 41
Schmitt, H. D. xlvii
Schult, H. 55
Schunck, K. D. 232
Schweizer, H. 28, 69
Sekine, M. 313
Selms, A. van 344, 349
Seters, J. van xxx, xxxi, xxxii, 160, 171, 298
Seybold, K. 234
Shafer, B. E. 28, 31
Shaheen, N. 296
Shea, W. H. 187, 194, 196, 198, 220, 230
Shenkel, J. D. xxxix, xliv, xlv, 3, 30, 84, 103, 151
Shiloh, Y. 359
Shils, E. xxxiii, xxxv, 327
Simons, J. xlvii, 181, 260, 262
Skinner, J. xlvi, 67, 84, 96, 101, 102, 104, 136, 137, 139, 140, 141, 169, 170, 178, 226, 229
Smend, R. xxii, xxiii, xlvii, 236
Smit, E. 104
Smith, C. C. 107, 116
Smith, D. A. xlvi, 65, 181, 204, 260, 261, 262, 291, 306, 327
Smith, W. R. 36
Snaith, N. H. xlvi, 84, 226, 231, 232, 236, 238, 247, 251, 254, 258, 300, 306, 313
Snijders, L. A. 187
Soden, W. von 130
Soggin, J. A. xxiii, xlvii, 133, 315
Sperber, D. 13
Stade, B. 135, 242, 246
Steck, O. H. 1, 8
Stern, E. 313, 337, 357, 365
Stinespring, W. 10, 155
Stolz, F. 21
Strange, J. 93, 104
Stuhlmueller, C. 264, 278

Tadmor, H. 187, 220, 229, 242, 255, 344, 355
Tadmor, H. and M. Cogan 207, 211, 214, 242
Talmon, S. xlviii, 220, 238, 297, 308, 344
Tawil, H. 264
Thackeray, H. St. J. xlvi, xlviii
Thenius, O. xlvi, 51
Thiel, W. xxii, xxxiii, xxxviii

Thiele, E. R. xxxix, xlii, xliii, xliv, 34, 103, 151, 168, 178, 180, 181, 185, 187, 193, 194, 195, 198, 201, 203, 205, 212, 228, 250, 289, 304
Thomas, D. W. xlviii, 127
Thompson, J. A. 118
Thompson, R. C. 52, 64, 65, 160, 169
Todd, E. W. 242
Torrey, C. C. 145, 154
Tov, E. xliv, xlv
Trever, J. C. 53
Tsevat, M. 357

Uffenheimer, B. 313
Ungnad, A. 242
Ussishkin, D. 173, 182, 242, 255, 272

Vanutelli, P. 316
Vattioni, F. 220
Vaughn, P. H. 173, 179
Vaux, R. de xlviii, 66, 100, 155, 181, 207, 213, 216, 217, 337
Vogelstein, M. xlviii
Vogt, E. 220, 242, 357

Wallis, G. 253, 275
Ward, J. M. 51
Warren, C. and C. R. Conder 284, 296
Watts, J. D. W. xlviii
Weidner, E. F. 357
Weinberg, W. 242, 258, 357
Weiner, H. M. 264
Weinfeld, M. xxii, xxxiii, xxxviii, xlviii, 213, 226, 227, 231, 233, 242, 252, 253, 278, 306, 313, 334, 338
Weippert, M. xlviii, 187
Wellhausen, J. 135, 148, 281
Welten, P. xlviii, 220
Wenham, G. J. 298
Wernberg-Møller, P. 133, 140
Werner, E. 115
Westermann, C. 10, 11, 85, 86
Wevers, J. W. xlviii, 21, 55, 139, 264, 270, 344
Whitelam, K. W. 100
Wifall, W. xlvi, xlviii
Wilch, J. R. 347
Wilkinson, J. 260, 284, 296, 313
Williams, G. 13, 21, 22, 26
Williams, R. J. 111, 136, 139, 162, 299
Willis, J. T. xlviii
Wilson, J. A. 230
Wilson, R. R. 327
Wiseman, D. J. 187, 202, 344, 348
Wishlicki, L. 41
Wolf, C. U. 101
Wolff, H. W. xxiii, 26
Würthwein, E. 313, 318

Yadin, Y. xlviii, 89, 90, 91, 118, 195, 200, 202, 294, 313, 334
Yamashita, T. xlvii
Yeivin, S. xlviii, 173, 220

Zakovitz, J. 284, 298
Zenger, E. 357

Index of Principal Subjects

Abanah River 65
Abelbeth-maacah 202
Abner 127
Accountant, king's 148
Achbor 320, 326
Adad-nirari III 167, 256
Adam, Bridge of 92
Adar (twelfth month) 348
Adramelek 239, 282
Ahab
  dynasty of 111
  king 10, 20, 31, 63, 69, 80, 103, 113, 138, 145, 213, 300, 305, 311, 320, 336
Ahaz (Jud.) 209–19, 228, 240, 248, 271, 335
  steps of 294
Ahaziah (Isr.) 33, 69, 296, 326
Ahaziah (Jud.) 99, 106, 125, 168, 182
Ahijah, the prophet 236
Ahikam 320, 324, 326
Altar 215–19, 251, 335
  bronze 216–17
Amarna Letters 50
Amaziah (Jud.) 212, 248, 251
Ammon 39, 363, 366
Amon (Jud.) 300, 309–10
Amorites 307
Amos 93, 165, 307
Anathoth 324
Anger of Yahweh 163, 166, 235, 301, 338–39, 354
Annals 246–47, 346
Anointing of Jehu 112, 114, 119, 123, 132, 169
Anthropomorphisms 278
Apostasy 12, 38, 117, 165, 180, 182, 212, 213, 217, 234, 235, 238, 246, 278, 297, 306, 311, 327, 333, 335, 355
Arabah
  road 362–63
  Wadi 35, 179, 180
Arabs 349–50
Arad 232, 339–40
  Letters 156, 350
Aramaic 258
Archives 106, 209, 213, 325
Argob & Areah 200–201
Armory 294
Army
  Israelite, formation 31, 168
  Israelite, Organization 10
  of Judah 182
  Persian 166
  Syrian 81, 348
Aroer 40, 131
Arpad 198, 260
Asa (Jud.) 132
Ascension of Elijah 17–18, 22
Asherahs 232, 306, 333
Ashima 238–39
Ashkelon 348, 349
Asshur 281, 322
Ashurbanipal 236, 272, 282–83, 304, 322
Asshurnadin-shumi 289

Assyria, Assyrians 90, 165, 184, 192, 236, 246, 270, 303–4, 321–22, 324, 339
Astral deities, Assyrian 219, 305–6, 322
Athaliah 103, 106, 136, 144, 151, 305, 320
Authority
  divine 12
  prophetic 5–7, 12, 18–19, 49, 324
  royal 4–7, 11, 12, 74
Ava 237
Azaryau of Iauda 194
Azekah 254, 276, 362

Baalism 117, 124, 125, 129, 132, 143, 144, 145, 305, 333
Baal-Shalishah 49, 53
Baal-zebub 8, 257
Baasha (Isr.) 113, 114, 118
Babylon 166, 192, 210, 236–37, 286, 288, 339, 342
Babylonian Chronicle 229, 289, 348, 349, 351, 352, 354
Babylonian King List 198
Ban, the 78
Baruch, the scribe 250
Beer Sheba 334
Bel-ibni 289
Ben Hadad, king of Syria 62, 63, 69, 75, 76, 78–79, 80, 98, 99–102, 105–6
Ben Hadad II of Syria 171
Beth Baal-meon 40
Beth Eked (Beit Qad) 127, 132
Beth Haggan (Jenin) 118, 128
Beth Horon 180
Beth Millo 156
Beth Shean 77, 92
Beth Shemesh (Galilee) 177
Beth Shemesh (Judah) 177
Bethel 19, 20, 131, 227, 333, 335
Bit-Yakin 294
Blasphemy 67
Blindness 78
Bloodshed 309
Body
  as symbol 292
  symbolism of 215
Book of Law 319–32
Bozkath 323
Bribes, bribery 214
Bureaucracy 60
Burnt offering 66
Byblos (Gebail) 202

Calendar
  Babylonian xliii
  Gezer xliii
Calves, golden 131, 234
Camps (encampments) 90
Cannibalism 80
Carchemish 317, 339
Carites (royal troops) 137, 139, 140
Carmel, Mount 18, 50, 51, 278
Carpenters 353
Cassius, Mount 157
Cavalry 257
Centralization of worship 151, 322

Centurion (captain of a hundred) 138
Chair (as symbol) 368
Chalcitis 230
Chaldeans 362
Chariot 89, 117, 128, 169, 279
Chariot of fire 21, 78
Chemosh 39–41, 166, 235, 258, 335
Cherubim 277
Chiasmus 87, 88, 99, 124
Chronicler 317, 337
Chronicles, book of 178, 340
Chronology xxxi, xxxvii–xliv, 104–5, 151, 178, 184–85, 192, 197, 211, 212, 228, 250, 254, 289–90, 304–5, 350
Cilicia 84, 90–91
Cimmerians 322
Cleansing 65
Co-regency (Jehoshaphat and Jehoram) 103
Coastal plain 255
Colloquialisms 116, 183
Comedy 74
Commandments 233, 291
Continuity 361
Corner Gate 181
Coronation 112, 142
Cosmetics 118
Covenant 240, 241, 322, 332
  between Jehoiada and the people 137
  with Abraham 171, 234
  with David xxiv, 103, 143, 282
Creation 235
Cult xxi
Cuthah (Tel Ibrahim) 237
Cycle, threefold narrative 113, 116
Cyrus 258
Cyrus Cylinder 166

Damascus 98, 101, 170, 183–84, 203, 211, 248
Damascus Gate 181
Dan 131
David xxiv, 34, 39, 82, 114, 127, 141, 158, 179, 186, 193, 212, 262, 278, 287, 290, 291, 294, 311, 323, 338, 343, 369
David and Syria 82
Dead Sea 37, 76, 335
Dead Sea Scrolls 84, 95, 325
Death and burial, formula 104
Debt 50–51
Deceit 61
Deir 'Alla 77
Deliverance 86, 282
Deliverer 167
Dependence upon Yahweh 75
Deportation 355–56, 365
Dervish, circle 163
Descent of Silla 156
Desertions 257, 364
Despair 283
Deutero-Isaiah 278, 280
Deuteronomist 38, 82, 93, 111, 131, 145, 168, 170, 179, 191, 227, 232, 237, 302, 309, 317, 364, 368

Index of Principal Subjects 375

Deuteronomy, book of xxiv, 69–106, 119, 176, 179, 213, 231, 252–53, 306, 307, 316, 322, 325–26, 339
Dibhan (Dibon) 34, 131
Diggers 364
Divination 235
Dothan 77, 92
Dynasty
 Davidic 144–45, 341
 of Jehu (end of) 172
 of Omri (end of) 119

Ecstatic behavior 115
Edom
 desert of 86
 nation of 7, 31, 33, 35, 37, 39, 93, 104, 178, 179, 180, 186, 211, 213, 214, 347, 355
Eglon 323
Egypt 90–91, 233, 263, 280, 310, 321, 339, 342, 367
Ekron 8–9, 254, 258
Elah, Valley of 276
Elam(ites) 289, 354
Elath 180, 209, 210, 211, 213–14, 219
Elders 80
Election 280
Elephantine Papyri 310
Eliakim 249
Elijah 1–28, 163, 274, 278, 287, 355
Elisha 13–120, 162, 287, 355
Elkanah 67
Elnathan 326
Enoch 21
Ephraim 67, 317, 337
Ephraim Gate 181
Esarhaddon 127, 236, 272, 282–83, 304
Etiology 227
Euphrates River 182, 340
Evil Merodach 367–68
Exile, Babylonian xxxiii, 105
Exodus 166, 279, 308
Eye (as symbol) 363
Ezekiel, the prophet 303
Ezion Geber 203
Ezra 325

Face (as symbol) 290
Faith 54
Faithfulness 39, 193, 259, 311
Famine 75, 79, 100, 362
Faria, Wadi 77, 92
Fear of Yahweh 50, 239
Feast days 52
Foundry, Temple 154
Furnishings 51
 of temple 154–55, 210, 218

Galilee 47, 180, 192, 211
Galilee, Sea of 76
Gate, city 89
Gath (Tel es-Safi) 155, 254, 262, 276, 343
Gath (Tell Sheikh el-Areini) 155
Gath Hepher 183
Gaza 202, 211, 253
Gazelle 151
Geba of Benjamin 334
Gedaliah 324, 359, 369
Gehazi 45, 51, 53, 58–59, 66, 68, 100, 101, 105
 later traditions of 48
Gezer 104, 215
Gibeon 193
Gideon 235

Gift 60, 63
Gihon, Spring 362
Gilboa, Mount 50, 77
Gilead 166
Gileadites 201
Gilgal 16, 19, 53, 64
Goliath 278
Gourds 53
Governors 126
Grass 281
Greatness of Yahweh 271
Guard, palace 138
Guards' Gate 144
Guilt offering 155
Gur, Ascent of 118

Habs, Wadi 179
Hadad 82
Hadad (storm god) 66
Hadadeser 38, 141
Halah 231
Hamath 183–84
Hammo of Gaza 253
Hand (as symbol of power) 36, 154, 170, 279
Haran 322
Harran 348
Haruspicy 217
Harutz 310
Hazael, king of Syria 82, 98, 99, 102, 150, 155, 159, 165, 166, 168, 171, 181, 248, 321
Hazor 200
Healing 4, 8–9, 23–24, 60, 68, 292–93
Hebron 104
Hezekiah (Jud.) 132, 145, 149, 151, 159, 166, 192, 210, 212, 227, 246–63, 269–97, 302, 304, 320, 338
High Priest 153, 324
High places 151, 178, 213, 232, 233, 334, 335
Highway, King's 35
Hilkiah the priest 217, 320, 324, 326
Hinnom, Valley of sons of 333, 334, 363
Hiram 217
History xxx, 12–13, 93, 119, 129, 173, 224, 233, 236, 248, 269, 276–77, 360
Hope 361, 369
Hophra, Pharaoh 367
Horonaim 40–41
 Way of 35
Horse of the sun 334–35
Hosea, the prophet 182, 229
Hoshea (Isr.) 225–41
Huldah 321
Huleh, Lake 202
Humiliation of Elisha 81
Hurrians 157

Ibleam (Bel 'almeh) 118
Iddo, the prophet 50
Idols, idolatry 232, 233, 307, 333
Idri-mi of Alalakh 156–58
Incense, burning of 333
Income, Temple 150–59
Inheritance, Naboth's 116
Inspiration, prophetic 36
Introductory formula to reigns 148–49, 246, 319, 323, 341, 342, 346–47
Inversion as a literary device 87
Iron, Nahal 340
Irony as a literary device 49, 259
Isaiah, memoirs 246

Isaiah, the prophet 194–95, 210, 270, 271, 274, 287–92, 294, 306, 356
Ishbosheth 127
Ishmael 366–67
Ishtar, Prayer of 166
Iskaka 197
Issachar, Tribe of 50

Jabesh-Gilead 195
Jachin and Boaz 232, 365
Jahaz 40
Janoach 202
Jar handle 193
Jehoahaz (Isr.) 63, 132, 162, 166, 340
Jehoash (Isr.) 63
Jehoiachin (Jud.) 295, 347–48, 352–55
Jehoiada, the priest 135, 217, 337
Jehoiadin 178
Jehoiakim (Jud.) 203, 341–42, 346–55
Jehonadab ben Recheb 125
Jehoram (Jud.) 34, 102–3, 106, 213, 250
Jehoshaphat (Jud.) 34, 132, 251
Jehosheba 136
Jehu, accession of 111–12
Jehu (Isr.) 63, 111–20, 126, 129, 130, 151, 159, 164, 320, 336, 337
Jeremiah 93, 213, 274, 303, 308, 324, 326, 360
Jericho 16, 19, 53, 363
Jeroboam I (Isr.) 113, 114, 130, 165, 213, 218, 236, 307, 311, 335, 336
Jeroboam II (Isr.) 132, 176, 209, 273
Jerusalem
 city 67, 150, 156, 177, 181, 182, 214, 231, 236, 246–63, 269–93, 301–2, 348, 351
 water supply 260–62, 295–96
Jerusalem-Zion tradition 279, 282, 303
Jezebel 20, 113, 114, 138, 145, 235
 death of 118
Jezreel, Plain of 50, 105, 106, 113, 118, 126, 340
Joab 127
Joah 249
Joash (Jud.) 112, 148–59, 165, 181, 248, 251, 320
Job 283
Joktheel 179
Jonah, the prophet 177, 274
Joppa 254
Joram (Isr.) 33, 76, 99–100, 113, 347
Jordan River 64, 73, 76, 91
Joseph 368
Joshua 19, 27, 67, 170
Josiah (Jud.) 145, 149, 151, 159, 232, 303, 312–43
Jotbah 310
Jotham (Jud.) 149, 212, 228, 251
Jubilee, year of 50, 138
Judean 258
Judges, Book of 12, 38, 163, 172
Judgment 73, 82, 86, 111, 114, 119, 163, 165, 172, 206, 263, 281, 297, 301, 303, 307–8, 311–12, 321, 338, 339, 350, 369
Justice 55, 309

Kab (weight) 79, 89
Kabal-am 195–96
Kadesh on the Orontes 89, 341
Karnaim 171
Kidron Valley 156, 333, 363
Kir 215
Kir Haresheth (el-Kerak) 38
Kiriathaim 40

Index of Principal Subjects

Kislev (ninth month) 348
Knowledge of Yahweh 281
Kuites 171

Lachish, Tel el-Duweir 104, 179–80, 182, 246, 254, 255, 256, 259, 323, 350, 360, 362
Lachish Letters 20, 51, 143, 195, 310, 362
Land
  as gift 171
  expropriation of 101
Laver 218
Law of Moses 131, 179, 233, 304, 309, 338
Lebanon 280, 284
Lebo-hamath 182
Legitimation
  of kings 209
  prophetic 98
Lending 50–51
Leper, leprosy 59, 64, 86–87, 92, 193, 194, 206
Letter, formal features in ANE 62, 125, 277
Libnah 7, 104, 254, 272, 276, 341
Limits 186
Litani River 182
Literary artistry 32, 46–47
Lo-debar 171
Luash 171
Lydda (Diospolis) 53

Madeba 40
Madness 115
Magic, sympathetic 76
Magistrate 100
Maktesh 327
Malhata Nahal 179
Man of God 5–6, 10–11, 45, 46, 73, 74, 114, 295, 297–312, 317, 321, 327, 335–37, 347
Manasseh (Jud.) 215, 235
Manasseh (tribe) 317
Marduk 166, 258
Mari 52
Mathaniah 354–63
Medes 231, 322
Medicine 287
Megiddo 118, 202, 317, 339, 340
Menahem (Isr.) 190–206, 210, 214
Mercenaries 90, 200, 340
Merodach Baladan 206, 288, 289, 292
Mesad Hashavyahu 339
Mesha of Moab 166, 235, 258, 277, 288
Mesha Stone 33–41, 67, 338
Micah, the prophet 273, 274, 303, 306, 308
Milcom 335
Military personnel 353
Ministry of Jesus 55, 69
Miracles, prophetic 17, 23, 37, 54, 63, 68, 73, 81, 164
Miriam the prophetess 327
Mishneh 327
Mizpah 366
Moab 5, 7, 31–41, 164, 170, 355, 363
Moabite Stone (see Mesha Stone)
Mockery 275, 279
Molten Sea 218
Monotheism 66
Moreh, Mount 50
Moses 19, 20–21, 27, 167, 168, 234, 252, 275, 332, 338
Murabbat Papyrus 151

Murder 308
Music and musicians 36, 142
Musri 84, 90–91, 229

Naaman 52, 58–69, 87, 93, 184, 365
Nabonidus 166
Nabopolassar 322, 339, 348
Naboth, crime against by Ahab 106, 127
Naphtali 192, 317, 337
Narrative writing 111
Nathan-melek 335
Nazareth 183
Nebo 40, 277
Nebuchadrezzar 230, 346–68
Nebuzaradan 364
Necho, Pharaoh 317, 322, 339, 340, 341, 350
Necromancy 306
Negev 179
Nehemiah 325
Nehushtan ("The Brass Thing") 251–52
Nergal 238
Neriglissar 367
Nibchaz 239
Nineveh 215, 231, 322, 339
Ninlil I 281
Nisrock 282
Noadiah, the prophetess 327

Oath 20, 66, 67, 113
Obadiah 50
Obedience 69
Offense, Mountain of 335
Officials, state 352
Omri 33, 36–39, 113–14, 124, 132, 235
Ophel 67, 309, 333
Ophel Inscription 293
Orphans 55

Palace bodyguard 130
Pashhur 93
Passover 316, 319, 321, 337
Pathos 80
Peasantry 353
Pekah (Isr.) 190–206, 209, 228, 347
Pekahiah (Isr.) 190–206
Pentateuch, dating of 315–16
People of the land 137, 142, 182, 310, 340, 341, 342, 362
Petra 179
Pharpar River 65
Philistines, Philistia 8, 50, 100, 211, 253, 254, 255, 262
Pillar 34, 130, 232, 255, 365
Plenty 86
Plot development 74, 320
Plowers 364
Polemic 234
Polytheism 235
Prayer 48, 65, 77–78, 270, 277, 290, 302–3
Prefiguring 105
Pride 65
Priest of Baal 143–44, 337
Priests 148, 332, 334, 365
Propaganda 123
Prophecy xxi, 233
Prophet
  and war 31–41
  characteristics 73
  from Samaria 336
  status of 18
Prophetess 327
Prophetic consciousness 233

Prophetic word
  fulfilment xxi, 47–48, 49, 78, 92, 93, 112, 206
  power of 93
Prophets of Baal 278
Prostitution, cultic 333–34
Protocol, regulations governing the king 141–42
Psammetichus I, Pharaoh 138, 322, 340
Psammetichus II, Pharaoh 348–49, 351
Punishment xxxvii–xxxviii, 66, 99, 103, 180
Purity xxxv–xxxvi

Qarqar, battle of 79, 168
Quivers 141

Rab-saris 249–63
Rab-shakeh 249–63, 272, 275–76
Rafia 230
Raiding parties 37, 63, 164, 170, 349
Ramat Rachel 194
Ramoth Gilead 82, 105, 106, 111, 114, 131
Ramses II, Pharaoh 89, 340
Raphia 253
Redaction, Double xxii, 273–74, 338
Reform
  Hezekiah's xxviii, 343
  Jehu's xxviii, 168
  Josiah's xxv, xxviii, 178, 311, 323–43
Rehoboam (Jud.) 212, 248
Remaliah 200
Remnant 281–82
Repentance 287
Resef 277
Restitution 155
Restoration 105
Resurrection 164
Revolt
  Jehoiakim's 349
  Jehu's 117, 132
  Mesha's 31–41, 131
  Zedekiah's 361–62
Rezin 192, 209
Rezon 82
Riblah 341, 361, 363
Rimmon 66
Ritual xxxvi, xxxvii
Role reversal 61, 67
Rumah 342

Sabbath(s) 52, 140, 218
Sacrifice
  and Offerings 129, 216, 217, 233
  child 38, 213
Salvation 172
Samaria 59, 74, 78, 89, 92, 125, 228–41, 253, 254, 260, 263
  Fall of 224–41, 284, 296, 337
Samarian Ostraca 196, 230
Samarians 228
Samaritanism 238
Samuel, the prophet 51, 93
Sappers 353
Sareser 282
Sargon II 116, 192, 228–41, 277, 289
Saul, king 50
Scarcity 86
Scenes, narrative 97, 111
Scribe 256, 324, 365
Sea Peoples 90
Sea of Reeds 257
Seah (weight) 89
Secretary, king's 149, 153, 159

Index of Principal Subjects 377

Seir 103
Sela 179
Selectivity, principle of 303, 309–10, 318
Self-confidence of Elisha 74
Sennacherib 192, 212, 230, 231, 248–63, 269–70, 321
Sepharvayim 237
Sequence
  narrative 112–13
  verb 111
Seraiah, the scribe 365
Shabaka, Pharaoh 229
Shallum (Isr.) 190–206
Shalmaneser III 99, 101, 115, 127, 131, 155, 168, 171, 282
Shalmaneser V 192, 224, 225–41, 277
Shamash 335
Shamash-shum-ukin 309
Shaphan 320, 324
Shebna 249
Shechem 53, 67, 92, 230
Shekel (weight) 63, 86
Shephelah 180, 254, 323, 341, 362
Shields 141
Shishak, Pharaoh 50, 248
Shofar 115, 142
Shunem 46, 50
Shunemite woman 67
Shutting of door 50, 52, 75, 80
Sibe 229
Sickness 4–7, 61, 98, 101, 286–87, 292–93
Sidon 304
Siege 92, 197, 230, 281, 351, 362
Sign 281
Simeon 317, 337
Sin xxxv–xxxvii
Siwan (third month) 348
Skepticism, Official 86, 87, 91
Skin malady 296
Slingers 37
Society xxxv–xxxviii
Solomon 34, 69, 92, 112, 212, 248, 250, 261, 338, 352
Sons of Prophets 25–27, 48–49, 50, 53, 54, 67, 75, 114
Soothsaying 306
Sorceries 235
Sorek, Valley of 180
Sources xxxii, 300–301, 346–47
Spears 141
Spirit of Yahweh 22–23, 275

Statutes 233
Steward, Chief 127
Style ix, xxvi–xxvii, 4, 191, 226
Succession, prophetic 15–28
Sur, Gate of 139
Symbolic action, prophetic 52, 163, 169, 172, 287
Syncretism 235
Syria
  king of 76
  nation 39, 62, 82, 209, 210, 219, 350
  wars with Israel 73, 98, 105, 162, 170

Tabeel 204
Talent (weight) 63, 255
Tartak 239
Tartan 256
Tax 199
Tefnakhte, Pharaoh 229
Tel Barnat (Libnah) 104
Tel Nagila 323
Tel Ramith (Ramoth Gilead) 105
Tell Beit Mirsim 350
Temple
  at Arad 251–52
  ceremonies 216
  Jerusalem xxi, 181, 219, 290–91, 301–2, 311
  of Baal 129, 136, 137, 143, 157
  plans 216
  records 210
  repairs 148–59
Tension as a literary device 32, 46, 47, 58
Text, 2 Kings xliv–xlv
Theophany 21
Threshold
  Keepers of 149, 325
  of Temple 149
Threshing floor 79–80
Thutmoses III, Pharaoh 50, 183, 340
Tiglath Pileser III 192–206, 210, 211–12, 213–15, 228–29, 277, 297, 347
Time xl–xli, 293, 297
Tiphsah 196–97
Tirhaka of Cush 269, 276
Tirzah 118, 196–97
Tishbite 9
Tombs, royal 296
Topheth 334
Tragedy 61
Treason 142

Treasures, palace and temple 289, 352
Tribute 229, 272
Tunnel, Hezekiah's 295
Tyre 355
Tyropean, Valley 327

Ululai (see Tiglath Pileser III)
Unfaithfulness 119, 229
Universalism 66
Unleavened Bread 337
Upper pool 256, 260–61
Uriah, the priest 212, 215–17
Utensils, temple 364–65
Uzza, Garden of 309, 350
Uzziah (Jud.) 165, 190–206, 209, 251

Vassal 214, 226, 246, 343, 347
Vendor's cry 86
Vengeance 117
Verb sequences in narratives 46, 111
Via Maris 203
Vision, prophetic 102

War, Holy 21, 37, 77, 78, 229, 257, 258, 276
Warfare
  defensive 257
  in the ANE 102, 197
Washing for ritual cleansing 64
Weapons 21
Widow 55
Wilderness motif 308
Wine vat 79–80
Wizardry 306
Word of Yahweh 89, 124, 164, 169, 191
  Fulfilment 11, 45, 54, 86, 88, 89, 92, 165, 177, 178, 283, 284, 303, 339
Workmen, skilled 154, 325, 354
Worship 65

Yakin 294
Yarmuk River 92

Zakir of Hamath 167, 333
Zechariah (Isr.) 190–206, 250
Zedekiah 295
Zedekiah (Jud.) 354–63
Zephaniah 332
  the prophet 307, 332
Zered, Nahal (Wadi Hasa) 37
Zibiah 151
Zimri 118
Zoar 103

Index of Biblical Texts

A. Old Testament

Genesis		*Exodus*		5:15	342
				5:15–19	155
1:5	252	2:11	289	5:18	342
3:6	215	2:23	289	5:25	342
3:24	277	3:4	22	6:25	363
3:32	26	3:7	183	10:4	345
4:8	37	3:7–8	279	13	63, 291
4:26	65	3:9	167, 288	13–14	64
5:5	198	3:12	293	13–15	68
6:2	26, 215	4:6–7	68	13:4	64
6:4	26, 290	5:6	342	13:5	64
7:22	15	6:23	128	13:27	217
12:15	215	7:8–13	54	13:33	217
13:10	103	7:19	52	13:46	147
14:6	104	9	291	14:6	65
15:1	275	9:3	36	14:8–9	64
15:2	26	12	282	14:12	65
17:21	51	12:1–13:16	337	16:24	216
18:10	51	12:22	154	18:3	231
18:14	51	13:4	xliii	18:21	213
19:8	76	14	19, 27	20:1–5	213
19:11	78	14:13–14	257	20:23	231
21:10	26	14:21	20	24:22	147
21:16	328	14:21–22	15	25:3–4	138
21:22	253, 294	15:4	84, 89	27:1–33	152
22:11	22	18:15	8	27:34	26
23:16	147	18:22	194		
23:18	26	19:10	130	*Numbers*	
24:7	229	20:5	179		
24:65	336	20:25	66	3:46	71
25–50	158	21:22	341	6:16	216
25:8	328	22:24–26	50	12:3	338
25:11	4	22:30	53	13:21	182
25:15	10	23:19	65	15:31	279
25:22	8	24:11	324	15:35	10
26:18	3	25:18–20	277	18:27	79
26:20	252	27:3	154	18:30	79
27:3	92	27:4	96	19:11	48
28:15	253	28:11	353	19:16–19	335
29:13	51	29:38–42	217	19:18	65
29:15–20	158	30	152	21:6–9	252
31:19–35	338	30:13–14	152	22:26	76
31:36	7	30:16	155	23:23	89
33:4	51	31:2	215	27:12–23	27
33:11	66	32	234	27:18–23	19
34:2	215	32:11	166	28	216
35:1	9	33:11	359	28:2–8	217
35:14	232			32:13	34
35:18	26	*Leviticus*		33:33	310
36:41–42	203			34:8	182
37–50	158	1–3	216	34:11	363
38:1	294	1:9	233		
38:2	215	1:13	233	*Deuteronomy*	
39:1	101	1:15	233		
40:3	364	1:17	233	1:16	114
40:5	256	2	216	1:41	92
41:14	368	2:1	50	2:13	37
43:33	76	2:2	233	2:36	126
44:16	91	2:3	155	3:4	200
44:34	328	2:6	50	3:12–16	126
46:2	22	2:9	233	3:14	200
47:15	324	2:13	23	3:20	306
48:10	51	2:16	233	4	240
50:1	162	3:13	26	4:4	252
50:5	290	4:13	155	4:5–18	252

Index of Biblical Texts

4:6–18	239	19:17	289	11:23	144
4:9	305	20:1	253	13:5	182
4:10	231	20:1–4	77	14:15	144
4:19	235, 333	20:8	114	15:8	331
4:20	143	20:19–20	37	15:26	156
4:23	137	21:8	308	15:38	179
4:25–28	12, 39	21:9	308	15:39	323
4:25–31	119	21:11	258	15:42	104
4:26	234	21:17	21	15:54	104
4:28	278	22:19	341	16:8	197
4:29	8, 335	23:7	69	17:15	67
4:30	91	24:10–13	50	19:13	176
4:34	259, 260	24:16	179, 326	19:18	50
5:6	231	26:3	289	19:50	67
5:29	231	26:5–9	163, 167, 288	20:7	67
5:32	323	26:7	167, 183	21:44	306
5:33	213	26:7–9	167	22:4	168
6	227	26:16	233	22:6	168
6:5	338	26:68	235	22:7	168
6:10	171	27–28	327	22:8	168
6:11	68	27:25	214, 308	23	227
6:17	332	28	291	23:6	325
6:24	231	28:14	323	24	332
7	227	28:34	115	24:3	171
7:5	232, 278, 335	28:56–57	80	24:6	325
7:6	137, 143	28:58	325	24:13	68
7:26	2	28:58–68	231	24:30	67
8	227	28:61	325		
8:7–9	259	29:20	325	*Judges*	
8:8	68	29:21	295, 325		
8:19	234	29:27	325	1:1	4
8:20	213, 234	30:10	325	1:17	252
10:7	310	30:19	234	2	227
10:17	214	31:11	302	2:14	166, 236
10:18	55	31:17	91	2:16	236
10:19	69	31:24	325	2:17	117
12:2	213	31:26	325	2:20	166
12:3	335	31:28	234	3	19
12:5–6	305	32:37	22	3:3	182
12:10	306	32:39	64	3:7–9	163
12:30	9	32:43	117	3:8	166
13:6	236	32:46	234	3:12–15	163
14:1	24	32:52	86	3:15	229
14:2	143	33:1	5	3:17	229
14:29	55	33:24	65	3:18	229
15:2	342	34:6	21	3:25	23
15:3	342	34:9	27	4:1–3	163
15:9	65	34:10–12	338	4:5	67
15:14	80			4:20	14
16	337	*Joshua*		5:11	197
16:8	129			5:13	197
16:11	55	1	227	5:28	8
16:13	80	1:1	4	6	235
16:14	55	1:8	325	6:1	163
16:19	214	1:12–18	126	6:3	35
16:21	232	3–4	27	6:7	163
16:21–22	335	3:17	15, 20	6:20	52, 336
17:3	235, 305	4:18	15	7:8	168
17:9	289	4:19	19	7:15	104
17:11	323	6:3	53	7:19	363
17:17	294	6:26	23	7:24	67
17:18	9, 325	7:1	166	8:10	95
17:20	323	7:1–26	179	8:20	104
18	317	7:20	63	8:21	104
18:6–8	334	8	91	8:30	126
18:9–14	305, 306	8:1	9, 275	8:33	117
18:10	213, 235	8:31	325	9	91
18:14	306	8:34	325	9:2–56	126
18:15–18	28	9:6	295	9:26	114
18:15–20	338	9:9	295	9:31	114
18:18	233	9:27	302	9:32	104
18:19	233	10:1	275	9:45	23
19:10	308	10:33	35, 197	9:46	114
19:11	104	11:6	89, 275	9:54	92
19:13	308	11:20	340	9:56	114

INDEX OF BIBLICAL TEXTS

10:1	67	17:51	67	1:17			168
10:7	166	18:17	26	1:20			169
10:14	274	19:5	309	1:24			169
11:18	36	19:13	338	1:27			169
13:12	10	19:16	338	1:29			274
13:23	89	21:8	14	1:30			169
17:1	67	21:13	115	1:34			115
17:5	338	22:7	130	1:35			169
18:11	92	25:22	115	1:38–39			112
18:14–20	338	25:24	53	1:38–40			112
18:16	92	26:24	274	1:46			169
18:17	92	28:3	306	1:48			169
19:22	197	28:4	50	2			143
20:1	366	30:8	63	2:1–2			338
20:44	71	30:15	63	2:1–4		xxiv, 103, 126, 131, 326
20:46	71	30:17	90	2:3			332
21:22	89	30:23	114	2:4			131, 290
				2:12			169, 185
Ruth		*2 Samuel*		2:19			169
				2:24			169
4:16	126	1:1	4	2:36			67
		1:10	141	2:42			67
1 Samuel		2:7	114	2:46			36, 179
		3:4	341	3:2			151, 251, 302
1:1	67	4	127	3:3			251
2:11	77	4:7	363	3:4			232
2:27	10	4:9	274	3:6			169, 290
2:31–34	290	5–6	311	4			143
2:34	293	5:3	143, 158	4:13			116
3:4	22	5:5	158	4:29			332
4:4	267	5:9	252	5			154
4:10	168, 180	6	158	5:1			229
4:20	89	6:2	267	5:4			189, 197
6:1	261	6:6–7	24	5:5			302
6:16–17	8	7	xxiv, xxxiv, 131, 143, 158, 311	5:17–18			325
7:16	366	7:8	114	6:1			xliii
8:3	214	7:12–17	103	6:11–13			xxiv, 338
8:12	10	7:13	302	6:19–36			277
8:14–17	68	7:14	xxiv, 76, 103	6:36			306
8:20	233	7:15	63	6:38			xliii
9	6, 53	8:2	34, 38, 78, 229	7:1			214
9:6	5, 11	8:6	38, 82	7:15			154
9:10	11	8:7	38, 141	7:17			8
9:16	89	8:12	7, 39	7:18			8
9:16–24	232	8:13	175, 179	7:20			8, 154
9:23	364	8:14	262	7:27–37			218
10	115	8:15	100	7:41			8
10:1	114	11:2	215	7:42			8
10:1–16	36	11:6	9	7:51			352
10:5	25	11:10	169	8			131, 291, 302
10:10	25	11:22	14	8:2			xliii
10:19	274	12–24	338	8:14			209
10:27	26	12:25	323	8:15			306
12:22	143	15:1	10, 139	8:17–20			302
12:24	290	15:12	229	8:20			169
13:2	180	18:1	10, 139	8:22			217
13:6	342	18:14	253	8:25			131, 169
13:12	166	18:17	180	8:25–26			338
13:20	71	18:20	91	8:29			302
14:1	52	19:4	22	8:33–34			302
14:16	139	19:8	152	8:41–43			69
14:27	65	20:23	139	8:43			302
14:48	236	21:18	197	8:44			302
14:52	26	22:30	37	8:44–51			302
15	93, 236	22:41	234	8:46			295
15:1–3	39	23:7	117	8:46–56			302
16–2 Sam 7	158	23:8	84	8:48			302
16:1–3	123	23:10	104	8:50			2, 7, 302
16:11	14			8:54			217
16:19	229	*1 Kings*		8:62–64			217
17:10	278			8:63			216
17:26	52	1:3	50	8:64			216, 217
17:36	278	1:5	10, 139	8:65			182
17:45	278	1:11	250	9			131, 143
17:46	23, 278, 279	1:13	168	9:1–9		xxiv, 103, 126, 131, 326, 338

Index of Biblical Texts

9:3	301, 302	16:31	7	22:46	119		
9:4	338	16:31–34	xxv, 305	22:48	103		
9:5	131	16:32	34, 129	22:51–52	4		
10:14	248	16:33	119, 129, 130	22:51–53	7, 12		
10:28	84	16:34	88, 131	22:53	7		
11	236	17:1	2, 9, 274				
11:1	7	17:8–16	46	*2 Kings*			
11:4	212	17:15–20	365				
11:5	335	17:15–22	365	1	xix, xxi, xxix, 5, 7, 8, 10, 12, 17,		
11:7	34, 335	17:15–50	364		18, 19, 46, 105, 164, 257, 271,		
11:13	302	17:16	88		279, 288, 296, 326, 327		
11:23	82	17:17–24	44, 53	1–2	xxi, xxix		
11:23–43	114	17:21	52	1–3	288		
11:25	82	17:27–37	365	1–8	xxvii		
11:29–39	xxiii	18	10, 12, 36, 261	1:1	2, 4, 31, 33, 38, 40, 211, 255, 288,		
11:32	223, 302	18:3	43, 50		349, 355		
11:33	7, 335	18:4	50, 54, 115	1:1–4	290		
11:34	302	18:12	22, 43	1:1–8	18		
11:36	103, 282, 301, 305	18:13	115	1:1–18	1		
11:39	xxiii	18:31	240	1:2	xxix, 6, 51, 95, 105, 359		
12	234	18:32	261	1:2–4	290		
12–14	11	18:35	261	1:3	9		
12:19	2, 7	18:37	218, 278	1:4	6, 58		
12:25–33	xxiii, 335	18:38	261	1:5	39		
12:31	251	18:43	51	1:5–8	260		
13	xxiv, xxv, 336	19–21	16	1:6	64		
13:2	22, 129, 251, 336	19:7	9	1:7	39, 237		
13:2–3	336	19:9	14	1:8	9, 24, 25, 28		
13:6	166	19:10	27	1:9	62, 113		
13:14–18	11	19:15	101, 114	1:9–15	18		
13:20–24	24	19:15–19	119	1:10	18, 270		
13:26	88	19:15–21	19	1:10–12	163		
13:32	251, 336	19:19	17, 22, 117	1:11	113, 305		
14:1–5	212	19:19–21	27	1:13	113, 270, 305, 336		
14:4–11	111	19:21	77	1:16–17	18		
14:6–11	114	20	78, 170	1:17	xxi, 4, 18, 24, 34, 58, 88,		
14:10	290, 301, 307	20:1–22	79		102, 103, 250, 282		
14:11	115, 118, 120	20:6	89	1:17–18	xxvi, xlii, 3		
14:18	11, 88	20:16–22	367	2	xix, xxix, 46, 81, 115, 288		
14:20	128	20:26–30	170	2–8	xxix		
14:21	301, 302, 305	20:35	25, 26, 75	2–13	61		
14:23	34, 213, 232	20:35–36	24	2:1	11, 53		
14:25–28	248, 255, 289	21	93, 119	2:1–18	16, 58		
14:26	352	21:4	290	2:1–24	16		
14:27	139, 214	21:10	128	2:1–25	13		
14:27–28	130	21:11	127	2:2	52		
15:1	xlii	21:17	9	2:2–3	113		
15:3	212	21:17–24	111	2:3	75		
15:4	103	21:19	113	2:4	14, 52		
15:11	212	21:19–24	118, 120	2:4–5	113		
15:12	233	21:20	235	2:5	75		
15:14	151	21:20–24	125, 129	2:6	52, 113		
15:18	79, 214	21:21	114	2:7	54		
15:23	132	21:23	113	2:8	44		
15:27	191	21:25	235	2:10	169		
15:28–33	4	21:27	260	2:10–11	169		
15:29	88	21:28	9	2:11	11		
15:34	103	22	25, 38, 39, 79, 82, 98,	2:15	7		
16:1–3	111		116, 119, 177, 310	2:16	54		
16:1–14	114	22:4	129	2:17	54		
16:4	118, 120	22:10	80, 169	2:19	73		
16:5	132	22:13	11	2:19–22	xxii, 59, 68, 73, 223		
16:8	203	22:19	169	2:20	307		
16:8–10	119, 200	22:20–24	118	2:20–22	291		
16:9–20	118	22:22	267, 275	2:21	58, 76		
16:10	191	22:26	126	2:22	11, 58, 88		
16:11	122	22:34	117	2:22–24	25, 58		
16:12	88	22:38	88, 118	2:22–5:27	58		
16:15–20	119, 196, 200	22:41	xli	2:23	73		
16:15–28	113	22:41–44	149	2:23–24	58, 59, 97, 128		
16:20	123, 229	22:41–50	119	2:23–25	16		
16:24	156, 331	22:42	102, 103	2:25	10		
16:27	132	22:43	251	2:38–41	73		
16:29	xli	22:44	119	3	xix, xxvii, xxxii, xxxix, 46,		
16:29–33	119	22:45	132		54, 98, 111, 119, 164, 171		

3–8	xix	5:16	63	9–25	xxvii
3:1	xlii, 102, 103, 136	5:20–28	101	9:1	25, 136
3:1–3	3	5:22	25, 26	9:1–10	169
3:1–27	28, 73	5:23	154	9:1–13	26
3:3	349	6	84, 92, 100, 101, 111,	9:1–37	106
3:4	184, 229, 325		164, 230, 258, 351	9:2	128
3:4–5	211	6–7	xxix	9:3	50
3:5	2, 4, 255	6:1	25, 26, 73	9:4	51
3:7	2, 129, 189, 340	6:1–7	16	9:6	50, 127
3:9	103	6:1–33	69	9:6–10	27
3:9–12	93	6:5	73, 200	9:7	25, 26, 233
3:11	7, 27, 64, 87, 91, 93	6:6	73, 123	9:12	63
3:11–12	6	6:7	21	9:14	99, 127
3:12	169	6:8	136	9:14–15	102
3:13	27	6:8–14	93	9:17–20	xl
3:14	62, 367	6:8–23	101	9:23	142
3:16	68	6:12	27, 87, 91, 114	9:25	129, 130, 200
3:20	86, 217	6:15	51	9:27	196
3:21	63, 349	6:18	88	9:32	295
3:22–24	86	6:21	25, 77, 102	9:34	122
3:24	104	6:24	62, 101, 340, 349	9:36	xxi, 9
4	xxix, 6, 26, 51, 58, 61, 62,	6:24–30	85	9:37	130
	81, 111, 172, 287	6:24–7:20	101	10	xxi, 164, 337
4:1	25, 73, 75, 128, 136	6:25	89, 199, 362	10:1	334
4:1–7	16, 59, 68, 73, 97, 98, 105	6:30	260	10:1–28	110
4:2	73	6:32	25, 26, 50	10:1–36	120
4:5	50, 336	6:32–33	85	10:5	245
4:7	73	6:33	85, 98	10:12–14	138
4:8	153	7	85, 106, 249	10:12–17	xxxii
4:8–37	16, 58, 59	7:1–2	273	10:13	114
4:12	63	7:1–20	66, 82	10:14	24
4:13	80, 100	7:2	80	10:15	199
4:14	100	7:4	364	10:17	11
4:15	63, 64	7:6	275	10:22	327
4:16	89	7:12	138	10:24	301
4:17	89	7:13	93	10:28–31	xxviii, 196
4:21	50	7:16	98	10:28–33	321
4:25	10, 331	7:18	98	10:29	110
4:26	67	7:20	98	10:30	165, 169
4:27	61, 68, 102	7:20–8:5	95	10:31	xxii
4:28	71	8	9, 51, 58, 111, 288	10:32	99, 236, 288
4:29	114	8–10	320	10:32–33	155, 159, 192, 211, 346
4:29–31	113, 169	8:1	77, 136	10:34–36	xx
4:32–34	113	8:1–6	16, 51, 58, 62, 68	11	xix, xx, xxi, xxviii, xxxii,
4:32–37	68, 169	8:1–29	93		xl, 103, 105, 156, 157, 305
4:33	50, 77	8:7	62, 294	11–12	156, 157, 158, 216
4:34	170	8:7–15	6, 32, 64	11:1	103
4:35–36	113	8:8	xxix, 6	11:1–20	133
4:38	25, 26, 66, 136	8:8–9	105	11:2	150
4:38–41	59, 73	8:9	6	11:4	130, 150, 234
4:39	261	8:10	6	11:9–12	112
4:39–41	16	8:11	23	11:12	112, 114, 234
4:41	76, 123	8:12	197	11:14	229, 260, 332
4:42	136	8:14	6	11:14–18	310
4:42–44	16, 59	8:15	65	11:17	234
5	xxvii, xxix, 9, 51, 54, 86, 90,	8:16	xli, xlii, 103	11:17–18	xxi
	101, 111, 164, 274, 277	8:16–17	212	11:17–19	337
5:1	10, 30, 82, 90, 93, 136, 234	8:16–24	303	11:17–20	320
5:1–2	345, 365, 367	8:17	314	11:18	157
5:1–14	73	8:18	7, 213	11:19	169
5:1–27	16, 55, 97	8:19	xxxvii, 144, 282, 321, 327, 347	12	xix, xxv, xxviii, xxxii, 105, 156,
5:2	37	8:20	xli, 2, 7, 347		217, 229, 320, 323, 324, 365
5:2–3	92	8:20–22	xxxii, 180	12:1–3	xx
5:3	7, 27, 150	8:21	180	12:1–4	xx
5:5	210	8:22	2, 7, 180	12:1–22	145
5:5–7	93, 125	8:25	118	12:2	229
5:5–8	xxix	8:26	320	12:4	251
5:7	326	8:27	7	12:5	342
5:7–8	260	8:28	114	12:7	324
5:8	27, 77	8:28–29	xix, 116	12:9–16	xxi
5:11	109	8:29	110, 112, 169, 294	12:10	325
5:13	87	8:29–9:36	32	12:10–16	323
5:13–14	92	9	xxi, xxix, 99, 119, 125,	12:10–17	324
5:14	88		127, 172, 271	12:10–19	210
5:15	6, 91	9–10	xxxii, 320	12:11	149, 314, 324, 326

Index of Biblical Texts 383

12:11–12	196	15:32–33	205	18:17–19:9	246, 248, 249, 268
12:12	325, 353	15:32–35	149	18:27	72, 79
12:12–13	325	15:35	251	18:29	276
12:14	365	15:38	205	18:34	277
12:15	325	16	192, 218, 263, 343	18:37	260
12:17	xix, 324	16:1	203, 205	19	245, 259, 263, 288
12:17–18	xxv, xxviii, 39, 99, 165, 180,	16:1–4	xx	19:1	249
	211, 248, 255, 288, 303	16:1–20	207	19:1–9	249
12:18	171, 199, 340	16:2	xxviii	19:1–37	264
12:19	214, 340	16:3	218, 228, 233, 235, 240, 306	19:2	290
12:19–21	xx, 165, 179, 181	16:3–4	xxii, 320	19:6	258
13	xxix, 79, 288	16:4	115, 232, 233	19:9	246, 255, 276, 305
13–15	184	16:5	203, 349	19:9–35	246, 248, 249
13:1	135	16:5–9	200	19:9–37	246
13:1–2	138	16:8–9	248, 255, 288	19:14	255
13:1–3	155	16:9	340	19:15	290, 307
13:1–25	159	16:10–16	xxi	19:15–20	293
13:3	76, 99	16:11	37	19:20	290, 291, 327
13:3–4	211	16:16	180	19:29	293
13:3–7	xix	17	xxi, 4, 12, 239, 246, 247,	19:31	295
13:4	177		253, 260, 277, 301, 360	19:32	261
13:5	183, 203	17–21	xix	19:34	291, 307, 339
13:5–7	183	17:1	205, 249	19:36–37	246
13:7	179	17:1–6	xx	19:37	246
13:8	132	17:1–23	xxiv	20	206, 246, 288, 291
13:10	184	17:1–41	219	20:1–11	xxxvi, xxxvii
13:10–11	138	17:2–23	xxii	20:1–21	284
13:12	132	17:3	199	20:2	209
13:12–13	xx, 177	17:3–6	xix	20:6	282
13:13	185	17:5	199, 254	20:8–11	xxii
13:14	21, 25, 102, 290	17:6	201, 232, 244, 254, 277, 305	20:11	335
13:14–19	xxii, xxxvii, 76	17:7	273	20:12–19	xxv, xxviii, 192, 303, 321
13:22	76, 99, 288	17:7–23	xx, xxv, 246, 254	20:14–19	210
13:23	177, 186, 234	17:7–24	307	20:16–19	xxii, 352
13:25	182	17:9	199, 253	20:17–18	xxiv
13:26–27	xx	17:10	213	20:18	305
14	165, 263, 311, 317, 343	17:11	251	20:19	159
14:1–4	xx, 138, 149	17:12	307	20:20	132, 261
14:1–15	303	17:13	303	20:21	347
14:1–29	173	17:13–14	xxii	21	xxi, 246, 303
14:2	151	17:14–18	246	21:1–26	297
14:3	xxviii, 193	17:16	7	21:2–15	xxiv
14:4	251	17:18	xxxvii, 273	21:3	xxv, xxviii, 235
14:5–6	xxii	17:19	xxiv	21:3–9	xxii
14:6	273	17:19–20	303	21:4	302
14:8	340	17:20–23	247	21:5	335
14:8–14	xix	17:23	214, 233, 350, 365	21:7	302, 339
14:11	340	17:24	277, 288	21:9	233
14:14	248, 255, 288	17:26	233	21:10	233
14:15–16	xx, 168	17:30–31	259	21:10–15	xxii
14:17	xx, 185	17:31	282	21:11	233
14:18	214	18	245, 261, 269, 270,	21:12	301, 327
14:22	214		274, 288, 320	21:16	129, 301, 350
14:23–29	194	18–19	xxviii, 186, 275, 296	21:18	193
14:25	274	18–20	xx, xxvii, xxxii, 315	21:20	301
14:25–27	xix, xxxvii	18:1–3	149	21:26–28	343
14:26	115	18:1–8	145, 320	22	xxi, 149, 151, 152, 154, 332, 338,
14:26–27	195, 288	18:1–37	241		342
14:28	132, 197	18:2	212, 289	22–23	xx, xxv, xxxii, 159, 315, 316,
15	240	18:3	xxviii, 193		317, 318, 319, 320, 322, 342
15–17	xxvii	18:3–6	288	22:1–2	212, 316, 317
15:1–4	149	18:4	159	22:1–7	149
15:1–38	186	18:4–5	xxi	22:1–20	312
15:2	151	18:4–6	xxii	22:1–23:25	xxiv
15:4	251	18:5	338, 343	22:2	193, 343
15:5	185, 203, 205	18:8	232	22:3	342, 366
15:10	4	18:9	35, 324	22:3–7	152, 159
15:14	4	18:9–12	212, 224, 338	22:3–23:3	316, 318, 319
15:19–20	205, 210	18:13	324	22:3–23:27	145
15:20	214	18:13–15	289	22:4	149, 153
15:23	xlii	18:13–19:7	268	22:5	147, 149
15:29	xix, xli, 205, 288, 347	18:15	295	22:6	149
15:29–30	210, 215	18:16	126	22:7	149
15:30	4, 228	18:17	101, 260, 261, 282	22:7–8	317
15:30–31	226	18:17–19	279	22:8	153, 317

384   Index of Biblical Texts

22:8–23:3		319	9:36	128	33:10–13	215
22:9		154	12:12	156	33:10–33	xl
22:11		260	26:18	335	33:11	295
22:12		366			33:11–17	309
22:16		307	*2 Chronicles*		33:19	232
22:19		260			34–35	315, 316, 317
22:21		317	3:7	76	34:1–2	316
23	xxi, xxii, 217, 315		9:29	50	34:1–29	317
23:1		342	11:12	335	34:3	317, 318
23:1–3		318	13:23	144	34:3–7	316
23:1–20		322	14:5	144	34:6	317, 337
23:1–37		328	16:1	35	34:6–7	339
23:2		317	17:18	156	34:8–31	316, 318
23:3		143	18	63	34:12	317
23:4	153, 317, 339		21:4	103	34:20	317
23:4–14		xxi	21:9	104	34:28–29	315
23:4–20	316, 318, 319		21:19	104	34:29–31	318
23:7		52	22:4	96	34:30	317, 330
23:8		126	22:6	96	34:32–33	316, 318
23:11	21, 278		22:11	134, 138	35:1–17	316, 318
23:13		2	23:5	134, 140	35:1–19	337
23:15		317	23:9	135, 141	35:18–19	316
23:16–20		318	23:12	142	35:19	331
23:20		129	23:13	135	35:20–27	316, 339, 340
23:21–23	xxxvi, 316, 319		23:18	143	35:22	218
23:21–25	318, 319		23:20	135	36:4	341
23:24		233	24	148, 151, 152, 153, 155, 156	36:5–8	350
23:24–27	316, 318, 319, 322		24:2	151	36:6–7	349
23:25		252	24:4–7	148	36:9	351
23:26–27	xxv, xxviii, xxxvii, 311, 321		24:7	138	36:10	354
23:27	236, 302, 350		24:11	147		
23:28	xx, 319		24:12	147	*Ezra*	
23:28–30	xxviii, 316		24:17–22	150		
23:29	xli, 37, 347		24:24–27	156	2:69	153
23:29–30	xx, xxv, 159, 317, 319		24:25	109, 156	6:22	218
23:29–31		322	24:26	109, 156	8:33	156
23:30		114	25	180, 181	9:26	53
23:31–32		346	25:1	175	10:21	9
23:31–35		xx	25:2	175	10:26	9
23:35		199	25:5–13	175	12:51	53
23:36–37		346	25:6–16	180		
24		295	25:19	175	*Nehemiah*	
24–25	xxvii, 12		25:20	175		
24:1	xli, 35, 368		25:23	175	3:25	342
24:1–20		343	25:24	175, 181	3:26	67
24:2	11, 233		26	190, 194	3:27	67
24:8–17		xx	26:5	195	5:11	68
24:9		342	26:5–21	193	8:4	342
24:13	214, 294		26:5–30	189	9:25	68
24:14		364	26:6–15	182, 184, 194	10:32	151, 152
24:17	143, 250		26:9	181	11:7	342
24:18–19		xx	27	204	11:9	327
24:19		342	27:3	67	11:17	327
24:20–25:7		xxxiii	28	211, 213	11:21	67
25	295, 349		28:5–8	211	12:38–43	181
25:1		201	28:18	211, 213	13:13	342
25:1–30		356	28:23	215		
25:8		xxxix	29:1	250	*Esther*	
25:8–17		xxi	29:3–6	255		
25:13		295	29:11	52	1:14	359, 365
25:17		8	30	337	8:3	53
25:18		332	32	247, 254, 292		
25:22		326	32:1–8	257	*Job*	
25:22–26		xxxiii	32:2–8	295		
25:27		xxxix	32:20	267	2	291
25:27–30		xxxiii	32:27–31	289	3:9	90
			32:27–33	295	6:6	23
1 Chronicles			32:30	295	7:4	90
			32:33	296	15:22	116
2:28		128	33	304	18:8	8
3:18		342	33:1	299	22:8	30
3:19		342	33:3	299	24:15	84
4:37		156	33:4	299	38:25	261
6		104	33:6	299	41:26	26
8:27		9	33:7	299, 306		

Index of Biblical Texts

Psalms

2	xxxiv, 279
4:5	281
8:5	26
17:6	278
18:11	277
22:6	26
22:8	279
27:4	209, 217
33:13	26
37:32	116
39:8	278
42:1	26
48	xxxiv, 302
60:4	24
66:7	116
68:14	310
71:2	278
72:1–19	55
79:11	26
80:12	53
80:15	2
81:3	115
86:1	278
89	xxxv
89:22	26
89:27–37	103
93:1	115
97:1	115
102:13	278
105	308
106	308
110	xxxiv
116:2	278
119:5	57
119:58	166
119:147	90
132	xxxiv
132:11–12	103
132:18	141
139:2	281

Proverbs

5:15–20	259
7:9	90
7:21	223
20:25	209, 217
23:27	76
24:10	76

Ecclesiastes

1:13	26
3:5	51
10:1	2, 8
10:20	77

Canticles

1:17	76
3:2	89
4:4	141

Isaiah

1–39	117
1:7–8	256
1:7–9	273
1:8	280
2:1–4	302
2:4	252
2:5	240
2:6	306
2:11	53
3:3	30
5:1	345
5:7	309
5:8	101
5:11	90
6:1	195
6:22	280
7	211, 213
7–9	210
7:1	213
7:1–8:8	203, 204
7:3	261
7:4	200
7:5	200
7:7–9	204
7:9	200
7:10	281
7:14	271
7:18	2, 8
8:1	281
8:2	215, 217
8:6	200, 261
8:23	89
9:1–11	281
9:6	282
10	280
10:5–11	281
10:5–19	263
10:13	63
10:27–32	254
11:15	65
13–23	39
13:14	151
14:2	342
14:13	279
14:22	104
15:5	35
16:7	37
17:6	110
20:22	256
21:4	90
22:9–11	261
22:16	127
23:17	278
27:9	232
28:17	307
29:1–4	273
30:1–7	295
30:2–4	257
30:28	65
31:1–3	295
31:3	257
32:14	67
36	244, 247, 248, 254, 255
36:2	245, 261
36:3	245
36:7	245
36:10	245
36:11	245
36:12	72
36:14	245
36:17	245
36:21	245
37	269, 270
37:6	267
37:7	267
37:9	267
37:11	267
37:12	267
37:13	267
37:14	267
37:15	267
37:17	267
37:18	267
37:20	267
37:21	268
37:21–35	279
37:23	268
37:24	268
37:25	268, 280
37:27	268
37:30	268
37:36	268
38	292, 293
38:2	285
38:4	286
38:5	286, 291
38:6	286, 291
38:8	294
38:21	286
39:1	286
39:2	286
39:5	286
40:2	152
40:6–8	281
40:9	23
40:18–24	271
40:27–31	271
41:2	281
42:3	257
42:8	278
43:13	278
43:25	278
44	278
44:6	278
45:18	278
49:20	76
50:10	90
55:1	281
56:8	69
57:14	261
58:3	342
60:17	342
61:5	95
62:10	261

Jeremiah

1–25	xxxviii
1:1–2	324
1:4–10	280
1:5	27
1:11–13	102
1:11–15	36
2–3	236, 307
2:1–8	308
2:1–13	117
2:4	89
2:6	231, 259
2:9–13	306
2:13	278
2:14–19	308
2:16	367
2:18	347
2:37	236
3:16	289
3:18	289
3:22	24
4:6	301
4:23–26	273
5:15	301
5:29	240
6:4	129
6:6	261
6:17	115
6:19	301
6:30	234, 236, 339
7:3	233
7:5	233

Index of Biblical Texts

7:6		308	29:26	115	*Lamentations*		
7:9		233	30–33	xxxviii	2:20		80
7:20		327	31:21	336	4:10		80
7:25		233	31:27–30	307	5:6–22		102
7:30		335	31:29–30	326			
7:31		213	31:40	143, 330	*Ezekiel*		
8:2	115, 305		32:35	213	1:3		36
8:8–12		93	32:37	86	3:12		23
10:1		89	32:44	105	3:14		23
11:2		89	33:11	105	4:12		233
11:11		301	33:26	105	5:10		80
11:13		233	34	231	6:4		233
11:17		233	34–35	xxxviii	6:5		233
11:19		222	34:1–3	354	6:6		233
12:7		308	34:7	362	7:22	218, 290
13:13		332	35	128	8:1	36, 76, 114
13:16		90	35:4	128	8:3		23
15:1		275	35:11	350	9:2		216
15:1–4		307	35:15	233	12:13		363
15:4		278	36	93, 320, 326	13:9		36
17:20		89	36:9–26	342	14:1	76, 114
18:11		233	36:12	324	16	236, 307
18:15		261	36:24	260	18:13		10
18:17		234	36:25	324	20:1	114, 355
19:3	89, 301		36:26	365	23:23		89
19:3–5		342	36:30	350	25–29		39
19:4		308	37:5	362, 367	27:11		141
19:5		213	37:6–10	354	27:12		89
19:11		24	38:11	130	27:14		89
19:13		335	38:17	361	27:16		89
20:1–6		93	38:17–23	354	27:18		89
20:4		86	38:19	90, 364	29:6		257
20:7		279	39	364	30:12		15
21:1	363, 365		39:1	358	31:4		261
21:1–10		354	39:1–10	359	33:11		233
21:4		218	39:8	358	34:11		217
21:11		89	40:5–9	359	34:12		217
22:2		89	40:5–41:10	324	39:15	331, 336
22:3		308	40:9	359	40:17–19		306
22:10–11		340	40:10	366	46:2		217
22:10–12		341	41	367	46:13–16		217
22:17		308	41:1–3	367	46:19		147
22:19	115, 350		41:1–18	359	47:8		24
22:28		175	44:4	233			
22:29		22	46–51	xxxviii, 39	*Daniel*		
22:30		11	46:2	339	3:6		xl
23:5–6		354	47:1	340	8:6		10
23:9–40	25, 27		47:5	340	8:13		71
23:10		37	48:31	37	8:20		10
24		324	48:34	35	9:13		71
24:9		278	48:36	37			
25:4		233	49:3	105	*Hosea*		
25:26		278	49:6	105	3:4–5		338
25:33		115	51:9	24	4:13		213
26		320	51:11	141	5:13		229
26:6		233	51:33	80	7:8–16		229
26:7		332	51:59	354	8:9		229
26:8		10	52	359	9:1–2		80
26:15		308	52:4–16	359	9:7		115
26:19		166	52:6	358, 362	9:10		335
26:20–23		342	52:7	362	10:5		333
26:24	324, 326, 366		52:12	358	10:9		26
27–28		355	52:13	358	10:14		102
27–29	361, 369		52:14	359	11		297
27–39		354	52:15	359	13:3		80
27:2–11		36	52:17–23	359, 360	14:1		102
27:4		363	52:22	365			
27:8		366	52:24–27	359	*Joel*		
27:13–19		342	52:28	352, 353	1:10		37
27:18		349	52:28–30	359, 360	1:14		129
27:19–22		352	52:30	231	2:15		129
29:10		126	52:31	359			
29:18		278	52:31–34	xxxiii			
29:19		233	52:32	359			
29:25		365	52:34	368			

Index of Biblical Texts

Amos		Micah		Zephaniah	
1–2	39	1:1	9	1:3	335
1:1	21, 35, 223	1:1–9	307	1:4	333
1:1–2:6	171	1:10–16	254, 276	1:6	305
1:3–5	166	2:1	89	1:11	262
1:5	215	3:1	89, 240		
2:8	341	3:5	129		
3:7	25, 27, 233	3:5–8	25, 115	*Haggai*	
3:13	240	3:9	89		
4:2	281	4:1–4	302	2:6	15
5:21	129	4:8	67		
5:26	235, 238, 333	4:12	80		
6:14	183	5:14	232	*Zechariah*	
7	93	6:1	89		
7:1–6	274	6:6	217	1:10	327
7:1–8:3	102	6:7	213	2:8	52
7:7–8	307	7:10	267	4:14	26
7:9	104	7:12	2	13:4	10
7:14	25, 26	7:18	308		
7:16–17	89				
7:17	259	*Nahum*		*Malachi*	
8:14	238				
9:1	102	3:4	117	3:2	261
9:7	63, 215, 281, 306	3:10	102	4:4–6	28

B. New Testament

Matthew				13:34	22
		5:36	54	14:28	186
11:21	306	6:30–44	55		
21:8	115	7:24–30	55		
		8:12	20	*John*	
		9:9–13	28		
		11:27–33	11	2:4	30
Mark		16:19	15	4	238
				20:31	xxx
2:1–12	293	*Luke*			
3:22	8			*Hebrews*	
5:21–24	55	4:27	28, 69		
5:24–34	55	7:11–17	55	11:37	308

C. Apocrypha

Sirach	
48:9	28
48:12	13
48:17	296

Index of Key Hebrew Words

אז	213	ירא	50, 231, 239	עופל	67
אלף	282	ישע	167, 183, 282	עזוב	183
אמונות	255			עם	127, 142, 144, 182
אמונים	126	כאב	37	עיר	130, 232, 253
אף	166, 338	כבס	261	עצור	183
ארגב	100	כהן	153	ערב	181
אריה	100	כלים	92		
אש	21	כסף	152–54	פצר	66
אשרה	232	כרי	139	פקעה	53
		כרמים	333		
בטח	252			צדקה	127
במות	232	מזכיר	256	ציון	336
בן	25–26, 128–29	מלא	156	צלחה	308
בעל	10	מכבר	96, 102	צעיר	103–4
בעל־זבוב	8	מנחה	216	צעק	37
בקר	217	מסגר	353	צר	76, 154
ברך	52	מסלה	261		
בת	104	מצבות	232	קב	79
		מצרע	63, 68, 193	קורה	76
גבים	364	משא	117		
גדוד	37, 63, 162, 170, 349	משגע	115	רוח	22–23
גרם	115	משח	114	רכב	128
		משנה	327	רפא	23–24
דלים	364	משפט	2	רצים	130, 139
חבל	234	נוקד	35	שבכה	8
חנה	84	נחשתן	252	שדמות	333
		נסך	216	שרים	126, 139, 352, 361
זבח	129	נפל	364		
זנונים	116	נשא	62	שבע	150–51
זקנים	80	נשא	50	שונה	50
				שחין	292–93
חבק	51	סאה	89	שכל	23
חי	20	סנורים	78	שלח	52
חיל	22	סערה	21	שלטים	141
חלה	166	סֵפֶר	325–26	שליש	89, 117, 130
חפא	232	סֹפֶר	256	שערים	334
חרש	353	סריס	101		
				תועבות	305
יום	290	עדות	141	תעלה	260–61
יצר	154	עולה	216	תשבי	9